Lecture Notes in Artificial Intelligence 4264

Edited by J. G. Carbonell and J. Siekmann

Subseries of Lecture Notes in Computer Science

T0216771

José L. Balcázar   Philip M. Long
Frank Stephan (Eds.)

Algorithmic
Learning Theory

17th International Conference, ALT 2006
Barcelona, Spain, October 7-10, 2006
Proceedings

 Springer

Series Editors

Jaime G. Carbonell, Carnegie Mellon University, Pittsburgh, PA, USA
Jörg Siekmann, University of Saarland, Saarbrücken, Germany

Volume Editors

José L. Balcázar
Universitat Politecnica de Catalunya, Dept. Llenguatges i Sistemes Informatics
c/ Jordi Girona, 1-3, 08034 Barcelona, Spain
E-mail: balqui@lsi.upc.edu

Philip M. Long
Google
1600 Amphitheatre Parkway, Mountain View, CA 94043, USA
E-mail: plong@google.com

Frank Stephan
National University of Singapore, Depts. of Mathematics and Computer Science
2 Science Drive 2, Singapore 117543, Singapore
E-mail: fstephan@comp.nus.edu.sg

Library of Congress Control Number: 2006933733

CR Subject Classification (1998): I.2.6, I.2.3, F.1, F.2, F.4, I.7

LNCS Sublibrary: SL 7 – Artificial Intelligence

ISSN	0302-9743
ISBN-10	3-540-46649-5 Springer Berlin Heidelberg New York
ISBN-13	978-3-540-46649-9 Springer Berlin Heidelberg New York

Springer is a part of Springer Science+Business Media

springer.com

© Springer-Verlag Berlin Heidelberg 2006
Printed in Germany

Typesetting: Camera-ready by author, data conversion by Scientific Publishing Services, Chennai, India
Printed on acid-free paper   SPIN: 11894841   06/3142   5 4 3 2 1 0

Preface

This volume contains the papers presented at the 17th Annual Internation Conference on Algorithmic Learning Theory (ALT 2006) which was held in Barcelona (Catalunya, Spain), October 7–10, 2006. The conference was organized with support from the PASCAL Network within the framework of PASCAL Dialogues 2006, which comprised three conferences:

Learning 2006 provided a forum for interdisciplinary study and discussion of the different aspects of learning and took place October 2–5, 2006 on the campus of Vilanova i La Geltrú.

ALT 2006 was dedicated to the theoretical foundations of machine learning and took place in the rooms of the Institute of Catalan Studies in Barcelona. ALT provides a forum for high-quality talks with a strong theoretical background and scientific interchange in areas such as query models, on-line learning, inductive inference, algorithmic forecasting, boosting, support vector machines, kernel methods, reinforcement learning and statistical learning models.

DS 2006 was the 9th International Conference on Discovery Science and focused on the development and analysis of methods for intelligent data analysis, knowledge discovery and machine learning, as well as their application to scientific knowledge discovery; as is already tradition, it was collocated and held in parallel with Algorithmic Learning Theory.

In addition to these three conferences, the European Workshop on Curricular Issues in Learning Theory initiated as the first regular meeting the Curriculum Development Programme of the PASCAL Network taking place on October 11, 2006.

The volume includes 24 contributions which the Programme Committee selected out of 53 submissions. It also contains descriptions of the five invited talks of ALT and DS; longer versions of the DS papers are available in the proceedings of DS 2006. These invited talks were presented to the audience of both conferences in joint sessions.

- Gunnar Rätsch (Friedrich Miescher Labor, Max Planck Gesellschaft, Tübingen, Germany): "Solving Semi-Infinite Linear Programs Using Boosting-Like Methods" (invited speaker for ALT 2006)
- Carole Goble (The University of Manchester, UK): "Putting Semantics into e-Science and the Grid" (invited speaker for DS 2006)
- Hans Ulrich Simon (Ruhr-Universität Bochum, Germany): "The Usage of the Spectral Norm in Learning Theory: Some Selected Topics" (invited speaker for ALT 2006)
- Padhraic Smyth (University of California at Irvine, USA): "Data-Driven Discovery Using Probabilistic Hidden Variable Models" (invited speaker for DS 2006)

– Andrew Ng (Stanford University, USA): "Reinforcement Learning and Apprenticeship Learning for Robotic Control" (invited speaker jointly of ALT 2006 and DS 2006)

Since 1999, ALT has been awarding the E. M. Gold Award for the most outstanding contribution by a student. This year the award was given to Alp Atici for his paper "Learning Unions of $\omega(1)$-Dimensional Rectangles," co-authored by Rocco A. Servedio. We would like to thank Google for sponsoring the E. M. Gold Award.

Algorithmic Learning Theory 2006 was the 17th in a series of annual conferences established in Japan in 1990. A second root is the conference series Analogical and Inductive Inference previously held in 1986, 1989, 1992 which merged with the conference series ALT after a collocation in the year 1994. From then on, ALT became an international conference series, which kept its strong links to Japan but was also regularly held at overseas destinations including Australia, Germany, Italy, Singapore, Spain and the USA.

Continuation of ALT 2006 was supervised by its Steering Committee consisting of Naoki Abe (IBM Thomas J. Watson Research Center, Yorktown, USA), Shai Ben-David (University of Waterloo, Canada), Roni Khardon (Tufts University, Medford, USA), Steffen Lange (FH Darmstadt, Germany), Philip M. Long (Google, Mountain View, USA), Hiroshi Motoda (Osaka University, Japan), Akira Maruoka (Tohoku University, Sendai, Japan), Takeshi Shinohara (Kyushu Institute of Technology, Iizuka, Japan), Osamu Watanabe (Tokyo Institute of Technology, Japan), Arun Sharma (Queensland University of Technology, Brisbane, Australia – Co-chair), Frank Stephan (National University of Singapore, Republic of Singapore) and Thomas Zeugmann (Hokkaido University, Japan – Chair).

We would in particular like to thank Thomas Zeugmann for his continuous support of the ALT conference series and in particular for running the ALT Web page and the ALT submission system which he programmed together with Frank Balbach and Jan Poland. Thomas Zeugmann assisted us in many questions with respect to running the conference and to preparing the proceedings.

The ALT 2006 conference was made possible by the financial and administrative support of the PASCAL network, which organized this meeting together with others in the framework of PASCAL Dialogues 2006. Furthermore, we acknowledge the support of Google by financing the E. M. Gold Award (the corresponding award at Discovery Science 2006 was sponsored by Yahoo). We are grateful for the dedication of the host, the Universitat Politécnica de Catalunya (UPC), who organized the conference with much dedication and contributed to ALT in many ways. We want to express our gratitude to the Local Arrangements Chair Ricard Gavaldà and all other colleagues from the UPC, UPF and UB, who put so much time into making ALT 2006 to a success. Here we want also acknowledge the local sponsor Idescat, Statistical Institute of Catalonia. Furthermore, the Institute for Theoretical Computer Science of the University of Lübeck as well as the Division of Computer Science, Hokkaido University, Sapporo, supported ALT 2006.

The conference series ALT was this year collocated with the series Discovery Science as in many previous years. We are greatful for this continuous collaboration and would like in particular to thank the conference Chair Klaus P. Jantke and the Programme Committee Chairs Nada Lavrac and Ljupco Todorovski of Discovery Science 2006.

We also want to thank the Programme Committee and the subreferees (both listed on the next pages) for their hard work in selecting a good programme for ALT 2006. Reviewing papers and checking the correctness of results are demanding in time and skills and we very much appreciated this contribution to the conference.

Last but not least we also want to thank the authors for choosing ALT 2006 as a forum to report on their research.

August 2006   Jose L. Balcázar
                                                               Philip M. Long
                                                               Frank Stephan

Organization

Conference Chair

Jose L. Balcázar   Universitat Politécnica de Catalunya, Barcelona, Spain

Program Committee

Shai Ben-David	University of Waterloo
Olivier Bousquet	Pertinence
Nader Bshouty	Technion
Nicolò Cesa-Bianchi	Universitá degli Studi di Milano
Henning Fernau	University of Hertfordshire
Bill Gasarch	University of Maryland
Sally Goldman	Washington University in St. Louis
Kouichi Hirata	Kyushu Institute of Technology, Iizuka
Marcus Hutter	IDSIA
Efim Kinber	Sacred Heart University
Philip M. Long	Google (Co-chair)
Shie Mannor	McGill University
Eric Martin	The University of New South Wales
Partha Niyogi	University of Chicago
Steffen Lange	Fachhochschule Darmstadt
Hans-Ulrich Simon	Ruhr-Universität Bochum
Frank Stephan	National University of Singapore (Co-chair)
Etsuji Tomita	The University of Electro-Communications
Sandra Zilles	DFKI

Local Arrangements

Ricard Gavaldà   Universitat Politécnica de Catalunya, Barcelona, Spain

Subreferees

Hiroki Arimura	Francisco Casacuberta
Amos Beimel	Alexey Chernov
Jochen Blath	Alexander Clark

Frank Drewes
Vitaly Feldman
Dmitry Gavinsky
Robert Glaubius
Gunter Grieser
Colin de la Higuera
Hiroki Ishizaka
Yuri Kalnishkan
Roni Khardon
Adam Klivans
Shigenobu Kobayashi
Shane Legg
Hanna Mazzawi
Tetsuhiro Miyahara
Sayan Mukherjee
Thomas Nichols
Jan Poland

Michael Richter
Sebastien Roch
Joseph Romano
Daniel Reidenbach
Cynthia Rudin
Daniil Ryabko
Hiroshi Sakamoto
Rocco Servedio
Takeshi Shinohara
William D. Smart
Yasuhiro Tajima
Eiji Takimoto
Franck Thollard
Vladimir Vovk
Mitsuo Wakatsuki
Osamu Watanabe

Sponsoring Institutions

Spanish Ministry of Science

Google

Pascal Network of Excellence

PASCAL Dialogues 2006

Universitat Politècnica de Calalunya

Idescat, Statistical Institute of Catalonia

Institut für Theoretische Informatik, Universität Lübeck

Division of Computer Science, Hokkaido University

Table of Contents

Invited Contributions

Regular Contributions

Editors' Introduction

Jose L. Balcázar, Philip M. Long, and Frank Stephan

The conference "Algorithmic Learning Theory 2006" is dedicated to studies of learning from a mathematical and algorithmic perspective. Researchers consider various abstract models of the problem of learning and investigate how the learning goal in such a setting can be formulated and achieved. These models describe ways to define

- the goal of learning,
- how the learner retrieves information about its environment,
- how to form of the learner's models of the world (in some cases).

Retrieving information is in some models is passive where the learner just views a stream of data. In other models, the learner is more active, asking questions or learning from its actions. Besides explicit formulation of hypotheses in an abstract language with respect to some indexing system, there are also more implicit methods like making predictions according to the current hypothesis on some arguments which then are evaluated with respect to their correctness and wrong predictions (coming from wrong hypotheses) incur some loss on the learner. In the following, a more detailed introduction is given to the five invited talks and then to the regular contributions.

Gunnar Rätsch works on boosting and support vector machines. His is also interested in online-learning, optimisation theory, new inference principles and new types of machine learning problems. He also applies his results to real word problems from computational biology and chemistry. In his invited talk for ALT 2006, Gunnar spoke about using boosting techniques to solve semi-infinite linear programs, which can be used to address a wide variety of learning problems, including learning to make complex predictions.

Carole Goble works on the World-Wide Web, particularly the Semantic Web and Electronic Science / Grids. As the name suggests, the Semantic Web aims to facilitate the expression and use of meaning on the World-Wide Web. Electronic Science is scientific investigation in which groups are distributed globally. In her invited lecture for DS 2006, Garole Goble presented these two areas and laid out why these two areas depend on each other.

Hans Ulrich Simon studies the complexity of learning, that is, how much of resources of various types are needed for solving theoretically formulated learning problems. In particular, he has worked on query-learning and statistical models. In his invited talk for ALT 2006, Hans Ulrich Simon described work on the learnability of function classes using statistical queries, in which an algorithm interacts with the environment by asking for estimates of probabilities. The model is motivated because previous work had shown that algorithms that obey such a restriction can be made robust against certain kinds of noise. For finite classes, Hans described connections between the complexity of learning with statistical queries

J.L. Balcázar, P.M. Long, and F. Stephan (Eds.): ALT 2006, LNAI 4264, pp. 1–9, 2006.

and the structure of the matrix of correlations between pairs of possible target functions. The structure is captured by the spectral norm of this matrix.

Padhraic Smyth works on all aspects linked to large scale databases as they are found in many applications. To extract and retrieve useful information from such large data bases is an important practical problem. For that reason, his research focusses on using large databases to build descriptive models that are both accurate and understandable. His invited talk for DS 2006 is on data-driven discovery with statistical approaches. Generative probabilistic models have already been proven a useful framework in machine learning from scientific data and the key ideas of this research include (a) representing complex stochastic phenomena using the structured language of graphical models, (b) using latent (hidden) variables for inference about unobserved phenomena and (c) leveraging Bayesian ideas for learning and predicting. Padhraic Smyth began his talk with a brief review of learning from data with hidden variables and then discussed some recent work in this area.

Andrew Y. Ng has research interests in machine learning and pattern recognition, statistical artificial intelligence, reinforcement learning and adaptive control algorithms for text and web data processing. He presented the joint invited talk of ALT 2006 and DS 2006. His talk was on algorithms for control that learn by observing the behaviors of competent agents, rather than through trial and error, the traditional reinforcement learning approach.

The Presentation for the E. M. Gold Award. The first contributed talk presented at ALT 2006 was the talk "Learning unions of $\omega(1)$-dimensional rectangles" by Alp Atici and Rocco Servedio for which the first author received the E. M. Gold Award, as the program committee felt it was the best contribution submitted to ALT 2006 which is co-authored by a student. Atici and Servedio study the learnability of unions of rectangles over $\{0, 1, \ldots, b-1\}^n$ in dependence of b and n. They give algorithms polynomial in n and $\log b$ to learn concepts which are the majority of polynomially many or the union of polylogarithmically many rectangles of dimension a bit below $\log(n \log b)$ and $\log^2(n \log b)$, respectively.

Query Learning. Query Learning is a learning model where a learner or pupil asks a teacher questions about the concept to be learned. One important component of this model is a formal query language used during the learning process; the teacher has to answer every query posed in this language correctly. In this model, the complexity of a learning problem is the maximum number of queries needed by the best learning algorithm provided that the answers of the teacher meet the given specifications; however the teacher himself can be adversary in the sense that he can make the learner to learn as slow as possible as long as he does not violate the constraints. In some settings, also probabilistic teachers are considered instead of adversarial ones.

Nader H. Bshouty and Ehab Wattad investigate the question of how to learn halfspaces with random consistent hypothesis. In their model, the learner combines in each round several randomly selected halfspaces consistent with all data seen so far by majority vote to one object and then queries the teacher whether these objects are correct. If so, the learner has succeeded; otherwise the teacher returns a counterexample where the hypothesis and the concept to be learnt disagree. In addition to the teacher, the learner has access to a random oracle returning half spaces consistent with the counterexamples seen so far. The authors show that this algorithm needs roughly only two thirds as many queries to the teacher as the best known previous algorithm working with single halfspaces as hypotheseses space.

Matti Kääriäinen deals with the setting where the learner receives mostly unlabeled data, but can actively ask a teacher to label some of the data. Most previous work on this topic has concerned the realizable case, in which some member of a concept class achieves perfect accuracy. Kääriäinen considers the effects of relaxing this constraint in different ways on what can be proved about active learning algorithms.

Jorge Castro extends the setting of exact learning with queries into the world of quantum mechanics. He obtains counterparts of a number of results on exact learning; the new results hold for algorithms that can ask queries that exploit quantum effects.

The complexity of teaching. Learning and teaching are viewing the learning process from two sides. While learning mainly focusses on the aspect of how to extract information from the teacher, teaching focusses on the question of how to help a pupil to learn fast; in the most pessimistic models, the teacher must *force* learning. In this model it can be more interesting to consider randomized or adversarial learners than cooperative ones; a teacher and a cooperative pupil might agree on some coding which permits rapid learning success. Nevertheless, the learner should have some type of consistency constraint since otherwise the teacher cannot force the learner to update wrong hypotheses.

Frank Balbach and Thomas Zeugmann consider in their paper a setting where the learning task consists only of finitely many concepts and the learner keeps any hypothesis until it becomes inconsistent with the current datum presented by the teacher; at that moment the learner revises the hypothesis to a new one chosen from all consistent hypothesis at random with respect to the uniform distribution. The authors show that it is NP-hard to find out whether a good teacher might force the learners to learn a given polynomial-sized class in a given time with high probability. Furthermore, the choice of the sequence on which the learners would succeed is hard; as otherwise one could simulate the learners on this sequence and retrieve their expected behaviour from that knowledge.

Inductive Inference and its complexity. Inductive inference is the learning-theoretic counterpart to recursion theory and studies the learnability of classes of recursive or recursively enumerable sets in the limit. Gold's fundamental paradigm is that such a class is given and that the learner sees an infinite sequence in arbitrary, perhaps adversary order containing all the elements of the set but nothing else except perhaps pause symbols. From these data and some implicit knowledge about the class the learner makes a finite sequence of conjectures such that the last one is an index for the set to be learned, that is, an algorithm which enumerates the members of the given set. Gold showed already that the class of all recursively enumerable sets is not learnable and since then many variants of his basic model have been addressed, which mainly tried to capture not only the learning process in principle but also its complexity. How many mind changes are needed, how much memory of data observed so far has to be kept, what types of revisions of the previous hypothesis to the current one is needed? An example for such an additional constraint is that some interesting classes but not all learnable ones can be identified by learners which never output a conjecture which is a proper subset of some previous conjecture.

Stephen Fenner and William Gasarch dedicated their paper to a specific learning problem, namely, given a language A find the minimum-state deterministic finite automaton accepting the language SUBSEQ(A) which consists of all substrings of strings contained in A; this language is always regular and thus the corresponding automaton exists. In their approach, the data is given as an informant which reveals not only the members of A but also the nonmembers of A. Nevertheless, SUBSEQ(A) can only be learned for restrictive classes of sets A like the class of all finite or the class of all regular sets. If the class is sufficiently rich, learning fails. For example there is no learner which learns SUBSEQ(A) for all polynomial time computable sets A. They show that for every recursive ordinal α there is a class such that one can learn SUBSEQ(A) from any given A in this class with α mind changes but not with β mind changes for any $\beta < \alpha$.

Matthew de Brecht and Akihiro Yamamoto show in their paper that the class of unbounded unions of languages of regular patterns with constant segment length bound is inferable from positive data with an ordinal mind change bound. The authors give depending on the length of the constant segments considered and the size of the alphabet bounds which are always between the ordinals ω^ω and ω^{ω^ω}. The authors claim that their class is the first natural class (besides those classes as in the previous paper obtained by coding ordinals) for which the mind change complexity is an ordinal beyond ω^ω. The authors discover that there is a link from their topic to proof theory.

Sanjay Jain and Efim Kinber contributed to ALT 2006 two joint papers. In their first paper they deal with the following requirement: If a a learner does not see a full text T of a language L to be learnt but just a text of some subset, then it should still converge to some hypothesis which is a superset of the content of the text T. There are several variants considered with respect how the language W_e generated by the hypothesis relates to L: in the first variant, $W_e \subseteq L$, in the second variant, $W_e \subseteq L'$ for some class L' in the class $\mathcal{C}$ of languages to be learnt; in the third variant, $W_e \in \mathcal{C}$. It is shown that these three models are different and it is characterised when a uniformly recursive class of languages is learnable under one of these criteria.

Sanjay Jain and Efim Kinber consider in their second paper iterative learning where the learner reads one by one the data and either ignores it or updates the current hypothesis to a new one which only depends on the previous hypothesis and the current datum. The authors extend in their work this model such that they permit the learner to test its current hypothesis with a teacher by a subset query and to use the negative information arising from the counterexample for the case that they are wrong. The authors consider three variants of their model with respect to the choice of the counterexample by the teacher: whether it is the least negative counterexample, bounded by the maximum size of input seen so far or just arbitrary. The authors compare these three notions with each other and also with other important models from the field of inductive inference.

Sanjay Jain, Steffen Lange and Sandra Zilles study incremental, that is, iterative learning from either positive data only or from positive and negative data. They focus on natural requirements such as conservativeness and consistency. Conservativeness requires that whenever the learner makes a mind change it has already seen a counterexample to this hypothesis. Consistency requires that the learner always outputs a hypothesis which generates all data seen so far and perhaps also some more. There are several variants of these requirements, for example with respect to the question what the learer is permitted or not permitted to do with data not coming from any language to be learnt. The authors study how these versions relate to iterative learning.

Online learning. The difference between online and offline learning is that the online learner has to react to data immediately while the offline learner reads all the data and then comes up with a programme for the function. The most popular online learning model can be viewed as a prediction game to learn a function f: in each of a series of rounds, the learner encounters an item x; the learner makes a prediction y for the value $f(x)$; the learner discovers the true value of $f(x)$. For each wrong prediction, the learner might suffer some loss. The overall goal is keep the total loss small.

In many settings of online learning, there is already a pool of experts whose advice (predictions) are heard by the learner before making the prediction. The learner takes this advice into account and also collects statistics on the realiability of the various experts. It is often advisable to combine the expert predictions, e.g. through some kind of weighted voted, rather than to greedily follow the expert that appears to be best at a given time. Evaluating and combining experts has become a discipline on its own inside the community of online learning.

Nader H. Bshouty and Iddo Bentov focus on the question of the dependence of the performance of a prediction algorithm on the way the data is presented: does the data where the learner has to make a prediction for a Boolean function come adversarily, from a uniform distribution or from a random walk? The authors consider a few particular exact learning models based on a random walk stochastic process. Such models are more restricted than the well known general exact learning models. They give positive and negative results as to whether learning in these particular models is easier than in the general learning models.

Eyal Even-Dar, Michael Kearns and Jennifer Wortman want to incorporate explicit risk considerations into standard models of worst-case online learning: they want to combine the forecasts of the experts not only with respect to the expected rewards but also by taking into account the risk in order to obtain the best trade-off between these two parameters. They consider two common measures balancing returns and risk: the Sharpe ratio and the mean-variance criterion of Markowitz. It turns out to be impossible to build no-regret algorithms under these measures. But the authors show that the algorithm of Cesa-Bianchi, Mansour and Stoltz achieves nontrivial performance when a modified risk-return measure is used.

Vladimir Vovk considers the experts as given by a pool of prediction strategies represented as functions in a normed function class. Considering mostly those strategies whose norm is not too large, it is well known that there is a "master prediction strategy" that performs almost as well as all of these strategies. The author constructs a "leading prediction strategy" which even serves as a standard for the prediction strategies in the pool: each of them suffers a small loss to the degree that its predictions resemble the leading stategy's prediction and only those strategies are successful which copycat it. This result is first given for quadratic loss functions and later extended to other loss functions like Bregman divergences.

Chamy Allenberg, Peter Auer, László Györfi and György Ottucsák study the sequential prediction problem of combining expert advice. They consider a multi-round scenario and unbounded loss where the aim of the learner is to lose on long term in each round not more than the best expert. Furthermore, the feedback received by the learner is not complete. Such a scenario is called "partial monitoring" and the learner is informed about the performance of the expert it wants to track only with a certain probability; the scenario is the combination of the label efficient and multi-armed bandit problem. The authors obtain for bounded and unbounded losses the following results. In the case of bounded losses, the authors develop an algorithm whose expected regret is more or less the square root of the loss of the best expert. In the case of unbounded losses, the authors' algorithm achieves Hannan consistency, in dependence of the average over the squared loss of all experts.

Forecasting. The next papers address general questions similar to those in online learning. For example, how much rewards can a forecaster receive in the limit or how can Solomonoff's nonrecursive forecaster be approximated? The settings considered include predictions of values of functions from $\mathbb{N}$ to $\mathbb{N}$ by deterministic machines as well as probabilistic forcasters dealing with functions of finite domains.

Marcus Hutter addresses mainly the question what can be said about the expected rewards on the long run. As they are less and less secure to be obtained, the author introduces some discounting factors for future rewards. He compares the average reward U received in the first m rounds with the discounted sum over all possible future rewards from some round k onwards. The author considers arbitrary discount and reward sequences; that is, the discounts need not to be geometric and the environments do not need to be Markov decision processes. He shows that the limits of U for $m \to \infty$ and V for $k \to \infty$ are equal whenever both limits exist. Indeed it can happen that only one limit exists or even none. Therefore, the author gives a criterion such that this criterion and the existence of the limit of U imply the existence of the limit of V. The author also provides such a criterion for the reverse implication.

Jan Poland investigates stochastic model selection. In particular he is interested in the use of the posterior (as used in Bayes' rule) for future predictions. There are three principle ways on how to do this which the author called "marginalization (integration over the hypotheses with respect to the posterior)", "MAP (taking the a posteriori most probable hypothesis)" and "stochastic model selection (selecting a hypothesis at random according to the posterior distribution)". For his work, the author makes two assumptions: that the hypothesis class is countable and that it contains the data generating the distribution. For the first two methods mentioned by the author (marginalization and MAP), strong consistency theorems are already known; these theorems guarantee almost sure convergence of the predictions to the truth and give bounds on the loss. The corresponding result was missing for the third method (stochastic model selection) and the author closes this gap.

Shane Legg dedicates his work to the question of how to overcome the principle problem, that Solomonoff's inductive learning model is not computable and thus not usable in the practice. Indeed people have tried from time to time to modify and weaken Solomonoff's rule such that one obtains general and powerful theories of prediction which are computable. Such algorithms exist indeed. The author analyses the Kolmogorov complexity of sequences and shows that the minimum Kolmogorov complexity of some recursive sequence not predicted by a predictor is approximately a lower bound for the Kolmogorov complexity of the predictor itself.

Boosting, Support Vector Machines and Kernel Methods. The next papers deal with specific algorithms or methods of learning. Support vector machines can be thought of as conducting linear classification using a large, even infinite, collection of features that are computed as a function of the raw inputs. A kernel provides inner products in the derived feature space, so efficiently computable kernels are useful for learning. Boosting is a method to improve a weak learner to a stronger one by identifying a collection of weak hypotheses that complement one another; this is often accomplished by training weak learners on data that has been reweighted to assign higher priority to certain examples.

Leonid Kontorovich, Corinna Cortes and Mehryar Mohri provide an embedding into feature space for which all members of the previously identified and expressive class of piecewise-testable languages are linearly separable. They also show that the kernel associated with this embedding can be computed in quadratic time.

Kohei Hatano investigates smooth boosting. Smooth boosting algorithms obey a constraint that they do not change the weight of examples by much; these have been shown to have a number of advantages. At the same time, a refinement of AdaBoost called InfoBoost, which takes a more detailed account of the strengths of the weak learners, has also been shown to have advantages. The author develops a new algorithm, GiniBoost, which incorporates both ideas. He provides a theoretical analysis and also adapts GiniBoost to the filtering framework.

Hsuan-Tien Lin and Ling Li investigate ordinal regression. This is a type of multiclass classification in which the classes are totally ordered (e.g. "one star, two stars, three stars,...”). The authors improve the theoretical treatment of this subject and construct two ORBoost algorithms which they compare with an adapted version of the algorithm RankBoost of Freund, Iyer, Shapire and Singer. Experiments were carried out to compare the two ORBoost algorithms with RankBoost, AdaBoost and support vector machines.

Reinforcement learning. In reinforcement learning, an agent can accrue immediate costs or benefits from its actions, but its actions also affect the environment, which can impact its prospects for long-term reward. One important effect is that, often, an agent only learns about actions that it takes, and, in constrast with other learning settings, not about actions that it could have taken.

Daniil Ryabko and Marcus Hutter consider reinforcement learning in the context where observations can have any form of stochastic dependence on past observations and actions. Such environments may be more general than Markov decision processes. The agent knows that its environment belongs to some given family of countably many environments, but the agent does not know in which of these environments it is. The agent tries – as usual – to achieve the best possible asymptotic reward. The authors study when there is an agent achieving asymptotically the best possible reward for any environment in the class and give some sufficient conditions on the class for the existence of such an agent.

Takeshi Shibata, Ryo Yoshinaka and Takashi Chikayama extend recent work on the learnability from positive data of some non-regular subclasses of context-free grammars to probabilistic languages. The authors introduce a new subclass of the simple grammars, called unifiable simple grammars. This is a superclass of the right-unique simple grammars, which Ryo Yoshinakai showed to be effeciently learnable from positive data in previous work. The authors show that the right-unique simple grammars are unifiable within their class of unifiable simple grammars. Furthermore, they generalise finite Markov decision processes to simple context-free decision processes. The authors apply their results on right-unique simple grammars and propose a reinforcement learning method on simple context-free decision proceeses.

Statistical Learning. Supervised learning means that the learner receives pairs $(x_0, y_0), (x_1, y_1), \ldots$ of items and their classifications. In the case of unsupervised learning, class designations are not provided. Nevertheless, in certain cases, it is still possible to extract from the distribution of the x_n useful information which either permits to reconstruct the y_n or to get information which is almost as useful as the original values y_n. Another field of learning is the construction of ranking functions: search machines like Google or Yahoo! must not only find on the internet the pages matching the requests of the users but also put them into an order such that those pages which the user searches are among the first ones displayed. Many of these ranking functions are not explicitly constructed but learned by analyzing the user behaviour, for example, by tracking down which links are accessed by the user and which not.

Andreas Maurer proposes a method of unsupervised learning from processes which are stationary and vector-valued. The learning method selects a low-dimensional subspace and tries to keep the data-variance high and the variance of the velocity vector low. The idea behind this is to make use of short-time dependencies of the process. In the theoretical part of the paper, the author obtains for absolutely regular processes error bounds which depend on the β-mixing coefficients and the consistency. The experimental part is done with image processing that the algorithm can learn feature maps which are geometrically invariant.

Atsuyoshi Nakamura studies the complexity of the class $\mathcal{C}$ of ranking functions which split the n-dimensional Euclidean space via $k-1$ parallel hyperplains into subsets mapped to $1, 2, \ldots, k$, respectively. He shows that the graph dimension of $\mathcal{C}$ is $\Theta(n+k)$, which is considerably smaller than the graph dimension of the corresponding decision list problem. The importance of the graph dimension is that it can be translated into an upper bound of the number of examples needed in PAC learning. The author also adapts his technique to show a risk bound for learning $\mathcal{C}$.

Solving Semi-infinite Linear Programs Using Boosting-Like Methods

Gunnar Rätsch

Friedrich Miescher Laboratory, Max Planck Society, Spemannstr. 39, 72076 Tübingen
Gunnar.Raetsch@tuebingen.mpg.de
http://www.fml.mpg.de/~raetsch

Linear optimization problems (LPs) with a very large or even infinite number of constraints frequently appear in many forms in machine learning. A linear program with m constraints can be written as

$$\min_{\mathbf{x} \in \mathcal{P}^n} \; \mathbf{c}^\top \mathbf{x}$$

$$\text{with} \;\; \mathbf{a}_j^\top \mathbf{x} \le b_j \quad \forall i = 1, \ldots, m,$$

where I assume for simplicity that the domain of $\mathbf{x}$ is the n dimensional probability simplex $\mathcal{P}^n$. Optimization problems with an infinite number of constraints of the form $\mathbf{a}_j^\top \mathbf{x} \le b_j$, for all $j \in J$, are called *semi-infinite*, when the index set J has infinitely many elements, e.g. $J = \mathbb{R}$. In the finite case the constraints can be described by a matrix with m rows and n columns that can be used to directly solve the LP. In semi-infinite linear programs (SILPs) the constraints are often given in a functional form depending on j or implicitly defined, for instance by the outcome of another algorithm.

In this work I consider several examples from machine learning where large LPs need to be solved. An important case is *boosting* – a method for combining classifiers in order to improve the accuracy (see [1] and references therein). The most well-known instance is AdaBoost [2]. Under certain assumptions it finds a separating hyperplane in an infinite dimensional feature space with a *large margin*, which amounts to solving a semi-infinite linear program. The algorithms that I will discuss to solve the SILPs have their roots in the AdaBoost algorithm. The second problem is the one of learning to predict structured outputs, which can be understood as a multi-class classification problem with a large number of classes. Here, every class and example generate a constraint leading to a huge optimization problem [3]. Such problems appear for instance in natural language processing, speech recognition as well as gene structure prediction [4]. Finally, I consider the case of learning the optimal convex combination of kernels for support vector machines [5, 6]. I show that it can be reduced to a semi-infinite linear program [7] that is equivalent to a semi-definite programming formulation proposed in [8].

I will review several methods to solve such optimization problems, while mainly focusing on three algorithms related to boosting: *LPBoost*, *AdaBoost** and *TotalBoost*. They work by iteratively selecting violated constraints while refining the solution of the SILP. The selection of violated constraints is done in a problem dependent manner: a so-called *base learning algorithm* is employed in boosting, dynamic programming is applied for structured output learning and a single

J.L. Balcázar, P.M. Long, and F. Stephan (Eds.): ALT 2006, LNAI 4264, pp. 10–11, 2006.
© Springer-Verlag Berlin Heidelberg 2006

kernel support vector machine is used for multiple kernel learning. The main difference between optimization strategies is how they determine intermediate solutions. The first and conceptually simplest algorithm is *LPBoost* [9] and works by iteratively adding violated constraints to a restricted LP. The algorithm is known to converge [10, 11, 12] under mild assumptions but no convergence rates could be proven. The second algorithm, *AdaBoost** [13], is closely related to AdaBoost and works by multiplicatively updating the iterate based on the violated constraint. It was shown that this algorithm solves the problem with accuracy ϵ in at most $\lceil 2 \log(n)/\epsilon^2 \rceil$ iterations. However, it turns out that *LPBoost*, which does not come with an iteration bound, is considerably faster than *AdaBoost** in practice. We have therefore worked on a new algorithm, called *TotalBoost* [14], that combines the advantages of both strategies: empirically it is at least as fast as *LPBoost* and it comes with the same convergence rates as AdaBoost*.

References

1. R. Meir and G. Rätsch. An introduction to boosting and leveraging. In S. Mendelson and A. Smola, editors, *Advanced Lectures on Machine Learning*, LNCS, pages 119–184. Springer, 2003.
2. Y. Freund and R.E. Schapire. A decision-theoretic generalization of on-line learning and an application to boosting. *Journal of Computer and System Sciences*, 55(1):119–139, 1997.
3. Y. Altun, I. Tsochantaridis, and T. Hofmann. Hidden Markov support vector machines. In *Proc. ICML'03*, pages 3–10. AAAI Press, 2003.
4. G. Rätsch, S. Sonnenburg, J. Srinivasan, H. Witte, K.-R. Müller, R. Sommer, and B. Schölkopf. Improving the C. elegans genome annotation using machine learning. *PLoS Computational Biology*, 2006. Under revision.
5. C. Cortes and V.N. Vapnik. Support vector networks. *Machine Learning*, 20:273–297, 1995.
6. G. Lanckriet, N. Cristianini, L. Ghaoui, P. Bartlett, and M. Jordan. Learning the kernel matrix with semidefinite programming. *Journal of Machine Learning Research*, 5:27–72, 2004.
7. S. Sonnenburg, G. Rätsch, C. Schäfer, and B. Schölkopf. Large scale multiple kernel learning. *Journal of Machine Learning Research*, pages 1531–1565, July 2006.
8. F. Bach, G. Lanckriet, and M. Jordan. Multiple kernel learning, conic duality, and the SMO algorithm. In C. E. Brodley, editor, *Proc. ICML'04*. ACM, 2004.
9. A. Demiriz, K.P. Bennett, and J. Shawe-Taylor. Linear programming boosting via column generation. *Machine Learning*, 46:225–254, 2002.
10. R. Hettich and K.O. Kortanek. Semi-infinite programming: Theory, methods and applications. *SIAM Review*, 3:380–429, September 1993.
11. G. Rätsch, A. Demiriz, and K. Bennett. Sparse regression ensembles in infinite and finite hypothesis spaces. *Machine Learning*, 48(1-3):193–221, 2002.
12. G. Rätsch. *Robust Boosting via Convex Optimization*. PhD thesis, University of Potsdam, Neues Palais 10, 14469 Potsdam, Germany, October 2001.
13. G. Rätsch and M.K. Warmuth. Efficient margin maximization with boosting. *Journal of Machine Learning Research*, 6:2131–2152, 2005.
14. M.K. Warmuth, J. Liao, and G. Rätsch. Totally corrective boosting algorithms that maximize the margin. In W. Cohen and A. Moore, editors, *Proc. ICML'06*, pages 1001–1008. ACM Press, 2006.

e-Science and the Semantic Web: A Symbiotic Relationship

Carole Goble[1], Oscar Corcho[1], Pinar Alper[1], and David De Roure[2]

[1] School of Computer Science
The University of Manchester
Manchester M13 9PL, UK
{carole, ocorcho, penpecip}@cs.man.ac.uk
[2] School of Electronics and Computer Science
University of Southampton
Southampton SO17 1BJ, UK
dder@ecs.soton.ac.uk

e-Science is scientific investigation performed through distributed global collaborations between scientists and their resources, and the computing infrastructure that enables this [4]. Scientific progress increasingly depends on pooling know-how and results; making connections between ideas, people, and data; and finding and reusing knowledge and resources generated by others in perhaps unintended ways. It is about harvesting and harnessing the "collective intelligence" of the scientific community. The Semantic Web is an extension of the current Web in which information is given well-defined meaning to facilitate sharing and reuse, better enabling computers and people to work in cooperation [1]. Applying the Semantic Web paradigm to e-Science [3] has the potential to bring significant benefits to scientific discovery [2]. We identify the benefits of lightweight and heavyweight approaches, based on our experiences in the Life Sciences.

References

1. T. Berners-Lee, J. Hendler, and O. Lassila. The semantic web. *Scientific American*, 284(5):34–43, 2001.
2. C. Goble. Using the semantic web for e-science: inspiration, incubation, irritation. *4th International Semantic Web Conference*, 2005.
3. J. Hendler. Science and the semantic web. *Science*, 299:520–521, 2003.
4. T. Hey. and A.E. Trefethen. Cyberinfrastructure for e-science. *Science*, 308(5723):817–821, 2005.

J.L. Balcázar, P.M. Long, and F. Stephan (Eds.): ALT 2006, LNAI 4264, p. 12, 2006.
© Springer-Verlag Berlin Heidelberg 2006

Spectral Norm in Learning Theory: Some Selected Topics*

Hans Ulrich Simon

Fakultät für Mathematik, Ruhr-Universität Bochum, 44780 Bochum, Germany
simon@lmi.rub.de

Abstract. In this paper, we review some known results that relate the statistical query complexity of a concept class to the spectral norm of its correlation matrix. Since spectral norms are widely used in various other areas, we are then able to put statistical query complexity in a broader context. We briefly describe some non-trivial connections to (seemingly) different topics in learning theory, complexity theory, and cryptography. A connection to the so-called Hidden Number Problem, which plays an important role for proving bit-security of cryptographic functions, will be discussed in somewhat more detail.

1 Introduction

Kearns' Statistical Query (SQ) model [7] is an elegant abstraction from Valiant's PAC learning model [14].[1] In this model, instead of having direct access to random examples (as in the PAC learning model) the learner obtains information about random examples via an oracle that provides estimates of various statistics about the unknown concept. Kearns showed that any learning algorithm that is successful in the SQ model can be converted, without much loss of efficiency, into a learning algorithm that is successful in the PAC learning model despite noise uniformly applied to the class labels of the examples. In the same paper where Kearns showed that SQ learnability implies noise-tolerant PAC learnability, he developed SQ algorithms for almost all function classes known to be efficiently learnable in the PAC learning model. This had raised the question of whether any concept class that is efficiently learnable by a noise-tolerant learner in the PAC learning model might already be efficiently learnable in the SQ model. This question was (at least partially) answered to the negative by Blum, Kalai, and Wasserman [3] who presented a concept class that has an efficient noise-tolerant[2] PAC learner but (provably) has no efficient SQ learner. However, classes that distinguish between the model of noise-tolerant PAC learning and SQ learning

---

* This work was supported in part by the IST Programme of the European Community, under the PASCAL Network of Excellence, IST-2002-506778. This publication only reflects the authors' views.
[1] The model of "Learning by Distances" [1] seems to be equivalent to the SQ model. For our purpose, the notation within the SQ model is more convenient.
[2] For noise rate bounded away from $1/2$.

seem to be extremely rare. Thus, the non-existence of an efficient SQ learner often indicates that finding an efficient and noise-tolerant PAC learner might also be hard to achieve.

Information-theoretic lower bounds in the PAC model are stated in terms of the VC-dimension. Information-theoretic lower bounds in the in the SQ model have a much different (more algebraic) flavor. Blum et al. [2] have shown that, roughly speaking, the number of statistical queries being necessary and sufficient for weakly learning a concept class is polynomially related to the largest number of pairwise "almost orthogonal" concepts from this class (the so-called SQ Dimension). Ke Yang [17] presented an alternative (stronger but polynomially equivalent) lower bound on the number of statistical queries. It is stated in terms of the eigenvalues of the correlation matrix C associated with the concept class. A simplified variant of this lower bound is stated in terms of the spectral norm (= largest eigenvalue) of C. There exist classes which are weakly learnable in the SQ model, but not strongly. Ke Yang [16, 17] invented a technique that allows to prove statements of this type (at least occasionally for specific classes). A variant of this technique [18] yields lower bounds in the so-called model of SQ Sampling (related to quantum computing). In this model, the goal of the learner is to find a positive example of the unknown target concept (again by means of statistical queries).

In the first part of this paper (up to section 5), we partially review the work about SQ learning in [2, 16, 17, 18]. In order to present the results in the technically simplest fashion, we introduce the Correlation Query (CQ) model that replaces statistical queries by correlation queries. Correlation queries deal with predicates on instances (whereas statistical queries deal with predicates on *labeled* instances). Upon a correlation query, the CQ oracle will return an estimate for the correlation between this predicate and the target concept. While the SQ and CQ oracle turn out to be equivalent in a rather strong sense, the CQ model will be much more convenient for our purposes.[3]

In the second part of the paper (beginning in section 6), we briefly describe some non-trivial connections to (seemingly) different topics in learning theory, complexity theory, and cryptography. A connection to the so-called Hidden Number Problem, which plays an important role for proving bit-security of cryptographic functions, will be discussed in somewhat more detail.

2   Definitions and Notations

Concept Learning: A *concept* is a function f of the form $f : X \to \{\pm 1\}$. A concept class, denoted as $\mathcal{F}$, is a set of concepts. Throughout this paper, X is a finite set called the *domain*. An element $x \in X$ is called an *instance*. A labeled instance $(x, b) \in X \times \{\pm 1\}$ is called an *example for f* if $b = f(x)$. $D : X \to [0, 1]$

---

[3] The relation between statistical queries and correlation queries is implicitly contained in some of the existing papers. But, since the equivalence is never stated explicitly, no paper exploits the potential for possible simplification to full extent.

denotes a mapping that assigns probabilities to instances such that $D(x) \geq 0$ for all $x \in X$ and $\sum_{x \in X} D(x) = 1$. Notations $\Pr_D[\cdot]$ and $\mathbb{E}_D[\cdot]$ refer to the probability of an event and to the expectation of a random variable, respectively. A function $h : X \to \{\pm 1\}$ (not necessarily from $\mathcal{F}$) is called a *hypothesis*. We say that h is ε-*accurate for* f if $\Pr_D[h(x) \neq f(x)] \leq \varepsilon$. Informally, the goal of a learner for concept class $\mathcal{F}$ is to infer an ε-accurate hypothesis for an unknown *target concept* $f \in \mathcal{F}$ from "partial information". There must be a uniform learning algorithm for all choices of $f \in \mathcal{F}$ and $\varepsilon > 0$ (and sometimes, but not in this paper, also for all choices of D and other relevant parameters). The formal notion of "partial information" depends on the learning model in consideration. We assume the reader to be familiar with the PAC learning model [14] where the information given to the learner consists of random examples for the unknown target concept. We will be mainly concerned with the SQ model that is outlined in the next paragraph.

Statistical Query Learning: In this model, the learner has access to random examples only indirectly through statistical queries that are answered by an oracle. A statistical query is of the form $SQ(\hbar, \tau)$ where $\hbar : X \times \{\pm 1\} \to \{\pm 1\}$ denotes a binary predicate on labeled instances and $\tau > 0$ is a *tolerance parameter*. Upon such a query, the oracle returns a τ-*approximation* for $\mathbb{E}_D[\hbar(x, f(x)]$, i.e., it returns a number d that satisfies

$$\mathbb{E}_D[\hbar(x, f(x)] - \tau \leq d \leq \mathbb{E}_D[\hbar(x, f(x)] + \tau .$$

We briefly note that

$$\mathbb{E}_D[\hbar(x, f(x)] = \Pr_D[\hbar(x, f(x)) = +1] - \Pr_D[\hbar(x, f(x)) = -1] .$$

We will measure the "efficiency" of the learner by the number of statistical queries, say q, that it passes to the oracle (in the worst-case), by the smallest tolerance parameter τ that is ever used during learning, and by the accuracy ε of the final hypothesis. It was shown by Kearns [7] that an SQ learner can be simulated by a noise-tolerant PAC learner that has access to $\text{poly}(q, 1/\tau, 1/\varepsilon)$ random examples.

Incidence and Correlation Matrix: The real-valued functions on domain X form an $|X|$-dimensional vector space that can be equipped with the following inner product:

$$\langle h_1, h_2 \rangle_D := \sum_{x \in X} D(x) h_1(x) h_2(x) = \mathbb{E}_D[h_1(x) h_2(x)]$$

With a concept class $\mathcal{F}$, we associate the *incidence matrix* $M \in \{\pm 1\}^{\mathcal{F} \times X}$ given by $M[f, x] := f(x)$ and the *correlation matrix* $C \in [-1, 1]^{\mathcal{F} \times \mathcal{F}}$ given by $C[f_1, f_2] := \langle f_1, f_2 \rangle_D$. Clearly, C is positive semidefinite. Let $\text{diag}(D) \in [0, 1]^{X \times X}$ denote the matrix with values $D(x)$ on the main diagonal and zeroes elsewhere. Then matrices C and M satisfy the relation $C = M \cdot \text{diag}(D) \cdot M^\top$. In particular, we have $C = \frac{1}{|X|} \cdot M \cdot M^\top$ if D is the uniform distribution.

Warning: We will use the analogous notations (and analogous remarks are valid) for the more general case, where $\mathcal{F}$ contains real-valued functions.

Correlation Query Learning: The definition of Correlation Query (CQ) learning is completely analogous to the definition of SQ learning with the only difference that we replace the SQ oracle by a CQ oracle. A correlation query is of the form $\mathrm{CQ}(h, \tau)$ for some function $h : X \to \{-1, 0, +1\}$ and $\tau > 0$. The oracle will return a τ-approximation of $\langle h, f \rangle_D$, where (as always) $f \in \mathcal{F}$ denotes the unknown target concept.

Warning: We will use this model (for technical reasons) also in the more general case where $\mathcal{F}$ contains real-valued functions.

Lower Bounds and Adversaries: The emphasis of this paper is on lower bounds. A well-known adversary argument for proving lower bounds is as follows. An adversary of the learner runs the learning algorithm, waits for queries, answers them in a malicious fashion and keeps track of the so-called *version space*. The latter, by definition, consists of all target concepts being consistent with all answers that have been returned so far to the learner. Intuitively, the adversary tries to keep the version space as "rich" as possible in order to slow down the progress made by the learner.

In order to make the lower bounds as strong as possible, we do not impose unnecessary restrictions on the learner. In particular, our lower bounds will be valid even in the following setting:

- The learner may output arbitrary functions $h : X \to \{-1, 0, +1\}$ as hypotheses.
- The learning algorithm need not be uniform w.r.t. domain distributions (since there is a fixed distribution D).
- The learner is already considered successful when its final hypothesis has a significant correlation, say γ, with the target concept. Note that a hypothesis whose correlation with f is γ is $(1/2 - \gamma/2)$-accurate for f, i.e., it has advantage $\gamma/2$ over random guessing.

Notations and Facts from Matrix Theory: Although we assume some familiarity with basic concepts from matrix theory, we provide the reader with a refreshment of his or her memory and fix some notation. The Euclidean norm of a vector $u \in \mathbb{R}^d$ is denoted as $\|u\|$. For a matrix M, $\|M\|$ denotes its spectral norm:

$$\|M\| = \sup_{u:\|u\|\leq 1} \|Mu\|$$

It is well-known that $\|M\|$ coincides with the largest singular value of M. If M is symmetric and positive semidefinite, then the largest singular value coincides with the largest eigenvalue. A matrix of the form $M \cdot M^\top$ (symmetric and positive semidefinite !) satisfies $\|M \cdot M^\top\| = \|M\|^2$. In particular, if M is an incidence matrix for a concept class $\mathcal{F}$ and $C = \frac{1}{|X|} M \cdot M^\top$ is the corresponding correlation matrix under the uniform distribution, we get the relation $\|C\| = \frac{1}{|X|} \|M\|^2$.

3   Statistical Queries Versus Correlation Queries

In this section we show that, from an information-theoretic point of view, statistical queries and correlation queries are equivalent: for any query of one kind, there is a query of the other kind that reveals precisely the same amount of information.

Consider a function $\hbar : X \times \{\pm 1\} \to \{\pm 1\}$. It induces the following split of the instance space:

$$X_0(\hbar) = \{x \in X \mid \hbar(x, +1) = \hbar(x, -1)\}$$
$$X_1(\hbar) = \{x \in X \mid \hbar(x, +1) \neq \hbar(x, -1)\}$$

Loosely speaking, $X_1(\hbar)$ contains the instances on which predicate $\hbar$ is "label-sensitive" whereas $\hbar$ is insensitive to labels of instances from $X_0(\hbar)$. With $\hbar$ we associate the following function $h : X \to \{-1, 0, +1\}$:

$$h(x) = \begin{cases} 0 & \text{if } x \in X_0(\hbar) \\ \hbar(x, 1) & \text{if } x \in X_1(\hbar) \end{cases}$$

Note that, for every $x \in X_1$ and every $b = \pm 1$,

$$\hbar(x, b) = b \cdot \hbar(x, 1) = b \cdot h(x) \ .$$

Now $\mathbb{E}_D[\hbar(x, f(x))]$ can be written in terms of $\langle h, f \rangle_D$ as follows:

$$\mathbb{E}_D[\hbar(x, f(x))] = \sum_{x \in X_0(\hbar)} D(x)\hbar(x, f(x)) + \sum_{x \in X_1(\hbar)} D(x)\hbar(x, f(x))$$

$$= \underbrace{\sum_{x \in X_0(\hbar)} D(x)\hbar(x, 1))}_{=:k(\hbar)} + \sum_{x \in X_1(\hbar)} D(x)f(x)h(x)$$

$$= k(\hbar) + \langle h, f \rangle_D \ ,$$

where $k(\hbar)$ depends on $\hbar$ only (and not on the target concept f).

Notice that the mapping $\hbar \mapsto h$ is surjective since any mapping $h : X \to \{-1, 0, +1\}$ has a pre-image, for instance the mapping $\hbar : X \times \{\pm 1\} \to \{\pm 1\}$ given by

$$\hbar(x, b) = \begin{cases} 1 & \text{if } h(x) = 0 \\ bh(x) & \text{otherwise} \end{cases} \ .$$

We conclude from these considerations, and in particular from the relation $\mathbb{E}_D[\hbar(x, f(x))] = k(\hbar) + \langle h, f \rangle_D$ that there are mutual simulations between an SQ-oracle and a CQ-oracle such that answers to $SQ(\hbar, \tau)$ and to $CQ(h, \tau)$ provide the same amount of information. Thus, we arrive at the following result:

Theorem 1. *There exists an algorithm that finds a ε-accurate hypothesis for every target concept $f \in \mathcal{F}$ by means of q statistical queries whose tolerance parameters are lower-bounded by τ respectively if and only if there exists an algorithm that finds a ε-accurate hypothesis for every target concept $f \in \mathcal{F}$ by means of q correlation queries whose tolerance parameters are lower-bounded by τ respectively.*

4   A Lower Bound in Terms of the Spectral Norm

In the sequel, we say "function class" (as opposed to "concept class") when we allow real function values different from ± 1.

Theorem 2 ([17]). *Consider a finite function class $\mathcal{F}$ (with correlation matrix C) and a learning algorithm for $\mathcal{F}$ in the CQ model with the following features:*

- *It outputs a hypothesis h satisfying $\langle h, f \rangle_D > \gamma$, where f denotes the target concept.*
- *It makes at most q statistical queries none of which uses a tolerance parameter smaller than τ.*

Let $\lambda_1(C) \geq \cdots \geq \lambda_{|\mathcal{F}|}(C)$ be the eigenvalues of C. Then,

$$\sum_{i=1}^{q+1} \lambda_i(C) \geq |\mathcal{F}| \cdot \min\{\gamma^2, \tau^2\} \ . \tag{1}$$

Proof. We basically present the proof of Ke Yang [17] (modulo some slight simplifications resulting from the more convenient CQ model).[4] Consider an adversary that returns 0 upon correlation queries as long as this does not lead to an empty version space. Choose $q' \leq q$ maximal such that the first q' queries of the learner, say $\mathrm{CQ}(h_1, \tau_1), \mathrm{CQ}(h_2, \tau_2), \ldots, \mathrm{CQ}(h_{q'}, \tau_{q'})$, are answered 0. Let $h_{q'+1}$ denote the query function of the next correlation query if $q > q'$, and let $h_{q'+1}$ denote the final hypothesis of the learner if $q = q'$. Let $\mathcal{V} \subseteq \mathcal{F}$ denote the version space resulting after "queries" with query functions $h_1, \ldots, h_{q'}, h_{q'+1}$. By definition of q', $\mathcal{V}$ is empty if $q > q'$. Let $\mathcal{Q}$ denote the (at most) $q' + 1$-dimensional vector space spanned by $h_1, \ldots, h_{q'}, h_{q'+1}$. For every function $f \in \mathcal{F}$, the following holds:

- If $f \in \mathcal{V}$, then $q = q'$. Since $h_{q'+1}$ is the final hypothesis of the learner, it follows that $\langle h_{q'+1}, f \rangle_D \geq \gamma$.
- If $f \notin \mathcal{V}$, then f was eliminated after one of the first $q' + 1$ "queries". Thus there exists some $i \in \{1, \ldots, q' + 1\}$ such that $\langle h_i, f \rangle_D \geq \tau$.

We use $f^{\mathcal{Q}}$ to denote the projection of f into subspace $\mathcal{Q}$ and conclude that

$$\sum_{f \in \mathcal{F}} \|f^{\mathcal{Q}}\|^2 \geq |\mathcal{F}| \cdot \min\{\gamma^2, \tau^2\} \ . \tag{2}$$

On the other hand, it is a well-known fact from matrix theory that

$$\sum_{f \in \mathcal{F}} \|f^{\mathcal{Q}}\|^2 \leq \sum_{i=1}^{q'+1} \lambda_i \leq \sum_{i=1}^{q+1} \lambda_i \ . \tag{3}$$

Solving (2) and (3) for $\sum_{i=1}^{q+1} \lambda_i$ yields the result. □

---

[4] He considered only classes $\mathcal{F}$ with ± 1-valued functions, but his argument holds in the more general case of real-valued functions. The adversary technique applied in the proof goes back to [2].

The following result is immediate from Theorem 2 and the fact that $\mathcal{F}$ is not easier to learn than a subclass $\mathcal{F}' \subseteq \mathcal{F}$ (with correlation matrix C').

Corollary 1. *The number q of queries needed to learn $\mathcal{F}$ in the sense of Theorem 2 satisfies the following condition:*

$$\forall \mathcal{F}' \subseteq \mathcal{F} : \sum_{i=1}^{q+1} \lambda_i(C') \geq |\mathcal{F}'| \cdot \min\{\gamma^2, \tau^2\} \ .$$

Since the spectral norm of C, $\|C\|$, coincides with the largest eigenvalue, λ_1, (1) implies the following inequality:

$$q \geq \frac{|\mathcal{F}| \cdot \min\{\gamma^2, \tau^2\}}{\|C\|} - 1 \ . \tag{4}$$

Define

$$L(\mathcal{F}) := \sup_{\mathcal{F}' \subseteq \mathcal{F}} \frac{|\mathcal{F}'|}{\|C'\|} \ , \tag{5}$$

where C' denotes the correlation matrix associated with $\mathcal{F}'$. If D is the uniform distribution on X and M' denotes the incidence matrix of $\mathcal{F}'$, we have $\|C'\| = \frac{1}{|X|}\|M'\|^2$ and can rewrite (5) as follows:

$$L(\mathcal{F}) = \sup_{\mathcal{F}' \subseteq \mathcal{F}} \frac{|\mathcal{F}'| \cdot |X|}{\|M'\|^2} \ . \tag{6}$$

Analogously to Corollary 1, we obtain

Corollary 2. $q \geq L(\mathcal{F}) \cdot \min\{\gamma^2, \tau^2\} - 1.$ [5]

5   Related Lower Bounds

The lower bounds from section 4 are tailored to weak learning in the SQ model. These bounds get trivial when a class is efficiently weakly, but not strongly, learnable. Ke Yang [16, 17] presented a technique that allows to reduce the problem of (better than weakly) learning a class consisting of "(almost) uniformly correlated" concepts to the problem of weakly learning a corresponding class of "(almost) uncorrelated" concepts. To the latter class, the bounds from section 4 *do* apply. In this section, we present another (and even older) technique that is slightly simpler and fits the same purpose.[6] Furthermore, both techniques (Yang's and the technique from this section) lead to lower bounds in the so-called SQ Sampling model.

Throughout this section, D is the uniform distribution on X (and we omit index D in the notation of probabilities, expectations, and inner products). Consider a concept class $\mathcal{F}$ with the following properties:

---

[5] Even a slightly stronger bound of the form $q \geq L(\mathcal{F})\tau^2 - (\tau^2/\gamma^2)$ is valid (and proven in the full paper).

[6] A nice feature of Yang's technique is that it applies even when the SQ oracle is assumed as "honest". We conjecture that the alternative technique (described in this section) applies to honest oracles as well.

Property 1. There exists a constant $0 < \rho < 1/2$ such that, for every $f \in \mathcal{F}$,
$\Pr[f(x) = 1] = \rho$.

Property 2. There exists a constant s such that the matrix M_s, given by

$$M_s[f, x] = \begin{cases} s & \text{if } f(x) = 1 \\ -1 & \text{if } f(x) = -1 \end{cases} \quad ,$$

has pairwise orthogonal rows.

It is easy to see that s and ρ must satisfy the relation $s \geq (1 - 2\rho)/\rho$. It is furthermore easy to infer from property 1 that the constant function -1 is positively correlated with every concept from $\mathcal{F}$:

$$\forall f \in \mathcal{F} : \langle f, -1 \rangle = (1 - \rho) - \rho = 1 - 2\rho \ .$$

We will pursue the question how many queries it takes to find a hypothesis whose correlation with the target concept is significantly greater than $1 - 2\rho$.

The first important observation is that we can consider M_s as the incidence matrix of the function class $\mathcal{F}_s = \{f_s \mid f \in \mathcal{F}\}$ where f_s is given by

$$f_s(x) = \begin{cases} s & \text{if } f(x) = 1 \\ -1 & \text{if } f(x) = -1 \end{cases} \quad .$$

Since M_s has pairwise orthogonal rows and every row vector has squared Euclidean length $\rho|X|s^2 + (1 - \rho)|X|$, the correlation matrix $C_s = \frac{1}{|X|} \cdot M_s M_s^\top$ satisfies

$$C_s = \mathrm{diag}(\rho s^2 + 1 - \rho, \ldots, \rho s^2 + 1 - \rho) \ .$$

Thus $\|C_s\| = \rho s^2 + 1 - \rho$. Note that Corollary 2 applies to $\mathcal{F}_s$ and leads to a lower bound of the form

$$\frac{|\mathcal{F}|}{\rho s^2 + 1 - \rho} \min\{\gamma^2, \tau^2\} - 1 \tag{7}$$

with the usual meaning of γ and τ.

The second important observation is that the problems of learning $\mathcal{F}$ and $\mathcal{F}_s$ by correlation queries exhibit a close relationship. For a query function g, consider the following calculation:

$$\mathbb{E}[f(x)g(x)] = \mathbb{E}[f(x)g(x)|f(x) = 1] \cdot \rho + \mathbb{E}[f(x)g(x)|f(x) = -1] \cdot (1 - \rho)$$
$$= \mathbb{E}[g(x)|f(x) = 1] \cdot \rho - \mathbb{E}[g(x)|f(x) = -1] \cdot (1 - \rho)$$
$$\mathbb{E}[f_s(x)g(x)] = \mathbb{E}[g(x)|f(x) = 1] \cdot \rho s - \mathbb{E}[g(x)|f(x) = -1] \cdot (1 - \rho)$$
$$\mathbb{E}[g(x)] = \mathbb{E}[g(x)|f(x) = 1] \cdot \rho + \mathbb{E}[g(x)|f(x) = -1] \cdot (1 - \rho)$$

Now an easy calculation shows that

$$\mathbb{E}[f(x)g(x)] - \frac{s-1}{s+1}\mathbb{E}[-g] = \frac{2}{s+1}\mathbb{E}[f_s(x)g(x)] \ . \tag{8}$$

According to (8), the following holds:

Lemma 1. *g has a correlation of at least $\alpha + \frac{s-1}{s+1}\mathbb{E}[-g]$ with f iff g has a correlation of at least $\frac{s+1}{2}\alpha$ with f_s.*

Since $\mathbb{E}[-g] \leq 1$ (with equality for $g = -1$), we obtain

Corollary 3. *If g has a correlation of at least $\alpha + \frac{s-1}{s+1}$ with f, then g has a correlation of at least $\frac{s+1}{2}\alpha$ with f_s.*

Since the latter two results are valid for tolerance parameter τ in the role of α and for final correlation γ in the role of α, we get

Corollary 4. *The number of correlation queries (with smallest tolerance τ) needed to achieve a correlation of at least $\frac{s-1}{s+1} + \gamma$ with an unknown target concept from $\mathcal{F}$ is not smaller than the number of correlation queries (with smallest tolerance $\frac{s+1}{2}\tau$) needed to achieve a correlation of at least $\frac{s+1}{2}\gamma$ with an unknown target function from $\mathcal{F}_s$.*

An application of the lower bound in (7) with $\frac{s+1}{2}\tau$ in the role of τ and $\frac{s+1}{2}\gamma$ in the role of γ finally leads to

Corollary 5. *The number of correlation queries (with smallest tolerance τ) needed to achieve a correlation of at least $\frac{s-1}{s+1} + \gamma$ with an unknown target concept from $\mathcal{F}$ is at least*

$$\frac{|\mathcal{F}|}{\rho s^2 + 1 - \rho} \frac{(s+1)^2}{4} \min\{\gamma^2, \tau^2\} \ .$$

Note $\frac{(s+1)^2}{4}\min\{\gamma^2, \tau^2\} \leq 1$ since $\frac{s-1}{s+1} + \gamma \leq 1$.

Here is a concrete example[7] to which Corollary 5 applies. Remember that the elements (projective points) of the $(n-1)$-dimensional projective space over $\mathbb{Z}_p$ are the 1-dimensional linear subspaces of $\mathbb{Z}_p^n$. We will represent projective points by elements in $\mathbb{Z}_p^n$. We say that a projective point Q is *orthogonal* to a projective point Q', denoted as $Q \perp Q'$, if $\langle Q, Q' \rangle = 0$. We view the matrix M such that

$$M[Q, Q'] = \begin{cases} 1 & \text{if } Q \perp Q' \\ -1 & \text{otherwise} \end{cases}$$

as the incidence matrix of a concept class $\mathrm{ORT}(p, n)$ (over domain $X = \mathrm{ORT}(p, n)$). According to results in [11], $\mathrm{ORT}(p, n)$ has properties 1 and 2, where

$$\rho = \frac{p^{n-1} - 1}{p^n - 1} \approx \frac{1}{p} \text{ and } s = \frac{(p-1)p^{n/2-1}}{1 + p^{n/2-1}} \approx p \ .$$

Combining this with $|\mathrm{ORT}(p, n)| = \frac{p^n - 1}{p - 1}$ and with Corollary 5, we get

Corollary 6. *The number of correlation queries (with smallest tolerance τ) needed to achieve a correlation of at least $1 - 2\frac{p^{n/2-1}}{p^{n/2}+1} + \gamma$ with an unknown target concept from $\mathcal{F}$ is asymptotically at least $p^{n-2}(p^2/4)\min\{\gamma^2, \tau^2\}$.*

Note that $\gamma \leq 2\frac{p^{n/2-1}}{p^{n/2}+1} \approx 2/p$ such that $(p^2/4)\min\{\gamma^2, \tau^2\}$ is asymptotically at most 1.

---

[7] Taken from [11] and used in connection with half-space embeddings in [6].

A Note on the SQ Sampling Model: A query in the SQ Sampling model has the same form as a query in the CQ model but is answered by a τ-approximation for $\mathbb{E}[g(x)|f(x) = 1]$. In the SQ sampling model, the learner pursues the goal to find a positive example for the unknown target concept. Blum and Yang [18] showed that the technique of Yang from [16, 17] leads to lower bounds in the SQ sampling model (when properly applied). The same remark is valid for the alternative technique that we have used in this section. It can be shown that classes with properties 1 and 2 are "hard" in the SQ Sampling model. For example, the retrieval of a positive example for an unknown concept from $\mathrm{ORT}(p, n)$ requires exponentially many queries. The corresponding results and proofs are found in the full paper. Here, we give only the equation that plays the the same key role for the SQ Sampling model as equation (8) for the SQ model:

$$\mathbb{E}[g(x)|f(x) = 1] - \frac{1}{\rho(s+1)}\mathbb{E}[g] = \frac{1}{\rho(s+1)}\mathbb{E}[f_s(x)g(x)] \ .$$

6   Characterizations of Statistical Query Learnability

As for this section, we pass to the parameterized scenario, where we consider ensembles of domains, distributions, and concept classes, respectively:

$$X = (X_n)_{n\geq1}, \ D = (D_n)_{n\geq1}, \ \text{and} \ \mathcal{F} = (\mathcal{F}_n)_{n\geq1} \ .$$

We furthermore focus on "weak polynomial" learners, i.e., the number of queries, q, the inverse of required correlation with the target concept, $1/\gamma$, and the inverse of the lower bound on the tolerance parameters, $1/\tau$, should be bounded by a polynomial in n, respectively.

Blum et al. [2] have shown that $\mathcal{F}$ has a weak polynomial learner in the SQ model if and only if $\mathrm{SQDim}(\mathcal{F}_n)$ is bounded by a polynomial in n, where $\mathrm{SQDim}(\mathcal{F}_n)$ denotes the so-called SQ dimension. In the full paper, we show that $L(\mathcal{F}_n)$ is polynomially related to $\mathrm{SQDim}(\mathcal{F}_n)$. Thus:

Corollary 7. *The following statements are equivalent:*

1. *$\mathcal{F}$ admits a weak polynomial learner in the SQ model.*
2. *$\mathrm{SQDim}(\mathcal{F}_n)$ is polynomially bounded in n.*
3. *$L(\mathcal{F}_n)$ is polynomially bounded in n.*

We close this section by listing some rather surprising connections between SQ learning and (seemingly) different questions in learning and complexity theory, respectively:

Corollary 8. *There is a weak polynomial SQ learner for $\mathcal{F} = (\mathcal{F}_n)_{n\geq1}$ under the uniform distribution if at least one of the following conditions is satisfied:*

- *There exists a $\mathrm{poly}(n)$-dimensional half-space embedding for $\mathcal{F}_n$.*
- *There exists a half-space embedding for $\mathcal{F}_n$ that achieves a margin whose inverse is polynomially bounded in n.*

- *The probabilistic communication complexity of the evaluation problem for $\mathcal{F}_n$ in the unbounded error model is logarithmically bounded in n.*
- *The evaluation problem for $\mathcal{F}_n$ can be solved by a depth-2 threshold circuit whose size and whose weights associated with nodes on the hidden layer are polynomially bounded in n (but the weights may be arbitrary at the top gate).*

Proof. It suffices to show that all conditions mentioned in the corollary will be violated if there is no weak polynomial learner for $\mathcal{F}$. According to Corollary 7, the non-existence of a weak polynomial learner implies that $L(\mathcal{F}_n)$ is super-polynomial in n. Since we assume a uniform distribution, we may apply (6) and write $L(\mathcal{F}_n)$ in the form $\frac{|\mathcal{F}_n| \cdot |X_n|}{\|M_n\|^2}$. The proof can now be completed by calling the following facts into mind:

- It was shown by Forster [5] that $\frac{\sqrt{|\mathcal{F}_n| \cdot |X_n|}}{\|M_n\|}$ is a lower bound on the smallest dimension and on the inverse of largest margin that can be achieved by a half-space embedding for $\mathcal{F}_n$.
- It is well-known [13] that the probabilistic communication complexity in the unbounded error model coincides (up to rounding) with the logarithm of the smallest Euclidean dimension that allows for a half-space embedding.
- It is furthermore well-known [6] that the smallest size of a threshold circuit (of the type described above) grows linearly with the smallest dimension that allows for a half-space embedding.   □

7   Hardness of Learning a "Hidden Number"

In the final section, we outline a relation between learning and the concept of bit-security in cryptography.

7.1   Hidden Number Problem and Bit Security

Let p be an n-bit prime, $(\mathbb{Z}_p, +, \cdot)$ be the field of integers modulo p, $(\mathbb{Z}_p^*, \cdot)$ be the (cyclic) group of prime residuals modulo p, and g be a generator of $\mathbb{Z}_p^*$. We will identify $\mathbb{Z}_p$ with $\{0, 1, \ldots, p-1\}$, the smallest residuals modulo p, and $\mathbb{Z}_p^*$ with $\{1, \ldots, p-1\}$.

Loosely speaking, the Hidden Number Problem (HNP) is the problem of inferring a hidden number $u \in \mathbb{Z}_p^*$ by means of an oracle that provides us with information about $u \cdot z$ for (known) random instances $z \in \mathbb{Z}_p^*$.[8]

In order to cast HNP as a learning problem, consider a binary predicate $B : \mathbb{Z}_p^* \to \{\pm 1\}$. Now we view the hidden number $u \in \mathbb{Z}_p^*$ as an unknown target concept that assigns label $B(u \cdot z)$ to instance z. We denote the resulting concept class $\mathrm{HNP}[B] = (\mathrm{HNP}[B]_n)_{n \geq 1}$ where n always denotes the bit-length of prime p.

The Hidden Number Problem is closely related to the cryptographic concept of bit security, a connection that we now outline briefly for motivational purposes.

---

[8] Terms involving elements from $\mathbb{Z}_p$ are always understood modulo p.

The Diffie-Hellman function (w.r.t. the cyclic group $\mathbb{Z}_p^*$) is given by

$$\mathrm{DH}(g^a, g^b) = g^{ab} \ .$$

It is widely believed that the evaluation of DH is computationally intractable. Even if DH cannot be efficiently evaluated, it might still be possible to compute some bits of information about g^{ab}. In fact, it is known that the Legendre symbol of g^{ab} is easy to compute from p, g, p^a, p^b. This bit of information is therefore "insecure". In order to show that a particular bit of a cryptographic function G is "secure", one typically proves that a general efficient procedure, which reliably predicts this bit, can be converted into an efficient procedure which evaluates G. Everybody who believes that the evaluation problem for G is intractable is therefore forced to believe that no such efficient procedure for the particular bit is conceivable. The analogous remarks are valid for the security of a particular collection of bits.[9]

The Hidden Number Problem was introduced by Boneh and Venkatesan [4] as a tool for showing that the collection of $\sqrt{n}$ unbiased most significant bits of the Diffie-Hellman function is secure. An error in the proof from [4] was spotted and corrected by Vasco and Shparlinski [15]. A technically simpler correction was outlined by Nguyen and Stern [12], but they had to assume that the evaluation problem for the Diffie-Hellman function remains intractable when the input p, g, g^a, g^b is augmented by the prime factorization of $p - 1$.

Here comes the central relation [15] that helps to understand the connection between the Hidden Number Problem and bit-security:

$$g^{(b+r)a} \cdot g^{(b+r)x} = g^{ab+ar+xb+xr} = g^{(a+x)(b+r)} = \mathrm{DH}\left(g^{a+x}, g^{b+r}\right) \qquad (9)$$

Note that $g^{(b+r)a}$ is as hard to compute as g^{ab} whereas g^{a+x}, g^{b+r} are easy to compute from input parameters g^a and g^b (assuming r and x are known). Because of (9), a reliable bit predictor for $B \circ \mathrm{DH}$ provides us with information about the "hidden number" $g^{(b+r)a}$. If we were able to efficiently infer the hidden number from this information, we would end up with a conversion of a bit-predictor for DH into an efficient algorithm that computes the whole function (thereby proving security for bit B of the Diffie-Hellman function).

As emphasized by [8], the Hidden Number Problem plays a central role for the bit-security of a variety of cryptosystems (not just systems employing the Diffie-Hellman function).

7.2   Hidden Number Problem and Learning

Consider a family $B = (B_p)$ of binary predicates $B_p : \mathbb{Z}_p^* \to \{\pm 1\}$. We say that B *distinguishes hidden numbers* if there exists a polynomial $P(n)$ such that

---

[9] Note that the security of a collection of bits is easier to show than the security of an individual bit because a predictor for a collection of bits is a more powerful tool for solving the evaluation problem for G than the predictor for only one individual bit of the collection.

the correlation between two different concepts u_1, u_2 from $\mathbb{Z}_p^*$ under the uniform distribution is at most $1 - 1/P(n)$:

$$\Pr[B(u_1 \cdot z) = B(u_2 \cdot z)] - \Pr[B(u_1 \cdot z) \neq B(u_2 \cdot z)] \leq 1 - \frac{1}{P(n)}$$

Here, z is drawn uniformly at random from $\mathbb{Z}_p^*$ and n denotes the bit-length of prime p.

The proof of the following theorem strongly builds on problem reductions performed in [15] and [12]. New is only the "compilation" in a learning-theoretic framework.

Theorem 3. *For every binary predicate B that distinguishes hidden numbers, the following holds. If* $\mathrm{HNP}[B]$ *is properly PAC learnable under the uniform distribution, then bit B of the Diffie-Hellman function is secure.*

Proof. Consider a fixed n-bit prime p and a generator g of $\mathbb{Z}_p^*$. We will show how a PAC learner and a reliable predictor for $B \circ \mathrm{DH}$ can be used to compute g^{ab} from p, g, g^a, g^b and the prime factorization of $p - 1$:

- Select repeatedly a random element r from $\{0, \ldots, p-2\}$ (independent drawings according to the uniform distribution) until g^{b+r} is a generator.[10]
- Simulate the PAC learner, say A, for target concept $g^{a(b+r)}$ and for "sufficiently small" parameters ε, δ. Whenever A asks for an example, temporarily suspend the simulation and do the following:
  - Select a random element x from $\{0, \ldots, p-2\}$ and compute $g^{a+x} = g^a g^x$ and $g^{b+r} = g^b g^r$.
  - Ask the reliable bit predictor for label $b = B(\mathrm{DH}(g^{a+x}, g^{b+r}))$ and return example (x, b) to the PAC learner.
  Receive finally a hypothesis, say $u \in \mathbb{Z}_p^*$, from the PAC learner.

Note that b correctly labels x w.r.t. target concept $g^{a(b+r)}$ because of the general equation (9). Thus, with probability at least $1 - \delta$, hypothesis u will be ε-accurate for concept $g^{a(b+r)}$. Let P be the polynomial such that either $u = g^{a(b+r)}$ or the correlation of u and $g^{a(b+r)}$ is bounded above by $1 - 1/P(n)$. In the latter case, the labels $B(uz)$ and $B(g^{a(b+r)}z)$ assigned to a random instance $z \in \mathbb{Z}_p^*$ are different with probability at least $1/(2P(n))$. Choosing $\varepsilon = 1/(3P(n))$, we can force the PAC learner to be probably *exactly* correct. Thus, with probability at least $1 - \delta$, $u = g^{a(b+r)}$. In this case, we can retrieve g^{ab} by making use of the equation $g^{ab} = g^{a(b+r)}(g^a)^{-r}$. $\qquad\square$

The *unbiased most significant bit* is the following predicate on $\mathbb{Z}_p^*$:

$$\mathrm{MSB}(z) = \begin{cases} 1 \text{ if } \frac{p+1}{2} \leq z \leq p-1 \\ 0 \text{ otherwise} \end{cases}$$

---

[10] Although we do not know b, we can easily test for the generator-property thanks to the factorization of $p - 1$.

Lemma 2 ([9]). *The unbiased most significant bit distinguishes hidden numbers in the following strong sense:*

$$\forall u_1, u_2 \in \mathbb{Z}_p^* : u_1 \neq u_2 \Rightarrow \Pr[\mathrm{MSB}(u_1 z) = \mathrm{MSB}(u_2 z)] \leq \frac{2}{3} .$$

The corresponding statement for the least significant bit was proven by Kiltz and Simon [9]. Because of $\mathrm{MSB}(x) = \mathrm{LSB}(2x)$, the result carries over to the unbiased most significant bit.

Corollary 9. *If* HNP[MSB] *is properly PAC learnable under the uniform distribution, then the unbiased most significant bit of the Diffie-Hellman function is secure.*

To the best of our knowledge, it is not known whether HNP[MSB] is properly PAC learnable under the uniform distribution. However, from our general lower bound on the number of statistical queries, we can infer the following result:

Lemma 3. *For every n-bit prime,* $L(\mathrm{HNP}[\mathrm{MSB}]_n) = p^{1-o(1)}$.

Proof. Consider the multiplication table $M \in (\mathbb{Z}_p^*)^{(p-1) \times (p-1)}$. i.e, $M[u_1, u_2] = u_1 \cdot u_2 \in \mathbb{Z}_p^*$ for all $u_1, u_2 \in \mathbb{Z}_p^*$. For any binary predicate $B : \mathbb{Z}_p \to \{\pm 1\}$, let $B \circ M$ denote the matrix given by $(B \circ M)[u_1, u_2] = B(u_1 \cdot u_2)$. It is shown by Kiltz and Simon (see Corollary 5.1 in [10]) that

$$\|B \circ M\| = p^{1/2+o(1)}$$

provided that predicate B is "balanced". For the purpose of this paper, we do not need to know the definition of "balanced" because it is also shown in the appendix of [10] that every predicate that can be represented by union of $o(\log n)$ intervals actually is balanced. Since MSB is represented by one interval, namely $\{(p+1)/2, \ldots, p-1\}$, it follows that

$$\|\mathrm{MSB} \circ M\| = p^{1/2+o(1)} .$$

Note that $\mathrm{MSB} \circ M$ is the incidence matrix for concept class $\mathrm{HNP}[\mathrm{MSB}]_n$. From (6), with the full concept class in the role of $\mathcal{F}'$, we conclude that

$$L(\mathrm{HNP}[\mathrm{MSB}]_n) \geq \frac{(p-1) \cdot (p-1)}{(p^{1/2+o(1)})^2} = p^{1-o(1)} .$$

$\square$

Since $p \approx 2^n$, we get the

Corollary 10. HNP[*MSB*] *is not weakly polynomially learnable in the SQ model.*

This result indicates that the same concept class might be hard to learn even in the PAC learning model.

References

1. Shai Ben-David, Alon Itai, and Eyal Kushilevitz. Learning by distances. *Information and Computation*, 117(2):240–250, 1995.
2. Avrim Blum, Merrick Furst, Jeffrey Jackson, Michael Kearns, Yishai Mansour, and Steven Rudich. Weakly learning DNF and characterizing statistical query learning using Fourier analysis. In *Proceedings of the 26th Annual Symposium on Theory of Computing*, pages 253–263, 1994.
3. Avrim Blum, Adam Kalai, and Hal Wasserman. Noise-tolerant learning, the parity problem, and the statistical query model. *Journal of the Association on Computing Machinery*, 50(4):506–519, 2003.
4. Dan Boneh and Ramarathnam Venkatesan. Hardness of computing the most significant bits of secret keys in Diffie-Hellman and related schemes. In *Proceedings of the Conference on Advances in Cryptology — CRYPTO '96*, pages 129–142, 1996.
5. Jürgen Forster. A linear lower bound on the unbounded error communication complexity. *Journal of Computer and System Sciences*, 65(4):612–625, 2002.
6. Jürgen Forster, Matthias Krause, Satyanarayana V. Lokam, Rustam Mubarakzjanov, Niels Schmitt, and Hans Ulrich Simon. Relations between communication complexity, linear arrangements, and computational complexity. In *Proceedings of the 21'st Annual Conference on the Foundations of Software Technology and Theoretical Computer Science*, pages 171–182, 2001.
7. Michael Kearns. Efficient noise-tolerant learning from statistical queries. *Journal of the Association on Computing Machinery*, 45(6):983–1006, 1998.
8. Eike Kiltz. A useful primitive to prove security of every bit and about hard core predicates and universal hash functions. In *Proceedings of the 14th International Symposium on Fundamentals of Computation Theory*, pages 388–392, 2001.
9. Eike Kiltz and Hans Ulrich Simon. Unpublished Manuscript about the Hidden Number Problem.
10. Eike Kiltz and Hans Ulrich Simon. Threshold circuit lower bounds on cryptographic functions. *Journal of Computer and System Sciences*, 71(2):185–212, 2005.
11. Matthias Krause and Stephan Waack. Variation ranks of communication matrices and lower bounds for depth two circuits having symmetric gates with unbounded fan-in. *Mathematical System Theory*, 28(6):553–564, 1995.
12. Phong Q. Nguyen and Jacques Stern. The two faces of lattices in cryptology. In *Proceedings of the International Conference on Cryptography and Lattices*, pages 146–180, 2001.
13. Ramamohan Paturi and Janos Simon. Probabilistic communication complexity. *Journal of Computer and System Sciences*, 33(1):106–123, 1986.
14. Leslie G. Valiant. A theory of the learnable. *Communications of the ACM*, 27(11):1134–1142, 1984.
15. Maria Isabel Gonzáles Vasco and Igor E. Shparlinski. On the security of Diffie–Hellman bits. In *Proceedings of the Workshop on Cryptography and Computational Number Theory*, pages 331–342, 2000.
16. Ke Yang. On learning correlated boolean functions using statistical query. In *Proceedings of the 12th International Conference on Algorithmic Learning Theory*, pages 59–76, 2001.
17. Ke Yang. New lower bounds for statistical query learning. In *Proceedings of the 15th Annual Conferene on Computational Learning Theory*, pages 229–243, 2002.
18. Ke Yang and Avrim Blum. On statistical query sampling and nmr quantum computing. In *Proceedings of the 18th Annual Conference on Computational Complexity*, pages 194–208, 2003.

Data-Driven Discovery Using Probabilistic Hidden Variable Models

Padhraic Smyth

Information and Computer Science
University of California
Irvine, CA 92697-3425, USA
`smyth@ics.uci.edu`

Generative probabilistic models have proven to be a very useful framework for machine learning from scientific data. Key ideas that underlie the generative approach include (a) representing complex stochastic phenomena using the structured language of graphical models, (b) using latent (hidden) variables to make inferences about unobserved phenomena, and (c) leveraging Bayesian ideas for learning and prediction. This talk will begin with a brief review of learning from data with hidden variables and then discuss some exciting recent work in this area that has direct application to a broad range of scientific problems. A number of different scientific data sets will be used as examples to illustrate the application of these ideas in probabilistic learning, such as time-course microarray expression data, functional magnetic resonance imaging (fMRI) data of the human brain, text documents from the biomedical literature, and sets of cyclone trajectories.

J.L. Balcázar, P.M. Long, and F. Stephan (Eds.): ALT 2006, LNAI 4264, p. 28, 2006.
© Springer-Verlag Berlin Heidelberg 2006

Reinforcement Learning and Apprenticeship Learning for Robotic Control

Andrew Y. Ng

Computer Science Department
Stanford University
Stanford CA 94304

Many robotic control problems, such as autonomous helicopter flight, legged robot locomotion, and autonomous driving, remain challenging even for modern reinforcement learning algorithms. Some of the reasons for these problems being challenging are (i) It can be hard to write down, in closed form, a formal specification of the control task (for example, what is the cost function for "driving well"?), (ii) It is often difficult to learn a good model of the robot's dynamics, (iii) Even given a complete specification of the problem, it is often computationally difficult to find good closed-loop controller for a high-dimensional, stochastic, control task. However, when we are allowed to learn from a human demonstration of a task—in other words, if we are in the apprenticeship learning[1] setting—then a number of efficient algorithms can be used to address each of these problems.

To motivate the first of the problems described above, consider the setting of teaching a young adult to drive, where rather than telling the student what the cost function is for driving, it is much easier and more natural to demonstrate driving to them, and have them learn from the demonstration. In practical applications, it is also (perhaps surprisingly) common practice to manually tweak cost functions until the correct behavior is obtained. Thus, we would like to devise algorithms that can learn from a teacher's demonstration, without needing to be explicitly told the cost function. For example, can we "guess" the teacher's cost function based on the demonstration, and use that in our own learning task? Ng and Russell [8] developed a set of *inverse reinforcement learning* algorithms for guessing the teacher's cost function. More recently, Abbeel and Ng [1] showed that even though the teacher's "true" cost function is ambiguous and thus can never be recovered, it is nevertheless possible to recover a cost function that allows us to learn a policy that has performance comparable to the teacher, where here performance is as evaluated on the teacher's *unknown (and unknowable) cost function*. Thus, access to a demonstration removes the need to explicitly write down a cost function.

A second challenge in the application of Markov decision processes (MDPs) and reinforcement learning to robotics lies in the need to estimate the robot's dynamics (more formally, the state transition probabilities). In order to learn a sufficiently rich model of the robot's dynamics, one has to have the robot *ex-*

---

[1] Also called learning by watching, imitation learning, or learning from demonstration (e.g., [6,4]).

J.L. Balcázar, P.M. Long, and F. Stephan (Eds.): ALT 2006, LNAI 4264, pp. 29–31, 2006.

plore its state space and try out a variety of actions from different states, so as to collect data for learning the dynamics. The state-of-the-art algorithm for doing this efficiently is Kearns and Singh's E^3-algorithm [5], which repeatedly applies an "exploration policy" to aggressively visit states whose transition dynamics are still inaccurately modeled. While the E^3 algorithm gives a polynomial time convergence guarantee, it is unacceptable for running on most real systems. For example, running E^3 on an autonomous helicopter would require executing policies that aggressively explore different parts of the state-space, including parts of it that would lead to crashing the helicopter. In contrast, Abbeel and Ng [2] showed that in the apprenticeship learning setting, there is no need to explicitly run these dangerous exploration policies. Specifically, suppose we are given a (polynomial length) human pilot demonstration of helicopter flight. Then, it suffices to only repeatedly run *exploitation* policies that try to fly the helicopter as well as we can, without ever explicitly taking dangerous exploration steps. After at most a polynomial number of iterations, such a procedure will converge to a controller whose performance is at least comparable to that of the pilot demonstrator's. [2] In other words, access to the demonstration removes the need to explicitly carry out dangerous exploration steps.

Finally, even when the MDP is fully specified, often it still remains a computationally challenging problem to find a good controller for it. Again exploiting the apprenticeship learning setting, Bagnell, Kakade, Ng and Schneider's "Policy search by dynamic programming" algorithm [3] uses knowledge of the distribution of states visited by a teacher to efficiently perform policy search, so as to find a good control policy. (See also [7].) Informally, we can view PSDP as using observations of the teacher to guide the search for a good controller, so that the problem of finding a good controller is reduced to that of solving a sequence of standard supervised learning tasks.

In summary, reinforcement learning holds great promise for a large number of robotic control tasks, but its practical application is still sometimes challenging because of the difficulty of specifying reward functions, the difficultly of exploration, and the computational expense of finding good policies. In this short paper, we outlined a few ways in which apprenticeship learning can used to address some of these challenges, both from a theoretical and from a practical point of view.

Acknowledgments

This represents joint work with Pieter Abbeel, J. Andrew Bagnell, Sham Kakade, and Jeff Schneider.

References

1. P. Abbeel and A. Y. Ng. Apprenticeship learning via inverse reinforcement learning. In *Proc. ICML*, 2004.
2. P. Abbeel and A. Y. Ng. Exploration and apprenticeship learning in reinforcement learning. In *Proc. ICML*, 2005.

3. J. Andrew Bagnell, Sham Kakade, Andrew Y. Ng, and Jeff Schneider. Policy search by dynamic programming. In *NIPS 16*, 2003.
4. J. Demiris and G. Hayes. A robot controller using learning by imitation, 1994.
5. Michael Kearns and Satinder Singh. Near-optimal reinforcement learning in polynomial time. *Machine Learning journal*, 2002.
6. Y. Kuniyoshi, M. Inaba, and H. Inoue. Learning by watching: Extracting reusable task knowledge from visual observation of human performance. *T-RA*, 10:799–822, 1994.
7. John Langford and Bianca Zadrozny. Relating reinforcement learning performance to classification performance. In *Proc. ICML*, 2005.
8. A. Y. Ng and S. Russell. Algorithms for inverse reinforcement learning. In *Proc. ICML*, 2000.

Learning Unions of $\omega(1)$-Dimensional Rectangles

Alp Atıcı and Rocco A. Servedio*

Columbia University, New York, NY, USA
{atici@math, rocco@cs}.columbia.edu

Abstract. We consider the problem of learning unions of rectangles over the domain $[b]^n$, in the uniform distribution membership query learning setting, where both b and n are "large". We obtain poly$(n, \log b)$-time algorithms for the following classes:

- poly$(n \log b)$-MAJORITY of $O(\frac{\log(n \log b)}{\log \log(n \log b)})$-dimensional rectangles.
- Unions of poly$(\log(n \log b))$ many rectangles with dimension
  $O(\frac{\log^2(n \log b)}{(\log \log(n \log b) \log \log \log(n \log b))^2})$.
- poly$(n \log b)$-MAJORITY of poly$(n \log b)$-OR of disjoint rectangles with dimension $O(\frac{\log(n \log b)}{\log \log(n \log b)})$.

Our main algorithmic tool is an extension of Jackson's boosting- and Fourier-based Harmonic Sieve algorithm [13] to the domain $[b]^n$, building on work of Akavia *et al.* [1]. Other ingredients used to obtain the results stated above are techniques from exact learning [4] and ideas from recent work on learning augmented AC^0 circuits [14] and on representing Boolean functions as thresholds of parities [16].

1 Introduction

Motivation. The learnability of Boolean valued functions defined over the domain $[b]^n = \{0, 1, \ldots, b-1\}^n$ has long elicited interest in computational learning theory literature. In particular, much research has been done on learning various classes of "unions of rectangles" over $[b]^n$ (see e.g. [4, 6, 7, 10, 13, 19]), where a rectangle is a conjunction of properties of the form "the value of attribute x_i lies in the range $[\alpha_i, \beta_i]$". One motivation for studying these classes is that they are a natural analogue of classes of DNF (Disjunctive Normal Form) formulae over $\{0, 1\}^n$; for instance, it is easy to see that in the case $b = 2$ any union of s rectangles is simply a DNF with s terms.

Since the description length of a point $x \in [b]^n$ is $n \log b$ bits, a natural goal in learning functions over $[b]^n$ is to obtain algorithms which run in time poly$(n \log b)$. Throughout the article we refer to such algorithms with poly$(n \log b)$ runtime as *efficient* algorithms. In this article we give efficient algorithms which can learn several interesting classes of unions of rectangles over $[b]^n$ in the model of uniform distribution learning with membership queries.

Previous results. In a breakthrough result a decade ago, Jackson [13] gave the Harmonic Sieve (HS) algorithm and proved that it can learn any s-term DNF

---

* Supported in part by NSF award CCF-0347282 and NSF award CCF-0523664.

formula over n Boolean variables in poly(n, s) time. In fact, Jackson showed that the algorithm can learn any s-way majority of parities in poly(n, s) time; this is a richer set of functions which includes all s-term DNF formulae. The HS algorithm works by boosting a Fourier-based weak learning algorithm, which is a modified version of an earlier algorithm due to Kushilevitz and Mansour [18].

In [13] Jackson also described an extension of the HS algorithm to the domain $[b]^n$. His main result for $[b]^n$ is an algorithm that can learn any union of s rectangles over $[b]^n$ in poly$(s^{b \log \log b}, n)$ time; note that this runtime is poly(n, s) if and only if b is $\Theta(1)$ (and the runtime is clearly exponential in b for any s).

There has also been substantial work on learning various classes of unions of rectangles over $[b]^n$ in the more demanding model of exact learning from membership and equivalence queries. Some of the subclasses of unions of rectangles which have been considered in this setting are

The dimension of each rectangle is $O(1)$: Beimel and Kushilevitz [4] give an algorithm learning any union of s $O(1)$-dimensional rectangles over $[b]^n$ in poly$(n, s, \log b)$ time steps, using equivalence queries only.

The number of rectangles is limited: An algorithm is given in [4] which exactly learns any union of $O(\log n)$ many rectangles in poly$(n, \log b)$ time using membership and equivalence queries. Earlier, Maass and Warmuth [19] gave an algorithm which uses only equivalence queries and can learn any union of $O(1)$ rectangles in poly$(n, \log b)$ time.

The rectangles are disjoint: If no input $x \in [b]^n$ belongs to more than one rectangle, then [4] can learn a union of s such rectangles in poly$(n, s, \log b)$ time with membership and equivalence queries.

Our techniques and results. Because efficient learnability is established for unions of $O(\log n)$ arbitrary dimensional rectangles by [4] in a more demanding model, we are interested in achieving positive results when the number of rectangles is strictly larger. Therefore all the cases we study involve at least poly$(\log(n \log b))$ and sometimes as many as poly$(n \log b)$ rectangles.

We start by describing a new variant of the Harmonic Sieve algorithm for learning functions defined over $[b]^n$; we call this new algorithm the Generalized Harmonic Sieve, or GHS. The key difference between GHS and Jackson's algorithm for $[b]^n$ is that whereas Jackson's algorithm used a weak learning algorithm whose runtime is poly(b), the GHS algorithm uses a poly$(\log b)$ time weak learning algorithm described in recent work of Akavia *et al.* [1].

We then apply GHS to learn various classes of functions defined in terms of "b-literals" (see Section 2 for a precise definition; roughly speaking a b-literal is like a 1-dimensional rectangle). We first show the following result:

Theorem 1. *The concept class $\mathfrak{C}$ of s-MAJORITY of r-PARITY of b-literals where $s = \text{poly}(n \log b)$, $r = O(\frac{\log(n \log b)}{\log \log(n \log b)})$ is efficiently learnable using* GHS.

Learning this class has immediate applications for our goal of "learning unions of rectangles"; in particular, it follows that

Theorem 2. *The concept class of s-MAJORITY of r-rectangles where $s = \text{poly}(n \log b)$, $r = O(\frac{\log(n \log b)}{\log \log(n \log b)})$ is efficiently learnable using* GHS.

This clearly implies efficient learnability for unions (as opposed to majorities) of s such rectangles as well.

We then employ a technique of restricting the domain $[b]^n$ to a much smaller set and adaptively expanding this set as required. This approach was used in the exact learning framework by Beimel and Kushilevitz [4]; by an appropriate modification we adapt the underlying idea to the uniform distribution membership query framework. Using this approach in conjunction with GHS we obtain almost a quadratic improvement in the dimension of the rectangles if the number of terms is guaranteed to be small:

Theorem 3. *The concept class of unions of* $s = \text{poly}(\log(n \log b))$ *many* r-*rectangles where* $r = O(\frac{\log^2(n \log b)}{(\log\log(n \log b) \log\log\log(n \log b))^2})$ *is efficiently learnable via Algorithm 1 (see Section 5).*

Finally we consider the case of disjoint rectangles (also studied by [4] as mentioned above), and improve the depth of our circuits by 1 provided that the rectangles connected to the same OR gate are disjoint:

Corollary 1. *The concept class of* s-MAJORITY *of* t-OR *of disjoint* r-*rectangles where* $s, t = \text{poly}(n \log b)$, $r = O(\frac{\log(n \log b)}{\log\log(n \log b)})$ *is efficiently learnable under* GHS.

Organization. In Section 3 we describe the Generalized Harmonic Sieve algorithm GHS which will be our main tool for learning unions of rectangles. In Section 4 we show that s-MAJORITY of r-PARITY of b-literals is efficiently learnable using GHS for suitable r, s; this concept class turns out to be quite useful for learning unions of rectangles. In Section 5 we improve over the results of Section 4 slightly if the number of terms is small, by adaptively selecting a small subset of $[b]$ in each dimension which is sufficient for learning, and invoke GHS over the restricted domain. In Section 6 we explore the consequences of the results in Sections 4 and 5 for the ultimate goal of learning unions of rectangles.

Because of space limitations some proofs are omitted; see [3] for a full version.

2   Preliminaries

The learning model. We are interested in Boolean functions defined over the domain $[b]^n$, where $[b] = \{0, 1, \ldots, b-1\}$. We view Boolean functions as mappings into $\{-1, 1\}$ where -1 is associated with TRUE and 1 with FALSE.

A *concept class* $\mathfrak{C}$ is a collection of classes (sets) of Boolean functions $\{C_{n,b}: n > 0, b > 1\}$ such that if $f \in C_{n,b}$ then $f: [b]^n \to \{-1, 1\}$. Throughout this article we view both n and b as asymptotic parameters, and our goal is to exhibit algorithms that learn various classes $C_{n,b}$ in $\text{poly}(n, \log b)$ time. We now describe the uniform distribution membership query learning model that we will consider.

A *membership oracle* MEM(f) is an oracle which, when queried with input x, outputs the label $f(x)$ assigned by the target f to the input. Let $f \in C_{n,b}$ be an unknown member of the concept class and let $\mathcal{A}$ be a randomized learning algorithm which takes as input accuracy and confidence parameters ϵ, δ and can invoke MEM(f). We say that $\mathcal{A}$ *learns* $\mathfrak{C}$ *under the uniform distribution on* $[b]^n$

provided that given any $0 < \epsilon, \delta < 1$ and access to $\mathsf{MEM}(f)$, with probability at least $1 - \delta$ $\mathcal{A}$ outputs an ϵ-approximating hypothesis $h \colon [b]^n \to \{-1, 1\}$ (which need not belong to $\mathfrak{C}$) such that $\mathrm{Pr}_{x \in [b]^n}[f(x) = h(x)] \geq 1 - \epsilon$.

We are interested in computationally efficient learning algorithms. We say that $\mathcal{A}$ *learns* $\mathfrak{C}$ *efficiently* if for any target concept $f \in C_{n,b}$,

- $\mathcal{A}$ runs for at most $\mathrm{poly}(n, \log b, 1/\epsilon, \log 1/\delta)$ steps;
- Any hypothesis h that $\mathcal{A}$ produces can be evaluated on any $x \in [b]^n$ in at most $\mathrm{poly}(n, \log b, 1/\epsilon, \log 1/\delta)$ time steps.

The functions we study. The reader might wonder which classes of Boolean valued functions over $[b]^n$ are interesting. In this article we study classes of functions that are defined in terms of "b-literals"; these include rectangles and unions of rectangles over $[b]^n$ as well as other richer classes. As described below, b-literals are a natural extension of Boolean literals to the domain $[b]^n$.

Definition 1. *A function* $\ell \colon [b] \to \{-1, 1\}$ *is a* basic b-literal *if for some* $\sigma \in \{-1, 1\}$ *and some* $\alpha \leq \beta$ *with* $\alpha, \beta \in [b]$ *we have* $\ell(x) = \sigma$ *if* $\alpha \leq x \leq \beta$, *and* $\ell(x) = -\sigma$ *otherwise. A function* $\ell \colon [b] \to \{-1, 1\}$ *is a* b-literal *if there exists a basic* b-literal ℓ' *and some fixed* $z \in [b]$, $\gcd(z, b) = 1$ *such that for all* $x \in [b]$ *we have* $\ell(x) = \ell'(xz \bmod b)$.

Basic b-literals are the most natural extension of Boolean literals to the domain $[b]^n$. General b-literals (not necessarily basic) were previously studied in [1] and are also quite natural; for example, if b is odd then the *least significant bit* function $lsb(x) \colon [b] \to \{-1, 1\}$ (defined by $lsb(x) = -1$ iff x is even) is a b-literal.

Definition 2. *A function* $f \colon [b]^n \to \{-1, 1\}$ *is a* k-rectangle *if it is an* AND *of* k *basic* b-literals $\ell_1, \ldots, \ell_k$ *over* k *distinct variables* $x_{i_1}, \ldots, x_{i_k}$. *If* f *is a* k-rectangle for some k then we may simply say that f is a rectangle. A union of s rectangles $R_1, \ldots, R_s$ is a function of the form $f(x) = \mathrm{OR}_{i=1}^{s} R_i(x)$.*

The class of unions of s rectangles over $[b]^n$ is a natural generalization of the class of s-term DNF over $\{0, 1\}^n$. Similarly MAJORITY of PARITY of basic b-literals generalizes the class of MAJORITY of PARITY of Boolean literals, a class which has been the subject of much research (see e.g. [13, 5, 16]).

If G is a logic gate with potentially unbounded fan-in (e.g. MAJORITY, PARITY, AND, etc.) we write "s-G" to indicate that the fan-in of G is restricted to be at most s. Thus, for example, an "s-MAJORITY of r-PARITY of b-literals" is a MAJORITY of at most s functions $g_1, \ldots, g_s$, each of which is a PARITY of at most r many b-literals. We will further assume that *any two b-literals which are inputs to the same gate depend on different variables*. This is a natural restriction to impose in light of our ultimate goal of learning unions of rectangles. Although our results hold without this assumption, it provides simplicity in the presentation.

Harmonic analysis of functions over $[b]^n$. We will make use of the Fourier expansion of complex valued functions over $[b]^n$.

Consider $f, g \colon [b]^n \to \mathbb{C}$ endowed with the inner product $\langle f, g \rangle = \mathbf{E}[f\bar{g}]$ and induced norm $\|f\| = \sqrt{\langle f, f \rangle}$. Let $\omega_b = e^{\frac{2\pi i}{b}}$ and for each $\alpha = (\alpha_1, \ldots, \alpha_n) \in [b]^n$, let $\chi_\alpha \colon [b]^n \to \mathbb{C}$ be defined as $\chi_\alpha(x) = \omega_b^{\alpha_1 x_1 + \cdots + \alpha_n x_n}$. Let $\mathcal{B}$ denote the set of functions $\mathcal{B} = \{\chi_\alpha \colon \alpha \in [b]^n\}$. It is easy to verify the following properties:

- For each $\alpha = (\alpha_1, \ldots, \alpha_n) \in [b]^n$, we have $\|\chi_\alpha\| = 1$.
- Elements in $\mathcal{B}$ are orthogonal: For $\alpha, \beta \in [b]^n$, $\langle \chi_\alpha, \chi_\beta \rangle = \begin{cases} 1 \text{ if } \alpha = \beta \\ 0 \text{ if } \alpha \neq \beta \end{cases}$.
- $\mathcal{B}$ constitutes an orthonormal basis for all functions $\{f \colon [b]^n \to \mathbb{C}\}$ considered as a vector space over $\mathbb{C}$, so every $f \colon [b]^n \to \mathbb{C}$ can be expressed uniquely as $f(x) = \sum_\alpha \hat{f}(\alpha) \chi_\alpha(x)$, which we refer to as the *Fourier expansion* or *Fourier transform* of f.

The values $\{\hat{f}(\alpha) \colon \alpha \in [b]^n\}$ are called the *Fourier coefficients* or the *Fourier spectrum* of f. As is well known, *Parseval's Identity* relates the values of the coefficients to the values of the function:

Lemma 1 (Parseval's Identity). $\sum_\alpha |\hat{f}(\alpha)|^2 = \mathbf{E}[|f|^2]$ *for any* $f \colon [b]^n \to \mathbb{C}$.

We write $L_1(f)$ to denote $\sum_\alpha |\hat{f}(\alpha)|$.

Additional tools: weak hypotheses and boosting. Let $f \colon [b]^n \to \{-1, 1\}$ and $\mathcal{D}$ be a probability distribution over $[b]^n$. A function $g \colon [b]^n \to \mathbb{R}$ is said to be a *weak hypothesis for f with advantage γ under $\mathcal{D}$* if $\mathbf{E}_\mathcal{D}[fg] \geq \gamma$.

The first *boosting* algorithm was described by Schapire [20] in 1990; since then boosting has been intensively studied (see [9] for an overview). The basic idea is that by combining a sequence of weak hypotheses $h_1, h_2, \ldots$ (the i-th of which has advantage γ with respect to a carefully chosen distribution $\mathcal{D}_i$) it is possible to obtain a high accuracy final hypothesis h which satisfies $\Pr[h(x) = f(x)] \geq 1 - \epsilon$. The following theorem gives a precise statement of the performance guarantees of a particular boosting algorithm, which we call Algorithm $\mathcal{B}$, due to Freund. Many similar statements are now known about a range of different boosting algorithms but this is sufficient for our purposes.

Theorem 4 (Boosting Algorithm [8]). *Suppose that Algorithm $\mathcal{B}$ is given:*

- $0 < \epsilon, \delta < 1$, *and membership query access* $\mathsf{MEM}(f)$ *to* $f \colon [b]^n \to \{-1, 1\}$;
- *access to an algorithm* WL *which has the following property: given a value* δ' *and access to* $\mathsf{MEM}(f)$ *and to* $\mathsf{EX}(f, \mathcal{D})$ *(the latter is an example oracle which generates random examples from* $[b]^n$ *drawn with respect to distribution $\mathcal{D}$), it constructs a weak hypothesis for f with advantage γ under $\mathcal{D}$ with probability at least* $1 - \delta'$ *in time polynomial in* n, $\log b$, $\log(1/\delta')$.

Then Algorithm $\mathcal{B}$ behaves as follows:

- *It runs for* $S = O(\log(1/\epsilon)/\gamma^2)$ *stages and runs in total time polynomial in* n, $\log b$, ϵ^{-1}, γ^{-1}, $\log(\delta^{-1})$.
- *At each stage* $1 \leq j \leq S$ *it constructs a distribution $\mathcal{D}_j$ such that* $L_\infty(\mathcal{D}_j) < \mathrm{poly}(\epsilon^{-1})/b^n$, *and simulates* $\mathsf{EX}(f, \mathcal{D}_j)$ *for* WL *in stage j. Moreover, there is a "pseudo-distribution" $\tilde{\mathcal{D}}_j$ satisfying $\tilde{\mathcal{D}}_j(x) = c\mathcal{D}_j(x)$ for all x (where $c \in [1/2, 3/2]$ is some fixed value) such that $\tilde{\mathcal{D}}_j(x)$ can be computed in time polynomial in $n \log b$ for each $x \in [b]^n$.*

- *It outputs a final hypothesis $h = \text{sign}(h_1 + h_2 + \ldots + h_S)$ which ϵ-approximates f under the uniform distribution with probability $1 - \delta$; here h_j is the output of WL at stage j invoked with simulated access to $\text{EX}(f, \mathcal{D}_j)$.*

We will sometimes informally refer to distributions $\mathcal{D}$ which satisfy the bound $L_\infty(\mathcal{D}) < \frac{\text{poly}(\epsilon^{-1})}{b^n}$ as *smooth* distributions.

In order to use boosting, it must be the case that there exists a suitable weak hypothesis with advantage γ. The "discriminator lemma" of Hajnal *et al.* [11] can often be used to assert that the desired weak hypothesis exists:

Lemma 2 (The Discriminator Lemma [11]). *Let $\mathfrak{H}$ be a class of ± 1-valued functions over $[b]^n$ and let $f: [b]^n \to \{-1, 1\}$ be expressible as $f = \text{MAJORITY}(h_1, \ldots, h_s)$ where each $h_i \in \mathfrak{H}$ and $h_1(x) + \ldots + h_s(x) \neq 0$ for all x. Then for any distribution $\mathcal{D}$ over $[b]^n$ there is some h_i such that $|\mathbf{E}_\mathcal{D}[fh_i]| \geq 1/s$.*

3   The Generalized Harmonic Sieve Algorithm

In this section our goal is to describe a variant of Jackson's Harmonic Sieve Algorithm and show that under suitable conditions it can efficiently learn certain functions $f: [b]^n \to \{-1, 1\}$. As mentioned earlier, our aim is to attain poly($\log b$) runtime dependence on b and consequently obtain efficient algorithms as described in Section 2. This goal precludes using Jackson's original Harmonic Sieve variant for $[b]^n$ since the runtime of his weak learner depends polynomially rather than polylogarithmically on b (see [13, Lemma 15]).

As we describe below, this poly($\log b$) runtime can be achieved by modifying the Harmonic Sieve over $[b]^n$ to use a weak learner due to Akavia *et al.* [1] which is more efficient than Jackson's weak learner. We shall call the resulting algorithm "The Generalized Harmonic Sieve" algorithm, or GHS for short.

Recall that in the Harmonic Sieve over the Boolean domain $\{-1, 1\}^n$, the weak hypotheses used are simply the Fourier basis elements over $\{-1, 1\}^n$, which correspond to the Boolean-valued parity functions. For $[b]^n$, we will use the real component of the complex-valued Fourier basis elements $\{\chi_\alpha, \alpha \in [b]^n\}$ as our weak hypotheses.

The following theorem of Akavia *et al.* [1, Theorem 5] plays a crucial role:

Theorem 5 (See [1]). *There is a learning algorithm that, given membership query access to $f: [b]^n \to \mathbb{C}$, $0 < \gamma$ and $0 < \delta < 1$, outputs a list L of indices such that with probability at least $1 - \delta$, we have $\{\alpha : |\hat{f}(\alpha)| > \gamma\} \subseteq L$ and $|\hat{f}(\beta)| \geq \frac{\gamma}{2}$ for every $\beta \in L$. The running time of the algorithm is polynomial in n, $\log b$, $\|f\|_\infty$, γ^{-1}, $\log(\delta^{-1})$.*

A weak learning algorithm can be obtained building on Theorem 5 (see [3] for details; because of space limitations the proof is omitted here), which combined with Theorem 4 gives rise to the following corollary:

Corollary 2 (The Generalized Harmonic Sieve). *Let $\mathfrak{C}$ be a concept class. Suppose that for any concept $f \in C_{n,b}$ and any distribution $\mathcal{D}$ over $[b]^n$ with $L_\infty(\mathcal{D}) < \text{poly}(\epsilon^{-1})/b^n$ there exists a Fourier basis element χ_α such that*

$$|\mathbf{E}_{\mathcal{D}}[f\overline{\chi_\alpha}]| \geq \gamma.$$

Then $\mathfrak{C}$ can be learned in time $\mathrm{poly}(n, \log b, \epsilon^{-1}, \gamma^{-1})$.

4   Learning Majority of Parity Using GHS

In this section we identify classes of functions which can be learned efficiently using the GHS algorithm and prove Theorem 1.

To prove Theorem 1, we show that for any concept $f \in \mathfrak{C}$ and under any smooth distribution there must be some Fourier basis element which has non-negligible correlation with f; this is the essential step which lets us apply the Generalized Harmonic Sieve. We prove this in Section 4.2. In Section 4.3 we give an alternate argument which yields a Theorem 1 analogue but with a slightly different bound on r, namely $r = O(\frac{\log(n\log b)}{\log\log b})$.

4.1   Setting the Stage

For ease of notation we will write $abs(\alpha)$ to denote $\min\{\alpha, b - \alpha\}$. We will use the following simple lemma (see [1] for proof) and corollary (see [3] for proof):

Lemma 3 (See [1]). *For all $0 \leq \ell \leq b$, we have $|\sum_{y=0}^{\ell-1} \omega_b^{\alpha y}| < b/abs(\alpha)$.*

Corollary 3. *Let $f\colon [b] \to \{-1, 1\}$ be a basic b-literal. Then if $\alpha = 0$, $|\hat{f}(\alpha)| < 1$, while if $\alpha \neq 0$, $|\hat{f}(\alpha)| < \frac{2}{abs(\alpha)}$.*

The following easy lemma (see [3] for proof) is useful for relating the Fourier transform of a b-literal to the corresponding basic b-literal:

Lemma 4. *For $f, g\colon [b] \to \mathbb{C}$ such that $g(x) = f(xz)$ where $\gcd(z, b) = 1$, we have $\hat{g}(\alpha) = \hat{f}(\alpha z^{-1})$.*

A natural way to approximate a b-literal is by truncating its Fourier representation. We make the following definition:

Definition 3. *Let k be a positive integer. For $f\colon [b] \to \{-1, 1\}$ a basic b-literal, the k-restriction of f is $\tilde{f}\colon [b] \to \mathbb{C}$, $\tilde{f}(x) = \sum_{abs(\alpha) \leq k} \hat{f}(\alpha)\chi_\alpha(x)$. More generally, for $f\colon [b] \to \{-1, 1\}$ a b-literal (so $f(x) = f'(xz)$ where f' is a basic b-literal) the k-restriction of f is $\tilde{f}\colon [b] \to \mathbb{C}$, $\tilde{f}(x) = \sum_{abs(\alpha z^{-1}) \leq k} \hat{f}(\alpha)\chi_\alpha(x) = \sum_{abs(\beta) \leq k} \widehat{f'}(\beta)\chi_\beta(x)$.*

4.2   Correlated Fourier Basis Elements for Functions in $\mathfrak{C}$

In this section we show that given any $f \in \mathfrak{C}$ and any smooth distribution $\mathcal{D}$, some Fourier basis element must have high correlation with f. We begin by bounding the error of the k-restriction of a basic b-literal (see [3] for proof):

Lemma 5. *For $f\colon [b] \to \{-1, 1\}$ a b-literal and $\tilde{f}$ the k-restriction of f, we have $\mathbf{E}[|f - \tilde{f}|^2] = O(1/k)$.*

Now suppose that f is an r-PARITY of b-literals $f_1, \ldots, f_r$. Since PARITY corresponds to multiplication over the domain $\{-1, 1\}$, this means that $f = \prod_{i=1}^{r} f_i$. It is natural to approximate f by the product of the k-restrictions $\prod_{i=1}^{r} \tilde{f}_i$. The following lemma bounds the error of this approximation:

Lemma 6. *For $i = 1, \ldots, r$, let $f_i \colon [b] \to \{-1, 1\}$ be a b-literal and let $\tilde{f}_i$ be its k-restriction. Then*

$$\mathbf{E}[|f_1(x_1)f_2(x_2) \ldots f_r(x_r) - \tilde{f}_1(x_1)\tilde{f}_2(x_2) \ldots \tilde{f}_r(x_r)|] < O(1) \cdot (e^{\frac{O(1)r}{\sqrt{k}}} - 1).$$

Proof. First note that by the non-negativity of variance and Lemma 5, we have that for each $i = 1, \ldots, r$:

$$\mathbf{E}_{x_i}[|f_i(x_i) - \tilde{f}_i(x_i)|] \leq \sqrt{\mathbf{E}_{x_i}[|f_i(x_i) - \tilde{f}_i(x_i)|^2]} = O(1/\sqrt{k}).$$

Therefore we also have for each $i = 1, \ldots, r$:

$$\mathbf{E}_{x_i}[|\tilde{f}_i(x_i)|] < \underbrace{\mathbf{E}_{x_i}[|\tilde{f}_i(x_i) - f_i(x_i)|]}_{<O(\frac{1}{\sqrt{k}})} + \underbrace{\mathbf{E}_{x_i}[|f_i(x_i)|]}_{=1} \leq 1 + \frac{O(1)}{\sqrt{k}}.$$

For any $(x_1, \ldots, x_r)$ we can bound the difference in the lemma as follows:

$$|f_1(x_1) \ldots f_r(x_r) - \tilde{f}_1(x_1) \ldots \tilde{f}_r(x_r)| \leq$$
$$|f_1(x_1) \ldots f_r(x_r) - f_1(x_1) \ldots f_{r-1}(x_{r-1})\tilde{f}_r(x_r)| +$$
$$|f_1(x_1) \ldots f_{r-1}(x_{r-1})\tilde{f}_r(x_r) - \tilde{f}_1(x_1) \ldots \tilde{f}_r(x_r)| \leq$$
$$|f_r(x_r) - \tilde{f}_r(x_r)| + |\tilde{f}_r(x_r)||f_1(x_1) \ldots f_{r-1}(x_{r-1}) - \tilde{f}_1(x_1) \ldots \tilde{f}_{r-1}(x_{r-1})|$$

Therefore the expectation in question is at most:

$$\underbrace{\mathbf{E}_{x_r}[|f_r(x_r) - \tilde{f}_r(x_r)|]}_{=O(\frac{1}{\sqrt{k}})} + \underbrace{\mathbf{E}_{x_r}[|\tilde{f}_r(x_r)|]}_{\leq 1 + \frac{O(1)}{\sqrt{k}}} \cdot \mathbf{E}_{(x_1, \ldots, x_{r-1})}[|f_1(x_1) \ldots f_{r-1}(x_{r-1}) - \tilde{f}_1(x_1) \ldots \tilde{f}_{r-1}(x_{r-1})|].$$

We can repeat this argument successively until the base case $\mathbf{E}_{x_1}[|f_1(x_1) - \tilde{f}_1(x_1)|] \leq O(\frac{1}{\sqrt{k}})$ is reached. Thus for some $K = O(1)$, $1 < L = 1 + \frac{O(1)}{\sqrt{k}}$:

$$\mathbf{E}[|f_1(x_1) \ldots f_r(x_r) - \tilde{f}_1(x_1) \ldots \tilde{f}_r(x_r)|] \leq \frac{K \sum_{i=0}^{r-1} L^i}{\sqrt{k}} < O(1) \cdot (e^{\frac{O(1)r}{\sqrt{k}}} - 1).\ \square$$

Now we are ready for the main theorem asserting the existence (under suitable conditions) of a highly correlated Fourier basis element. The basic approach of the following proof is reminiscent of the main technical lemma from [14].

Theorem 6. *Let τ be a parameter to be specified later and $\mathfrak{C}$ be the concept class consisting of s-MAJORITY of r-PARITY of b-literals where $s = \text{poly}(\tau)$ and $r = O(\frac{\log(\tau)}{\log\log(\tau)})$. Then for any $f \in C_{n,b}$ and any distribution $\mathcal{D}$ over $[b]^n$ with $L_\infty(\mathcal{D}) = \text{poly}(\tau)/b^n$, there exists a Fourier basis element χ_α such that $|\mathbf{E}_{\mathcal{D}}[f\overline{\chi_\alpha}]| > \Omega(1/\text{poly}(\tau))$.*

Proof. Assume f is a MAJORITY of $h_1, \ldots, h_s$ each of which is a r-PARITY of b-literals. Then Lemma 2 implies that there exists h_i such that $|\mathbf{E}_{\mathcal{D}}[fh_i]| \geq 1/s$. Let h_i be PARITY of the b-literals $\ell_1, \ldots, \ell_r$.

Since s and $b^n \cdot L_\infty(\mathcal{D})$ are both at most $\text{poly}(\tau)$ and $r = O(\frac{\log(\tau)}{\log\log(\tau)})$, Lemma 6 implies that there are absolute constants C_1, C_2 such that if we consider the k-restrictions $\tilde{\ell}_1, \ldots, \tilde{\ell}_r$ of $\ell_1, \ldots, \ell_r$ for $k = C_1 \cdot \tau^{C_2}$, we will have $\mathbf{E}[|h_i - \prod_{j=1}^r \tilde{\ell}_j|] \leq 1/(2sb^n L_\infty(\mathcal{D}))$ where the expectation on the left hand side is with respect to the uniform distribution on $[b]^n$. This in turn implies that $\mathbf{E}_{\mathcal{D}}[|h_i - \prod_{j=1}^r \tilde{\ell}_j|] \leq 1/2s$. Let us write h' to denote $\prod_{j=1}^r \tilde{\ell}_j$. We then have

$$|\mathbf{E}_{\mathcal{D}}[f\overline{h'}]| \geq |\mathbf{E}_{\mathcal{D}}[f\overline{h_i}]| - |\mathbf{E}_{\mathcal{D}}[f\overline{(h_i - h')}]| \geq |\mathbf{E}_{\mathcal{D}}[f\overline{h_i}]| - |\mathbf{E}_{\mathcal{D}}[|f\overline{(h_i - h')}|]|$$
$$= |\mathbf{E}_{\mathcal{D}}[fh_i]| - \mathbf{E}_{\mathcal{D}}[|h_i - h'|] \geq 1/s - 1/2s = 1/2s.$$

Now observe that we additionally have

$$|\mathbf{E}_{\mathcal{D}}[f\overline{h'}]| = |\mathbf{E}_{\mathcal{D}}[f\overline{\sum_\alpha \hat{h}'(\alpha)\chi_\alpha}]| = |\sum_\alpha \overline{\hat{h}'(\alpha)}\mathbf{E}_{\mathcal{D}}[f\overline{\chi_\alpha}]| \leq L_1(h') \max_\alpha |\mathbf{E}_{\mathcal{D}}[f\overline{\chi_\alpha}]|$$

Moreover, for each $j = 1, \ldots, r$ we have the following (where we write ℓ'_j to denote the basic b-literal associated with the b-literal ℓ_j):

$$L_1(\tilde{\ell}_j) = \sum_{abs(\alpha) \leq k} |\widehat{\ell'_j}(\alpha)| \underbrace{=}_{\text{by Corollary 3}} 1 + \sum_{\alpha=1}^k O(1)/\alpha = O(\log k).$$

Therefore, for some absolute constant $c > 0$ we have $L_1(h') \leq \prod_{j=1}^r L_1(\tilde{\ell}_j) \leq (c \log k)^r$, where the first inequality holds since the L_1 norm of a product is at most the product of the L_1 norms. Combining inequalities, we obtain our goal:

$$\max_\alpha |\mathbf{E}_{\mathcal{D}}[f\overline{\chi_\alpha}]| \geq 1/(2s(c \log k)^r) = \Omega(1/\text{poly}(\tau)). \qquad \square$$

Since we are interested in algorithms with runtime $\text{poly}(n, \log b, \epsilon^{-1})$, setting $\tau = n\epsilon^{-1} \log b$ in Theorem 6 and combining its result with Corollary 2, gives rise to Theorem 1.

4.3   The Second Approach

A different analysis, similar to that which Jackson uses in the proof of [13, Fact 14], gives us an alternate bound to Theorem 6 (see [3] for proof):

Lemma 7. *Let $\mathfrak{C}$ be the concept class consisting of s-MAJORITY of r-PARITY of b-literals. Then for any $f \in C_{n,b}$ and any distribution $\mathcal{D}$ over $[b]^n$, there exists a Fourier basis element χ_α such that $|\mathbf{E}_{\mathcal{D}}[f\overline{\chi_\alpha}]| = \Omega(1/s(\log b)^r)$.*

Combining this result with that of Corollary 2 we obtain the following result:

Theorem 7. *The concept class $\mathfrak{C}$ consisting of s-MAJORITY of r-PARITY of b-literals can be learned in time $\text{poly}(s, n, (\log b)^r)$ using the GHS algorithm.*

As an immediate corollary we obtain the following close analogue of Theorem 1:

Theorem 8. *The concept class $\mathfrak{C}$ consisting of s-MAJORITY of r-PARITY of b-literals where $s = \mathrm{poly}(n \log b)$, $r = O(\frac{\log(n \log b)}{\log \log b})$ is efficiently learnable using the GHS algorithm.*

5 Locating Sensitive Elements and Learning with GHS on a Restricted Grid

In this section we consider an extension of the GHS algorithm which lets us achieve slightly better bounds when we are dealing only with basic b-literals. Following an idea from [4], the new algorithm works by identifying a subset of "sensitive" elements from $[b]$ for each of the n dimensions.

Definition 4 (See [4]). *A value $\sigma \in [b]$ is called i-sensitive with respect to $f : [b]^n \to \{-1, 1\}$ if there exist values $c_1, c_2, \ldots, c_{i-1}, c_{i+1}, \ldots, c_n \in [b]$ such that $f(c_1, \ldots, c_{i-1}, \sigma - 1, c_{i+1}, \ldots, c_n) \neq f(c_1, \ldots, c_{i-1}, \sigma, c_{i+1}, \ldots, c_n)$. A value σ is called sensitive with respect to f if σ is i-sensitive for some i. If there is no i-sensitive value with respect to f, we say index i is* trivial.

The main idea is to run GHS over a restricted subset of the original domain $[b]^n$, which is the grid formed by the sensitive values and a few more additional values, and therefore lower the algorithm's complexity.

Definition 5. *A grid in $[b]^n$ is a set $\mathcal{S} = L_1 \times L_2 \times \cdots \times L_n$ with $0 \in L_i \subseteq [b]$ for each i. We refer to the elements of $\mathcal{S}$ as corners. The region covered by a corner $(x_1, \ldots, x_n) \in \mathcal{S}$ is defined to be the set $\{(y_1, \ldots, y_n) \in [b]^n : \forall i, x_i \leq y_i < \lceil x_i \rceil\}$ where $\lceil x_i \rceil$ denotes the smallest value in L_i which is larger than x_i (by convention $\lceil x_i \rceil := b$ if no such value exists). The area covered by the corner $(x_1, \ldots, x_n) \in \mathcal{S}$ is therefore defined to be $\prod_{i=1}^n (\lceil x_i \rceil - x_i)$. A refinement of $\mathcal{S}$ is a grid in $[b]^n$ of the form $L'_1 \times L'_2 \times \cdots \times L'_n$ where each $L_i \subseteq L'_i$.*

The following lemma is proved in [3].

Lemma 8. *Let $\mathcal{S}$ be a grid $L_1 \times L_2 \times \cdots \times L_n$ in $[b]^n$ such that each $|L_i| \leq \ell$. Let $\mathcal{I}_{\mathcal{S}}$ denote the set of indices for which $L_i \neq \{0\}$. If $|\mathcal{I}_{\mathcal{S}}| \leq \kappa$, then $\mathcal{S}$ admits a refinement $\mathcal{S}' = L'_1 \times L'_2 \times \cdots \times L'_n$ such that*

1. *All of the sets L'_i which contain more than one element have the same number of elements: $\mathbf{L_{max}}$, which is at most $\ell + C\kappa\ell$, where $C = \frac{b}{\kappa\ell} \cdot \frac{1}{\lfloor b/4\kappa\ell \rfloor} \geq 4$.*
2. *Given a list of the sets $L_1, \ldots, L_n$ as input, a list of the sets $L'_1, \ldots, L'_n$ can be generated by an algorithm with a running time of $O(n\kappa\ell \log b)$.*
3. *$L'_i = \{0\}$ whenever $L_i = \{0\}$.*
4. *Any ϵ fraction of the corners in $\mathcal{S}'$ cover a combined area of at most $2\epsilon b^n$.*

The following lemma is easy and useful; similar statements are given in [4]. Note that the lemma critically relies on the b-literals being basic.

Lemma 9. Let $f\colon [b]^n \to \{-1,1\}$ be expressed as an s-MAJORITY of PARITY of basic b-literals. Then for each index $1 \le i \le n$, there are at most $2s$ i-sensitive values with respect to f.

Proof. A literal ℓ on variable x_i induces two i-sensitive values. The lemma follows directly from our assumption (see Section 2) that for each variable x_i, each of the s PARITY gates has at most one incoming literal which depends on x_i. □

Algorithm 1. An improved algorithm for learning MAJORITY of PARITY of basic b-literals.

1: $L_1 \leftarrow \{0\}, L_2 \leftarrow \{0\}, \ldots, L_n \leftarrow \{0\}$.
2: **loop**
3:    $\mathcal{S} \leftarrow L_1 \times L_2 \times \cdots \times L_n$.
4:    $\mathcal{S}' \leftarrow$ the output of refinement algorithm with input $\mathcal{S}$.
5:    One can express $\mathcal{S}' = L_1' \times L_2' \times \cdots \times L_n'$. If $L_i \ne \{0\}$ then $L_i' = \{x_0^i, x_1^i \ldots, x_{(\mathbf{L_{max}}-1)}^i\}$. Let $x_0^i < x_1^i < \cdots < x_{t-1}^i$ and let $\tau_i : \mathbb{Z}_{\mathbf{L_{max}}} \to L_i'$ be the translation function such that $\tau_i(j) = x_j^i$. If $L_i = L_i' = \{0\}$ then τ_i is the function simply mapping 0 to 0.
6:    Invoke GHS over $f|_{\mathcal{S}'}$ with accuracy $\epsilon/8$. This is done by simulating $\mathsf{MEM}(f|_{\mathcal{S}'}(x_1,\ldots,x_n))$ with $\mathsf{MEM}(f(\tau_1(x_1),\tau_2(x_2),\ldots,\tau_n(x_n)))$. Let the output of the algorithm be g.
7:    Let h be a hypothesis function over $[b]^n$ such that $h(x_1,\ldots,x_n) = g(\tau_1^{-1}(\lfloor x_1 \rfloor),\ldots,\tau_n^{-1}(\lfloor x_n \rfloor))$ ($\lfloor x_i \rfloor$ denotes largest value in L_i' less than or equal to x_i).
8:    **if** h ϵ-approximates f **then**
9:        Output h and terminate.
10:   **end if**
11:   Perform random membership queries until an element $(x_1,\ldots,x_n) \in [b]^n$ is found such that $f(\lfloor x_1 \rfloor,\ldots,\lfloor x_n \rfloor) \ne f(x_1,\ldots,x_n)$.
12:   Find an index $1 \le i \le n$ such that

$$f(\lfloor x_1 \rfloor,\ldots,\lfloor x_{i-1} \rfloor, x_i,\ldots,x_n) \ne f(\lfloor x_1 \rfloor,\ldots,\lfloor x_{i-1} \rfloor,\lfloor x_i \rfloor, x_{i+1},\ldots,x_n).$$

This requires $O(\log n)$ membership queries using binary search.
13:   Find a value σ such that $\lfloor x_i \rfloor + 1 \le \sigma \le x_i$ and $f(\lfloor x_1 \rfloor,\ldots,\lfloor x_{i-1} \rfloor, \sigma - 1, x_{i+1},\ldots,x_n) \ne f(\lfloor x_1 \rfloor,\ldots,\lfloor x_{i-1} \rfloor, \sigma, x_{i+1},\ldots,x_n)$. This requires $O(\log b)$ membership queries using binary search.
14:   $L_i \leftarrow L_i \cup \{\sigma\}$.
15: **end loop**

Algorithm 1 is our extension of the GHS algorithm. It essentially works by repeatedly running GHS on the target function f but restricted to a small (relative to $[b]^n$) grid. To upper bound the number of steps in each of these invocations we will be referring to the result of Theorem 8. After each execution of GHS, the hypothesis defined over the grid is extended to $[b]^n$ in a natural way and is tested for ϵ-accuracy. If h is not ϵ-accurate, then a point where h is incorrect is used to identify a new sensitive value and this value is used to refine the grid for the next iteration. The bound on the number of sensitive values from Lemma 9 lets us bound the number of iterations. Our theorem about Algorithm 1's performance is the following:

Theorem 9. *Let concept class $\mathfrak{C}$ consist of s-MAJORITY of r-PARITY of basic b-literals such that $s = \text{poly}(n \log b)$ and each $f \in C_{n,b}$ has at most $\kappa(n,b)$ non-trivial indices and at most $\ell(n,b)$ i-sensitive values for each $i = 1, \ldots, n$. Then $\mathfrak{C}$ is efficiently learnable if $r = O(\frac{\log(n \log b)}{\log \log \kappa \ell})$.*

Proof. We assume $b = \omega(\kappa \ell)$ without loss of generality. Otherwise one immediately obtains the result with a direct application of GHS through Theorem 8.

We clearly have $\kappa \leq n$ and $\ell \leq 2s$. By Lemma 9 there are at most $\kappa \ell = O(ns)$ sensitive values. We will show that the algorithm finds a new sensitive value at each iteration and terminates before all sensitive values are found. Therefore the number of iterations will be upper bounded by $O(ns)$. We will also show that each iteration runs in $\text{poly}(n, \log b, \epsilon^{-1})$ steps. This will give the desired result.

Let us first establish that step 6 takes at most $\text{poly}(n, \log b, \epsilon^{-1})$ steps. To obtain this it is sufficient to combine the following facts:

- By Lemma 8, for every non-trivial index i of f, L_i' has fixed cardinality $= \mathbf{L_{max}}$. Therefore GHS could be invoked over the restriction of f onto the grid, $f|_{\mathcal{S}'}$, without any trouble.
- If f is s-MAJORITY of r-PARITY of basic b-literals, then the function obtained by restricting it onto the grid: $f|_{\mathcal{S}'}$ could be expressed as t-MAJORITY of u-PARITY of basic L-literals where $t \leq s$, $u \leq r$ and $L \leq O(\kappa \ell)$ (due to the 1st property of the refinement).
- Running GHS over a grid with alphabet size $O(\kappa \ell)$ in each non-trivial index takes $\text{poly}(n, \log b, \epsilon^{-1})$ time if the dimension of the rectangles are $r = O(\frac{\log(n \log b)}{\log \log \kappa \ell})$ due to Theorem 8. (The key idea here is that running GHS over this $\kappa \ell$-size alphabet lets us replace the "b" in Theorem 8 with "$\kappa \ell$".)

To check whether if h ϵ-approximates f at step 8, we may draw $O(1/\epsilon) \cdot \log(1/\delta)$ uniform random examples and use the membership oracle to empirically estimate h's accuracy on these examples. Standard bounds on sampling show that if the true error rate of h is less than (say) $\epsilon/2$, then the empirical error rate on such a sample will be less than ϵ with probability $1 - \delta$. Observe that if all the sensitive values are recovered by the algorithm, h will ϵ-approximate f with high probability. Indeed, since g $(\epsilon/8)$-approximates $f|_{\mathcal{S}'}$, Property 4 of the refinement guarantees that misclassifying the function at $\epsilon/8$ fraction of the corners could at most incur an overall error of $2\epsilon/8 = \epsilon/4$. This is because when all the sensitive elements are recovered, for every corner in $\mathcal{S}'$, h either agrees with f or disagrees with f in the entire region covered by that corner. Thus h will be an $\epsilon/4$ approximator to f with high probability. This establishes that the algorithm must terminate within $O(ns)$ iterations of the outer loop.

Locating another sensitive value occurs at steps 11, 12 and 13. Note that h is not an ϵ-approximator to f because the algorithm moved beyond step 8. Even if we were to correct all the mistakes in g this would alter at most $\epsilon/8$ fraction of the corners in the grid $\mathcal{S}'$ and therefore $\epsilon/4$ fraction of the values in h – again due to the 4th property of the refinement and the way h is generated. Therefore for at least $3\epsilon/4$ fraction of the domain we ought to have $f(\lfloor x_1 \rfloor, \ldots, \lfloor x_n \rfloor) \neq f(x_1, \ldots, x_n)$ where $\lfloor x_i \rfloor$ denotes largest value in L'_i less than or equal to x_i. Thus the algorithm requires at most $O(1/\epsilon)$ random queries to find such an input in step 11.

We have seen that steps 6, 8, 11, 12, 13 take at most poly$(n, \log b, \epsilon^{-1})$ time, so each iteration of Algorithm 2 runs in poly$(n, \log b, \epsilon^{-1})$ steps as claimed.

We note that we have been somewhat cavalier in our treatment of the failure probabilities for various events (such as the possibility of getting an inaccurate estimate of h's error rate in step 9, or not finding a suitable element $(x_1, \ldots, x_n)$ soon enough in step 11). A standard analysis shows that all these failure probabilities can be made suitably small so that the overall failure probability is at most δ within the claimed runtime.   □

6   Applications to Learning Unions of Rectangles

In this section we apply the results we have obtained in Sections 4 and 5 to obtain results on learning unions of rectangles and related classes.

6.1   Learning Majorities of Many Low-Dimensional Rectangles

The following lemma will let us apply our algorithm for learning MAJORITY of PARITY of b-literals to learn MAJORITY of AND of b-literals:

Lemma 10. *Let $f\colon \{-1,1\}^n \to \{-1,1\}$ be expressible as an s-MAJORITY of r-AND of Boolean literals. Then f is also expressible as a $O(ns^2)$-MAJORITY of r-PARITY of Boolean literals.*

We note that Krause and Pudlák gave a related but slightly weaker bound in [17]; they used a probabilistic argument to show that any s-MAJORITY of AND of Boolean literals can be expressed as an $O(n^2s^4)$-MAJORITY of PARITY. Our boosting-based argument below closely follows that of [13, Corollary 13].

Proof of Lemma 10: Let f be the MAJORITY of $h_1, \ldots, h_s$ where each h_i is an AND gate of fan-in r. By Lemma 2, given any distribution $\mathcal{D}$ there is some AND function h_j such that $|\mathbf{E}_\mathcal{D}[fh_j]| \geq 1/s$. It is not hard to show that the L_1-norm of any AND function is at most 4 (see, e.g., [18, Lemma 5.1] for a somewhat more general result), so we have $L_1(h_j) \leq 4$. Now the argument from the proof of Lemma 7 shows that there must be some parity function χ_a such that $|\mathbf{E}_\mathcal{D}[f\chi_a]| \geq 1/4s$, where the variables in χ_a are a subset of the variables in h_j – and thus χ_a is a parity of at most r literals. Consequently, we can apply the boosting algorithm of [8] stated in Theorem 4, choosing the weak hypothesis to be a PARITY with fan-in at most r at each stage of boosting, and be assured that each weak hypothesis has advantage at least $1/4s$ at every stage of boosting. If we boost to accuracy $\epsilon = \frac{1}{2^n+1}$, then the resulting final hypothesis will have zero error with respect to f and will be a MAJORITY of $O(\log(1/\epsilon)/s^2) = O(ns^2)$ many r-PARITY functions. Note that while this argument does not lead to a computationally efficient construction of the desired MAJORITY of r-PARITY, it does establish its existence, which is all we need.   □

Note that clearly any union (OR) of s many r-rectangles can be expressed as an $O(s)$-MAJORITY of r-rectangles as well.

Theorem 1 and Lemma 10 together give us Theorem 2. (In fact, these results give us learnability of s-MAJORITY of r-AND of b-literals which need not necessarily be basic.)

6.2   Learning Unions of Fewer Rectangles of Higher Dimension

We now show that the number of rectangles s and the dimension bound r of each rectangle can be traded off against each other in Theorem 2 to a limited extent. We state the results below for the case $s = \text{poly}(\log(n \log b))$, but one could obtain analogous results for a range of different choices of s.

We require the following lemma:

Lemma 11. *Any s-term r-DNF can be expressed as an $r^{O(\sqrt{r} \log s)}$-MAJORITY of $O(\sqrt{r} \log s)$-PARITY of Boolean literals.*

Proof. [16, Corollary 13] states that any s-term r-DNF can be expressed as an $r^{O(\sqrt{r} \log s)}$-MAJORITY of $O(\sqrt{r} \log s)$-ANDs. By considering the Fourier representation of an AND, it is clear that each t-AND in the MAJORITY can be replaced by at most $2^{O(t)}$ many t-PARITYs, corresponding to the parities in the Fourier representation of the AND. This gives the lemma.   □

Now we can prove Theorem 3, which gives us roughly a quadratic improvement in the dimension r of rectangles over Theorem 2 if $s = \text{poly}(\log(n \log b))$.

Proof of Theorem 3: First note that by Lemma 9, any function in $C_{n,b}$ can have at most $\kappa = O(rs) = \text{poly}(\log(n \log b))$ non-trivial indices, and at most $\ell = O(s) = \text{poly}(\log(n \log b))$ many i-sensitive values for all $i = 1, \ldots, n$. Now use Lemma 11 to express any function in $C_{n,b}$ as an s'-MAJORITY of r'-PARITY of basic b-literals where $s' = r^{O(\sqrt{r} \log s)} = \text{poly}(n \log b)$ and $r' = O(\sqrt{r} \log s) = O(\frac{\log(n \log b)}{\log \log \log(n \log b)})$. Finally, apply Theorem 9 to obtain the desired result.   □

Note that it is possible to obtain a similar result for learning $\text{poly}(\log(n \log b))$ union of $O(\frac{\log^2(n \log b)}{(\log \log(n \log b))^4})$-AND of b-literals if one were to invoke Theorem 1.

6.3   Learning Majorities of Unions of Disjoint Rectangles

A set $\{R_1, \ldots, R_s\}$ of rectangles is said to be *disjoint* if every input $x \in [b]^n$ satisfies at most one of the rectangles. Learning unions of disjoint rectangles over $[b]^n$ was studied by [4], and is a natural analogue over $[b]^n$ of learning "disjoint DNF" which has been well studied in the Boolean domain (see e.g. [15, 2]).

We observe that when disjoint rectangles are considered Theorem 2 extends to the concept class of majority of unions of disjoint rectangles; enabling us to improve the depth of our circuits by 1. This extension relies on the easily verified fact that if $f_1, \ldots, f_t$ are functions from $[b]^n$ to $\{-1, 1\}^n$ such that each x satisfies at most one f_i, then the function $\text{OR}(f_1, \ldots, f_t)$ satisfies $L_1(\text{OR}(f_1, \ldots, f_t)) = O(L_1(f_1) + \cdots + L_1(f(t)))$. This fact lets us apply the argument behind Theorem 6 without modification, and we obtain Corollary 1. Note that only the rectangles connected to the same OR gate must be disjoint in order to invoke Corollary 1.

7 Conclusions and Future Work

For future work, besides the obvious goals of strengthening our positive results, we feel that it would be interesting to explore the limitations of current techniques for learning unions of rectangles over $[b]^n$. At this point we cannot rule out the possibility that the Generalized Harmonic Sieve algorithm is in fact a $\text{poly}(n, s, \log b)$-time algorithm for learning unions of s arbitrary rectangles over $[b]^n$. Can evidence for or against this possibility be given? For example, can one show that the representational power of the hypotheses which the Generalized Harmonic Sieve algorithm produces (when run for $\text{poly}(n, s, \log b)$ many stages) is – or is not – sufficient to express high-accuracy approximators to arbitrary unions of s rectangles over $[b]^n$?

References

[1] A. Akavia, S. Goldwasser, S. Safra, *Proving Hard Core Predicates Using List Decoding*, Proc. **44**th IEEE Found. Comp. Sci.: 146–156 (2003).

[2] H. Aizenstein, A. Blum, R. Khardon, E. Kushilevitz, L. Pitt, D. Roth, *On Learning Read-k Satisfy-j* DNF, SIAM Journal on Computing, **27**(6): 1515–1530 (1998).

[3] A. Atıcı and R. Servedio, *Learning Unions of $\omega(1)$-Dimensional Rectangles*, available at http://arxiv.org/abs/cs.LG/0510038

[4] A. Beimel, E. Kushilevitz, *Learning Boxes in High Dimension*, Algorithmica, **22**(1/2): 76–90 (1998).

[5] J. Bruck. *Harmonic Analysis of Polynomial Threshold Functions*, SIAM Journal on Discrete Mathematics, **3**(2): 168–177 (1990).

[6] Z. Chen and S. Homer, *The Bounded Injury Priority Method and The Learnability of Unions of Rectangles*, Annals of Pure and Applied Logic, **77**(2): 143–168 (1996).

[7] Z. Chen and W. Maass, *On-line Learning of Rectangles and Unions of Rectangles*, Machine Learning, **17**(2/3): 23–50 (1994).

[8] Y. Freund, *Boosting a Weak Learning Algorithm by Majority*, Information and Computation, **121**(2): 256–285 (1995).

[9] Y. Freund and R. Schapire. *A Short Introduction to Boosting*, Journal of the Japanese Society for Artificial Intelligence, **14**(5): 771–780 (1999).

[10] P. W. Goldberg, S. A. Goldman, H. D. Mathias, *Learning Unions of Boxes with Membership and Equivalence Queries*, COLT '94: Proc. of the **7**th annual conference on computational learning theory: 198 – 207 (1994).

[11] A. Hajnal, W. Maass, P. Pudlák, M. Szegedy, G. Turan, *Threshold Circuits of Bounded Depth*, J. Comp. & Syst. Sci. **46**: 129–154 (1993).

[12] J. Håstad, *Computational Limitations for Small Depth Circuits*, MIT Press, Cambridge, MA (1986).

[13] J. C. Jackson, *An Efficient Membership-Query Algorithm for Learning* DNF *with Respect to the Uniform Distribution*, J. Comp. & Syst. Sci. **55**(3): 414–440 (1997).

[14] J. C. Jackson, A. R. Klivans, R. A. Servedio, *Learnability Beyond* AC^0, Proc. of the **34**th annual ACM symposium on theory of computing (STOC): 776–784 (2002).

[15] R. Khardon. *On Using the Fourier Transform to Learn Disjoint* DNF, Information Processing Letters,**49**(5): 219–222 (1994).

[16] A. R. Klivans, R. A. Servedio, *Learning* DNF *in Time* $2^{\tilde{O}(n^{1/3})}$, J. Comp. & Syst. Sci. **68**(2): 303–318 (2004).

[17] M. Krause and P. Pudlák, *Computing Boolean Functions by Polynomials and Threshold Circuits*, Computational Complexity **7**(4): 346–370 (1998).

[18] E. Kushilevitz and Y. Mansour, *Learning Decision Trees using the Fourier Spectrum*, SIAM Journal on Computing **22**(6): 1331-1348 (1993).

[19] W. Maass and M. K. Warmuth, *Efficient Learning with Virtual Threshold Gates*, Information and Computation, **141**(1): 66–83 (1998).

[20] R. E. Schapire, *The Strength of Weak Learnability*, Machine Learning **5**: 197–227 (1990).

On Exact Learning Halfspaces with Random Consistent Hypothesis Oracle

(Extended Abstract)

Nader H. Bshouty and Ehab Wattad

Department of Computer Science
Technion, Haifa, 32000, Israel.
{bshouty, wattad}@cs.technion.ac.il

Abstract. We study exact learning of halfspaces from equivalence queries. The algorithm uses an oracle RCH that returns a random consistent hypothesis to the counterexamples received from the equivalence query oracle. We use the RCH oracle to give a new polynomial time algorithm for exact learning halfspaces from majority of halfspaces and show that its query complexity is less (by some constant factor) than the best known algorithm that learns halfspaces from halfspaces.

1 Introduction

In this paper we consider learning strategies for exact learning halfspaces, HS_n^d, over the domain $\{0, 1, \ldots, n-1\}^d$ from equivalence queries and study the query complexity and the time complexity of exact learning using those strategies. Our strategies are based on two basic oracles. An RCH_C-oracle that chooses a uniform random consistent (to the counterexamples) halfspace from HS_n^d and an RCH-oracle that chooses a random consistent halfspace over $\Re^d$ (uniform random halfspace from the dual space of all consistent halfspaces). The advantage of the RCH-oracle over the RCH_C-oracle is that it can be simulated in polynomial time [L98].

We study exact learning halfspaces using both oracles. We first show that the Halving algorithm can be performed using a number of calls to RCH_C-oracle that depends only on the dimension of the space d. We then give a new polynomial time exact learning algorithm that uses the RCH-oracle for learning halfspaces from majority of halfspaces. We show that the latter algorithm runs in polynomial time with query complexity that is less (by some constant factor) than the best known algorithm that learns halfspaces from halfspaces.

2 Preliminaries

In this section we give some preliminaries and introduce some terms and concepts that will be used throughout the paper.

J.L. Balcázar, P.M. Long, and F. Stephan (Eds.): ALT 2006, LNAI 4264, pp. 48–62, 2006.

2.1   Probability

Let F be a Boolean functions $F : X \to \{0,1\}$ and D a distribution on X. Let $\mathcal{U}$ be the uniform distribution over X. For $S \subseteq X$, we will write $x \in_D S$ when we want to indicate that x is chosen from S according to the distribution D. Suppose we randomly and independently choose $S = \{x^{(1)}, \ldots, x^{(m)}\}$ from X, each $x^{(i)}$ according to the distribution D. We will write E_X for $E_{x \in_D X}$ and E_S for $E_{x \in_{\mathcal{U}} S}$. We say that $\mathcal{S} = (X, C)$ is a *range space* if C is a set of Boolean functions $f : X \to \{0,1\}$. Each function in C can be also regarded as a subset of X. We will also call C a *concept class*. For a Boolean function $F \in C$ and a subset $A \subseteq X$ the *projection of F on A* is the Boolean function $F_{|_A} : A \to \{0,1\}$, such that, for every $x \in A$ we have $F_{|_A}(x) = F(x)$. For a subset $A \subseteq X$ we define the *projection of C on A* to be the set $P_C(A) = \{F_{|_A} \mid F \in C\}$. If $P_C(A)$ contains all the functions, 2^A, then we say that A is *shattered*. The *Vapnik-Chervonenkis dimension* (or VC-dimension) of $\mathcal{S}$, denoted by $\mathrm{VCdim}(\mathcal{S})$, is the maximum cardinality of a subset S of X that is shattered.

Let (X, C) be a range space and D be a distribution on X. We say that a set of points $S \subseteq X$ is an ϵ-*net* if for any $F \in C$ that satisfies $E_X[F(x)] > \epsilon$, S contains at least one *positive point for F*, i.e., a point y in S such that $F(y) = 1$. Notice that $E_S[F(x)] = 0$ if and only if S contains no positive point for F. Therefore, S is not an ϵ-net if and only if

$$(\exists F \in C) \; E_X[F(x)] > \epsilon \text{ and } E_S[F(x)] = 0.$$

We say that S is ϵ-*sample* if

$$(\forall F \in C) \; |E_X[F(x)] - E_S[F(x)]| \le \epsilon.$$

Notice that an ϵ-sample is an ϵ-net. We now list few results from the literature

Lemma 1. *Let $F : X \to \{0,1\}$ be a Boolean function. Suppose we randomly and independently choose $S = \{x^{(1)}, \ldots, x^{(m)}\}$ from X according to the distribution D.*
Bernoulli *For $m = \frac{1}{\epsilon} \ln \frac{1}{\delta}$ we have*

$$\Pr\left[E_X[F(x)] > \epsilon \text{ and } E_S[F(x)] = 0\right] \le \delta.$$

Chernoff *(Additive form) For $m = \frac{1}{2\epsilon^2} \ln \frac{2}{\delta}$ we have*

$$\Pr\left[|E_X[F(x)] - E_S[F(x)]| > \epsilon\right] \le 2e^{-2\epsilon^2 m} = \delta.$$

It follows from Lemma 1

Lemma 2. *Let C be a concept class of Boolean functions $F : X \to \{0,1\}$. Suppose we randomly and independently choose $S = \{x^{(1)}, \ldots, x^{(m)}\}$ from X according to the distribution D.*
Bernoulli *For any finite concept class C and*

$$m = \frac{1}{\epsilon}\left(\ln |C| + \ln \frac{1}{\delta}\right)$$

we have $\Pr\left[(\exists F \in C)\ E_X[F(x)] > \epsilon \text{ and } E_S[F(x)] = 0\right] \le \delta.$

That is, with probability at least $1 - \delta$, *the set* S *is* ϵ-*net.*

Chernoff *(Additive form) For any finite concept class* C *and*

$$m = \frac{1}{2\epsilon^2}\left(\ln|C| + \ln\frac{2}{\delta}\right)$$

we have $\Pr\left[(\exists F \in C)\ |E_X[F(x)] - E_S[F(x)]| > \epsilon\right] \le \delta.$

That is, with probability at least $1 - \delta$, *the set* S *is* ϵ-*sample.*

The following uses the VCdim and for many concept classes C gives a better bound

Lemma 3. *Let* C *be a concept class of Boolean functions* $F : X \to \{0,1\}$. *Suppose we randomly and independently choose* $S = \{x^{(1)}, \ldots, x^{(m)}\}$ *from* X *according to the distribution* D.

ϵ-**Net** *([HW87], [BEHW89]) There is a constant* c_{Net} *such that for any concept class* C *and*

$$m = \frac{c_{Net}}{\epsilon}\left(VCdim(C)\log\frac{1}{\epsilon} + \log\frac{1}{\delta}\right)$$

we have $\Pr\left[(\exists F \in C)\ E_X[F(x)] > \epsilon \text{ and } E_S[F(x)] = 0\right] \le \delta.$

That is, with probability at least $1 - \delta$, *the set* S *is* ϵ-*net.*

ϵ-**Sample** *([VC71]) There is a constant* c_{VC} *such that for any concept class* C *and*

$$m = \frac{c_{VC}}{\epsilon^2}\left(VCdim(C)\log\frac{VCdim(C)}{\epsilon} + \log\frac{1}{\delta}\right)$$

we have $\Pr\left[(\exists F \in C)\ |E_X[F(x)] - E_S[F(x)]| > \epsilon\right] \le \delta.$

That is, with probability at least $1 - \delta$, *the set* S *is* ϵ-*sample.*

2.2   Halfspace

A halfspace is a simple model of neuron activity. A simplified account of how neuron works can be found in [P94] Chapter 3.

Let $w = (w_1, \ldots, w_d) \in \Re^d$ and $t \in \Re$. We define the *halfspace* $f_{w,t}$ over $X \subseteq \Re^d$ (also called *linear threshold function* [P94] and *Perceptron* [MP43]) as follows:

$$f_{w,t}(x) = \begin{cases} 1 \text{ if } w^T x \ge t \\ 0 \text{ otherwise} \end{cases}$$

for every $x \in X$. We will also use the notation $f_{w,t} = [w^T x \ge t]$. The constants $w = (w_1, \ldots, w_d)$ are called the *weights* and t is called the *threshold* value. The class HS_X^d is the class of all halfspace functions over X. For the sake of notational convenience when $X = [n]^d = \{0, 1, \ldots, n-1\}^d$ we denote HS_X^d by HS_n^d and when $X = \Re$ we denote it by HS^d. When $n = 2$ we call $f_{w,t} \in \mathrm{HS}_2^d$ a *threshold* Boolean function. When the threshold value $t = 0$ we write f_w for $f_{w,t}$ and call it *zero halfspace* (also called *zero threshold* [P94]).

It is known that the VC-dimension of HS_X^d is at most $d + 1$ and of HS_2^d is exactly $d + 1$, [WD81].

We will now give some results for halfspaces that will be used in the sequel. We start with the following

Lemma 4. *([P94]) We have* $n^{d^2+d} > |HS_n^d| > n^{d(d-1)/2}$.

The proof in ([P94]) is for HS_2^d. The same proof is also true for HS_n^d. Notice also that the upper bound follows immediately from Sauer's Lemma

Lemma 5. *([P94]) For every* $f \in HS_2^d$ *there is* $w \in Z^d$ *and* $t \in Z$ *such that* $f_{w,t} \equiv f$ *and for all* $1 \le i \le n$,

$$|w_i| \le \frac{(d + 1)^{(d+1)/2}}{2^d} = d^{\frac{d}{2} - \frac{d}{\log d} + o(1)}.$$

Hastad [H94] showed that this bound is tight for d that is power of 2. That is, for any integer k and for $d = 2^k$ there is a halfspace f such that for any $f_{w,t} \equiv f$ there is $1 \le i \le n$ with $|w_i| \ge d^{\frac{d}{2} - \frac{d}{\log d}}$. For HS_n^d and d that is power of 2, Hastad achieves the bound

$$|w_i| \ge (n - 1)^d d^{\frac{d}{2} - \frac{d}{\log d}}.$$

On the other hand, we have

Lemma 6. *([MT94]) For every* $f \in HS_n^d$ *there is* $w \in Z^d$ *and* $t \in Z$ *such that* $f \equiv f_{w,t}$ *and for every* $1 \le i \le n$, $|w_i| \le 3n^{2(d+1)}(2d + 2)^{d+2}$.

Using a similar technique as in [P94] we prove in the full paper the following

Lemma 7. *For every* $f \in HS_n^d$ *there is* $w \in Z^d$ *and* $t \in Z$ *such that* $f \equiv f_{w,t}$ *and for every* $1 \le i \le n$,

$$|w_i| \le \frac{(n - 1)^{d-1}(d + 1)^{(d+1)/2}}{2^d},$$

$$|t| < (n - 1)\sum_i |w_i| = \frac{(n - 1)^d d(d + 1)^{(d+1)/2}}{2^d}.$$

2.3   Dual Domain

Define a map $\phi : \Re^{d+1} \to HS_X^d$ where $\phi(w, t) = f_{w,t}$. Notice that two different points (w_1, t_1) and (w_2, t_2) may map into the same halfspace, i.e., $\phi(w_1, t_1) \equiv \phi(w_2, t_2)$. We call the domain $\Re^{d+1}$ in ϕ the *coefficients domain* or the *dual domain*. For $f \in HS_X^d$, we call $\phi^{-1}(f) \in \Re^{d+1}$ the polytope that corresponds to f in the dual space. For a d-hypercube $U_R = [-R, R]^{d+1}$ we say that U_R *covers* HS_X^d if for every $f_{w,t} \in HS_X^d$ there is $(u, t') \in U_R$ such that $\phi(u, t') = f_{u,t'} \equiv f_{w,t}$. For a hypercube U_R that covers HS_X^d we define

$$V_{min}(R) = \min_{f \in HS_X^d} \text{Vol}(U_R \cap \phi^{-1}(f)),$$

where Vol() is the volume in the $(d+1)$-dimensional space. This is the minimal volume of polytope in U_R that corresponds to $f \in \mathrm{HS}_X^d$.

By Lemma 7 we can choose for HS_n^d,

$$R = \frac{(n-1)^d d(d+1)^{(d+1)/2}}{2^d}. \tag{1}$$

Lemma 8. *For R in (1) we have*

$$V_{min}(R) \geq \frac{1}{2^{d+1}(d(n-1))^d}.$$

The proof is in the full paper.

2.4 Convex Set

A subset $K \subset \Re^d$ is called *convex set* if for every $x, y \in K$ and every $0 \leq \lambda \leq 1$ we have $\lambda x + (1 - \lambda)y \in K$, i.e., the line connecting the two points x and y is in K.

An *affine transformation* is $\phi_{A,B} : x \mapsto Ax + B$ where A and B are $d \times d$ matrices and A is nonsingular $(det(A) \neq 0)$. The affine transformation changes the volume of any subset by the same factor $\alpha = |det(A)|$. In particular,

$$\mathrm{Vol}(\phi_{A,B}(K)) = |det(A)|\mathrm{Vol}(K).$$

For a uniform random point x in K the *centroid (center of gravity)* is $E_K[x]$ and the covariant matrix is $E_K[xx^T]$. A convex set K in $\Re^d$ is said to be in *isotropic position* if:

1. The centroid of K is the origin, i.e., $E_K[x] = 0$
2. The covariant matrix of K is the identity, i.e., $E_K[xx^T] = I$.

For any full-dimensional $(\mathrm{Vol}(K) \neq 0$ in $\Re^d)$ convex set, there exists an affine transformation that puts the set in isotropic position.

It is known from [G60]

Lemma 9. *For a convex set K, any cut through its centroid by a halfspace has at least $1/e$ of the volume on each side.*

In [BV02], Bertsimas and Vempala show

Lemma 10. *Let K be a convex set in isotropic position and z be a point at distance t from its centroid. Then any halfspace containing z also contains at least $\frac{1}{e} - t$ of the volume of K.*

In the full paper we use the above with Lemma 10 to prove the following

Lemma 11. *Let K be a convex set in $\Re^d$. Let z be the average of kd random uniform points in K. Then with probability at least $1 - \delta$ any halfspace containing z also contains at least $\frac{1}{e} - \frac{1}{\sqrt{k\delta}}$ of the volume of K.*

3   Learning Models

In the *online learning model* [L88] the learning task is to identify an unknown *target* halfspace f that is chosen by a *teacher* from HS_X^d. At each *trial*, the teacher sends a point $x \in X$ to the *learner* and the learner has to predict $f(x)$. The learner returns to the teacher a prediction y. If $f(x) \neq y$ then the teacher returns "mistake" to the learner. The goal of the learner is to minimize the number of prediction mistakes.

In the online learning model we say that algorithm $\mathcal{A}$ of the learner *online learns* the class HS_X^d if for any $f \in \mathrm{HS}_X^d$ and for any δ, algorithm $\mathcal{A}(\delta)$ with probability at least $1 - \delta$ makes a bounded number of mistakes. We say that HS_X^d is *online learnable* with t mistakes if the number of mistakes is bounded by t. We say that HS_X^d is *efficiently online learnable* with t mistakes if the number of mistakes is bounded by t and the running time of the learner for each prediction is $poly(1/\delta, d, \log |X|)$. The bound of the number of mistakes t of an online learning algorithm is also called *the mistake bound* of the algorithm.

In the *exact learning model* [A88] the learning task is to identify an unknown *target* halfspace f, that is chosen by a *teacher* from HS_X^d, from *queries*. The learner at each trial sends the teacher a hypothesis h from some class of hypothesis H and asks the teacher whether this hypothesis is equivalent to the target function (this is called the *equivalence query*). The teacher either sends back a "YES" indicating that h is equivalent to the target function f or, otherwise, it sends a counterexample a. That is, an instance $a \in X$ such that $h(a) \neq f(a)$.

In the exact learning model we say that algorithm $\mathcal{A}$ of the learner *exactly learns* the class HS_X^d from H if for any $f \in \mathrm{HS}_X^d$ and for any δ, algorithm $\mathcal{A}(\delta)$ with probability at least $1 - \delta$ makes a bounded number of equivalence queries and finds a hypothesis in H that is equivalent to the target function f. We say that HS_X^d is *exactly learnable* from H with t equivalence queries if the number of equivalence queries is bounded by t. We say that HS_X^d is *efficiently exactly learnable* from H with t equivalence queries if the number of equivalence queries is bounded by t and the running time of the learner is $poly(1/\delta, d, \log |X|)$.

It is known [A88] that if HS_X^d is exactly learnable from H with t equivalence queries then HS_X^d is online learnable with $t - 1$ mistakes. If HS_X^d is efficiently exactly learnable from H with t equivalence queries and elements of H are efficiently computable (for each $h \in H$ and $x \in X$ we can compute $h(x)$ in polynomial time) then HS_X^d is efficiently online learnable with $t - 1$ mistakes.

4   Old and New Results

In this paper we consider different learning strategies for exact learning halfspaces and study the query complexity and time complexity of learning with those strategies. Our strategies are based on two basic oracles:

1. An RCH-oracle that chooses a uniform random halfspace in the dual domain that is consistent to the counterexamples seen so far.

2. An RCH_C-oracle that chooses a uniform random hypothesis from the class being learned C that is consistent to the counterexamples seen so far.

We will study the query complexity as well as the number of calls to the RCH-oracles and RCH_C-oracle.

The RCH-oracle can be simulated in polynomial time, [L98], and therefore all the algorithms in this paper that uses this oracle runs in polynomial time. On the other hand, it is not known how to simulate the RCH_C-oracle in polynomial time.

The first algorithm considered in this paper in the Halving algorithm [A88, L88]. In the Halving algorithm the learner chooses at each trial the majority of all the halfspaces in C that are consistent with the examples seen so far. Then it asks equivalence query with this hypothesis. Each counterexample for this hypothesis eliminates at least half of the consistent halfspaces. Therefore, by Lemma 4 the query complexity of the Halving algorithm is at most

$$\log |\mathrm{HS}_n^d| \le d^2 \log n + d \log n.$$

The randomized Halving algorithm [BC+96] uses the RCH_C-oracle and asks on average $(1+c)d^2 \log n$ equivalence queries[1] for any constant $c > 0$. For each query it takes the majority of $t = O(d \log n)$ uniform random halfspaces from C that are consistent to the counterexamples seen so far. This requires $t = O(d \log n)$ calls to the RCH_C-oracle. In the next section we will show that

$$t = O(d \min(\log d, \log n))$$

calls to the RCH_C-oracle suffices. Notice that, for large n the number of calls $O(d \log d)$ is independent of n. This significantly improves the number of calls to the RCH_C-oracle. In particular, for constant dimensional space, the number of calls to the oracle is $O(1)$. Unfortunately, we do not know if the RCH_C-oracle can be simulated in polynomial time and therefore this algorithm will not give a polynomial time learning algorithm for halfspaces.

The first (exponential time) learning algorithm for halfspaces was the Perceptron learning algorithm PLA [R62]. The algorithm asks equivalence query with (initially any) hypothesis $h_u(x) = [u^T x \ge 0]$. For a positive counterexample $(a, 1)$ it updates the hypothesis to h_{u+a} and for a negative counterexample it updates the hypothesis to h_{u-a}.

The equivalence query complexity of this algorithm is known to be $\|w\|^2 \delta_{max}/ \delta_{min}^2$ where $\delta_{min} = \min_{x \in X} |w^T x|$ and $\delta_{max} = \max_{x \in X} \|x\|^2$ where f_w is the target function. For HS_2^d the above query complexity is less than (see [M94])

$$d^{2+d/2}.$$

Therefore the running time of PLA is exponential.

Littlestone [L88] gave another algorithm (Winnow 2) for learning halfspaces. It is known from [S02] that Winnow 2 learning algorithm runs in exponential time.

---

[1] The complexity is $d^2 \log n + o(d^2 \log n)$ if we take $t = \omega(d \log n)$.

The first polynomial time learning algorithm was given by Maass and Turan [MT94]. They show that there is an Exact learning algorithm for HS_n^d that runs in polynomial time and asks

$$O(d^2(\log n + \log d))$$

equivalence queries with hypotheses that are halfspaces. Using recent results in linear programming we show that this algorithm uses

$$1.512 \cdot d^2 \left(\log n + \frac{\log d}{2}\right)$$

equivalence queries and $O(d)$ calls to the RCH-oracle in each trial.

In this paper we use a different approach and achieve a learning algorithm that uses

$$d^2 \left(\log n + \frac{\log d}{2}\right) \tag{2}$$

equivalence queries with hypotheses that are majority of halfspaces. Our algorithm uses $O(d \log d)$ calls to the RCH-oracle in each trial. Since the RCH-oracle can be simulated in polynomial time, our algorithm runs in polynomial time.

In [MT94] Maass and Turan also gave a lower bound of

$$\binom{d}{2} \log n \leq \frac{1}{2} d^2 \log n. \tag{3}$$

on the number of equivalence queries needed to learn HS_n^d with any learning algorithm that has unlimited computational power and that can ask equivalence query with any hypothesis.

5   Learning with Halving Algorithm

In this section we study the query complexity and the hypothesis size of the standard randomized Halving algorithm [BC+96]. We show

Theorem 1. *The randomized halving algorithm uses on average* $(1+c)d^2 \log n$ *equivalence queries for any constant* $c > 0$ *where each hypothesis to the equivalence query is the majority of* $t = O(d \min(\log d, \log n))$ *uniform random consistent halfspaces. That is, with* t *calls to the* RCH_C*-oracle in each trial.*

In the next subsection we give a general framework that proves a more general Theorem.

5.1   The Dual Concept Class

Let C be a concept class of functions $f : X \rightarrow \{0, 1\}$. We define the *dual class* $C^\perp$ of C, the set of all Boolean functions $F_x : C \rightarrow \{0, 1\}$ where, for

$x \in X$, we have $F_x(f) = f(x)$ for every $f \in C$. The *dual VC-dimension* of C, $\mathrm{VCdim}^{\perp}(C)$ is defined to be the VC-dimension of the dual class of C, i.e., $\mathrm{VCdim}^{\perp}(C) = \mathrm{VCdim}(C^{\perp})$.

The connection between the VC-dimension of C and its dual is given in the following

Lemma 12. *[BBK97] We have*

$$\lfloor \log VCdim(C) \rfloor \leq VCdim^{\perp}(C) \leq 2^{VCdim(C)+1}.$$

Since the dual of HS_n^d is subset of HS^{d+1}, we have $\mathrm{VCdim}^{\perp}(\mathrm{HS}_n^d) \leq d+2$.

For a concept class C of Boolean functions $f : X \to \{0,1\}$ we define the function

$$Maj(C)(x) = \begin{cases} 1 & \Pr_{f \in_{\mathcal{U}} C}[f(x) = 1] \geq \frac{1}{2} \\ 0 & \text{otherwise} \end{cases}$$

where the probability is over the uniform distribution over C. We write $g =_{\eta} Maj(C)$ if $g(x) = Maj(C)(x)$ for all points x that satisfies

$$\Delta(x) \stackrel{def}{=} |\Pr_f[f(x) = 1] - \Pr_f[f(x) = 0]| \geq \eta.$$

We now show

Lemma 13. *Let $f_1, \ldots, f_m$ be m independently uniform random functions from C where*

$$m = \frac{2}{\eta^2}\left(\ln|X| + \ln\frac{2}{\delta}\right).$$

Then with probability at least $1 - \delta$ we have $Maj(f_1, \ldots, f_m) =_{\eta} Maj(C)$.

Proof. We use Lemma 2. Consider the set $W = \{x \,|\, \Delta(x) \geq \eta\}$. Let the domain be $\mathcal{X} = C$, the concept class be $\mathcal{C} = \{F_x | x \in W\}$.

Consider the sample $S = \{f_1, \ldots, f_m\}$. Then by Lemma 2

$$\begin{aligned} \Pr[Maj(S) \neq_{\eta} Maj(C)] &= \Pr[(\exists x \in W)\ Maj(f_1(x), \ldots, f_m(x)) \neq Maj(C)(x)] \\ &\leq \Pr[(\exists x \in W)\ |E_{f \in \mathcal{X}}[f(x)] - E_{f \in S}[f(x)]| \geq \eta/2] \\ &\leq \Pr[(\exists F_x \in \mathcal{C})\ |E_{f \in \mathcal{X}}[F_x(f)] - E_{f \in S}[F_x(f)]| \geq \eta/2] \\ &\leq \delta. \qquad \blacksquare \end{aligned}$$

Notice that in Lemma 13 when X is infinite then m is infinite. In the next lemma we show that the sample is finite when the dual VC-dimension is finite.

Lemma 14. *Let $f_1, \ldots, f_m$ be m independently uniform random functions from C where*

$$m = \frac{c_{VC}}{\eta^2}\left(VCdim^{\perp}(C)\log\frac{VCdim^{\perp}(C)}{\eta} + \ln\frac{1}{\delta}\right).$$

Then with probability at least $1 - \delta$ we have $Maj(f_1, \ldots, f_m) =_{\eta} Maj(C)$.

Proof. We use Lemma 3 and the same proof as in Lemma 13. $\blacksquare$

5.2   The Randomized Halving Algorithm

In this subsection we prove the following result

Theorem 2. *Let C be a concept class. The randomized Halving algorithm for C asks on average*

$$(1 + c) \log |C|$$

equivalence queries for any constant c, where for each query it takes the majority of

$$m = O(\min(\log |X|, VCdim^{\perp}(C) \log VCdim^{\perp}(C))) \tag{4}$$

uniform random consistent functions from C.

We note here that the constant of m in the order of equation (4) depends on c.
Since $\text{VCdim}^{\perp}(HS_n^d) \leq d + 2$, Theorem 1 follows.

Proof of Theorem 2. We will show that if we choose

$$m = \min\left(\frac{2}{\eta^2} \left(\ln |X| + \ln \frac{2}{\delta} \right), \frac{c_{VC}}{\eta^2} \left(\text{VCdim}^{\perp}(C) \log \frac{\text{VCdim}^{\perp}(C)}{\eta} + \ln \frac{1}{\delta} \right) \right)$$

uniform random functions $f_1, \ldots, f_m$ from C then with probability at least $1 - \delta$ the equivalence query with $Maj(f_1, \ldots, f_m)$ returns a counterexample that eliminates at least $1/2 - \eta/2$ of the elements of C. This implies that on average the number of equivalence queries is

$$\frac{\log |C|}{(1 - \delta)(1 - \log(1 + \eta))} \leq (1 + c) \log |C|$$

for some constants η and δ. Then for constant η and δ we have

$$m = O(\min(\log |X|, \text{VCdim}^{\perp}(C) \log \text{VCdim}^{\perp}(C)).$$

To prove the above, let (x_0, y_0) be a counterexample received by the equivalence query oracle. We have two cases: If $\Delta(x_0) > \eta$ then with probability at least $1 - \delta$, $Maj(f_1(x_0), \ldots, f_m(x_0)) = Maj(C)(x_0)$ and then (as in the Halving algorithm) this counterexample eliminates at least half of the functions in C. If $\Delta(x_0) < \eta$ then by the definition of Δ at least $1/2 - \eta/2$ of the functions in C are not equal to y_0 on x_0 and therefore this counterexample eliminates at least $1/2 - \eta/2$ of the elements of C.   ∎

6   Polynomial Time Learning Halfspaces

In this section we describe Maass and Turan algorithm using the new linear programming results from the literature. We give the analysis of the complexity of the algorithm and then give our new algorithm and analyse its complexity.

6.1   Maass-Turan Algorithm

Following Maass and Turan techniques [MT94]: By Lemma 7 we may assume
that the target function $f_{w,t}$ satisfies: $w \in Z^d$ and $t \in Z$,

$$|w_i| \leq \frac{(n-1)^{d-1}(d+1)^{(d+1)/2}}{2^d},$$

for every $1 \leq i \leq n$ and

$$|t| < (n-1)\sum_i |w_i| = \frac{(n-1)^d d(d+1)^{(d+1)/2}}{2^d}.$$

Those inequalities define a domain for (w,t) in the dual domain $\Re^{d+1}$. Denote
this domain by W_0. Also, each counterexample $(x^{(i)}, f(x^{(i)}))$, $i = 1,\ldots,t$ received by an equivalence query defines a halfspace in the dual domain $\Re^{d+1}$,

$$\begin{cases} w^T x^{(i)} \geq 0 \text{ for } f(x^{(i)}) = 1 \\ w^T x^{(i)} < 0 \text{ for } f(x^{(i)}) = 0 \end{cases}$$

Let S be the set of counterexamples received from the first ℓ equivalence queries.
Suppose W_ℓ is the domain in the dual domain defined by $S = \{(x^{(i)}, f(x^{(i)})) \mid i = 1,\ldots,\ell\}$ and W_0. Any hypothesis $f_{w',t'}$ that is chosen for the $\ell + 1$ equivalence query is a point (w',t') in the dual domain. Any counterexample $p = (x^{(\ell+1)}, f(x^{(\ell+1)}))$ for $f_{w',t'}$ defines a new halfspace in the dual domain that
does not contain the point (w',t'). If the volume of any cut through the point
(w',t') has at least $1 - \alpha$ of the volume of W_ℓ then any counterexample will
define a new domain $W_{\ell+1}$ such that $\text{Vol}(W_{\ell+1}) \leq \alpha\text{Vol}(W_\ell)$. By Lemma 8 if
the volume $\text{Vol}(W_\ell)$ is less than

$$V_{min} \overset{\Delta}{=} \frac{1}{2^{d+1}(d(n-1))^d},$$

then any point (w',t') in the domain gives a unique halfspace. Since

$$Vol(W_0) = \frac{(n-1)^{d^2} d(d+1)^{\frac{(d+1)^2}{2}}}{2^{(d-1)(d+1)}}$$

and

$$Vol(W_{\ell+1}) \leq \alpha Vol(W_\ell),$$

the number of equivalence queries in this algorithm is

$$\frac{\log \frac{Vol(W_0)}{V_{min}}}{\log \frac{1}{\alpha}} = c_\alpha d^2 \left(\log n + \frac{\log d}{2}\right) + O(d(\log n + \log d)) \tag{5}$$

where

$$c_\alpha = \frac{1}{\log \frac{1}{\alpha}}.$$

This algorithm is equivalent to the algorithms that finds a point in a convex set using a separation oracle. Today there are many methods for solving this problem [V96, BV02, DV04].

If we choose (w', t') to be the centroid of W_ℓ then by Lemma 9 we have $\alpha = 1 - e^{-1}$ and $c_\alpha = 1.512$. Since there is no polynomial time algorithm that find the centroid we use Lemma 11. We use the RCH-oracle to choose $kd = O(d)$ random uniform points in W_ℓ and take the average point $z = (w'', t'')$. Then by Lemma 11 with probability at least $1 - \delta$ any halfspace (counterexample) containing z also contains at least $1/e - 1/\sqrt{k\delta}$ of the volume of W_ℓ. Therefore in each trial we have with probability at least $1 - \delta$, $\alpha = 1 - e^{-1} + 1/\sqrt{k\delta}$. Now for appropriate constants k and δ the query complexity is on average

$$(1.512 + c) \cdot d^2 \left(\log n + \frac{\log d}{2} \right)$$

for any constant $c > 0$.

In this paper we use a different approach and achieve a learning algorithm that uses on average

$$(1 + c) \cdot d^2 \left(\log n + \frac{\log d}{2} \right)$$

equivalence queries for any constant $c > 0$ using $O(d \log d)$ calls to the RCH-oracle. Since RCH can be simulated in polynomial time, our algorithm runs in polynomial time.

6.2 Our Algorithm

Our algorithm simply uses the Randomized Halving algorithm but with the RCH-oracle instead of the RCH_C-oracle. Since the RCH-oracle can be simulated in polynomial time, the algorithm runs in polynomial time.

We first show the following

Lemma 15. *Let $W \subseteq \Re^{d+1}$ be any domain of volume V and consider all the halfspaces over W, HS_W^{d+1}. Let S be a set of m uniform random points in W where*

$$m = \frac{c_{VC}}{\epsilon^2} \left((d+2) \log \frac{d+2}{\epsilon} + \log \frac{1}{\delta} \right).$$

Then with probability at least $1 - \delta$ any cut (by a halfspace) in W that contains at most $m/2$ points is of volume at most $(1/2 + \epsilon)V$.

Proof. This Lemma follows from the ϵ-Sample in Lemma 3. Consider $X = W$ and $C = HS_W^{d+1}$. Then for a halfspace F, $E_X[F(x)]$ is equal to the volume V_{cut} of the cut (of this halfspace) over the volume of W and for the desired cut $E_S[F(x)] < 1/2$. Now since VC-dimension of HS_W^{d+1} is at most $d+2$ we have with probability at least $1 - \delta$,

$$|V_{cut}/V - 1/2| < \epsilon.$$

This follows the result. ∎

We now give the algorithm:

Algorithm **RanHalv**
1. $S \leftarrow \emptyset$.
2. $W(S) = W_0 \cap$ The halfspaces defined by S.
3. Choose $m = \frac{c_{VC}}{\epsilon^2}\left((d+2)\log\frac{d+2}{\epsilon} + \log\frac{1}{\delta}\right)$ uniform random functions $F = \{f_{w_1,t_1}, \ldots, f_{w_m,t_m}\}$ using the RCH-oracle on the domain $W(S)$.
4. Ask $EQ(Maj(F)) \rightarrow b$.
5. If $b=$"Yes"
6.   then output($Maj(F)$)
7.   else $S \leftarrow S \cup \{(b, \overline{Maj(F)(b)})\}$
8. Goto 2

Fig. 1. Randomized Halving using the RCH-oracle

The algorithm **RanHalv** in Figure 1 is the randomized halving algorithm but instead of using the RCH_C-oracle it uses the RCH-oracle. We prove the following

Theorem 3. *Algorithm* **RanHalv** *learns the class* HS_n^d *with, on average,*

$$(1+c) \cdot d^2 \left(\log n + \frac{\log d}{2}\right)$$

equivalence queries for any constant $c > 0$ *using* $m = O(d\log d)$ *calls to the RCH-oracle in each trial.*

Proof. Let $f_{w_1,t_1}, \ldots, f_{w_m,t_m}$ be

$$m = \frac{c_{VC}}{\epsilon^2}\left((d+2)\log\frac{d+2}{\epsilon} + \log\frac{1}{\delta}\right)$$

uniform random consistent functions in HS_n^d. Let $W_\ell \subset \Re^{d+1}$ be as defined in subsection 6.1. Then the points $L = \{(w_1, t_1), \ldots, (w_m, t_m)\}$ are random points in W_ℓ. The counterexample (b, y) for $Maj(f_{w_1,t_1}, \ldots, f_{w_m,t_m})$ must be a counterexample for at least $m/2$ function in $F = \{f_{w_1,t_1}, \ldots, f_{w_m,t_m}\}$. This means that the cut $W_{\ell+1}$ in W_ℓ caused by this counterexample contains at most $m/2$ points from L. By Lemma 15 with probability at least $1 - \delta$ this cut satisfies

$$\text{Vol}(W_{\ell+1}) \leq \left(\frac{1}{2} + \epsilon\right)\text{Vol}(W_\ell).$$

Therefore, the number of equivalence queries is, on average,

$$\frac{1}{1-\delta} \frac{\log\frac{Vol(W_0)}{Vol(V_{min})}}{\log\frac{2}{1+2\epsilon}} \leq (1+c) \cdot d^2 \left(\log n + \frac{\log d}{2}\right)$$

and $m = O(d\log d)$ for sufficient small constants ϵ and δ. $\blacksquare$

Note that $c = O(\epsilon + \delta)$ and can be made $o(1)$ with respect to d and n for any $1/\epsilon, 1/\delta = \omega(1)$.

7   Open Problems

In this paper we use a new technique and achieve a learning algorithm for half-spaces that uses on average

$$(1 + c) \cdot d^2 \left(\log n + \frac{\log d}{2} \right)$$

equivalence queries for any constant $c > 0$ using $O(d \log d)$ calls to the RCH-oracle.

In [MT94] Maass and Turan show a lower bound of

$$\binom{d}{2} \log n \leq \frac{1}{2} d^2 \log n.$$

on the number of equivalence queries needed to learn HS_n^d with any learning algorithm that has unlimited computational power that can ask equivalence query with any hypothesis. It is an open problem to

1. Close the gap between this lower bound and the new upper bound.
2. Get rid of the term $(d^2 \log d)/2$ in the upper bound.
3. Show that RCH_C can be simulated in polynomial time. This will give a polynomial time learning algorithm for HS_n^d with $d^2 \log n$ equivalence queries.

Another interesting question is whether parallel algorithms can speed up learning Halfspaces. From [B97], if there is a parallel algorithm with e processors that asks t parallel equivalence queries then there is a sequential algorithm that asks $t \log e$ equivalence queries. Now since $t \log e > (1/2)d^2 \log n$ and $e = poly(d, \log n)$, any efficient parallel algorithm for learning halfspaces will ask at least

$$\Omega \left(\frac{d^2 \log n}{\log d + \log \log n} \right)$$

parallel equivalence queries. Is there such algorithm?

It is also interesting to study learning Halfspaces in other models. See for example [BJT02, BG02].

References

[A88]   D. Angluin. Queries and concept learning. *Machine Learning*, 2, pp. 319-342, 1987.

[B97]   N. H. Bshouty. Exact learning of formulas in parallel. *Machine Learning*, 26, pp. 25-41, 1997.

[BBK97]   S. Ben-David, N. H. Bshouty, E. Kushilevitz. A Composition Theorem for Learning Algorithms with Applications to Geometric Concept Classes. STOC 97, pp. 324-333, 1997.

[BC+96]   N. H. Bshouty, R. Cleve, R. Gavaldà, S. Kannan, C. Tamon. Oracles and Queries That Are Sufficient for Exact Learning. *Journal of Computer and System Sciences*, 52(3): pp. 421-433, 1996.

[BEHW89]   A. Blumer, A. Ehrenfeucht, D. Haussler, M. K. Warmuth. Learnability
            and the Vapnik-Chervonenkis dimension. J. ACM 36(4): 929-965 (1989)
[BG02]   N. H. Bshouty and D. Gavinsky. PAC=PAExact and other equivalent
            models. FOCS 02. pp. 167-176, 2002.
[BJT02]   N. H. Bshouty, J. Jackson and C. Tamon, Exploring learnability between
            exact and PAC. COLT 02, pp. 244-254, 2002.
[BV02]   D. Bertsimas, S. Vempala. Solving convex programs by random walks.
            STOC 02: pp. 109-115, 2002.
[DV04]   J. Dunagan and S. Vempala. A simple polynomial-time rescaling algorithm
            for solving linear programs. STOC 04, pp. 315-320, 2004.
[G60]   B. Grunbaum. Partitions of mass-distributions and convex bodies by hy-
            perplanes. *Pacific J. Math*, 10, pp. 1257-1261, 1960.
[H94]   J. Hastad. On the Size of Weights for Threshold Gates. *SIAM Journal on
            Discrete Mathematics*, (7) 3, pp. 484-492, 1994.
[HW87]   D. Haussler and E. Welzl. Epsilon-nets and simplex range queries. *Discrete
            Comput. Geom.*, 2: pp. 127-151, 1987.
[L88]   N. Littlestone. Learning when irrelevant attributes abound: A new linear-
            threshold algorithm. *Machine Learning*, 2, pp. 285-318, 1988.
[L98]   L. Lovász. Hit-and-run mixes fast. *Mathematical Programming*, 86, pp.
            443-461, 1998.
[M94]   W. Maass. Perspectives of current research about the complexity of learn-
            ing on neural nets. In V. P. Roychowdhury, K. Y. Siu, and A. Orlitsky,
            editors, Theoretical Advances in Neural Computation and Learning, pp.
            295-336. Kluwer Academic Publishers (Boston), 1994.
[MP43]   W. S. McCulloch and W. Pitts. A logical calculus of ideas immanent in
            nervous activity. Bulletin of mathematical biophysics, 5:115-133, 1943.
[MT94]   W. Maass and G. Turan. How fast can a threshold gate learn. In S. J.
            Hanson, G. A. Drastal, and R. L. Rivest, editors, Computational Learning
            Theory and Natural Learning System: Constraints and Prospects, MIT
            Press (Cambridge), pp. 381-414, 1994.
[P94]   I. Parberry. Circuit complexity and neural networks. The MIT press
            (1994).
[R62]   F. Rosenblatt, Principles of neurodynamics: Perceptrons and the theory
            of brain mechanisms, Spartan Books, New York, 1962.
[S02]   R. Servedio. Perceptron, Winnow, and PAC Learning. *SIAM Journal on
            Computing*, 31(5), pp. 1358-1369, 2002.
[V96]   P. M. Vaidya. new algorithm for minimizing convex functions over convex
            sets. *Mathematical Programming*, pp. 291-341, 1996.
[V84]   L. Valiant. A theory of the learnable. *Communications of the ACM*,
            27(11), pp. 1134-1142, 1984.
[VC71]   V. N. Vapnik, A. Y. Chervonenkis, On the uniform convergence of relative
            frequencies of events to their probabilities. *theory of Probability and its
            Applications*, 16(2), pp. 264-280, 1971.
[W]   E. W. Weisstein. Gamma Function. From MathWorld–A Wolfram Web
            Resource. http://mathworld.wolfram.com/GammaFunction.html.
[WD81]   R. S. Wenocur, R. M. Dudley. Some special Vapnik-Chervonenkis classes,
            Discrete Math., 33, pp. 313-318, 1981.

Active Learning in the Non-realizable Case

Matti Kääriäinen

Department of Computer Science
University of Helsinki
matti.kaariainen@cs.helsinki.fi

Abstract. Most of the existing active learning algorithms are based on
the realizability assumption: The learner's hypothesis class is assumed
to contain a target function that perfectly classifies all training and test
examples. This assumption can hardly ever be justified in practice. In
this paper, we study how relaxing the realizability assumption affects
the sample complexity of active learning. First, we extend existing results on query learning to show that any active learning algorithm for
the realizable case can be transformed to tolerate random bounded rate
class noise. Thus, bounded rate class noise adds little extra complica-
tions to active learning, and in particular exponential label complexity
savings over passive learning are still possible. However, it is questionable
whether this noise model is any more realistic in practice than assuming
no noise at all.

Our second result shows that if we move to the truly non-realizable
model of statistical learning theory, then the label complexity of active
learning has the same dependence $\Omega(1/\epsilon^2)$ on the accuracy parameter ϵ
as the passive learning label complexity. More specifically, we show that
under the assumption that the best classifier in the learner's hypothesis class has generalization error at most $\beta > 0$, the label complexity
of active learning is $\Omega(\beta^2/\epsilon^2 \log(1/\delta))$, where the accuracy parameter
ϵ measures how close to optimal within the hypothesis class the active
learner has to get and δ is the confidence parameter. The implication of
this lower bound is that exponential savings should not be expected in
realistic models of active learning, and thus the label complexity goals
in active learning should be refined.

1 Introduction

In standard passive (semi)supervised learning, the labeled (sub)sample of training examples is generated randomly by an unknown distribution defining the
learning problem. In contrast, an active learner has some control over which examples are to be labeled during the training phase. Depending on the specifics
of the learning model, the examples to be labeled can be selected from a pool of
unlabeled data, filtered online from a stream of unlabeled examples, or synthe-
sized by the learner. The motivation for active learning is that label information
is often expensive, and so training costs can potentially be reduced significantly
by concentrating the labeling efforts on examples that the learner considers useful. This hope is supported by both theoretical and practical evidence: There

J.L. Balcázar, P.M. Long, and F. Stephan (Eds.): ALT 2006, LNAI 4264, pp. 63–77, 2006.

exist active learning algorithms that in certain restricted settings give provably exponential savings in label complexity [1, 2, 3, 4], and also a variety of heuristic methods that at least sometimes give significant label complexity savings in practice (see, e.g., [5] and the references therein).

Unfortunately, there is a huge gap between the theory and the practice of active learning, even without considering computational complexity issues. The theoretical methods rely on unrealistic assumptions that render them (or at least their analysis) inapplicable to real life learning problems, while the practically motivated heuristics have no associated theoretical guarantees and indeed often fail miserably. One of the most unrealistic assumptions common to virtually all theoretical work in active learning is the realizability (or PAC) assumption, i.e., the assumption that the correct labeling is given by a target function belonging to a known hypothesis class F. The realizability assumption is never true in practice — at least we are aware of no real world problem in which it could be justified — and seems to lead to fragile learning algorithms that may and often do completely break down when the problem turns out to be non-realizable. Thus, relaxing the realizability assumption is a necessary first step in making the theory of active learning relevant to practice.

Many relaxations to the realizability assumption have been studied in passive learning, but it is not at all clear which of them leads to the best model for active learning. If the assumptions are relaxed too little, the theory may remain inapplicable. On the other hand, if no restrictions on noise are imposed, learning becomes impossible. In this paper, we try to chart where exactly the fruitful regime for active learning resides on the on the range between full realizability and arbitrary adversarial noise. To this end, we study two relaxations to the realizability assumption, both adapted to active learning from passive learning.

First, we show that in the model of bounded rate class noise [6], active learning is essentially as easy as in the realizable case, provided that the noise is non-persistent, i.e., each label query is corrupted independently at random. The key idea is to cancel out the noise by repeating each query a sufficient number of times and using the majority of the answers as a proxy for the true label. This way, any active learning algorithm for the realizable case can be transformed to tolerate bounded rate class noise with the cost of increasing the label complexity by a factor that has optimal dependence on the noise rate and logarithmic dependence on the original label complexity in the realizable case. Applying the transformation to an optimal algorithm for the realizable case yields a close to optimal algorithm for the bounded rate class noise case, so there is no need to design active learning algorithms for the bounded rate class noise model separately. Our strategy of repeated queries is a simplification of a similar strategy independently proposed in the query learning context [7], but unlike the earlier solution, our adaptive sampling based strategy requires no prior knowledge on the noise rate nor a separate step for estimating an upper bound for it.

The noise cancelling transformation makes the bounded rate class noise model look quite suspicious: In theory, the strategy of repeated queries is close to optimal, yet in practice it would most likely fail. The reason for the likely failure is of course that in reality non-realizability is rarely caused by random noise alone. Instead, non-realizability typically arises also from the aspects of the learning problem that are not sufficiently well understood or well-behaved to be modelled accurately. In case none of the models fits the learning problem perfectly, justifying assumptions on how exactly the modelling assumptions (say, linear separability in feature space) are violated is hard. To cope with such deviations, a more general model for non-realizability is needed.

In the model of statistical learning theory [8] the data is assumed to be generated iid by some unknown distribution that defines the learning problem, but the relationship between the objects and the labels is only implicitly assumed to be approximately representable by some classifier in the learner's hypothesis class. This model has been very fruitful in passive learning: Not only has it resulted in a body of new interesting theory, but also in many successful algorithms (e.g., soft-margin SVMs) that indeed seem to handle the types of non-realizability encountered in practice quite nicely. We believe similar success is possible also in active learning. Firstly, the empirical observation that the statistical learning theory model fits nicely into many real learning problems (in the sense that the algorithms developed within the model work well in practice) remains true in the active learning case, as the learning problems are more or less the same. Secondly, recent results show that the model is benevolent enough to make non-trivial positive results in active learning possible. In particular, [4] presents an algorithm for the statistical learning theory framework that exhibits exponential label complexity savings, but only until a certain accuracy threshold is reached. Whether exponential savings are possible on all accuracy levels, i.e., whether active learning can improve the learning rate in the statistical learning theory framework, is an open question.

The main contribution of this paper is to show that the kind of exponential label complexity savings that can sometimes be obtained in the realizable case[1] are not possible if true non-realizable as in the statistical learning theory model is allowed. We show that if the realizability assumption is relaxed by assuming that the learning problem is such that the generalization error of the best classifier in the hypothesis class F is at most β, then the expected label complexity on some such problems has to be at least $\Omega(\beta^2/\epsilon^2)$ to guarantee that the generalization error of the hypothesis output by the active learner is within ϵ of optimal in F. We show this even in the noise-free case, i.e., when the labels are fully determined by a target function (possibly outside F), thus showing that the lower bound arises from non-realizability per se and not random noise as is the case with the lower bound for learning with membership queries in [9]. Also, the lower bound remains true even when the unlabeled examples are uniformly distributed.

If only the dependence on ϵ is concerned, the lower bound matches the upper bound $O(1/\epsilon^2)$ for passive learning. Thus, allowing true non-realizability makes active learning require the same order of labeled examples as passive learning does, which is in huge contrast to the realizable case in which exponential savings are sometimes known to be possible. This justifies our choice of not studying

---

[1] And in the bounded rate class noise case by our noise-cancelling transformation.

the more adversarial models of malicious noise that have been studied in passive learning, since already allowing arbitrary non-malicious errors seems to kill most of the potential of active learning. Our lower bound matches the above mentioned upper bound proved in [4] that shows that active learning can drop the label complexity exponentially even in the truly non-realizable case when the target accuracy ϵ is large in comparison to β. Combined, the results show that active learning can indeed help exponentially much in the initial phase of learning, after which the gains deteriorate and the speed of learning drops to match that of passive learning. This prediction is well in line with the empirical observations that active learning heuristics tend to initially clearly outperform passive learning algorithms, but become less useful or even harmful as the learning progresses.

In contrast to the recent label complexity lower bounds of $\Omega(1/\epsilon)$ for active learning in the realizable case [3], our lower bound does not depend on special properties of F or the data distribution, but applies whenever F contains at least two classifiers that sometimes agree and that disagree on an unbounded set. Also, our lower bound is better by a factor of $1/\epsilon$, which is to be expected due to non-realizability.

The rest of the paper is organized as follows. In Section 2, we introduce the active learning framework used in this paper. Section 3 is devoted to our positive result, showing how bounded rate class noise can be dealt with. Then, we move on to the more realistic full non-realizability assumption and prove our lower bound for that case in Section 4. Finally, the conclusions are presented in Section 5.

2   Learning Model

Throughout the following, we assume that the learning problem is modeled by a probability distribution P on (object, label) pairs $(X, Y) \in \mathcal{X} \times \mathcal{Y}$, whose marginal on $\mathcal{X}$ is denoted by P_X. The goal of the active learning algorithm is to find a classifier f with small generalization error $\varepsilon(f) = \mathbb{P}(f(X) \neq Y)$ with respect to this distribution. We compare the generalization error of the learned classifier to $\min_{f \in F} \varepsilon(f)$. Here, the hypothesis class F is used only as a comparison class, so the learner is not restricted to select its classifier from F. The realizable case is the special case where $\mathbb{P}(Y = f(X)) = 1$ for some $f \in F$.

What differentiates active learning from passive learning is that we assume that the active learner can choose the examples whose labels it wants to query. The amount and type of control in choosing the queries varies among different active learning models and ranges from complete freedom (query learning with membership queries), to selecting the query points from a pool of unlabeled data (pool-based active learning), to deciding online which queries to make while observing a stream of unlabeled data (filtering based active learning). Out of these variants, different flavors of the last two are considered the central active learning models.

Each variant of active learning has its own motivation, and since we do not have to, we will not commit to any one of them. Instead, we formulate our results so that they apply to a template active learning algorithm that is flexible enough to cover all the above mentioned active learning models simultaneously. The template is presented in Figure 1. Here, Teacher(x) denotes the label oracle, which according to our assumption of the data being iid samples from P implies that Teacher(x) $\sim P(Y|X = x)$, and that the answers of the teacher are independent given the query points.

ActiveLearn(ϵ, δ)
U = pool of unlabeled data sampled iid from P_X
do
    choose query point $x \in U$
    query y = Teacher(x)
    add more points to U by sampling from P_X
while (!stopping_condition)
output $f \in F$

Fig. 1. Template for active learning algorithms

The template defines how the active learner can access P. As long as P is not accessed except as seen in Figure 1, the active learner can be completely arbitrary and possibly randomized. The gray parts are optional, and the inclusion or exclusion thereof leads to different restricted models of active learning. More specifically, including all the gray parts corresponds to the general active learning algorithm in [3], including the constraint on query points being chosen from U which itself is not updated corresponds to pool-based active learning, and the case in which arbitrary label queries are allowed corresponds to query learning.

An active learning algorithm is defined to be (ϵ, δ)-successful with respect to a class of learning problems $\mathcal{P}$ and a hypothesis class F if, for all learning problems $P \in \mathcal{P}$, the generalization error of the classifier f output by the active learner is with probability at least $1 - \delta$ (over the examples and the randomness in the learner) within ϵ of the generalization error of the best classifier in F. The key quantities of interest to us are the random number $n(\epsilon, \delta)$ of queries to Teacher, also known as the active learning label complexity, and the number of unlabeled examples $m(\epsilon, \delta)$ the active learner samples from P_X. Even though labeled examples are typically assumed to be far more expensive than unlabeled examples, the latter cannot be assumed to be completely free (since already processing them costs something). Thus, the goal is to be successful with as small (expected) $n(\epsilon, \delta)$ as possible, while keeping the (expectation of) $m(\epsilon, \delta)$ non-astronomical.

Of course, the difficulty of active learning depends on what we assume of the underlying task P and also on what we compare our performance to. In our definition, these are controlled by the choice of $\mathcal{P}$ and the comparison class F. One extreme is the realizability assumption that corresponds to the assumption that

$$\mathcal{P}_F = \{P \mid \exists f \in F : P(f(X) = Y) = 1\},$$

and choosing the comparison class to be the same F in which the target is assumed to reside. As already mentioned, in this special case exponential savings are possible in case F is the class of threshold functions in one dimension [1]. Also, if F is the class of linear separators going through the origin in R^d, and in addition to realizability we assume that the distribution P_X is uniform on the unit sphere of R^d, successful active learning is possible with and $n = O(\log(1/\epsilon))$ label queries and $m = O(1/\epsilon)$ unlabeled examples, whereas the same task requires $n = \Omega(1/\epsilon)$ labeled examples in passive learning. Here, the dependence on all other parameters like d and δ has been abstracted away, so only the rate as a function of the accuracy parameter ϵ is considered. For algorithms achieving the above mentioned rates, see [2, 3].

The above cited results for the realizable case show that active learning can in some special cases give exponential savings, and this has lead some researchers to believe that such savings might be possible also for other function classes, without assumptions on P_X, and also without the realizability assumption. However, there is little concrete evidence supporting such beliefs.

3   Positive Result

Let us first replace the realizability assumption by the bounded rate class noise assumption introduced in the case of passive learning in [6]. More specifically, we assume that there exists a function $f \in F$ such that $\mathbb{P}(Y = f(X)|X) = 1 - \eta(X)$, where $\eta(X) < 1/2$ is the noise rate given X. Since $\eta(X) < 1/2$, the optimal Bayes classifier is in F.

The main technique we use to deal with the noise is applying an adaptive sampler to find out the "true" labels based on the teacher's noisy answers. In contrast to passive sampling, the sample size in adaptive sampling is a random quantity that may depend on the already seen samples (more technically, a stopping time). Adaptive samplers have been studied before in [10] in more generality, but they give no explicit bounds on the number of samples needed in the special case of interest to us here. To get such, we present a refined and simplified version of their general results that applies to our setting.

Lemma 1. *Suppose we have a coin with an unknown probability p of heads. Let $\delta > 0$. There is an adaptive procedure for tossing the coin such that, with probability at least $1 - \delta$*

1. *The number of coin tosses is at most*

$$\frac{\ln(2/\delta)}{4(1/2 - p)^2} \log \left(\frac{\ln(2/\delta)}{4(1/2 - p)^2} \right) = \tilde{O} \left(\frac{\ln(2/\delta)}{4(1/2 - p)^2} \right).$$

2. *The procedure reports correctly whether heads or tails is more likely.*

Proof. Consider the algorithm of Figure 2. By the Hoeffding bound, $p \in I_k$ with probability at least $1 - \delta/2^{k+1}$, and thus by the union bound the invariant $p \in I_k$ is true for all k with probability at least $1 - \delta$. Provided that this invariant is true, the algorithm clearly cannot output an incorrect answer. And by the same

AdaptiveQuery(δ)
set $n_0 = 1$ and toss the coin once;
for $k = 0, 1, \ldots$
    p_k = frequency of heads in all tosses so far
    $I_k = [p_k - \sqrt{\frac{(k+1)\ln(2/\delta)}{2^k}}, p_k + \sqrt{\frac{(k+1)\ln(2/\delta)}{2^k}}]$
    if$(0.5 \notin I_k)$ **break**
    toss the coin n_k more times, and set $n_{k+1} = 2n_k$
end
if$(I_k \subset [-\infty, 0.5])$ output TAILS
else output HEADS

Fig. 2. Procedure for determining the more likely outcome of a coin

invariant, due to the length of I_k decreasing toward zero, the algorithm will output something after at most the claimed number of coin tosses (in the special case $p = 1/2$ the algorithm will keep tossing the coin indefinitely, but in this case the bound on the number of tosses is also infinite).   □

Note that the adaptive sampler of the above lemma is almost as efficient as passive sampling would be if $|p - 1/2|$ was known in advance. Our positive result presented in the next theorem uses the adaptive sampler as a noise-cancelling subroutine. A similar method for cancelling class noise by repeated queries was independently presented in the query learning context in [7]. However, their strategy uses passive sampling, and thus either requires prior knowledge on $|p - 1/2|$ or a separate step for estimating a lower bound for it. Due to their method needing extra samples in this separate estimation step, our proposed solution will have a smaller total sample complexity.

Theorem 1. *Let A be an active learning algorithm for F that requires $n(\epsilon, \delta)$ label queries and $m(\epsilon, \delta)$ unlabeled examples to be (ϵ, δ)-successful in the realizable case. Then A can be transformed into a noise-tolerant (ϵ, δ)-successful active learner A' for the class of distributions obtained by adding bounded rate class noise to the distributions on which A is successful. With probability at least $1 - \delta$, the unlabeled sample complexity $m'(\epsilon, \delta)$ of A' is $m(\epsilon, \delta/3)$, and if the noise rate is upper bounded by $\alpha < 1/2$, then the label complexity $n'(\epsilon, \delta)$ of A' is at most*

$$n'(\epsilon, \delta) = \tilde{O}\left(\frac{\ln(\frac{18\mathbb{E}[n(\epsilon, \delta/3)]}{\delta^2})}{4(1/2 - \alpha)^2}\right) n(\epsilon, \delta/3).$$

Proof. We transform A to A' by replacing each label query Teacher(x) made by A by a call to **AdaptiveQuery**(δ'), where the role of the coin is played by the teacher that is corrupted by noise. By choosing δ' appropriately, we can ensure that if A does not make too many label queries, then all calls to **AdaptiveQuery** give the correct answer with sufficiently high probability, and thus A' outputs exactly the same answer in the noisy case as A would have done in the realizable case. We next show how this can be done in detail.

First split δ into three equal parts, covering the three ways in which the modified active learner A' simulating the behavior of A may fail. The simulation

A' may fail because A fails in the realizable case, A makes dramatically more label queries than expected, or one or more invocations to the adaptive sampling procedure of Lemma 1 used in the simulation fails. The first case can be covered by setting the parameters of A in the simulation to $(\epsilon, \delta/3)$. For the second case, we use Markov's inequality which implies that the probability of the inequality $n(\epsilon, \delta/3) \leq 3/\delta \cdot \mathbb{E}[n(\epsilon, \delta/3)]$ failing is at most $\delta/3$. In case it does not fail, we have an upper bound for the number of invocations to Lemma 1, and so splitting the remaining $\delta/3$ to the invocations of the adaptive sampler lets us choose its confidence parameter to be $\delta' = \delta^2/(9\mathbb{E}[n(\epsilon, \delta/3)])$. A simple application of the union bound then shows that the total probability of any of the failures happening is at most δ.

In case the no bad event happens, Lemma 1 shows that each of its invocations requires at most

$$\tilde{O}\left(\frac{\ln(\frac{18\mathbb{E}[n(\epsilon, \delta/3)]}{\delta^2})}{4(1/2 - \alpha)^2}\right)$$

calls to the noisy teacher. Also, if all these invocations give the correct answer, then A' behaves exactly as A, so the total number of label queries will be the label complexity $n(\epsilon, \delta/3)$ of A in the realizable case times the above, giving the label complexity in the theorem statement. By the same argument of identical behavior, the number of unlabeled examples $m'(\epsilon, \delta)$ required by A' is $m(\epsilon, \delta/3)$.

To complete the proof, it remains to observe that since the noise rate is bounded, the true target $f \in F$ in the realizable case is still the best possible classifier in the bounded class noise rate case. Thus, provided that none of the bad events happens, the fact that A provides an ϵ-approximation to the target in the realizable case directly implies that A' provides an ϵ-approximation to the best function in F in the noisy case.   □

The above theorem shows that allowing bounded rate class noise increases the active learning label complexity only by at most a multiplicative factor determined by the bound on the noise rate α and the logarithm of the label complexity of the active learning algorithm for the realizable case. Thus, for $\alpha < 1/2$ and neglecting logarithmic factors, the order of label complexity as a function of ϵ is unaffected by this kind of noise, so exponentially small label complexity is still possible. As the lower bound presented in the next section shows that the dependence on α is optimal, at most a logarithmic factor could be gained by designing active learners for the bounded rate class noise model directly instead of using the transformation.

Interestingly, it has been recently shown that if the noise rate is not bounded away from $1/2$ but may approach it near the class boundary, then exponential label complexity savings are no longer possible [11]. Thus, relaxing the conditions on the noise in this dimension any more is not possible without sacrificing the exponential savings: the optimal classifier being in F is not enough, but the noise rate really has to be bounded.

It can be claimed that the way A' deals with class noise is an abuse of the learning and/or noise model, that is, that A' cheats by making repeated queries.

It may be, for example, that repeated queries are not possible due to practical reasons (e.g., teacher destroys the objects as a side effect of determining the label). Also, it might be more natural to assume that the teacher makes random errors, but is persistent in the sense that it always gives the same answer when asked the same question. However, such persistently noisy answers define a deterministic labelling rule for all objects, so once the teacher is fixed, there is no randomness left in the noise. Thus, this kind of persistent noise is more naturally dealt with in the model of statistical learning theory that allows true non-realizability.

While the strategy of repeated queries looks suspicious and unlikely to have wide applicability in practice, we believe it is an artifact of suspicious modelling assumptions and should not be prohibited explicitly without additional reasons. It seems to us that even strategies that are not explicitly designed to use repeated queries may actually choose to do so, and thus great care should be taken in their analysis if repetitions are not permissible in the intended applications. As a special case, the number of times an object appears in the pool or stream of unlabeled data should not be automatically taken as an upper bound for the number of queries to the object's label — the original motivation for restricting label queries to unlabeled objects that occur in the sample from P_X was to control the difficulty of the queries [1], and repetitions hardly make a query more difficult. It is also noteworthy that in the regression setting the analogous phenomenon of repeated experiments is more a rule than an exception in optimal solutions to experimental and sequential design problems [12], whereas nonrepeatable experiments are handled as a separate special case [13]. The success of the experimental design approach suggests that maybe there is place for repeatable queries in active learning, too, and that repeatable and nonrepeatable queries definitely deserve separate treatment. While it is unclear to us how the case of nonrepeatable queries can be dealt with efficiently, the next section provides some idea of the difficulties arising there.

4   Negative Result

Let's now move on to true non-realizability and assume only that the learning task P is such that F contains a classifier with a small generalization error of at most β on P. That is, the class of distributions on which we wish the active learner to be successful is

$$\mathcal{P}_{F,\beta} = \{P \mid \exists f \in F : P(f(X) \neq Y) \leq \beta\}.$$

This class allows the target Y to behave completely arbitrarily at least on a set of objects with probability β. A related class of interest to us is

$$\mathcal{P}_{F,\beta}^{\mathrm{det}} = \{P \in \mathcal{P}_{F,\beta} \mid \exists g : P(Y = g(X)) = 1\},$$

in which random noise is excluded by postulating that Y is a function of X. This class models a situation in which the phenomenon to be learned is known to be deterministic, but only approximable by F (e.g., learning the conditions on inputs under which a deterministic computer program crashes).

The role of β is very similar to the role of the bound α on the noise rate in the previous section. While β has a natural interpretation as the best generalization performance achievable by F, it should not be thought of as a parameter known to the learner. Rather, the idea is to study active learning under the unrestricted non-realizability assumption (corresponding to the case $\beta = 1$), and just express the lower bounds of such methods in terms of β.

The question we analyze in this section is the following: Assuming $P \in \mathcal{P}_{F,\beta}$ or $P \in \mathcal{P}_{F,\beta}^{\text{det}}$, what is the expected number of label queries needed to actively learn a classifier from F whose generalization error is with probability at least $1 - \delta$ within ϵ from the optimum in F?

4.1   Lower Bound for the Noisy Case

In this section we introduce the ideas needed for the lower bound in the case of deterministic non-realizability by considering the simpler case in which random noise is allowed. The special case $\beta = 1/2 - \epsilon$ follows directly from lower bounds for learning with membership queries presented in [9], but the case of general $\beta > 0$ is to our knowledge new even when random noise is allowed.

The problem we study is predicting whether a coin with bias $1/2 \pm \epsilon$ is biased toward heads or tails[2]. This corresponds to the case where $\beta = 1/2 - \epsilon$ and P_X is concentrated on a single point $x_0 \in \mathcal{X}$ on which not all the classifiers in F agree. We further assume that $P(Y|X = x)$ for $x \neq x_0$ is the same for both possibilities of $P(Y|X = x_0)$ and that the learner knows it only has to distinguish between the two remaining alternative distributions P, so queries to objects other than x_0 provide no new information.

Intuitively, it seems clear that an active learner cannot do much here, since there is nothing but x_0 to query and so the only control the learner has is the number of queries. Indeed, by a known result from adaptive sampling mentioned in [10], an active learner still needs an expected number of $\Omega(1/\epsilon^2)$ label queries in this case, and thus has no advantage over passive learning.

The above argument gives a lower bound for the special case $P \in \mathcal{P}_{F,1/2}$, provided $|F| \geq 2$. Adapting the argument for general β can be done as follows. Suppose F contains two classifiers, say, f_0 and f_1, that sometimes agree and sometimes disagree with each other — this is always true if $|F| > 2$. Place P_X-probability 2β on an object x_0 on which f_0 and f_1 disagree, and the remaining P_X-probability $1 - 2\beta$ on an object x_1 on which they agree. Now, embed the above coin tossing problem with ϵ/β in place of ϵ to the object x_0 on which f_0 and f_1 disagree, and let both f_0 and f_1 be always correct on x_1. This way, the best classifier in F has error at most β — the better of the classifiers f_0 and f_1 errs at most half the time on x_0 and neither errs on x_1. By the coin tossing lower bound, $\Omega(\beta^2/\epsilon^2)$ label queries are needed to find out whether f_0 or f_1 is better,

---

[2] This learning problem is also a simple example of a case in which prohibiting repeated queries or insisting on persistence of noise makes no sense.

even assuming the learner never wastes efforts on querying any other points. As the active learner fails to achieve accuracy ϵ if it chooses incorrectly between f_0 and f_1, a lower bound $\Omega(\beta^2/\epsilon^2)$ for active learning for $P \in \mathcal{P}_{F,\beta}$ follows.

The above lower bound leaves open the possibility that the difficulties for active learning are caused by high noise rates, not by non-realizability per se. This is a significant weakness, since even though non-realizability can rarely be circumvented in practice, noise-free problems are quite common, e.g., in the verification domain. In such cases, it is reasonable to assume that there really exists a deterministic target, but that it cannot be expected to lie in any sufficiently small F. In the next section, we will extend our lower bound to such cases by essentially derandomizing the arguments outlined above.

4.2   Lower Bound for Deterministic Targets

The lower bound for deterministic targets builds on the techniques used in proving a lower bound for adaptive sampling [14]. In adaptive sampling, the task is to estimate the fraction of inputs that make an unknown boolean function output 1 by querying the values of the function on inputs chosen by an arbitrary adaptive randomized algorithm. Such adaptive samplers can be used, e.g., to estimate the number of rows returned by a query to a database without going through the whole database.

By viewing the unknown boolean function whose bias is to be estimated as the target and assuming P_X is uniform on the domain of this function, it can be seen that adaptive sampling is very close to active learning with queries under uniform distribution. The only difference is that to be (ϵ, δ)-successful, an adaptive sampler is required to output an ϵ-approximation of the bias of the unknown function with probability at least $1 - \delta$, whereas an active learner has to approximate the unknown function and not only its bias.

It is clear that an active learner can be used to solve the seemingly easier task of adaptive sampling, but the other direction that we would need here is less obvious. Hence, we take a different route and instead look directly at the problem that underlies the difficulty of adaptive sampling according to the proof in [14]. Using our terminology, the lower bound for adaptive sampling is proved there through the following result:

Theorem 2. *Let $\epsilon \leq \frac{1}{8}$, $\delta \leq \frac{1}{6}$, and assume the sample complexity n of the sampler is at most $\sqrt{M}/4$ for some large enough M. Let P_X be the uniform distribution on a set $\mathcal{X}$ of size M. Consider target functions*

$$g \in G = \left\{ g \colon \mathcal{X} \to \{0,1\} \mid P_X(g(X) = 1) = \frac{1}{2} \pm \epsilon \right\}$$

Then any randomized adaptive sampling algorithm for the task of determining the bias of any such target $g \in G$ correctly with probability at least $1 - \delta$ requires on some $g \in G$ an expected sample complexity of at least $\Omega\left(\frac{1}{\epsilon^2} \ln \frac{1}{\delta}\right)$.

Theorem 2 implies a lower bound for adaptive sampling, since an (ϵ, δ)-successful adaptive sampler solves the above decision problem as a special case. However, in case of active learning, we need a strengthened version of Theorem 2 that is fortunately also implied by exactly the same proof presented in [14] (see especially the beginning of the proof of Theorem 1 therein). Namely, the proof in [14] shows that the lower bound applies also to the version of the decision problem in which the adaptive sampler is required only to give the correct answer with probability at least $1 - \delta$ with respect to its internal randomness *and* the choice of g from the uniform distribution on G. To solve this modified problem, even the simplistic strategy of first running an active learner that outputs an f and then predicting that $P_X(g(X) = 1) = 1/2 + \epsilon$ iff $P_X(f(X) = 1) > 1/2$ suffices. More exactly, it can be shown that the probability of the event that the bias of the learned f differs from that of the randomly chosen target $g \in G$ is at most δ. This is accomplished by the following lemma, in which the boundedness assumption on label complexity can be replaced by an application of Markov's inequality if desired.

Lemma 2. *Let A be an $(\epsilon/2, \delta/2)$-successful active learning algorithm for $\mathcal{P}^{det}_{F,1/2-\epsilon}$, where F contains the constant classifiers 0 and 1. Suppose that the label complexity $n(\epsilon/2, \delta/2)$ of A is bounded by $N < \infty$. Suppose $\mathcal{X}$ is infinite and P_X is a uniform distribution on a sufficiently large finite set $\mathcal{X}_0 \subset \mathcal{X}$. Then, the probability that the bias of the classifier f output by A is the same as the bias of the target chosen uniformly at random from*

$$G_0 = \{g \colon \mathcal{X} \to \{0,1\} \mid P_X(g(X) = 1) = \frac{1}{2} \pm \epsilon \text{ and } g(x) = 0 \text{ for } x \notin \mathcal{X}_0 \}$$

is at most δ.

Proof (Sketch). As F contains the constant classifiers 0 and 1, the minimal generalization error achievable using F is always at most $1/2 - \epsilon$ on any target $g \in G_0$. Thus, for each such $g \in G_0$, A can output a classifier f with generalization error larger than $1/2 - \epsilon/2$ on the learning problem defined by P_X and g with probability at most δ. Since this holds for each $g \in G_0$, we can let g be chosen randomly to get $\mathbb{P}(\varepsilon(f) \geq 1/2 - \epsilon/2) \leq \delta$, where $\mathbb{P}$ now denotes probability with respect to randomness in A (internal and that caused by the random choice of U if such is used) and the choice of g from the uniform distribution over G_0.

Let B denote whether a classifier is biased toward 0 or 1, i.e., $B(f) = 1$ iff $P_X(f(X) = 1) \geq 1/2$ and $B(f) = 0$ otherwise. Conditioning on whether $B(f) = B(g)$ or not, we get from the previous inequality that

$$\delta \geq \mathbb{P}\left(\varepsilon(f) \geq \frac{1}{2} - \frac{\epsilon}{2}\right) = \mathbb{P}\left(\varepsilon(f) \geq \frac{1}{2} - \frac{\epsilon}{2} \middle| B(f) = B(g)\right) \mathbb{P}\left(B(f) = B(g)\right)$$

$$+ \mathbb{P}\left(\varepsilon(f) \geq \frac{1}{2} - \frac{\epsilon}{2} \middle| B(f) \neq B(g)\right) \mathbb{P}\left(B(f) \neq B(g)\right)$$

$$\geq \mathbb{P}\left(\varepsilon(f) \geq \frac{1}{2} - \frac{\epsilon}{2} \middle| B(f) \neq B(g)\right) \mathbb{P}\left(B(f) \neq B(g)\right),$$

implying $\mathbb{P}(B(f) \neq B(g)) \leq \frac{\delta}{\mathbb{P}(\varepsilon(f) \geq 1/2 - \epsilon/2 | B(f) \neq B(g))}$. Thus, to show that the probability of the event $B(f) \neq B(g)$ — that is, the event that using the strategy of predicting that the bias of g is that of f fails — has probability at most 2δ, it suffices to show that

$$\mathbb{P}(\varepsilon(f) \geq 1/2 - \epsilon/2 | B(f) \neq B(g)) \geq 1/2. \qquad (1)$$

We outline an argument showing this next.

Let $S \subset \mathcal{X}$ denote the (random) set of points that A queries. We can assume that $S \subset \mathcal{X}_0$, since points outside $\mathcal{X}_0$ provide no information about g and can thus be ignored in the analysis. Also, since we assume $|S| \leq N$, we can take $\mathcal{X}_0$ so large that fraction of $|S|/|\mathcal{X}_0|$ is arbitrarily small. Note that f can depend on the values of the target g on S only, but not on its values outside S as these are never observed by A. Thus, for each choice of f, S, and the values of g on S observed by A, the number of errors f makes on $\mathcal{X}_0 \setminus S$ is a random variable whose distribution is induced by the distribution of g conditioned on the values of g on S and the underlying conditioning event $B(g) \neq B(f)$.

Now we apply the fact that $\mathcal{X}_0$ can be made so large in comparison to S that the values of g and f on S do not affect their biases on $\mathcal{X}_0 \setminus S$ by much. Consider any $x \in \mathcal{X}_0 \setminus S$. If $f(x) = B(f)$, the probability over the choice of g of the event $f(x) \neq g(x)$ is (about) $1/2 + \epsilon$, and if $f(x) \neq B(f)$, the corresponding probability is (about) $1/2 - \epsilon$. Thus, since the former case is more probable provided $\mathcal{X}_0$ is large, the expected error of f on $\mathcal{X}_0 \setminus S$ is at least almost $1/2$. The contribution of the error of f on S to its overall error can be made arbitrarily small again by taking $\mathcal{X}_0$ large enough, from which it follows that the expected generalization error of f is, say, at least $1/2 - \epsilon/4$ for large enough $\mathcal{X}_0$. Furthermore, by noting that the distribution of the error of f on $\mathcal{X}_0 \setminus S$ can be expressed in terms of a hypergeometric distribution whose variance goes to zero as $\mathcal{X}_0$ is increased, it finally follows by Chebysev's inequality that the probability of the error of f being larger than $1/2 - \epsilon/2$ can be made to be at least $1/2$. The details in all these arguments can be made precise by filling in the calculations on how much the behavior of f and g on S can affect their behavior outside S given that $|S|/|\mathcal{X}_0|$ is small, but we omit the tedious details in this draft.

Since the above is true whatever set S the algorithm A decides to query, whatever answers it receives, and what classifier f it chooses, we get inequality (1), finally concluding the proof. $\qquad \Box$

The above lemma shows how an $(\epsilon/2, \delta/2)$-successful active learner for the class of distributions $\mathcal{P}_{F,1/2-\epsilon}^{\text{det}}$ can be used to solve the average-case version of the decision problem of Theorem 2 discussed after the theorem statement, provided that F contains the constant classifiers 0 and 1. This assumption can be replaced by assuming F contains any two classifiers that are complements of each other, since detecting which of these is closer to the target is equivalent to detecting the bias. Furthermore, we can move the target to within β of F by the same trick we used in Section 3 by embedding the bias detection problem to a subset of $\mathcal{X}$ that has probability 2β, and putting the rest of the probability mass on a point on which the classifiers agree. These steps together give us the desired lower bound stated below:

Theorem 3. *Let A be an active learning algorithm. Let $\epsilon \leq 1/8$, $\delta \leq 1/6$, suppose the label complexity $n(\epsilon, \delta)$ of A is uniformly bounded for each (ϵ, δ), and let the unlabeled label complexity $m(\epsilon, \delta)$ be arbitrary. Suppose F is such that it contains two functions f_0, f_1 that agree at least on one point and disagree on infinitely many points. Let $\beta > 0$ and suppose A is successful for $\mathcal{P}_{F,\beta}^{det}$. Then, for some P_X and target function g, the expected number of $n(\epsilon, \delta)$ is*

$$\Omega\left(\frac{\beta^2}{\epsilon^2} \ln \frac{1}{\delta}\right).$$

The lower bound applies to all active learning algorithms and is not specific to, say, empirical risk minimization, or to any specific hypothesis class. Also, it is easy to see by replacing the point masses in $\mathcal{X}_0$ by a partition of $\{x \in \mathcal{X} \mid f_0(x) \neq f_1(x)\}$ into equiprobable sets that the lower bound immediately extends to a wide range of distributions P_X (including, e.g., all continuous distributions), and remains true even if P_X is known in advance. Thus, the lower bound does not result from any specific properties of P_X, and cannot be circumvented by any amount of unlabeled data. As an interesting special case, the lower bound applies to learning linear separators with uniform distribution, the best known case in which exponential savings are possible under the realizability assumption. However, the lower bound becomes interesting only when $\epsilon \ll \beta$, so it does not rule out exponential speed-ups in the low accuracy regime. This fits perfectly together with the label complexity upper bounds for an active learning algorithm for linear thresholds presented in [4], where it is shown that exponential speed-ups are indeed possible when $\epsilon > \text{const} \cdot \beta$, after which their upper bound on the learning speed degrades to match the above lower bound (up to constants).

The fact that the lower bound depends on β is unavoidable, since if the target is only slightly outside F, the learner will with high probability fail to even notice the non-realizability. This case is of real importance when using the covering approach for active learning in the realizable case [3]. Making the covering finer as a function of ϵ corresponds to enlarging the covering of the underlying F that the algorithm uses as its hypothesis class so that β goes to zero as the accuracy requirements get stricter. This eliminates the effects of the lower bound, but is of course only possible if we know a suitably small class F for which the problem is realizable in advance. In case the target is truly unknown, circumventing the lower bound by extending F is not possible.

5   Conclusions

We have shown that bounded rate class noise can be relatively easily dealt with by using repeated label queries to cancel the effects of the noise, but that in the truly non-realizable case active learning does not give better rates of sample complexity than passive learning when only the dependence on the accuracy and confidence parameters is considered. However, even though the lower bound rules out exponential savings in the non-realizable case, the bound leaves open the possibility of reducing the label complexity by at least a factor of β^2 or more as the complexity of F is not reflected in the lower bound. In practice, even such savings would be of great value. Thus, the lower bound should not be interpreted to mean that active learning does not help in reducing the label complexity in the non-realizable case. Instead, the lower bound only means that the reductions will not be exponential, and that the goal of active learning should be readjusted accordingly.

The results in this paper are only a first step toward a full understanding of the label complexity of active learning under various noise models. In particular, it would be interesting to see how the complexity of F and other kinds of noise (noise in objects, malicious noise, . . .) affect the active learning label complexity.

References

1. Yoav Freund, H. Sebastian Seung, Eli Shamir, and Naftali Tishby. Selective sampling using the query by committee algorithm. *Machine Learning*, 28(2-3):133–168, 1997.
2. Sanjoy Dasgupta, Adam Tauman Kalai, and Claire Monteleoni. Analysis of perceptron-based active learning. In *COLT'05*, pages 249–263. Springer-Verlag, 2005.
3. Sanjoy Dasgupta. Coarse sample complexity bounds for active learning. In *NIPS'05*, 2005.
4. Nina Balcan, Alina Beygelzimer, and John Langford. Agnostic active learning. In *ICML*, 2006. Accepted.
5. Simon Tong and Daphne Koller. Support vector machine active learning with applications to text classification. *Journal of Machine Learning Research*, 2:45–66, 2002.
6. Dana Angluin and Philip Laird. Learning from noisy examples. *Machine Learning*, 2(4):343–370, 1987.
7. Yasubumi Sakakibara. On learning from queries and counterexamples in the presence of noise. *Information Processing Letters*, 37(5):279–284, 1991.
8. Vladimir N. Vapnik. *Estimation of Dependencies Based on Empirical Data*. Springer-Verlag, 1982.
9. Claudio Gentile and David P. Helmbold. Improved lower bounds for learning from noisy examples: an information-theoretic approach. In *COLT'98*, pages 104–115. ACM Press, 1998.
10. Carlos Domingo, Ricard Gavaldà, and Osamu Watanabe. Adaptive sampling methods for scaling up knowledge discovery algorithms. In *DS'99*, pages 172–183. Springer-Verlag, 1999.
11. Rui Castro, March 2006. Personal communication.
12. Samuel D. Silvey. *Optimal Design*. Chapman and Hall, London, 1980.
13. Gustaf Elfving. Selection of nonrepeatable observations for estimation. In *Proceedings of the 3rd Berkeley Symposium on Mathematical Statistics and Probability*, volume 1, pages 69–75, 1956.
14. Ran Canetti, Guy Even, and Oded Goldreich. Lower bounds for sampling algorithms for estimating the average. *Information Processing Letters*, 53(1):17–25, 1995.

How Many Query Superpositions Are Needed to Learn?

Jorge Castro

Software Department. Universitat Politècnica de Catalunya. Campus Nord, 08034
Barcelona, Spain
castro@lsi.upc.edu

Abstract. This paper introduces a framework for quantum exact learning via queries, the so-called quantum protocol. It is shown that usual protocols in the classical learning setting have quantum counterparts. A combinatorial notion, the general halving dimension, is also introduced. Given a quantum protocol and a target concept class, the general halving dimension provides lower and upper bounds on the number of queries that a quantum algorithm needs to learn. For usual protocols, the lower bound is also valid even if only involution oracle teachers are considered. Under some protocols, the quantum upper bound improves the classical one. The general halving dimension also approximates the query complexity of ordinary randomized learners. From these bounds we conclude that quantum devices can allow moderate improvements on the query complexity. However, any quantum polynomially query learnable concept class must be also polynomially learnable in the classical setting.

1 Introduction

A central topic in quantum computation concerns the query complexity of oracle machines. Often it is assumed that a quantum device can get partial information about an unknown function making some type of oracle calls. The broad goal is to take advantage of quantum mechanic effects in order to improve the number of queries (or oracle calls) that an ordinary algorithm needs to find out some characteristic of the hidden function. In some cases it has been proved that exponentially fewer black-box oracle calls (also called membership queries) are required in the quantum model, see for instance [13, 18]. On the other hand, there are tasks that do not accept huge improvements on the query complexity. For example, it is known that the quadratic speedup of Grover's quantum algorithm for database search is optimal [14]. Furthermore, quite general lower bounds on the number of oracle interactions have been also obtained [1, 7, 9].

Quantum concept learning can bee seen as a special case of this type of research where the goal of the algorithm is to figure out which the hidden function is. Here several results are known. Bshouty and Jackson [12] define a quantum version of the PAC model and provide a quantum learning algorithm for DNF that does not require memberships, a type of queries used by its classical counterpart. Servedio and Gortler [17] show lower bounds on the number of oracle

J.L. Balcázar, P.M. Long, and F. Stephan (Eds.): ALT 2006, LNAI 4264, pp. 78–92, 2006.

calls required to learn on the quantum PAC setting and on the more demanding scenario of exact learning from membership queries. For both specific learning settings they conclude that dramatic improvements on the number of oracle interactions are not possible. Ambainis et al. [2] and Atici and Servedio [4] give non-trivial upper bounds for quantum exact learning from membership queries. Finally, Hunziker et al. [16] show a general technique for quantum learning from memberships and restricted equivalences that is shown to need, in a couple of specific cases, less number of queries than is possible classically.

This paper has two goals. The first one is to introduce a general framework for quantum exact learning via queries which sets when a class of queries can be considered to define a learning game played by quantum devices. We note that, as far as we know, the only queries that have been used in the literature have been memberships [2, 4, 16, 17] and restricted equivalences [16]. This contrasts with the classical setting where a rich variety of queries have been considered, see for instance Angluin [3]. The second goal is to study the number of queries (or query complexity) required by exact learners. Our aim is to obtain lower and upper bounds on the query complexity that are valid under any choice of queries defining the learning game.

According to the first goal, we introduce in Sect. 3 the quantum protocol concept, a notion that allows us to define a learning game played by quantum machines where popular queries from the classical setting, as memberships, equivalences, subsets and others defined in [3] have natural quantum counterparts. Specific quantum protocols for these queries are presented. Learning games defined by quantum protocols for memberships and memberships and restricted equivalences agree with learning settings present in the literature [2, 4, 16, 17].

With respect to the second goal, we define in Sect. 4 a combinatorial function, the general halving dimension, GHdim, having some nice features. In the quantum learning scenario, we show a lower bound for the query complexity in terms of GHdim that is valid for any quantum protocol and for any target concept class (Theorem 9). We also show a generic quantum algorithm that achieves learning on many quantum protocols and provides an upper bound for the query complexity in terms of GHdim (Theorem 14). These lower and upper bounds extend the previous ones in [4, 17] for the specific protocol of membership queries. In the classical learning model, we prove that GHdim approximates the query complexity of randomized learners (Theorems 11 and 15). This characterization extends the previous ones provided by Simon [19] for the specific ordinary protocols of membership and membership and equivalence queries.

From previous results we state in Sect. 5 the following conclusion. Given an arbitrary set of queries, quantum learners can allow some gain on the number of queries needed to learn but huge improvements are not possible. Specifically, we show that any quantum polynomially query learnable concept class must be also polynomially learnable in the ordinary setting (Theorem 16). This fact was only known for membership queries [17].

2   Preliminaries

2.1   Basic Definitions

Given a complex number α, we denote by α^* its complex conjugate and by $|\alpha|$ its module. For complex vectors v and w, the l_2-norm (Euclidean norm) of v is expressed by $\|v\|$, the l_1-norm by $\|v\|_1$ and the inner product of v and w by $\langle v|w \rangle$. Note that $\|v\| = \langle v|v \rangle^{1/2}$. Abusing notation, we also denote the cardinality of a set A by $|A|$. For $b, d \in \{0, 1\}$ we write $b \oplus d$ to denote $b + d \pmod 2$. For n-bit strings $x = (x_1, \ldots, x_n)$ and $y = (y_1, \ldots, y_n)$ we write $x \oplus y$ to denote $(x_1 \oplus y_1, \ldots, x_n \oplus y_n)$. The set of all Boolean functions on $\{0, 1\}^n$ is denoted by B_n. A *concept* f is a function of B_n. Equivalently, a concept f can be viewed as the subset $\{x \in \{0, 1\}^n \mid f(x) = 1\}$. A *concept class* C is a subset of B_n.

2.2   Classical Exact Learning

In query learning two players, the *learner* and the *teacher*, play a game. The learner is a (classical) randomized algorithm and the teacher is an oracle function. Some concept class C (the *target* concept class) is known to both players and the teacher chooses a concept in C (the target concept) that is unknown to the learner. The goal of the learner is to find out what concept is, asking the teacher some type of queries.

A query is a question that the learner poses to the teacher. The most popular in the literature are *membership queries* and *equivalence queries*. Other type of queries, as subsets, supersets and restricted equivalences, have been defined, see [3]. In general, the setting of the learning game is complete when the learning *protocol* is defined. The protocol is the agreement about which the admissible queries are and, for each target concept, which the possible answers for such queries are. Answers provide a property of the target. A teacher is valid for the target concept f and the protocol P if it replies to each query q choosing one of the admissible answers in P for q and f.

A concept class C is learnable with k queries under protocol P if there is a randomized learning algorithm L such that for any $f \in C$ and for any valid teacher T that answers with respect to f using P, with probability at least $2/3$ L outputs a circuit h such that $h(x) = f(x)$ for all $x \in \{0, 1\}^n$ after at most k interactions with T. For a class $C \subseteq B_n$ and a protocol P, the *query complexity*, is the smallest k such that C is learnable with k queries under P.

2.3   Quantum Computation

Detailed descriptions of quantum Turing machines and quantum oracle computations are provided in [9, 10]. In spite of assuming the reader is familiar with basic aspects of quantum computers, we provide below a short summary of essential elements.

To each quantum Turing machine M corresponds an inner-product vector space S. The vectors of S are *superpositions* (i.e. finite complex linear combinations) of configurations of M. The complex coefficients defining a vector of S are called *amplitudes*. The inner-product is defined by given an orthonormal basis for S, the vectors of this basis are the configurations of M. The time evolution operator of a quantum Turing machine M is determined by an unitary matrix U_M, which defines a linear operator on S that conserves the distance.

At step j of the computation of M, the time evolution operator U_M is applied to a superposition of configurations (a vector $|v_j\rangle$ of S). The initial superposition $|v_0\rangle$ is the linear combination of configurations having all amplitude value 0 except the only one corresponding to the initial configuration of the machine that has value 1.

A quantum Turing machine M finishes at step t if the corresponding superposition $|v_t\rangle$ only has nonzero amplitudes on final configurations (those whose state is a final one) and previous superpositions $|v_j\rangle$ where $j < t$ give amplitude zero to each final configuration. Let us assume that M finishes at step t and that $|v_t\rangle = \sum_x \alpha_x |x\rangle$ is the corresponding superposition. Now the machine M chooses to be in a single configuration rather than in a superposition of configurations making an *observation* (or *measurement*). The superposition is then changed so that a single configuration has amplitude 1 and all others are 0. Formally, the observation operation provides configuration $|x\rangle$ with probability $|\alpha_x|^2$. Note that $\sum_x |\alpha_x|^2 = 1$ because $|v_t\rangle$ has norm 1 (it is obtained by applying an unitary operator to an initial superposition $|v_0\rangle$ that has norm 1).

Oracle Quantum Turing Machine. We follow definitions in [9]. An oracle quantum Turing machine has a special query tape (that has to accomplish some rules of behaviour, see [9]) and two distinguished internal states: a pre-query state p_1 and a post-query state p_2. A query is executed whenever the machine enters the pre-query state. In this case, it applies a fixed unitary operator U to the current contents $|q\rangle$ of the query tape, replacing it by $U|q\rangle$. In order to ensure that a single machine cycle ought not to make infinite changes in the tape, we require that $U|q\rangle$ have amplitude zero on all but finitely many basis vectors. The use of this kind of unitary oracles still provide unitary time evolution for, in other aspects, well-defined quantum Turing machines. Another natural restriction one may wish to impose upon U is that it be an involution, $U^2 = I$, so that the effect of an oracle call can be undone by a further call on the same oracle. This may be crucial to allow proper interference to take place.

3 Quantum Exact Learning

The learning game is similar to the classical one but now the learner is a quantum algorithm and the teacher is a quantum oracle function. The game is completely defined when the learning protocol is provided.

3.1 Quantum Protocols

We show here how to adapt the learning protocol notion [5, 6] to the quantum setting. A protocol P specifies which the admissible queries are and, for each query, which the valid answers are. Queries belong to a finite set Q, answers are from a finite set A and P is a subset of $Q \times A$. To each tuple (q, a) of P corresponds a subset of B_n so-called *consistent set* and denoted by σ_q^a. Functions in σ_q^a are said to be consistent with tuple (q, a). In the learning game defined by protocol P, answer a to query q provides the information that the target function belongs to σ_q^a. We also denote by Σ_q the set of consistent sets defined by the valid answers to query q, so $\Sigma_q = \{\sigma_q^a \mid a$ is an answer for q in $P\}$.

Discussion above encompasses any type of protocol, classical or quantum. A distinguishing feature of quantum protocols is that different queries can provide the same information. This is an useless characteristic in the classical scenario, but it makes possible to define teachers that as quantum oracles, in addition to be unitary operators are also involutions, a property that one may wish to impose to a quantum oracle to allow proper interference to take place, as we have noted in Section 2.3. Queries showing the same information are said to be *equivalent*. Formally, given a protocol $P \subseteq Q \times A$, queries q_i and q_j are equivalent if their respective sets of consistent function sets defined by their (respective) valid answers coincide, in short $\Sigma_{q_i} = \Sigma_{q_j}$. The equivalence class of query q is denoted by $[q]$ and the set of equivalence classes by $[Q]$.

Definition 1. *A subset P of $Q \times A$ defines a quantum protocol iff P satisfies the following requirements,*

1. *Completeness: Given a query q of Q and a function f in B_n there exists an answer a such that (q, a) is a tuple of P and function f is consistent with (q, a) (in short, $f \in \sigma_q^a$).*
2. *If q_i and q_j are non-equivalent queries then they do not share any valid answer.*
3. *If a is a valid answer for two different queries q_i and q_j then the consistent sets of (q_i, a) and (q_j, a), respectively $\sigma_{q_i}^a$ and $\sigma_{q_j}^a$, are different.*

The completeness requirement is the only one necessary in order to define a classical protocol. Its justification can be found in [5, 6]. On the other hand, last two requirements in Definition 1 are specific for the quantum setting and they impose some compatible behaviour of P with respect to the equivalence relation it defines on Q. Both are considered by technical convenience (see Lemmas 3 and 4 below).

As first example we consider the protocol consisting of quantum membership queries (or quantum black-box oracle calls). A quantum black-box oracle for function f in B_n transforms $(x, b) \in \{0,1\}^n \times \{0,1\}$ to $(x, b \oplus f(x))$. Thus, in the corresponding protocol the set of queries and the set of answers are both $\{0,1\}^n \times \{0,1\}$. Valid answers to query (x, b) are $(x, 0)$ and $(x, 1)$. So, tuples of the protocol are $((x, b), (x, b'))$ for all x in $\{0,1\}^n$ and for all b and b' in $\{0,1\}$. The consistent set of answer (x, b') to query (x, b) is the set of functions that evaluate to $b' \oplus b$ on x. Queries (x, b) and (y, d) are equivalent whenever $x = y$. Note that the quantum protocol requirements are trivially satisfied.

A quantum version of the classical equivalence query protocol can be defined as follows. Given a hypothesis class H, where H is a subset of B_n, queries and answers are tuples (h, x, b) belonging to $H \times \{0,1\}^n \times \{0,1\}$. Valid answers to query (h, x, b) are $(h, x \oplus y, b)$ for any $y \in \{0,1\}^n$ and $(h, x, 1 \oplus b)$. The consistent set corresponding to answer $(h, x \oplus y, b)$ are those Boolean functions f such that $f(y) \neq h(y)$. The consistent set of answer $(h, x, 1 \oplus b)$ has only a single element, the function h. Note that queries (h, x, b) and (g, z, d) are equivalent whenever $h = g$. It is straightforward to see that this defines a quantum protocol. Quantum protocols for subsets, restricted equivalences, memberships and equivalences, and other type of popular queries can be defined in a similar way.

3.2 Quantum Teachers

Let $P \subseteq Q \times A$ be a quantum protocol. We associate to the set of queries Q a Hilbert space S_Q defined as follows. Vectors of S_Q are superpositions of query vectors $|q\rangle$ where q is a query of Q. The inner product of S_Q is the one defined by considering the set of query vectors $\{|q\rangle \mid q \in Q\}$ as an orthonormal basis. In a similar way, we also define a Hilbert space S_A corresponding to the set of answers A.

Let f be a Boolean function. A *quantum teacher* for f under protocol P is an unitary operator T transforming each basis query vector $|q\rangle$ to a superposition in S_A of valid answers according to P that are consistent with f. Quantum teacher T for f is said to be a *permutation teacher* whenever it transforms each basis query $|q\rangle$ to a consistent basis answer $|a\rangle$. When $S_Q = S_A$ and the quantum teacher operator T holds that $T^2 = I$, we say that T is an *involution teacher*. Involution teachers shall correspond with involution oracle gates.

We highlight that classical deterministic teachers for memberships, equivalences, subsets and other popular queries trivially define corresponding permutation teachers in the quantum setting. Note that they are also involution teachers.

3.3 Query Complexity

A superposition $|\phi\rangle$ of an oracle quantum machine is said to be a *query superposition* if there is a configuration with nonzero amplitude in $|\phi\rangle$ whose state is the pre-query one. Let P be a quantum protocol. A concept class $C \subseteq B_n$ is learnable under protocol P with m query superpositions if there exists an oracle quantum Turing machine L –so-called learner– such that for any target function f in C and for any quantum teacher T for f under P:

1. L^T gets a final superposition and with probability at least $2/3$, outputs a circuit for f.
2. The computation of L^T yields at most m query superpositions.

For target class C and quantum protocol P we define the *quantum query complexity*, $\mathrm{QC}(C, P)$, as the smallest m such that C is learnable with m query superpositions under P. We note that this query complexity notion is consistent with the definition given in Beals et al. [7] (see also Servedio et al. [17]) for quantum networks.

3.4   Answering Schemes

Let $P \subseteq Q \times A$ be a quantum protocol.

Definition 2. *A subset T of P is said to be an answering scheme if:*

1. *For any query $q \in Q$ there is exactly one answer a such that (q, a) belongs to T.*
2. *If (q_i, a_i) and (q_j, a_j) are tuples of T and q_i and q_j are equivalent queries then (q_i, a_i) and (q_j, a_j) define the same consistent set of Boolean functions.*

The following lemma is an immediate consequence of the quantum protocol and the answering scheme definitions.

Lemma 3. *Answers of an answering scheme are all different.*

Thus, observe that answering schemes extend naturally to unitary transformations from S_Q to S_A (see Sect. 3.2 above) and they can be considered as quantum oracle functions. However, for an answering scheme T it is possible that there is no function in B_n consistent with all tuples in T. This contrasts with the quantum teacher notion introduced above where there is always a consistent Boolean function with all teacher answers. As we will see later, answering schemes have an adversary role in our arguments in Section 4.2.

Let L be a quantum learner under protocol P and let T be an answering scheme of P. We consider the computation of L when oracle calls are solved according to T and we denote by L^T the resulting quantum oracle machine. Let $|\phi\rangle$ be a valid superposition of L^T. We define the *query magnitude* of q in $|\phi\rangle$, denoted by $w_q(|\phi\rangle)$, as the weight of query q in superposition $|\phi\rangle$; formally, $w_q(|\phi\rangle) = \sum_c |\alpha_c|^2$ where the sum extends over configurations c querying q and α_c denotes the amplitude of c in $|\phi\rangle$. We naturally extend the query magnitude concept to query classes: $w_{[q]}(|\phi\rangle)$ is the sum of query magnitudes $w_{q'}(|\phi\rangle)$ where q' is any query equivalent to q.

For the specific case of membership queries Bennet *et al.* (Theorem 3.3 in [9]) showed that the final outcome of L's computations cannot depend very much on the oracle's answers to queries of little magnitude. We extend this result to any quantum protocol in Theorem 5 below. We provide some proof details for two reasons. First, we think that it is a non-trivial extension of the original theorem statement. Second, as we point out later, there is an incorrect assertion in the proof shown in [9]. In the rest of this section, we assume an arbitrary underlying quantum protocol is given.

Lemma 4. *Let $|\phi\rangle$ be a valid superposition of L^T. Let $G \subseteq [Q]$ be a set of query classes and let $\tilde{T}$ be any answering scheme that agrees with T on any query q such that $[q] \notin G$. Let U and $\tilde{U}$ be, respectively, the unitary time operators of L^T and $L^{\tilde{T}}$. Then, $\|U|\phi\rangle - \tilde{U}|\phi\rangle\|^2 \le 4 \sum_{[q] \in G} w_{[q]}(|\phi\rangle)$.*

Proof. Let $|E\rangle = U|\phi\rangle - \tilde{U}|\phi\rangle$ be the error vector. Assume that $|\phi\rangle = \sum_{c \in I^G} \alpha_c c + |\varphi\rangle$ where I^G is the set of configurations querying some query equivalent to those defined by G and $|\varphi\rangle$ is a superposition of configurations with no query in G. Then,

$$\||E\rangle\|^2 = \sum_{c,d \in I^G} \alpha_c \alpha_d^* \langle Uc|Ud \rangle + \sum_{c,d \in I^G} \alpha_c \alpha_d^* \langle \tilde{U}c|\tilde{U}d \rangle$$
$$- \sum_{c,d \in I^G} \alpha_c \alpha_d^* \langle Uc|\tilde{U}d \rangle - \sum_{c,d \in I^G} \alpha_c \alpha_d^* \langle \tilde{U}c|Ud \rangle.$$

In this expression, by orthogonality the first two summands are both equal to $\sum_{[q] \in G} w_{[q]}(|\phi\rangle)$. For the last two summands observe that all scalar products are zero except for those configurations c and d such that $Uc = \tilde{U}d$. Given a configuration c_0 there is at most one d_0 where this equality happens because the answers of an answering scheme are all different, see Lemma 3. Thus, denoting by J the set of configuration pairs (c_0, d_0) such that $c_0, d_0 \in I^G$ and $Uc_0 = \tilde{U}d_0$, it holds that

$$\left| \sum_{c,d \in I^G} \alpha_c \alpha_d^* \langle Uc|\tilde{U}d \rangle + \sum_{c,d \in I^G} \alpha_c \alpha_d^* \langle \tilde{U}c|Ud \rangle \right| = \left| \sum_{(c_0,d_0) \in J} \alpha_{c_0} \alpha_{d_0}^* + \sum_{(c_0,d_0) \in J} \alpha_{d_0} \alpha_{c_0}^* \right| =$$

$$\left| \sum_{(c_0,d_0) \in J} 2\mathrm{Re}(\alpha_{c_0} \alpha_{d_0}^*) \right| \le \sum_{(c_0,d_0) \in J} 2|\alpha_{c_0}||\alpha_{d_0}^*| \le \sum_{(c_0,d_0) \in J} |\alpha_{c_0}|^2 + |\alpha_{d_0}|^2 \le 2 \sum_{[q] \in G} w_{[q]}(|\phi\rangle).$$

Therefore, $\||E\rangle\|^2 \le 4 \sum_{[q] \in G} w_{[q]}(|\phi\rangle)$.   □

We note that the proof of Theorem 3.3 in [9] states (see first line in the last paragraph of the proof) that $\||E\rangle\|^2 = 2 \sum_{[q] \in G} w_{[q]}(|\phi\rangle)$, that is a better characterization than the inequality given by Lemma 4. However, a counterexample for this equality can be provided under the membership query protocol (which is the protocol considered in [9]). Interested readers can download such counterexample at http://www.lsi.upc.edu/~castro/counter.pdf.

Theorem 5. *Let $|\phi_i\rangle$ be the superposition of L^T at time i. Let $\epsilon > 0$. Let $F \subseteq \{0, \ldots, t-1\} \times [Q]$ be a set of time-query class pairs such that $\sum_{(i,[q]) \in F} w_{[q]}(|\phi_i\rangle) \le \frac{\epsilon^2}{4t}$. For each i, let $\tilde{T}_i$ be any answering scheme that agrees with T on any query q such that $(i, [q]) \notin F$. Let $|\tilde{\phi}_t\rangle$ be the time t superposition that L will get if the answer to each query instance $(i, [q]) \in F$ is modified according to $\tilde{T}_i$. Then, $\||\phi_t\rangle - |\tilde{\phi}_t\rangle\| < \epsilon$.*

4   The Query Complexity of Exact Learners

4.1   The General Halving Dimension

Let $C \subseteq B_n$ be a concept class and let P be a protocol. We associate the parameter $\mathrm{ghdim}(V, P)$ to each subset V of C with $|V| > 1$. This parameter is the smallest non-negative integer d satisfying the following predicate: for any answering scheme T from P there exists a subset $S \subseteq T$ of cardinality d such that at most half of the functions in V are consistent with all tuples in S. When there is no integer d satisfying the predicate, $\mathrm{ghdim}(V, P)$ is defined to be ∞.

Definition 6. *The* general halving dimension *of C under P, $GHdim(C, P)$, is the maximum of parameters $ghdim(V, P)$. Thus,*

$$GHdim(C, P) = \max\{ghdim(V, P) \mid V \subseteq C \land |V| > 1\}.$$

The general halving dimension has two ancestors. One is the general dimension concept — which is in turn an extension of the certificate size notion introduced by Hellerstein *et al.* [15]— that is shown to be a nice characterization of the query complexity of deterministic learners in the ordinary learning scenario (see [5]). The other one is the halving complexity notion defined by Simon [19], that approximates the query complexity of randomized learners in the classical setting. We prove below several bounds of the query complexity in terms of the general halving dimension as much for quantum protocols as for classical ones.

4.2   A Lower Bound for the Quantum Query Complexity

Lemma 7. *Let us assume $GHdim(C, P) > l \geq 1$. There exists a set of concepts $V \subseteq C$ with $|V| > 1$ and an answering scheme $\mathcal{T}$ such that for any tuple $(q, a) \in \mathcal{T}$ less than $\frac{|V|}{l}$ concepts from V are not consistent with (q, a).*

Proof. For the sake of contradiction suppose that for each subset V of C with $|V| > 1$ and for any answering scheme $\mathcal{T}$ there exists a tuple $(q, a) \in \mathcal{T}$ such that at least $\frac{|V|}{l}$ concepts from V are not consistent with (q, a). Fix $V = V_0$ and let $\mathcal{T}$ be an answering scheme. Thus, it corresponds to V_0 a tuple $(q_0, a_0) \in \mathcal{T}$ such that at least $\frac{|V_0|}{l}$ concepts from V_0 are not consistent with (q_0, a_0). Let V_1 be the subset of V_0 consistent with (q_0, a_0). By assumption, $|V_1| \leq |V|(1 - 1/l)$. We repeat this process with V_1 instead of V_0 and so on and so forth. After l iterations we get a subset V_l of V with $|V_l| \leq |V|/2$. This implies that $ghdim(V, P) \leq l$. $\square$

Let l be such that $1 \leq l < GHdim(C, P)$ and let V and $\mathcal{T}$ be respectively the subset of C and the answering scheme promised by Lemma 7. Inspired by Servedio et al. [17], we define the *difference matrix* M as the $|V| \times |Q|$ zero/one matrix where rows are indexed by concepts in V, columns are indexed by queries in Q, and $M_{f,q} = 1$ iff the Boolean function f is not consistent with the answer a of q in $\mathcal{T}$. By our choice of V and $\mathcal{T}$, each column of M has less than $\frac{|V|}{l}$ ones. Thus, the l_1 matrix norm of M is $\|M\|_1 < \frac{|V|}{l}$. The following lemma, which is a technical generalization of Lemma 6 from [17], shows that no quantum learning algorithm L with small query complexity can effectively distinguish many concepts in V.

Lemma 8. *Let L be a quantum learner with query complexity m. Let $\epsilon > 0$. There are a set $W \subseteq V$ and quantum teachers T_f for concepts f in W such that:*

1. *$|W| > |V|(1 - \frac{8m^2}{l\epsilon^2})$*
2. *If $|\phi^{T_f}\rangle$ denotes the final superposition of L^{T_f} then, for any pair of concepts f and g of W, it holds $\||\phi^{T_f}\rangle - |\phi^{T_g}\rangle\| < \epsilon$.*

Proof. Let $\mathcal{T}$ be the answering scheme promised by Lemma 7. We define a permutation teacher T_f for each $f \in V$ in the following way. Teacher T_f answers to query q with the answer a such that $(q, a) \in \mathcal{T}$ whenever f is consistent with (q, a). Otherwise, any consistent basis answer is chosen in such a way that equivalent queries have equivalent answers. Note that such permutation teacher can always be constructed and it defines a valid answering scheme.

Let $|\phi_i^{\mathcal{T}}\rangle$ be the i-th query superposition of $L^{\mathcal{T}}$. Let $w(|\phi_i^{\mathcal{T}}\rangle) \in \mathbb{R}^{|Q|}$ be the $|Q|$-dimensional vector which has entries indexed by queries $q \in Q$ and which has $w_q(|\phi_i^{\mathcal{T}}\rangle)$ as its q-th entry.

Let $w_f(|\phi_i^{\mathcal{T}}\rangle)$ be the sum of all query magnitudes $w_q(|\phi_i^{\mathcal{T}}\rangle)$ where query q is such that f is not consistent with its corresponding tuple $(q, a) \in \mathcal{T}$. Note that $w_f(|\phi_i^{\mathcal{T}}\rangle)$ is the magnitude in superposition $|\phi_i^{\mathcal{T}}\rangle$ of those queries where answering schemes T_f and $\mathcal{T}$ are different. Moreover, observe that $Mw(|\phi_i^{\mathcal{T}}\rangle) \in \mathbb{R}^{|V|}$ is a $|V|$-dimensional vector whose f-th entry is precisely $w_f(|\phi_i^{\mathcal{T}}\rangle)$. Since $\|M\|_1 < \frac{|V|}{l}$ and $\|w(|\phi_i^{\mathcal{T}}\rangle)\|_1 \leq 1$ we have that $\|Mw(|\phi_i^{\mathcal{T}}\rangle)\|_1 < \frac{|V|}{l}$, i. e. $\sum_{f \in V} w_f(|\phi_i^{\mathcal{T}}\rangle) < \frac{|V|}{l}$. Hence

$$\sum_{i=1}^{m} \sum_{f \in V} w_f(|\phi_i^{\mathcal{T}}\rangle) < \frac{m|V|}{l}. \tag{1}$$

Let us define the subset of concepts $W = \{f \in V \mid \sum_{i=1}^{m} w_f(|\phi_i^{\mathcal{T}}\rangle) \leq \epsilon^2/8m\}$. From (1), it follows that $|V \backslash W| < \frac{8m^2|V|}{l\epsilon^2}$. Finally, for any $f \in W$, Theorem 5 implies that $\||\phi_m^{T_f}\rangle - |\phi_m^{\mathcal{T}}\rangle\| < \epsilon/2$. $\qquad\square$

Given $\epsilon = 1/8$, a non-learnability result arises from Lemma 8 whenever $|W| > 1$. Thus, it follows

Theorem 9. *Let P be a quantum protocol and let C be a target concept class. The learning query complexity of C under P holds that*

$$QC(C, P) \geq \frac{\sqrt{GHdim(C, P)}}{32}.$$

We finally note that teachers used in this discussion are permutation teachers. Thus, for popular protocols as the ones in Sect. 3.1, the statement of Theorem 9 is also valid even if only involution teachers are considered as valid oracle functions.

4.3   Upper Bounds for the Query Complexity

First in this section we provide an upper bound for deterministic learners under classical protocols in terms of the general halving dimension. This immediately yields a trivial upper bound for the quantum query complexity. Afterwards, we show a quantum algorithm that, under many quantum protocols, achieves learning improving the trivial upper bound. Lemma 10 and Theorem 11 below can be easily proved using arguments similar to those in [5, 6]. Here, P denotes any (classical) protocol.

Lemma 10. *Let $GHdim(C, P) = d$. Then, any subset V of C with $|V| > 1$ accomplish the following predicate. There exists a query q such that for any valid answer a at least $\frac{|V|}{2d}$ concepts from V are not consistent with (q, a).*

From Lemma 10 we get an upper bound for the query complexity.

Theorem 11. *There is a deterministic learner for the class C under protocol P whose query complexity is bounded by $\lceil 2 \ln |C| \, GHdim(C, P) \rceil$.*

As any quantum protocol is also a classical one and since reversible Turing machines can simulate any deterministic algorithm [8], the upper bound in Theorem 11 also applies to the quantum query complexity.

Let us consider now a quantum protocol P satisfying the following *test property*. Given a tuple (q, a) of P there is a query q' such that for any valid answer a' it is either the case that all functions consistent with (q', a') are also consistent with (q, a) or (q', a') does not share any consistent function with (q, a). It is easy to check that protocols consisting of memberships, restricted equivalences, memberships and equivalences, and memberships and subsets hold the test property. Other protocols can also satisfy it under some specific settings. For instance, when the hypothesis class contains all singleton functions the subset protocol also holds it. On the other hand, the equivalence query protocol is one popular protocol that does not satisfy the test property.

The test property allows us to evaluate the consistency of the target function f with respect to a superposition of tuples in P by asking a query superposition. The following lemma formalizes this fact.

Lemma 12. *Let P be a quantum protocol that satisfies the test property. There is a quantum algorithm that, making a single query superposition, computes the operator that transforms the superposition of P-tuples $\sum_{p \in P} \alpha_p |p\rangle$ into $\sum_{p \in P} (-1)^{b_p} \alpha_p |p\rangle$, where $b_p = 1$ when f is not consistent with tuple p and $b_p = 0$ otherwise.*

The Grover search [14] is a nice quantum algorithm that performs a search over a space S using $O(\sqrt{|S|})$ oracle calls. We consider here an extended version of this algorithm that performs a search for a non-consistent tuple for the target f with small probability error. Lemma 13 below can be easily shown by using results in [11] and Lemma 12.

Lemma 13. *Let P be as in the previous lemma and let K be a subset of P. There is a quantum algorithm, denoted by Extended_GS, that provided as inputs set K and a positive integer m, makes at most $17m\sqrt{|K|}$ query superpositions, and outputs a boolean value success and a tuple $k \in K$ satisfying the following predicate. With error probability bounded by 2^{-m}, success points out if there is a non-consistent tuple in K for f and tuple k is a non-consistent one when success is true.*

We are ready to show a quantum learning algorithm that achieves learning under any quantum protocol holding the test property. It is inspired on previous membership queries quantum learning algorithms by Ambainis et al. [2] and Atici et al. [4]. Its query complexity will improve the trivial upper bound provided by Theorem 11 whenever GHdim is not very small.

Theorem 14. *Let P be a quantum protocol that satisfies the test property. It holds that $QC(C,P) \leq \tau \log |C| \log \log |C| \sqrt{GHdim(C,P)}$, where τ denotes a constant.*

Proof. (sketch) Let $d = \text{GHdim}(C, P)$ and let us consider the procedure Qlearner below. This procedure keeps a set of candidate functions V formed by those functions from C that have not yet been ruled out. Initially, set V agrees with C and the algorithm finishes when $|V| = 1$. We will show that at each iteration of the while loop at least $|V|/2$ functions of V are eliminated. Thus, Qlearner performs at most $\log |C|$ iterations before finishing.

procedure Qlearner (P, C)
1:   $V \leftarrow C$
2:   **while** $|V| \neq 1$
3:       $b \leftarrow$ Is_There_a_PowerfulQuery?(P, V)
4:       **if** b **then**
5:            Let q be a powerful query.
6:            Ask the basis query q and perform an observation
               on the teacher answer. Let a be the observation result.
7:            $W \leftarrow \{g \in V \mid g$ is not consistent with $(q, a)\}$
               $// By\ the\ choice\ of\ q,\ |W| \geq |V|/2$
8:            $V \leftarrow V \setminus W$
9:       **else**
10:          Let T be an answering scheme s.t. for all $(q, a) \in T$ at least
             $|V|/2$ functions of V are consistent with (q, a).
11:          $K \leftarrow$ CandidateSetCover(V, T)
12:          $\langle$succes, $(q, a)\rangle \leftarrow$ Extended_GS$(K, \lceil \log(3 \log |C|) \rceil)$
13:          **if** success **then**
14:                  $W \leftarrow \{g \in V \mid g$ is consistent with $(q, a)\}$
                     $// By\ hypothesis\ on\ T,\ |W| \geq |V|/2$
15:                  $V \leftarrow V \setminus W$
16:          **else**
17:                  $W \leftarrow \{g \in V \mid \exists k \in K$ st g is not consitent with $k\}$
                     $// W\ is\ the\ subset\ of\ functions\ covered\ by\ K,$
                     $// by\ construction\ of\ K,\ |W| \geq |V|/2$
18:                  $V \leftarrow V \setminus W$
19:          **endif**
20:       **endif**
21: **endwhile**
22: **return** V

Procedure Qlearner considers two cases in order to shrink set V. The first one —which corresponds to program lines from 5 to 8— assumes that there is a basis query q such that for any valid basis answer a at most half of the functions in V

are consistent with (q, a). Note that such q is a powerful query because asking q and making and observation on the teacher answer we can rule out at least half of the functions in V.

The second case —program lines from 10 to 19— assumes that there is no powerful query. So, for each query q there is valid answer a such that at least half of the functions in V are consistent with (q, a). An answering scheme $\mathcal{T}$ formed by this type of elements is considered and a subset K of $\mathcal{T}$ that satisfies a covering property is computed at line 11 by calling procedure CandidateSetCover below. The covering property we are interested in states that at least half of the functions in V have some non-consistency witness in K. Here, $(q, a) \in K$ is a non-consistency witness for the function $g \in V$ iff g is not consistent with (q, a).

procedure CandidateSetCover$(V, \mathcal{T})$
    $U \leftarrow V$
    $K \leftarrow \emptyset$
    while $|U| > |V|/2$
        Let $(q, a) \in \mathcal{T}$ be such that at least $\frac{|U|}{2d}$ concepts
        from U do not satisfy (q, a).
        //By Lemma 10 such (q, a) always exists
        $W \leftarrow \{g \in U \mid g$ is not consistent with $(q, a)\}$
        $U \leftarrow U \setminus W$
        $K \leftarrow K \cup \{(q, a)\}$
    endwhile
    return K
    //it holds that $|K| \leq 2d$

By using Lemma 10, it is straightforward to show that the covering set K returned by CandidateSetCover has cardinality bounded by $2d$.

By Lemma 13, the procedure call to Extended_GS at line 12 yields, with error probability bounded by $\frac{1}{3 \log |C|}$, information about if there is a non-consistency witness in K for the target and returns a such witness if there is any. Moreover, this procedure makes at most $\tau \log \log |C| \sqrt{d}$ queries, where τ denotes a constant. Accordingly with the search success, program lines from 13 to 19 removes at least half of the functions from V.

Summarizing the results from the two cases we have considered, we conclude that, with error probability $1/3$, procedure Qlearner identifies the target concept after $\log |C|$ iterations of the while loop. □

4.4   The General Halving Dimension and the Query Complexity of Randomized Learners

We show below that the general halving dimension also provides a lower bound for the query complexity of randomized learners under classical protocols. The results in this section are straightforward extensions of results by Simon [19].

Given a classical protocol P and a target concept class C, Simon defines a *halving game* between two deterministic players and associates a complexity to each halving game, the *halving complexity*. It can be easily shown that GHdim provides a tight characterization of this complexity. Specifically, the halving complexity is always between the value d of GHdim and $2d$. Theorem 3.1 in [19] shows a lower bound of the query complexity of randomized learners in terms of the halving complexity. This theorem immediately yields the following lower bound in terms of the general halving dimension –where the constant is different from the one in the original version because Simon defines the query complexity as an expected value–.

Theorem 15. *Any randomized learner for the target class C under protocol P with success probability 2/3 makes at least $\frac{1}{4}$ GHdim(C, P) queries.*

5 Polynomial Learnability

We assume in this section some arbitrary underlying protocol. In order to discuss the polynomial learnability, we need to extend the concept class notion used until now. In this section a concept class C will be the union of former concept classes, i.e. $C = \cup_n C_n$ where C_n is a subset of B_n. We also need a length notion l defined on concepts in C. For instance, the length can be the circuit size. In this case, the length of concept f, denoted by $l(f)$, is the length of the minimum circuit description for function f. We assume that length notions are so that at most 2^s concepts from C have length less than s.

Given a concept class $C = \cup_n C_n$ and a length notion l, a learner L for C and l is an algorithm that accomplish the following predicate. For each n and for any target concept $f \in C_n$, given as inputs $s = l(f)$ and n and provided that a valid teacher answers the queries according to f, the algorithm L learns f. Moreover, L is a polynomial query learner when its query complexity — as a function of s and n— is bounded by a polynomial. A concept class is polynomially query learnable when it has a polynomial query learner. The following theorem, which states that any quantum polynomially learnable concept class is also polynomially learnable in the classical setting, is immediate from Theorems 9 and 11.

Theorem 16. *Let C be a concept class and let $q(s, n)$ be its quantum query complexity function. Then, there exists a deterministic learner for C whose query complexity function is $O(sq^2(s, n))$.*

Under the membership query protocol Servedio and Gortler show a $O(nq^3(s, n))$ upper bound for the query complexity of deterministic learners ([17], Theorem 12). We note that this bound also follows from Theorem 16 and the $\Omega(s/n)$ lower bound for $q(s, n)$ in the membership case provided by Theorem 10 in [17].

Acknowledgments. This work was supported in part by the IST Programme of the European Community, under the PASCAL Network of Excellence, IST-2002-506778, and by the spanish MCYT research project TRANGRAM, TIN2004-07925-C03-02. This publication only reflects the authors' views.

References

[1] A. Ambainis. Quantum lower bounds by quantum arguments. *J. Comput. Syst. Sci*, 64(4):750–767, 2002.

[2] A. Ambainis, K. Iwama, A. Kawachi, H. Masuda, R. H. Putra, and S. Yamashita. Quantum identification of boolean oracles. In *STACS*, pages 105–116, 2004.

[3] D. Angluin. Queries and concept learning. *Machine Learning*, 2:319–342, 1988.

[4] A. Atici and R. A. Servedio. Improved bounds on quantum learning algorithms. *Quantum Information Processing*, 4(5):355–386, 2005.

[5] J. L. Balcázar, J. Castro, and D. Guijarro. A general dimension for exact learning. In *Proceedings of the 14th Annual Conference on Computational Learning Theory*, volume 2111 of *LNAI*, pages 354–367. Springer, 2001.

[6] J. L. Balcázar, J. Castro, and D. Guijarro. A new abstract combinatorial dimension for exact learning via queries. *J. Comput. Syst. Sci.*, 64(1):2–21, 2002.

[7] R. Beals, H. Buhrman, R. Cleve, M. Mosca, and R. de Wolf. Quantum lower bounds by polynomials. *J. ACM*, 48(4):778–797, 2001.

[8] C. H. Bennett. Logical reversibility of computation. *IBM Journal of Research and Development*, 17:525–532, 1973.

[9] C. H. Bennett, E. Bernstein, G. Brassard, and U. V. Vazirani. Strengths and weaknesses of quantum computing. *SIAM J. Comput.*, 26(5):1510–1523, 1997.

[10] E. Bernstein and U. V. Vazirani. Quantum complexity theory. *SIAM J. Comput.*, 26(5):1411–1473, 1997.

[11] M. Boyer, G. Brassard, P. Hyer, and A. Tapp. Tight bounds on quantum searching. *Fortschritte der Physik*, 46(4-5):493–505, 1998.

[12] N. H. Bshouty and J. C. Jackson. Learning DNF over the uniform distribution using a quantum example oracle. *SIAM Journal on Computing*, 28(3):1136–1153, 1999.

[13] D. Deutsch and R. Jozsa. Rapid solution of problems by quantum computation. *Proc Roy Soc Lond A*, 439:553–558, 1992.

[14] L. K. Grover. A fast quantum mechanical algorithm for database search. In *STOC*, pages 212–219, 1996.

[15] L. Hellerstein, K. Pillaipakkamnatt, V. Raghavan, and D. Wilkins. How many queries are needed to learn? *Journal of the ACM*, 43(5):840–862, Sept. 1996.

[16] M. Hunziker, D. A. Meyer, J. Park, J. Pommersheim, and M. Rothstein. The geometry of quantum learning. *arXiv:quant-ph/0309059*, 2003. To appear in Quantum Information Processing.

[17] R. A. Servedio and S. J. Gortler. Equivalences and separations between quantum and classical learnability. *SIAM J. Comput.*, 33(5):1067–1092, 2004.

[18] D. R. Simon. On the power of quantum computation. *SIAM J. Comput.*, 26(5):1474–1483, 1997.

[19] H. U. Simon. How many queries are needed to learn one bit of information? *Annals of Mathematics and Artificial Intelligence*, 39:333–343, 2003.

Teaching Memoryless Randomized Learners Without Feedback

Frank J. Balbach[1] and Thomas Zeugmann[2],*

[1] Institut für Theoretische Informatik, Universität zu Lübeck
Ratzeburger Allee 160, 23538 Lübeck, Germany
balbach@tcs.uni-luebeck.de
[2] Division of Computer Science
Hokkaido University, N-14, W-9, Sapporo 060-0814, Japan
thomas@ist.hokudai.ac.jp

Abstract. The present paper mainly studies the expected teaching time of memoryless randomized learners without feedback.

First, a characterization of optimal randomized learners is provided and, based on it, optimal teaching teaching times for certain classes are established. Second, the problem of determining the *optimal teaching time* is shown to be $\mathcal{NP}$-hard. Third, an algorithm for approximating the optimal teaching time is given. Finally, two heuristics for teaching are studied, i.e., cyclic teachers and greedy teachers.

1 Introduction

Teaching studies scenarios in which a teacher gives examples of a target concept c, chosen from a prespecified concept class $\mathcal{C}$, to a student or a set of students with the aim that the student or all students, respectively, eventually hypothesize c. Classically, the admissible students are deterministic learning algorithms and the teaching performance is measured with respect to the worst case student.

Several models have been proposed to formalize these ideas mathematically. In the inductive inference framework, Freivalds *et al.* [8] and Jain *et al.* [14] developed a model of learning from good examples. Jackson and Tomkins [13] as well as Goldman and Mathias [11, 18] defined models of teacher/learner pairs where teachers and learners are constructed explicitly. In all these models, some kind of adversary disturbing the teaching process is necessary to avoid collusion between the teacher and the learner. Angluin and Kriķis' [1, 2] model prevents collusion by giving incompatible hypothesis spaces to teacher and learner.

Further approaches differ from the ones mentioned above by not constructing the learner but assume a learner or a set of learners is given. In Shinohara and Miyano's [20] model the students are all consistent deterministic learning algorithms and the teacher provides a set of examples for the target concept c such that c is the only concept in the class that is consistent with these examples.

---

* This work has been supported by the MEXT Grand-in-Aid for Scientific Research on Priority Areas under Grant No. 18049001.

J.L. Balcázar, P.M. Long, and F. Stephan (Eds.): ALT 2006, LNAI 4264, pp. 93–108, 2006.

Goldman *et al.* [12] and Goldman and Kearns [10] also consider a helpful teacher within the online learning model and investigate how many mistakes a consistent learner can make in the worst case. This number equals the size of the smallest sample in Shinohara and Miyano's [20] model. This number is called the *teaching dimension* of the target. Then, the difficulty of teaching a class C is the maximum of the teaching dimensions taken over all $c \in C$. Because of this similarity we will from now on refer to both models as the *teaching dimension (TD-)model*. The teaching dimension has been studied as a measure for the difficulty to teach a concept class. However, this measure does not always coincide with our intuition, since it can be as large as the maximum value possible, i.e., equal to size of the set of all examples (see, e.g., [4] for an illustrative example).

So, instead of looking at the worst-case, one has also studied the *average teaching dimension* (cf., e.g., [3, 4, 15, 16]). Nevertheless, the resulting model still does not allow to study interesting aspects of teaching such as teaching learners with limited memory or to investigate the difference to teach learners providing and not providing feedback, respectively (cf. [5] for a more detailed discussion). Therefore, in [5] we have introduced a new model for teaching randomized learners. This model is based on the *TD*-model but the set of deterministic learners is replaced by a single randomized one. The teacher gives in each round an example of the target concept to the randomized learner that in turn builds hypotheses. Moreover, the memory of the randomized learner may range from memoryless (just the example received can be used) to unlimited (all examples received so far are available). Additionally, the learner may or may not give feedback by showing its actual guess to the teacher. The teacher's goal is to make the learner to hypothesize the target and to maintain it as quickly as possible. Now, the teaching performance is measured by the *expected* teaching time (cf. Sect. 2).

In [5] we showed that feedback is provably useful and that varying the learner's memory size sensibly influences the expected teaching time. Thus, in this paper we focus our attention to randomized learners without feedback and limited memory. If there is *no* feedback, then the teacher can only present an infinite sequence of examples. Teaching infinite sequences introduces difficulties not present in the variant with feedback. As there are uncountably many teachers, there is no way to represent them all finitely. Also their teaching time cannot, in general, be calculated exactly. Finding optimal teachers in the set of all teachers also seems hard; it is not even clear that always an optimal one exists.

So, for getting started, we analyze the model of *memoryless* learners without feedback and ask occasionally which results generalize to any fixed constant memory size. First, we derive a characterization of optimal learners thereby showing that there is always an optimal one (Sect. 3). This enables us to calculate optimal teaching times for certain classes.

We then look at the computational problem of determining the optimal teaching time. No algorithm is known to solve this problem. We show that it is $\mathcal{NP}$-hard, and there is an (inefficient) algorithm to approximate this value (Sect. 4). Since optimal teachers are hard to find, we study two heuristics for teaching. The greedy one is sometimes optimal (checkable via the characterization in

Sect. 3), but can be arbitrarily far off the optimum (Sect. 5.2). In contrast, teachers iterating over the same sequence of examples forever can come arbitrarily close to optimal, but it is hard to determine whether they in fact *are* optimal (Sect. 5.1).

2 Preliminaries

2.1 Notations

Let X be a finite *instance space* and $\mathcal{X} = X \times \{0, 1\}$ the corresponding set of *examples*. A *concept class* is a set $\mathcal{C} \subseteq 2^X$ of *concepts* $c \subseteq X$. An example (x, v) is *positive* if $v = 1$ and *negative* if $v = 0$. We denote the set of all examples for a concept c by $\mathcal{X}(c) = \{(x, v) \mid v = 1 \iff x \in c\}$ and the set of all concepts *consistent* with an example z by $\mathcal{C}(z) = \{c \in \mathcal{C} \mid z \in \mathcal{X}(c)\}$.

A set $Z \subseteq \mathcal{X}$ is a *teaching set* for a concept $c \in \mathcal{C}$ with respect to a class $\mathcal{C}$ iff c is the only concept in $\mathcal{C}$ consistent with all examples in Z, i.e., $\bigcap_{z \in Z} \mathcal{C}(z) = \{c\}$.

For any set S, we denote by S^* the set of all finite lists of elements from S and by S^ℓ the set of all lists with length ℓ. By $[a, b]$ we mean $\{a, a + 1, \ldots, b\}$.

We denote by $\mathcal{M}_n$ the concept class of *monomials* over $X = \{0, 1\}^n$, that is conjunctions of Boolean literals over n variables. We exclude the empty concept from $\mathcal{M}_n$ and can thus identify each monomial with a string from $\{0, 1, *\}^n$ and vice versa. The concept classes $\mathcal{S}_n$ over $X = [1, n]$ are defined as $\mathcal{S}_n = \{[1, n] \setminus \{x\} \mid x \in [1, n]\} \cup \{[1, n]\}$.

2.2 The Teaching Model

The teaching process is divided into rounds. In each round the teacher gives the learner an example of a target concept. The learner chooses a new hypothesis based on this example and on its current hypothesis.

The Learner. As a minimum requirement we demand that the learner's hypothesis is consistent with the example received in the last round. But the hypothesis is chosen at random from all consistent ones.

We define the goal of teaching as making the learner hypothesize the target *and maintain it*. Consistency alone cannot ensure this, since there may be several consistent hypotheses at every time and the learner would oscillate between them rather than maintaining a single one. To avoid this, the learner has to maintain its hypothesis as long as it is consistent to the new examples (*conservativeness*).

The following algorithm describes the choice of the next hypothesis by the *memoryless randomized learner* in one round of the teaching process.

> **Input**: Current Hypothesis $h \in \mathcal{C}$, example $z \in \mathcal{X}$.
> **Output**: Next Hypothesis $h' \in \mathcal{C}$.
> 1. **if** $z \notin \mathcal{X}(h)$ **then** pick h' uniformly at random from $\mathcal{C}(z)$;
> 2.   **else** $h' := h$;

In the following the term "learner" refers to the memoryless randomized learner.

In order to make our results depend on $\mathcal{C}$ alone, rather than on an arbitrary initial hypothesis from $\mathcal{C}$, we stipulate a special initial hypothesis, denoted *init*. We consider every example inconsistent with *init* and thus *init* is automatically left after the first example and never reached again.

The definition of the learner contains implicitly a function $p\colon (\mathcal{C} \cup \{init\}) \times \mathcal{X} \times (\mathcal{C} \cup \{init\}) \to [0,1]$ with $p(h,z,h')$ specifying the probability of a transition from hypothesis h to h' when receiving example z.

The Teacher. A teacher is an algorithm that is given a target concept c^* in the beginning and then outputs an example for c^* in each round. A teacher for c^* can thus be regarded as a function $T\colon \mathbb{N} \to \mathcal{X}(c^*)$.

Definition 1. *Let $\mathcal{C}$ be a concept class and $c^* \in \mathcal{C}$. Let $T\colon \mathbb{N} \to \mathcal{X}(c^*)$ be a teacher and $(h_t)_{t\in\mathbb{N}}$ be the series of random variables for the learner's hypothesis at round t. The event "teaching success in round t," denoted by G_t, is defined as*

$$h_{t-1} \neq c^* \quad \wedge \quad \forall t' \geq t\colon h_{t'} = c^* \ .$$

The success probability *of T is $\Pr\left[\bigcup_{t\geq 1} G_t\right]$. A teacher is* successful *iff the success probability is 1. For such a teacher we therefore define the* teaching time *as $E_T(c^*,\mathcal{C}) := \sum_{t\geq 1} t \cdot \Pr[G_t]$. Then the* teaching time *for the concept c^* is*

$$E(c^*,\mathcal{C}) := \inf_T E_T(c^*,\mathcal{C}) \ .$$

Although the teacher cannot observe the hypotheses, it can at least calculate the probability distribution $\delta\colon \mathcal{C} \cup \{init\} \to [0,1]$ over all possible hypotheses. Such a δ contains all knowledge of the teacher about the situation. The probability of being in c^*, however, is irrelevant for the teacher's decision. Only the relations of the probabilities for non-target states are important. Normalizing these probabilities yields a probability distribution $\gamma\colon \mathcal{C} \cup \{init\} \setminus \{c^*\} \to [0,1]$ over $\widehat{\mathcal{C}} := \mathcal{C} \cup \{init\} \setminus \{c^*\}$. Following Patek [19] we call γ an *information state*. We denote by $\gamma^{(0)}$ the initial information state, that is $\gamma^{(0)}(init) = 1$.

The definition of the learner defines implicitly a *state transition function* $f\colon \Gamma \times \mathcal{X} \to \Gamma$, that is $f(\gamma,z)$ is the follow-up information state after teaching example z to a learner in state γ.

It is possible to describe teachers as functions $\tilde{T}\colon \Gamma \to \mathcal{X}(c^*)$ where Γ is the set of all information states. Such a teacher $\tilde{T}$, when applied to the initial state $\gamma^{(0)}$ and subsequently to all emerging states, yields a teacher $T\colon \mathbb{N} \to \mathcal{X}(c^*)$.

Remark. If we assume that the learner's hypothesis is observable as feedback then teachers become functions $T\colon \mathcal{C} \cup \{init\} \to \mathcal{X}(c^*)$. In this model variant *with* feedback, teachers are finite objects (see Balbach and Zeugmann [5]).

Our teaching model without (with) feedback is a special case of an *unobservable (observable) stochastic shortest path problem*, (U)SSPP. Stochastic shortest path problems are more general in that they allow arbitrary transition probabilities and arbitrary costs assigned to each transition. In our teaching models, the transition probabilities are restricted to p and each example has unit cost. For more details on SSPPs see e.g., Bertsekas [6].

3 Existence of Optimal Teachers

The most interesting property of a target concept in our model is its optimal teaching time $E(c^*, \mathcal{C})$. One way to calculate $E(c^*, \mathcal{C})$ is to calculate $E_T(c^*, \mathcal{C})$ for an optimal teacher T. However, as there are uncountably many teachers, it is not even clear whether an optimal teacher exists at all. In this section we derive a characterization of optimal teachers which shows that there is always one. Moreover, it allows us to check whether a given teacher is optimal.

Our result is based on a characterization of optimal "policies" in USSPPs presented by Patek [19] that is applicable to USSPPs satisfying certain assumptions. As our teaching model is a special case of USSPPs, where "policies" correspond to teachers, we have to show that these assumptions hold in our teaching model.

To state Patek's [19] characterization and the assumptions under which it works, it is inevitable to introduce some further technical notation. Moreover, the optimality criterion is based on information state teachers $\tilde{T} \colon \Gamma \to \mathcal{X}(c^*)$ rather than sequential teachers $T \colon \mathbb{N} \to \mathcal{X}(c^*)$.

Following Patek [19], we consider series $(\tilde{T}_t)_{t \in \mathbb{N}}$ of teachers. Such a series is called *stationary* if all teachers in it are identical. For such a series $(\tilde{T}_t)_{t \in \mathbb{N}}$, we denote by $\mathrm{Pr}^m(\gamma, \tilde{T})$ the probability that a learner reaches c^* within m rounds when it is started in $\gamma \in \Gamma$ and is taught by teacher $\tilde{T}_t$ in round $t = 0, 1, \dots$.

We also need two so called *dynamic programming operators* D and $D_{\tilde{T}}$ mapping functions $G \colon \Gamma \to \mathbb{R}$ to functions of the same type:

$$[D_{\tilde{T}} G](\gamma) = 1 + G(f(\gamma, \tilde{T}(\gamma))) \cdot \sum_{c, d \in \widehat{\mathcal{C}}} \gamma(c) \cdot p(c, \tilde{T}(\gamma), d) \,,$$

$$[DG](\gamma) = \min_{z \in \mathcal{X}(c^*)} \left(1 + G(f(\gamma, z)) \cdot \sum_{c, d \in \widehat{\mathcal{C}}} \gamma(c) \cdot p(c, z, d) \right).$$

The sum $\sum_{c, d \in \widehat{\mathcal{C}}} \gamma(c) \cdot p(c, \tilde{T}(\gamma), d)$ yields the probability for *not* reaching c^* in the next round after being taught $\tilde{T}(\gamma)$ in state γ. To get an intuition about above formulas, it is helpful to think of a value $G(\gamma)$ as the expected number of rounds to reach the target when the learner starts in state γ. Then $[D_{\tilde{T}} G](\gamma)$ specifies for every initial state γ the expected number of rounds under teacher $\tilde{T}$, assuming that for all other states the expectations are given by G.

Given a teacher series $(\tilde{T}_t)_{t \in \mathbb{N}}$, the expected time to reach the target when starting in $\gamma \in \Gamma$ is denoted by $G_{\tilde{T}}(\gamma)$. This yields a function $G_{\tilde{T}} \colon \Gamma \to \mathbb{R}$.

The characterization, in terms of the randomized teaching model, now is:

Theorem 2 ([19]). *Let $\mathcal{C}$ be a concept class and $c^* \in \mathcal{C}$ a target. Assume that*

(a) *There is a stationary series $(\tilde{T}_t)_{t \in \mathbb{N}}$ with $\lim_{m \to \infty} \mathrm{Pr}^m(\gamma, \tilde{T}) = 1$ for all $\gamma \in \Gamma$.*

(b) *For every series $(\tilde{T}_t)_{t \in \mathbb{N}}$ not satisfying (a), a subsequence of*

$$\left([D_{\tilde{T}_0} D_{\tilde{T}_1} \cdots D_{\tilde{T}_t} \mathbf{0}](\gamma) \right)_{t=0}^{\infty} \quad \textit{tends to infinity for some } \gamma \in \Gamma \,.$$

Then

1. *The operator D has a fixed point G, that is $DG = G$.*
2. *A teacher $\tilde{T} \colon \Gamma \to \mathcal{X}(c^*)$ is optimal (i.e., has minimal teaching time) iff there is a $G \colon \Gamma \to \mathbb{R}$ such that $DG = G$ and $D_{\tilde{T}}G = G$.*

Roughly speaking, Theorem 2 says: If (a) there is a teacher successful from every initial state and if (b) every non-successful teacher has an infinite teaching time from at least one initial state, then there is an optimal teacher and its teaching time G is just the fixed point of the operator D.

We now show that conditions (a) and (b) hold for all classes and targets in our model. For condition (a) we show that a greedy teacher is always successful.

Definition 3. *A teacher $\tilde{T}$ for $c^* \in \mathcal{C}$ is called* greedy *iff for all $\gamma \in \Gamma$*

$$\tilde{T}(\gamma) \in \operatorname*{argmax}_{z \in \mathcal{X}(c^*)} \sum_{c \in \hat{\mathcal{C}}} \gamma(c) \cdot p(c, z, c^*) \, .$$

Note that replacing γ with δ and $\hat{\mathcal{C}}$ with $\mathcal{C} \cup \{init\}$ yields an equivalent definition.

Lemma 4. *Let $\mathcal{C}$ be a concept class and $c^* \in \mathcal{C}$. Let T be the sequential teacher for some greedy teacher $\tilde{T}$. Then T is successful for c^*.*

Proof. We denote by $\delta_t \colon \mathcal{C} \cup \{init\} \to [0, 1]$ the probabilities of the hypotheses in round t under teacher T. In each round t, T picks an example z maximizing $\sum_{c \in \mathcal{C} \cup \{init\}} \delta_t(c) \cdot p(c, z, c^*)$. We lower bound this value.

There is a concept $c' \neq c^*$ with $\delta_t(c') \geq (1 - \delta_t(c^*))/|\mathcal{C}|$. Let z' be an example inconsistent with c'. Then $p(c', z, c^*) \geq 1/|\mathcal{C}|$ and therefore $\sum_c \delta_t(c) \cdot p(c, z', c^*) \geq (1 - \delta_t(c^*))/|\mathcal{C}|^2$. As T maximizes this sum, we have also for $z = T(t)$ that $\sum_c \delta_t(c) \cdot p(c, z, c^*) \geq (1 - \delta_t(c^*))/|\mathcal{C}|^2$. This sum also equals $\delta_{t+1}(c^*) - \delta_t(c^*)$ and therefore

$$1 - \delta_{t+1}(c^*) \leq (1 - 1/|\mathcal{C}|^2) \cdot (1 - \delta_t(c^*)) \, .$$

Hence, $1 - \delta_t(c^*) \to 0$ as $t \to \infty$ and the probability $\delta_t(c^*)$ tends to one. □

We only sketch the technical proof that condition (b) is satisfied too.

Lemma 5. *Let $\mathcal{C}$ be a concept class and $c^* \in \mathcal{C}$ a target. Then (b) holds.*

Proof. (Sketch) Let $(\tilde{T}_t)_{t \in \mathbb{N}}$ be a series that does not satisfy condition (a). Then there is a γ with $\lim_{m \to \infty} \Pr^m(\gamma, \tilde{T}) < 1$. This means $\lim_{m \to \infty} \delta_m(c^*) < 1$, where $(\delta_t)_{t \in \mathbb{N}}$ is the series resulting from application of $\tilde{T}$ to γ. The expected number of rounds to reach c^* is infinite in this case. Patek [19] shows that this expectation is also $\liminf_{t \to \infty} [D_{\tilde{T}_0} \cdots D_{\tilde{T}_t} \mathbf{0}](\gamma)$, where $\mathbf{0} \colon \Gamma \to \mathbb{R}$ is the zero function.

Hence the sequence $([D_{\tilde{T}_0} D_{\tilde{T}_1} \cdots D_{\tilde{T}_t} \mathbf{0}](\gamma))_{t=0}^{\infty}$ tends to infinity. □

Theorem 2 requires us to find a $G \colon \Gamma \to \mathbb{R}$ and to define a teacher $\tilde{T} \colon \Gamma \to \mathcal{X}(c^*)$. However, most of the states in Γ cannot be reached from the initial state $\gamma^{(0)}$ and it seems unnecessary to specify $\tilde{T}$'s behavior for the unreachable states too. As a matter of fact, it suffices to define G and $\tilde{T}$ for the *reachable states* in Γ denoted by $\Gamma_0 = \{\gamma \in \Gamma \mid \exists t \, \exists z_0, \ldots, z_t \colon \gamma = f(\ldots f(f(\gamma^{(0)}, z_0), z_1) \ldots, z_t)\}$. We omit the proof thereof and state the final version of the characterization.

Corollary 6. *Let $\mathcal{C}$ be a concept class and $c^* \in \mathcal{C}$ a target. A teacher $\tilde{T} \colon \Gamma_0 \to \mathcal{X}(c^*)$ is optimal iff there is a $G \colon \Gamma_0 \to \mathbb{R}$ such that $DG = G$ and $D_{\tilde{T}} G = G$, where D and $D_{\tilde{T}}$ have to be restricted suitably to work on functions $G \colon \Gamma_0 \to \mathbb{R}$.*

One advantage of using Γ_0 instead of Γ is that we have to consider only one state with $\gamma(init) > 0$, namely the initial state $\gamma^{(0)}$. For illustration, we apply Corollary 6 to the class $\mathcal{S}_n$ in order to find an optimal teacher for $[1, n]$.

Fact 7. *Let $c^* = [1, n] \in \mathcal{S}_n$. Then the teacher $T \colon \mathbb{N} \to \mathcal{X}(c^*)$ with $T(i) = (1 + (i \bmod n), 1)$ is an optimal teacher for c^* with teaching time $n(n-1)/2 + 1$.*

Proof. The proof proceeds in several steps. First we define a teacher $\tilde{T} \colon \Gamma_0 \to \mathcal{X}(c^*)$ and a function $G \colon \Gamma_0 \to \mathbb{R}$. Then we show that $DG = G$ and $D_{\tilde{T}} = D$ from which we conclude that $\tilde{T}$ is optimal. Finally we show that $\tilde{T}$, when applied to $\gamma^{(0)}$, generates the same example sequence as T.

For a $\gamma \in \Gamma$ and $i \in [1, n]$ we set as shortcut $\gamma_i := \gamma(c)$ for $c = [1, n] \setminus \{i\}$. A positive example $(x, 1)$ is inconsistent only with the concept $[1, n] \setminus \{x\}$. Teaching $(x, 1)$ in a state $\gamma \neq \gamma^{(0)}$ results in a state $f(\gamma, (x, 1)) = \hat{\gamma}$ with $\hat{\gamma}_i = \frac{\gamma_i + \gamma_x/n}{1 - \gamma_x/n}$ for $i \neq x$, and $\hat{\gamma}_x = 0$. For $\gamma = \gamma^{(0)}$ we have $\hat{\gamma}_i = 1/(n-1)$ for all $i \neq x$ and $\hat{\gamma}_x = 0$.

We define $\tilde{T}$ to be a greedy teacher. If there are several equally "greedy" examples, $\tilde{T}$ picks the one with smallest instance. As every example is inconsistent with exactly one concept, $\tilde{T}$ greedily picks an example that is inconsistent with a most probable hypothesis.

For defining G, let $\gamma \in \Gamma_0 \setminus \{\gamma^{(0)}\}$ and assume without loss of generality $\gamma_1 \geq \gamma_2 \geq \cdots \geq \gamma_n$. Let $F = \frac{(n-1)n}{2}$. Then we define

$$G(\gamma) := F + \sum_{i=1}^n \gamma_i \cdot i \qquad \text{and} \qquad G(\gamma^{(0)}) := F + 1 \ .$$

Next we show $DG = G$. Let $\gamma \in \Gamma_0 \setminus \{\gamma^{(0)}\}$ and recall that $\gamma_1 \geq \cdots \geq \gamma_n$. We have to show that $[DG](\gamma) = G(\gamma)$, in other words that $1 + \min_{(x,1) \in \mathcal{X}} G(f(\gamma, (x, 1))) \cdot \sum_{c, d \in \hat{c}} p(c, (x, 1), d) = G(\gamma)$. Since $\sum_{c, d} p(c, (x, 1), d) = 1 - \gamma_x/n$ this means

$$1 + \min_{(x,1) \in \mathcal{X}} G(f(\gamma, (x, 1))) \cdot (1 - \gamma_x/n) = G(\gamma) \ . \tag{1}$$

Let $z = (x, 1) \in \mathcal{X}$ and $\hat{\gamma} = f(\gamma, z)$. Then $\hat{\gamma}_1 \geq \cdots \geq \hat{\gamma}_{z-1} \geq \hat{\gamma}_{z+1} \geq \cdots \geq \hat{\gamma}_n \geq \hat{\gamma}_z = 0$. The expression to be minimized is

$$\left(1 - \frac{\gamma_x}{n}\right) \cdot G(\hat{\gamma}) = \left(1 - \frac{\gamma_x}{n}\right) \cdot \left(F + \sum_{i \leq x-1} i\hat{\gamma}_i + \sum_{i \geq x+1} (i-1)\hat{\gamma}_i\right)$$

$$= \left(1 - \frac{\gamma_x}{n}\right) \cdot \left(F + \sum_{i \leq x-1} i \cdot \frac{\gamma_i + \gamma_x/n}{1 - \gamma_x/n} + \sum_{i \geq x+1} (i-1) \frac{\gamma_i + \gamma_x/n}{1 - \gamma_x/n}\right)$$

$$= F + \sum_{i=1}^n i\gamma_i - \left(x \cdot \gamma_x + \sum_{i \geq x+1} \gamma_i\right) \ . \tag{$*$}$$

From $\gamma_1 \geq \cdots \geq \gamma_n$, it follows $1\gamma_1 + \sum_{i \geq 2} \gamma_i \geq 2\gamma_2 + \sum_{i \geq 3} \gamma_i \geq \cdots \geq n\gamma_n$. This means that the expression $(*)$ is minimal for $x = 1$, or $\gamma_x = \gamma_1$. Setting $x = 1$ yields $\min_{(x,1)} G(f(\gamma,(x,1))) \cdot (1 - \gamma_x/n) = F - 1 + \sum_{i=1}^{n} i\gamma_i = G(\gamma) - 1$ and thus Equation (1) is satisfied.

It remains to show $[DG](\gamma^{(0)}) = G(\gamma^{(0)})$. For all examples $(x,1) \in \mathcal{X}$ we have
$[DG](\gamma^{(0)}) = 1 + (1 - \frac{1}{n})G(f(\gamma^{(0)},(x,1))) = 1 + (1 - \frac{1}{n}) \cdot \left(F + \sum_{i=1}^{n-1} i \frac{1/n}{1-1/n} \right) =$
$1 + \frac{n-1}{n} \cdot \left(F + \frac{1}{n-1} \cdot \frac{n(n-1)}{2} \right) = 1 + \frac{n(n-1)}{2} = F + 1 = G(\gamma^{(0)})$.

It follows that $[DG](\gamma) = G(\gamma)$ for all $\gamma \in \varGamma_0$. Moreover, teacher $\tilde{T}$ always picks the example $(x,1)$ minimizing the term in Equation (1), thus $D_{\tilde{T}}G = G$ and $\tilde{T}$ is optimal according to Corollary 6.

The teacher $\tilde{T}$, when started in $\gamma^{(0)}$, generates the same sequence of examples as T. By the definition of $\tilde{T}$, $\tilde{T}(\gamma^{(0)}) = (1,1)$ and for $\gamma \neq \gamma^{(0)}$ with $\gamma_1 \geq \cdots \geq \gamma_n$ (w.l.o.g.) $\tilde{T}$ chooses example $(1,1)$ and the next information state is $\hat{\gamma}$ with $\hat{\gamma}_2 \geq \cdots \geq \hat{\gamma}_n \geq \hat{\gamma}_1 = 0$. Therefore, $\tilde{T}$ chooses $(2,1)$ next and so on. □

With *feedback* $[1,n] \in \mathcal{S}_n$ can be taught in expected n rounds: A teacher T observing the learner's hypothesis can always choose an inconsistent example. Under T, the learner has in each round a probability of $1/n$ of reaching the target. But teaching $[1,n] \in \mathcal{S}_n$ *without* feedback requires $\Omega(n^2)$ rounds (cf. Fact 7).

As the previous fact also shows, to prove the optimality of a sequential teacher, we have to take a detour via information state teachers. Thus finding the "right" information state teacher is the crucial step in applying Corollary 6.

4   Finding Optimal Teachers

Now that we know that there is always an optimal teacher, we ask how to find one effectively. But as these teachers are infinite sequences of examples, it is unclear how an "optimal teacher finding"-algorithm should output one. Alternatively, we could seek a *generic optimal teacher*, that is an algorithm receiving a class, a target c^*, and a finite example sequence, and outputting an example such that its repeated application yields an optimal teacher for c^*.

A closely related task is to determine the teaching time of an optimal teacher, that is $E(c^*, \mathcal{C})$.

Definition 8. *We call the following problem* OPT-TEACHING-TIME.
   Input: Concept class $\mathcal{C}$, *concept* $c^* \in \mathcal{C}$, *rational number* F.
   Question: Is $E(c^*, \mathcal{C}) \leq F$?

In the more general setting of USSPPs the analog problem is undecidable (see Madani *et al.* [17] and Blondel and Canterini [7]). This can be seen as evidence for the undecidability of OPT-TEACHING-TIME. On the other hand, USSPPs differ from our model in some complexity aspects. For example, deciding whether there is a teacher with at least a given success probability is easy (because there is always one), whereas the analog problem for USSPPs is undecidable [17, 7].

$B = \{1, 2, 3, 4, 5, 6\},$
$A_1 = \{2, 4, 5\},$
$A_2 = \{1, 3, 5\},$
$A_3 = \{1, 3, 6\}$

$\longrightarrow$

	x_1	x_2	x_3	y_1	y_2	y_3	y_4	y_5	y_6
c^*	1	1	1	1	1	1	1	1	1
c_1	1	0	0	0	1	1	1	1	1
c_2	0	1	1	1	0	1	1	1	1
c_3	1	0	0	1	1	0	1	1	1
c_4	0	1	1	1	1	1	0	1	1
c_5	0	0	1	1	1	1	1	0	1
c_6	1	1	0	1	1	1	1	1	0

Fig. 1. Illustration of the reduction from X3C to OPT-TEACHING-TIME. Every example on the left is inconsistent with exactly three concepts; $y_1, \ldots, y_6$ are "dummy" instances making all concepts unique. The examples $(x_1, 1), (x_3, 1)$ have the X3C property.

Although the decidability of OPT-TEACHING-TIME is open, we can at least show it is $\mathcal{NP}$-hard. So even if there is an algorithm, it is presumably inefficient.

The proof is by reduction from the EXACT-3-COVER (X3C) problem [9]. The following algorithm computes OPT-TEACHING-TIME instances from X3C instances in polynomial time (see Fig.1 for an example).

Input: Set $B = [1, 3n]$ ($n \in \mathbb{N}$), sets $A_1, \ldots, A_m \subseteq B$ with $|A_i| = 3$.
1. $X := \{x_1, \ldots, x_m\} \cup \{y_1, \ldots, y_{3n}\}$
2. $c_j := \{x_i \mid j \notin A_i\} \cup \{y_i \mid i \neq j\}$ for $j = 1, \ldots, 3n$
3. $c^* := X$
4. $\mathcal{C} := \{c^*, c_1, \ldots, c_{3n}\}$
5. **Output** $\langle \mathcal{C}, c^*, 1 + \frac{3}{2}n(n-1) \rangle$

We call a concept class $\mathcal{C}$ output by this algorithm a *positive* or *negative X3C class* depending on whether the input was a positive or negative X3C instance.

An X3C class is positive iff there are examples $z_1, \ldots, z_n \in \mathcal{X}(c^*)$ such that the sets $\mathcal{C} \backslash \mathcal{C}(z_j)$ are pairwise disjoint for $j = 1, \ldots, n$ and $\bigcup_j (\mathcal{C} \backslash \mathcal{C}(z_j)) = \mathcal{C} \backslash \{c^*\}$. Examples $z_1, \ldots, z_n$ satisfying the property just stated have the *X3C property*.

If $A_1, \ldots, A_m$ consists of all $m = \binom{3n}{3}$ subsets of B we call the class a *full X3C class*. Every full X3C class is a positive X3C class.

Of all X3C classes, the full X3C classes are easiest to analyze because of their intrinsic symmetries. Moreover, the optimal teachers are just the greedy teachers, which simplifies the application of our optimality criterion. Note that for arbitrary X3C classes a greedy teacher need not to be optimal.

Lemma 9. *Let $n \geq 2$, let $\mathcal{C}$ be a full X3C class for n and c^* be the concept containing all instances. Then a teacher $\tilde{T} \colon \Gamma_0 \to \mathcal{X}(c^*)$ is optimal if and only if $\tilde{T}$ is greedy. The teaching time, when starting in $\gamma^{(0)}$, is $1 + \frac{3}{2}n(n-1)$.*

Proof. (sketch) The class $\mathcal{C}$ is similar to the class $\mathcal{S}$ only with three zeros per column instead of one. Consequently the proof that all greedy teachers are optimal is similar to that of Fact 7. That the "dummy" examples are never chosen by an optimal teacher and that all optimal teachers are greedy can be proved by straightforward but technically involved application of Corollary 6. $\square$

The next lemma describes the optimal teachers as example sequences rather than in terms of the information states.

Lemma 10. *Let $n \geq 2$, let C be a full X3C class for n and c^* be the concept containing all instances. A teacher $T: \mathbb{N} \to \mathcal{X}(c^*)$ is optimal if and only if $T(t) = z_{t \bmod n}$ for all t with the examples $z_0, \ldots, z_{n-1}$ having the X3C property.*

Proof. This proof is similar to the last paragraph of the proof of Fact 7. We omit the technical details. □

So far, we have characterized the optimal teachers for *full* X3C classes.

Lemma 11. *Let C be an X3C class. Then $E(c^*, C) = 1 + \frac{3}{2}n(n-1)$ if and only if C is a positive X3C class.*

Proof. For the if-direction, let $z_1, \ldots, z_n \in \mathcal{X}(c^*)$ have the X3C property.

The teacher T defined by $T(t) = z_{t \bmod n}$ has a teaching time of $1 + \frac{3}{2}n(n-1)$. This follows similar to Lemma 10. If there was a better teacher, this teacher would also have a smaller teaching time when applied to the full X3C class, thus contradicting Lemma 10.

For the only-if direction, assume $E(c^*, C) = 1 + \frac{3}{2}n(n-1)$ and suppose that C is a negative X3C class. Then there is a teacher T for c^* with teaching time $1 + \frac{3}{2}n(n-1)$, but not iterating over a sequence of examples $z_1, \ldots, z_n \in \mathcal{X}(c^*)$ with the X3C property (because negative X3C classes have no such examples). The teacher T would then have the same teaching time with respect to a full X3C class, too. Hence, T would be an optimal teacher for the full X3C class, a contradiction to Lemma 10. □

Using Lemma 11 we can show our main result.

Theorem 12. *The problem* OPT-TEACHING-TIME *is $\mathcal{NP}$-hard.*

Proof. Let $\langle B, A_1, \ldots, A_m \rangle$ with $B = [1, 3n]$ be an instance of X3C and let $\langle C, c^*, 1 + \frac{3}{2}n(n-1) \rangle$ be the instance of OPT-TEACHING-TIME resulting from the polynomial time reduction on Page 101.

By definition $\langle B, A_1, \ldots, A_m \rangle$ is a positive instance of X3C iff C is a positive X3C class. The latter holds iff $E(c^*, C) = 1 + \frac{3}{2}n(n-1)$ (by Lemma 11). This in turn holds iff $\langle C, c^*, 1 + \frac{3}{2}n(n-1) \rangle$ is a positive OPT-TEACHING-TIME instance. □

The last theorem implies that no polynomial time generic optimal teacher exists (unless $\mathcal{P} = \mathcal{NP}$).

In our teaching model it is at least possible to effectively approximate E with arbitrary precision.

Fact 13. *There is an algorithm with:*
Input: *Concept class C, concept $c \in C$, precision $\varepsilon > 0$.*
Output: *$F \in \mathbb{R}$ with $|F - E(c, C)| < \varepsilon$.*

Input: Concept class $\mathcal{C}$, concept $c \in \mathcal{C}$, rational number $\varepsilon > 0$.

1. $D := |X| \cdot |\mathcal{C}|$
2. **for** $\ell = 1, 2, \ldots$:
3.   **for all** $\alpha \in \mathcal{X}(c)^\ell$:
        // denote with h_i $(i = 1, \ldots, \ell)$ the random variable for the
        // hypothesis the teacher after round i when taught α.
4. $b(\alpha) := \sum_{i=1}^{\ell} i \cdot \Pr[h_i = c \wedge h_{i-1} \neq c] + (\ell + 1) \cdot \Pr[h_\ell \neq c]$
5. $B(\alpha) := \sum_{i=1}^{\ell} i \cdot \Pr[h_i = c \wedge h_{i-1} \neq c] + (\ell + D) \cdot \Pr[h_\ell \neq c]$
6. $b_\ell := \min\{b(\alpha) \mid \alpha \in \mathcal{X}(c)^\ell\}$
7.   **if** $\exists \alpha \in \mathcal{X}(c)^\ell : B(\alpha) - b_\ell < \varepsilon$:
8.   **Output** $B(\alpha)$.

Fig. 2. Algorithm computing an approximation of $E(c^*, \mathcal{C})$

Proof. Roughly speaking, the probability for not being in the target state tends to zero as the sequence of examples given by the teacher grows. The idea of the algorithm in Fig. 2 is to approximate the expectations for growing finite sequences of examples until the probability of not being in the target state becomes negligibly small.

The values $\Pr[h_i = c \wedge h_{i-1} \neq c]$ can be calculated according to the state transition function f. Its values are always rational numbers which can be calculated and stored exactly. The value D is an upper bound for the expected number of rounds to reach c regardless of the initial state of the learner. That means that in every state of the learner teaching can be continued such that the target is reached in expected at most D rounds.

The values $b(\alpha)$ and $B(\alpha)$ are a lower and an upper bound for the teaching time of a teacher starting with example sequence α. To verify this note that $\sum_{i=1}^{\ell} i \cdot \Pr[h_i = c \wedge h_{i-1} \neq c]$ is the expectation considering the first ℓ rounds only. The remaining probability mass $Pr[h_\ell \neq c]$ needs at least 1 and at most D additional rounds, which yields $b(\alpha)$ and $B(\alpha)$, respectively.

It follows that $B(\alpha) \geq E(c, \mathcal{C})$ for all $\alpha \in \mathcal{X}(c)^*$. Moreover, since every teacher starts with some example series $\alpha \in \mathcal{X}(c)^\ell$, the values b_ℓ are all lower bounds for $E(c, \mathcal{C})$, that is $b_\ell \leq E(c, \mathcal{C})$ for all $\ell \geq 1$. Therefore the output $B(\alpha)$ with $B(\alpha) - b_\ell < \varepsilon$ is an ε-approximation for $E(c, \mathcal{C})$.

It remains to show the termination of the algorithm. To this end we show:

Claim. $\lim_{\ell \to \infty} b_\ell = E(c, \mathcal{C})$.
Proof. Let $\delta > 0$ and set $\ell_0 := (D \cdot E(c, \mathcal{C}))/\delta$. We show that for all $\ell \geq \ell_0$, $|E(c, \mathcal{C}) - b_\ell| < \delta$. Let $\ell \geq \ell_0$. Then $\ell \geq (D \cdot E(c, \mathcal{C}))/\delta$.

Let $\alpha \in \mathcal{X}(c)^\ell$ such that $b(\alpha) = b_\ell$. Then $b(\alpha) \leq E(c, \mathcal{C})$ and therefore $(\ell + 1) \cdot \Pr[h_\ell \neq c] \leq E(c, \mathcal{C})$. It follows $\Pr[h_\ell \neq c] \leq E(c, \mathcal{C})/(\ell + 1)$.

For $B(\alpha)$ we have

$$B(\alpha) = b(\alpha) + \Pr[h_\ell \neq c] \cdot (D - 1) \leq b(\alpha) + \frac{E(c,\mathcal{C})}{\ell+1} \cdot (D - 1) < b(\alpha) + \frac{E(c,\mathcal{C})}{\ell} \cdot D.$$

Using $1/\ell \leq \delta/(D \cdot E(c, \mathcal{C}))$, we get $B(\alpha) < b(\alpha) + \delta$.

On the other hand, $E(c, \mathcal{C}) \leq B(\alpha)$ and therefore $E(c, \mathcal{C}) < b(\alpha) + \delta$, hence $E(c, \mathcal{C}) - b_\ell = E(c, \mathcal{C}) - b(\alpha) < \delta$. $\square$ Claim

To prove the termination of the algorithm we have to show that there is an α such that $B(\alpha) - b_\ell < \varepsilon$. Let $T \colon \mathbb{N} \to \mathcal{X}(c)$ be an optimal teacher and denote $\langle T(0), \ldots, T(\ell - 1) \rangle \in \mathcal{X}(c)^\ell$ by $T_{0:\ell}$. Then $\lim_{\ell \to \infty} B(T_{0:\ell}) = E(c, \mathcal{C})$. Together with $\lim_{\ell \to \infty} b_\ell = E(c, \mathcal{C})$ it follows $\lim_{\ell \to \infty} (B(T_{0:\ell}) - b_\ell) = 0$. That means for sufficiently long $\alpha = T_{0:\ell}$, the condition $B(T_{0:\ell}) - b_\ell < \varepsilon$ is satisfied. $\square$

5   Heuristics for Teaching

As it seems difficult to find an optimal teacher, next we study teaching heuristics.

5.1   Cyclic Teachers

Probably the simplest teachers are those that give the same sequence of examples over and over again. Such a *cyclic teacher* is identified with the sequence $(z_0, \ldots, z_{m-1}) \in \mathcal{X}^m$ of examples it teaches.

Fact 14. *Let $\mathcal{C}$ be a concept class and $c^* \in \mathcal{C}$ a target concept. A cyclic teacher $(z_0, \ldots, z_{m-1})$ is successful iff $\{z_0, \ldots, z_{m-1}\}$ is a teaching set for c^* wrt. $\mathcal{C}$.*

Not only is success of a cyclic teacher easy to decide, the teaching time is also efficiently computable.

Lemma 15. *The teaching time of a cyclic teacher can be computed from the sequence of examples that the teacher repeats.*

Proof. Let $\mathcal{C}$ be a concept class and let $c^* \in \mathcal{C}$. Let T be a cyclic teacher repeating $z_0, \ldots, z_{m-1}$. We assume that the examples constitute a teaching set.

Teaching will be successful no matter at which of the examples z_i the loop starts. We denote by F_i ($0 \leq i < m$) the teaching time for the teacher $T_i \colon T(t) = z_{(i+t) \bmod m}$ starting with example z_i. For $h \in \mathcal{C}$ we denote by $F_i(h)$ the teaching time for teacher T_i when the learner's initial hypothesis is h. For convenience throughout this proof all subscripts of T, z, and F are to be taken modulo m.

We can now state a linear equation for F_i involving all F_j with $j \neq i$. Consider the teacher T_i and the learner's state δ after the first example, z_i, has been given. The learner assumes all hypotheses $h \in \mathcal{C}(z_i)$ with equal probability $\delta(h) = 1/|\mathcal{C}(z_i)|$ and all other hypotheses with probability $\delta(h) = 0$.

The expectation F_i is one plus the expectation for teacher T_{i+1} when the learner starts in state δ. This expectation equals the weighted sum of the expectations of teacher T_{i+1} starting in state h, that is

$$F_i = 1 + \sum_{h \in \mathcal{C} \setminus \{c^*\}} \delta(h) \cdot F_{i+1}(h) \ .$$

We now determine $F_{i+1}(h)$. Consider a learner in state $h \neq c^*$ and a teacher giving $z_{i+1}, z_{i+2}, \ldots$. The learner will change its state only when the first example inconsistent with h arrives (such an example exists since the z_i's form a teaching set for c^*). Let z_{i+k} be this example. Beginning with z_{i+k}, teaching proceeds as if teacher T_{i+k} had started from the *init* state. Therefore $F_{i+1}(h) = (k-1) + F_{i+k}$.

If we denote for $i = 0, \ldots, m-1$ and for $k = 1, \ldots, m$,

$$\mathcal{C}_{i,k} = \{ h \in \mathcal{C} \setminus \{c^*\} \mid h \in \mathcal{C}(z_i), h \notin \mathcal{C}(z_{i+1}), \ldots, h \notin \mathcal{C}(z_{i+k-1}), h \in \mathcal{C}(z_{i+k}) \},$$

then we get the following linear equation for F_i:

$$F_i = 1 + \sum_{k=1}^{m} \frac{|\mathcal{C}_{i,k}|}{|\mathcal{C}(z_i)|} \cdot ((k-1) + F_{i+k}) \, .$$

In this manner we get m linear equations in the variables $F_0, \ldots, F_{m-1}$. Denoting the solution vector by $\boldsymbol{F}$ we get a linear equation system of the form $(\mathbf{1} - C) \cdot \boldsymbol{F} = U$, where $\mathbf{1}$ is the $m \times m$ unit matrix, C is a substochastic matrix composed of entries of the form $|\mathcal{C}_{i,k}|/|\mathcal{C}(z_i)|$ and zeros. Thus $\mathbf{1} - C$ is invertible and the values $F_0, \ldots, F_{m-1}$ are uniquely determined by the equation system. F_0 is the sought teaching time. □

The algorithm in Fig. 2 computes an $\alpha \in \mathcal{X}^*$ such that every extension of α yields a teacher ε-close to optimal. In particular, this holds for the cyclic teacher α. Hence, cyclic teachers can be arbitrarily close to the optimal teacher.

A drawback of cyclic teachers T is that they do not directly yield an information state teacher $\tilde{T}$. Thus the optimality criterion cannot immediately be applied. But cyclic teachers can be used to calculate upper bounds on $E(c^*, \mathcal{C})$.

Fact 16. *Let $k \geq 3$, $n \geq k$. The monomial $1^k *^{n-k}$ has a teaching time of at most* $\frac{-2 + 2^{k+1} + 7 \cdot 2^n - 2^{n+k+2} + 2^{2+k} \cdot 3^n + 2^{n+2} \cdot 3^n - 2 \cdot 3^{n+1} - 4^{n+1} - 2(2^k - 2^{n+1} + 2 \cdot 3^n)k}{2 \cdot 3^n - 2^{n+1} + 2^k}$.

Proof. This teaching time is achieved by the following cyclic teacher T. The teacher provides alternately positive and negative examples. The positive examples alternate between the two complementary examples $1^k 0^{n-k}$ and $1^k 1^{n-k}$.

The first k characters of the negative examples iterate through $01^{k-1}, 101^{k-2}, \ldots, 1^{k-1}0$, the last $n-k$ characters equal the last $n-k$ characters of the immediately preceding positive example. For example, let $k = 3$ and $n = 5$. Then the example sequence is $(11100, 1), (01100, 0), (11111, 1), (10111, 0), (11100, 1), (11000, 0), (11111, 1), (01111, 0), (11100, 1), (10100, 0), (11111, 1), (11011, 0)$.

Applying the method of the proof of Lemma 15, the expected teaching time of this teacher can be calculated. We omit the details. □

For comparison, the optimal teaching time for monomials in the scenario *with* feedback is $\frac{(3^n - 2^n)(2^n + 2^k) - 2^{n+k-1} + 2^{n+1} - 3^n}{3^n - 2^n + 2^{k-1}}$ (see [5]). A tedious analysis would show that the value given in Fact 16 is at most twice as high. Thus, teaching monomials without feedback takes at most twice as long as with feedback.

Corollary 17. *The following problem* OPT-CYCLIC-TEACHING-TIME *is $\mathcal{NP}$-hard.*

   Input: *Concept class $\mathcal{C}$, concept $c^* \in \mathcal{C}$, rational number F.*

   Question: *Is there a cyclic teacher with teaching time at most F?*

5.2 Greedy Teachers

We know from Lemma 4 that a greedy teacher is always successful. Moreover, in contrast to cyclic teachers, they allow a direct application of the optimality criterion. Thus we were able to prove their optimality in Fact 7. However, they can be arbitrarily far off the optimal teacher.

Fact 18. *For every $d > 1$ there is a class $\mathcal{C}$ and a target c^* such that for all greedy teachers T, $E_T(c^*, \mathcal{C}) > d \cdot E(c^*, \mathcal{C})$.*

	x_1 x_2 x_3	y_1 ... ... y_n
c^*	1 1 1	1 1
c_1	0 1 1	1 1
c_2	1 0 1	1 1
c_3	1 1 0	1 1
c_4	0 0 1	0 1 ... 1 1
	⋮ ⋮ ⋮	1 0 1 ... 1
	⋮ ⋮ ⋮	⋮ 1 ⋱ ⋮
	⋮ ⋮ ⋮	⋮ ⋮ ⋱ 1
c_{3+n}	0 0 1	1 1 ... 1 0

Fig. 3. For growing n, the greedy teacher for c^* becomes arbitrarily worse than the optimal teacher. See Fact 18. The examples on the right are "dummy" examples.

Proof. Figure 3 shows a family of classes parameterized by n. We sketch the main steps of the proof.

(1) The cyclic teacher $((x_1, 1), (x_2, 1), (x_3, 1))$ has a teaching time of $(16 + 5n)/(4 + n) < 5$. Therefore $E(c^*, \mathcal{C}) < 5$. This can be shown using Lemma 15.

(2) Setting $n := \frac{3}{2}(3^{2\ell-1} - 3) + 1$ makes the greedy teacher be a cyclic teacher of the form $(((x_1, 1), (x_2, 1))^\ell, (x_3, 1))$ or $(((x_2, 1), (x_1, 1))^\ell, (x_3, 1))$ giving ℓ times x_1, x_2 before giving x_3. The value ℓ becomes larger with growing n because, intuitively, the example x_3 becomes less attractive for the greedy teacher.

(3) For given ℓ the cyclic teacher has $\dfrac{-n + 9^\ell(16 + 5n) + 4\ell(1 + 3^{2\ell+1} + 9^\ell n)}{2(-1 + 9^\ell)(4 + n)}$ as teaching time. The proof is again an application of Lemma 15.

(4) For n as in (2) the greedy learner is cyclic with $\ell = \log(7 + 2n)/\log(9)$ and according to (3) with a teaching time of

$$\frac{(56 + n(33 + 5n))\log(3) + (22 + n(13 + 2n))\log(7 + 2n)}{(3 + n)(4 + n)\log(9)}$$

which is not bounded from above and can be larger than 5 by any factor d. □

In general there can be more than one greedy teacher for a given class and concept. It is $\mathcal{NP}$-hard to compute the teaching time of the optimal one.

Corollary 19. *The following problem* OPT-GREEDY-TEACHING-TIME *is $\mathcal{NP}$-hard.*
Input: *Concept class $\mathcal{C}$, concept $c^* \in \mathcal{C}$, rational number F.*
Question: *Is there a greedy teacher with teaching time at most F?*

Conclusion. We presented a model for teaching randomized memoryless learners without feedback, characterized optimal learners, and analyzed the expected teaching time of certain classes. We showed the problem of determining the optimal teaching time to be $\mathcal{NP}$-hard and studied useful heuristics for teaching.

Acknowledgment. The authors are very grateful to the ALT 2006 PC members for their many valuable comments.

References

[1] D. Angluin and M. Kriķis. Teachers, learners and black boxes. In *Proc. 10th Ann. Conf. on Comput. Learning Theory*, pp. 285–297. ACM Press, New York, 1997.

[2] D. Angluin and M. Kriķis. Learning from different teachers. *Machine Learning*, 51(2):137–163, 2003.

[3] M. Anthony, G. Brightwell, D. Cohen, and J. Shawe-Taylor. On exact specification by examples. In *Proc. 5th Ann. ACM Works. on Comput. Learning Theory*, pp. 311–318. ACM Press, New York, NY, 1992.

[4] F. J. Balbach. Teaching Classes with High Teaching Dimension Using Few Examples. In *Learning Theory, 18th Ann. Conf. on Learning Theory, COLT 2005, Bertinoro, Italy, June 2005, Proc.*, LNAI 3559, pp. 668–683, Springer, 2005.

[5] F. J. Balbach and T. Zeugmann. Teaching randomized learners. In *Learning Theory, 19th Ann. Conf. on Learning Theory, COLT 2006, Pittsburgh, PA, USA, June 2006, Proc.*, LNAI 4005, pp. 229–243, Springer, 2006.

[6] D. P. Bertsekas. *Dynamic Programming and Optimal Control.* Athena Sci., 2005.

[7] V. D. Blondel and V. Canterini. Undecidable problems for probabilistic automata of fixed dimension. *Theory of Computing Systems*, 36(3):231–245, 2003.

[8] R. Freivalds, E. B. Kinber, and R. Wiehagen. On the power of inductive inference from good examples. *Theoret. Comput. Sci.*, 110(1):131–144, 1993.

[9] M. R. Garey and D. S. Johnson. *Computers and Intractability: A Guide to the Theory of NP-Completeness.* W. H. Freeman, San Francisco, 1979.

[10] S. A. Goldman and M. J. Kearns. On the complexity of teaching. *J. of Comput. Syst. Sci.*, 50(1):20–31, 1995.

[11] S. A. Goldman and H. D. Mathias. Teaching a smarter learner. *J. of Comput. Syst. Sci.*, 52(2):255–267, 1996.

[12] S. A. Goldman, R. L. Rivest, and R. E. Schapire. Learning binary relations and total orders. *SIAM J. Comput.*, 22(5):1006–1034, 1993.

[13] J. Jackson and A. Tomkins. A computational model of teaching. In *Proc. 5th Ann. ACM Works. on Comput. Learning Theory*, pp. 319–326. ACM Press, 1992.

[14] S. Jain, S. Lange, and J. Nessel. On the learnability of recursively enumerable languages from good examples. *Theoret. Comput. Sci.*, 261(1):3–29, 2001.

[15] C. Kuhlmann. On Teaching and Learning Intersection-Closed Concept Classes. In *Computat. Learning Theory, 4th European Conf., EuroCOLT '99, Nordkirchen, Germany, March 29-31, 1999, Proc.*, LNAI 1572, pp. 168–182, Springer, 1999.

[16] H. Lee, R.A. Servedio, and A. Wan. DNF Are Teachable in the Average Case. In *Learning Theory, 19th Ann. Conf. on Learning Theory, COLT 2006, Pittsburgh, PA, USA, June 2006, Proc.*, *LNAI* 4005, pp. 214–228, Springer, 2006.

[17] O. Madani, S. Hanks, and A. Condon. On the undecidability of probabilistic planning and infinite-horizon partially observable markov decision problems. In *Proc. 16th Nat. Conf. on Artificial Intelligence & 11th Conf. on Innovative Applications of Artificial Intelligence*, pp. 541–548, AAAI Press/MIT Press, 1999.

[18] H. D. Mathias. A model of interactive teaching. *J. of Comput. Syst. Sci.*, 54(3): 487–501, 1997.

[19] S. D. Patek. On partially observed stochastic shortest path problems. In *Proc. of the 40-th IEEE Conf. on Decision and Control*, pp. 5050–5055, 2001.

[20] A. Shinohara and S. Miyano. Teachability in computational learning. *New Generation Computing*, 8(4):337–348, 1991.

The Complexity of Learning SUBSEQ(A)

Stephen Fenner[1,*] and William Gasarch[2,**]

[1] University of South Carolina
Dept. of Computer Science and Engineering, Columbia, SC 29208
`fenner@cse.sc.edu`
[2] University of Maryland at College Park
Dept. of Computer Science and UMIACS, College Park, MD 20742
`gasarch@cs.umd.edu`

Abstract. Higman showed[1] that if A is *any* language then SUBSEQ(A) is regular, where SUBSEQ(A) is the language of all subsequences of strings in A. We consider the following inductive inference problem: given $A(\varepsilon), A(0), A(1), A(00), \ldots$ learn, in the limit, a DFA for SUBSEQ(A). We consider this model of learning and the variants of it that are usually studied in inductive inference: anomalies, mindchanges, and teams.

1 Introduction

In Inductive Inference [2, 4, 15] the basic model of learning is as follows.

Definition 1.1. A class $\mathcal{A}$ of decidable sets of strings[2] is in EX if there is a Turing machine M (the learner) such that if M is given $A(\varepsilon)$, $A(0)$, $A(1)$, $A(00)$, $A(01)$, $A(10)$, $A(11)$, $A(000)$, ..., where $A \in \mathcal{A}$, then M will output $e_1, e_2, e_3, \ldots$ such that $\lim_s e_s = e$ and e is an index for a Turing machine that decides A.

Note that the set A must be computable and the learner learns a Turing machine index for it. There are variants [1, 11, 13] where the set need not be computable and the learner learns something about the set (e.g., "Is it infinite?" or some other question).

Our work is based on the following remarkable theorem of Higman's [16][3]. *Convention:* Σ is a finite alphabet.

Definition 1.2. Let $x, y \in \Sigma^*$. We say that x is a *subsequence* of y if $x = x_1 \cdots x_n$ and $y \in \Sigma^* x_1 \Sigma^* x_2 \cdots x_{n-1} \Sigma^* x_n \Sigma^*$. We denote this by $x \preceq y$.

Notation 1.3. If A is a set of strings, then SUBSEQ(A) is the set of subsequences of strings in A.

---

[*] Partially supported by NSF grant CCF-05-15269.
[**] Partially supported by NSF grant CCR-01-05413.

[1] The result we attribute to Higman is actually an easy consequence of his work. We explain in the journal version.

[2] The basic model is usually described in terms of learning computable functions; however, virtually all of the results hold in the setting of decidable sets.

[3] See footnote 1.

Theorem 1.4 (Higman [16]). *If A is any language over Σ^*, then $\mathrm{SUBSEQ}(A)$ is regular. In fact, for any language A there is a unique minimum finite set S of strings such that*

$$\mathrm{SUBSEQ}(A) = \{x \in \Sigma^* : (\forall z \in S)[z \not\preceq x]\}. \tag{1}$$

Note that A is *any language whatsoever*. Hence we can investigate the following learning problem.

Notation 1.5. We let $s_1, s_2, s_3, \ldots$ be the standard length-first lexicographic enumeration of Σ^*. We refer to Turing machines as TMs.

Definition 1.6. A class $\mathcal{A}$ of sets of strings in Σ^* is in SUBSEQ-EX if there is a TM M (the learner) such that if M is given $A(s_1), A(s_2), A(s_3), \ldots$ where $A \in \mathcal{A}$, then M will output $e_1, e_2, e_3, \ldots$ such that $\lim_s e_s = e$ and e is an index for a DFA that recognizes $\mathrm{SUBSEQ}(A)$. It is easy to see that we can take e to be the least index of the minimum state DFA that recognizes $\mathrm{SUBSEQ}(A)$. Formally, we will refer to $A(s_1)A(s_2)A(s_3)\cdots$ as being on an auxiliary tape.

This problem is part of a general theme of research: given a language A, rather than try to learn the language (which may be undecidable) learn some aspect of it. In this case we learn $\mathrm{SUBSEQ}(A)$. Note that we learn $\mathrm{SUBSEQ}(A)$ in a very strong way in that we have a DFA for it.

If $\mathcal{A} \in \mathrm{EX}$, then a TM can infer a Turing index for any $A \in \mathcal{A}$. The index is useful if you want to determine membership of particular strings, but not useful if you want most global properties (e.g., "Is A infinite?"). If $\mathcal{A} \in \mathrm{SUBSEQ\text{-}EX}$, then a TM can infer a DFA for $\mathrm{SUBSEQ}(A)$. The index is useful if you want to determine virtually any property of $\mathrm{SUBSEQ}(A)$ (e.g., "Is $\mathrm{SUBSEQ}(A)$ infinite?") but not useful if you want to answer almost any question about A.

We look at anomalies, mind-changes, and teams (standard Inductive Inference variants) in this context. We prove the following results.

1. $\mathcal{A} \in \mathrm{SUBSEQ\text{-}EX}^a$ means that the final DFA may be wrong on $\leq a$ strings. $\mathcal{A} \in \mathrm{SUBSEQ\text{-}EX}^*$ mean that the final DFA may be wrong on a finite number of strings. The anomaly hierarchy collapses: that is $\mathrm{SUBSEQ\text{-}EX} = \mathrm{SUBSEQ\text{-}EX}^*$. This contrasts sharply with the case of EX^a.
2. Let $\mathcal{A} \in \mathrm{SUBSEQ\text{-}EX}_n$ mean that the TM makes at most $n+1$ conjectures (and hence changes its mind at most n times). The mind-change hierarchy separates: that is, for all n, $\mathrm{SUBSEQ\text{-}EX}_n \subset \mathrm{SUBSEQ\text{-}EX}_{n+1}$.
3. The mind-change hierarchy also separates if you allow a transfinite number of mind-changes, up to ω_1^{CK}.
4. Let $\mathcal{A} \in [a,b]\mathrm{SUBSEQ\text{-}EX}$ mean that there are b TMs trying to learn the DFA, and we demand that at least a of them succeed (it may be a different a machines for different $A \in \mathcal{A}$).
   (a) If $1 \leq a \leq b$ and $q = \lfloor b/a \rfloor$, then $[a,b]\mathrm{SUBSEQ\text{-}EX} = [1,q]\mathrm{SUBSEQ\text{-}EX}$. Hence we need only look at team learning of the form $[1,n]\mathrm{SUBSEQ\text{-}EX}$.
   (b) The team hierarchy separates. That is, for all b, $[1,b]\mathrm{SUBSEQ\text{-}EX} \subset [1,b+1]\mathrm{SUBSEQ\text{-}EX}$.

Note 1.7. PEX [4, 3] is like EX except that the conjectures must be for total TMs. The class SUBSEQ-EX is similar in that all the machines are total (in fact, DFAs) but different in that we learn the subsequence language, and the input need not be computable. The anomaly hierarchy for SUBSEQ-EX collapses just as it does for PEX; however the team hierarchy for SUBSEQ-EX is proper, unlike for PEX.

2 Definitions

2.1 Definitions About Subsequences

Notation 2.1. We let $\mathbb{N} = \{0, 1, 2, \ldots\}$. For $n \in \mathbb{N}$ and alphabet Σ, we let $\Sigma^{=n}$ denote the set of all strings over Σ of length n. We also define $\Sigma^{\leq n} = \bigcup_{i \leq n} \Sigma^{=i}$ and $\Sigma^{<n} = \bigcup_{i<n} \Sigma^{=i}$.

Notation 2.2. Given a language A, we call the unique minimum set S satisfying (1) the *obstruction set* of A and denote it by $os(A)$. In this case, we also say that S *obstructs* A.

The following facts are obvious:

- The $\preceq$ relation is computable.
- For every string x there are finitely many $y \preceq x$, and given x one can compute a canonical index for the set of all such y.
- By various facts from automata theory, including the Myhill-Nerode minimization theorem: given a DFA, NFA, or regular expression for a language A, one can effectively compute the unique minimum state DFA recognizing A. (The minimum state DFA is given in some canonical form.)
- Given DFAs F and G, one can effectively compute DFAs for $\overline{L(F)}$, $L(F) \cup L(G)$, $L(F) \cap L(G)$, $L(F) - L(G)$, and $L(F) \triangle L(G)$ (symmetric difference). One can also effectively determine whether or not $L(F) = \emptyset$ and whether or not $L(F)$ is finite.
- For any language A, the set SUBSEQ(A) is completely determined by $os(A)$, and in fact, $os(A) = os(\text{SUBSEQ}(A))$.
- The strings in the obstruction set of a language must be pairwise $\preceq$-incomparable (i.e., the obstruction set is an $\preceq$-antichain). Conversely, any $\preceq$-antichain obstructs some language. For any $S \subseteq \Sigma^*$ define

$$\text{obsby}(S) = \{x \in \Sigma^* : (\forall z \in S)[z \not\preceq x]\}.$$

The term obsby(S) is an abbreviation for 'obstructed by S'. Note that $os(\text{obsby}(S)) \subseteq S$, and equality holds iff S is an $\preceq$-antichain.

Definition 2.3. A language $A \subseteq \Sigma^*$ is $\preceq$-*closed* if SUBSEQ(A) = A.

Observation 2.4. A language A is $\preceq$-closed if and only if there exists a language B such that $A = \text{SUBSEQ}(B)$.

Observation 2.5. Any infinite $\preceq$-closed set contains strings of every length.

The next proposition implies that finding $os(A)$ is computationally equivalent to finding a DFA for $\mathrm{SUBSEQ}(A)$. We omit the easy proof.

Proposition 2.6. *The following tasks are computable:*

1. *Given a DFA F, find a DFA G such that $L(G) = \mathrm{SUBSEQ}(L(F))$.*
2. *Given the canonical index of a finite language $D \subseteq \Sigma^*$, compute a regular expression for (and hence the minimum state DFA recognizing) the language* $\mathrm{obsby}(D) = \{x \in \Sigma^* : (\forall z \in D)[z \npreceq x]\}$.
3. *Given a DFA F, decide whether or not $L(F)$ is $\preceq$-closed.*
4. *Given a DFA F, compute the canonical index of $os(L(F))$.*

2.2   Classes of Languages

We define classes of languages via the types of machines that recognize them.

Notation 2.7.

1. $D_1, D_2, \ldots$ is a standard enumeration of finite languages. (e is the *canonical index* of D_e.)
2. $F_1, F_2, \ldots$ is a standard enumeration of minimized DFAs, presented in some canonical form, so that for all i and j, if $L(F_i) = L(F_j)$ then $F_i = F_j$. (We might have $i \neq j$ and $F_i = F_j$, however.) Let $\mathrm{REG} = \{L(F_1), L(F_2), \ldots\}$.
3. $P_1, P_2, \ldots$ is a standard enumeration of $\{0,1\}$-valued polynomial-time TMs. Let $\mathrm{P} = \{L(P_1), L(P_2), \ldots\}$. Note that these are total.
4. $M_1, M_2, \ldots$ is a standard enumeration of Turing machines. We let $\mathrm{CE} = \{L(M_1), L(M_2), \ldots\}$, where $L(M_i)$ is the set of all x such that $M_i(x)$ halts with output 1 (i.e., $M_i(x)$ *accepts*). CE stands for "computably enumerable."
5. We let $\mathrm{DEC} = \{L(N) : N$ is a total TM$\}$.

For the notation that relates to computability theory, our reference is [20]. For separation results, we will often construct tally sets, i.e., subsets of 0^*.

Notation 2.8.

1. The empty string is denoted by ε.
2. For $m \in \mathbb{N}$, we define $J_m = \{0^i : i < m\}$.
3. If $A \subseteq 0^*$ is finite, we let $m(A)$ denote the least m such that $A \subseteq J_m$, and we observe that $\mathrm{SUBSEQ}(A) = J_{m(A)}$.
4. If A is a set then $\mathcal{P}(A)$ is the powerset of A.

If $A, B \subseteq 0^*$ and A is finite, we define a "shifted join" of A and B as follows:

$$A \uplus B = \{0^{2n+1} : 0^n \in A\} \cup \{0^{2(m(A)+n)} : 0^n \in B\}.$$

In $A \uplus B$, all the elements from A have odd length and are shorter than the elements from B, which have even length.

2.3   Variants on SUBSEQ-EX

There are several variations on the definition of SUBSEQ-EX.

Definition 2.9. Let $e_1, e_2, \ldots$ be the output sequence of some learner M on some language A. Let $t > 1$. We say that M *changes its mind at time t* if $e_t \neq e_{t-1}$. For fixed $n \geq 0$, let SUBSEQ-EX$_n$ be the same as SUBSEQ-EX except that we restrict the learner to change its mind no more than n times, for any language $A \in \mathcal{C}$.

Obviously,

$$\text{SUBSEQ-EX}_0 \subseteq \text{SUBSEQ-EX}_1 \subseteq \text{SUBSEQ-EX}_2 \subseteq \cdots \subseteq \text{SUBSEQ-EX}. \quad (2)$$

We will extend this definition into the transfinite later.

Definition 2.10. Let $a \in \mathbb{N}$, let M be a TM, and let $A \subseteq \Sigma^*$ be any language. The machine M *learns* SUBSEQ(A) *with at most a anomalies* (respectively, with *finitely many anomalies*) if it behaves as follows: when you feed $A(s_1)$, $A(s_2)$, $A(s_3)$, ... and M outputs $e_1, e_2, e_3, \ldots$, then $e = \lim_{n \to \infty} e_n$ exists, and $|L(F_e) \triangle \text{SUBSEQ}(A)| \leq a$ (respectively, $L(F_e) \triangle \text{SUBSEQ}(A)$ is finite). For $a \in \mathbb{N}$ let SUBSEQ-EX^a be the same as SUBSEQ-EX except that we allow the learner to learn SUBSEQ(A) with at most a anomalies. Let SUBSEQ-EX* be the same as SUBSEQ-EX except that we allow the learner to learn SUBSEQ(A) with finitely many anomalies. Note that in the latter case, the number of anomalies may vary with the language being learned.

Clearly,

$$\text{SUBSEQ-EX} = \text{SUBSEQ-EX}^0 \subseteq \text{SUBSEQ-EX}^1 \subseteq \cdots \subseteq \text{SUBSEQ-EX}^*. \quad (3)$$

Definition 2.11. For integers $1 \leq a \leq b$, we say that a class $\mathcal{C}$ of languages is in $[a, b]$SUBSEQ-EX iff there are learners $M_1, \ldots, M_b$ such that for any $A \in \mathcal{C}$, at least a of the learners learn SUBSEQ(A).

Evidently, if $a \geq c$ and $b \leq d$, then $[a, b]$SUBSEQ-EX $\subseteq [c, d]$SUBSEQ-EX.

Definition 2.12. If $X \subseteq \mathbb{N}$, then SUBSEQ-EX^X is the same as SUBSEQ-EX except that we allow the learner to be an oracle TM using oracle X.

We may combine these variants in a large variety of ways.

3   Main Results

3.1   Standard Learning

It was essentially shown in [6] that DEC $\notin$ SUBSEQ-EX. The proof there can be tweaked to show the stronger result that P $\notin$ SUBSEQ-EX. We omit the proof; however, it will appear in the full version.

Theorem 3.1 ([6]). *There is a computable function g such that for all e, setting $A = L(P_{g(e)})$, we have $A \subseteq 0^*$ and* SUBSEQ(A) *is not learned by M_e.*

Corollary 3.2. P $\notin$ SUBSEQ-EX. *In fact,* P $\cap \mathcal{P}(0^*) \notin$ SUBSEQ-EX.

We now show some classes that are in SUBSEQ-EX. An additional example is given in Section 4.

Definition 3.3. Let $\mathcal{F} = \{A \subseteq \Sigma^* : A \text{ is finite}\}$.

Proposition 3.4. $\mathcal{F} \in$ SUBSEQ-EX.

Proof. Let M be a learner that, when $A \in \mathcal{F}$ is on the tape, outputs $k_1, k_2, \ldots$, where each k_i is the least index of a DFA recognizing SUBSEQ$(A \cap \Sigma^{\leq i})$. Clearly, M learns SUBSEQ(A). $\square$

More generally, we have

Proposition 3.5. REG $\in$ SUBSEQ-EX.

Proof. When A is on the tape, $n = 0, 1, 2, \ldots$, the learner M

1. finds the least k such that $A \cap \Sigma^{<n} = L(F_k) \cap \Sigma^{<n}$, then
2. outputs the least ℓ such that $L(F_\ell) = $ SUBSEQ$(L(F_k))$.

If A is regular, then clearly M will converge to the least k such that $A = L(F_k)$, whence M will converge to the least ℓ such that $L(F_\ell) = $ SUBSEQ(A). $\square$

3.2 Anomalies

The next theorem shows that the hierarchy of (3) collapses completely.

Theorem 3.6. SUBSEQ-EX $=$ SUBSEQ-EX*. *In fact, there is a computable h such that for all e and languages A, if M_e learns* SUBSEQ(A) *with finitely many anomalies, then $M_{h(e)}$ learns* SUBSEQ(A) *(with zero anomalies).*

Proof. Given e, let $M = M_{h(e)}$ be the following learner:
    When a language A is on the tape:

1. Run M_e with A. Wait for M_e to output something.
2. Whenever M_e outputs some index k do the following:
   (a) Let n be the number of outputs of M_e thus far.
   (b) Build a finite set E of anomalies as follows:
       i. Initially, $E := \emptyset$.
       ii. For each $w \in \Sigma^{<n}$, define $S(w) = \{z \in \Sigma^* : w \preceq z\}$.
           – If F_k rejects w but $S(w) \cap \Sigma^{\leq n} \cap A \neq \emptyset$, then put w into E. (w is a "false negative.")
           – If F_k accepts w but $S(w) \cap \Sigma^{\leq n} \cap A = \emptyset$ and $S(w) \cap \Sigma^{=n} \cap L(F_k) = \emptyset$, then put w into E. (w is a "potentially false positive.")
   (c) Output the least index for a DFA G such that $L(G) = L(F_k) \triangle E$.

If M_e learns SUBSEQ(A) with finite anomalies, then there is a DFA F such that for all large enough n the nth output of M_e is an index for F, and moreover, SUBSEQ(A) $\triangle L(F) \subseteq \Sigma^{<n}$ (all anomalies are of length less than n). We claim that for all large enough n the anomaly set E built in step 2b is exactly SUBSEQ(A) $\triangle L(F)$, and hence SUBSEQ(A) $= L(G)$, where G is output by M in step 2c. The theorem follows once we prove the claim.

Let n be large enough as above, and let w be any string in $\Sigma^{<n}$. There are four cases to consider:

- $w \notin$ SUBSEQ(A) $\cup L(F)$. Then $F(w)$ rejects and $S(w) \cap A = \emptyset$, so we don't put w into E. (w is a "true negative.")
- $w \in$ SUBSEQ(A) $- L(F)$. Then $F(w)$ rejects, but there is some $z \in S(w) \cap A$. So as long as $n \geq |z|$, i.e., $z \in \Sigma^{\leq n}$, we will put w into E.
- $w \in L(F)$ $-$ SUBSEQ(A). Then $F(w)$ accepts, and $S(w) \cap A = \emptyset$. Furthermore, $S(w) \cap$ SUBSEQ(A) $= \emptyset$ as well, and since there are no anomalies of length n, we must also have $S(w) \cap \Sigma^{=n} \cap L(F) = \emptyset$. Thus we put w into E.
- $w \in$ SUBSEQ(A) $\cap L(F)$. Then $F(w)$ accepts. Since $w \in$ SUBSEQ(A), there is a $z \in S(w) \cap A$. If $|z| \leq n$, then $S(w) \cap \Sigma^{\leq n} \cap A \neq \emptyset$, and we would not put w into E. If $|z| > n$, then there is some $y \in \Sigma^{=n}$ with $w \preceq y \preceq z$. Thus we have $y \in$ SUBSEQ(A), and since there are no anomalies of length n, we also have $y \in L(F)$. Therefore, $y \in S(w) \cap \Sigma^{=n} \cap L(F) \neq \emptyset$, and so we don't put w into E.

Thus $E = ($SUBSEQ(A) $\triangle L(F)) \cap \Sigma^{<n} =$ SUBSEQ(A) $\triangle L(F)$ for all large enough n. The claim follows. $\square$

3.3   Mind Changes

The next theorems show that the hierarchy (2) separates.

Definition 3.7. For every $i > 0$, define the class $\mathcal{C}_i = \{A \subseteq \Sigma^* : |A| \leq i\}$.

Theorem 3.8. $\mathcal{C}_i \in$ SUBSEQ-EX$_i$ for all $i \in \mathbb{N}$. In fact, there is a single learner M that for each i learns SUBSEQ(A) for every $A \in \mathcal{C}_i$ with at most i mind-changes.

Proof. Let M be as in the proof of Proposition 3.4. Clearly, M learns any $A \in \mathcal{C}_i$ with at most $|A|$ mind-changes. $\square$

Theorem 3.9. For each $i > 0$, $\mathcal{C}_i \cap \mathcal{P}(0^*) \notin$ SUBSEQ-EX$_{i-1}$. In fact, there is a computable function ℓ such that, for each e and $i > 0$, $M_{\ell(e,i)}$ is total and decides a unary language $A_{e,i} = L(M_{\ell(e,i)}) \subseteq 0^*$ such that $|A_{e,i}| \leq i$ and M_e does not learn SUBSEQ($A_{e,i}$) with fewer than i mind-changes.

Proof. Given e and $i > 0$ we use the Recursion Theorem with Parameters to construct a machine $N = M_{\ell(e,i)}$ that implements the following recursive algorithm to compute $A_{e,i}$:

Given input x,

1. If $x \notin 0^*$, then reject. (This ensures that $A_{e,i} \subseteq 0^*$.) Otherwise, let $x = 0^n$.
2. Recursively compute $R_n = A_{e,i} \cap J_n$.
3. Simulate M_e for $n - 1$ steps with R_n on the tape. (Note that M_e does not have time to read any of the tape corresponding to inputs $0^{n'}$ for $n' \geq n$.) If M_e does not output anything within this time, then reject.
4. Let k be the most recent output of M_e in the previous step, and let c be the number of mind-changes that M_e has made up to this point. If $c < i$ and $L(F_k) = \text{SUBSEQ}(R_n)$, then accept; else reject.

In step 3 of the algorithm, M_e behaves the same with R_n on its tape as it would with $A_{e,i}$ on its tape, given the limit on its running time.

Let $A_{e,i} = \{0^{z_0}, 0^{z_1}, \ldots\}$, where $z_0 < z_1 < \cdots$ are natural numbers.

Claim 3.10. For $0 \leq j$, if z_j exists, then M_e (with $A_{e,i}$ on its tape) must output a DFA for $\text{SUBSEQ}(R_{z_j})$ within $z_j - 1$ steps, having changed its mind at least j times when this occurs.

Proof (of the claim). We proceed by induction on j: For $j = 0$, the string 0^{z_0} is accepted by N only if within $z_0 - 1$ steps M_e outputs a k where $L(F_k) = \emptyset = \text{SUBSEQ}(R_{z_0})$; no mind-changes are required. Now assume that $j \geq 0$ and z_{j+1} exists, and also (for the inductive hypothesis) that within $z_j - 1$ steps M_e outputs a DFA for $\text{SUBSEQ}(R_{z_j})$ after at least j mind-changes. We have $R_{z_j} \subseteq J_{z_j}$ but $0^{z_j} \in R_{z_{j+1}}$, and so $\text{SUBSEQ}(R_{z_j}) \neq \text{SUBSEQ}(R_{z_{j+1}})$. Since N accepts $0^{z_{j+1}}$, it must be because M_e has just output a DFA for $\text{SUBSEQ}(R_{z_{j+1}})$ within $z_{j+1} - 1$ steps, thus having changed its mind at least once since the z_jth step of its computation, making at least $j + 1$ mind-changes in all. So the claim holds for $j + 1$. This ends the proof of the claim. □

First we show that $A_{e,i} \in \mathcal{C}_i$. Indeed, by Claim 3.10, z_i cannot exist, because the algorithm would explicitly reject such a string 0^{z_i} if M_e made at least i mind-changes in the first $z_i - 1$ steps. Thus we have $|A_{e,i}| \leq i$, and so $A_{e,i} \in \mathcal{C}_i$.

Next we show that M_e cannot learn $A_{e,i}$ with fewer than i mind-changes. Suppose that with $A_{e,i}$ on its tape, M_e makes fewer than i mind-changes. Suppose also that there is a DFA F such that cofinitely many of M_e's outputs are indices for F. Let t be least such that $t \geq m(A_{e,i})$ and M_e outputs an index for F within $t - 1$ steps. Then $L(F) \neq \text{SUBSEQ}(A_{e,i})$, for otherwise the algorithm would accept 0^t and so $0^t \in A_{e,i}$, contradicting the choice of t. It follows that M_e cannot learn $A_{e,i}$ with fewer than i mind-changes. □

Transfinite Mind Changes and Procrastination. We extend the results of this section into the transfinite. Freivalds & Smith defined EX_α for all constructive ordinals α [8]. When $\alpha < \omega$, the definition is the same as the finite mind-change case above. If $\alpha \geq \omega$, then the learner may revise its bound on the number of mind changes during the computation. The learner may be able to revise more than once, or even compute a bound on the number of future revisions, and this bound itself could be revised, etc., depending on the size of α.

We define SUBSEQ-EX$_\alpha$ for all constructive α, then describe (without proof) how this transfinite hierarchy separates. Our definition is slightly different from, but equivalent to, the definition in [8]. For general background on constructive ordinals, see [18, 19].

Definition 3.11. A *procrastinating learner* is a learner M equipped with an additional *ordinal tape*, whose contents is always a constructive ordinal. Given a language on its input tape, M runs forever, producing infinitely many outputs as usual, except that just before M changes its mind, if α is currently on its ordinal tape, M is required to compute some ordinal $\beta < \alpha$ and replace the contents of the ordinal tape with β before proceeding to change its mind. (So if $\alpha = 0$, no mind-change may take place.) M may alter its ordinal tape at any other time, but the only allowed change is replacement with a lesser ordinal.

Thus a procrastinating learner must decrease its ordinal tape before each mind-change. We abuse notation and let $M_1, M_2, \ldots$ be a standard enumeration of procrastinating learners. Such an effective enumeration can be shown to exist.

Definition 3.12. Let M be a procrastinating learner, α a constructive ordinal, and A a language. We say that M *learns* SUBSEQ(A) *with α mind-changes* if M learns SUBSEQ(A) with α initially on its ordinal tape.

If $\mathcal{C}$ is a class of languages, we say that $\mathcal{C} \in$ SUBSEQ-EX$_\alpha$ if there is a procrastinating learner that learns every language in $\mathcal{C}$ with α mind-changes.

The following is straightforward and given without proof.

Proposition 3.13. *If $\alpha < \omega$, then SUBSEQ-EX$_\alpha$ is equal to the corresponding class in Definition 2.9.*

Proposition 3.14. *For all $\alpha < \beta < \omega_1^{\mathrm{CK}}$,*

$$\text{SUBSEQ-EX}_\alpha \subseteq \text{SUBSEQ-EX}_\beta \subseteq \text{SUBSEQ-EX}.$$

Proof. The first containment follows from the fact that any procrastinating learner allowed α mind-changes can be simulated by a procrastinating learner, allowed β mind-changes, that first decreases its ordinal tape from β to α before the simulation. (α is hard-coded into the simulator.)

The second containment is trivial; any procrastinating learner is also a regular learner. □

In [8], Freivalds and Smith showed that the EX$_\alpha$ hierarchy separates using classes of languages constructed entirely by diagonalization. We take a different approach and define more "natural" (using the term loosely) classes of languages that separate the SUBSEQ-EX$_\alpha$ hierarchy.

Definition 3.15. For every $\alpha < \omega_1^{\mathrm{CK}}$, we define the class $\mathcal{F}_\alpha$ inductively as follows: Let n and λ uniquely satisfy $n < \omega$, λ is not a successor, and $\lambda + n = \alpha$.

– If $\lambda = 0$, let $\mathcal{F}_\alpha = \mathcal{F}_n = \{A \uplus \emptyset : (A \subseteq 0^*) \wedge (|A| \leq n)\}$.

− If $\lambda > 0$, then λ has notation $3 \cdot 5^e$ for some TM index e (see [19]). Let

$$\mathcal{F}_\alpha = \{A \uplus B : (A, B \subseteq 0^*) \wedge (|A| \leq n + 1) \wedge (B \in \mathcal{F}_{M_e(m(A))})\}.$$

It is evident by induction on α that $\mathcal{F}_\alpha$ consists only of finite unary languages, and that $\emptyset \in \mathcal{F}_\alpha$. Note that in the case of finite α we have the condition that $|A| \leq n$, but in the case of $\alpha \geq \omega$ we have the condition that $|A| \leq n + 1$. This is not a mistake.

The next two theorems have proofs that are similar to the finite mind-change case in some ways, but very different in others. Unfortunately we have to omit the proofs for this version.

Theorem 3.16. *For every constructive α, $\mathcal{F}_\alpha \in$ SUBSEQ-EX$_\alpha$. In fact, there is a single procrastinating learner N such that for every α, N learns every language in $\mathcal{F}_\alpha$ with α mind-changes.*

Theorem 3.17. *For all $\beta < \alpha < \omega_1^{CK}$, $\mathcal{F}_\alpha \notin$ SUBSEQ-EX$_\beta$. In fact, there is a computable function r such that, for each e and $\beta < \alpha < \omega_1^{CK}$, $M_{r(e,\alpha,\beta)}$ is total and decides a language $A_{e,\alpha,\beta} = L(M_{r(e,\alpha,\beta)}) \in \mathcal{F}_\alpha$ such that M_e does not learn SUBSEQ$(A_{e,\alpha,\beta})$ with β mind-changes.*

We end with an easy observation.

Corollary 3.18. SUBSEQ-EX $\not\subseteq \bigcup_{\alpha < \omega_1^{CK}}$ SUBSEQ-EX$_\alpha$.

Proof. Let $\mathcal{F} \in$ SUBSEQ-EX be the class of Definition 3.3. For all $\alpha < \omega_1^{CK}$, we clearly have $\mathcal{F}_{\alpha+1} \subseteq \mathcal{F}$, and so $\mathcal{F} \notin$ SUBSEQ-EX$_\alpha$ by Theorem 3.17.   □

3.4   Teams

In this section, we show that $[a, b]$SUBSEQ-EX depends only on $\lfloor b/a \rfloor$. Recall that $b \leq c$ implies $[a, b]$SUBSEQ-EX $\subseteq [a, c]$SUBSEQ-EX.

Lemma 3.19. *For all $1 \leq a \leq b$, $[a, b]$SUBSEQ-EX $= [1, \lfloor b/a \rfloor]$SUBSEQ-EX.*

Proof. Let $q = \lfloor b/a \rfloor$. To show that $[1, q]$SUBSEQ-EX $\subseteq [a, b]$SUBSEQ-EX, let $\mathcal{C} \in [1, q]$SUBSEQ-EX. Then there are learners $Q_1, \ldots, Q_q$ such that for all $A \in \mathcal{C}$ there is some Q_i that learns SUBSEQ(A). For all $1 \leq i \leq q$ and $1 \leq j \leq a$, let $N_{i,j} = Q_i$. Then clearly, $\mathcal{C} \in [a, qa]$SUBSEQ-EX as witnessed by the $N_{i,j}$. Thus, $\mathcal{C} \in [a, b]$SUBSEQ-EX, since $b \geq qa$.

To show the reverse containment, suppose that $\mathcal{D} \in [a, b]$SUBSEQ-EX. Let $Q_1, \ldots, Q_b$ be learners such that for each $A \in \mathcal{D}$, at least a of the Q_i's learn SUBSEQ(A). We define learners $N_1, \ldots, N_q$ to behave as follows.

Each N_j runs all of $Q_1, \ldots, Q_b$. At any time t, let $k_1(t), \ldots, k_b(t)$ be the most recent outputs of $Q_1, \ldots, Q_b$, respectively, after running for t steps (if some machine Q_i has not yet output anything in t steps, let $k_i(t) = 0$).

Define a *consensus value at time t* to be a value that shows up at least a times in the list $k_1(t), \ldots, k_b(t)$. There can be at most q many different consensus values at any given time. The idea is that the machines N_j output consensus values. If k_{correct} is the least index of a DFA recognizing SUBSEQ(A), then k_{correct} will be a consensus value at all sufficiently large times t, and so we hope that k_{correct} will eventually always be output by some N_j. We could simply assign each consensus value at time t to be output by one of the machines $N_1, \ldots, N_q$ to guarantee that k_{correct} is eventually always output by one or another of the N_j, but this does not suffice, because it may be output by different N_j at different times. The tricky part is to ensure that k_{correct} is eventually output not only by some N_j, but also by the *same* N_j each time. To make sure of this, we hold a popularity contest among the consensus values.

For $1 \leq j \leq q$ and $t = 1, 2, 3, \ldots$, each machine N_j computes $k_1(t'), \ldots, k_b(t')$ and all the consensus values at time t' for all $t' \leq t$. For each $v \in \mathbb{N}$, let $p_v(t)$ be the number of times $\leq t$ at which v is a consensus value. We call $p_v(t)$ the *popularity* of v at time t. We rank all the consensus values found so far (at all times $t' \leq t$) in order of decreasing popularity; if there is a tie, i.e., some $u \neq v$ such that $p_u(t) = p_v(t)$, then we consider the smaller value to be more popular. As its t'th output, N_j outputs the j'th most popular consensus value at time t.

This ends the description of the machines $N_1, \ldots, N_q$.

We'll be done if we can show that there is a $1 \leq j \leq q$ such that N_j outputs k_{correct} cofinitely often.

Let t_0 be least such that k_{correct} is a consensus value at time t for all $t \geq t_0$. We claim that

- from t_0 on, k_{correct} will never lose ground in the popularity rankings, and
- eventually k_{correct} will be one of the q most popular consensus values.

For all $t \geq t_0$, let $P(t)$ be the set of all values that are at least as popular as k_{correct} at time t. That is,

$$P(t) = \{v \in \mathbb{N} : \text{either } p_v(t) > p_{k_{\text{correct}}}(t) \text{ or } p_v(t) = p_{k_{\text{correct}}}(t) \text{ and } v \leq k_{\text{correct}}\}.$$

We claim that $P(t_0) \supseteq P(t_0 + 1) \supseteq P(t_0 + 2) \supseteq \cdots$. This holds because the only way for a value v to go from being less popular than k_{correct} to being more popular than k_{correct} is for there to be a time $t \geq t_0$ when v is a consensus value but k_{correct} is not, but this never happens.

Since the $P(t)$ are clearly all finite, there is a $t_1 \geq t_0$ such that $P(t_1) = P(t_1 + 1) = P(t_1 + 2) = \cdots = \bigcap_t P(t)$. Set $P = P(t_1)$, and let $r = |P|$. It suffices to show that $r \leq q$, for then N_r outputs k_{correct} for all $t \geq t_1$ and so N_r learns SUBSEQ(A).

Suppose $r > q$. Let $v_1, \ldots, v_{r-1} \in P$ be the values in P other than k_{correct}. For each $t \geq t_1$, there can be at most q consensus values at time t, and one of these is k_{correct}, so at least one of $v_1, \ldots, v_{r-1}$ does not appear as a consensus value at time t. By the pigeon hole principle, there is some v_i that does not appear as a consensus value at time t for infinitely many $t \geq t_1$. For every $t \geq t_1$ we have $p_{k_{\text{correct}}}(t + 1) = p_{k_{\text{correct}}}(t) + 1$, and

$$p_{v_i}(t + 1) = \begin{cases} p_{v_i}(t) + 1 & \text{if } v_i \text{ is a consensus value at time } t + 1, \\ p_{v_i}(t) & \text{otherwise,} \end{cases}$$

and the second case occurs infinitely often. Thus there is some $t_2 \geq t_1$ such that $p_{v_i}(t_2) < p_{k_{\text{correct}}}(t_2)$, making v_i less popular than k_{correct} at time t_2. Thus $v_i \notin P$, which is a contradiction. Hence, $r \leq q$, and we are done.   □

To prove a separation, we describe classes $\mathcal{A}_1, \mathcal{A}_2, \ldots$ and prove that for any $n > 1$, $\mathcal{A}_n \in [1, n]\text{SUBSEQ-EX} - [1, n - 1]\text{SUBSEQ-EX}$.

Notation 3.20. For languages $A, B \subseteq \Sigma^*$, we write $A \subseteq^* B$ to mean that $A - B$ is finite.

Definition 3.21. For $i \geq 1$, let R_i be the language $(0^*1^*)^i$, and define

$$\mathcal{Q}_i = \{A \subseteq \{0,1\}^* : R_i \subseteq \text{SUBSEQ}(A) \subseteq^* R_i\}.$$

For all $n \geq 1$, define $\mathcal{A}_n = \mathcal{Q}_1 \cup \mathcal{Q}_2 \cup \cdots \cup \mathcal{Q}_n$.

Note that $R_1 \subseteq R_2 \subseteq R_3 \subseteq \cdots$, but $R_{i+1} \not\subseteq^* R_i$ for any $i \geq 1$. This means that the $\mathcal{Q}_i$ are all pairwise disjoint. Also note that $\text{SUBSEQ}(R_i) = R_i$ for all $i \geq 1$. Finally, note that $A \in \mathcal{Q}_i$ implies $\text{SUBSEQ}(A) \in \mathcal{Q}_i$.

Lemma 3.22. *For all $n > 1$, $\mathcal{A}_n \in [1, n]\text{SUBSEQ-EX}$ and $\mathcal{A}_n \cap \text{DEC} \notin [1, n - 1]\text{SUBSEQ-EX}$. In fact, there is a computable function $d(s)$ such that for all $n > 1$ and all $e_1, \ldots, e_{n-1}$, the machine $M_{d([e_1,\ldots,e_{n-1}])}$ decides a language $A_{[e_1,\ldots,e_{n-1}]} \in \mathcal{A}_n$ that is not learned by any of $M_{e_1}, \ldots, M_{e_{n-1}}$.*[4]

Proof. To see that $\mathcal{A}_n \in [1, n]\text{SUBSEQ-EX}$, let $Q_1, \ldots, Q_n$ be learners that behave as follows given a language A on their tapes: For $1 \leq i \leq n$, Q_i outputs $k_{i,1}, k_{i,2}, k_{i,3}, \ldots$, where $k_{i,j}$ is the least index of a DFA recognizing $R_i \cup \text{SUBSEQ}(A \cap \Sigma^{\leq j})$. Suppose $A \in \mathcal{Q}_i$ for some $1 \leq i \leq n$. We claim that Q_i learns $\text{SUBSEQ}(A)$. Since $A \in \mathcal{Q}_i$, there is a finite set D such that $\text{SUBSEQ}(A) = R_i \cup D$. For every $x \in D$, there is a $y \in A$ with $x \preceq y$. Because D is finite, this implies that $D \subseteq \text{SUBSEQ}(A \cap \Sigma^{\leq j})$ for all large enough j. Then for all such j,

$$\text{SUBSEQ}(A) = R_i \cup D \subseteq$$
$$R_i \cup \text{SUBSEQ}(A \cap \Sigma^{\leq j}) \subseteq \text{SUBSEQ}(A) \cup \text{SUBSEQ}(A) = \text{SUBSEQ}(A),$$

and thus $\text{SUBSEQ}(A) = R_i \cup \text{SUBSEQ}(A \cap \Sigma^{\leq j})$ for all large enough j. This proves the claim, and shows that $\mathcal{A}_n \in [1, n]\text{SUBSEQ-EX}$.

To show that $\mathcal{A}_n \notin [1, n - 1]\text{SUBSEQ-EX}$ effectively, we use the Recursion Theorem with Parameters to define a computable function $d(s)$ such that for all $n > 1$ and $e_1, \ldots, e_{n-1}$, the machine $M_{d([e_1,\ldots,e_{n-1}])}$ is total and decides a language $A = A_{[e_1,\ldots,e_{n-1}]} \in \mathcal{A}_n$, and $\text{SUBSEQ}(A)$ is not learned by any of $M_{e_1}, \ldots, M_{e_{n-1}}$. The machine $M_{d([e_1,\ldots,e_{n-1}])}$ has some input alphabet Σ such that $0, 1 \in \Sigma$, and it decides A via the following recursive algorithm:

---

[4] $[e_1, e_2, \ldots, e_{n-1}]$ is a natural number encoding the finite sequence $e_1, e_2, \ldots, e_{n-1}$.

On input $x \in \Sigma^*$:

1. If x is not of the form $(0^t 1^t)^i$, where $t \geq 1$ and $1 \leq i \leq n$, then reject. (This ensures that $A \subseteq \{(0^t 1^t)^i : (t \geq 1) \wedge (1 \leq i \leq n)\}$.) Otherwise, let t and i be such that $x = (0^t 1^t)^i$.
2. Recursively compute $B_t := A \cap \{(0^s 1^s)^\ell : (1 \leq s < t) \wedge (1 \leq \ell \leq n)\}$.
3. Compute $k_1(t), \ldots, k_{n-1}(t)$, the most recent outputs of $M_{e_1}, \ldots, M_{e_{n-1}}$, respectively, after running for t steps with B_t on their tapes. If some M_{e_j} has not yet output anything within t steps, then set $k_j(t) = 0$. (None of these machines has time to scan any tape cells corresponding to strings of the form $(0^u 1^u)^\ell$ where $\ell \geq 1$ and $u \geq t$, so the machines' behaviors with B_t on their tapes are the same as with A on their tapes.)
4. Let $1 \leq i_t \leq n$ be least such that there is no $1 \leq j \leq n-1$ such that $L(F_{k_j(t)}) \in \mathcal{Q}_{i_t}$. (Such an i_t exists by the disjointness of the $\mathcal{Q}_i$ and by the pigeon hole principle, and we can compute such an i_t.)
5. If $i = i_t$, then accept; else reject.

By the pigeon hole principle, there is some largest $i_{\max}$ that is found in step 4 for infinitely many values of t. That is, $i_t = i_{\max}$ for infinitely many t, and $i_t > i_{\max}$ for only finitely many t.

We first claim that $A \in \mathcal{Q}_{i_{\max}}$, and hence $A \in \mathcal{A}_n$. Since A contains strings of the form $(0^t 1^t)^{i_{\max}}$ for arbitrarily large t, it is clear that $R_{i_{\max}} \subseteq \mathrm{SUBSEQ}(A)$. By the choice of $i_{\max}$, there is a t_0 such that A contains no strings of the form $(0^t 1^t)^i$ where $i > i_{\max}$ and $t > t_0$. Therefore the set $D = A - R_{i_{\max}}$ is finite, and we also have $\mathrm{SUBSEQ}(A) = R_{i_{\max}} \cup \mathrm{SUBSEQ}(D)$. Thus $\mathrm{SUBSEQ}(A) \subseteq^* R_{i_{\max}}$, and so we have $A \in \mathcal{Q}_{i_{\max}}$, which in turn implies $\mathrm{SUBSEQ}(A) \in \mathcal{Q}_{i_{\max}}$.

We next claim that no M_{e_j} learns $\mathrm{SUBSEQ}(A)$ for any $1 \leq j \leq n-1$. This is immediate by the choice of $i_{\max}$: For infinitely many t, none of the $k_j(t)$ satisfies $L(F_{k_j(t)}) \in \mathcal{Q}_{i_{\max}}$, and so none of the M_{e_j} can learn $\mathrm{SUBSEQ}(A)$. $\square$

Lemmas 3.19 and 3.22 combine to show the following general theorem, which completely characterizes the containment relationships between the various team learning classes $[a, b]\mathrm{SUBSEQ\text{-}EX}$.

Theorem 3.23. *For every $1 \leq a \leq b$ and $1 \leq c \leq d$, $[a, b]\mathrm{SUBSEQ\text{-}EX} \subseteq [c, d]\mathrm{SUBSEQ\text{-}EX}$ if and only if $\lfloor b/a \rfloor \leq \lfloor d/c \rfloor$.*

Proof. Let $p = \lfloor b/a \rfloor$ and let $q = \lfloor d/c \rfloor$. By Lemma 3.19, $[a, b]\mathrm{SUBSEQ\text{-}EX} = [1, p]\mathrm{SUBSEQ\text{-}EX}$ and $[c, d]\mathrm{SUBSEQ\text{-}EX} = [1, q]\mathrm{SUBSEQ\text{-}EX}$. By Lemma 3.22, $[1, p]\mathrm{SUBSEQ\text{-}EX} \subseteq [1, q]\mathrm{SUBSEQ\text{-}EX}$ if and only if $p \leq q$. $\square$

4 Rich Classes

Are there classes in SUBSEQ-EX containing languages of arbitrary complexity? Yes, trivially.

Proposition 4.1. *There is a $\mathcal{C} \in \mathrm{SUBSEQ\text{-}EX}_0$ such that for all $A \subseteq \mathbb{N}$, there is a $B \in \mathcal{C}$ with $B \equiv_\mathrm{T} A$.*

Proof. Let $\mathcal{C} = \{A \subseteq \Sigma^* : |A| = \infty \land (\forall x, y \in \Sigma^*)[x \in A \land |x| = |y| \to y \in A]\}$. That is, $\mathcal{C}$ is the class of all infinite languages, membership in whom depends only on a string's length.

For any $A \subseteq \mathbb{N}$, define

$$L_A = \begin{cases} \Sigma^* & \text{if } A \text{ is finite,} \\ \bigcup_{n \in A} \Sigma^{=n} & \text{otherwise.} \end{cases}$$

Clearly, $L_A \in \mathcal{C}$ and $A \equiv_T L_A$. Furthermore, $\mathrm{SUBSEQ}(L_A) = \Sigma^*$, and so $\mathcal{C} \in \mathrm{SUBSEQ\text{-}EX}_0$ witnessed by a learner that always outputs a DFA for Σ^*. $\qquad\square$

In Proposition 3.5 we showed that $\mathrm{REG} \in \mathrm{SUBSEQ\text{-}EX}$. Note that the $A \in \mathrm{REG}$ are trivial in terms of computability, but the languages in $\mathrm{SUBSEQ}(\mathrm{REG})$ can be rather complex (large obstruction sets, arbitrary $\preceq$-closed sets). By contrast, in Proposition 4.1, we show that there can be $\mathcal{A} \in \mathrm{SUBSEQ\text{-}EX}$ of arbitrarily high Turing degree but $\mathrm{SUBSEQ}(\mathcal{A})$ is trivial. Can we obtain classes $\mathcal{A} \in \mathrm{SUBSEQ\text{-}EX}$ where $A \in \mathcal{A}$ has arbitrary Turing degree and $\mathrm{SUBSEQ}(\mathcal{A})$ has arbitrary $\preceq$-closed sets independently? Yes, subject to an obvious restriction.

Definition 4.2. A class $\mathcal{C}$ of languages is *rich* if for every $A \subseteq \mathbb{N}$ and $\preceq$-closed $S \subseteq \Sigma^*$, there is a $B \in \mathcal{C}$ such that $\mathrm{SUBSEQ}(B) = S$ and, provided S is infinite, $B \equiv_T A$.

Definition 4.3. Let $\mathcal{G}$ be the class of all languages $A \subseteq \Sigma^*$ for which there exists a length $c = c(A) \in \mathbb{N}$ (necessarily unique) such that

1. $A \cap \Sigma^{=c} = \emptyset$,
2. $A \cap \Sigma^{=n} \neq \emptyset$ for all $n < c$, and
3. $os(A) = os(A \cap \Sigma^{\leq c+1}) \cap \Sigma^{\leq c}$.

In the full paper, we show the following:

Proposition 4.4. $\mathcal{G} \in \mathrm{SUBSEQ\text{-}EX}_0$ *and* $\mathcal{G}$ *is rich.*

5   Open Questions

We can combine teams, mindchanges, and anomalies in different ways. For example, for which a, b, c, d, e, f, g is $[a, b]\mathrm{SUBSEQ\text{-}EX}_c^d \subseteq [e, f]\mathrm{SUBSEQ\text{-}EX}_g^h$? This problem has been difficult in the standard case of EX though there have been some very interesting results [9, 5]. The setting of SUBSEQ-EX may be easier since all the machines that are output are total.

We can also combine the two notions of queries with SUBSEQ-EX and its variants. The two notions are allowing queries *about the set* [14, 12, 10] and allowing queries *to an undecidable set* [7, 17]. In the full paper, we show that $\mathrm{CE} \in \mathrm{SUBSEQ\text{-}EX}^{\emptyset'}$, where $\emptyset'$ is the halting problem and CE is the class of computably enumerable sets.[5]

---

[5] These sets used to be called recursively enumerable.

References

1. G. Baliga and J. Case. Learning with higher order additional information. In *Proc. 5th Int. Workshop on Algorithmic Learning Theory*, pages 64–75. Springer-Verlag, 1994.

2. L. Blum and M. Blum. Towards a mathematical theory of inductive inference. *Information and Computation*, 28:125–155, 1975.

3. J. Case, S. Jain, and S. N. Manguelle. Refinements of inductive inference by Popperian and reliable machines. *Kybernetika*, 30–1:23–52, 1994.

4. J. Case and C. H. Smith. Comparison of identification criteria for machine inductive inference. *Theoretical Computer Science*, 25:193–220, 1983.

5. R. Daley, B. Kalyanasundaram, and M. Velauthapillai. Breaking the probability 1/2 barrier in FIN-type learning. *Journal of Computer and System Sciences*, 50:574–599, 1995.

6. S. Fenner, W. Gasarch, and B. Postow. The complexity of finding SUBSEQ(L), 2006. Unpublished manuscript.

7. L. Fortnow, S. Jain, W. Gasarch, E. Kinber, M. Kummer, S. Kurtz, M. Pleszkoch, T. Slaman, F. Stephan, and R. Solovay. Extremes in the degrees of inferability. *Annals of Pure and Applied Logic*, 66:21–276, 1994.

8. R. Freivalds and C. H. Smith. On the role of procrastination for machine learning. *Information and Computation*, 107(2):237–271, 1993.

9. R. Freivalds, C. H. Smith, and M. Velauthapillai. Trade-off among parameters affecting inductive inference. *Information and Computation*, 82(3):323–349, Sept. 1989.

10. W. Gasarch, E. Kinber, M. Pleszkoch, C. H. Smith, and T. Zeugmann. Learning via queries, teams, and anomalies. *Fundamenta Informaticae*, 23:67–89, 1995. Prior version in *Computational Learning Theory (COLT)*, 1990.

11. W. Gasarch and A. Lee. Inferring answers to queries. In *Proceedings of* 10th *Annual ACM Conference on Computational Learning Theory*, pages 275–284, 1997. Long version on Gasarch's home page, in progress, much expanded.

12. W. Gasarch, M. Pleszkoch, and R. Solovay. Learning via queries to $[+, <]$. *Journal of Symbolic Logic*, 57(1):53–81, Mar. 1992.

13. W. Gasarch, M. Pleszkoch, F. Stephan, and M. Velauthapillai. Classification using information. *Annals of Math and AI*, pages 147–168, 1998. Earlier version in *Proc. 5th Int. Workshop on Algorithmic Learning Theory*, 1994, 290–300.

14. W. Gasarch and C. H. Smith. Learning via queries. *Journal of the ACM*, 39(3):649–675, July 1992. Prior version in *IEEE Sym. on Found. of Comp. Sci. (FOCS)*, 1988.

15. E. M. Gold. Language identification in the limit. *Information and Computation*, 10(10):447–474, 1967.

16. A. G. Higman. Ordering by divisibility in abstract algebra. *Proc. of the London Math Society*, 3:326–336, 1952.

17. M. Kummer and F. Stephan. On the structure of the degrees of inferability. *Journal of Computer and System Sciences*, 52(2):214–238, 1996. Prior version in *Sixth Annual Conference on Computational Learning Theory (COLT)*, 1993.

18. H. Rogers. *Theory of Recursive Functions and Effective Computability*. McGraw-Hill, 1967. Reprinted by MIT Press, 1987.

19. G. E. Sacks. *Higher Recursion Theory*. Perspectives in Mathematical Logic. Springer-Verlag, Berlin, 1990.

20. R. Soare. *Recursively Enumerable Sets and Degrees*. Perspectives in Mathematical Logic. Springer-Verlag, Berlin, 1987.

Mind Change Complexity of Inferring Unbounded Unions of Pattern Languages from Positive Data

Matthew de Brecht and Akihiro Yamamoto

Graduate School of Informatics, Kyoto University
Yoshida Honmachi, Sakyo-ku, Kyoto, Japan 606-8501
matthew@mbox.kudpc.kyoto-u.ac.jp,
akihiro@i.kyoto-u.ac.jp

Abstract. This paper gives a proof that the class of unbounded unions of languages of regular patterns with constant segment length bound is inferable from positive data with mind change bound between ω^ω and ω^{ω^ω}. We give a very tight bound on the mind change complexity based on the length of the constant segments and the size of the alphabet of the pattern languages. This is, to the authors' knowledge, the first time a natural class of languages has been shown to be inferable with mind change complexity above ω^ω. The proof uses the notion of closure operators on a class of languages, and also uses the order type of well-partial-orderings to obtain a mind change bound. The inference algorithm presented can be easily applied to a wide range of classes of languages. Finally, we show an interesting connection between proof theory and mind change complexity.

1 Introduction

Ordinal mind change complexity was proposed by Freivalds and Smith [8] as a means of measuring the complexity of inferring classes of languages in the limit. This notion was later used to show the complexity of inferring various classes of pattern languages [1, 14], elementary formal systems [14], and various algebraic structures [25], to name just a few results. In this paper, we give upper and lower bounds on the mind change complexity of inferring unbounded unions of regular pattern languages with a constant segment bound [23].

Jain and Sharma [14] have shown that the class formed by taking up to n unions of pattern languages is inferable with optimal mind change complexity of ω^n. In this paper, we consider a subclass of pattern languages, $L(\mathbf{RP}_l)$, which are pattern languages formed from patterns that contain constant segments of length at most l and in which each variable occurs in the pattern at most once. The class $L(\mathbf{RP}_l)^\omega$, formed by taking any finite number of unions of languages from $L(\mathbf{RP}_l)$, was proved to be inferable from positive data by Shinohara and Arimura [23]. The present paper proves that for any $l \geq 1$ and any alphabet Σ containing at least 3 elements, $L(\mathbf{RP}_l)^\omega$ is inferable from positive data with mind change bound $\omega^{\omega^{2l|\Sigma|-1}} + |\Sigma^{\leq l}|$, and that it is not inferable with bound

J.L. Balcázar, P.M. Long, and F. Stephan (Eds.): ALT 2006, LNAI 4264, pp. 124–138, 2006.

less than $\omega^{\omega^{l^{|\Sigma|-1}-1}}$. This is the first time, to the authors' knowledge, that a mind change bound has been given to a class of unbounded unions of languages, and the first time that a mind change bound has been shown to be greater than ω^ω for a natural class of languages. The proof uses closure operators on classes of languages and connections between mind change complexity and the order type of well-partial-orderings. The results in this paper can be easily applied to a wide range of learning problems, and give new insight into the role of topological properties of language classes in inductive inference.

Furthermore, we show a connection between proof theory and mind change complexity. Based on results by Simpson [24], we prove that within the weak axiom system RCA_0, the claim that $L(\mathbf{RP}_l)^\omega$ is inferable from positive data by a confident learner is equivalent to the claim that the ordinal ω^{ω^ω} is well-ordered. This means that the mind change complexity of a class of languages is related to the logical strength of the claim that the class is inferable from positive data. This holds interesting implications of connections between inductive inference and proof theory.

The outline of this paper is as follows. In Section 2, we give preliminary definitions and results concerning inductive inference from positive data, well-partial-orders, unions of languages, mind change complexity, and pattern languages. In Section 3, we introduce closure operators and show some of their properties. In Section 4, we give tight upper and lower mind change bounds for inferring $L(\mathbf{RP}_l)^\omega$ from positive data. In Section 5, we show the connection between the mind change complexity of $L(\mathbf{RP}_l)^\omega$ and the logical strength of the assertion that it is inferable from positive data by a confident learner. We discuss and conclude in Section 6.

2   Preliminaries

In this paper we only consider indexed classes of recursive languages over some finite alphabet Σ. We assume that for an indexed class of recursive languages $\mathcal{L}$, there is a recursive characteristic function f such that $f(n,s) = 0$ if $s \notin L_n$ and $f(n,s) = 1$ if $s \in L_n$ for all $L_n \in \mathcal{L}$. For simplicity, we will often refer to $\mathcal{L}$ as simply a class of languages. We use $\subseteq$ to represent the subset relation, and $\subset$ to represent the strict subset relation. Given an alphabet Σ, we use $\Sigma^{<l}$, $\Sigma^{\leq l}$, $\Sigma^{=l}$, Σ^*, to denote the set of all strings of Σ of length less than l, less than or equal to l, exactly equal to l, or of finite length, respectively.

2.1   Inductive Inference from Positive Data

We consider identification of languages in the limit as proposed by Gold [10] (see also [13]). Let L be some recursive language over Σ^*. An infinite sequence $\sigma = s_0, s_1, s_2, \ldots$ such that $L = \{s_i \mid s_i \in \sigma\}$ is called a *positive presentation* of L. An *inference machine* $\mathbf{M}$ is an algorithm that incrementally receives elements of a presentation of a language and occasionally outputs a positive integer representing the index of a language. We say that the output of $\mathbf{M}$ converges to an integer j if $\mathbf{M}$'s output is infinite and all but finitely many integers equal j, or if $\mathbf{M}$'s output is finite and the last integer equals j. If for any positive presentation of a set L, the output of $\mathbf{M}$ converges to an integer j such that $L_j = L$, then we say $\mathbf{M}$ *infers L from positive data*. If an inference algorithm $\mathbf{M}$ exists that infers from positive data every $L \in \mathcal{L}$, then we say $\mathcal{L}$ *is inferable from positive data*.

A *finite tell-tale* of $L \in \mathcal{L}$ is a finite set T such that $T \subseteq L$ and for all $L' \in \mathcal{L}$, $T \subseteq L'$ implies that $L' \not\subset L$ (Angluin [2]). A *characteristic set* of $L \in \mathcal{L}$ is a finite set F such that $F \subseteq L$ and for all $L' \in \mathcal{L}$ such that $F \subseteq L'$ implies that $L \subseteq L'$ (Kobayashi [17]). A class of sets $\mathcal{L}$ has *infinite elasticity* if and only if there exists an infinite sequence of sets $L_1, L_2, L_3, \ldots$ in $\mathcal{L}$ and elements $s_0, s_1, s_2, \ldots$ such that $\{s_0, \ldots, s_{n-1}\} \subseteq L_n$ but $s_n \notin L_n$. $\mathcal{L}$ has *finite elasticity* if and only if it does not have infinite elasticity (Wright [26], Motoki et al. [19]). $\mathcal{L}$ has *finite thickness* if and only if every element of Σ^* is contained in at most a finite number of languages of $\mathcal{L}$ (Angluin [2]).

Theorem 1 ((Angluin [2])). *An indexed class of recursive sets $\mathcal{L}$ is inferable from positive data if and only if there exists a procedure to enumerate the elements of the finite tell-tale of every $L \in \mathcal{L}$.*

Theorem 2 ((Kobayashi [17])). *If every $L \in \mathcal{L}$ has a characteristic set, then $\mathcal{L}$ is inferable from positive data.*

Theorem 3 ((Wright [26])). *If $\mathcal{L}$ has finite elasticity, then $\mathcal{L}$ is inferable from positive data.*

Theorem 4 ((Angluin [2])). *If $\mathcal{L}$ has finite thickness, then $\mathcal{L}$ is inferable from positive data.*

Finite thickness implies finite elasticity which implies that every language has a characteristic set which implies that a procedure exists that enumerates a finite tell-tale for every language. However, the reverse implications do not hold in general.

2.2   Well-Partial-Orders

Let $\langle A, \leq_A \rangle$ be a partial order. An *anti-chain* of A is a subset $S \subseteq A$ of elements that are mutually incomparable with respect to $\leq_A$. That is, for all $a, b \in S$ such that $a \neq b$, neither $a \leq_A b$ nor $b \leq_A a$ holds.

Lemma 5. *Let $\leq_A$ and $\sqsubseteq_A$ be two partial orders on A such that for $a, b \in A$, $a \leq_A b$ implies that $a \sqsubseteq_A b$. If there are no infinite anti-chains in A with respect to $\leq_A$, then there are no infinite anti-chains in A with respect to $\sqsubseteq_A$.*

Proof. Obviously, if a and b are incomparable with respect to $\sqsubseteq_A$ then they are incomparable with respect to $\leq_A$, so any infinite anti-chain with respect to $\sqsubseteq_A$ is an infinite anti-chain with respect to $\leq_A$.   □

A is said to be *well-partially-ordered* if and only if A contains no infinitely descending chains and no infinite anti-chains with respect to $\leq_A$. A finite or infinite sequence $a_0, a_1, \ldots$ of elements of A is said to be *bad* if for all i and j such that $i < j$, $a_i \not\leq_A a_j$. Note that A is well-partially-ordered if and only if it does not contain any infinite bad sequences. We will define $Bad(A)$ to be the set of all bad sequences of A.

Given a partial order $\langle A, \leq_A \rangle$, let A^* be the set of finite ordered sequences of elements of A. We will write $s\langle a \rangle$ to represent the concatenation of an element $a \in A$ to the end of a sequence $s \in A^*$. A *Higman embedding*, $\preceq_H$, is a partial ordering on A^* such that for $a, b \in A^*$, $a \preceq_H b$ if and only if $a = \langle s_0, \ldots, s_n \rangle$ and $\langle t_0, \ldots, t_m \rangle$ and there exists $j_0 < \cdots < j_n \leq m$ such that $s_0 \leq_A t_{j_0}, \ldots, s_n \leq_A t_{j_n}$. A *subsequence relation*, $\preceq_S$, on A^* is defined similarly, with the stronger requirement that $a \preceq_S b$ if and only if there exists $j_0 < \cdots < j_n \leq m$ such that $s_0 = t_{j_0}, \ldots, s_n = t_{j_n}$.

Lemma 6 ((Higman [12]. See also [9])). *If $\leq_A$ is a well-partial-ordering on A, then $\preceq_H$ is a well-partial-ordering on A^*.*

2.3 Unbounded Unions of Languages

Given two language classes $\mathcal{L}$ and $\mathcal{M}$, define the union of $\mathcal{L}$ and $\mathcal{M}$, $\mathcal{L} \tilde{\cup} \mathcal{M}$, to be:

$$\mathcal{L} \tilde{\cup} \mathcal{M} = \{L \cup M \mid L \in \mathcal{L}, M \in \mathcal{M}\}.$$

Wright [26] showed that if $\mathcal{L}$ and $\mathcal{M}$ have finite elasticity, then $\mathcal{L} \tilde{\cup} \mathcal{M}$ has finite elasticity, and is therefore inferable from positive data.

The concept of unions of language classes was expanded to unbounded unions of languages by Shinohara and Arimura [23]. Given a class of languages $\mathcal{L}$, define the class of unbounded unions $\mathcal{L}^\omega$ to be the class of all finite unions of languages of $\mathcal{L}$. Formally, $\mathcal{L}^\omega$ is defined as:

$$\mathcal{L}^\omega = \{\bigcup_{i \in I} L_i \mid L_i \in \mathcal{L}, I \subset \mathbf{N}, 1 \leq |I| < \infty\},$$

where $\mathbf{N}$ is the set of integers greater than or equal to zero. It can be shown that if $\mathcal{L}$ has finite thickness and no infinite anti-chains with respect to subset inclusion, then $\mathcal{L}^\omega$ is inferable from positive data [23].

2.4 Mind Change Complexity

Let α be a constructive ordinal number [16, 21]. An inference machine $\mathbf{M}$ infers a class of languages $\mathcal{L}$ from positive data with mind change bound α if and only if $\mathbf{M}$ infers $\mathcal{L}$ from positive data, and every time $\mathbf{M}$ outputs a new hypothesis it counts down its ordinal without ever falling below zero. Ordinal mind change complexity was originally proposed by Freivalds and Smith [8]. For more on inductive inference with mind change bounds and results on the complexity of certain languages classes, see [1, 14, 22, 25].

We assume that ordinal addition and multiplication are commutative. Arithmetic for ordinals with positive integer exponents can be thought of as being similar to polynomials of the variable ω, however we consider ordinals with very large exponents in this paper. For example, the ordinal ω^ω is the limit of the sequence $\omega, \omega^2, \omega^3, \ldots$, and ω^{ω^ω} is the limit of the sequence $\omega^\omega, \omega^{\omega^2}, \omega^{\omega^3}, \ldots$. So if an inference machine has the mind change counter set to ω^{ω^2} and makes a mind change, it must decrease the counter to some $\alpha_0 \omega^{\beta_0 \omega + \gamma_0} + \cdots + \alpha_n \omega^{\beta_n \omega + \gamma_n}$, where n is finite and the α_i, β_i, and γ_i are all less than ω. Note that ω^0 is defined to be 1.

When defining a function from or to a set of ordinals, we will treat each ordinal to be a set containing every strictly smaller ordinal. So $f : \omega \to \omega$ is a function from natural numbers to natural numbers, and $g : \omega + 1 \to \omega$ is a function from the set of natural numbers and the ordinal ω to the set of natural numbers.

2.5   Pattern Languages

We will mainly be concerned with the inference of pattern languages in this paper, although the techniques used are easily applied to other classes of languages. Pattern languages were originally introduced into inductive inference by Angluin [2] and later became a rich field of research. See [23] for more on the inductive inference of pattern languages and their applications. Let Σ be a finite alphabet and let $V = x_0, x_1, \ldots$ be a countably infinite set of symbols disjoint from Σ. A finite string of elements of Σ is called a *constant segment* and elements of V are called *variables*. A *pattern* is a non-empty finite string over $\Sigma \cup V$. A pattern p is said to be *regular* if every variable x_i appearing in p occurs only once. Let **RP** be the set of regular patterns, and let $\mathbf{RP}_l$ be the set of regular patterns which contain constant segments of length no longer than l.

The language of a pattern p, denoted $L(p)$, is the subset of Σ^* that can be obtained by substituting a non-empty constant segment $s_i \in \Sigma^+$ for each occurrence of the variable x_i in p for all $i \geq 0$. For example, if $\Sigma = \{a, b\}$ and $p = a x_1 b$, then $L(p)$ is the subset of Σ^* of strings beginning with "a", ending with "b", and of length greater than or equal to three. For a set of patterns P, we define $L(P) = \{L(p) \,|\, p \in P\}$.

The next two theorems will be useful for showing the mind change complexity of $L(\mathbf{RP}_l)^\omega$, the class of unbounded unions of languages of regular patterns with constant segment length bound l.

Theorem 7 ((Shinohara and Arimura [23])). *For any $l \geq 1$, $L(\mathbf{RP}_l)$ has finite thickness and contains no infinite anti-chains with respect to set inclusion.*

Theorem 8 ((Shinohara and Arimura [23])). *For any $l \geq 1$, $L(\mathbf{RP}_l)^\omega$ is inferable from positive data.*

3   Closed Set Systems

We now introduce closure operators, which we will use later to define an inference algorithm for $L(\mathbf{RP}_l)^\omega$.

A mapping $C : 2^U \rightarrow 2^U$ is called a *closure operator* on U if and only if for all subsets X and Y of U, $C(\cdot)$ has the following properties:

1. $X \subseteq C(X)$,
2. $C(C(X)) = C(X)$,
3. $X \subseteq Y \Rightarrow C(X) \subseteq C(Y)$.

A *closed set* is a set $X \subseteq U$ such that $X = C(X)$. $\mathcal{C} = \{X \mid X = C(X)\}$ is called the *closed set system* defined by $C(\cdot)$. It is easy to see that a collection of sets is a closed set system for some closure operator if and only if it is closed under arbitrary intersections. Closed set systems form a complete lattice ordered by set inclusion, where $\bigwedge_{i \in I} C(X_i) = \bigcap_{i \in I} C(X_i)$ and $\bigvee_{i \in I} C(X_i) = C(\bigcup_{i \in I} X_i)$ [3, 5].

For any class of languages $\mathcal{L}$ over Σ^* and any $X \subseteq \Sigma^*$, let $C_{\mathcal{L}}(X) = \bigcap\{L \mid X \subseteq L, L \in \mathcal{L}\}$. It is easy to see that $C_{\mathcal{L}} : 2^{\Sigma^*} \rightarrow 2^{\Sigma^*}$ is a closure operator on Σ^*, and that $\mathcal{C}_{\mathcal{L}}$, the set of all closed sets of $C_{\mathcal{L}}(\cdot)$, is the smallest closed set system that contains $\mathcal{L}$ [4]. Note that for all $L \in \mathcal{L}$, $L = C_{\mathcal{L}}(L)$, although not every closed set is in $\mathcal{L}$.

In the following, we will assume that $\mathcal{L}$ is an indexed family of recursive sets, and that $\mathcal{C}_{\mathcal{L}}$ is the corresponding closed set system.

A closed set system is said to be *Noetherian* if and only if it contains no infinite strictly ascending chains of closed sets.

Lemma 9. *$\mathcal{L}$ has finite elasticity if and only if $\mathcal{C}_{\mathcal{L}}$ is Noetherian.*

Proof. Assume an infinitely increasing chain of closed sets $X_0 \subset X_1 \subset \cdots$ exists in $\mathcal{C}_{\mathcal{L}}$. Let s_0 be any element of X_0, and for each $i \geq 0$ choose $s_i \in X_{i+1}$ such that $s_i \notin X_i$. Then $s_i \notin \bigcap\{L \mid X_i \subseteq L, L \in \mathcal{L}\}$, but $s_i \in \bigcap\{L \mid X_{i+1} \subseteq L, L \in \mathcal{L}\}$, therefore there exists some $L \in \mathcal{L}$ such that $X_i \subseteq L$ and $s_i \notin L$. For all $j \geq i+1$, $s_i \in X_j$, so $\{s_0, \ldots, s_{i-1}\} \subseteq X_i \subseteq L$ and $s_i \notin L$. Since i was arbitrary, this shows that $\mathcal{L}$ has infinite elasticity.

For the converse, assume that the languages $L_1, L_2, L_3, \ldots$ and elements $s_0, s_1, s_2, \ldots$ show the infinite elasticity of $\mathcal{L}$. From the definition of infinite elasticity, $\{s_0, \ldots, s_{n-1}\} \subseteq C(\{s_0, \ldots, s_{n-1}\}) \subseteq L_n$, but $s_n \notin L_n$ so $C(\{s_0, \ldots, s_{n-1}\}) \subset C(\{s_0, \ldots, s_n\})$. Since n was arbitrary, $C(\{s_0, \ldots, s_i\})$ $(i \geq 0)$ is an infinite strictly ascending chain, and thus $\mathcal{C}_{\mathcal{L}}$ is not Noetherian.   □

Lemma 10. *Let $\mathcal{L}$ be a class of languages with finite thickness. $\mathcal{L}$ contains no infinite anti-chains with respect to set inclusion if and only if $\mathcal{C}_{\mathcal{L}}$ contains no infinite anti-chains.*

Proof. From the definition of finite thickness, any set of elements is contained in at most a finite number of languages of $\mathcal{L}$. Therefore, there exists an irredundant representation of any closed set $X_i \in \mathcal{C}_{\mathcal{L}}$ as the intersection of a finite number of languages of $\mathcal{L}$, so let $X_i = L_0^i \cap \cdots \cap L_{n_i}^i$. Define the ordering $\leq'$ over elements of $\mathcal{L}$ such that $L_j^i \leq' L_{j'}^{i'}$ if and only if $L_j^i \supseteq L_{j'}^{i'}$. The finite thickness and absence of anti-chains in $\mathcal{L}$ guarantee that $\leq'$ is a well-partial-order.

Define a mapping $f : \mathcal{C}_{\mathcal{L}} \to \mathcal{L}^*$ such that $f(X_i) = \langle L_0^i, \ldots, L_{n_i}^i \rangle$. We order $\mathcal{L}^*$ by the Higman embedding $\preceq_H$ based on the ordering $\leq'$. Lemma 6 guarantees that $\preceq_H$ is a well-partial-order on $\mathcal{L}^*$, and therefore contains no infinite anti-chains.

We now show that $f(X_i) \preceq_H f(X_j)$ implies that $X_i \supseteq X_j$. Assume that $f(X_i) \preceq_H f(X_j)$, then there exists $k_0 < \cdots < k_{n_i} \leq n_j$ such that $L_0^i \leq' L_{k_0}^j, \ldots, L_{n_i}^i \leq' L_{k_{n_i}}^j$. This implies that $L_0^i \cap \cdots \cap L_{n_i}^i \supseteq L_{k_0}^j \cap \cdots \cap L_{k_{n_i}}^j$. Since $L_{k_0}^j \cap \cdots \cap L_{k_{n_i}}^j \supseteq L_0^j \cap \cdots \cap L_{n_j}^j$, it follows that $X_i \supseteq X_j$. From Lemma 5, it follows that there are no infinite anti-chains in $\mathcal{C}_{\mathcal{L}}$ with respect to set inclusion. The converse follows immediately since $\mathcal{L}$ is a subset of $\mathcal{C}_{\mathcal{L}}$. $\square$

4   Upper and Lower Mind Change Bounds for $L(\mathbf{RP}_l)^{\omega}$

We now proceed to show the mind change complexity of inferring $L(\mathbf{RP}_l)^{\omega}$ from positive data. The results are largely based on the following two lemmas.

Lemma 11 ((Simpson [24])). *Let A be a finite set containing exactly k elements. Then there exists a recursive mapping $g : \omega^{\omega^{k-1}} \to A^*$ with the property that $\alpha \nleq \beta$ implies $g(\alpha) \nleq_S g(\beta)$.*

Lemma 12 ((Simpson [24], Hasegawa [11])). *Let A be a finite set containing exactly k elements. Then there exists a recursive mapping $f : Bad(A^*) \to \omega^{\omega^{k-1}} + 1$ with the property that $f(s\langle a \rangle) < f(s)$ for all $s, s\langle a \rangle \in Bad(A^*)$.*

The mapping f in Lemma 12 is known as a *reification*. If A is a well-partially-ordered set, and α is the smallest possible ordinal such that a (not necessarily recursive) reification $f : A \to \alpha + 1$ exists, then we say that A has *order type* α (see [24, 11] for a more detailed discussion).

We will use Lemma 11 to find a lower bound of the mind change complexity of $L(\mathbf{RP}_l)^{\omega}$ and use Lemma 12 and closure operators to find an upper bound.

Let Σ be an alphabet containing at least three elements. Let $\Sigma_{-c} = \Sigma - \{c\}$, where c is some element of Σ. We define $x(\mathbf{RP}'_{=l})y$ to be the subset of $\mathbf{RP}_l$ of patterns that begin and end with a variable, do not contain any occurrences of the constant element c, and only have constant segments of length exactly equal to l. Note that although no $p \in x(\mathbf{RP}'_{=l})y$ contains the element c, $L(p)$ is defined over Σ, so c may occur in some elements of the language $L(p)$.

Next we define a mapping $P : (\Sigma_{-c}^{=l})^* \to x(\mathbf{RP}'_{=l})y$ so that $P(\langle w_1, \ldots, w_n \rangle) = x_1 w_1 \cdots x_n w_n x_{n+1}$. Let $\preceq'_S$ be the subsequence relation on $(\Sigma_{-c}^{=l})^*$. The following lemma is related to a theorem proved by Mukouchi [20].

Lemma 13. *Let $\sigma, \tau_1, \ldots, \tau_n \in (\Sigma_{-c}^{=l})^*$ for $n \geq 1$. If for all i $(1 \leq i \leq n)$, $\tau_i \npreceq'_S \sigma$, then $L(P(\sigma)) \nsubseteq \bigcup_{1 \leq i \leq n} L(P(\tau_i))$.*

Proof. Let $\sigma = \langle w_1, \ldots, w_m \rangle$, and let $s = cw_1 c \cdots cw_m c$, where c is the constant in $\Sigma - \Sigma_{-c}$. Obviously $s \in L(P(\sigma))$. Assume $s \in \bigcup_{1 \leq i \leq n} L(P(\tau_i))$, then for some j, $s \in L(P(\tau_j))$. Assume $\tau_j = \langle u_1, \ldots, u_{m'} \rangle$, so $P(\tau_j) = x_1 u_1 \cdots x_{m'} u_{m'} x_{m'+1}$.

Each constant segment $u_{i'}$ $(1 \leq i' \leq m')$ in $P(\tau_j)$ must map to a segment in s, but since $u_{i'}$ does not contain c, $u_{i'}$ must appear within some $w_{k_{i'}}$ $(1 \leq k_{i'} \leq m)$. Since $|u_{i'}| = |w_{k_{i'}}| = l$, it follows that $u_{i'} = w_{k_{i'}}$. Furthermore, the ordering of the mapping must be preserved, so $k_{i'} < k_{i'+1}$ for $i' < m'$. But this shows that $\tau_j \preceq'_s \sigma$, which contradicts the hypothesis. □

Since $|\Sigma^{=l}_{-c}| = l^{|\Sigma-c|} = l^{|\Sigma|-1}$, we can use Lemma 11 to define a mapping $g :$ $\omega^{\omega^{l^{|\Sigma|-1}-1}} \rightarrow (\Sigma^{=l}_{-c})^*$ with the property that $\alpha > \beta$ implies $g(\alpha) \npreceq'_s g(\beta)$. We now define $g' : \omega^{\omega^{l^{|\Sigma|-1}-1}} \rightarrow L(x(\mathbf{RP}'_{=l})y)$ to be $g'(\alpha) = L(P(g(\alpha)))$. It follows from Lemma 13 that if $\omega^{\omega^{l^{|\Sigma|-1}-1}} > \alpha_0 > \cdots > \alpha_n > \beta$ for finite n, then $g'(\beta) \nsubseteq \bigcup_{0 \leq i \leq n} g'(\alpha_i)$.

Theorem 14. $L(\mathbf{RP}_l)^\omega$ *is not inferable from positive data with mind change bound less than* $\omega^{\omega^{l^{|\Sigma|-1}-1}}$ *for* $l \geq 1$ *and for* Σ *containing at least* 3 *elements.*

Proof. Let $\mathbf{M}$ be an inference machine with mind change counter initially set at $\alpha_0 < \omega^{\omega^{l^{|\Sigma|-1}-1}}$. Use the mapping g' defined above to start enumerating elements of the language $L_0 = g'(\alpha_0 + 1)$.

If $\mathbf{M}$ ever changes its hypothesis to include L_n, then its mind change counter drops to some $\alpha_{n+1} < \alpha_n$, and we start enumerating elements of $L_{n+1} = L_n \cup g'(\alpha_{n+1} + 1)$. Note that $L_{n+1} \supset L_n$.

At some point, $\mathbf{M}$ must stop making mind changes, but since we are still enumerating the elements of some language $L_{n'} \in L(x(\mathbf{RP}'_{=l})y)^\omega$ that is different from $\mathbf{M}$'s hypothesis, we see that $\mathbf{M}$ fails to infer a language in $L(\mathbf{RP}_l)^\omega$. □

We now move on to give an upper bound on the mind change complexity of $L(\mathbf{RP}_l)^\omega$. Let $\mathcal{L}$ be a class of recursive languages, and let $C_\mathcal{L}(X) = \bigcap\{L \mid X \subseteq L, L \in \mathcal{L}\}$ be the corresponding closure operator. Given a finite subset X of some unknown language L_*, any language $L \in \mathcal{L}$ that contains X also contains $C_\mathcal{L}(X)$, and $C_\mathcal{L}(X)$ is the largest subset containing X that has this property. Therefore we have the very natural interpretation that $C_\mathcal{L}(X)$ is the most information about L_* that we can unambiguously extract from X. If X contains only the single element s, then we will abbreviate $C_\mathcal{L}(X)$ as $C_\mathcal{L}(s)$. We can define a quasi-ordering[1] $\leq_\mathcal{L}$ on Σ^* such that $s \leq_\mathcal{L} t$ if and only if $t \in C_\mathcal{L}(s)$. If $\mathcal{L}$ has finite thickness and no infinite anti-chains, then $\langle \Sigma^*, \leq_\mathcal{L} \rangle$ is a well-quasi-order. If we define an inference machine that only changes its hypothesis when it receives elements of a bad sequence of $\langle \Sigma^*, \leq_\mathcal{L} \rangle$ (i.e. if it sees an element that is not in the closure of any of the elements it has already seen), then the order type of $\langle \Sigma^*, \leq_\mathcal{L} \rangle$ will give an upper bound on the mind change complexity of $\mathcal{L}$. We now show how this is done for $L(\mathbf{RP}_l)^\omega$.

Let $C_{RP_l}(X) = \bigcap\{L \mid X \subseteq L, L \in L(\mathbf{RP}_l)\}$ for any subset X of Σ^*, and let $\mathcal{C}_{RP_l}$ be the set of all closed sets of $C_{RP_l}(\cdot)$. From Theorem 7 and Lemmas 9 and 10, $\mathcal{C}_{RP_l}$ is Noetherian and contains no infinite anti-chains with respect to subset inclusion.

---

[1] Quasi-orders are relations that are reflexive and transitive, but not necessarily anti-symmetric. Well-quasi-orders are defined in the same way as well-partial-orders.

Lemma 15. *For any finite $X \subseteq \Sigma^*$ and $s \in \Sigma^+$, the containment problem "is $s \in C_{RP_l}(X)$?" is computable.*

Proof. If X is a subset of the language of a pattern p, then the length of p must be less than the length of the shortest element in X. Only a finite number of such p exist, so an algorithm can check whether or not s is in every pattern language that contains X. □

Let Σ be an alphabet containing at least three elements, and let $\#$ be a new symbol not in Σ. Define $\Sigma_{\#}^{=l}$ to be the set of elements of $\Sigma^{=l}$ with the symbol $\#$ appended to the beginning or end. We define a mapping $h : \Sigma^{>l} \rightarrow (\Sigma_{\#}^{=l})^*$ such that for $s = a_1 \cdots a_n$ $(n > l)$, $h(s) = \langle \#a_1 \cdots a_l, a_2 \cdots a_{l+1}\#, \ldots, \#a_{n-l+1} \cdots a_n \rangle$, where $\#$ appears on the left side of the initial and final segments, and $\#$ appears on the right of all other segments.

Lemma 16. *If $|s| \leq l$ and $s = t$ or if $h(s)$ is a subsequence of $h(t)$, then $t \in C_{RP_l}(\{s\})$.*

Proof. The case where $s = t$ is obvious, so assume $s = a_1 \cdots a_n$, $t = b_1 \cdots b_{n'}$, and that $h(s)$ is a subsequence of $h(t)$. It follows that each segment $a_i' = a_i \cdots a_{i+l-1}$ $(1 \leq i \leq n - l + 1)$ in s is equal to some segment $b_{j_i}' = b_{j_i} \cdots b_{j_i+l-1}$ $(1 \leq j_i \leq n' - l + 1)$ in t. Also, note that the placement of the $\#$ symbols guarantee that $a_1' = b_1'$ and $a_{n-l+1}' = b_{n'-l+1}'$, meaning the first and last l elements of s and t are the same.

Let $p = w_1 x_1 \cdots w_m x_m w_{m+1}$ be a pattern in $\mathbf{RP}_l$ such that $s \in L(p)$, where the x_i's are variables and the w_i's are in $\Sigma^{\leq l}$. For each w_i $(1 \leq i \leq m + 1)$ in p, w_i is mapped to a segment in s, so let k_i be the position in s where the first element of w_i is mapped. Note that $k_{i+1} \geq k_i + |w_i| + 1$ for $i \leq m$.

If $k_i < n - l + 1$, then w_i maps to the prefix of a_{k_i}' which is mapped to $b_{j_{k_i}}'$, so w_i appears in t at position j_{k_i}. Also, $j_{k_{i-1}} < j_{k_{i-1}+1} < \cdots < j_{k_i}$ for $i > 1$, and therefore $j_{k_i} \geq j_{k_{i-1}} + |w_{i-1}| + 1$, so there is at least one element between the segments w_i and w_{i-1} in t.

If $k_i < n - l + 1$ and $k_{i+1} \geq n - l + 1$, then $j_{n-l+1} - j_{k_i} \geq (n - l + 1) - k_i$, and since w_{i+1} is mapped to the same segment of the last l elements in s and t, $k_{i+1} - (n-l+1)$ equals the difference between $j_{n-l+1} = n' - l + 1$ and the position of w_{i+1} in t. Therefore, w_i and w_{i+1} are separated by at least one element in t.

If $k_i \geq n - l + 1$, then w_i is mapped within the last l elements of s, which are equal to t, so if $i < m + 1$ then w_i and w_{i+1} are separated by at least one element in t.

Therefore, each constant segment of p matches a segment in t, and are separated by at least one element. Since the initial and final constant segments of p and t also match, it is easily seen that $t \in L(p)$. □

Theorem 17. *$L(\mathbf{RP}_l)^{\omega}$ is inferable from positive data with mind change bound $\omega^{\omega^{2^{l|\Sigma|-1}}} + |\Sigma^{\leq l}|$ for any $l \geq 1$ and Σ containing at least 3 elements.*

Proof. The following algorithm receives a positive presentation of an unknown language $L_* \in L(\mathbf{RP}_l)^{\omega}$ and outputs hypotheses of the form $H = \{w_0, \ldots, w_k\} \subseteq$

Σ^+ such that $L(H)$, the language corresponding to the hypothesis H, is defined as $C_{RP_l}(w_0) \cup \cdots \cup C_{RP_l}(w_k)$.

Set $counter = \omega^{\omega^{2l|\Sigma|-1}} + |\Sigma^{\leq l}|$ and initialize the set $H = \emptyset$. Initialize the ordered list B to be empty. Let $s_n \in \Sigma^+$ be the nth input, and assume $H = \{w_0, \ldots, w_m\}$.

1. If $s_n \in C_{RP_l}(w_i)$ for some $w_i \in H$, then do nothing and proceed to read in the next input.
2. If there is any $w_i \in H$ such that $w_i \in C_{RP_l}(s_n)$ and $s_n \notin C_{RP_l}(w_i)$ (i.e. $C_{RP_l}(w_i) \subset C_{RP_l}(s_n)$), replace the w_i in H with s_n. For every other $w_j \in H$ $(j \neq i)$ such that $w_j \in C_{RP_l}(s_n)$, remove w_j from H. Update $counter$ and output the new hypothesis H. Read in the next input.
3. Otherwise, $C_{RP_l}(s_n)$ is incomparable with every $C_{RP_l}(w_i)$ $(w_i \in H)$, so redefine H to be $H \cup \{s_i\}$, update $counter$, and output the new hypothesis H. Read in the next input.

In cases 2 and 3, $counter$ is updated in the following way. If $|s_n| \leq l$ then reduce what remains of the $|\Sigma^{\leq l}|$ portion of $counter$ by one. Otherwise, redefine B to be $B\langle h(s_n)\rangle$, where $h: \Sigma^{>l} \to (\Sigma_{\#}^{=l})^*$ is the mapping defined above. Since elements are added to B only when they have length longer than l and are not included in the closure of any of the previous elements, Lemma 16 shows that B is a bad sequence of elements of $(\Sigma_{\#}^{=l})^*$. We can then use the mapping $f: Bad((\Sigma_{\#}^{=l})^*) \to \omega^{\omega^{2l|\Sigma|-1}} + 1$ based on Lemma 12 to set what remains of the $\omega^{\omega^{2l|\Sigma|-1}}$ portion of $counter$ to $f(B)$.

Every time H changes, either an element of H is replaced with one that generates a strictly larger closed set, or else a new incomparable closed set is found. Therefore, since $\mathcal{C}_{RP_l}$ is Noetherian and contains no infinite anti-chains, H changes only a finite number of times. Assume that the algorithm converges to some H'. Any pattern language that contains $w_i \in H'$ will contain $C_{RP_l}(w_i)$, so $L(H') \subseteq L_*$. If there is any element $s \in L_*$ that is not in $L(H')$, then eventually s will appear in the presentation, and since $s \notin C_{RP_l}(w_i)$ for all $w_i \in H'$, the hypothesis will be updated, contradicting the choice of H'. Therefore $L(H') = L_*$, and so the above algorithm infers $L(\mathbf{RP}_l)^\omega$ from positive data.

Since there are only $|\Sigma^{\leq l}| - 1$ (empty string not included) elements of length less than or equal to l, the $|\Sigma^{\leq l}|$ portion of $counter$ will not be reduced below zero. All other elements that induce a mind change can be mapped to a part of a bad sequence of $(\Sigma_{\#}^{=l})^*$, so Lemma 12 ensures that the $\omega^{\omega^{2l|\Sigma|-1}}$ portion of $counter$ decreases after every mind change but does not fall below zero. Therefore the algorithm infers $L(\mathbf{RP}_l)^\omega$ with mind change bound $\omega^{\omega^{2l|\Sigma|-1}} + |\Sigma^{\leq l}|$. $\square$

5   Mind Change Bounds and Reverse Mathematics

Reverse Mathematics is a field of research dedicated to finding which axioms are necessary and sufficient to prove theorems in second order arithmetic. In general, the base axiom system RCA_0 is used to compare the logical strength of different axioms. RCA_0 is a weak system that basically only asserts the existence of recursive sets, a weak form of induction, and the basic axioms of arithmetic. WKA_0 (Weak König's Lemma) is a slightly stronger system which is defined to be RCA_0 with an additional axiom asserting König's Lemma for binary trees. ACA_0 (Arithmetical Comprehension Axiom) is stronger than WKA_0, and is a conservative extension of Peano Arithmetic. See [7] for further discussion on these systems and their relation to various theorems in countable algebra.

The basic idea is that if we have two theorems, Theorem A and Theorem B, and we can show that by assuming Theorem A as an axiom along with the axioms of RCA_0 then we can prove Theorem B, and conversely by assuming Theorem B as an axiom we can prove Theorem A, then we can say that Theorem A and Theorem B are equivalent within RCA_0. This kind of reasoning is similar to the equivalence of Zorn's Lemma and the Axiom of Choice within the Zermelo-Fraenkel axiom system.

The purpose of this section is to show the relationship within RCA_0 of asserting the inferability of certain classes of languages with asserting the well-orderedness[2] of certain ordinal numbers. The result is important because it shows some connections between proof theory and the theory of inductive inference.

Proposition 18 ((Simpson [24])). ω^{ω^ω} cannot be proved to be well-ordered within RCA_0. However, RCA_0 does prove that ω^{ω^ω} is well-ordered if and only if ω^{ω^m} is well-ordered for all m.

The next theorem follows directly from Theorems 14 and 17, and the work of Simpson [24]. Simpson showed that the Hilbert basis theorem is equivalent to the well-orderedness of ω^ω, and that Robson's generalization of the Hilbert basis theorem is equivalent to the well-orderedness of ω^{ω^ω}.

An inference machine is said to be *confident* if it only makes a finite number of mind changes on any presentation of a language, even if the language is not one that the inference machine infers in the limit. The next theorem basically shows that the logical strength of asserting the inferability of $L(\mathbf{RP}_l)^\omega$ by a confident learner is related to the mind change complexity of $L(\mathbf{RP}_l)^\omega$.

Theorem 19. *The following are equivalent within RCA_0:*

1. ω^{ω^ω} is well-ordered.
2. $L(\mathbf{RP}_l)^\omega$ is inferable from positive data by a confident learner for any $l \geq 1$ and any Σ containing at least three elements.

Proof. First, we note that the mappings in Lemmas 11 and 12 are defined within RCA_0 [24], and since we only consider computable inference machines in Theorems 14 and 17, they are also definable in RCA_0.

To show that 1 implies 2, fix $m > 2$ and assume that $\omega^{\omega^{m-1}}$ is well-ordered. Assume that there is some l and Σ such that $2l^{|\Sigma|} < m$ and that $L(\mathbf{RP}_l)^\omega$ is

---

[2] Recall that a totally ordered set A is well-ordered if and only if there is no infinitely decreasing sequence of elements in A.

not inferable from positive data. Since the algorithm in Theorem 17 will always expand its hypothesis to include new elements not already accounted for, and since it will never output an overgeneralized hypothesis, the only way $L(\mathbf{RP}_l)^\omega$ would not be inferable is if the inference machine never converges. Therefore the mind change counter of the machine gives an infinitely descending chain of ordinals less than $\omega^{\omega^{m-1}}$, which contradicts the assumption that $\omega^{\omega^{m-1}}$ is well-ordered.

To show that 2 implies 1, fix $l \geq 1$ and Σ to contain at least three elements, and assume that $L(\mathbf{RP}_l)^\omega$ is inferable from positive data. If $\omega^{\omega^{m-1}}$ is not well-ordered for some $m < l^{|\Sigma|-1}$, then we can use the same technique as in Theorem 14 to convert an infinitely descending sequence in $\omega^{\omega^{m-1}}$ to an infinitely increasing (with respect to $\subset$) sequence of languages in $L(\mathbf{RP}_l)^\omega$. Therefore we can show that any inference machine either fails to infer some language in $L(\mathbf{RP}_l)^\omega$, or else it makes an infinite number of mind changes on some text, in either case a contradiction.   □

This result can be applied to most proofs involving mind change complexity. For example, Stephan and Ventsov [25] showed that ideals of the ring of polynomials with n variables is inferable with optimal mind change bound ω^n. This result can easily be converted into another proof that the Hilbert basis theorem is equivalent to the well-orderedness of ω^ω.

6   Discussion and Conclusion

This paper contains several new results. First, we introduced closure operators on arbitrary language classes, which can be interpreted as representing the amount of information contained in a subset of an unknown language. We also showed that the minimal closed set system containing a class of languages preserves several topological properties of the class. We showed how closure operators can be used to define an ordering on Σ^*, and how the order type of this ordering is related to mind change complexity. We also give an inference algorithm that can easily be applied to the inductive inference of a wide variety of classes of languages provided that the closure operation is computable. As a practical application, we used these techniques to show that $L(\mathbf{RP}_l)^\omega$ is inferable from positive data with mind change bound $\omega^{\omega^{2l^{|\Sigma|-1}}} + |\Sigma^{\leq l}|$, and that it is not inferable with mind change bound less than $\omega^{\omega^{l^{|\Sigma|-1}-1}}$. Finally, we showed an interesting connection between proof theory and mind change complexity.

Our approach of applying well-partial-orderings to mind change complexity seems to be related to the work in [18] which uses point-set topology to show the relationship between accumulation order and mind change complexity. A generalization of ordinal mind change complexity, as proposed in [22], considers using recursive partially ordered sets as mind change counters. This notion is similar to the role well-partial-orderings play in mind change complexity in our paper. Since we use ordinal mind change complexity, our results would be considered as a Type 2 mind change bound, although our methods may give insight into the differences between the mind change bound types.

A simple modification of the inference algorithm in Theorem 17 will work for inferring any class of languages $\mathcal{L}$ if every language in $\mathcal{L}$ has a characteristic set and if the closure operator $C_{\mathcal{L}}(\cdot)$ of $\mathcal{C}_{\mathcal{L}}$ is computable for finite sets. In this case we would only keep one closed set $C_{\mathcal{L}}(X)$, where X is a subset of the presentation seen so far, and only add an element s to X if $s \notin C_{\mathcal{L}}(X)$. If a language in $\mathcal{L}$ has a characteristic set then it can be shown that it is a finitely generated closed set in $\mathcal{C}_{\mathcal{L}}$, so we can be sure that $C_{\mathcal{L}}(X)$ does not grow without bound. Also it is clear that $C_{\mathcal{L}}(X)$ will converge to the unknown language. However, we will not be guaranteed a mind change bound in this case.

Note that if a class of languages $\mathcal{L}$ contains a language L that has a finite tell-tale but no characteristic set, then L within $\mathcal{C}_{\mathcal{L}}$ will equal the union of an infinitely increasing chain of closed sets. Therefore, the algorithm in Theorem 17 will not converge. This shows a fundamental difference in inferring languages that only have finite tell-tales, because the inference machine will be forced to choose a hypothesis from a set of incomparable languages that are all minimal with respect to the current presentation.

One should also notice the similarities between the algorithm in Theorem 17 with Buchberger's algorithm to compute the Groebner basis of an ideal of a polynomial ring [6]. In Buchberger's algorithm, polynomial division is used to check if a polynomial is in the closure of the current basis, and then expand the basis to include the polynomial if it is not. Since much research has gone into finding efficient versions of Buchberger's algorithm, some of those results may be useful for creating more efficient inference algorithms.

Theorem 19 uses Reverse Mathematics to show that the mind change complexity of a class of languages gives a concrete upper bound to the logical strength of the claim that the class is inferable from positive data. Ambainis et al. [1] have already shown that a confident learner that infers a class $\mathcal{L}$ from positive data can do so with some mind change bound α for some constructive ordinal notation, and Stephan and Ventsov [25] pointed out that the converse holds. However, the result in Theorem 19 shows that the two notions are actually logically equivalent with respect to the weak base system RCA_0. It can be shown that the smallest ordinal that cannot be proven well-ordered in the three systems mentioned previously is ω^ω for RCA_0 and WKL_0, and ϵ_0 for ACA_0. Therefore, we conjecture that if a class of languages $\mathcal{L}$ can be shown within WKL_0 to be confidently learnable, then the class should not have an optimal mind change bound greater than ω^ω. Furthermore, ACA_0 would not be sufficient to prove that a class of languages has optimal mind change bound greater than ϵ_0.

Therefore, classes of languages with increasingly large mind change bounds will require increasingly strong axiom systems to prove them confidently inferable. This is apparent in the case of $L(\mathbf{RP}_l)^\omega$, since it relies heavily on Higman's lemma, but is also seen in Wright's theorem, which is used to prove the inferability of finite unions of pattern languages, and relies on a weak form of Ramsey's theorem.

It may be possible to extend these proof theoretical results even further by using reductions between language classes [15], although care must be taken on the complexity of the proof of the reduction.

Some classes of languages, such as FIN, the class of all finite sets of natural numbers, are not inferable with a mind change bound [1], and yet the inference algorithm is trivial, simply output the finite sequence seen so far. Although the inference algorithm for FIN is simple, and it is trivial to prove its success, FIN is often considered a difficult learning problem because mind changes cannot be bounded. This suggests that it is necessary to further clarify the differences between the complexity of inference algorithms and the complexity of the proof of inferability.

Acknowledgements

We would like to thank Professor Hiroki Arimura and the anonymous reviewers for their helpful comments.

References

1. A. Ambainis, S. Jain, A. Sharma: Ordinal Mind Change Complexity of Language Identification. Theoretical Computer Science **220** (1999) 323–343.
2. D. Angluin: Inductive Inference of Formal Languages from Positive Data. Information and Control **45** (1980) 117–135.
3. G. Birkhoff: Lattice Theory, Third Edition. American Mathematical Society (1967).
4. D. J. Brown, R. Suszko: Abstract Logics. Dissertationes Mathematicae **102** (1973) 9–41.
5. S. Burris, H. P. Sankappanavar: A Course in Universal Algebra. Springer-Verlag (1981).
6. D. Cox, J. Little, D. O'Shea: Ideals, Varieties, and Algorithms, Second Edition. Springer-Verlag (1996).
7. H. Friedman, S. G. Simpson, R. L. Smith: Countable Algebra and Set Existence Axioms. Annals of Pure and Applied Logic **25** (1983) 141–181.
8. R. Freivalds, C. H. Smith: On the Role of Procrastination for Machine Learning. Information and Computation **107** (1993) 237–271.
9. J. H. Gallier: What's So Special About Kruskal's Theorem and the Ordinal Γ_0? A survey of some results in proof theory. Annals of Pure and Applied Logic **53** (1991) 199–260.
10. E. M. Gold: Language Identification in the Limit. Information and Control **10** (1967) 447–474.
11. R. Hasegawa: Well-ordering of Algebras and Kruskal's Theorem. Logic, Language and Computation, Lecture Notes in Computer Science **792** (1994) 133–172.
12. G. Higman: Ordering by Divisibility in Abstract Algebras. Proceedings of the London Mathematical Society, Third Series **2** (1952) 326–336.
13. S. Jain, D. Osherson, J. S. Royer, A. Sharma: Systems That Learn, Second Edition. MIT Press (1999).
14. S. Jain, A. Sharma: Elementary Formal Systems, Intrinsic Complexity, and Procrastination. Proceedings of COLT '96 (1996) 181–192.

15. S. Jain, A. Sharma: The Structure of Intrinsic Complexity of Learning. Journal of Symbolic Logic **62** (1997) 1187–1201.
16. S. C. Kleene: Notations for Ordinal Numbers. Journal of Symbolic Logic **3** (1938) 150–155.
17. S. Kobayashi: Approximate Identification, Finite Elasticity and Lattice Structure of Hypothesis Space. Technical Report, CSIM 96-04, Dept. of Compt. Sci. and Inform. Math., Univ. of Electro- Communications (1996).
18. W. Luo, O. Schulte: Mind Change Efficient Learning. Proceedings of COLT 2005 (2005) 398–412.
19. T. Motoki, T. Shinohara, and K. Wright: The Correct Definition of Finite Elasticity: Corrigendum to Identification of Unions. Proceedings of COLT '91 **375** (1991).
20. Y. Mukouchi: Containment Problems for Pattern Languages. IEICE Trans. Inform. Systems E75-D (1992) 420–425.
21. G. E. Sacks: Higher Recursion Theory. Springer-Verlag (1990).
22. A. Sharma, F. Stephan, Y. Ventsov: Generalized Notions of Mind Change Complexity. Information and Computation **189** (2004) 235–262.
23. T. Shinohara, H. Arimura: Inductive Inference of Unbounded Unions of Pattern Languages From Positive Data. Theoretical Computer Science **241** (2000) 191–209.
24. S. G. Simpson: Ordinal Numbers and the Hilbert Basis Theorem. Journal of Symbolic Logic **53** (1988) 961–974.
25. F. Stephan, Y. Ventsov: Learning Algebraic Structures from Text. Theoretical Computer Science **268** (2001) 221–273.
26. K. Wright: Identification of Unions of Languages Drawn from an Identifiable Class. Proc. 2nd Workshop on Computational Learning Theory (1989) 328–333.

Learning and Extending Sublanguages

Sanjay Jain[1,*] and Efim Kinber[2]

[1] School of Computing, National University of Singapore, Singapore 117543
sanjay@comp.nus.edu.sg
[2] Department of Computer Science, Sacred Heart University, Fairfield, CT
06432-1000, U.S.A.
kinbere@sacredheart.edu

Abstract. A number of natural models for learning in the limit is introduced to deal with the situation when a learner is required to provide a grammar covering the input even if only a part of the target language is available. Examples of language families are exhibited that are learnable in one model and not learnable in another one. Some characterizations for learnability of algorithmically enumerable families of languages for the models in question are obtained. Since learnability of any part of the target language does not imply *monotonicity* of the learning process, we consider also our models under additional monotonicity constraint.

1 Introduction

Models of algorithmic learning in the limit have been used for quite a while for study of learning potentially infinite languages. In the widely used mathematical paradigm of learning in the limit, as suggested by Gold in his seminal article [Gol67], the learner eventually gets all positive examples of the language in question, and the sequence of its conjectures converges in the limit to a correct description. However, in Gold's original model, the learner is not required to produce any reasonable description for partial data — whereas real learning process of languages by humans is rather a sort of incremental process: the learner first actually finds grammatical forms — in the beginning, probably, quite primitive — that describe partial data, and refines conjectures when more data becomes available. Moreover, if some data never becomes available, a successful learner still can eventually come up with a feasible useful description of the part of the language it has learned so far. This situation can be well understood by those who have been exposed to a foreign language for a long time, but then stopped learning it. For example, English has many common grammatical forms with Russian, which makes them relatively easy to learn. However, the system of tenses in English is much more complex than in Russian, and remains a tough nut to crack for many adult Russians who mustered English otherwise relatively well. Similar argument can be made for many other situations when even partial descriptions based on partial input data might be important: diagnosing the complete health status of a

---

* Supported in part by NUS grant number R252-000-127-112.

J.L. Balcázar, P.M. Long, and F. Stephan (Eds.): ALT 2006, LNAI 4264, pp. 139–153, 2006.
© Springer-Verlag Berlin Heidelberg 2006

patient versus detecting only some of his/her deficiencies, forecasting weather for a whole region, or just for some small towns, etc.

In this paper, we introduce several variants of the Gold's model for learning languages in the limit requiring the learner to converge to a reasonable description for just a *sublanguage* if the data from this sublanguage only is available (this approach to learning recursive functions in the limit was studied in [JKW04]). In particular, we consider

(1) a model, where, for any input representing a part P of a language L from the learnable class $\mathcal{L}$, the learner converges to a grammar describing a part of L containing P;

(2) a model, where for any input representing a part P of some language L in the learnable class $\mathcal{L}$, the learner converges to a grammar describing a part (containing P) of some (maybe other) language L' in $\mathcal{L}$. The reason for considering this model is that the first model maybe viewed as too restrictive — partial data P seen by the learner can belong to several different languages, and in such a case, the learner, following the model (1), must produce a grammar describing a part P and being a part of ALL languages in $\mathcal{L}$ which contain P;

(3) a model, similar to the above, but the language L' containing the part P of a language on the input is required to be a *minimal* language in the class $\mathcal{L}$ which contains P.

For all three models, we also consider the variant where the final conjecture itself is required to be a grammar describing a language in the class $\mathcal{L}$ (rather than being a subset of such a language, as in the original models (1) — (3)). (A slightly different variants of the models (1) and (3), with a slightly different motivation, and in somewhat different forms, were introduced in [Muk94] and [KY95]).

We also consider a weaker variant of all the above models: for a learner to be able to learn just a part of the language, the part must be *infinite* (sometimes, we may be interested in learning just potentially infinite languages – in this case, correct learning of just a finite fragment of a target language may be inessential).

We compare all these models, examining when one model has advantages over the other. This gives us opportunity to build some interesting examples of learnable families of languages, for which learnability of a part is possible in one sense, but not possible in the other. We also look at how requirement of being able to learn all (or just infinite) parts fairs against other known models of learnability — in particular, the one that requires the learner to be *consistent* with the input seen so far. We obtain some characterizations for learnability within our models when the final conjecture is required to be a member of the learnable class of languages.

Some of our examples separating one model from another use the fact that, while in general learning increasing parts of an input language can be perceived as incremental process, actual learning strategies can, in fact, be *nonmonotonic* — each next conjecture is not required to contain every data item covered by the prior conjecture. Consequently, we also consider how our models of learnability fair in the context where monotonicity is explicitly required.

2   Notation and Preliminaries

Any unexplained recursion theoretic notation is from [Rog67]. N denotes the set of natural numbers, $\{0, 1, 2, 3, \ldots\}$. $\emptyset$ denotes the empty set. $\subseteq, \subset, \supseteq, \supset$ respectively denote subset, proper subset, superset and proper superset. D_x denotes the finite set with canonical index x [Rog67]. We sometimes identify finite sets with their canonical indices. The quantifier '$\forall^\infty$' means 'for all but finitely many'.

$\uparrow$ denotes undefined. $\max(\cdot), \min(\cdot)$ denotes the maximum and minimum of a set, respectively, where $\max(\emptyset) = 0$ and $\min(\emptyset) = \uparrow$. $\langle \cdot, \cdot \rangle$ stands for an arbitrary, computable, one-to-one encoding of all pairs of natural numbers onto N [Rog67]. Similarly we can define $\langle \cdot, \ldots, \cdot \rangle$ for encoding tuples of natural numbers onto N. π_k^n denotes the k-th projection for the pairing function for n-tuples, i.e., $\pi_k^n(\langle x_1, \ldots, x_n \rangle) = x_k$.

φ_i denotes the partial computable function computed by program i in a fixed *acceptable* programming system φ (see [Rog67]). W_i denotes domain(φ_i). W_i is, then, the recursively enumerable (r.e.) set/language ($\subseteq N$) accepted (or equivalently, generated) by the φ-program i. $\mathcal{E}$ will denote the set of all r.e. languages. L, with or without subscripts and superscripts, ranges over $\mathcal{E}$. $\mathcal{L}$, with or without subscripts and superscripts, ranges over subsets of $\mathcal{E}$.

A class $\mathcal{L} = \{L_0, L_1, \ldots\}$ is said to be an *indexed family* [Ang80b] of recursive languages (with indexing $L_0, L_1, \ldots$), iff there exists a recursive function f such that $f(i, x) = 1$ iff $x \in L_i$. When learning indexed families $\mathcal{L}$, we often consider hypothesis space being $\mathcal{L}$ itself. In such cases, $\mathcal{L}$-grammar i is a grammar for L_i.

We now consider some basic notions in language learning. We first introduce the concept of data that is presented to a learner. A *text* T is a mapping from N into $(N \cup \{\#\})$ (see [Gol67]). The *content* of a text T, denoted content(T), is the set of natural numbers in the range of T. T is a text for L iff content(T) = L. $T[n]$ denotes the initial segment of T of length n. We let T, with or without superscripts, range over texts. Intuitively, #'s in the texts denote pauses in the presentation of data. For example, the only text for the empty language is just an infinite sequence of #'s.

A finite sequence σ is an initial segment of a text. content(σ) is the set of natural numbers in the range of σ. $|\sigma|$ denotes the length of σ, and if $n \le |\sigma|$, then $\sigma[n]$ denotes the initial segment of σ of length n. $\sigma\tau$ denotes the concatenation of σ and τ.

A *language learning machine* is an algorithmic device which computes a mapping from finite initial segments of texts into $N \cup \{?\}$. (Here ? intuitively denotes the fact that $\mathbf{M}$ does not wish to output a conjecture on a particular input). We let $\mathbf{M}$, with or without subscripts and superscripts, range over learning machines. We say that $\mathbf{M}(T)\!\downarrow = i \Leftrightarrow (\forall^\infty n)[\mathbf{M}(T[n]) = i]$.

We now introduce criteria for a learning machine to be considered *successful* on languages. Our first criterion is based on learner, given a text for the language, converging to a grammar for the language.

Definition 1. [Gol67] (a) $\mathbf{M}$ **TxtEx**-*identifies* L (written: $L \in \mathbf{TxtEx}(\mathbf{M})$) $\Leftrightarrow$ ($\forall$ texts T for L)($\exists i \mid W_i = L$)[$\mathbf{M}(T)\!\downarrow = i$].

(b) **M TxtEx**-*identifies* $\mathcal{L}$, if it **TxtEx**-identifies each $L \in \mathcal{L}$.
(c) **TxtEx** = $\{\mathcal{L} \mid (\exists \mathbf{M})[\mathcal{L} \subseteq \mathbf{TxtEx(M)}]\}$.

The influence of Gold's paradigm [Gol67] to analyze human language learning is discussed by various authors, for example [OSW86].

Note that the hypothesis space used for interpreting the conjectures of the learner in the above definition is the acceptable numbering $W_0, W_1, \ldots$. In some cases we use special hypothesis spaces (for example when learning indexed families, we often use the class $\mathcal{L}$ itself as hypothesis space). We will make it explicit when we use such an hypothesis space.

Gold [Gol67] also considered the case when the learner is required to learn a language without making any mind changes.

Definition 2. [Gol67] (a) **M Fin**-*identifies* L (written: $L \in \mathbf{Fin(M)}$) $\Leftrightarrow$ ($\forall$ texts T for L)$(\exists i \mid W_i = L)(\exists n)[\mathbf{M}(T[n]) = i \ \wedge \ (\forall m < n)[\mathbf{M}(T[m]) = ?]]$.
(b) **M Fin**-identifies $\mathcal{L}$, if it **Fin**-identifies each $L \in \mathcal{L}$.
(c) **Fin** = $\{\mathcal{L} \mid (\exists \mathbf{M})[\mathcal{L} \subseteq \mathbf{Fin(M)}]\}$.

The following definition is based on a learner semantically rather than syntactically converging to a grammar (or grammars) for an input language. Here note that equivalence of grammars is non-computable. The corresponding notion for learning functions was introduced by [Bār74b, CS83].

Definition 3. [CL82, OW82a].
(a) **M TxtBc**-*identifies* L (written: $L \in \mathbf{TxtBc(M)}$) $\Leftrightarrow$ ($\forall$ texts T for L)$(\forall^\infty n)[W_{\mathbf{M}(T[n])} = L]$.
(b) **M TxtBc**-identifies $\mathcal{L}$, if it **TxtBc**-identifies each $L \in \mathcal{L}$.
(c) **TxtBc** = $\{\mathcal{L} \mid (\exists \mathbf{M})[\mathcal{L} \subseteq \mathbf{TxtBc(M)}]\}$.

It can be shown that **TxtEx** $\subset$ **TxtBc** (for example, see [CL82, OW82a]).

The following concept is useful for proving some of our results.

Definition 4.
(a) [Ful85] σ is a **TxtEx**-*stabilizing sequence for* **M** *on* L just in case content$(\sigma) \subseteq L$ and $(\forall \tau \mid \text{content}(\tau) \subseteq L \wedge \sigma \subseteq \tau)[\mathbf{M}(\tau) = \mathbf{M}(\sigma)]$.
(b) [BB75, OW82b] σ is a **TxtEx**-*locking sequence for* **M** *on* L just in case σ is a **TxtEx**-stabilizing sequence for **M** on L and $W_{\mathbf{M}(\sigma)} = L$.

Lemma 1. *[BB75] If* **M TxtEx**-*identifies* L, *then there exists a* **TxtEx**-*locking sequence for* **M** *on* L. *Furthermore, all stabilizing sequences of* **M** *on* L *are locking sequences for* **M** *on* L.

Similarly one can define a **TxtBc**-stabilizing sequence and a **TxtBc**-locking sequence for **M** on L. A lemma similar to Lemma 1 can be established for **TxtBc**-learning as well as other criteria of inference considered below. We often drop **TxtEx**- (**TxtBc**-, etc.) from **TxtEx**-(**TxtBc**-, etc.)-stabilizing sequence, when it is clear from context.

Definition 5. [Bār74a, Ang80b] (a) **M** is *consistent* on σ iff content$(\sigma) \subseteq W_{\mathbf{M}(\sigma)}$.

(b) **M** is *consistent* on L iff it is consistent on all σ such that content$(\sigma) \subseteq L$.

(c) **M Cons**-identifies $\mathcal{L}$ iff it is consistent on each $L \in \mathcal{L}$ and **M TxtEx**-identifies $\mathcal{L}$.

Cons $= \{\mathcal{L} \mid$ some **M Cons**-identifies $\mathcal{L}\}$.

3   Learning Sublanguages: Definitions and Separations

Below we define our three models for learning sublanguages, as explained in the Introduction, as well as their variants reflecting the requirement of the final correct conjecture describing a language in the learnable class. We give our definitions for the **Ex** and **Bc** paradigms of learnability in the limit.

Intuitively, we vary three parameters in our learning criteria (in addition to the base criterion such as **Ex** or **Bc**): (a) whether we want the extensions to be subsets of *every* language in the class of which the input is a subset (denoted by **Sub** in the name of the criterion), or of a *minimal* language in the class of which the input is a subset (denoted by **MWSub** in the name of the criterion), or *only one* of the languages in the class of which the input is a subset (denoted by **WSub** in the name of the criterion), (b) whether *all* sublanguages are to be extended (denoted by **All** in the name of the criterion), or only the *infinite* ones (denoted by **Inf** in the name of the criterion), and (c) whether we require the final hypothesis extending the input to be *within the class* or not (denoted by presence or absence of **Res** in the name of the criterion).

A language $L \in \mathcal{L}$ is said to be a *minimal language* [Muk94] containing S in $\mathcal{L}$, iff $S \subseteq L$, and no $L' \in \mathcal{L}$ satisfies $S \subseteq L' \subset L$.

Below, **Sub** denotes learning subsets, **WSub**, denotes weak learning of subsets, and **MWSub** denotes minimal weak learning of subsets. We first consider extending all subsets.

Definition 6. (a) **M AllSubEx**-*identifies* $\mathcal{L}$, iff for all $L \in \mathcal{L}$, for all texts T such that content$(T) \subseteq L$, **M**(T) converges to a grammar i such that content$(T) \subseteq W_i \subseteq L$.

(b) **M AllWSubEx**-*identifies* $\mathcal{L}$, iff **M TxtEx**-identifies $\mathcal{L}$ and for all $L \in \mathcal{L}$, for all texts T such that content$(T) \subseteq L$, **M**(T) converges to a grammar i such that content$(T) \subseteq W_i \subseteq L'$, for some $L' \in \mathcal{L}$.

(c) **M AllMWSubEx**-*identifies* $\mathcal{L}$, iff for all $L \in \mathcal{L}$, for all texts T such that content$(T) \subseteq L$, **M**(T) converges to a grammar i such that content$(T) \subseteq W_i \subseteq L'$, for some $L' \in \mathcal{L}$, such that L' is a minimal language containing content(T) in $\mathcal{L}$.

(d) For **I** $\in$ {**AllSubEx, AllWSubEx, AllMWSubEx**}, we say that **M ResI**-identifies $\mathcal{L}$, iff **M I**-identifies $\mathcal{L}$, and for all $L \in \mathcal{L}$, for all texts T such that content$(T) \subseteq L$, $W_{\mathbf{M}(T)} \in \mathcal{L}$.

As for the latter part of the above definition, it must be noted that Mukouchi [Muk94] considered a variation of **ResAllMWSubEx** for indexed families and provided some sufficient conditions for learnability in the model. Essentially his model allowed a learner to diverge if the input language did not have any minimal extension in $\mathcal{L}$. Kobayashi and Yokomori [KY95] considered a variation of **ResAllSubEx** learning (and briefly also **ResAllMWSubEx** learning) for indexed families of recursive languages and provided some characterizations. Essentially, they required a learner to learn on all inputs, even those which may not be contained in any language in the class (in other words, they required N to be a member of the class). Mukouchi and Kobayashi and Yokomori arrived at their definitions via a slightly different motivation (to find minimal extensions within the class), and, thus, had definitions somewhat different from ours. Here note that Kobayashi and Yokomori's techinque also gives that the class of pattern languages [Ang80a] belongs to **AllSubEx**.

Note also that learning from incomplete texts (with just finite amount of data missing) was studied in the context, where the final grammar still was required to be a correct (or nearly correct) description of the full target language (see, for example, [OSW86, FJ96]). This is incomparable with our approach, in general.

In part (b) of the above definition, we explicitly added **TxtEx**-identifiability as the rest of the definition in part (b) does not imply **TxtEx**-identifiability (for parts (a) and (c), this was not needed, as the conditions imply **TxtEx**-identifiability).

Definition 7. (a) **M AllSubBc**-*identifies* $\mathcal{L}$, iff for all $L \in \mathcal{L}$, for all texts T such that content$(T) \subseteq L$, for all but finitely many n, content$(T) \subseteq W_{M(T[n])} \subseteq L$.

(b) **M AllWSubBc**-*identifies* $\mathcal{L}$, iff **M TxtBc**-identifies $\mathcal{L}$ and for all $L \in \mathcal{L}$, for all texts T such that content$(T) \subseteq L$, for all but finitely many n, for some $L' \in \mathcal{L}$, content$(T) \subseteq W_{M(T[n])} \subseteq L'$.

(c) **M AllMWSubBc**-*identifies* $\mathcal{L}$, iff for all $L \in \mathcal{L}$, for all texts T such that content$(T) \subseteq L$, for all but finitely many n, for some $L' \in \mathcal{L}$ such that L' is a minimal superset of content(T) in L, content$(T) \subseteq W_{M(T[n])} \subseteq L'$.

(d) For $\mathbf{I} \in \{\mathbf{AllSubBc, AllWSubBc, AllMWSubBc}\}$, we say that **M ResI**-identifies $\mathcal{L}$, iff **M I**-identifies $\mathcal{L}$, and for all $L \in \mathcal{L}$, for all texts T such that content$(T) \subseteq L$, for all but finitely many n, $W_{M(T[n])} \in \mathcal{L}$.

In the above definitions, when we only require extending infinite subsets, then we replace **All** by **Inf** in the name of the criterion (for example, **InfSubEx**).

Our first proposition establishes a number of simple relationships between our different models that easily follow from the definitions. In particular, we formally establish that our model (1) is more restrictive than model (3), and model (3) is more restrictive than model (2) (we refer here, and in the sequel, to the models described in the Introduction).

Proposition 1. *Suppose* $\mathbf{I} \in \{\mathbf{All, Inf}\}$, $\mathbf{J} \in \{\mathbf{Sub, WSub, MWSub}\}$, $\mathbf{K} \in \{\mathbf{Ex, Bc}\}$.
(a) **ResIJK** $\subseteq$ **IJK**.
(b) **AllJK** $\subseteq$ **InfJK**.
(c) **ISubK** $\subseteq$ **IMWSubK** $\subseteq$ **IWSubK**.
(d) **IJEx** $\subseteq$ **IJBc**.
(b), (c), (d) *above hold for* **Res** *versions too.*

Results below would show that above inclusions are proper. They give the advantages of having a weaker restriction, such as final conjecture not being required to be within the class (Theorem 1), **WSub** vs **MWSub** vs **Sub** (Theorems 3 and 2) and **Inf** vs **All** (Theorem 4).

First we show that the requirement of the last correct conjecture(s) being a member of the learnable class makes a difference for the sublanguage learners: there are classes of languages learnable in our most restrictive model, **AllSubEx**, and not learnable in the least restrictive model **ResInfWSubBc** satisfying this requirement.

Theorem 1. AllSubEx – ResInfWSubBc $\neq \emptyset$.

Proof. Let $L_f = \{\langle x, f(x) \rangle \mid x \in N\}$. Let $\mathcal{L} = \{L_f \mid f \in \mathcal{R} \;\wedge\; \mathrm{card}(\mathrm{range}(f)) < \infty \;\wedge\; (\forall e \in \mathrm{range}(f))[W_e = f^{-1}(e)]\}$. It is easy to verify that $\mathcal{L} \in$ **AllSubEx**. However $\mathcal{L}$ is not in **ResInfWSubBc** (proof of Theorem 23 in [JKW04] can be easily adapted to show this). ∎

On the other hand, an **AllMWSubEx**-learner, even satisfying **Res** variant of sublanguage learnability, can sometimes do more than any **SubBc**-learner even if just learnability of only infinite sublanguages is required.

Theorem 2. ResAllMWSubEx – InfSubBc $\neq \emptyset$.

Proof. Let $Y = \{\langle 1, x \rangle \mid x \in N\}$. Let $Z_e = \{\langle 1, x \rangle \mid x \le e\} \cup \{\langle 1, 2x \rangle \mid x \in N\} \cup \{\langle 0, 0 \rangle\}$. Let $\mathcal{L} = \{Y\} \cup \{Z_e \mid e > 0\}$.

Note that Y is not contained in any other language in the class, nor contains any other language of the class.

$\mathcal{L} \in$ **ResAllMWSubEx** as on input σ, a learner can output as follows. If content$(\sigma) \subseteq Y$, then output a (standard) grammar for Y. If content(σ) contains just $\langle 0, 0 \rangle$, then output a standard grammar for $\{\langle 0, 0 \rangle\}$. Otherwise output Z_e, where e is the maximum odd number such that $\langle 1, e \rangle \in$ content(σ) (if there is no such odd number, then one takes e to be 1).

On the other hand, suppose by way of contradiction that $\mathcal{L} \in$ **InfSubBc** as witnessed by **M**. Let σ be a **Bc**-locking sequence for **M** on Y (that is, content$(\sigma) \subseteq Y$, and on any τ such that $\sigma \subseteq \tau$ and content$(\tau) \subseteq Y$, **M** outputs a grammar for Y). Now, let e be the largest odd number such that $\langle 1, x \rangle \in$ content(σ) (we assume without loss of generality that there does exist such an odd number). Now let $L' = Y \cap Z_e$. So **M** on any text for L' extending σ, should output (in the limit) grammars for L' rather than Y, a contradiction. ∎

Similarly to the above result, a **ResAllWSubEx**-learner can learn sometimes more than any **MWSubBc**-learner even if learnability for just infinite sublanguages is required.

Theorem 3. ResAllWSubEx – InfMWSubBc $\neq \emptyset$.

Proof. Let $L_0^k = \{\langle k, i, x \rangle \mid i > 0, x \in N\} \cup \{\langle k, 0, 0 \rangle\}$.
For $j \in N$, let $L_{j+1}^k = \{\langle k, i, x \rangle \mid i > 0, x \le j\} \cup \{\langle k, 0, j+1 \rangle\}$.

Let $\mathcal{L} = \{N\} \cup \{L_{r_k}^k \mid k \in N\}$, where we will determine r_k below.
First we show that, irrespective of the values of r_k, $\mathcal{L} \in \textbf{ResAllWSubEx}$. $\textbf{M}$
is defined as follows. Let g_N be a grammar for N, and g_j^k be a grammar for L_j^k.

$$
\textbf{M}(\sigma) = \begin{cases} g_j^k, & \text{if content}(\sigma) \cap \{\langle i, 0, x\rangle \mid i, x \in N\} = \{\langle k, 0, j\rangle\} \text{ and} \\ & \text{content}(\sigma) \subseteq L_j^k; \\ g_N, & \text{otherwise.} \end{cases}
$$

Above $\textbf{M}$ witnesses that $\mathcal{L} \in \textbf{ResAllWSubEx}$, as except for N, all languages
in the class are minimal languages in the class, containing exactly one element
from $\{\langle i, 0, x\rangle \mid i, x \in N\}$.

Now we select r_k appropriately to show that $\textbf{M}_k$ does not $\textbf{InfMWSubBc}$-
identify $\mathcal{L}$. Consider the behaviour of $\textbf{M}_k$ on inputs being $S_j^k = L_j^k - \{\langle k, 0, j\rangle\}$.
Note that $\textbf{M}_k$ cannot $\textbf{TxtBc}^1$-identify the class $\{S_j^k \mid j \in N\}$ (based on
[Gol67]; here $\textbf{TxtBc}^1$-identification is similar to $\textbf{TxtBc}$-identification except
that on texts for language L, $\textbf{M}$ is allowed to output grammars which enumerate L, except for upto one error (of either omission or commission)). Pick
r_k such that $\textbf{M}_k$ does not $\textbf{TxtBc}^1$-identify $S_{r_k}^k$. Now, on input language being
$S_{r_k}^k$, $\textbf{M}_k$, in the limit, is supposed to output grammars for either $S_{r_k}^k$ or $L_{r_k}^k$,
and thus $\textbf{TxtBc}^1$-identify $S_{r_k}^k$, a contradiction. Since k was arbitrary, theorem
follows. ∎

Now we show that limiting learnability to just infinite sublanguages, even in the
most restrictive model, can give us sometimes more than learners in the least
restrictive model (2) required to learn descriptions for *all* sublanguages.

Theorem 4. ResInfSubEx − AllWSubBc $\neq \emptyset$.

Proof. Using Kleene's Recursion Theorem [Rog67], for any i, let e_i be such
that $W_{e_i} = \{\langle i, e_i, x\rangle \mid x \in N\}$. If $\textbf{M}_i$ does not $\textbf{TxtBc}$-identify W_{e_i}, then let
$L_i = W_{e_i}$. Else, let σ^i be a $\textbf{TxtBc}$-locking sequence for $\textbf{M}_i$ on W_{e_i}. Without loss
of generality assume that content$(\sigma^i) \neq \emptyset$. Using Kleene's Recursion Theorem
[Rog67], let $e_i' > e_i$ be such that $W_{e_i'} = \text{content}(\sigma^i) \cup \{\langle i, e_i', x\rangle \mid x \in N\}$, and
then let $L_i = W_{e_i'}$.

Let $\mathcal{L} = \{L_i \mid i \in N\}$. Now clearly, $\mathcal{L}$ is in $\textbf{ResInfSubEx}$, as the learner can
just output the maximum value of $\pi_2^3(x)$, where x is in the input language.

We now show $\mathcal{L} \notin \textbf{AllWSubBc}$. For any i either $\textbf{M}_i$ does not $\textbf{TxtBc}$-
identify $W_{e_i} = L_i$ or on any text extending σ^i for content$(\sigma^i) \subseteq L_i$, beyond σ^i,
$\textbf{M}_i$ outputs only grammars for W_{e_i} — which is not contained in any $L \in \mathcal{L}$.
It follows that $\textbf{M}_i$ does not $\textbf{AllWSubBc}$-identify $\mathcal{L}$. Since i was arbitrary, the
theorem follows. ∎

We now note that not all classes learnable within the traditional paradigm of
algorithmic learning are learnable in our weakest model even if learnability of
only infinite sublanguages is required.

Theorem 5. Fin − InfWSubBc $\neq \emptyset$.

Proof. Let $L_e = \{\langle 1, e \rangle\} \cup \{\langle 0, x \rangle \mid x \in W_e\}$. Let $\mathcal{L} = \{L_e \mid e \in N\}$. It is easy to verify that $\mathcal{L} \in$ **Fin**. However $\mathcal{L} \in$ **InfWSubBc** implies that for any text T for $L_e − \{\langle 1, e \rangle\}$, the learner must either (i) output grammars for L_e on almost all initial segments of T, or (ii) output grammars for $L_e − \{\langle 1, e \rangle\}$ on almost all initial segments of T. Thus, an easy modification of this learner would give us that $\mathcal{E} \in$ **TxtBc**, a contradiction to a result from [CL82]. ∎

Following theorem gives yet another cost of learning sublanguages requirement: increase in mind changes.

Theorem 6. *There exists $\mathcal{L} \in$ **AllSubEx** $\cap$ **Fin** $\cap$ **ResAllMWSubEx**, which cannot be **InfSubEx**-identified by any learner making at most n mind changes.*

On the other hand, **Bc**-learners in the most restrictive model of sublanguage learnability can sometimes learn more than traditional **Ex**-learners that are not required to learn sublanguages.

Theorem 7. ResAllSubBc − TxtEx $\neq \emptyset$.

Proof. Let $\mathcal{L} = \{\emptyset\} \cup \{S_i \mid i \in N\}$, where S_i would be defined below. Let $L_i = \{\langle i, x \rangle \mid x \in N\}$. For some e_i, S_i will satisfy the following two properties:
   A) $\emptyset \subset S_i \subseteq L_{e_i}$,
   B) W_{e_i} enumerates an infinite set of elements such that all but finitely many of these are grammars for S_i.
   It follows immediately from above that $\mathcal{L} \in$ **ResAllSubBc**, as on an input being a nonempty subset of L_{e_i}, a learner can just output an increasing sequence of elements from W_{e_i}.
   We now define S_i such that $\mathbf{M}_i$ does not **TxtEx**-identify S_i. By implicit use of Kleene's Recursion Theorem [Rog67], there exists an e_i such that W_{e_i} may be defined as follows.
   Let $X = \{\sigma \mid \text{content}(\sigma) \subseteq L_{e_i} \wedge \emptyset \subset \text{content}(\sigma) \subset W_{\mathbf{M}_i(\sigma)}\}$.
   Let $Y = \{\sigma \mid \text{content}(\sigma) \subseteq L_{e_i} \wedge (\exists \tau \mid \sigma \subseteq \tau)[\text{content}(\tau) \subseteq L_{e_i} \wedge \mathbf{M}_i(\sigma) \neq \mathbf{M}_i(\tau)]\}$.
   Note that both X and Y are recursively enumerable. We assume without loss of generality that X is not empty. Let $\tau_0, \tau_1, \ldots$ be an infinite recursive sequence such that $\{\tau_j \mid j \in N\} = X$. Let $Y_0, Y_1, \ldots$ be a sequence of recursive approximations to Y such that $Y_j \subseteq Y_{j+1}$ and $\bigcup_{j \in N} Y_j = Y$.
   We now define W_{e_i} as follows. Let g_j be defined such that

$$W_{g_j} = \begin{cases} \text{content}(\tau_j), & \text{if } \tau_j \notin Y; \\ L_{e_i}, & \text{otherwise.} \end{cases}$$

   Let $s_r = \max(\{j \leq r \mid (\forall j' < j)[\tau_{j'} \in Y_r]\})$.
   Now, if $\mathbf{M}_i$ does not have a stabilizing sequence, belonging to X, for L_{e_i}, then every g_r is a grammar for L_{e_i}, which is not **TxtEx**-identified by $\mathbf{M}_i$. In this case, let $S_i = L_{e_i}$. On the other hand, if j is the least number such that

τ_j is a stabilizing sequence for $\mathbf{M}_i$ on L_{e_i}, then $\lim_{r \to \infty} s_r = j$, and W_{g_j} is a grammar for content(τ_j), which is not **TxtEx**-identified by $\mathbf{M}_i$. In this case let $S_i = $ content(τ_j). Clearly, (A) is satisfied and $\mathbf{M}_i$ does not **TxtEx**-identify S_i.

Let *pad* be a 1–1 recursive function such that $W_{pad(i,j)} = W_i$, for all i, j. Let $W_{e_i} = \{pad(g_{s_r}, r) \mid r \in N\}$. It is easy to verify that (B) is satisfied. The theorem follows. ∎

Our next result shows that learners in all our models that are required to learn *all* sublanguages can be made *consistent* (with the input seen so far). This can be proved in a way similar to Theorem 28 in [JKW04].

Theorem 8. *Suppose* $\mathbf{I} \in \{\mathbf{Sub}, \mathbf{WSub}, \mathbf{MWSub}\}$.
  (a) **AllIEx** $\subseteq$ **AllICons**.
  (b) **ResAllIEx** $\subseteq$ **ResAllICons**.

On the other hand, if learnability of infinite sublanguages only is required, consistency cannot be achieved sometimes.

Theorem 9. **ResInfSubEx** – **Cons** $\neq \emptyset$.

Proof. Let $\mathcal{L} = \{L \mid \text{card}(L) = \infty$ and $(\exists e)[W_e = L$ and $(\forall^\infty x \in L)[\pi_1^2(x) = e]]\}$. It is easy to verify that $\mathcal{L} \in$ **ResInfSubEx**. The proof of Proposition 29 in [JKW04] can be adapted to show that $\mathcal{L} \notin$ **Cons**. ∎

4   Some Characterizations

In this section, we suggest some characterizations for sublanguage learnability of indexed classes. First, we get a characterization of **ResAllSubEx** in terms of requirements that must be imposed on regular **TxtEx**-learnability.

Theorem 10. *Suppose* $\mathcal{L} = \{L_0, L_1, \ldots\}$ *is an indexed family of recursive languages. Then* $\mathcal{L} \in$ **ResAllSubEx** *iff (a) to (d) below hold.*
  (a) $\mathcal{L} \in$ **TxtEx***;*
  (b) $\mathcal{L}$ *is closed under non-empty infinite intersections (that is, for any non-empty* $\mathcal{L}' \subseteq \mathcal{L}$, $\bigcap_{L \in \mathcal{L}'} L \in \mathcal{L}$*);*
  For any set S, *let* $Min_{\mathcal{L}}(S)$ *denote the minimal language in* $\mathcal{L}$ *which contains* S, *if any (note that due to closure under intersections, there is a unique minimal language containing* S *in* $\mathcal{L}$, *if any).*
  (c) For all finite S *such that for some* $L \in \mathcal{L}$, $S \subseteq L$, *one can effectively find in the limit a* $\mathcal{L}$-*grammar for* $Min_{\mathcal{L}}(S)$*;*
  (d) For all infinite S *which are contained in some* $L \in \mathcal{L}$, $Min_{\mathcal{L}}(S) = Min_{\mathcal{L}}(X)$, *for some finite subset* X *of* S.

Proof. ($\Longrightarrow$) Suppose $\mathcal{L} \in$ **ResAllSubEx** as witnessed by $\mathbf{M}$.
(a) and (b) follow using the definition of **ResAllSubEx**.
(c): Given any finite set S which is contained in some language in $\mathcal{L}$, for any text T_S for S, $\mathbf{M}(T_S)$ converges to a (r.e.) grammar for the minimal language

in $\mathcal{L}$. This r.e. grammar can now be easily converted to a $\mathcal{L}$-grammar using **TxtEx**-identifiability of $\mathcal{L}$ (note that for an indexed family of recursive languages, **TxtEx** learnability implies learnability using the hypothesis space $\mathcal{L}$).

(d): Suppose by way of contradiction that (d) does not hold. We then construct a text for S on which M does not converge to $Min_{\mathcal{L}}(S)$. Let $(X_i)_{i \in N}$ be a family of non-empty and finite sets such that $\bigcup_{i \in N} X_i = S$ and $X_i \subseteq X_{i+1}$ for all i. Define $\sigma_0 = \Lambda$. Let σ_{i+1} be an extension of σ_i such that content$(\sigma_{i+1}) = X_i$, and $M(\sigma_{i+1})$ is a grammar for $Min_{\mathcal{L}}(X_i)$ (note that there exists such a σ_{i+1} as M on any text for X_i converges to a grammar for $Min_{\mathcal{L}}(X_i)$). Now let $T = \bigcup_{i \in N} \sigma_i$. Clearly, T is a text for S. However, $M(T)$ does not converge to a grammar for $Min_{\mathcal{L}}(S)$, as $Min_{\mathcal{L}}(X_i) \neq Min_{\mathcal{L}}(S)$, for all i (by assumption about (d) not holding). A contradiction to M **ResAllSubEx**-identifying $\mathcal{L}$. Thus, (d) must hold.

($\Longleftarrow$) Suppose (a) to (d) are satisfied. Let f be a recursive function such that for all finite S, $\lim_{t \to \infty} f(S, t)$ is an $\mathcal{L}$-grammar for $Min_{\mathcal{L}}(S)$ (by clause (c), there exists such an f). Then, define M' as follows. M' on any input $T[n]$, computes $i_j^n = f(\text{content}(T[j]), n)$, for $j \leq n$. Then it outputs i_j^n, for minimal j such that content$(T[n]) \subseteq L_{i_j^n}$. By definition of f, for each j, $i_j = \lim_{n \to \infty} i_j^n$ is defined and is a $\mathcal{L}$-grammar for $Min_{\mathcal{L}}(\text{content}(T[j]))$. As for all but finitely many j, $Min_{\mathcal{L}}(\text{content}(T[j])) = Min_{\mathcal{L}}(\text{content}(T))$ (by clause (d)), we have that M' will converge on T to i_k, where k is minimal such j. It follows that $M'(T)$ converges to a $\mathcal{L}$-grammar for $Min_{\mathcal{L}}(\text{content}(T))$. Note that this also implies **TxtEx**-identifiability of $\mathcal{L}$ by M'. ∎

Our next theorem shows that if an indexed class is learnable within models (2) or (3) under the requirement that the last (correct) conjecture is a member of the learnable class $\mathcal{L}$, then the learner can use conjectures from the class $\mathcal{L}$ itself. In particular, this result will be used in our next characterizations.

Theorem 11. *Suppose* $\mathcal{L} = \{L_0, L_1, \ldots\}$ *is an indexed family of recursive languages. Then* $\mathcal{L} \in$ **ResAllWSubEx** *(***ResInfWSubEx**, **ResAllMWSubEx**, **ResInfMWSubEx***) iff there exists a machine* **M** *such that* **M** **ResAllWSubEx**-*identifies (***ResInfWSubEx**-*identifies,* **ResAllMWSubEx**-*identifies,* **ResInfMWSubEx**-*identifies)* $\mathcal{L}$ *using* $\mathcal{L}$ *as a hypothesis space.*

Now we show that learnability within the model **ResAllWSubEx** is equivalent to regular learnability **TxtEx** if a learner just stabilizes on every input sublanguage of every language in the learnable indexed family $\mathcal{L}$.

Theorem 12. *Suppose* $\mathcal{L} = \{L_0, L_1, \ldots\}$ *is an indexed family of recursive languages. Then* $\mathcal{L} \in$ **ResAllWSubEx** *iff there exists a machine* **M** *such that:*
(a) **M** **TxtEx**-*identifies* $\mathcal{L}$ *using hypothesis space* $\mathcal{L}$.
(b) *For all texts* T *such that, for some* $L \in \mathcal{L}$, content$(T) \subseteq L$, *we have:* $M(T)\downarrow$.

Proof. ($\Longrightarrow$) If $\mathcal{L} \in$ **ResAllWSubEx**, then (a) and (b) follow from the definition of **ResAllWSubEx** and Theorem 11.

($\Longleftarrow$) Suppose $\mathbf{M}$ is given such that (a) and (b) hold. Define $\mathbf{M}'$ as follows:

$$\mathbf{M}'(\sigma) = \begin{cases} \mathbf{M}(\sigma), & \text{if content}(\sigma) \subseteq L_{M(\sigma)}; \\ j, & \text{otherwise, where } j = \min(\{|\sigma|\} \cup \{i : \text{content}(\sigma) \subseteq L_i\}). \end{cases}$$

The first clause ensures $\mathbf{TxtEx}$ learnability of $\mathcal{L}$ by $\mathbf{M}'$ using the hypothesis space $\mathcal{L}$. Now consider any text T for $L' \subseteq L$ where $L \in \mathcal{L}$. Since $\mathbf{M}$ converges on T, let i be such that $\mathbf{M}(T) = i$. If content$(T) \subseteq L_i$, then clearly $\mathbf{M}'(T) = i$ too. On the other hand, if content$(T) \not\subseteq L_i$, then by the second clause in the definition of $\mathbf{M}'$, $\mathbf{M}'(T)$ will converge to the least j such that content$(T) \subseteq L_j$. It follows that $\mathbf{M}'$ $\mathbf{ResAllWSubEx}$-identifies $\mathcal{L}$ using the hypothesis space $\mathcal{L}$. ∎

Proof technique used for Theorem 12 can also be used to show the following.

Theorem 13. *Suppose $\mathcal{L} = \{L_0, L_1, \ldots\}$ is an indexed family of recursive languages. Then $\mathcal{L} \in \mathbf{ResInfWSubEx}$ iff there exists a machine $\mathbf{M}$ such that:*
(a) $\mathbf{M}$ $\mathbf{TxtEx}$-identifies $\mathcal{L}$ using the hypothesis space $\mathcal{L}$.
(b) For all texts T such that content(T) is infinite and content$(T) \subseteq L$ for some $L \in \mathcal{L}$, $\mathbf{M}(T)\!\downarrow$.

The next theorem presents a simple natural condition sufficient for learnability of indexed classes in the model $\mathbf{ResAllWSubEx}$.

Theorem 14. *Suppose $\mathcal{L}$ is an indexed family of recursive languages such that for any distinct languages L_1, L_2 in $\mathcal{L}$, $L_1 \not\subseteq L_2$. Then, $\mathcal{L} \in \mathbf{ResAllWSubEx}$.*

Proof. Suppose $\mathcal{L} = \{L_0, L_1, \ldots\}$. Then, $\mathbf{M}$ on input σ outputs the least i such that content$(\sigma) \subseteq L_i$. It is easy to verify that $\mathbf{M}$ $\mathbf{ResAllWSubEx}$-identifies $\mathcal{L}$. ∎

5   Monotonicity Constraints

In this section we consider sublanguage learnability satisfying monotonicity constraints. Our primary goal is to explore how so-called *strong monotonicity* ([Jan91]) affects sublanguage learnability: the learners are strongly monotonic for the criteria discussed in this paper in the sense that when we get more data in the text, then the languages conjectured are larger.

Definition 8. [Jan91] (a) $\mathbf{M}$ is said to be *strong-monotonic* on L just in case $(\forall \sigma, \tau \mid \sigma \subseteq \tau \wedge \text{content}(\tau) \subseteq L)[\mathbf{M}(\sigma) =? \vee W_{\mathbf{M}(\sigma)} \subseteq W_{\mathbf{M}(\tau)}]$.
(b) $\mathbf{M}$ is said to be *strong-monotonic* on $\mathcal{L}$ just in case $\mathbf{M}$ is strong-monotonic on each $L \in \mathcal{L}$.
(c) $\mathbf{SMon} = \{\mathcal{L} \mid (\exists \mathbf{M})[\mathbf{M}$ is strong-monotonic on $\mathcal{L}$ and $\mathcal{L} \subseteq \mathbf{TxtEx}(\mathbf{M})]\}$.

Let $\mathbf{AllWSubSMon}$, etc, denote the corresponding learning criteria. In those criteria, $\mathbf{Ex}$-type of learnability is assumed by default, unless $\mathbf{Bc}$ is explicitly added at the end.

Unlike the general case of sublanguage learning, strong monotonicity requirement forces all variants of the least restrictive model (2) to collapse to the most restrictive model (1). For **Bc**-learning, it can also be shown that there is no difference whether only infinite sublanguages are required to be learned, or all sublanguages. This later result though does not hold when we consider **Ex**-learning, or require the learners to converge to grammars for a language within the class.

Theorem 15. *(a)* **AllWSubSMon** $\subseteq$ **AllSubSMon**.
  (b) **InfWSubSMon** $\subseteq$ **InfSubSMon**.
  (c) **AllWSubSMonBc** $\subseteq$ **AllSubSMonBc**.
  (d) **InfWSubSMonBc** $\subseteq$ **InfSubSMonBc**.
  (e) **InfSubSMonBc** $\subseteq$ **AllSubSMonBc**.
  (a) to (d) above hold for **Res** *versions too.*

Proof. We show (a). (b) to (e) (and **Res** versions for (a) to (d)) can be proved similarly. Suppose **M** **AllWSubSMon**-identifies $\mathcal{L}$. We first note that for all $L \in \mathcal{L}$, for all σ such that content$(\sigma) \subseteq L$, $W_{\mathbf{M}(\sigma)} \subseteq L$. This is so, since otherwise for any text T for L which extends σ, **M** does not output a grammar contained in L for any extension of σ, due to strong monotonicity of **M**. This, along with **AllWSubSMon**-identifiability of $\mathcal{L}$ by **M**, implies **AllSubSMon**-identifiability of $\mathcal{L}$ by **M**. ∎

Similar result as Theorem 15 holds (essentially by definition) if, instead of requiring strong monotonicity of the learner, one requires that for all $L \in \mathcal{L}$, for all σ such that content$(\sigma) \subseteq L$, $W_{\mathbf{M}(\sigma)} \subseteq L$.

Note that the proof of Theorem 15 is not able to show **InfSubSMon** $\subseteq$ **AllSubSMon**, as an **InfSubSMon**-learner may not converge on finite sets. Similarly, we do not get **ResInfSubSMonBc** $\subseteq$ **ResAllSubSMonBc** using the above proof. The following two theorems show that the above failure is not avoidable.

Theorem 16. ResInfSubSMon − **AllSubSMon** $\neq \emptyset$.

Proof. Let $X_{i,j} = \{\langle i, j, x \rangle \mid x \in N\}$. Using Kleene's Recursion Theorem [Rog67], for any i, let e_i be such that W_{e_i} is defined as follows. If there is no **TxtEx**-stabilizing sequence for $\mathbf{M}_i$ on X_{i,e_i}, then $W_{e_i} = X_{i,e_i}$. Otherwise, W_{e_i} is a finite set such that content$(\sigma^i) \subseteq W_{e_i} \subseteq X_{i,e_i}$, where σ^i is the least **TxtEx**-stabilizing sequence for $\mathbf{M}_i$ on X_{i,e_i} (here, without loss of generality we assume that content$(\sigma^i) \neq \emptyset$). Note that one can define such W_{e_i} as one can find the least **TxtEx**-stabilizing sequence, if any, in the limit.

If $\mathbf{M}_i$ does not have a **TxtEx**-stabilizing sequence on X_{i,e_i}, then let $L_i = W_{e_i}$. Otherwise, let σ^i be the least **TxtEx**-stabilizing sequence for $\mathbf{M}_i$ on X_{i,e_i}. Define S_i based on following two cases.

Case 1: $W_{\mathbf{M}_i(\sigma^i)}$ contains an infinite subset of X_{i,e_i}. In this case let $S_i =$ content(σ^i).

Case 2: Not case 1. In this case, let S_i be a finite set such that content$(\sigma^i) \subseteq S_i \subseteq X_{i,e_i}$ and $S_i \not\subseteq W_{\mathbf{M}_i(\sigma^i)}$.

Using Kleene's Recursion Theorem [Rog67], let $e_i' > e_i$ be such that $W_{e_i'} = S_i \cup W_{e_i} \cup \{\langle i, e_i', x \rangle \mid x \in N\}$, and then let $L_i = W_{e_i'}$.

Let $\mathcal{L} = \{L_i \mid i \in N\}$. Now clearly, $\mathcal{L}$ is in **ResInfSubSMon**, as (on an input with non-empty content) the learner can just output the maximum value of $\pi_2^3(x)$, where x is in the input language.

Now suppose by way of contradiction that $\mathbf{M}_i$ **AllSubSMon**-identifies $\mathcal{L}$. If $\mathbf{M}_i$ does not have a **TxtEx**-stabilizing sequence on X_{i,e_i}, then $\mathbf{M}_i$ does not **TxtEx**-identify $L_i = W_{e_i} = X_{i,e_i} \in \mathcal{L}$. Thus $\mathbf{M}_i$ cannot **AllSubSMon**-identify $\mathcal{L}$.

On the other hand, if $\mathbf{M}_i$ has σ^i as the least **TxtEx**-stabilizing sequence on X_{i,e_i}, then: in Case 1 above, $\mathbf{M}_i$ cannot **SMon**-identify L_i, as $W_{\mathbf{M}_i(\sigma^i)}$ is not a subset of L_i; in Case 2 above, $\mathbf{M}_i$ on any text for S_i, which extends σ^i, converges to $W_{\mathbf{M}_i(\sigma^i)}$, which is not a superset of S_i.

It follows that $\mathcal{L} \notin$ **AllSubSMon**.   ∎

Theorem 17. ResInfSubSMon − ResAllSubBc $\neq \emptyset$.

Proof. Suppose $\mathbf{M}_0, \mathbf{M}_1, \ldots$ is a recursive enumeration of all inductive inference machines. Define L_i as follows. Let T_i be a text for $\{\langle i, 0 \rangle\}$. If $\mathbf{M}_i(T_i)$ infinitely often outputs a grammar containing $\langle i, 2x \rangle$, for some $x > 0$, then let $L_i = \{\langle i, 0 \rangle\} \cup \{\langle i, 2x+1 \rangle \mid x \in N\}$. Otherwise, let $L_i = \{\langle i, 0 \rangle\} \cup \{\langle i, 2x \rangle \mid x \in N\}$.

Let $\mathcal{L} = \{L_i \mid i \in N\}$.

By construction of L_i, $\mathbf{M}_i$ on T_i infinitely often outputs a grammar different from the grammar for L_i, the only language in $\mathcal{L}$ which contains content(T_i). Thus, $\mathcal{L} \notin$ **ResAllSubBc**.

On the other hand, it is easy to verify that $\mathcal{L} \in$ **ResInfSubSMon** (as one can easily determine L_i from a text for any subset of L_i, which contains at least one element other than $\langle i, 0 \rangle$).   ∎

Our proof of Theorem 1 also shows

Theorem 18. AllSubSMon − ResInfWSubBc $\neq \emptyset$.

Acknowledgements. We thank the anonymous referees of ALT for several helpful comments.

References

[Ang80a] D. Angluin. Finding patterns common to a set of strings. *Journal of Computer and System Sciences*, 21:46–62, 1980.

[Ang80b] D. Angluin. Inductive inference of formal languages from positive data. *Information and Control*, 45:117–135, 1980.

[Bār74a] J. Bārzdiņš. Inductive inference of automata, functions and programs. In *Int. Math. Congress, Vancouver*, pages 771–776, 1974.

[Bär74b]   J. Bārzdiņš. Two theorems on the limiting synthesis of functions. In *Theory of Algorithms and Programs, vol. 1*, pages 82–88. Latvian State University, 1974. In Russian.

[BB75]   L. Blum and M. Blum. Toward a mathematical theory of inductive inference. *Information and Control*, 28:125–155, 1975.

[CL82]   J. Case and C. Lynes. Machine inductive inference and language identification. In M. Nielsen and E. M. Schmidt, editors, *Proceedings of the 9th International Colloquium on Automata, Languages and Programming*, volume 140 of *Lecture Notes in Computer Science*, pages 107–115. Springer-Verlag, 1982.

[CS83]   J. Case and C. Smith. Comparison of identification criteria for machine inductive inference. *Theoretical Computer Science*, 25:193–220, 1983.

[FJ96]   M. Fulk and S. Jain. Learning in the presence of inaccurate information. *Theoretical Computer Science A*, 161:235–261, 1996.

[Ful85]   M. Fulk. *A Study of Inductive Inference Machines*. PhD thesis, SUNY/Buffalo, 1985.

[Gol67]   E. M. Gold. Language identification in the limit. *Information and Control*, 10:447–474, 1967.

[Jan91]   K. Jantke. Monotonic and non-monotonic inductive inference. *New Generation Computing*, 8:349–360, 1991.

[JKW04]   S. Jain, E. Kinber, and R. Wiehagen. Learning all subfunctions of a function. *Information and Computation*, 192(2):185–215, August 2004.

[KY95]   S. Kobayashi and T. Yokomori. On approximately identifying concept classes in the limit. In K. Jantke, T. Shinohara, and T. Zeugmann, editors, *Algorithmic Learning Theory: Sixth International Workshop (ALT '95)*, volume 997 of *Lecture Notes in Artificial Intelligence*, pages 298–312. Springer-Verlag, 1995.

[Muk94]   Y. Mukouchi. Inductive inference of an approximate concept from positive data. In S. Arikawa and K. Jantke, editors, *Algorithmic Learning Theory: Fourth International Workshop on Analogical and Inductive Inference (AII '94) and Fifth International Workshop on Algorithmic Learning Theory (ALT '94)*, volume 872 of *Lecture Notes in Artificial Intelligence*, pages 484–499. Springer-Verlag, 1994.

[OSW86]   D. Osherson, M. Stob, and S. Weinstein. *Systems that Learn: An Introduction to Learning Theory for Cognitive and Computer Scientists*. MIT Press, 1986.

[OW82a]   D. Osherson and S. Weinstein. Criteria of language learning. *Information and Control*, 52:123–138, 1982.

[OW82b]   D. Osherson and S. Weinstein. A note on formal learning theory. *Cognition*, 11:77–88, 1982.

[Rog67]   H. Rogers. *Theory of Recursive Functions and Effective Computability*. McGraw-Hill, 1967. Reprinted by MIT Press in 1987.

Iterative Learning from Positive Data and Negative Counterexamples

Sanjay Jain[1,*] and Efim Kinber[2]

[1] School of Computing, National University of Singapore, Singapore 117543
sanjay@comp.nus.edu.sg
[2] Department of Computer Science, Sacred Heart University, Fairfield, CT
06432-1000, U.S.A.
kinbere@sacredheart.edu

Abstract. A model for learning in the limit is defined where a (so-called *iterative*) learner gets all positive examples from the target language, tests every new conjecture with a teacher (oracle) if it is a subset of the target language (and if it is not, then it receives a negative counterexample), and uses only limited long-term memory (incorporated in conjectures). Three variants of this model are compared: when a learner receives least negative counterexamples, the ones whose size is bounded by the maximum size of input seen so far, and arbitrary ones. We also compare our learnability model with other relevant models of learnability in the limit, study how our model works for indexed classes of recursive languages, and show that learners in our model can work in *non-U-shaped* way — never abandoning the first right conjecture.

1 Introduction

In 1967 E. M. Gold [Gol67] suggested an algorithmic model for learning languages and other possibly infinite concepts. This model, **TxtEx**, where a learner gets all *positive* examples and stabilizes on the right description (a grammar) for the target concept, was adopted by computer and cognitive scientists (see, for example, [Pin79]) as a basis for discussion on algorithmic modeling of certain cognitive processes. Since then other different formal models of algorithmic learning in the limit have been defined and discussed in the literature. One of the major questions stimulating this discussion is what type of input information can be considered reasonable in various potentially infinite learning processes. Another important question is what amount of input data a learner can store in its (long-term) memory. Yet another issue is the way how input data is communicated to the learner. In Gold's original model the learner is able to store potentially *all* input (positive) examples in its long-term memory; still, the latter assumption may be unrealistic for certain learning processes. Gold also considered a variant of his model where the learner receives all positive and *all negative* examples. However, while it is natural to assume that *some* negative data may be available to the

---

* Supported in part by NUS grant number R252-000-127-112.

learner, this variant, **InfEx**, though interesting from theoretical standpoint (for example, it can be used as a formal model for learning classes of functions, see [JORS99]), can hardly be regarded as adequate for most of the learning processes in question. R. Wiehagen in [Wie76] (see also [LZ96]) suggested a variant of the Gold's original model, so-called *iterative* learners, whose long-term memory cannot grow indefinitely (in fact, it is incorporated into the learner's conjectures). This model has been considered for learnability from all positive examples (denoted as **TxtIt**) and from all positive and all negative examples (**InfIt**). In her paper [Ang88], D. Angluin suggested a model of learnability, where data about the target concept is communicated to a learner in a way different from the Gold's model – it is supplied to the learner by a *minimally adequate teacher* (oracle) in response to *queries* from a learner. Angluin considered different type of queries, in particular, *membership* queries, where the learner asks if a particular word is in the target concept, and *subset* queries, where the learner tests if the current conjecture is a subset of the target language — if not, then the learner may get a *negative counterexample* from a teacher (subset queries and corresponding counterexamples help a learner to refute *overgeneralizing* wrong conjectures; K. Popper [Pop68] regarded refutation of overgeneralizing conjectures as a vital part of learning and discovery processes).

In [JK04], the authors introduced the model (**NCEx**) combining the Gold's model, **TxtEx**, and the Angluin's model: a **NCEx**-learner receives all positive examples of the target concept and makes subset query about each conjecture — receiving a negative counterexample if the answer is negative. This model is along the line of research related to the Gold's model for learnability from positive data in presence of *some* negative data (see also [Mot91, BCJ95]). Three variants of negative examples supplied by the teacher were considered: negative counterexamples of arbitrary size, if any (the main model **NCEx**), least counterexamples (**LNCEx**), and counterexamples whose size would be bounded by the maximum size of positive input data seen so far (**BNCEx**) — thus, reflecting complexity issues that the teacher might have. In this paper, we incorporate the limitation on the long-term memory reflected in the **It**-approach into all three above variants of learning from positive data and negative counterexamples: in our new model, **NCIt** (and its variations), the learner gets full positive data and asks a subset query about every conjecture, however, the long-term memory is a part of a conjecture, and, thus, cannot store indefinitely growing amount of input data (since, otherwise, the learner cannot stabilize to a single right conjecture). Thus, the learners in our model, while still getting full positive data, get just as many negative examples as necessary (a finite number, if the learner succeeds) and can use only a finite amount of long-term memory. We explore different aspects of our model. In particular, we compare all three variants between themselves and with other relevant models of algorithmic learning in the limit discussed above. We also study how our model works in the context of learning *indexed* (that is, effectively enumerable) classes of recursive languages (such popular classes as *pattern* languages (see [Ang80]) and regular languages are among them). In the end, we present a result that learners in our model can work in *non-U-shaped* way — not ever abandoning a right conjecture.

The paper is structured as follows. In Sections 2 and 3 we introduce necessary notation and formally introduce our and other relevant learnability models and establish trivial relationships between them. Section 4 is devoted to relationships between the three above mentioned variants of **NCIt**. First, we present a result that least examples do not have advantage over arbitrary ones — this result is similar to the corresponding result for **NCEx** obtained in [JK04], however, the (omitted) proof is more complex. Then we show that capabilities of iterative learners getting counterexamples of arbitrary size and those getting short counterexamples are incomparable. The fact that short counterexamples can sometimes help more than arbitrary ones is quite surprising: if a short counterexample is available, then an arbitrary one is trivially available, but not vice versa — this circumstance can be easily used by **NCEx**-learners to simulate **BNCEx**-learners, but not vice versa, as shown in [JK04]. However, it turns out that iterative learners can sometimes use the fact that a short counterexample *is not* available to learn concepts, for which arbitrary counterexamples are of no help at all!

Section 5 compares our models with other popular models of learnability in the limit. First, **TxtEx**-learners, capable of storing potentially all positive input data, can learn sometimes more than **NCIt**-learners, even if the latter ones are allowed to make a finite number of errors in the final conjecture. On the other hand, **NCIt**-learners can sometimes do more than the **TxtEx**-learners (being able to store all positive data). We also establish a difference between **NCIt** and **TxtEx** on yet another level: it turns out that adding an arbitrary recursive language to a **NCIt**-learnable class preserves its **NCIt**-learnability, while it is trivially not true for **TxtEx**-learners. An interesting — and quite unexpected — result is that **NCIt**-learners can simulate any **InfIt**-learner. Note that **InfIt** gets access to *full* negative data, whereas an **NCIt**-learner gets only finite number of negative counterexamples (although both of them are not capable of storing all input data)! Moreover, **NCIt**-learners can sometimes learn more than any **InfIt**-learner. The fact that **NCIt**-learners receive negative counterexamples to wrong "overinclusive" conjectures (that is conjectures which include elments outside the language) is exploited in the relevant proof. Here note that for **NCEx** and **InfEx**-learning where all data can be remembered, $\mathbf{NCEx} \subset \mathbf{InfEx}$. So the relationship between negative counterexamples and complete negative data differs quite a bit from the noniterative case.

In Section 6, we consider **NCIt**-learnability of indexed classes of recursive languages. Our main result here is that all such classes are **NCIt**-learnable. Note that it is typically not the case when just positive data is available — even with unbounded long-term memory. On the other hand, interestingly, there are indexed classes that are not learnable if a learner uses the set of programs computing just the languages from the given class as its hypotheses space (so-called *class-preserving* type of learning, see [ZL95]). That is, full learning power of **NCIt**-learners on indexed classes can only be reached, if subset queries can be posed for conjectures representing languages outside the class. Dependability of learning via queries in dependence of hypothesis space has been studied, in particular, in [LZ04].

In Section 7, we present a result that **NCIt**-learning can be done so that a learner never abandons a right conjecture (so-called *non-U-shaped* learning, see [BCM⁺05], became a popular subject in developmental psychology, see [Bow82]).

Due to space restrictions, some proofs are omitted. We refer the reader to [JK06a] for details.

2 Notation and Preliminaries

Any unexplained recursion theoretic notation is from [Rog67]. The symbol N denotes the set of natural numbers, $\{0, 1, 2, 3, \ldots\}$. Symbols $\emptyset$, $\subseteq$, $\subset$, $\supseteq$, and $\supset$ denote empty set, subset, proper subset, superset, and proper superset, respectively. Cardinality of a set S is denoted by $\mathrm{card}(S)$. The maximum and minimum of a set are denoted by $\max(\cdot), \min(\cdot)$, respectively, where $\max(\emptyset) = 0$ and $\min(\emptyset) = \infty$. $L_1 \boldsymbol{\Delta} L_2$ denotes the symmetric difference of L_1 and L_2, that is $L_1 \boldsymbol{\Delta} L_2 = (L_1 - L_2) \cup (L_2 - L_1)$. For a natural number a, we say that $L_1 =^a L_2$, iff $\mathrm{card}(L_1 \boldsymbol{\Delta} L_2) \leq a$. We say that $L_1 =^* L_2$, iff $\mathrm{card}(L_1 \boldsymbol{\Delta} L_2) < \infty$. Thus, we take $n < * < \infty$, for all $n \in N$. If $L_1 =^a L_2$, then we say that L_1 is an a-variant of L_2.

We let $\langle \cdot, \cdot \rangle$ stand for an arbitrary, computable, bijective mapping from $N \times N$ onto N [Rog67]. We assume without loss of generality that $\langle \cdot, \cdot \rangle$ is monotonically increasing in both of its arguments. Let $\mathrm{cyl}_i = \{\langle i, x \rangle \mid x \in N\}$.

By W_i we denote the i-th recursively enumerable set in some fixed acceptable numbering. We also say that i is a grammar for W_i. Symbol $\mathcal{E}$ will denote the set of all r.e. languages. Symbol L, with or without decorations, ranges over $\mathcal{E}$. By χ_L we denote the characteristic function of L. By $\overline{L}$, we denote the complement of L, that is $N - L$. Symbol $\mathcal{L}$, with or without decorations, ranges over subsets of $\mathcal{E}$. By $W_{i,s}$ we denote the set of elements enumerated in W_i within s steps. We assume without loss of generality that $W_{i,s} \subseteq \{x \mid x \leq s\}$.

We often need to use padding to be able to attach some relevant information to a grammar. $pad(j, \cdot, \cdot, \ldots)$ denotes a 1–1 recursive function (of appropriate number of arguments) such that $W_{pad(j, \cdot, \cdot, \ldots)} = W_j$. Such recursive functions can easily be shown to exist [Rog67].

We now present concepts from language learning theory. First, we introduce the concept of a *sequence* of data. A *sequence* σ is a mapping from an initial segment of N into $(N \cup \{\#\})$. The empty sequence is denoted by Λ. The *content* of a sequence σ, denoted $\mathrm{content}(\sigma)$, is the set of natural numbers in the range of σ. The *length* of σ, denoted by $|\sigma|$, is the number of elements in σ. So, $|\Lambda| = 0$. For $n \leq |\sigma|$, the initial sequence of σ of length n is denoted by $\sigma[n]$. So, $\sigma[0]$ is Λ.

Intuitively, $\#$'s represent pauses in the presentation of data. We let σ, τ, and γ, with or without decorations, range over finite sequences. We denote the sequence formed by the concatenation of τ at the end of σ by $\sigma \diamond \tau$. For simplicity of notation, sometimes we omit $\diamond$, when it is clear that concatenation is meant. SEQ denotes the set of all finite sequences.

A *text* (see [Gol67]) T for a language L is a mapping from N into $(N \cup \{\#\})$ such that L is the set of natural numbers in the range of T. $T(i)$ represents the $(i+1)$-th element in the text. The *content* of a text T, denoted by content(T), is the set of natural numbers in the range of T; that is, the language which T is a text for. $T[n]$ denotes the finite initial sequence of T with length n.

A *language learning machine from texts* [Gol67] is an algorithmic device which computes a (possibly partial) mapping from SEQ into N.

An *informant* (see [Gol67]) I is a mapping from N to $(N \times \{0,1\}) \cup \#$ such that for no $x \in N$, both $(x,0)$ and $(x,1)$ are in the range of I. content$(I) =$ set of pairs in the range of I (that is range$(I) - \{\#\}$). We say that a I is *an informant* for L iff content$(I) = \{(x, \chi_L(x)) \mid x \in N\}$. A *canonical informant* for L is the informant $(0, \chi_L(0))(1, \chi_L(1)) \ldots$. Intuitively, informants give both all positive and all negative data for the language being learned. $I[n]$ is the first n elements of the informant I. One can similarly define language learning machines from informants.

We let $\mathbf{M}$, with or without decorations, range over learning machines. $\mathbf{M}(T[n])$ (or $\mathbf{M}(I[n])$) is interpreted as the grammar (index for an accepting program) conjectured by the learning machine $\mathbf{M}$ on the initial sequence $T[n]$ (or $I[n]$). We say that $\mathbf{M}$ converges on T to i, (written: $\mathbf{M}(T)\!\downarrow = i$) iff $(\forall^\infty n)[\mathbf{M}(T[n]) = i]$. Convergence on informants is similarly defined.

There are several criteria for a learning machine to be successful on a language. Below we define some of them. All of the criteria defined below are variants of the **Ex**-style learning described in Introduction and its extension, *behaviourally correct*, or **Bc**-style learning (where a learner produces conjectures, almost all of which are correct, but not necessarily the same, see [CL82] for formal definition); in addition, they allow a finite number of errors in almost all conjectures (uniformly bounded number, or arbitrary).

Definition 1. [Gol67, CL82] Suppose $a \in N \cup \{*\}$.

(a) $\mathbf{M}$ $\mathbf{TxtEx}^a$-*identifies* a language L (written: $L \in \mathbf{TxtEx}^a(\mathbf{M})$) just in case, for all texts T for L, $(\exists i \mid W_i =^a L)$ $(\forall^\infty n)[\mathbf{M}(T[n]) = i]$.

(b) $\mathbf{M}$ $\mathbf{TxtEx}^a$-*identifies* a class $\mathcal{L}$ of r.e. languages (written: $\mathcal{L} \subseteq \mathbf{TxtEx}^a(\mathbf{M})$) just in case $\mathbf{M}$ $\mathbf{TxtEx}^a$-identifies each $L \in \mathcal{L}$.

(c) $\mathbf{TxtEx}^a = \{\mathcal{L} \subseteq \mathcal{E} \mid (\exists \mathbf{M})[\mathcal{L} \subseteq \mathbf{TxtEx}^a(\mathbf{M})]\}$.

If instead of convergence to a grammar on text T, we just require that all but finitely many grammars output by $\mathbf{M}$ on T are for an a-variant of content(T), (that is, $(\forall^\infty n)[W_{\mathbf{M}(T[n])} =^a L]$), then we get $\mathbf{TxtBc}^a$-identification. We refer the reader to [CL82] or [JORS99] for details.

Definition 2. [Gol67, CL82] Suppose $a \in N \cup \{*\}$.

(a) $\mathbf{M}$ $\mathbf{InfEx}^a$-*identifies* L (written: $L \in \mathbf{InfEx}^a(L)$), just in case for all informants I for L, $(\exists i \mid W_i =^a L)$ $(\forall^\infty n)[\mathbf{M}(I[n]) = i]$.

(b) $\mathbf{M}$ $\mathbf{InfEx}^a$-*identifies a class $\mathcal{L}$ of r.e. languages* (written: $\mathcal{L} \subseteq \mathbf{InfEx}^a(\mathbf{M})$) just in case $\mathbf{M}$ $\mathbf{InfEx}^a$-identifies each language from $\mathcal{L}$.

(c) $\mathbf{InfEx}^a = \{\mathcal{L} \subseteq \mathcal{E} \mid (\exists \mathbf{M})[\mathcal{L} \subseteq \mathbf{InfEx}^a(\mathbf{M})]\}$.

One can similarly define $\mathbf{InfBc}^a$-identification [CL82].

Intuitively, an iterative learner [Wie76, LZ96] is a learner whose hypothesis depends only on its last conjecture and current input. That is, for $n \geq 0$, $\mathbf{M}(T[n+1])$ can be computed algorithmically from $\mathbf{M}(T[n])$ and $T(n)$. Thus, one can describe the behaviour of $\mathbf{M}$ via a partial recursive function $F(p, x)$, where $\mathbf{M}(T[n+1]) = F(\mathbf{M}(T[n]), T(n))$. Here, note that $\mathbf{M}(T[0])$ is predefined to be some constant value. We will often identify F above with $\mathbf{M}$ (that is use $\mathbf{M}(p, x)$ to describe $\mathbf{M}(T[n+1])$, where $p = \mathbf{M}(T[n])$ and $x = T(n)$). This is for ease of notation.

Below we formally define $\mathbf{TxtIt}^a$. $\mathbf{InfIt}^a$ can be defined similarly.

Definition 3. [Wie76, LZ96]

(a) $\mathbf{M}$ $\mathbf{TxtIt}^a$-*identifies* $\mathcal{L}$, iff $\mathbf{M}$ $\mathbf{TxtEx}^a$-identifies $\mathcal{L}$, and for all σ, τ and x, if $\mathbf{M}(\sigma) = \mathbf{M}(\tau)$, then $\mathbf{M}(\sigma x) = \mathbf{M}(\tau x)$. We further assume that $\mathbf{M}(\sigma)$ is defined for all σ such that for some $L \in \mathcal{L}$, content$(\sigma) \subseteq L$.

(b) $\mathbf{TxtIt}^a = \{\mathcal{L} \mid (\exists \mathbf{M})[\mathbf{M}\ \mathbf{TxtIt}^a\text{-identifies } \mathcal{L}]\}$.

For $\mathbf{Ex}^a$ and $\mathbf{Bc}^a$ models of learning (for learning from texts or informants or their variants when learning from negative examples, as defined below), one may assume without loss of generality that the learners are total. However for iterative learning one cannot assume so. Thus, we explicitly require in the definition that iterative learners are defined on all inputs which are initial segments of texts (informants) for a language in the class.

Note that, although it is not stated explicitly, an $\mathbf{It}$-type learner might store some input data in its conjecture (thus serving as a limited long-term memory). However, the amount of stored data cannot grow indefinitely, as the learner must stabilize to one (right) conjecture

For $a = 0$, we often write $\mathbf{TxtEx}, \mathbf{TxtBc}, \mathbf{TxtIt}, \mathbf{InfEx}, \mathbf{InfBc}, \mathbf{InfIt}$ instead of $\mathbf{TxtEx}^0, \mathbf{TxtBc}^0, \mathbf{TxtIt}^0, \mathbf{InfEx}^0, \mathbf{InfBc}^0, \mathbf{InfIt}^0$, respectively.

Definition 4. [Ful90] σ is said to be a $\mathbf{TxtEx}$-*stabilizing sequence* for $\mathbf{M}$ on L, iff (a) content$(\sigma) \subseteq L$, and (b) for all τ such that content$(\tau) \subseteq L$, $\mathbf{M}(\sigma\tau) = \mathbf{M}(\sigma)$.

Definition 5. [BB75, Ful90] σ is said to be a $\mathbf{TxtEx}$-*locking sequence* for $\mathbf{M}$ on L, iff (a) σ is a $\mathbf{TxtEx}$-stabilizing sequence for $\mathbf{M}$ on L and (b) $W_{\mathbf{M}(\sigma)} = L$.

If $\mathbf{M}$ $\mathbf{TxtEx}$-identifies L, then every $\mathbf{TxtEx}$-stabilizing sequence for $\mathbf{M}$ on L is a $\mathbf{TxtEx}$-locking sequence for $\mathbf{M}$ on L. Furthermore, one can show that if $\mathbf{M}$ $\mathbf{TxtEx}$-identifies L, then for every σ such that content$(\sigma) \subseteq L$, there exists a $\mathbf{TxtEx}$-locking sequence, which extends σ, for $\mathbf{M}$ on L (see [BB75, Ful90]).

Similar result can be shown for $\mathbf{InfEx}, \mathbf{TxtBc}, \mathbf{InfBc}$ and other criteria of learning discussed in this paper. We will often drop $\mathbf{TxtEx}$ (and other criteria notation) from $\mathbf{TxtEx}$-stabilizing sequence and $\mathbf{TxtEx}$-locking sequence, when the criterion is clear from context.

$\mathcal{L}$ is said to be an *indexed family* of languages iff there exists an indexing $L_0, L_1, \ldots$ of languages in $\mathcal{L}$ such that the question $x \in L_i$ is uniformly decidable (i.e., there exists a recursive function f such that $f(i, x) = \chi_{L_i}(x)$).

3   Learning with Negative Counterexamples

In this section we formally define our models of learning from full positive data and negative counterexamples as given by [JK04]. Intuitively, for learning with negative counterexamples, we may consider the learner being provided a text, one element at a time, along with a negative counterexample to the latest conjecture, if any. (One may view this negative counterexample as a response of the teacher to the *subset query* when it is tested if the language generated by the conjecture is a subset of the target language). One may model the list of negative counterexamples as a second text for negative counterexamples being provided to the learner. Thus the learning machines get as input two texts, one for positive data, and other for negative counterexamples.

We say that $\mathbf{M}(T, T')$ converges to a grammar i, iff for all but finitely many n, $\mathbf{M}(T[n], T'[n]) = i$.

First, we define the basic model of learning from positive data and negative counterexamples. In this model, if a conjecture contains elements not in the target language, then a negative counterexample is provided to the learner. **NC** in the definition below stands for *negative counterexample*.

Definition 6. [JK04] Suppose $a \in N \cup \{*\}$.

(a) $\mathbf{M}$ **NCEx**^{a}*-identifies a language* L (written: $L \in \mathbf{NCEx}^a(\mathbf{M})$) iff for all texts T for L, and for all T' satisfying the condition:

$$T'(n) \in S_n, \text{ if } S_n \neq \emptyset \text{ and } T'(n) = \#, \text{ if } S_n = \emptyset,$$
$$\text{where } S_n = \overline{L} \cap W_{\mathbf{M}(T[n], T'[n])}$$

$\mathbf{M}(T, T')$ converges to a grammar i such that $W_i =^a L$.

(b) $\mathbf{M}$ **NCEx**^{a}*-identifies a class* $\mathcal{L}$ *of languages* (written: $\mathcal{L} \subseteq \mathbf{NCEx}^a(\mathbf{M})$), iff $\mathbf{M}$ **NCEx**^{a}-identifies each language in the class.

(c) $\mathbf{NCEx}^a = \{\mathcal{L} \mid (\exists \mathbf{M})[\mathcal{L} \subseteq \mathbf{NCEx}^a(\mathbf{M})]\}$.

For ease of notation, we sometimes define $\mathbf{M}(T[n], T'[n])$ also as $\mathbf{M}(T[n])$, where we separately describe how the counterexamples $T'(n)$ are presented to the conjecture of $\mathbf{M}$ on input $T[n]$.

One can similarly define **NCIt**^{a}-learning, where the learner's output depends only on the previous conjecture and the latest positive data and counterexample provided. In these cases, we sometimes denote the output $\mathbf{M}(T[n+1], T'[n+1])$, with $\mathbf{M}(p, T(n), T'(n))$, where $p = \mathbf{M}(T[n], T'[n])$ (here note that $\mathbf{M}(T[0], T'[0])$ is some predefined constant p_0).

As an example, consider the class $\{S \mid S \text{ is finite}\} \cup \{N\}$. This class is known not to be in **TxtEx**. One can learn the above class in **NCIt** as follows: Initially (on empty data) conjecture a grammar for N. If there is no counterexample, then we are done. Otherwise, one can just follow the strategy for learning finite sets, by storing all the input data.

Jain and Kinber [JK04] also considered the cases where

(i) negative counterexamples provided are the least ones (that is, in Definition 6(a), one uses $T'(n) = \min(S_n)$, instead of $T'(n) \in S_n$); The corresponding learning criterion is referred to as **LNCEx**^{a}, and

(ii) negative counterexamples are provided iff they are bounded by the largest element seen in $T[n]$ (that is, in Definition 6(a), one uses $S_n = \overline{L} \cap W_{\mathbf{M}(T[n],T'[n])} \cap \{x \mid x \leq \max(\text{content}(T[n]))\}$); The corresponding learning criterion is referred to as $\mathbf{BNCEx}^a$.

We refer the reader to [JK04] for details. One can similarly define $\mathbf{LNCIt}^a$, $\mathbf{BNCIt}^a$, and $\mathbf{BNCBc}^a$, $\mathbf{LNCBc}^a$, $\mathbf{BNCBc}^a$ criteria of learning.

It is easy to verify that, for $\mathbf{I} \in \{\mathbf{Ex}^a, \mathbf{Bc}^a, \mathbf{It}^a\}$, $\mathbf{TxtI} \subseteq \mathbf{BNCI}$, and $\mathbf{TxtI} \subseteq \mathbf{NCI} \subseteq \mathbf{LNCI}$. Also for $\mathbf{J} \in \{\mathbf{BNC}, \mathbf{NC}, \mathbf{LNC}\}$, for $a \in N \cup \{*\}$, $\mathbf{JIt}^a \subseteq \mathbf{JEx}^a \subseteq \mathbf{JBc}^a$.

4   Relationship Among Different Variations of NCIt-Criteria

In this section we compare all three variants of iterative learners using negative counterexamples. Our first result shows that least counterexamples do not give advantage to learners in our model. This result is similar to the corresponding result for $\mathbf{NCEx}$-learners ([JK04]), however, the omitted proof is more complex.

Theorem 1. *For all $a \in N \cup \{*\}$, $\mathbf{LNCIt}^a = \mathbf{NCIt}^a$.*

One of the variants of teacher's answers to subset queries in [Ang88] was just "yes" or "no". That is, the teacher just tells the learner that a counterexample exists, but does not provide it. The above result can be extended to work under these conditions also.

Now we will compare $\mathbf{NCIt}$-learning with its variant where the size of counterexamples is limited by the maximum size of the input seen so far. First we show that, surprisingly, short counterexamples can sometimes help to iteratively learn classes of languages not learnable by any $\mathbf{NCIt}$-learner. The proof exploits the fact that sometimes actually *absence* of short counterexamples can help in a situation when arbitrary counterexamples are useless!

Theorem 2. $\mathbf{BNCIt} - \mathbf{NCIt}^* \neq \emptyset$.

Proof. (sketch) Let $\mathcal{L}_1 = \{\{\langle 0, x \rangle \mid x \in W_e\} \mid e = \min(W_e), e \in N\}$.
Let $\mathcal{L}_2 = \{L \mid (\exists i, j \in N)[\text{card}(L \cap \text{cyl}_0) < \infty \text{ and } L \cap \text{cyl}_1 = \{\langle 1, \langle i, j \rangle \rangle\} \text{ and } (\forall w)[\langle 0, \langle i, w \rangle \rangle \notin L] \text{ and } (L - (\text{cyl}_0 \cup \text{cyl}_1)) = \{\langle 2, \langle x, k \rangle \rangle \mid x \in W_j, k \in N\}]\}$.
Let $\mathcal{L}_3 = \{L \mid (\exists i, j \in N, \text{ finite set } D)[$
$\text{card}(L \cap \text{cyl}_0) < \infty \text{ and } L \cap \text{cyl}_1 = \{\langle 1, \langle i, j \rangle \rangle\} \text{ and } (\exists w)[\langle 0, \langle i, w \rangle \rangle \in L] \text{ and } (L - (\text{cyl}_0 \cup \text{cyl}_1)) = \{\langle 2, \langle x, k \rangle \rangle \mid x \in D, k \in N\}]\}$.
   Let $\mathcal{L} = \mathcal{L}_1 \cup \mathcal{L}_2 \cup \mathcal{L}_3$.
   $\mathcal{L}$ can be shown to be in $\mathbf{BNCIt} - \mathbf{NCIt}^*$. Due to lack of space, we omit the details.   ∎

The next theorem shows that $\mathbf{NCIt}$-learners can sometimes do more than any $\mathbf{BNCBc}$-learner, even if the latter one is allowed to make finite number of errors in almost all conjectures.

Theorem 3. $(\mathbf{NCIt} \cap \mathbf{InfIt}) - \mathbf{BNCBc}^* \neq \emptyset$.

It can also be shown that there exists a class consisting of infinite languages which separates $\mathbf{NCIt}$ and $\mathbf{BNCIt}$. Note that $\mathbf{NCEx}$ and $\mathbf{BNCEx}$ have same power for classes consisting of infinite languages, as established in [JK06b].

One can also show anomaly hierarchy for the variations of $\mathbf{NCIt}^a$ criteria: $\mathbf{TxtIt}^{n+1} - \mathbf{LNCIt}^n \neq \emptyset$. This result follows directly from $\mathbf{TxtIt}^{n+1} - \mathbf{InfEx}^n \neq \emptyset$ (see [CS83]).

5   Comparison with Other Criteria of Learning

In this section we compare our model with other close relevant models of learnability in the limit. Our next two results show that learners that can store in their long-term memory potentially all positive data can sometimes learn more than any $\mathbf{BNCIt}/\mathbf{NCIt}$-learner.

Theorem 4. $\mathbf{TxtEx} - \mathbf{BNCIt}^* \neq \emptyset$.

Theorem 5. $\mathbf{TxtEx} - \mathbf{NCIt}^* \neq \emptyset$.

Proof. $\mathcal{L}$ used in Theorem 2 is also in $\mathbf{TxtEx}$.   ∎

The following theorem gives that $\mathbf{NCIt}$-learners (even $\mathbf{BNCIt}$-learners) can sometimes be more powerful than any $\mathbf{TxtBc}^*$-learner.

Theorem 6. $(\mathbf{BNCIt} \cap \mathbf{NCIt}) - \mathbf{TxtBc}^* \neq \emptyset$.

Now we will compare our model with iterative learners from informants. First, we show that there are $\mathbf{BNCIt}$-learnable ($\mathbf{NCIt}$-learnable) classes that cannot be learned from informants by any iterative learner. Thus, even just finite number of short negative data (received when necessary) can help iterative learners sometimes more than full negative data (most of it being forgotten by the learner).

Theorem 7. $(\mathbf{BNCIt} \cap \mathbf{NCIt}) - \mathbf{InfIt}^* \neq \emptyset$.

Proof. We give the proof only for $(\mathbf{BNCIt} \cap \mathbf{NCIt}) - \mathbf{InfIt} \neq \emptyset$. A complicated modification of this proof can be used to show that $(\mathbf{BNCIt} \cap \mathbf{NCIt}) - \mathbf{InfIt}^* \neq \emptyset$.

Let $\mathcal{L} = \{\{\langle 0, x \rangle \mid x \in W_e\} \mid e = \min(W_e), e \in N\} \cup \{L \mid (\exists x)[\langle 1, x \rangle \in L$ and $L - \{\langle 1, x \rangle\} \subseteq \{\langle 0, y \rangle \mid \langle 0, y \rangle \leq \langle 1, x \rangle\}]\}$.

It is easy to verify that the above class is in $\mathbf{BNCIt} \cap \mathbf{NCIt}$. (Initially just output a grammar for $\{\langle 0, x \rangle \mid x \in W_e\}$, for the minimal e such that $\langle 0, e \rangle$ is in the input, until it is found that the input language contains $\langle 1, x \rangle$ for some x. Then using the conjectures for $\{\langle 0, y \rangle\}$, for $\langle 0, y \rangle \leq \langle 1, x \rangle$, one can determine the elements of L.)

$\mathcal{L} \notin \mathbf{InfIt}$ can be shown as follows. Suppose by way of contradiction that $\mathbf{M}$ $\mathbf{InfIt}$-identifies $\mathcal{L}$. Note that $\mathbf{M}$ must be defined on all information segments σ such that $\{x \mid (x, 1) \in \text{content}(\sigma)\} \subseteq \{\langle 0, y \rangle \mid y \in N\}$, as $\mathbf{M}$ is defined on the information segments for languages in $\mathcal{L}$. Now, by implicit use of Kleene Recursion Theorem [Rog67], there exists an e such that W_e may be described as follows. Initially, $e \in W_e$. Let σ_0 be an information segment such that content$(\sigma_0) = \{(\langle 0, x \rangle, 0) \mid x < e\} \cup \{(\langle 0, e \rangle, 1)\}$. Let $z_0, z_1, \ldots$ be an enumeration of elements of $N - \{\langle 0, x \rangle \mid x \in N\}$. Suppose σ_s has been defined. Define σ_{s+1} as follows. If one of $\mathbf{M}(\sigma_s \diamond (z_s, 0) \diamond (\langle 0, e + s + 1 \rangle, 0))$ and $\mathbf{M}(\sigma_s \diamond (z_s, 0) \diamond (\langle 0, e + s + 1 \rangle, 1))$ is different from $\mathbf{M}(\sigma_s)$, then (i) let σ_{s+1} be $\sigma_s \diamond (z_s, 0) \diamond (\langle 0, e + s + 1 \rangle, w)$, where $w \in \{0, 1\}$ and $\mathbf{M}(\sigma_s) \neq \mathbf{M}(\sigma_{s+1})$ and (ii) enumerate $e + s + 1$ in W_e iff w chosen above is 1.

Now if σ_s is defined, for all s, then $\mathbf{M}$ diverges on $\bigcup_{s \in N} \sigma_s$, an informant for $\{\langle 0, x \rangle \mid x \in W_e\}$. On the other hand, if σ_{s+1} does not get defined (but σ_s does get defined), then fix k such that $\langle 1, k \rangle > \max(\{\langle 0, x \rangle \mid x \leq e + s + 1\} \cup \{z_r \mid r \leq s\})$, and let I be such that content$(I) = \{(\langle 0, x \rangle, 0) \mid x > e + s + 1\} \cup \{(z_r, 0) \mid r \in N, z_r \neq \langle 1, k \rangle\}$. Let $I_w = \sigma_s \diamond (z_s, 0) \diamond (\langle 0, e + s + 1 \rangle, w)(\langle 1, k \rangle, 1)I$. Note that I_1 is an informant for $L_1 = \{\langle 0, x \rangle \mid x \in W_e\} \cup \{\langle 1, k \rangle\} \cup \{\langle 0, e + s + 1 \rangle\}$ and I_0 is an informant for $L_0 = \{\langle 0, x \rangle \mid x \in W_e\} \cup \{\langle 1, k \rangle\}$.

It is easy to verify that $\mathbf{M}$ behaves in the same way on both of the above informants, and thus fails to **InfIt**-identify at least one of L_0 and L_1, both of which are in $\mathcal{L}$. ∎

Our next result, together with the above theorem, shows that **NCIt** is a proper superset of **InfIt**. Thus, just finite number of negative counterexamples received when the learner attempts to be "overinclusive" can do more than all negative counterexamples! Note that this is not true for **BNCIt**-learners, as, **InfIt** − **BNCIt** $\neq \emptyset$ follows from Theorem 3 (as **BNCIt** $\subseteq$ **BNCBc**, by definition). Below, an *initial information segment for L* denotes an initial information segment of canonical informant for L. First, we prove a useful technical lemma.

Lemma 1. *Suppose $\mathbf{M}$ **InfIt**^{a}-identifies L. Then for any initial information segment σ for L, if the following properties (a) to (c) are satisfied, then $W_{\mathbf{M}(\sigma)} =^a L$.*

(a) For all $x \in L$ such that $(x, 1) \notin$ content(σ), for some $\tau \subseteq \sigma$, $\mathbf{M}(\tau \diamond (x, 1)) = \mathbf{M}(\tau)$.

(b) For all but finitely many $x \in L$, $\mathbf{M}(\sigma \diamond (x, 1)) = \mathbf{M}(\sigma)$,

(c) $\{x \mid (x, 0) \notin$ content(σ) and $\mathbf{M}(\sigma \diamond (x, 0)) \downarrow \neq \mathbf{M}(\sigma) \downarrow\} \subseteq L$.

Proof. Let $S = \{x \in L \mid \mathbf{M}(\sigma \diamond (x, 1)) = \mathbf{M}(\sigma)\}$. Now $L - S$ is finite (by clause (b)). Let τ be a sequence formed by inserting each element $x \in L - S$ such that $(x, 1) \notin$ content(σ), in σ at places so that it does not cause a mind change (i.e., $x \in L - S$ such that $(x, 1) \notin$ content(σ) is inserted after $\sigma' \subseteq \sigma$, such that $\mathbf{M}(\sigma' \diamond (x, 1)) = \mathbf{M}(\sigma')$). Note that for all $x \in L - S$ such that $(x, 1) \notin$ content(σ), there exists such a σ' by clause (a). Now consider the information sequence $I = \tau I'$, where content$(I') = \{(x, 1) \mid x \in S\} \cup \{x, 0) \mid (x, 0) \notin$ content(σ) and $x \notin L\}$. Thus, I is an information sequence for L. Using the definition of S and (c), it is easy to verify that $\mathbf{M}(I) = \mathbf{M}(\sigma)$. Thus, $W_{\mathbf{M}(\sigma)} = W_{\mathbf{M}(I)} =^a L$, as $\mathbf{M}$ **InfIt**^{a}-identifies L. ∎

Now we show that any **InfIt**-learner can be simulated by a **NCIt**-learner.

Theorem 8. InfIt^a $\subseteq$ NCIt^a.

Proof. Suppose **M** **InfIt^a**-identifies $\mathcal{L}$. We construct **M$'$** which **NCIt^a**-identifies $\mathcal{L}$. Given a text T for $L \in \mathcal{L}$, the aim is to construct a σ satisfying (a) to (c) of Lemma 1.

Output of **M$'$** on $T[m]$ will be of form $pad(p_m, q_m, R_m, \sigma_m)$. The following invariants will be satisfied for all m.

(A) σ_m is an initial information segment for L. Moreover, $\sigma_m \subseteq \sigma_{m+1}$.

(B) $R_m \subseteq$ content($T[m]$), and for all $x \in$ content($T[m]$) $- R_m$, either $(x, 1) \in$ content(σ_m) or for some $\tau \subseteq \sigma_m$, $\mathbf{M}(\tau \diamond (x, 1)) = \mathbf{M}(\tau)$.

(C) If $q_m = 0$, then p_m is a grammar for the set $\{|\sigma_m|\}$. Note that $|\sigma_m|$ is the least element x such that neither $(x, 0)$ nor $(x, 1)$ belongs to content(σ_m).

(D) If $q_m = 1$, then p_m is a grammar for $\{x \mid (x, 0) \notin$ content(σ_m) and $\mathbf{M}(\sigma_m \diamond (x, 0)) \downarrow \neq \mathbf{M}(\sigma_m) \downarrow\}$. In this case, we will have additionally that $R_m = \emptyset$.

(E) If $q_m = 2$, then we have already tested that $\{x \mid (x, 0) \notin$ content(σ_m) and $\mathbf{M}(\sigma_m \diamond (x, 0)) \downarrow \neq \mathbf{M}(\sigma_m) \downarrow\} \subseteq L$. Additionally, $R_m = \emptyset$. Also in this case, $p_m = \mathbf{M}(\sigma_m)$.

Intuitively, we eventually want to search for σ_m which satisfies Lemma 1. We want to make sure that elements of L satisfy clause (a) in Lemma 1. R_m intuitively denotes the set of elements which may not (and thus need to be taken care of by extending σ_m). Note that we need to remember this set, as iterative learner could lose data. q_m intuitively keeps track of whether we are building up larger and larger σ_m or whether we are checking clause (c) in Lemma 1, or if this checking has already been done.

Initially on input Λ, **M$'$** outputs $(p, 1, \emptyset, \Lambda)$, where p is a grammar for $\{x \mid \mathbf{M}((x, 0)) \neq \mathbf{M}(\Lambda)\}$. Clearly, invariants (A) to (E) are satisfied.

Now **M$'$**, on the input $x = T(m)$, a counterexample y (on the conjecture of **M$'$** on $T[m]$) with previous conjecture being $pad(p_m, q_m, R_m, \sigma_m)$, outputs $pad(p_{m+1}, q_{m+1}, R_{m+1}, \sigma_{m+1})$ where the parameters $p_{m+1}, q_{m+1}, R_{m+1}, \sigma_{m+1}$ are defined as follows.

Case 1: $q_m = 0$.

Let $\sigma_{m+1} = \sigma_m \diamond (|\sigma_m|, w)$, where w is 1 or 0 based on whether the counterexample is $\#$ or a numerical value. Note that p_m was a grammar for $\{|\sigma_m|\}$.

Let $R_{m+1} = (R_m \cup \{x\}) - (\{\#\} \cup \{x' \mid (x', 1) \in$ content(σ_{m+1})$\} \cup \{x' \mid \mathbf{M}(\sigma_{m+1} \diamond (x', 1)) = \mathbf{M}(\sigma_{m+1})\})$.

If R_{m+1} is $\emptyset$, then let $q_{m+1} = 1$ and p_{m+1} be a grammar for $\{x' \mid (x', 0) \notin$ content(σ_{m+1}) and $\mathbf{M}(\sigma_{m+1} \diamond (x', 0)) \downarrow \neq \mathbf{M}(\sigma_{m+1}) \downarrow\}$. Else, let $q_{m+1} = 0$ and p_{m+1} be a grammar for $\{|\sigma_{m+1}|\}$.

Invariants (A), (C), (D) and (E) are easily seen to be satisfied. To see that invariant (B) is satisfied, note that by induction all $z \in$ content($T[m]$) $- R_m$, satisfied $[(z, 1) \in$ content(σ_m) or for some $\tau \subseteq \sigma_m$, $\mathbf{M}(\tau \diamond (z, 1)) = \mathbf{M}(\tau)]$. On the other hand if $z = T(m) = x, z \neq \#$ or if $z \in R_m$, then z is missing from R_{m+1} iff $(z, 1) \in$ content(σ_m) or $\mathbf{M}(\sigma_{m+1}\diamond(z, 1)) = \mathbf{M}(\sigma_{m+1})$. Thus, (B) is satisfied.

Case 2: $q_m = 1$.

Let $\sigma_{m+1} = \sigma_m$.

If there was a counterexample (i.e., $y \neq \#$), or $[x \neq \#$ and $(x, 1) \notin$ content(σ_m) and $\mathbf{M}(\sigma_m\diamond(x, 1)) \neq \mathbf{M}(\sigma_m)]$, then let $R_{m+1} = \{x\} - \{\#\}$, $q_{m+1} = 0$, and p_{m+1} be a grammar for $\{|\sigma_{m+1}|\}$.

Else (i.e., $y = \#$, and $[x = \#$ or $(x, 1) \in$ content(σ_m) or $\mathbf{M}(\sigma_m\diamond(x, 1)) = \mathbf{M}(\sigma_m)]$), then let $R_{m+1} = \emptyset$, $q_{m+1} = 2$, and $p_{m+1} = \mathbf{M}(\sigma_m)$.

Invariants (A), (C), (D) and (E) are easily seen to be satisfied. To see that invariant (B) is satisfied, note that by induction all $z \in$ content$(T[m])$, satisfied $(z, 1) \in$ content(σ_m) or for some $\tau \subseteq \sigma_m$, $\mathbf{M}(\tau\diamond(z, 1)) = \mathbf{M}(\tau)$. Also, $T(m) = x$ is placed in R_{m+1} if $(x \neq \#$ and $(x, 1) \notin$ content(σ_m) and $\mathbf{M}(\sigma_m\diamond(x, 1)) \neq \mathbf{M}(\sigma_m))$. Thus invariant (B) is also satisfied.

Case 3: $q_m = 2$.

Let $\sigma_{m+1} = \sigma_m$.

If $x \neq \#$ and $(x, 1) \notin$ content(σ_m) and $\mathbf{M}(\sigma_m\diamond(x, 1)) \neq \mathbf{M}(\sigma_m)$, then let $R_{m+1} = \{x\}$, $q_{m+1} = 0$ and p_{m+1} be a grammar for $\{|\sigma_{m+1}|\}$.

Else, let $R_{m+1} = \emptyset$, $q_{m+1} = 2$, and $p_{m+1} = \mathbf{M}(\sigma_m)$.

Invariants (A), (C), (D) are easily seen to be satisfied. If $q_{m+1} = 2$, then (E) also remains satisfied since q_m was also 2. To see that invariant (B) is satisfied, note that by induction all $z \in$ content$(T[m])$ satisfied $(z, 1) \in$ content(σ_m) or for some $\tau \subseteq \sigma_m$, $\mathbf{M}(\tau\diamond(z, 1)) = \mathbf{M}(\tau)$. Also, $T(m) = x$ is placed in R_{m+1} if $(x \neq \#$ and $(x, 1) \notin$ content(σ_m) and $\mathbf{M}(\sigma_m\diamond(x, 1)) \neq \mathbf{M}(\sigma_m))$. Thus invariant (B) is also satisfied.

Thus, the invariants are satisfied in all cases. Moreover, $\lim_{m\to\infty} \sigma_m$ converges, as for a large enough initial information segment σ_m for L, $\mathbf{M}(\sigma_m(x, \chi_L(x))) = \mathbf{M}(\sigma_m)$, for $(x, \chi_L(x)) \notin$ content(σ_m).

Also, it is easy to verify that if $q_m = 0$, then $\sigma_m \subset \sigma_{m+1}$. Thus, for all but finitely many m, $q_m \neq 0$. Also, if $q_m = 1$ or 2, then either $q_{m+1} = 2$ or $q_{m+1} = 0$. It follows that $\lim_{m\to\infty} q_m = 2$. Thus, by property (E), $\lim_{m\to\infty} R_m = \emptyset$. Hence, $\mathbf{M}'$ stabilizes to a conjecture of the form $(p, 2, \emptyset, \sigma)$, for some initial information segment σ for L — this σ satisfies (a) — (c) in Lemma 1, as otherwise Case 3 (along with properties (B) and (E)) would eventually ensure change of q_m, and the conjecture. Thus, $\mathbf{M}'$ $\mathbf{NCIt}^a$-identifies L, as it converges to a padded version of grammar $\mathbf{M}(\sigma)$. ∎

We already established that learners from full positive data with indefinitely growing long-term memory ($\mathbf{TxtEx}$) can sometimes learn more than any $\mathbf{NCIt}$-learner (Theorem 5). Now we consider this difference on yet another level. It can be easily demonstrated that adding a recursive language to a $\mathbf{TxtEx}$-learnable class does not always preserve its **TxtEx**-learnability (see, for example, [Gol67]). Our next result shows that adding one recursive language to a class in **NCIt**, still leaves it in **NCIt**. (Note that the same result was obtained in [JK04] for **NCEx**-learners, however, the algorithm witnessing the simulation there was nearly trivial — unlike our simulation in the omitted proof of the following theorem).

Theorem 9. *If $\mathcal{L} \in$ **NCIt** and X is recursive, then $\mathcal{L} \cup \{X\} \in$ **NCIt**.*

This result cannot be extended to r.e. X. For all r.e., but non-recursive sets A, $\{A \cup \{x\} \mid x \notin A\}$ is in **NCIt**. However [JK04] showed that, for r.e. but non-recursive A, $\{A\} \cup \{A \cup \{x\} \mid x \notin A\}$ is not in **LNCEx**.

6   Results Related to Indexed Families

In this section we consider **NCIt**-learning for indexed classes of recursive languages — one of the popular learning tasks (as it was mentioned in the Introduction, such popular subjects of learning as *patterns* and *regular languages* are examples of indexed classes). Note that these classes are often not learnable if only (full) positive and no negative data is available even if a learner can potentially hold all input in the long-term memory, as was established yet by Gold ([Gol67]). Note also that there exist indexed families which are not in **BNCBc*** (see [JK04]). Our main result in this section is that all such classes are **NCIt**-learnable.

Theorem 10. *Every indexed family $\mathcal{L}$ is in **NCIt**.*

The complexity of the algorithm witnessing the Theorem above is underscored by the following result showing that **NCIt**-learning of some indexed classes $\mathcal{L}$ becomes impossible if a learner wants to use a class preserving hypothesis space [ZL95] (that is, uses a hypothesis space $H_0, H_1, \ldots$ such that $\{H_i \mid i \in N\} = \mathcal{L}$, and for all i, x, one can effectively decide in i and x whether $x \in H_i$).

Theorem 11. *There exists an indexed family $\mathcal{L}$ such that $\mathcal{L}$ is not **NCIt**-learnable using a class preserving hypothesis space.*

Note that if we only consider indexed families consisting of infinite languages, then class preserving learning can be done.

By Theorem 7, in the general case, **NCIt**-learners can sometimes do more than **InfIt***-learners. However, as the next theorem shows, their capabilities on indexed classes are the same. Still, **InfIt**^{n}-learners cannot learn some indexed classes.

Theorem 12. *(a) If $\mathcal{L}$ is an indexed family, then $\mathcal{L} \in$ **InfIt***.
(b) $\mathcal{L} = \{\mathrm{cyl}_0 \cup \mathrm{cyl}_1\} \cup \{\mathrm{cyl}_0 \cup D \mid D \subseteq \mathrm{cyl}_1, \mathrm{card}(D) < \infty\} \notin \bigcup_{n \in N}$ **InfIt**^{n}.*

7 Non-U-shaped Learning

A learner is said to be *non-U-shaped* if it does not abandon a correct hypothesis ([BCM⁺05]). That is, its sequence of conjectures does not show a pattern of ..., correct conjecture, wrong conjecture, ..., correct conjecture.

We can show that the requirement of being non-U-shaped does not hurt **NCIt**-learning.

Theorem 13. LNCIt $\subseteq$ NUNCIt.

Acknowledgements. We thank the anonymous referees of ALT for several helpful comments.

References

[Ang80]   D. Angluin. Finding patterns common to a set of strings. *Journal of Computer and System Sciences*, 21:46–62, 1980.

[Ang88]   D. Angluin. Queries and concept learning. *Machine Learning*, 2:319–342, 1988.

[BB75]   L. Blum and M. Blum. Toward a mathematical theory of inductive inference. *Information and Control*, 28:125–155, 1975.

[BCJ95]   G. Baliga, J. Case, and S. Jain. Language learning with some negative information. *Journal of Computer and System Sciences*, 51(5):273–285, 1995.

[BCM⁺05] G. Baliga, J. Case, W. Merkle, F. Stephan, and R. Wiehagen. When unlearning helps. Manuscript, http://www.cis.udel.edu/~case/papers/decisive.ps, 2005.

[Bow82]   M. Bowerman. Starting to talk worse: Clues to language acquisition from children's late speech errors. In S. Strauss and R. Stavy, editors, *U-Shaped Behavioral Growth*. Developmental Psychology Series. Academic Press, New York, 1982.

[CL82]   J. Case and C. Lynes. Machine inductive inference and language identification. In M. Nielsen and E. M. Schmidt, editors, *Proceedings of the 9th International Colloquium on Automata, Languages and Programming*, volume 140 of *Lecture Notes in Computer Science*, pages 107–115. Springer-Verlag, 1982.

[CS83]   J. Case and C. Smith. Comparison of identification criteria for machine inductive inference. *Theoretical Computer Science*, 25:193–220, 1983.

[Ful90]   M. Fulk. Prudence and other conditions on formal language learning. *Information and Computation*, 85:1–11, 1990.

[Gol67]   E. M. Gold. Language identification in the limit. *Information and Control*, 10:447–474, 1967.

[JK04]   S. Jain and E. Kinber. Learning languages from positive data and negative counterexamples. In Shai Ben-David, John Case, and Akira Maruoka, editors, *Algorithmic Learning Theory: Fifteenth International Conference (ALT' 2004)*, volume 3244 of *Lecture Notes in Artificial Intelligence*, pages 54–68. Springer-Verlag, 2004.

[JK06a]   S. Jain and E. Kinber. Iterative learning from positive data and nega-
             tive counterexamples. Technical Report TRA3/06, School of Computing,
             National University of Singapore, 2006.

[JK06b]   S. Jain and E. Kinber. Learning languages from positive data and negative
             counterexamples. *Journal of Computer and System Sciences*, 2006. To
             appear.

[JORS99]   S. Jain, D. Osherson, J. Royer, and A. Sharma. *Systems that Learn: An
             Introduction to Learning Theory.* MIT Press, Cambridge, Mass., second
             edition, 1999.

[LZ96]   S. Lange and T. Zeugmann. Incremental learning from positive data.
             Journal of Computer and System Sciences, 53:88–103, 1996.

[LZ04]   S. Lange and S. Zilles. Comparison of query learning and Gold-style learn-
             ing in dependence of the hypothesis space. In Shai Ben-David, John Case,
             and Akira Maruoka, editors, *Algorithmic Learning Theory: Fifteenth In-
             ternational Conference (ALT' 2004)*, volume 3244 of *Lecture Notes in Ar-
             tificial Intelligence*, pages 99–113. Springer-Verlag, 2004.

[Mot91]   T. Motoki. Inductive inference from all positive and some negative data.
             Information Processing Letters, 39(4):177–182, 1991.

[Pin79]   S. Pinker. Formal models of language learning. *Cognition*, 7:217–283,
             1979.

[Pop68]   K. Popper. *The Logic of Scientific Discovery.* Harper Torch Books, New
             York, second edition, 1968.

[Rog67]   H. Rogers. *Theory of Recursive Functions and Effective Computability.*
             McGraw-Hill, 1967. Reprinted by MIT Press in 1987.

[Wie76]   R. Wiehagen. Limes-Erkennung rekursiver Funktionen durch spezielle
             Strategien. *Journal of Information Processing and Cybernetics (EIK)*,
             12:93–99, 1976.

[ZL95]   T. Zeugmann and S. Lange. A guided tour across the boundaries of learn-
             ing recursive languages. In K. Jantke and S. Lange, editors, *Algorithmic
             Learning for Knowledge-Based Systems*, volume 961 of *Lecture Notes in
             Artificial Intelligence*, pages 190–258. Springer-Verlag, 1995.

Towards a Better Understanding of Incremental Learning

Sanjay Jain[1,*], Steffen Lange[2], and Sandra Zilles[3]

[1] School of Computing, National University of Singapore, Singapore 117543
sanjay@comp.nus.edu.sg
[2] FB Informatik, Hochschule Darmstadt, Haardtring 100, D–64295 Darmstadt
slange@fbi.h-da.de
[3] DFKI GmbH, Erwin-Schrödinger-Str. 57, D–67663 Kaiserslautern
zilles@dfki.de

Abstract. The present study aims at insights into the nature of incremental learning in the context of Gold's model of identification in the limit. With a focus on natural requirements such as consistency and conservativeness, incremental learning is analysed both for learning from positive examples and for learning from positive and negative examples. The results obtained illustrate in which way different consistency and conservativeness demands can affect the capabilities of incremental learners. These results may serve as a first step towards characterising the structure of typical classes learnable incrementally and thus towards elaborating uniform incremental learning methods.

1 Introduction

Considering data mining tasks, where specific knowledge has to be induced from a huge amount of more or less unstructured data, several approaches have been studied empirically in machine learning and formally in the field of learning theory. These approaches differ in terms of the form of interaction between the learning machine and its environment. For instance, scenarios have been analysed, where the learner receives instances of some target concept to be identified or where the learner may pose queries concerning the target concept [6, 2, 11]. For learning from examples, one critical aspect is the limitation of a learning machine in terms of its memory capacity. In particular, if huge amounts of data have to be processed, it is conceivable that this capacity is too low to memorise all relevant information during the whole learning process. This has motivated the analysis of so-called *incremental learning*, cf. [4, 5, 7, 8, 9, 12], where in each step of the learning process, the learner has access only to a limited number of examples. Thus, in each step, its hypothesis can be built upon these examples and its former hypothesis, only. Other examples seen before have to be 'forgotten'.

It has been analysed how such constraints affect the capabilities of learning machines, thus revealing models in which certain classes of target concepts are

---

* Supported in part by NUS grant number R252-000-127-112 and R252-000-212-112.

J.L. Balcázar, P.M. Long, and F. Stephan (Eds.): ALT 2006, LNAI 4264, pp. 169–183, 2006.

learnable, but not learnable in an incremental manner. However, some quite natural constraints for successful learning have mainly been neglected in the corresponding studies. These constraints are (a) the requirement for *consistent* learning, i. e., the demand that none of the intermediate hypotheses a learner explicates should contradict the data processed so far, and (b) the requirement for *conservative* learning, i. e., the demand that each intermediate hypothesis should be maintained as long as it is consistent with the data seen.

The fact that there is no comprehensive analysis of how these demands affect the capabilities of incremental learners can be traced back to a lack of knowledge about the nature of incremental learning. In particular, there is no formal basis explaining typical or uniform ways for solving learning tasks in an incremental way. In terms of learning theory, incremental learning is one of the very few models, for which no characterisation of the typical structure of learnable classes is known. For other models of learning from examples, characterisations and uniform learning methods have often been the outcome of analysing the impact of consistency or conservativeness, see, e. g., [13]. Thus, also in the context of incremental learning, it is conceivable that studying these natural requirements may yield insights into typical learning methods. In other words, analysing consistency and conservativeness may be the key for a better understanding of the nature of incremental learning and may thus, in the long term, provide characterisations of learnable classes and uniform incremental learning methods.

The present study aims at insights into the nature of incremental learning in the context of Gold's model of learning in the limit from examples [6]. For that purpose, we analyse Wiehagen's version of incremental learning, namely *iterative learning* [12] with a focus on consistent and conservative learners. In Gold's approach, learning is considered as an infinite process, where in each step the learner is presented an example e_n for the target concept and is supposed to return an intermediate hypothesis. In the limit, the hypotheses must stabilise on a correct representation of the target concept. Here, in step $n+1$ of the learning process, the learner has access to all examples $e_0, \ldots, e_n$ provided up to step n plus the current example e_{n+1}. In contrast, an iterative learner has no capacities for memorising any examples seen so far, i. e., its hypothesis h_{n+1} in step $n+1$ is built only upon the example e_{n+1} and its previous hypothesis h_n.

The present paper addresses consistency and conservativeness in the context of iterative learning. Here several possible ways to formalise the demands for consistency and conservativeness become apparent. Assume an iterative learner has processed the examples $e_0, \ldots, e_{n+1}$ for some target concept and returns some hypothesis h_{n+1} in step $n+1$. From a global perspective, one would define h_{n+1} consistent, if it agrees with the examples $e_0, \ldots, e_{n+1}$. But since the learner has not memorised $e_0, \ldots, e_n$, it might be considered natural to just demand that h_{n+1} agrees with the current example e_{n+1}. This is justified from a rather local perspective. Similarly, when defining conservativeness from a global point of view, one might demand that $h_{n+1} = h_n$ in case h_n does not contradict any of the examples $e_0, \ldots, e_{n+1}$, whereas a local variant of conservativeness would mean to require that $h_{n+1} = h_n$ in case h_n does not contradict the current example e_{n+1}.

Note that local consistency is a weaker requirement than global consistency, whereas local conservativeness is stronger than global conservativeness.

In the present paper, we restrict our focus on recursive languages as target concepts [1, 13]. In particular, the target classes are required to be indexable, i.e., there exist algorithms deciding the membership problem uniformly for all possible target languages. This restriction is motivated by the fact that many classes of target concepts relevant for typical learning tasks are indexable.

The paper is structured as follows. In Section 2, we provide the definitions and notations necessary for our formal analysis. Then Section 3 is concerned with a case study of iterative learning of regular erasing pattern languages – a quite natural and simple to define indexable class which has shown to be suitable for representing target concepts in many application scenarios. This case study shows how consistency and conservativeness may affect the learnability of such pattern languages in case quite natural hypothesis spaces are chosen for learning. Section 4 focuses on consistency in iterative learning. It has turned out, that iterative learners can be normalised to work in a locally consistent way, whereas global consistency is a constraint reducing the capabilities of iterative learners. Both results hold for learning from positive examples as well as for learning from both positive and negative examples. Section 5 then is concerned with conservativeness. Here we show that, in the scenario of learning from only positive examples, the effects of global conservativeness demands and local conservativeness demands are equal, as far as the capabilities of iterative learners are concerned. In contrast to that there are classes which can be learned iteratively from positive and negative examples by a globally conservative learner, but not in a locally conservative manner. Concerning the effect of weak conservativeness demands (i.e., of global conservativeness), we can show that they strictly reduce the capabilities of iterative learners which are given both positive and negative examples as information. However, the corresponding comparison in the case of learning from only positive examples is still open. In our point of view, not only the mere results presented here, but in particular the proof constructions and separating classes give an impression of characteristic methods of iterative learning and characteristic properties of iteratively learnable classes, even though we cannot provide a formal characterisation yet. Section 6 contains our conclusions.

2   Preliminaries

Let Σ be a fixed finite alphabet, Σ^* the set of all finite strings over Σ, and Σ^+ its subset excluding the empty string. $|w|$ denotes the length of a string w. Any non-empty subset of Σ^* is called a *language*. For any language L, $co(L) = \Sigma^* \setminus L$. $\mathbb{N}$ is the set of all natural numbers. If L is a language, then any infinite sequence $t = (w_j)_{j \in \mathbb{N}}$ with $\{w_j \mid j \in \mathbb{N}\} = L$ is called a *text* for L. Moreover, any infinite sequence $i = ((w_j, b_j))_{j \in \mathbb{N}}$ over $\Sigma^* \times \{+, -\}$ such that $\{w_j \mid j \in \mathbb{N}\} = \Sigma^*$, $\{w_j \mid j \in \mathbb{N}, b_j = +\} = L$, and $\{w_j \mid j \in \mathbb{N}, b_j = -\} = co(L)$ is referred to as an *informant* for L. Then, for any $n \in \mathbb{N}$, $t[n]$ and $i[n]$ denote the initial segment of t and i of length $n + 1$, while $t(n) = w_n$ and $i(n) = (w_n, b_n)$.

Furthermore, $content(t[n]) = \{w_j \mid j \leq n\}$. Let $content(i[n])$, $content^+(i[n])$, and $content^-(i[n])$ denote the sets $\{(w_j, b_j) \mid j \leq n\}$, $\{w_j \mid j \leq n, b_j = +\}$, and $\{w_j \mid j \leq n, b_j = -\}$.

A family $(L_j)_{j\in\mathbb{N}}$ of languages is called an *indexing* for a class $\mathcal{C}$ of recursive languages, if $\mathcal{C} = \{L_j \mid j \in \mathbb{N}\}$ and there is a recursive function f such that $L_j = \{w \in \Sigma^* \mid f(j, w) = 1\}$ for all $j \in \mathbb{N}$. $\mathcal{C}$ is called an *indexable class* (of recursive languages), if $\mathcal{C}$ possesses an indexing.

In our proofs, we will use a fixed Gödel numbering $(\varphi_j)_{j\in\mathbb{N}}$ of all (and only all) partial recursive functions over $\mathbb{N}$ as well as an associated complexity measure $(\Phi_j)_{j\in\mathbb{N}}$, see [3]. Then, for $k, x \in \mathbb{N}$, φ_k is the partial recursive function computed by program k and we write $\varphi_k(x) \downarrow (\varphi_k(x) \uparrow)$, if $\varphi_k(x)$ is defined (undefined).

2.1   Learning from Text

Let $\mathcal{C}$ be an indexable class, $\mathcal{H} = (L_j)_{j\in\mathbb{N}}$ any indexing of some $\mathcal{C}' \supseteq \mathcal{C}$ (called *hypothesis space*), and $L \in \mathcal{C}$. An *inductive inference machine* (*IIM* for short) M is an algorithmic device that reads longer and longer initial segments σ of a text and outputs numbers $M(\sigma)$ as its hypotheses. An IIM M returning some j is construed to hypothesise the language L_j. The following definition of learning from positive data is based on Gold [6]. Given a text t for L, M *learns L from t with respect to* $\mathcal{H}$, if (a) the sequence of hypotheses output by M, when fed t, stabilises on a number j (* i. e., past some point M always outputs the hypothesis j *) and (b) this number j fulfils $L_j = L$.

An *iterative inductive inference machines* is only allowed to use its previous hypothesis and the current string in a text for computing its current hypothesis. More formally, an *iterative* IIM M is an algorithmic device that maps elements from $\mathbb{N} \cup \{init\} \times \Sigma^*$ into $\mathbb{N}$, where $init$ denotes a fixed initial 'hypothesis' which the IIM may never output. Let $t = (w_n)_{n\in\mathbb{N}}$ be any text for some language $L \subseteq \Sigma^*$. Then we denote by $(M[init, t[n]])_{n\in\mathbb{N}}$ the sequence of hypotheses generated by M when processing t, i.e., $M[init, w_0] = M(init, w_0)$ and, for all $n \in \mathbb{N}$, $M[init, t[n+1]] = M(M[init, t[n]], w_{n+1})$.

Definition 1. *[12] Let $\mathcal{C}$ be an indexable class, $\mathcal{H} = (L_j)_{j\in\mathbb{N}}$ a hypothesis space, and $L \in \mathcal{C}$. An iterative IIM M learns L from text with respect to $\mathcal{H}$ iff, for any text $t = (w_n)_{n\in\mathbb{N}}$ for L, the sequence $(M[init, t[n]])_{n\in\mathbb{N}}$ stabilises on a number j with $L_j = L$. Moreover, M learns $\mathcal{C}$ from text with respect to $\mathcal{H}$, if it identifies every $L' \in \mathcal{C}$ from text with respect to $\mathcal{H}$. Finally, It Txt denotes the collection of all indexable classes $\mathcal{C}'$ for which there is a hypothesis space $\mathcal{H}'$ and an iterative IIM learning $\mathcal{C}'$ from text with respect to $\mathcal{H}'$.*

In the definition of *consistent learning*, a hypothesis of a learner is said to be consistent, if it reflects the data it was built upon correctly. Since an iterative IIM M, when processing some text t, is only allowed to use its previous hypothesis, say $L_{j'}$, and the current string v in t for computing its current hypothesis L_j, it is quite natural to distinguish two variants of consistent learning. In the first case, it is demanded that L_j contains all elements of t seen so far, while, in the second case, it is only required that L_j contains the string v.

Definition 2. *Let C be an indexable class, $\mathcal{H} = (L_j)_{j\in\mathbb{N}}$ a hypothesis space, and M an iterative IIM. M is globally (locally) consistent for C iff content$(t[n]) \subseteq L_{M[init,t[n]]}$ $(t(n) \in L_{M[init,t[n]]})$ for every text segment $t[n]$ for some $L \in C$. Finally, ItGConsTxt (ItLConsTxt) denotes the collection of all indexable classes C' for which there is a hypothesis space $\mathcal{H}'$ and an iterative IIM which is globally (locally) consistent for C' and learns C' from text with respect to $\mathcal{H}'$.*

Finally we consider *conservative learning*. Informally speaking, a conservative learner maintains its current hypothesis as long as the latter does not contradict any data seen. Hence, whenever a conservative IIM changes its recent hypothesis, this must be justified by data having occurred which prove an inconsistency of its recent hypothesis. Similarly to the case of consistent iterative learning, it is quite natural to distinguish two variants of conservativeness.

Definition 3. *Let C be an indexable class, $\mathcal{H} = (L_j)_{j\in\mathbb{N}}$ be a hypothesis space, and M be an iterative IIM. M is globally (locally) conservative for C iff, for every text segment $t[n+1]$ for some $L \in C$, $M[init,t[n+1]] \neq M[init,t[n]]$ implies content$(t[n+1]) \nsubseteq L_{M[init,t[n]]}$ (implies $t(n+1) \notin L_{M[init,t[n]]}$). Finally, ItGConvTxt (ItLConvTxt) denotes the collection of all indexable classes C' for which there is a hypothesis space $\mathcal{H}'$ and an iterative IIM which is globally (locally) conservative for C' and learns C' from text with respect to $\mathcal{H}'$.*

Note that we allow a mind change from *init* after the first input data is received.

2.2   Learning from Informant

For all variants of *ItTxt* considered so far we define corresponding models capturing the case of learning from informant. Now an iterative IIM M maps $\mathbb{N} \times (\Sigma^* \times \{+, -\})$ into $\mathbb{N}$. Let $i = (w_n, b_n)_{n\in\mathbb{N}}$ be any informant for some language L, and let *init* be a fixed initial hypothesis. Then $(M[init, i[n]])_{n\in\mathbb{N}}$ is the sequence of hypotheses by M processing i, i.e., $M[init, (w_0, b_0)] = M(init, (w_0, b_0))$ and, for all $n \in \mathbb{N}$, $M[init, i[n+1]] = M(M[init, i[n]], (w_{n+1}, b_{n+1}))$.

Definition 4. *[12] Let C be an indexable class, $\mathcal{H} = (L_j)_{j\in\mathbb{N}}$ a hypothesis space, and $L \in C$. An iterative IIM M learns L from informant with respect to $\mathcal{H}$, iff for every informant i for L, the sequence $(M[init, i[n]])_{n\in\mathbb{N}}$ stabilises on a number j with $L_j = L$. Moreover, M learns C from informant with respect to $\mathcal{H}$, if M learns every $L' \in C$ from informant with respect to $\mathcal{H}$.*

The notion *ItInf* is defined similarly to the text case. Now also the consistency and conservativeness demands can be formalised. For instance, for consistency, let C be an indexable class, $\mathcal{H} = (L_j)_{j\in\mathbb{N}}$ a hypothesis space, and M an iterative IIM. M is globally (locally) consistent for C iff content$^+(i[n]) \subseteq L_{M[init,i[n]]}$ and content$^-(i[n]) \subseteq co(L_{M[init,i[n]]})$ ($b = +$ for $w \in L_{M[init,i[n]]}$ and $b = -$ for $w \notin L_{M[init,i[n]]}$) for every informant segment $i[n]$ for some $L \in C$, where $i(n) = (w, b)$. Finally, the definitions of *ItGConsInf, ItLConsInf, ItGConvInf, ItLConvInf* can be adapted from the text case to the informant case.

3   A Case Study: The Regular Erasing Pattern Languages

Let Σ be any fixed finite alphabet. Let $X = \{x_1, x_2, \ldots\}$ be an infinite set of variables, disjoint with Σ. A *regular pattern* α is a string from $(\Sigma \cup X)^+$ which contains every variable at most once. Let α be a regular pattern. Then $L_\varepsilon(\alpha)$, the *regular erasing pattern language* generated by α, contains all strings in Σ^* that can be obtained by replacing the variables in α by strings from Σ^*, see, e.g., [10]. Note that $L_\varepsilon(\alpha)$ constitutes a regular language. Subsequently, let $\mathcal{C}_{\mathrm{rp}}$ denote the collection of all regular erasing pattern languages.

Our first result can be achieved by adapting a standard idea, see, e.g., [4].

Theorem 1. *There is a learner witnessing both* $\mathcal{C}_{\mathrm{rp}} \in \mathit{ItGConsTxt}$ *and* $\mathcal{C}_{\mathrm{rp}} \in \mathit{ItLConvTxt}$.

Sketch of the proof. Let $(D_j)_{j \in \mathbb{N}}$ be the canonical enumeration of all finite subsets of $\mathbb{N}$ and $(L_\varepsilon(\alpha_j))_{j \in \mathbb{N}}$ be an effective, repetition-free indexing of $\mathcal{C}_{\mathrm{rp}}$. Moreover let $L'_j = \bigcap_{z \in D_j} L_\varepsilon(\alpha_z)$. Hence $(L'_j)_{j \in \mathbb{N}}$ is an indexing comprising the class $\mathcal{C}_{\mathrm{rp}}$. The proof is essentially based on the following fact.

Fact 1. *There is an algorithm A which, given any string $w \in \Sigma^+$ as input, outputs an index j such that* $D_j = \{z \in \mathbb{N} \mid w \in L_\varepsilon(\alpha_z)\}$.

A learner M witnessing $\mathcal{C}_{\mathrm{rp}} \in \mathit{ItGConsTxt}$ and $\mathcal{C}_{\mathrm{rp}} \in \mathit{ItLConvTxt}$ with respect to $(L')_{j \in \mathbb{N}}$ may simply work as follows:

Initially, if the first string w appears, M starts its subroutine A, determines $j = A(w)$, and guesses the language L'_j, i.e., $M(init, w) = j$. Next M, when receiving a new string v, refines its recent hypothesis, say j', as follows. M determines the canonical index j of the set $\{z \mid z \in D_{j'}, v \in L_\varepsilon(\alpha_z)\} \subseteq D_{j'}$ and guesses the languages L'_j, i.e., $M(j', v) = j$.

It is not hard to see that M learns as required.   □

Although the iterative learner M used in this proof is locally conservative and globally consistent, M has the disadvantage of guessing languages not contained in the class of all regular erasing pattern languages. At first glance, it might seem that this weakness can easily be compensated, since the final guess returned by M is always a regular erasing pattern language and, moreover, one can effectively determine whether or not the recent guess of M equals a regular erasing pattern language. Surprisingly, even under this quite 'perfect' circumstances, it is impossible to replace M by an iterative, locally conservative, and globally consistent learner for $\mathcal{C}_{\mathrm{rp}}$ that hypothesises languages in $\mathcal{C}_{\mathrm{rp}}$, exclusively.

Theorem 2. *Let* $card(\Sigma) \geq 2$. *Let* $(L_j)_{j \in \mathbb{N}}$ *be any indexing of* $\mathcal{C}_{\mathrm{rp}}$. *Then there is no learner M witnessing both* $\mathcal{C}_{\mathrm{rp}} \in \mathit{ItGConsTxt}$ *and* $\mathcal{C}_{\mathrm{rp}} \in \mathit{ItLConvTxt}$ *with respect to* $(L_j)_{j \in \mathbb{N}}$.

Proof. Let $\{a, b\} \subseteq \Sigma$. Assume to the contrary that there is an iterative learner M which learns $\mathcal{C}_{\mathrm{rp}}$ locally conservatively and globally consistently, hypothesising only regular erasing pattern languages. Consider M for any text of some $L \in \mathcal{C}_{\mathrm{rp}}$ with the initial segment $\sigma = aba, aab$. Since M must avoid overgeneralised hypotheses, there are only two possible semantically different hypotheses which are globally consistent with σ, namely x_1abx_2 and ax_1ax_2. Distinguish two cases:

Case (a). $L_{M[init,\sigma]} = L_\varepsilon(x_1abx_2)$.

Consider M processing $\sigma_1 = \sigma ab, aa$ and $\sigma_2 = \sigma aa$. Since $ab \in L_\varepsilon(x_1abx_2)$ and M is locally conservative for $\mathcal{C}_{\mathrm{rp}}$, we obtain $M[init, \sigma ab] = M[init, \sigma]$. For reasons of global consistency, $L_{M[init,\sigma_1]} = L_\varepsilon(ax_1)$. Now, since $M[init, \sigma ab] = M[init, \sigma]$, this yields $L_{M[init,\sigma_2]} = L_\varepsilon(ax_1)$. However, σ_2 can be extended to a text for $L_\varepsilon(ax_1ax_2)$, on which M will fail to learn locally conservatively, since $M[init, \sigma_2]$ overgeneralises the target. This contradicts the assumptions on M.

Case (b). $L_{M[init,\sigma]} = L_\varepsilon(ax_1ax_2)$.

Here a similar contradiction can be obtained for M processing $\sigma_1 = \sigma aa, ab$ and $\sigma_2 = \sigma ab$.

Both cases yield a contradiction and thus the theorem is verified. $\square$

However, as Theorems 3 and 4 show, each of our natural requirements, in its stronger formulation, can be achieved separately, if an appropriate indexing of the regular erasing pattern languages is used as a hypothesis space. We provide the proof only for the first result; a similar idea can be used also for Theorem 4.

Theorem 3. *There is an indexing $(L_j^*)_{j\in\mathbb{N}}$ of $\mathcal{C}_{\mathrm{rp}}$ and a learner M witnessing $\mathcal{C}_{\mathrm{rp}} \in ItLConvTxt$ with respect to $(L_j^*)_{j\in\mathbb{N}}$.*

Proof. As in the proof of Theorem 1, let $(D_j)_{j\in\mathbb{N}}$ be the canonical enumeration of all finite subsets of $\mathbb{N}$ and $(L_\varepsilon(\alpha_j))_{j\in\mathbb{N}}$ an effective, repetition-free indexing of $\mathcal{C}_{\mathrm{rp}}$. Moreover let $L'_j = \bigcap_{z\in D_j} L_\varepsilon(\alpha_z)$ for all $j \in \mathbb{N}$. Hence $(L'_j)_{j\in\mathbb{N}}$ is an indexing comprising the class $\mathcal{C}_{\mathrm{rp}}$. The proof is based on the following fact.

Fact 2. *There is an algorithm A' which, given any index j as input, outputs an index k with $L_\varepsilon(\alpha_k) = L'_j$, if such an index exists, and 'no', otherwise.*

(* Since every regular erasing pattern language is a regular language and both the inclusion problem as well as the equivalence problem for regular languages are decidable, such an algorithm A' exists. *)

The required iterative learner uses the algorithm A' and the iterative learner M from the demonstration of Theorem 1 as its subroutines. Let $(L_{\langle k,j\rangle}^*)_{k,j\in\mathbb{N}}$ be an indexing of $\mathcal{C}_{\mathrm{rp}}$ with $L_{\langle k,j\rangle}^* = L_\varepsilon(\alpha_k)$ for all $k, j \in \mathbb{N}$. We define an iterative learner M' for $\mathcal{C}_{\mathrm{rp}}$ that uses the hypothesis space $(L_{\langle k,j\rangle}^*)_{k,j\in\mathbb{N}}$.

Initially, if the first string w appears, M' determines the canonical index k of the regular erasing pattern language $L_\varepsilon(w)$ as well as $j = M(init, w)$, and outputs the hypothesis $\langle k, j\rangle$, i.e., $M'(init, w) = \langle k, j\rangle$. Next M', when receiving a string v, refines its recent hypothesis, say $\langle k', j'\rangle$, as follows. First, if $v \in L_{\langle k',j'\rangle}^*$, M' repeats its recent hypothesis, i.e., $M'(\langle k', j'\rangle, v) = \langle k', j'\rangle$. (* Note that $j' = M(j', v)$, too. *) Second, if $v \notin L_{\langle k',j'\rangle}^*$, M' determines $j = M(j', v)$ and runs A' on input j. If A' returns some $k \in \mathbb{N}$, M' returns $\langle k, j\rangle$, i.e., $M'(\langle k', j'\rangle, v) = \langle k, j\rangle$. If A' returns 'no', M' determines the canonical index k of the regular erasing pattern language $L_\varepsilon(v)$ and returns $\langle k, j\rangle$, i.e., $M'(\langle k', j'\rangle, v) = \langle k, j\rangle$.

By definition, M' is an iterative and locally conservative learner. Let t be any text for any $L \in \mathcal{C}_{\mathrm{rp}}$. Since M learns L, there is some n such that $M[init, t[n]] = j$ with $L'_j = L$. By definition, for $\langle k, j \rangle = M'[init, t[n]]$, we have $L_\varepsilon(\alpha_k) = L'_j$. Thus $L^*_{\langle k,j \rangle} = L_\varepsilon(\alpha_k)$. Since M' is a locally conservative learner, M' learns L, too. $\square$

Theorem 4. *There is an indexing $(L_j)_{j \in \mathbb{N}}$ of $\mathcal{C}_{\mathrm{rp}}$ and a learner M witnessing $\mathcal{C}_{\mathrm{rp}} \in It\,GCons\,Txt$ with respect to $(L_j)_{j \in \mathbb{N}}$.*

This case study shows that the necessity of auxiliary hypotheses representing languages outside the target class may depend on whether both global consistency and local conservativeness or only one of these properties is required. In what follows, we analyse the impact of consistency and conservativeness separately in a more general context, assuming that auxiliary hypotheses are allowed.

4   Incremental Learning and Consistency

This section is concerned with the impact of consistency demands in iterative learning. In the case of learning from text, the weaker consistency demand, namely local consistency, does not restrict the capabilities of iterative learners.

Theorem 5. *$It\,LCons\,Txt = It\,Txt$.*

Proof. By definition, $It\,LCons\,Txt \subseteq It\,Txt$. To prove $It\,Txt \subseteq It\,LCons\,Txt$, fix an indexable class $\mathcal{C} \in It\,Txt$. Let $(L_j)_{j \in \mathbb{N}}$ be an indexing comprising $\mathcal{C}$ and M an iterative learner for $\mathcal{C}$ with respect to $(L_j)_{j \in \mathbb{N}}$.

The required learner M' uses the indexing $(L'_{\langle j,w \rangle})_{j \in \mathbb{N}, w \in \Sigma^*}$, where $L'_{\langle j,w \rangle} = L_j \cup \{w\}$ for all $j \in \mathbb{N}$, $w \in \Sigma^*$. Initially, $M'(init, w) = \langle j, w \rangle$ for $j = M(init, w)$. Next M', upon a string v, refines its recent hypothesis, say $\langle j', w' \rangle$, as follows. First, M' determines $j = M(j', v)$. Second, if $v \in L_j$, M returns $\langle j, w' \rangle$; otherwise, it returns $\langle j, v \rangle$. Obviously, M' witnesses $\mathcal{C} \in It\,LCons\,Txt$. $\square$

In contrast to that, requiring local consistency results in a loss of learning potential, as the following theorem shows.

Theorem 6. *$It\,GCons\,Txt \subset It\,Txt$.*

Proof. By definition, $It\,GCons\,Txt \subseteq It\,Txt$. It remains to provide a separating class $\mathcal{C}$ that witnesses $It\,Txt \setminus It\,GCons\,Txt \neq \emptyset$.

Let $\Sigma = \{a, b\}$ and let $(A_j)_{j \in \mathbb{N}}$ be the canonical enumeration of all finite subsets of $\{a\}^+$. Now $\mathcal{C}$ contains the language $L = \{a\}^+$ and, for all $j \in \mathbb{N}$, the finite language $L_j = A_j \cup \{b^z \mid z \leq j\}$.

Claim 1. $\mathcal{C} \in It\,Txt$.

The required iterative learner M may work as follows. As long as exclusively strings from $\{a\}^+$ appear, M just guesses L. If a string of form b^j appears for the first time, M guesses L_j. Past that point, M, when receiving a string v, refines its recent guess, say L_k, as follows. If $v \in L$ or $v = b^z$ for some $z \leq k$, M repeats its guess L_k. If $v = b^z$ for some $z > k$, M guesses L_z.

It is not hard to verify that M is an iterative learner that learns $\mathcal{C}$ as required.

Claim 2. $\mathcal{C} \notin ItGConsTxt$.

Suppose to the contrary that there is an indexing $(L'_j)_{j \in \mathbb{N}}$ comprising $\mathcal{C}$ and a learner M witnessing $\mathcal{C} \in ItGConsTxt$ with respect to $(L'_j)_{j \in \mathbb{N}}$.

Consider M when processing the text $t = a^1, a^2, \ldots$ for L. Since M is a learner for $\mathcal{C}$, there has to be some n such that $M[init, t[n]] = M[init, t[n+m]]$ for all $m \geq 1$. (* Note that $M[init, t[n]] = M[init, t[n]a^z]$ for all $z > n+1$. *)

Now let j be fixed such that $A_j = content(t[n]) = \{a^1, \ldots, a^{n+1}\}$. Consider M when processing any text $\hat{t}$ for L_j with $\hat{t}[n] = t[n]$. Since M is a learner for $\mathcal{C}$, there is some $n' > n$ such that $content(\hat{t}[n']) = L_j$ as well as $L'_k = L_j$ for $k = M[init, \hat{t}[n']]$. (* Note that there is some finite sequence σ with $\hat{t}[n'] = t[n]\sigma$. *)

Next let $j' > j$ be fixed such that $A_j \subset A_{j'}$. Moreover fix any string a^z in $A_{j'} \setminus A_j$. (* Note that $z > n+1$ and $a^z \notin L_j$. *) Consider M when processing any text $\tilde{t}$ for the language $L_{j'}$ having the initial segment $\tilde{t}[n'+1] = t[n]a^z\sigma$. Since $M[init, t[n]] = M[init, t[n]a^z]$, one obtains $M[init, \tilde{t}[n+1]] = M[init, \hat{t}[n]]$. Finally since M is an iterative learner, $\hat{t}[n'] = \hat{t}[n]\sigma$, and $\tilde{t}[n'+1] = \tilde{t}[n+1]\sigma$, one may conclude that $M[init, \tilde{t}[n'+1]] = M[init, \hat{t}[n']] = k$. But $L'_k = L_j$, and therefore $a^z \notin L'_k$. The latter implies $content(\tilde{t}[n'+1]) \not\subseteq L'_k$, contradicting the assumption that M is an iterative and globally consistent learner for $\mathcal{C}$.   □

In the case of learning from informant, the results obtained are parallel to those in the text case. Theorem 7 can be verified similarly to Theorem 5.

Theorem 7. *ItLConsInf = ItConsInf.*

Considering the stronger consistency requirement, there are even classes learnable iteratively from text, but not globally consistently from informant.

Theorem 8. *It Txt \ It GConsInf $\neq \emptyset$.*

Proof. It suffices to provide a class $\mathcal{C} \in ItTxt \setminus ItGConsInf$.

Let $\Sigma = \{a, b\}$ and let $(A_j)_{j \in \mathbb{N}}$ be the canonical enumeration of all finite subsets of $\{a\}^+$. Now $\mathcal{C}$ contains the language $L = \{a\}^+$ and, for all $j, k \in \mathbb{N}$, the finite language $L_{\langle j, k \rangle} = A_j \cup A_k \cup \{b^j, b^k\}$.

Claim 1. $\mathcal{C} \in ItTxt$.

The required iterative learner M may work as follows. As long as only strings from $\{a\}^+$ appear, M guesses L. If a string of form b^z appears for the first time, M guesses $L_{\langle z, z \rangle}$. Past that point, M refines its recent guess, say $L_{\langle j', k' \rangle}$, when receiving a string v as follows. If $j' = k'$ and $v = b^z$ with $z \neq j'$, M guesses $L_{\langle j', z \rangle}$. In all other cases, M repeats its guess $L_{\langle j', k' \rangle}$.

It is not hard to verify that M is an iterative learner that learns $\mathcal{C}$ as required.

Claim 2. $\mathcal{C} \notin ItGConsInf$.

Suppose to the contrary that there is an indexing $(L'_j)_{j \in \mathbb{N}}$ comprising $\mathcal{C}$ and a learner M witnessing $\mathcal{C} \in ItGConsInf$ with respect to $(L'_j)_{j \in \mathbb{N}}$.

Consider an informant $i = ((w_n, b_n)_{n \in \mathbb{N}})$ for L such that $|w_n| \leq n$ for all $n \in \mathbb{N}$. Since M is a learner for $\mathcal{C}$, there has to be some n such that $M[init, i[n]] = M[init, i[n+m]]$ for all $m \geq 1$. (* Note that $M[init, i[n]] = M[init, i[n](a^z, +)]$ for all $z > n+1$. *)

Let j be fixed such that $content^+(i[n]) \subseteq A_j$ and $b^j \notin content^-(i[n])$. Now consider M when processing an informant $\hat{\imath}$ for $L_{\langle j,j \rangle}$ with $\hat{\imath}[n] = i[n]$. Since M is a learner for $\mathcal{C}$, there has to be some $n' > n$ such that $content(\hat{\imath}[n']) = L_{\langle j,j \rangle}$ and $L'_k = L_{\langle j,j \rangle}$ for $k = M[init, \hat{\imath}[n']]$. (* Note that there is some finite sequence σ such that $\hat{\imath}[n'] = i[n]\sigma$. *)

Now let $k' > j$ be fixed such that $A_j \subset A_{k'}$, $content^-(\hat{\imath}[n]) \cap A_{k'} = \emptyset$, and $b^{k'} \notin content^-(\hat{\imath}[n])$. Let a^z be any string in $A_{k'} \setminus A_j$. (* Note that $z > n+1$ and $a^z \notin L_{\langle j,j \rangle}$. *) Consider M when processing any informant $\tilde{\imath}$ for the language $L_{\langle j,k' \rangle}$ with $\tilde{\imath}[n'+1] = i[n](a^z, +)\sigma$. Since $M[init, i[n]] = M[init, i[n](a^z, +)]$, one obtains $M[init, \tilde{\imath}[n+1]] = M[init, \hat{\imath}[n]]$. Finally since M is an iterative learner, $\hat{\imath}[n'] = \hat{\imath}[n]\sigma$, and $\tilde{\imath}[n'+1] = \tilde{\imath}[n+1]\sigma$, one may conclude that $M[init, \tilde{\imath}[n'+1]] = M[init, \hat{\imath}[n']] = k$. But $L'_k = L_{\langle j,j \rangle}$, and therefore $a^z \notin L'_k$. The latter implies $content^+(\tilde{\imath}[n'+1]) \not\subseteq L'_k$, contradicting the assumption that M is an iterative and globally consistent learner for $\mathcal{C}$.   □

Obviously $It\,Txt \subseteq It\,Inf$, and thus we obtain the following corollary.

Corollary 1. $It\,GConsInf \subset It\,Inf$.

5   Incremental Learning and Conservativeness

This section deals with conservativeness in the context of iterative learning. Here the results for learning from text differ from those for the informant case.

5.1   The Case of Learning from Text

Let us first discuss the different conservativeness definitions in the context of learning from positive examples only. By definition, local conservativeness is a stronger demand, since the learner is required to maintain a hypothesis if it is consistent with the most recent piece of information, even if it contradicts some previously processed examples. However, it turns out that this demand does not have any negative effect on the capabilities of iterative learners. Intuitively, a globally conservative learner may change mind depending on inconsistency with only a limited set of examples, which can be coded within the hypothesis.

Theorem 9. $It\,GConv\,Txt = It\,LConv\,Txt$.

Proof. By definition, $It\,LConv\,Txt \subseteq It\,GConv\,Txt$. Fix an indexable class $\mathcal{C} \in It\,GConv\,Txt$; let $(L_j)_{j \in \mathbb{N}}$ be an indexing and M an iterative IIM identifying $\mathcal{C}$ globally conservatively with respect to $(L_j)_{j \in \mathbb{N}}$. It remains to prove $\mathcal{C} \in It\,LConv\,Txt$. For that purpose, we need the following notion and technical claim.

Notion. For any text t and any $n \in \mathbb{N}$, let $mc(t[n], M)$ denote the set $\{t(0)\} \cup \{t(m) \mid 1 \leq m \leq n$ and $M[init, t[m-1]] \neq M[init, t[m]]\}$ of all strings in $content(t[n])$, which force M to change its mind when processing $t[n]$.

Technical claim. Let $L \in \mathcal{C}$, t a text for L, and $n \in \mathbb{N}$. Let $j = M[init, t[n]]$. If $t(n+1) \cup mc(t[n], M) \subseteq L_j$, then $M[init, t[n+1]] = M[init, t[n]]$.

Proof. Let $W = content(t[n + 1]) \setminus L_j$. As $t(n + 1) \cup mc(t[n], M) \subseteq L_j$, then $M[init, t[m + 1]] = M[init, t[m]]$ for all $m < n$ with $t(m + 1) \in W$. Now let τ be the subsequence of $t[n]$ obtained by deleting all $w \in W$ from $t[n]$. Obviously, $M[init, \tau] = M[init, t[n]]$ and $mc(t[n], M) \subseteq content(\tau) \subseteq L_j$. This implies

$$M[init, t[n + 1]] = M[init, \tau t(n + 1)] = M[init, \tau] = M[init, t[n]],$$

because M is globally conservative for L. (QED, technical claim).

Define an indexing $(L'_j)_{j \in \mathbb{N}}$ by $L'_{2\langle j,k\rangle} = L_j$ and $L'_{2\langle j,k\rangle+1} = \emptyset$ for all $j, k \in \mathbb{N}$.

We now define an IIM M' (witnessing $\mathcal{C} \in ItLConvTxt$ using $(L'_j)_{j \in \mathbb{N}}$), such that, on any finite text segment σ for some $L \in \mathcal{C}$, the following invariant holds:

$M'[init, \sigma] = 2\langle M[init, \sigma], k\rangle + y$ for some $k \in \mathbb{N}$, $y \in \{0, 1\}$, such that
- $D_k = mc(\sigma, M)$ (* and thus $D_k \subseteq content(\sigma)$ *).
- If $y = 0$, then $D_k \subseteq L_{M[init, \sigma]}$.

The reader may check that this invariant holds, if M' is defined as follows:
Definition of $M'(init, w)$, for $w \in \Sigma^*$: Let $j = M(init, w)$.

- If $w \in L_j$, let $M'(init, w) = 2\langle j, k\rangle$, where $D_k = \{w\}$.
- If $w \notin L_j$, let $M'(init, w) = 2\langle j, k\rangle + 1$, where $D_k = \{w\}$.

Definition of $M'(2\langle j, k\rangle + 1, w)$, for $w \in \Sigma^*$, $j, k \in \mathbb{N}$: Let $j' = M(j, w)$.

- If $j = j'$ and $D_k \subseteq L_j$, let $M'(2\langle j, k\rangle + 1, w) = 2\langle j, k\rangle$.
- If $j = j'$ and $D_k \nsubseteq L_j$, let $M'(2\langle j, k\rangle + 1, w) = 2\langle j, k\rangle + 1$.
- If $j \neq j'$, let $M'(2\langle j, k\rangle + 1, w) = 2\langle j', k'\rangle + 1$, where $D_{k'} = D_k \cup \{w\}$.

Definition of $M'(2\langle j, k\rangle, w)$, for $w \in \Sigma^*$, $j, k \in \mathbb{N}$: Let $j' = M(j, w)$.

- If $w \notin L_j$ and $j = j'$, let $M'(2\langle j, k\rangle, w) = 2\langle j, k\rangle + 1$.
- If $w \notin L_j$ and $j \neq j'$, let $M'(2\langle j, k\rangle, w) = 2\langle j', k'\rangle + 1$, where $D_{k'} = D_k \cup \{w\}$.
- If $w \in L_j$ (* by the invariant, there is some text segment σ with $M[init, \sigma] = j$ and $D_k = mc(\sigma, M) \subseteq L_j$; hence $D_k \cup \{w\} \subseteq L_j$ and $j = j'$ by the technical claim *), let $M'(2\langle j, k\rangle, w) = 2\langle j, k\rangle$.

By definition, M' is locally conservative with respect to $(L'_j)_{j \in \mathbb{N}}$. Since M is globally conservative for $\mathcal{C}$ with respect to $(L_j)_{j \in \mathbb{N}}$ and because of the invariant, it is not hard to verify that M' learns $\mathcal{C}$ iteratively. Thus $\mathcal{C} \in ItLConvTxt$. □

So local and global conservativeness are equal constraints for iterative text learners. Whether they reduce the capabilities of iterative text learners in general, i.e., whether $ItGConvTxt$ and $ItTxt$ coincide, remains an open question.

5.2   The Case of Learning from Informant

First, comparing the two versions of conservativeness, the informant case yields results different from those in the text case, namely that globally conservative iterative learners cannot be normalised to being locally conservative. In particular, the property that globally conservative learners can code all previously seen examples, for which their current hypothesis is inconsistent, no longer holds in the informant case.

Theorem 10. *ItLConvInf $\subset$ ItGConvInf.*

Proof. By definition, *ItLConvInf $\subseteq$ ItGConvInf*. Thus it remains to provide a separating class $\mathcal{C}$ that witnesses *ItGConvInf* \ *ItLConvInf* $\neq \emptyset$.

Let $\Sigma = \{a\}$ and $(D_j)_{j\in\mathbb{N}}$ the canonical enumeration of all finite subsets of $\{a\}^+$. Assume $D_0 = \emptyset$. For all $j \in \mathbb{N}$, set $L_j = \{a^0\} \cup D_j$ and $L'_j = \{a\}^+ \setminus D_j$. Let $\mathcal{C}$ be the collection of all finite languages L_j and all co-finite languages L'_j.

Claim 1. $\mathcal{C} \in$ *ItGConvInf.*

For all $j, k, z \in \mathbb{N}$, let $H_{2\langle j,k,z\rangle} = \{a\}^+ \setminus \{a^z\}$ and $H_{2\langle j,k,z\rangle+1} = \{a^z\}$. Now the required iterative learner M, processing an informant $i = ((w_n, b_n))_{n\in\mathbb{N}}$ for some $L \in \mathcal{C}$ may work as follows.

(i) As long as neither $(a^0, +)$ nor $(a^0, -)$ appear, M guesses — depending on whether or not $(w_0, b_0) = (a^z, +)$ or $(w_0, b_0) = (a^z, -)$ — in the first case $H_{2\langle j,k,z\rangle}$, in the second case $H_{2\langle j,k,z\rangle+1}$, where $D_j = content^+(i[n])$ and $D_k = content^-(i[n])$ (* The recent guess of M is inconsistent, so M can change its mind without violating the global conservativeness demand. *)

(ii) If $(a^0, +)$ or $(a^0, -)$ appears for the first time, the following cases will be distinguished. If $w_0 = a^0$ and $b_0 = +$, M guesses L_0. If $w_0 = a^0$ and $b_0 = -$, M guesses L'_0. Otherwise, let $j' = 2\langle j, k, z\rangle + y$, $y \in \{0,1\}$, denote the recent guess of M. If $(a^0, +)$ appears, M' guesses the finite language L_j. If $(a^0, -)$ appears, M' guesses the co-finite language L'_k.

(iii) Then M refines its recent guess as follows. If a positive example $(a^z, +)$ appears, the recent guess of M is $L_{j'}$, and $a^z \notin L_{j'}$, M guesses $L_j = L_{j'} \cup \{a^z\}$. If a negative example $(a^z, -)$ appears, the recent guess of M is $L'_{k'}$, and $a^z \in L'_{k'}$, M guesses $L'_k = L'_{k'} \setminus \{a^z\}$. Else M repeats its recent guess.

It is not hard to verify that M is an iterative learner that learns $\mathcal{C}$ as required.

Claim 2. $\mathcal{C} \notin$ *ItLConvInf.*

Suppose to the contrary that there is an indexing $(L^*_j)_{j\in\mathbb{N}}$ comprising $\mathcal{C}$ and a learner M which locally conservatively identifies $\mathcal{C}$ with respect to $(L^*_j)_{j\in\mathbb{N}}$.

Let $j = M(init, (a, +))$. We distinguish the following cases:

Case 1. $L^*_j \cap \{a\}^+$ is infinite.

Choose $a^r \in L^*_j$ with $r > 1$ and $L = \{a^0, a^1, a^r\}$. Consider M on the informant $i = (a, +), (a^r, +), (a^0, +), (a^2, -), \ldots, (a^{r-1}, -), (a^{r+1}, -), (a^{r+2}, -), \ldots$ for L. As M learns $\mathcal{C}$, there is an $n \geq 2$ with $M[init, i[n]] = M[init, i[n + m]]$ for all $m \geq 1$. (* $M[init, i[n](a^s, -)] = M[init, i[n]]$ for all a^s with $a^s \notin (content^+(i[n]) \cup content^-(i[n]))$. *) Let a^s be any string in L^*_j with $s > r + 1$, $a^s \notin (content^+(i[n]) \cup content^-(i[n]))$. As $L_j \cap \{a\}^+$ is infinite, such a^s exists. (* There is some σ with $i = (a, +), (a^r, +)\sigma(a^{s-1}, -), (a^s, -), (a^{s+1}, -), \ldots$ *)

Next let $\hat{\imath} = (a^1, +), (a^r, +), (a^s, +)\sigma(a^{s-1}, -), (a^{s+1}, -), (a^{s+2}, -), \ldots$ Consider M when processing the informant $\hat{\imath}$ for $L' = \{a^0, a^1, a^r, a^s\}$. Since M is locally conservative and $a^s \in L^*_j$, $M[init, \hat{\imath}[2]] = M[init, i[1]]$. As M is an iterative learner, $M[init, \hat{\imath}[n + 1]] = M[init, i[n]]$. Past step $n + 1$, M receives only negative examples $(a^z, -)$ with $a^z \notin (content^+(i[n]) \cup content^-(i[n]))$. Hence M converges on $\hat{\imath}$ to the same hypothesis j as on i, namely to $j = M[init, i[n]]$. Finally because $L \neq L'$, M cannot learn both finite languages L and L'.

Case 2. $L_j^* \cap \{a\}^+$ is finite.

An argumentation similar to that used in Case 1 shows that M must fail to learn some co-finite language in $\mathcal{C}$. We omit the relevant details. $\qquad \square$

The observed difference in the above theorem can now even be extended to a proper hierarchy of iterative learning from informant; globally conservative learners in general outperform locally conservative ones, but are not capable of solving all the learning tasks a general iterative learner can cope with. So there are classes in *ItInf* which cannot be learned by any iterative, globally conservative learner.

Theorem 11. *ItGConvInf* $\subset$ *ItInf*.

Proof. By definition, *ItGConvInf* $\subseteq$ *ItInf*. Thus it remains to provide a separating class $\mathcal{C}$ that witnesses *ItInf* \ *ItGConvInf* $\neq \emptyset$.

Let $(D_j)_{j \in \mathbb{N}}$ be the canonical enumeration of all finite subsets of $\mathbb{N}$.

Let $\mathcal{C} = \bigcup_{k \in \mathbb{N}} \mathcal{C}_k$, where $\mathcal{C}_k$ are defined below based on following cases.

Case (a). If $\varphi_k(k) \uparrow$, then $\mathcal{C}_k$ contains just one language, namely $L_k = \{a^k\}$.

Case (b). If $\varphi_k(k) \downarrow$, then $\mathcal{C}_k$ contains infinitely many languages. Let $s = \Phi_k(k)$. For all $j \in \mathbb{N}$, $\mathcal{C}_k$ contains the language $L_{\langle k,j \rangle} = L_k \cup \{b^s\} \cup \{c^{s+z} \mid z \in D_j\}$ as well as the language $L'_{\langle k,j \rangle} = L_k \cup \{c^{s+z} \mid z \notin D_j\}$. (* Note that $L_{\langle k,j \rangle}$ contains a finite subset of $\{c\}^*$, whereas $L'_{\langle k,j \rangle}$ contains a co-finite subset of $\{c\}^*$. *)

It is not hard to verify that $\mathcal{C}$ constitutes an indexable class.

Claim 1. $\mathcal{C} \in$ *ItInf*.

Let $i = ((w_n, b_n))_{n \in \mathbb{N}}$ be an informant for some $L \in \mathcal{C}$. A corresponding iterative learner M may be informally defined as follows:

(i) As long as no positive example $(a^k, +)$ appears, M' encodes in its guess all examples seen so far.

(ii) If some positive example $(a^k, +)$ appears, M' tests whether or not $\Phi_k(k) \leq |w|$, where w is the longest string seen so far. In case that $\varphi_k(k) \downarrow$ has been verified, M' guesses L_k, where in its hypothesis all examples seen so far are encoded. Subsequently, M' behaves according to *(iv)*. In case that $\Phi_k(k) > |w|$, M' guesses L_k, where the encoded examples can be simply ignored. Afterwards, M' behaves according to *(iii)*.

(iii) As long as M' guesses L_k, M' uses the recent example (w_n, b_n) to check whether or not $\Phi_k(k) \leq |w_n|$. In the positive case, M' behaves as in *(iv)*. Else M' repeats its recent guess, without encoding any further example.

(iv) Let $s = \Phi_k(k)$. As long as $(b^s, +)$ and $(b^s, -)$ neither appear nor belong to the examples encoded in the recent guess, M' adds the new example into the encoding of examples in the recent guess. If $(b^s, +)$ (or $(b^s, -)$) appears or is encoded, M' guesses a language $L_{\langle k,j \rangle}$ (or $L'_{\langle k,j \rangle}$, respectively) that is consistent with all examples encoded. Past that point, M' works like the iterative learner M used in the proof of Theorem 10, Claim 1.

It is not hard to see that M' is an iterative learner for $\mathcal{C}$.

Claim 2. $C \notin ItGConvInf$.

Suppose the converse. That is, there is an indexing $(L_j^*)_{j\in\mathbb{N}}$ comprising C and an iterative learner M which globally conservatively identifies C with respect to $(L_j^*)_{j\in\mathbb{N}}$. We shall show that M can be utilised to solve the halting problem.

Algorithm $\mathcal{A}$: Let k be given. Let $i = (w_n, b_n)_{n\in\mathbb{N}}$ be a repetition-free informant for L_k with $w_0 = a^k$ and $b_0 = +$ such that, for all $n \in \mathbb{N}$, $w_m = b^n$ implies $m < n$. For $m = 0, 1, 2, \ldots$ test in parallel whether $(\alpha 1)$ or $(\alpha 2)$ happens.

$(\alpha 1)$ $\Phi_k(k) \le m$.

$(\alpha 2)$ An index $j_m = M(init, i[m])$ is output such that $content^+(i[m]) \subseteq L_{j_m}^*$ and $content^-(i[m]) \cap L_{j_m}^* = \emptyset$.

If $(\alpha 1)$ happens first, output "$\varphi_k(k) \downarrow$." Otherwise, i.e., $(\alpha 2)$ happens first, output "$\varphi_k(k) \uparrow$."

Fact 1. On every input k, algorithm $\mathcal{A}$ terminates.

It suffices to show that either $(\alpha 1)$ or $(\alpha 2)$ happens. Suppose, $(\alpha 1)$ does not happen, and thus $\varphi_k(k) \uparrow$. Hence, $L_k \in C_k \subseteq C$. Consequently, M, when processing the informant i for L_k, eventually returns a hypothesis $j_m = M(init, i[m])$ such that $L_{j_m}^* = L_k$. Thus, $(\alpha 2)$ must happen.

Fact 2. Algorithm $\mathcal{A}$ decides the halting problem.

Obviously, if $(\alpha 1)$ happens then $\varphi_k(k)$ is indeed defined. Suppose $(\alpha 2)$ happens. We have to show that $\varphi_k(k) \uparrow$. Assume $\varphi_k(k) \downarrow$. Then, $\Phi_k(k) = s$ for some $s \in \mathbb{N}$. Since $(\alpha 2)$ happens, there is an $m < s$ such that $j_m = M(init, i[m])$ as well as $content^+(i[m]) \subseteq L_{j_m}^*$ and $content^-(i[m]) \cap L_{j_m}^* = \emptyset$. (* Note that neither $(b^s, +)$ nor $(b^s, -)$ appears in the initial segment $i[m]$. *)

Now, similarly to the proof of Theorem 10, Claim 2 one has to distinguish two cases: (i) $L_{j_m}^*$ contains infinitely many strings from $\{c\}^*$ and (ii) $L_{j_m}^*$ contains only finitely many strings of from $\{c\}^*$. In both cases, an argumentation similar to that used in the proof of Theorem 10, Claim 2 can be utilised to show that M fails to learn at least one language in C_k which contain a finite (co-finite) subset of $\{c\}^*$. We omit the relevant details. Since M is supposed to learn C, the latter contradicts our assumption that $\varphi_k(k) \downarrow$, and thus Fact 2 follows.

Since the halting problem is undecidable, $C \notin ItGConvInf$.   □

6   Some Concluding Remarks

We have studied iterative learning with two versions of consistency and conservativeness. In fact, a third version is conceivable. Note that an iterative learner M may use a redundant hypothesis space for coding in its current hypothesis all examples, upon which M has previously changed its guess. So one may think of mind changes as 'memorising examples' and repeating hypotheses as 'forgetting examples'. One might call a hypothesis consistent with the examples seen, if it does not contradict the 'memorised' examples, i.e., those upon which M has changed its hypothesis. Similarly, M may be considered conservative, if M sticks to its recent hypothesis, as long as it agrees with the 'memorised' examples.

Obviously, this version of consistency is equivalent to local consistency – the proof is essentially the same as for Theorem 5 and the fact is not surprising.

However, the third version of conservativeness is worth considering a little closer. For iterative learning from text Theorem 9 immediately implies that this notion is equivalent to both global and local conservativeness. The idea is quite simple: a conservative learner really has to 'know' that it is allowed to change its hypothesis! Thus being inconsistent with forgotten positive examples doesn't help at all, because the learner cannot memorise the forgotten examples and thus not justify its mind change. In this sense, 'forgotten' examples are really examples without any relevance for the learner on the given text. This intuition is already reflected in the technical claim used in the proof of Theorem 9.

Many similar insights may be taken from the proofs above to obtain further results. For instance, the separating classes provided in the proofs of Theorems 6 and 8, additionally lift our results to a more general case of incremental learning, where the learner has a k-bounded memory, i. e., the capacity for memorising up to k examples during the learning process, cf. [9]. Note that among our results we did not have a characterisation of the structure of classes learnable iteratively, however, our analysis will hopefully serve as a first step into this direction.

References

1. Angluin, D., Inductive inference of formal languages from positive data, *Information and Control* **45**, 117–135, 1980.
2. Angluin, D., Queries and concept learning, *Machine Learning* **2**, 319–342, 1988.
3. Blum, M., A machine independent theory of the complexity of recursive functions, *Journal of the ACM* **14**, 322–336, 1967.
4. Case, J., Jain, S., Lange, S., and Zeugmann, T., Incremental concept learning for bounded data mining, *Information and Computation* **152**, 74–110, 1999.
5. Gennari, J.H., Langley, P., and Fisher, D., Models of incremental concept formation, *Artificial Intelligence* **40**, 11–61, 1989.
6. Gold, E.M., Language identification in the limit, *Information and Control* **10**, 447–474, 1967.
7. Kinber, E. and Stephan, F., Language learning from texts: Mind changes, limited memory and monotonicity, *Information and Computation* **123**, 224–241, 1995.
8. Lange, S. and Grieser, G., On the power of incremental learning, *Theoretical Computer Science* **288**, 277-307, 2002.
9. Lange, S. and Zeugmann, T., Incremental learning from positive data, *Journal of Computer and System Sciences* **53**, 88–103, 1996.
10. Shinohara, T., Polynomial time inference of extended regular pattern languages, *in: Proc. RIMS Symposium on Software Science and Engineering*, LNCS, Vol. 147, pp. 115–127, Springer-Verlag, 1983.
11. Valiant, L.G., A theory of the learnable, *Communications of the ACM* **27**, 1134–1142, 1984.
12. Wiehagen, R., Limes-Erkennung rekursiver Funktionen durch spezielle Strategien, *Journal of Information Processing and Cybernetics (EIK)* **12** , 93–99, 1976.
13. Zeugmann, T. and Lange, S., A guided tour across the boundaries of learning recursive languages, *in: Algorithmic Learning for Knowledge-Based Systems*, LNAI, Vol. 961, pp. 190–258, Springer-Verlag, 1995.

On Exact Learning from Random Walk

Nader H. Bshouty and Iddo Bentov

Department of Computer Science
Technion, Haifa, 32000, Israel
bshouty@cs.technion.ac.il, sidddo@t2.technion.ac.il
http://www.cs.technion.ac.il/

Abstract. We consider a few particular exact learning models based on a random walk stochastic process, and thus more restricted than the well known general exact learning models. We give positive and negative results as to whether learning in these particular models is easier than in the general learning models.

1 Introduction

While there are numerous results in the literature with regard to the well known exact learning models such as Angluin Exact learning model [A88] and Littlestone Online learning model [L87], it may also be interesting to investigate more particular models such as the uniform Online model (UROnline) [B97], the random walk online model (RWOnline) [BFH95], and the uniform random walk online model (URWOnline) [BFH95].

All models investigated in this paper are over the boolean domain $\{0,1\}^n$, and the goal of the learning algorithm is to *exactly* identify the target function with a polynomial mistake bound and in polynomial time for each prediction.

The UROnline is the Online model where examples are generated independently and uniformly randomly. In the RWOnline model successive examples differ by exactly one bit, and in the URWOnline model the examples are generated by a uniform random walk on $\{0,1\}^n$. Obviously, learnability in the Online model implies learnability in all the other models with the same mistake bound. Also, learnability in the RWOnline model implies learnability in the URWOnline model with the same mistake bound. By using the results in [BFH95, BMOS03], it is easy to show that learnability in the UROnline model with a mistake bound q implies learnability in the URWOnline model with a mistake bound $\tilde{O}(qn)$. Therefore we have the following:

$$\begin{array}{ccc} \text{Online} & \Rightarrow & \text{RWOnline} \\ \Downarrow & & \Downarrow \\ \text{UROnline} & \Rightarrow & \text{URWOnline} \end{array}$$

In [BFH95] Bartlett et. al. developed efficient algorithms for exact learning boolean threshold functions, 2-term Ring-Sum-Expansion (2-term RSE is the parity of two monotone monomials) and 2-term DNF in the RWOnline model. Those

J.L. Balcázar, P.M. Long, and F. Stephan (Eds.): ALT 2006, LNAI 4264, pp. 184–198, 2006.
© Springer-Verlag Berlin Heidelberg 2006

classes are already known to be learnable in the Online model [L87, FS92] (and therefore in the RWOnline model), but the algorithms in [BFH95] (for threshold functions) achieve a better mistake bound. In this paper a negative result will be presented, showing that for all classes that possess a simple natural property, if the class is learnable in the RWOnline model, then it is learnable in the Online model with the same (asymptotic) mistake bound. Those classes include: read-once DNF, k-term DNF, k-term RSE, decision list, decision tree, DFA and halfspaces.

To study the relationship between the UROnline model and the URWOnline model, we then focus our efforts on studying the learnability of some classes in the URWOnline model that are not known to be polynomially learnable in the UROnline model. For example, it is unknown whether the class of functions of $O(\log n)$ relevant variables can be learned in the UROnline model with a poly-nomial mistake bound (this is an open problem even for $\omega(1)$ relevant variables [MDS03]), but it is known that this class can be learned with a polynomial num-ber of membership queries. We will present a positive result, showing that the information gathered from consecutive examples that are generated by a random walk process can be used in a similar fashion to the information gathered from membership queries, and thus we will prove that this class is learnable in the URWOnline model.

We then establish another result which shows that learning in the URWOnline model can indeed be easier than in the UROnline model, by proving that the class of read-once monotone DNF formulas can be learned in the URWOnline model. It is of course a major open question whether this class can be learned in the Online model, as that implies that the general DNF class can also be learned in the Online and PAC models [PW90, KLPV87]. Therefore, this result separates the Online and the RWOnline models from the URWOnline model, unless DNF is Online learnable. We now have (with the aforementioned learnability hardness assumptions)

$$
\begin{array}{ccc}
\text{Online} & \equiv & \text{RWOnline} \\
\Downarrow & & \Downarrow\!\!\!\not{} \\
\text{UROnline} & \overset{\not{}}{\underset{\Rightarrow}{}} & \text{URWOnline}
\end{array}
$$

We note that results such as [HM91] show that the read-once DNF class can be learned in a *uniform distribution* PAC model, but that does not imply URWOnline learning since the learning is not exact. Also, in [BMOS03], Bshouty et. al. show that DNF is learnable in the *uniform random walk* PAC model, but here again, that does not imply that DNF is learnable in the URWOnline model since the learning is not exact.

2   Learning Models and Definitions

Let n be a positive integer and $X_n = \{0, 1\}^n$. We consider the learning of classes in the form $C = \cup_{n=1}^{\infty} C_n$, where each C_n is a class of boolean functions defined on X_n. Each function $f \in C$ has some string representation $R(f)$ over some alphabet Σ. The length $|R(f)|$ is denoted by $size(f)$.

In the *Online learning model* (Online) [L87], the learning task is to *exactly* identify an unknown *target* function f that is chosen by a *teacher* from C. At each *trial*, the teacher sends a point $x \in X_n$ to the *learner* and the learner has to predict $f(x)$. The learner returns to the teacher the prediction y. If $f(x) \neq y$ then the teacher returns "mistake" to the learner. The goal of the learner is to minimize the number of prediction mistakes.

In the Online learning model we say that algorithm **A** of the learner *Online learns* the class C with a *mistake bound t* if for any $f \in C$ algorithm **A** makes no more than t mistakes. The *hypothesis* of the learner is denoted by h, and the learning is called *exact* because we require that $h \equiv f$ after t mistakes. We say that C is *Online learnable* if there exists a learner that Online learns C with a polynomial mistake bound, and the running time of the learner for each prediction is $poly(n, size(f))$. The learner may depend on a *confidence* parameter δ, by having a mistake bound $t = poly(n, size(f), \log \frac{1}{\delta})$, and probability that $h \not\equiv f$ after t mistakes smaller than δ.

We now define the particular learning models that we consider in this paper. The following models are identical to the above Online model, with various constraints on successive examples that are presented by the teacher at each trial:

Uniform Random Online (UROnline) In this model successive examples are independent and randomly uniformly chosen from X_n.

Random Walk Online (RWOnline) In this model successive examples differ by exactly one bit.

Uniform Random Walk Online (URWOnline) This model is identical to the RWOnline learning model, with the added restriction that

$$\Pr(x^{(t+1)} = y \mid x^{(t)}) = \begin{cases} \frac{1}{n} & \text{if } \text{Ham}(y, x^{(t)}) = 1 \\ 0 & \text{otherwise} \end{cases}$$

where $x^{(t)}$ and $x^{(t+1)}$ are successive examples for a function that depends on n bits, and the Hamming distance $\text{Ham}(y, x^{(t)})$ is the number of bits of y and $x^{(t)}$ that differ.

3   Negative Results for Random Walk Learning

In [BFH95] Bartlett et. al. developed efficient algorithms for exact learning boolean threshold functions, 2-term Ring-Sum-Expansion and 2-term DNF in the RWOnline model. Those classes are already known to be learnable in the Online model [L87, FS92] (and therefore in the RWOnline model) but the algorithm in [BFH95] for boolean threshold functions achieves a better mistake bound. They show that this class can be learned by making no more than $n + 1$

mistakes in the URWOnline model, improving on the $O(n \log n)$ bound for the Online model proven by Littlestone in [L87].

Can we achieve a better mistake bound for other concept classes? We present a negative result, showing that for all classes that possess a simple natural property, the RWOnline model and the Online models have the same asymptotic mistake bound. Those classes include: read-once DNF, k-term DNF, k-term RSE, decision list, decision tree, DFA and halfspaces.

We first give the following.

Definition 1. *A class of boolean functions C has the* one variable override *property if for every $f(x_1, ..., x_n) \in C$ there exist constants $c_0, c_1 \in \{0, 1\}$ and $g(x_1, ..., x_{n+1}) \in C$ such that*

$$g \equiv \begin{cases} c_1 & x_{n+1} = c_0 \\ f & otherwise \end{cases}.$$

Common classes do possess the one variable override property. We give here a few examples.

Consider the class of read-once DNF. Define for each function $f(x_1, \ldots, x_n)$, $g(x_1, \ldots, x_{n+1}) = x_{n+1} \vee f(x_1, \ldots, x_n)$. Then g is read-once DNF, $g(x, 1) = 1$ and $g(x, 0) = f(x)$. The construction is also good for decision list, decision tree and DFA. For k-term DNF and k-term RSE we can take $g = x_{n+1} \wedge f$. For halfspace, consider the function $f(x_1, \ldots, x_n) = [\sum_{i=1}^{n} a_i x_i \geq b]$. Then $g(x_1, \ldots, x_{n+1}) = x_{n+1} \vee f(x_1, \ldots, x_n)$ can be expressed as $g(x_1, \ldots, x_{n+1}) = [(b + \sum_{i=1}^{n} |a_i|) x_{n+1} + \sum_{i=1}^{n} a_i x_i \geq b]$. Notice that the class of boolean threshold functions $f(x_1, \ldots, x_n) = [\sum_{i=1}^{n} a_i x_i \geq b]$ where $a_i \in \{0, 1\}$ does not have the one variable override property.

In order to show equivalence between the RWOnline and Online models, we notice that a malicious teacher could set a certain variable to override the function's value, then choose arbitrary values for the other variables via random walk, and then reset this certain variable and ask the learner to make a prediction. Using this idea, we now prove

Theorem 1. *Let C be a class that has the one variable override property. If C is learnable in the* RWOnline *model with a mistake bound $T(n)$ then C is learnable in the* Online *model with a mistake bound $4T(n + 1)$.*

Proof. Suppose C is learnable in the RWOnline model by some algorithm **A**, which has a mistake bound of $T(n)$. Let $f(x_1, ..., x_n) \in C$ and construct

$$g(x_1, ..., x_{n+1}) \equiv \begin{cases} c_1 & x_{n+1} = c_0 \\ f & otherwise \end{cases}$$

using the constants c_0, c_1 that exist due to the one variable override property of C. An algorithm **B** for the Online model will learn f by using algorithm **A** simulated on g according to these steps:

1. At the first trial
    (a) Receive $x^{(1)}$ from the teacher.
    (b) Send $(x^{(1)}, \overline{c_0})$ to **A** and receive the answer y.
    (c) Send the answer y to the teacher, and inform **A** in case of a mistake.
2. At trial t
    (a) receive $x^{(t)}$ from the teacher.
    (b) $\tilde{x}^{(t-1)} \leftarrow (x_1^{(t-1)}, x_2^{(t-1)}, ..., x_n^{(t-1)}, c_0)$, $\tilde{x}^{(t)} \leftarrow (x_1^{(t)}, x_2^{(t)}, ..., x_n^{(t)}, c_0)$
    (c) Walk from $\tilde{x}^{(t-1)}$ to $\tilde{x}^{(t)}$, asking **A** for predictions, and informing **A** of mistakes in case it fails to predict c_1 after each bit flip.
    (d) Send $(x^{(t)}, \overline{c_0})$ to **A**.
    (e) Let y be the answer of **A** on $(x^{(t)}, \overline{c_0})$.
    (f) Send the answer y to the teacher, and inform **A** in case of a mistake.

Obviously, successive examples given to **A** differ by exactly one bit, and the teacher that we simulated for **A** provides it with the correct "mistake" messages, since $g(x^{(t)}, \overline{c_0}) = f(x^{(t)})$. Therefore, algorithm **A** will learn g exactly after $T(n+1)$ mistakes at the most, and thus **B** also makes no more than $T(n+1)$ mistakes.

In case the two constants c_0, c_1 cannot easily be determined, it is possible to repeat this process after more than $T(n+1)$ mistakes were received, by choosing different constants. Thus the mistake bound in the worst case is $4T(n+1)$. □

4   Positive Results for Random Walk Learning

4.1   Learning Boolean Functions That Depend on $\log n$ Variables

In this section we present a probabilistic algorithm for the URWOnline model that learns the class of functions of k relevant variables, i.e, functions that depend on at most k variables. We show that the algorithm makes no more than $poly(2^k, \log \frac{1}{\delta})$ mistakes, and thus in particular for $k = O(\log n)$ the number of mistakes is polynomially bounded. It is unknown whether it is possible to learn this class in polynomial time in the UROnline model even for $k = \omega(1)$ [MDS03].

The Online learning algorithm RVL(δ), shown in figure 1, receives an example $x^{(t)}$ at each trial $t = 1, 2, 3, ...$ from the teacher, and makes a prediction for $f(x^{(t)})$.

4.1.1   Complexity of RVL(δ)
In this section we investigate the complexity of the algorithm. Define

$$\alpha(k, \delta) = \frac{k(k+1)}{4} 2^k \log(k 2^{2k+2}) \log \frac{k}{\delta}.$$

The maximal number of prediction mistakes in phase 1 before each time a new relevant variable is discovered is $\alpha(k, \delta)$, and therefore the total number of prediction mistakes possible in phase 1 is at most $k\alpha(k, \delta)$. We will show in the

RVL(δ):

1. $S \leftarrow \emptyset$
2. At the first trial, make an arbitrary prediction for $f(x^{(1)})$
3. Phase 1 - find relevant variables as follows:
   (a) At trial t, predict $h(x^{(t)}) = f(x^{(t-1)})$
   (b) In case of a prediction mistake, find the unique i such that $x^{(t-1)}$ and $x^{(t)}$ differ on the ith bit, and perform $S \leftarrow S \cup \{x_i\}$
   (c) If S hasn't been modified after $\alpha(k, \delta)$ consecutive prediction mistakes, then assume that S contains all the relevant variables and goto (4)
   (d) If $|S| = k$ then goto (4), else goto (3.a)
4. Phase 2 - learn the target function:
   (a) Prepare a truth table with $2^{|S|}$ entries for all the possible assignments of the relevant variables
   (b) At trial t, predict on $x^{(t)}$ as follows:
      i. If $f(x^{(t)})$ is yet unknown because the entry in the table for the relevant variables of $x^{(t)}$ hasn't been determined yet, then make an arbitrary prediction and then update that table entry with the correct value of $f(x^{(t)})$
      ii. If the entry for the relevant variables of $f(x^{(t)})$ has already been set in the table, then predict $f(x^{(t)})$ according to the table value

Fig. 1. The RVL(δ) Algorithm - Relevant Variables Learner

next subsection that with probability of at least $1 - \delta$ the first phase finds all the relevant variables.

The maximal number of prediction mistakes in phase 2 is 2^k. Thus the overall number of prediction mistakes that RVL(δ) can make is bounded by

$$2^k + k\alpha(k, \delta) \le 2^k poly\left(k, \log\frac{1}{\delta}\right).$$

This implies

Corollary 1. *For $k = O(\log n)$, the number of mistakes that RVL(δ) makes is bounded by poly $\left(n, \log\frac{1}{\delta}\right)$.*

4.1.2 Correctness of RVL(δ)

We will show that the probability that the hypothesis generated by RVL(δ) is not equivalent to the target function is less than δ. This will be done using the fact that a uniform random walk stochastic process is similar to the uniform distribution. We first require the following definition.

Definition 2. *Let U_n be the uniform distribution on X_n. A stochastic process $P = (Y_1, Y_2, Y_3, ...)$ is said to be γ-close to uniform if*

$$P_{m|x}(b) = \Pr(Y_{m+1} = b \mid Y_i = x_i, i = 1, 2, ..., m)$$

is defined for all $m \in \mathbb{N}$, for all $b \in X_n$, and for all $x \in X_n^{\mathbb{N}}$, and

$$\sum_{b \in X_n} |P_{m|x}(b) - U_n(b)| \leq \gamma$$

for all $m \in \mathbb{N}$ and for all $x \in X_n^{\mathbb{N}}$.

We now quote the following lemma, that is proven in [DGM90]:

Lemma 1. *For any uniform random walk stochastic process P and $0 < \gamma < 1$, let Q_m be the stochastic process that corresponds to sampling P after at least m steps. Then Q_m is γ-close to uniform for*

$$m = \frac{n+1}{4} \log \frac{n}{\log(\gamma^2/2 + 1)}.$$

Suppose the target function f depends on k variables. We can consider the 2^n possible assignments as 2^k equivalence classes of assignments, where each equivalence class consists of 2^{n-k} assignments under which f has the same value. If x_i is a relevant variable, then there exist at least two equivalence classes such that flipping the ith bit in any assignment of one of these equivalence classes will change the value of the target function f. We note that flipping an irrelevant variable x_i will not change the value of f, and therefore a prediction mistakes cannot occur in this case. Hence, we can ignore the irrelevant variables and analyze a random walk stochastic process on the cube $\{0,1\}^k$ of the relevant variables. Let us choose the following values

$$\gamma = \frac{1}{2^k}, \quad m = \frac{k+1}{4} \log \frac{k}{\log(\gamma^2/2 + 1)} = \frac{k+1}{4} \log \frac{k}{\log(1/2^{2k+1} + 1)}.$$

Now, let us ignore all the prediction mistakes that occur during m consecutive trials, and consider the first subsequent trial in which an assignment $x^{(t)}$ caused a prediction mistake to occur. By using Lemma 1, we obtain that the probability that $x^{(t)}$ belongs to an equivalence class in which flipping the ith bit changes the value of f is at least $\frac{2}{2^k} - \gamma = \frac{1}{2^k}$. Since the probability that x_i flipped between $x^{(t-1)}$ and $x^{(t)}$ is $\frac{1}{k}$, the probability to discover a certain relevant variable x_i in this trial is at least $\frac{1}{k}\frac{1}{2^k}$.

In order to get the probability that x_i would not be discovered after t such prediction mistakes lower than $\frac{\delta}{k}$, we require

$$\left(1 - \frac{1}{k2^k}\right)^t \leq \frac{\delta}{k},$$

and using the fact that $1 - x \leq e^{-x}$, we get that

$$t = k2^k \log \frac{k}{\delta}$$

will suffice.

Therefore, if we allow $k2^k m \log \frac{k}{\delta}$ prediction mistakes while trying to discover x_i, the probability of a failure is at most $\frac{\delta}{k}$. Now,

$$\Pr(\{\mathrm{RVL}(\delta) \text{ fails}\}) = \Pr(\{\text{finding } x_{i_1} \text{ fails}\} \vee ... \vee \{\text{finding } x_{i_k} \text{ fails}\})$$

$$\leq \sum_{q=1}^{k} \Pr(\{\text{finding } x_{i_q} \text{ fails}\})$$

$$\leq \sum_{q=1}^{k} \Pr(\{\text{finding } x_{i_k} \text{ fails}\}) \leq k\frac{\delta}{k} = \delta.$$

Using the fact that for every $q \in \mathbb{N}$, $\frac{1}{\log(1/q+1)} \leq q + \frac{1}{2}$, we observe that

$$
\begin{aligned}
k2^k m \log \frac{k}{\delta} &= \frac{k(k+1)}{4} 2^k \log \frac{k}{\log(1/2^{2k+1}+1)} \log \frac{k}{\delta} \\
&\leq \frac{k(k+1)}{4} 2^k \log\left(k\left(2^{2k+1} + \frac{1}{2}\right)\right) \log \frac{k}{\delta} \\
&\leq \frac{k(k+1)}{4} 2^k \log(k2^{2k+2}) \log \frac{k}{\delta} = \alpha(k,\delta).
\end{aligned}
$$

This is the maximal amount of prediction mistakes that the algorithm is set to allow while trying to discover a relevant variable, and thus the proof of the correctness of $\mathrm{RVL}(\delta)$ is complete. □

4.2   Learning Read-Once Monotone DNF Functions

We now consider the Read-Once Monotone DNF (ROM-DNF) class of boolean functions, i.e. DNF formulas in which each variable appears at most once, and none of the variables are negated.

If it is possible to learn this class in the Online model, then it can be shown using the Composition Lemma [PW90, KLPV87] that the general class of DNF functions is also learnable in the Online model. Since we have shown that proving such a result is not easier in the RWOnline model than in the Online model, we will now prove that we can learn the ROM-DNF class in the URWOnline model. This will give further evidence that learnability in the URWOnline can indeed be easier than in the RWOnline and Online models.

The Online learning algorithm **ROM-DNF-L**(δ), shown in figure 2, receives an example $x^{(t)}$ at each trial $t = 1, 2, 3, ...$ from the teacher, and makes a prediction for $f(x^{(t)})$. The algorithm begins by initializing sets T_{x_i}, which can be regarded as terms. At each trial and for each variable x_i, the term set T_{x_i} of the algorithm will be a superset of the set of variables that belong to the term $T_{x_i}^f$ in f that contains x_i. The initial set T_{x_i} is $\{x_1, x_2, ..., x_n\}$ for every i, which corresponds to the full term $x_1 \wedge x_2 \wedge \cdots \wedge x_n$. We will use the notation of terms interchangeably with these sets, e.g. $T_{x_j}(x^{(t)})$ denotes whether all the variables of the assignment $x^{(t)}$ that belong to T_{x_j} are satisfied.

In the algorithm we have the following eight cases:

Case I: $T_{x_i} = \emptyset$. Step 6 in the algorithm. In this case x_i is not a relevant variable so flipping x_i will not change the value of the target. So the algorithm predicts $h(x^{(t)}) = f(x^{(t-1)})$. No mistake will be received.

Case II: $f(x^{(t-1)}) = 0$, $x_i^{(t-1)} = 1$ and $x_i^{(t)} = 0$. Step (7a) in the algorithm. In this case $x^{(t)} < x^{(t-1)}$ and since f is monotone $f(x^{(t)}) = 0$. So the algorithm predicts 0. No mistake will be received.

Case III: $f(x^{(t-1)}) = 0$, $x_i^{(t-1)} = 0$, $x_i^{(t)} = 1$ and $T_{x_i}(x^{(t)}) = 1$. Step (7(b)i) in the algorithm. Since T_{x_i} is a superset of $T_{x_i}^f$ in f and $T_{x_i}(x^{(t)}) = 1$ then $T_{x_i}^f(x^{(t)}) = 1$ (if it exists in f) and $f(x^{(t)}) = 1$. So the algorithm predicts 1. If a mistake is received by the teacher then the algorithm knows that f is independent of x_i and then it sets $T_{x_i} \leftarrow \emptyset$ and removes x_i from all the other terms.

Case IV: $f(x^{(t-1)}) = 0$, $x_i^{(t-1)} = 0$, $x_i^{(t)} = 1$ and $T_{x_i}(x^{(t)}) = 0$. Step (7(b)ii) in the algorithm. Notice that since $f(x^{(t-1)}) = 0$, all the terms in f are 0 in $x^{(t-1)}$ and in particular $T_{x_i}^f(x^{(t-1)}) = 0$. If flipping the bit x_i from 0 to 1 changes the value of the function f to 1 then $T_{x_i}^f(x^{(t)}) = 1$. The algorithm predicts 0. In case of a mistake, we have $T_{x_i}(x^{(t)}) = 0$ and $T_{x_i}^f(x^{(t)}) = 1$ and therefore we can remove every variable x_j in T_{x_i} that satisfies $x_j^{(t)} = 0$. Notice that there is at least one such variable, and that after removing all such variables the condition that T_{x_i} is a superset of $T_{x_i}^f$ still holds. Also, if x_k is not in $T_{x_i}^f$ then x_i is not in $T_{x_k}^f$, so we can also remove x_i from any such set T_{x_k}.

Case V: $f(x^{(t-1)}) = 1$, $x_i^{(t-1)} = 0$ and $x_i^{(t)} = 1$. Step (8a) in the algorithm. In this case $x^{(t)} > x^{(t-1)}$ and since f is monotone $f(x^{(t)}) = 1$. So the algorithm predicts 1. No mistake will be received.

Case VI: $f(x^{(t-1)}) = 1$, $x_i^{(t-1)} = 1$, $x_i^{(t)} = 0$ and there is k such that $T_{x_k}(x^{(t)}) = 1$. Step (8(b)i) in the algorithm. This is similar to Case III.

Case VII: $f(x^{(t-1)}) = 1$, $x_i^{(t-1)} = 1$, $x_i^{(t)} = 0$, for every k, $T_{x_k}(x^{(t)}) = 0$ and $T_{x_i}(x^{(t-1)}) = 0$. Step (8(b)ii) in the algorithm. In this case if $f(x^{(t)}) = 0$ then since $f(x^{(t-1)}) = 1$, we must have $T_{x_i}^f(x^{(t-1)}) = 1$. So this is similar to Case IV.

Case VIII: $f(x^{(t-1)}) = 1$, $x_i^{(t-1)} = 1$, $x_i^{(t)} = 0$, for every k, $T_{x_k}(x^{(t)}) = 0$ and $T_{x_i}(x^{(t-1)}) = 1$. Step (8(b)iii) in the algorithm. In this case the algorithm can be in two modes, "A" or "B". The algorithm begins in mode "A", which assumes that T_{x_k} is correct, i.e. $T_{x_k}^f = T_{x_k}$ for every k. With this assumption $f(x^{(t)}) = \vee_k T_{x_k}^f(x^{(t)}) = \vee_k T_{x_k}(x^{(t)}) = 0$ and the algorithm predicts 0. In case of a prediction mistake, we alternate between mode "A" and mode "B", where mode "B" assumes the opposite, i.e. it assumes that our lack of knowledge prevents us from seeing that some terms are indeed satisfied, so when we don't know whether some terms are satisfied while operating under mode "B", we assert that they are satisfied and set the algorithm to predict 1.

The most extreme possibility that requires mode "A" in order not to make too many mistakes is in case $f(x_1, x_2, \ldots, x_n) = x_1 \wedge x_2 \wedge \cdots \wedge x_n$. The most extreme possibility that requires mode "B" in order not to make too many mistakes is

---

ROM-DNF-L(δ):

1. For each variable x_i, $1 \le i \le n$, create the set $T_{x_i} \leftarrow \{x_1, x_2, x_3, ..., x_n\}$
2. $MODE \leftarrow$ "A"
3. **First Trial**: Make an arbitrary prediction for $f(x^{(1)})$.
4. **Trial t:** See whether the teacher sent a "mistake" message, and thus determine $f(x^{(t-1)})$
5. Find the variable x_i on which the assignments $x^{(t-1)}$ and $x^{(t)}$ differ
6. If $T_{x_i} = \emptyset$ (meaning: x_i is not a relevant variable), then predict $h(x^{(t)}) = f(x^{(t-1)})$
7. Otherwise, if $f(x^{(t-1)}) = 0$
   (a) If x_i flipped $1 \to 0$, then predict 0
   (b) Otherwise, x_i flipped $0 \to 1$
      i. If $T_{x_i}(x^{(t)}) = 1$, then predict 1
         On mistake do: $T_{x_i} \leftarrow \emptyset$, and update the other term sets by removing x_i from them.
      ii. Otherwise, predict 0
         On mistake do: update the set T_{x_i} by removing the unsatisfied variables of $x^{(t)}$ from it, since they are unneeded, and update the rest of the term sets by removing x_i from any term set T_{x_k} such that x_k was an unneeded variable in T_{x_i}
8. Otherwise, $f(x^{(t-1)}) = 1$
   (a) If x_i flipped $0 \to 1$, then predict 1
   (b) Otherwise, x_i flipped $1 \to 0$
      i. If some $T_{x_k}(x^{(t)}) = 1$, then predict 1
         On mistake do: for each k such that $T_{x_k}(x^{(t)}) = 1$, do $T_{x_k} \leftarrow \emptyset$, and remove the irrelevant variable x_k from the rest of the term sets
      ii. If $T_{x_i}(x^{(t-1)}) = 0$, then predict 1
         On mistake do: update the set T_{x_i} by removing the unsatisfied variables of $x^{(t-1)}$ from it, since they are unneeded, and update the rest of the term sets by removing x_i in any term set T_{x_k} such that x_k was an unneeded variable in T_{x_i}
      iii. If $MODE =$ "A", then predict 0
         On mistake do: $MODE \leftarrow$ "B"
         If $MODE =$ "B", then predict 1
         On mistake do: $MODE \leftarrow$ "A"
9. Goto 4

Fig. 2. The ROM-DNF-L(δ) Algorithm - ROM-DNF Learner

in case $f(x_1, x_2, \ldots, x_n) = x_1 \vee x_2 \vee \cdots \vee x_n$. After the algorithm has completed the learning and $h \equiv f$, it will always remain in mode "A", as the sets T_{x_i} will be accurate.

4.2.1 Correctness of ROM-DNF-L(δ)

We will find a $p = poly(n, \log \frac{1}{\delta})$ such that the probability of ROM-DNF-L(δ) making more than p mistakes is less than δ.

We note that the only prediction mistakes that ROM-DNF-L(δ) makes in which no new information is gained occur at step (8(b)iii). We will now bound the ratio between the number of assignments that could cause noninformative mistakes and the number of assignments that could cause informative mistakes during any stage of the learning process.

An assignment $x^{(t)}$ is called an *informative assignment* at trial t if there exists $x^{(t-1)}$ such that $x^{(t-1)} \to x^{(t)}$ is a possible random walk that forces the algorithm to make a mistake and to eliminate at least one variable from one of the term sets. An assignment $x^{(t)}$ is called a *noninformative assignment* at trial t if there exists $x^{(t-1)}$ such that $x^{(t-1)} \to x^{(t)}$ is a possible random walk that forces the algorithm to make a mistake in step (8(b)iii). Notice that $x^{(t)}$ can be informative and noninformative at the same time.

At trial t, let N be the number of informative assignments and N_A and N_B be the number of noninformative assignment in case the algorithm operates in mode "A" and "B", respectively. We want to show that $\min(N_A/N, N_B/N) \le N_0$ for some constant N_0. This will show that for at least one of the modes "A" or "B", there is a constant probability that a prediction mistake can lead to progress in the learning, and thus the algorithm achieves a polynomial mistake bound.

At trial t let $f = f_1 \vee f_2$ where

1. $f_1 = \hat{T}_1^f \vee \hat{T}_2^f \vee \cdots \hat{T}_{k_1}^f$ are the terms in f where for every term $\hat{T}_\ell^f$ there exists a variable x_j in that term such that $T_{x_j} = \hat{T}_\ell^f$. Those are the terms that have been discovered by the algorithm.
2. $f_2 = T_1^f \vee T_2^f \vee \cdots \vee T_{k_2}^f$ are the terms in f where for every term T_ℓ^f and every variable x_j in that term, we have that T_{x_j} is proper super-term of T_ℓ^f. Those are the terms of f that haven't been discovered yet by the algorithm. In other words, for each variable x_i that belongs to such a term, the set T_{x_i} contains unneeded variables.

Denote by X_1 and X_2 the set of variables of f_1 and f_2, respectively, and let X_3 be the set of irrelevant variables. Let $a_\ell = |\hat{T}_\ell^f|$ be the number of variables in $\hat{T}_\ell^f$, $b_\ell = |T_\ell^f|$ be the number of variables in T_ℓ^f, and $d = |X_3|$ be the number of irrelevant variables.

First, let us assume that the algorithm now operates in mode "A". Noninformative mistakes can occur only when: $f(x^{(t-1)}) = 1$, $x_i^{(t-1)} = 1$, $x_i^{(t)} = 0$, for every k, $T_{x_k}(x^{(t)}) = 0$ and $T_{x_i}(x^{(t-1)}) = 1$. The algorithm predict 0 but $f(x^{(t)}) = 1$.

We will bound from above N_A, the number of possible assignments $x^{(t)}$ that satisfy the latter conditions. Since $T_{x_k}(x^{(t)}) = 0$ for every k and for every $\hat{T}_\ell^f$ there is x_j such that $\hat{T}_\ell^f = T_{x_j}$, we must have $\hat{T}_\ell^f(x^{(t)}) = 0$ for every ℓ, and therefore $f_1(x^{(t)}) = 0$. Since $1 = f(x^{(t)}) = f_1(x^{(t)}) \vee f_2(x^{(t)})$, we must have $f_2(x^{(t)}) = 1$. Therefore, the number of such assignments is at most

$$N_A \le |\{x^{(t)} \in X_n \mid f_1(x^{(t)}) = 0 \text{ and } f_2(x^{(t)}) = 1\}|$$
$$= c2^d \left(\prod_{i=1}^{k_2} 2^{b_i} - \prod_{i=1}^{k_2} (2^{b_i} - 1) \right).$$

Here $c = \prod_{i=1}^{k_1}(2^{a_i} - 1)$ is the number of assignments to X_1 where $f_1(x) = 0$, 2^d is the number of assignments to X_3, and $\prod_{i=1}^{k_2} 2^{b_i} - \prod_{i=1}^{k_2}(2^{b_i} - 1)$ is the number of assignments to X_2 where $f_2(x) = 1$.

We now show that the number of informative assignments is at least

$$N \geq \frac{1}{2}c2^d \sum_{j=1}^{k_2} \prod_{i \neq j}^{k_2}(2^{b_i} - 1) \tag{1}$$

and therefore

$$\frac{N_A}{N} \leq \frac{c2^d \left(\prod_{i=1}^{k_2} 2^{b_i} - \prod_{i=1}^{k_2}(2^{b_i} - 1) \right)}{\frac{1}{2}c2^d \sum_{j=1}^{k_2} \prod_{i \neq j}^{k_2}(2^{b_i} - 1)}$$

$$= \frac{2(\prod_{i=1}^{k_2} 2^{b_i} - \prod_{i=1}^{k_2}(2^{b_i} - 1))}{\sum_{j=1}^{k_2} \prod_{i \neq j}^{k_2}(2^{b_i} - 1)}.$$

To prove (1), consider (Case IV) which corresponds to step (7(b)ii) in the algorithm. In case $x^{(t)}$ is informative there exist i and $x^{(t-1)}$ such that $f(x^{(t-1)}) = 0$, $x_i^{(t-1)} = 0$, $x_i^{(t)} = 1$, $T_{x_i}(x^{(t)}) = 0$, and $f(x^{(t)}) = 1$. Notice that since $f(x^{(t-1)}) = 0$, all the terms $T_{x_\ell}^f$ satisfy $T_{x_\ell}^f(x^{(t-1)}) = 0$, and therefore all the term sets T_{x_ℓ} satisfy $T_{x_\ell}(x^{(t-1)}) = 0$. Since $f(x^{(t)}) = 1$ and $x^{(t)}$ differ from $x^{(t-1)}$ only in x_i, it follows that $T_{x_i}^f$ is the only term that satisfies $T_{x_i}^f(x^{(t)}) = 1$.

One case in which this may occur is when $f_1(x^{(t)}) = 0$, and exactly one term $T_{x_i}^f \equiv T_\ell^f$ in f_2 satisfies $x^{(t)}$, and some variable x_j that is in T_{x_i} and is not in $T_{x_i}^f$ is 0 in $x^{(t)}$. We will call such an assignment a *perfect* assignment. An assignment $x^{(t)}$ where $f_1(x^{(t)}) = 0$ and exactly one term $T_{x_i}^f \equiv T_\ell^f$ in f_2 satisfies $x^{(t)}$ is called a *good* assignment. Notice that since f is monotone, for every good assignment $x^{(t)}$ in which every x_j that is in T_{x_i} and is not in T_{x_i} is 1 in $x^{(t)}$, we can choose the smallest index j_0 such that x_{j_0} is in T_{x_i} and is not in $T_{x_i}^f$, and flip x_{j_0} to 0 in order to get a perfect assignment. Therefore, the number of perfect assignments is at least $1/2$ the number of good assignments.

To count the number of good assignments, we note that $\sum_{j=1}^{k} \prod_{i \neq j}^{k}(2^{b_i} - 1)$ is the number of assignments to X_2 in which exactly one of the terms in f_2 is satisfied. As previously denoted, c is the number of assignments to X_1 in which $f_1 = 0$, and 2^d is the number of assignments to the irrelevant variables. This gives (1).

Second, let us assume that the algorithm now operates in mode "B". Again, Noninformative mistakes can occur only when: $f(x^{(t-1)}) = 1$, $x_i^{(t-1)} = 1$, $x_i^{(t)} = 0$, for every k, $T_{x_k}(x^{(t)}) = 0$ and $T_{x_i}(x^{(t-1)}) = 1$. But now the algorithm predict 1 though $f(x^{(t)}) = 0$.

Using the same reasoning, an upper bound for N_B can be obtained when neither f_1 nor f_2 are satisfied, thus

$$N_B \leq |\{x^{(t)} \in X_n \mid f_1(x^{(t)}) = 0 \text{ and } f_2(x^{(t)}) = 0\}| = c2^d \prod_{i=1}^{k_2}(2^{b_i} - 1).$$

And therefore we have

$$\frac{N_B}{N} \le \frac{c2^d \prod_{i=1}^{k_2}(2^{b_i}-1)}{\frac{1}{2}c2^d \sum_{j=1}^{k_2} \prod_{i\ne j}^{k_2}(2^{b_i}-1)}$$

$$= \frac{2 \prod_{i=1}^{k_2}(2^{b_i}-1)}{\sum_{j=1}^{k_2} \prod_{i\ne j}^{k_2}(2^{b_i}-1)}.$$

We now show that at least one of the above bounds is smaller than 3. Therefore, in at least one of the two modes, the probability to select a noninformative assignment is at most 3 times greater than the probability to select an informative assignment under the uniform distribution.

Consider

$$w_i := 2^{b_i}-1, \quad \alpha := \frac{\prod_{i=1}^{k}(w_i+1) - \prod_{i=1}^{k} w_i}{\sum_{j=1}^{k} \prod_{i\ne j}^{k} w_i}, \quad \beta := \frac{\prod_{i=1}^{k} w_i}{\sum_{j=1}^{k} \prod_{i\ne j}^{k} w_i}.$$

Then

$$\beta = \frac{\prod_{i=1}^{k} w_i}{\prod_{i=1}^{k} w_i \sum_{i=1}^{k} \frac{1}{w_i}} = \frac{1}{\sum_{i=1}^{k} \frac{1}{w_i}}$$

and

$$\alpha = \frac{\prod_{i=1}^{k}(w_i+1) - \prod_{i=1}^{k} w_i}{\prod_{i=1}^{k} w_i \sum_{i=1}^{k} \frac{1}{w_i}}$$

$$= \frac{1}{\sum_{i=1}^{k} \frac{1}{w_i}} \left(\frac{\prod_{i=1}^{k}(w_i+1)}{\prod_{i=1}^{k} w_i} - 1 \right)$$

$$= \beta \left(\prod_{i=1}^{k}(1+\frac{1}{w_i}) - 1 \right)$$

$$\le \beta \left(\prod_{i=1}^{k} e^{\frac{1}{w_i}} - 1 \right)$$

$$= \beta \left(e^{\sum_{i=1}^{k} \frac{1}{w_i}} - 1 \right) = \beta(e^{\frac{1}{\beta}} - 1).$$

Therefore

$$\min(N_A/N, N_B/N) = 2\min(\alpha,\beta) \le 2\min(\beta(e^{\frac{1}{\beta}}-1),\beta) \le 2 \times 1.443 < 3.$$

4.2.2   The Analysis for δ

Let P_U be the probability under the uniform distribution that an assignment that caused a prediction mistake is informative. We have shown that during any trial, in at least one of the modes "A" or "B", we have $P_U \ge \frac{1}{4}$.

For Lemma 1, let us now choose $\gamma = \frac{1}{8}$, and thus

$$m = \frac{n+1}{4} \log \frac{n}{\log(1/(2 \cdot 8^2) + 1)} = \frac{n+1}{4} \log(C_0 n), \quad C_0 \approx 128.5 .$$

When looking at prediction mistakes that occur after at least m trials, we will be γ-close to the uniform distribution. Therefore, in the algorithm the probability P_A that corresponds to P_U is at least

$$P_A \geq P_U - \gamma \geq \frac{1}{8}.$$

For the analysis, if we only examine prediction mistakes that occur after m trials, in case only noninformative mistakes occur, either the first or the second prediction mistake would be made while operating under a mode with the bounded uniform distribution failure probablity, since we switch between modes after a noninformative mistake. So for one of these two trials, the probability that a noninformative mistake indeed occured in that trial is $(1 - \frac{1}{n}P_A)$ at the most. This is because the probability that a variable whose flip in the previous trial would cause an informative mistake is at least $\frac{1}{n}P_A$. Therefore, the probability that no new information will be gained for $(m+1)t$ consecutive trials is at most

$$\left(1 - \frac{1}{n}P_A\right)^t = \left(1 - \frac{1}{8n}\right)^t .$$

In order to obtain a suitable bound by finding t that is large enough we require

$$\left(1 - \frac{1}{8n}\right)^t \leq \frac{\delta}{n^2},$$

and therefore

$$t = 8n \left(2 \log n + \log \frac{1}{\delta}\right).$$

Therefore, after a phase of $(m+1)t$ prediction mistakes, the probability of failure to gain information is at most δ/n^2.

We now get

$$\Pr(\{\text{ROM-DNF-L}(\delta) \text{ fails}\}) \leq \Pr(\{\text{phase 1 fails}\} \vee ... \vee \{\text{phase } n^2 \text{ fails}\})$$
$$\leq n^2 \Pr(\{\text{phase 1 fails}\})$$
$$\leq n^2 \frac{\delta}{n^2} = \delta,$$

and the total number of mistakes that ROM-DNF-L(δ) makes is bounded by

$$n^2(m+1)t = n^2 \left(\frac{n+1}{4} \log(C_0 n) + 1\right) 8n \left(2 \log n + \log \frac{1}{\delta}\right)$$
$$= poly\left(n, \log \frac{1}{\delta}\right).$$

$\square$

References

[A88]   D. Angluin. Queries and concept learning. *Machine Learning*, 2, pp. 319-342, 1987.

[B97]   N. H. Bshouty: Simple Learning Algorithms Using Divide and Conquer. *Computational Complexity*, 6(2): 174-194 (1997)

[BFH95]   P. L. Bartlett, P. Fischer and K. Höffgen. Exploiting Random Walks for Learning. *Information and Computation*, 176: 121-135 (2002).

[BMOS03]   N. H. Bshouty, E. Mossel, R. O'Donnell and R. A. Servedio. Learning DNF from Random Walks. FOCS 2003: 189-

[DGM90]   P. Diaconis, R. Graham, and J. Morrison. Asymptotic analysis of a random walk on a hypercube with many dimensions. *Random Structures and Algorithms*, 1:51-72, 1990.

[FS92]   P. Ficher and H. Simon. On learning ring-sum expansions. *SIAM J. Comput.* 21: 181–192, 1992.

[HM91]   T. Hancock and Y. Mansour. Learning Monotone $k\mu$ DNF Formulas on Product Distributions. *Proc. 4th Ann. Workshop on Comp. Learning Theory* (1991), 179-183.

[KLPV87]   M. Kearns, M. Li, L. Pitt, and L. Valiant. On the Learnability of Boolean Formulae. In Proceedings of the 19th ACM Symposium on the Theory of Computing, 285-195, 1987.

[L87]   N. Littlestone. Learning Quickly When Irrelevant Attributes Abound: A New Linear-Threshold Algorithm. *Machine Learning*, **2**, No. 4, 285–318, 1987.

[MDS03]   E. Mossel, R. O'Donnell and R. A. Servedio. Learning juntas. STOC 2003: 206-212. Learning functions of k relevant variables. *Journal of Computer and System Sciences* 69(3), 2004, pp. 421-434

[PW90]   L. Pitt and M. K. Warmuth. Prediction-preserving reducibility. *Journal of Computer and System Science*, 41(3), pp. 430–467, (1990).

Risk-Sensitive Online Learning

Eyal Even-Dar, Michael Kearns, and Jennifer Wortman

Department of Computer and Information Science
University of Pennsylvania, Philadelphia, PA 19104

Abstract. We consider the problem of online learning in settings in which we want to compete not simply with the rewards of the best expert or stock, but with the best trade-off between rewards and *risk*. Motivated by finance applications, we consider two common measures balancing returns and risk: the *Sharpe ratio* [9] and the *mean-variance* criterion of Markowitz [8]. We first provide negative results establishing the impossibility of no-regret algorithms under these measures, thus providing a stark contrast with the returns-only setting. We then show that the recent algorithm of Cesa-Bianchi et al. [5] achieves nontrivial performance under a modified bicriteria risk-return measure, and give a modified best expert algorithm that achieves no regret for a "localized" version of the mean-variance criterion. We perform experimental comparisons of traditional online algorithms and the new risk-sensitive algorithms on a recent six-year S&P 500 data set and find that the modified best expert algorithm outperforms the traditional with respect to Sharpe ratio, MV, and accumulated wealth. To our knowledge this paper initiates the investigation of explicit risk considerations in the standard models of worst-case online learning.

1 Introduction

Despite the large literature on online learning and the rich collection of algorithms with guaranteed worst-case regret bounds, virtually no attention has been given to the risk (as measured by the volatility in returns or profits) incurred by such algorithms. Partial exceptions are the recent work of Cesa-Bianchi et al. [5] which we analyze in our framework, and the work of Warmuth and Kuzmin [10] which assumes that a covariance matrix is revealed at each time step and focuses on minimizing only risk, ignoring returns. Especially in finance-related applications [6], where consideration of various measures of the volatility of a portfolio are often given equal footing with the returns themselves, this omission is particularly glaring.

It is natural to ask why one would like explicit consideration of volatility or risk in online learning given that we are already blessed with algorithms providing performance guarantees that track various benchmarks (e.g. best single stock or expert) with absolute certainty. However, in many natural circumstances the benchmark may not be sufficiently strong (e.g. tracking the best stock, as opposed to a richer class of strategies) or the guarantees may be sufficiently loose that realistic application of the existing online algorithms will require one

J.L. Balcázar, P.M. Long, and F. Stephan (Eds.): ALT 2006, LNAI 4264, pp. 199–213, 2006.

to incorporate additional, more traditional, risk criteria. For example, if one applies the standard EG portfolio management algorithm [6] to the S&P 500 over a recent six year period, its returns are actually worse (for all positive learning rates) than that of the simple uniform constant rebalanced portfolio (UCRP), despite the theoretical guarantees on EG performance. In contrast, a risk-sensitive online algorithm can considerably outperform the UCRP (see Section 7). Thus for a variety of reasons, we are motivated to find algorithms that can enjoy guarantees similar to those of the "traditional" approaches such as EG, but that deliberately incorporate risk-return trade-offs. More generally, since such trade-offs are an inherent part of the way Wall Street and the finance community view investment performance, it is interesting to consider online learning through the same lens.

The finance literature on balancing risk and return, and the proposed metrics for doing so, are far too large to survey here (see [2], chapter 4 for a nice overview). Among the most common methods are the *Sharpe ratio* [9], and the *mean-variance (MV)* criterion of which Markowitz was the first proponent [8]. Let $r_t \in [-1, \infty)$ be the return of any given financial instrument (a stock, bond, portfolio, trading strategy, etc.) during time period t. That is, if v_t represents the dollar value of the instrument immediately after period t, we have $v_t = (1+r_t)v_{t-1}$. Negative values of r_t (down to -1, representing the limiting case of the instrument losing all of its value) are losses, and positive values are gains. For a sequence of returns $r = (r_1, \ldots, r_T)$, suppose $\mu(r)$ denotes the (arithmetic) mean and $\sigma(r)$ denotes the standard deviation. Then the Sharpe ratio of the instrument on the sequence is simply $\mu(r)/\sigma(r)$,[1] while the MV is $\mu(r)-\sigma(r)$. (The term mean-variance is slightly misleading since the risk is actually measured by the standard deviation, but we use it to adhere to convention.)

A common alternative is to use the mean and standard deviation not of the r_t but of the $\log(1 + r_t)$, which corresponds to geometric rather than arithmetic averaging of returns; we shall refer to the resulting measures as the *geometric* Sharpe ratio and MV. Note that when r_t is close to 0, (as it is generally in finance applications) it is a good approximation of $\log(1 + r_t)$, so maximizing the arithmetic Sharpe ratio or MV is approximately equivalent to maximizing their geometric counterparts. Although it is tempting to claim that $\log(1 + r_t)$ approximates r_t minus the variance of r_t, it actually approximates $r_t - r_t^2/2$, which can be quite different even in financial applications.

Both the Sharpe ratio and the MV are natural, if somewhat different, methods for specifying a trade-off between the risk and returns of a financial instrument. Note that if we have an algorithm (like Weighted Majority [7, 4]) that maintains a dynamically weighted and rebalanced portfolio over K constituent stocks, this algorithm itself has a sequence of returns and thus its own Sharpe ratio and MV. A natural hope for online learning would be to replicate the kind of no-regret results to which we have become accustomed, but for regret in these risk-return

---

[1] The original definition of the Sharpe ratio also considers the return of a risk-free investment. This term can be safely ignored in analysis if we view returns as already having been shifted by the rate of the risk-free investment.

measures. Thus (for example) we would like an algorithm whose Sharpe ratio or MV at sufficiently long time scales is arbitrarily close to the *best* Sharpe ratio or MV of any of the K stocks. The prospects for these and similar results are the topic of this paper.

Our first results are negative, and show that the specific hope articulated in the last paragraph is unattainable. More precisely, we show that for either the Sharpe ratio or MV, any online learning algorithm must suffer *constant* regret, even when $K = 2$. This is in sharp contrast to the literature on returns alone, where it is known that zero regret can be approached rapidly with increasing time. Furthermore, and perhaps surprisingly, for the case of the Sharpe ratio the proof shows that constant regret is inevitable even for an *offline* algorithm (which knows in advance the specific sequence of returns for the two stocks, but still must compete with the best Sharpe ratio on all time scales).

The fundamental insight in these impossibility results is that the risk term in the different risk-return metrics introduces a "switching cost" not present in the standard return-only settings. Intuitively, in the return-only setting, no matter what decisions an algorithm has made up to time t, it can choose (for instance) to move all of its capital to one stock at time t and *immediately* begin enjoying the *same* returns as that stock from that time forward. However, under the risk-return metrics, if the returns of the algorithm up to time t have been quite different (either higher or lower) than those of the stock, the algorithm pays a "volatility penalty" not suffered by the stock itself.

These strong impossibility results force us to revise our expectations for online learning for risk-return settings. In the second part of the paper, we examine two different approaches to algorithms for MV-like metrics. First we analyze the recent algorithm of Cesa-Bianchi et al. [5] and show that it exhibits a trade-off balancing returns with variance (as opposed to standard deviation) that is additively comparable to a trade-off exhibited by the best stock. This approximation is weaker than competitive ratio or no-regret, but remains nontrivial, especially in light of the strong negative results mentioned above. In the second approach, we give a general transformation of the instantaneous gains given to algorithms (such as Weighted Majority) meeting standard returns-only no-regret criteria. This transformation permits us to incorporate a recent moving window of variance into the gains, yielding an algorithm competitive with a "localized" version of MV in which we are penalized only for volatility on short time scales.

In Section 7 we show the results of an experimental comparison of traditional online algorithms with the risk-sensitive algorithms mentioned above on a six-year S&P 500 data set. We find that the modified no-regret algorithm outperforms the others with respect to Sharpe ratio, MV, and cumulative wealth.

2 Preliminaries

We denote the set of experts as integers $\mathcal{K} = \{1, \ldots, K\}$. For each expert $k \in \mathcal{K}$, we denote its *reward* at time $t \in \{1, \ldots, T\}$ as x_t^k. At each time step t, an algorithm A assigns a weight $w_t^k \geq 0$ to each expert k such that $\sum_{k=1}^{K} w_t^k = 1$. Based on these weights, the algorithm then receives a reward $x_t^A = \sum_{k=1}^{K} w_t^k x_t^k$.

There are multiple ways to define the aforementioned rewards. In a financial setting it is common to define them to be the *simple returns* of some underlying investment. Thus if v_t represents the dollar value of an investment following period t, and $v_t = (1 + r_t)v_{t-1}$ where $r_t \in [-1, \infty)$, one choice is to let $x_t = r_t$. When r_t is close to 0, it is also a good approximation of $\log(1 + r_t)$, so maximizing the arithmetic average of rewards will be very close to maximizing the geometric average. We assume that daily rewards lie in the range $[-M, M]$ for some constant M; some of our bounds depend on M.

Two well-known measures of volatility that we will refer to often are variance and standard deviation. Formally, if $\bar{R}_t(k, \boldsymbol{x})$ is the average reward of expert k on the reward sequence $\boldsymbol{x}$ at time t, then

$$Var_t(k, \boldsymbol{x}) = \frac{1}{t} \sum_{t'=1}^{t} (x_{t'}^k - \bar{R}_t(k, \boldsymbol{x}))^2, \qquad \sigma_t(k, \boldsymbol{x}) = \sqrt{Var_t(k, \boldsymbol{x})}$$

We define $R_t(k, \boldsymbol{x})$ to be the sum of rewards of expert k at times $1, \ldots, t$.

Traditionally in online learning the objective of an algorithm A has been to achieve an average reward at least as good as the best expert over time, yielding results of the form

$$\bar{R}_T(A, \boldsymbol{x}) = \sum_{t=1}^{T} \frac{x_t^A}{T} \geq \max_{k \in \mathcal{K}} \sum_{t=1}^{T} \frac{x_t^k}{T} - \sqrt{\frac{\log K}{T}} = \max_{k \in \mathcal{K}} \bar{R}_T(k, \boldsymbol{x}) - \sqrt{\frac{\log K}{T}}$$

An algorithm achieving this goal is often referred to as a "no regret" algorithm.

Now we are ready to define two standard risk-reward balancing criteria, the Sharpe ratio [9] and the MV of expert k at time t.

$$Sharpe_t(k, \boldsymbol{x}) = \frac{\bar{R}_t(k, \boldsymbol{x})}{\sigma_t(k, \boldsymbol{x})}, \qquad MV_t(k, \boldsymbol{x}) = \bar{R}_t(k, \boldsymbol{x}) - \sigma_t(k, \boldsymbol{x})$$

In the following definitions we use the MV, but all apply mutatis mutandis to Sharpe ratio. We say that an algorithm has *no regret* with respect to MV if

$$MV_t(A, \boldsymbol{x}) \geq \max_{k \in \mathcal{K}} MV_t(k, \boldsymbol{x}) - Regret(t)$$

where $Regret(t)$ is a function that goes to 0 as t approaches infinity. We say that an algorithm A has *constant regret* C for some constant $C > 0$ (that does not depend on time but may depend on M) if for any large t there exists a $t' \geq t$ and a sequence $\boldsymbol{x}$ of expert rewards for which the following is satisfied:

$$MV_{t'}(A, \boldsymbol{x}) > \max_{k \in \mathcal{K}} MV_{t'}(k, \boldsymbol{x}) - C$$

Finally, the *competitive ratio* of an algorithm A is defined as

$$\inf_{\boldsymbol{x}} \inf_{t} \frac{MV_t(A, \boldsymbol{x})}{\max_{k \in \mathcal{K}} MV_t(k, \boldsymbol{x})}$$

where $\boldsymbol{x}$ can be any reward sequence generated for K experts. We sometimes refer to $MV_t(A, \boldsymbol{x}) / \max_{k \in \mathcal{K}} MV_t(k, \boldsymbol{x})$ as the *competitive ratio on $\boldsymbol{x}$ at time t*.

Note that for negative concepts like constant regret, it is sufficient to consider a single sequence of expert rewards for which *no* algorithm can perform well.

3   A Lower Bound for the Sharpe Ratio

In this section we show that even an offline policy cannot compete with the best expert with respect to the Sharpe ratio, even when there are only two experts.

Theorem 1. *Any offline algorithm has constant regret with respect to Sharpe ratio. Furthermore, for any $T \geq 30$, there exists an expert reward sequence x of length T and two points in time such that no algorithm can attain more than a $1 - C$ competitive ratio on x at both points, for some constant $C > 0$.*

We give a brief overview the proof here; details are provided in Appendix A.

The lower bound is proved in a setting where there are only two experts and the performance of the algorithm is tested at only two points. The reward sequence used is simple with each expert's reward changing only twice. The performance of the algorithm is tested when the second change occurs and at the end of the sequence. If the algorithm reward at the first checkpoint is too high, it will be the case that the competitive ratio at that point is bad. If it is lower, the competitive ratio at the second checkpoint will be bad. We characterize the optimal offline algorithm and show that it cannot compete with the best stock on this sequence. This, of course, implies that no algorithm can compete.

4   A Lower Bound for MV

A similar bound can be shown for our additive risk-reward measure, the MV.

Theorem 2. *Any online algorithm has constant regret with respect to the MV.*

The proof will again be based on specific sequences that will serve as counterexamples to show that in general it is not possible to compete with the best expert in terms of the MV. We begin by describing how these sequences are generated. Again we consider a scenario in which there are only two experts. For the first n time steps, the first expert receives at each time step a reward of 2 with probability $1/2$ or a reward of 0 with probability $1/2$, while at times $n + 1, ..., 2n$ the reward is always 1. The second expert's reward is always $1/4$ throughout the entire sequence. The algorithm's performance will be tested only at times n and $2n$, and the algorithm is assumed to know the process by which these expert rewards are generated.

This lower bound construction is not a single sequence but is a set of sequences generated according to the distribution over the first expert's rewards. We will refer to the set of all sequences that can be generated by this distribution as S. For any specific sequence in S, the optimal offline algorithm would suffer no regret, but we will show by the probabilistic method that there is no online algorithm that can perform well on all sequences in S at both checkpoints. In contrast to "standard" experts, there are now two randomness sources: the internal randomness of the algorithm and the randomness of the rewards.

We now give a high level overview. First we will consider a "balanced sequence" in S in which expert 1 receives an equal number of rewards that are 2 and rewards that are 0. Assuming such a sequence, it will be the case that the best expert at time

n is expert 2 with reward $1/4$ and standard deviation 0, while the best expert at time $2n$ is expert 1 with reward 1 and standard deviation $1/\sqrt{2}$. Note that any algorithm that has average reward $1/4$ at time n in this scenario will be unable to overcome this start and will have a constant regret at time $2n$. Yet it might be the case on such sequences that a sophisticated adaptive algorithm could have an average reward higher than $1/4$ at time n and still suffer no regret at time n. Hence, for the balanced sequence we first look at the case in which the *algorithm* is "balanced" as well, i.e. the weight it puts on expert 1 on days with reward 2 is equal to the weight it puts on expert 1 on days with reward 0. We can later drop this requirement.

In our analysis we show that most sequences in S are "close" to the balanced sequence. If the average reward of an algorithm over all sequences is less than $1/4 + \delta$, for some constant δ, then by the probabilistic method there exists a sequence for which the algorithm will have constant regret at time $2n$. If not, then there exists a sequence for which at time n the algorithm's standard deviation will be larger than δ by some constant factor, so the algorithm will have regret at time n. This argument will also be probabilistic, preventing the algorithm from constantly being "lucky." Details of this proof are given in Appendix B.

In fact we can extend this theorem to the broader class of objective functions of the form $\bar{R}_t(k, \boldsymbol{x}) - \alpha \sigma_t(A, \boldsymbol{x})$, where $\alpha > 0$ is constant. The proof, which is similar to the proof of Theorem 2, is omitted due to space limits. Both the constant and the length of the sequence will depend on α.

Theorem 3. *Let $\alpha \geq 0$ be a constant. The regret of any online algorithm with respect to the metric $\bar{R}_t(k, \boldsymbol{x}) - \alpha \sigma_t(A, \boldsymbol{x})$ is constant for some positive constant that depends on α.*

5   A Bicriteria Upper Bound

In this section we show that the recent algorithm of Cesa-Bianchi et al. [5] can yield a risk-reward balancing bound. Their original result expressed a no-regret bound with respect to *rewards* only, but the regret itself involved a variance term. Here we give an alternate analysis demonstrating that the algorithm actually respects a risk-reward trade-off. The quality of the results here depends on the bound M on the absolute value of expert rewards as we will show.

We first describe the algorithm Prod which takes one parameter η. It maintains a set of K weights, one for each expert. The (unnormalized) weights $\tilde{w}_t^k$ are initialized with $\tilde{w}_1^k = 1$ for every expert k and updated at each time step according to $\tilde{w}_t^k \leftarrow \tilde{w}_{t-1}^k(1 + \eta x_{t-1}^k)$. The normalized weights at each time step are then defined as $w_t^k = \tilde{w}_t^k / \tilde{W}_t$ where $\tilde{W}_t = \sum_{j=1}^k \tilde{w}_t^j$.

Theorem 4. *For any expert $k \in \mathcal{K}$, for the algorithm Prod with $\eta = 1/(LM)$ where $L > 2$ we have at time t*

$$\left(\frac{L\bar{R}_t(A, \boldsymbol{x})}{L-1} - \frac{\eta(3L-2)Var_t(A, \boldsymbol{x})}{6L} \right) \geq \left(\frac{L\bar{R}_t(k, \boldsymbol{x})}{L+1} - \frac{\eta(3L+2)Var_t(k, \boldsymbol{x})}{6L} \right) - \frac{\ln K}{\eta}$$

for any sequence $\boldsymbol{x}$ in which the absolute value of each reward is bounded by M.

The proof is given in Appendix C. The two large expressions in parentheses in Theorem 4 additively balance rewards and variance of rewards, but with different coefficients. It is tempting but apparently not possible to convert this inequality into a competitive ratio. Nevertheless certain natural settings of the parameters cause the two expressions to give quantitatively similar trade-offs. For example, let $\boldsymbol{x}$ be any sequence of rewards which are bounded in $[-0.1, 0.1]$ and let A be Prod for $\eta = 1$. Then for any time t and expert k we have

$$1.11\bar{R}_t(A, \boldsymbol{x}) - 0.466 Var_t(A, \boldsymbol{x}) \geq 0.91\bar{R}_t(k, \boldsymbol{x}) - 0.533 Var_t(k, \boldsymbol{x}) - (10\ln K)/t$$

This gives a relatively even balance between rewards and variance on both sides. We note that the choice of a "reasonable" bound on the rewards magnitudes should be related to the time scale of the process — for instance, returns on the order of $\pm 1\%$ might be entirely reasonable daily but not annually.

6   No-Regret Results for Localized Risk

We now show a no-regret result for an algorithm optimizing an alternative objective function that incorporates both risk and reward. The primary leverage of this alternative objective is that risk is now measured only "locally." The goal is to balance immediate rewards with how far these immediate rewards deviate from the average rewards over some "recent" past. In addition to allowing us to skirt the strong impossibility results for no-regret in the standard risk-return measures, we note that our new objective may be of independent interest, as it incorporates other notions of risk that are commonly considered in finance where short-term volatility is usually of greater concern than long-term. For example, this objective has the flavor of what is sometimes called "maximum draw-down," the largest decline in the price of a stock over a given, usually short, time period.

Consider the following risk measure for an expert k on a reward sequence $\boldsymbol{x}$:

$$P_t(k, \boldsymbol{x}) = \sum_{t'=2}^{t}(x_{t'}^k - \text{AVG}_\ell^*(x_1^k, ..., x_{t'}^k))^2$$

where $\text{AVG}_\ell^*(x_1^k, .., x_t^k) = \sum_{t'=t-\ell+1}^{t}(x_{t'}^k/\ell)$ is the fixed window size average for some window size $\ell > 0$. The new risk-sensitive criterion at time t will be

$$G_t(A, \boldsymbol{x}) = \bar{R}_t(A, \boldsymbol{x}) - P_t(A, \boldsymbol{x})/t.$$

Observe that the measure of risk defined here is very similar to variance. In particular, if for every expert $k \in \mathcal{K}$ we let $p_t^k = (x_t^k - \text{AVG}_t^*(x_1^k, .., x_t^k))^2$, then

$$P_t(k, \boldsymbol{x})/t = \sum_{t'=2}^{t}\frac{p_{t'}^k}{t}, \qquad Var_t(k, \boldsymbol{x}) = \sum_{t'=2}^{n}\frac{p_{t'}^k}{t}\left(1 + \frac{1}{t'-1}\right)$$

Our measure differs from the variance in two aspects. The variance of the sequence will be affected by rewards in the past and the future, whereas our measure depends only on rewards in the past, and for our measure the current reward is compared only to the rewards in the recent past, and not to all past rewards. While both differences are exploited in the proof, the fixed window size is key. The main obstacle of the algorithms in the previous sections was the "memory" of the variance, which prevented switching between experts. The memory of the penalty is now ℓ and our results will be meaningful when $\ell = o(\sqrt{T})$.

The algorithm we discuss will work by feeding modified instantaneous gains to any best experts algorithm that satisfies the assumption below. This assumption is met by algorithms such as Weighted Majority [7, 4].

Definition 1. *An optimized best expert algorithm is an algorithm that guarantees that for any sequence of reward vectors $\boldsymbol{x}$ over experts $\mathcal{K} = \{1, \ldots, K\}$, the algorithm selects a distribution $\boldsymbol{w_t}$ over $\mathcal{K}$ (using only the previous reward functions) such that*

$$\sum_{t=1}^{T} \sum_{k=1}^{K} w_t^k x_t^k \geq \sum_{t=1}^{T} x_t^k - \sqrt{TM \log K},$$

where $|x_t^k| \leq M$ and k is any expert. Furthermore, we also assume that decision distributions do not change quickly: $\|\boldsymbol{w_t} - \boldsymbol{w_{t+1}}\|_1 \leq \sqrt{\log(K)/t}$.

Since the risk function now has shorter memory, there is hope that a standard best expert algorithm will work. Therefore, we would like to incorporate this risk term into the instantaneous rewards fed to the best experts algorithm. We will define this instantaneous quantity, the *gain* of expert k at time t to be $g_t^k = x_t^k - (x_t^k - AVG_\ell^*(x_1^k, ..., x_{t-1}^k))^2 = x_t^k - p_t^k$, where p_t^k is the *penalty* for expert k at time t. Similarly the penalty for an algorithm A can be defined as $p_t^A = (x_t^A - AVG_\ell^*(x_1^A, ..., x_{t-1}^A))^2$. It is natural to wonder whether $p_t^A = \sum_{k=1}^{K} w_t^k p_t^k$; unfortunately, this is not the case, but they are similar. To formalize the connection between the measures, we let $\hat{P}(A, \boldsymbol{x}) = \sum_{t=1}^{T} \sum_{k=1}^{K} w_t^k p_t^k$ be the weighted penalty function of the experts, and $P(A, \boldsymbol{x}) = \sum_{t=1}^{T} p_t^A$ be the penalty function observed by the algorithm. The next lemma relates these quantities.

Lemma 1. *Let $\boldsymbol{x}$ be any reward sequence such that all rewards are bounded by M. Then $\hat{P}^T(A, \boldsymbol{x}) \geq P_T(A, \boldsymbol{x}) - 2TM^2\ell\sqrt{\frac{\log K}{T-\ell}}$.*

Proof

$$\hat{P}^T(A, \boldsymbol{x}) = \sum_{t=1}^{T} \sum_{k=1}^{K} w_t^k (x_t^k - AVG_\ell^*(x_1^k, .., x_t^k))^2$$

$$\geq \sum_{t=1}^{T} \left(\sum_{k=1}^{K} w_t^k \left(x_t^k - \frac{\sum_{j=1}^{\ell} x_{t-j+1}^k}{\ell} \right) \right)^2$$

$$= \sum_{t=1}^{T} \left(\sum_{k=1}^{K} w_t^k x_t^k - \frac{\sum_{k=1}^{K} \sum_{j=1}^{\ell} (w_t^k - w_{t-j+1}^k + w_{t-j+1}^k) x_{t-j+1}^k}{\ell} \right)^2$$

$$= \sum_{t=1}^{T} \left(\left(\sum_{k=1}^{K} w_t^k x_t^k - \frac{\sum_{k=1}^{K} \sum_{j=1}^{\ell} w_{t-j+1}^k x_{t-j+1}^k}{\ell} \right)^2 + \left(\frac{\sum_{k=1}^{K} \sum_{j=1}^{\ell} \epsilon_j^k x_{t-j+1}^k}{\ell} \right)^2 \right.$$

$$-2\left(\frac{\sum_{k=1}^{K}\sum_{j=1}^{\ell}\epsilon_j^k x_{t-j+1}^k}{\ell}\right)\left(\sum_{k=1}^{K}w_t^k x_t^k - \frac{\sum_{k=1}^{K}\sum_{j=1}^{\ell}w_{t-j+1}^k x_{t-j+1}^k}{\ell}\right)\right)$$

$$\geq P_T(A,\boldsymbol{x}) - \sum_{t=1}^{T}\left(2M\frac{\sum_{k=1}^{K}\sum_{j=1}^{\ell}|\epsilon_j^k|M}{\ell}\right) \geq P_T(A,\boldsymbol{x}) - 2M^2\ell T\sqrt{\frac{\log K}{T-\ell}}$$

where $\epsilon_j^k = w_t^k - w_{t-j+1}^k$. The first inequality is an application of Jensen's inequality using the convexity of x^2. The third inequality follows from the fact that $\sum_{k=1}^{K}|\epsilon_j^k|$ is bounded by $j\sqrt{\frac{\log K}{T-j}}$ using our best expert assumption.   □

The following theorem is the main result of this section, describing a no-regret algorithm with respect to the risk-sensitive function G_T.

Theorem 5. *Let A be a best expert algorithm that satisfies Definition 1 with instantaneous gain function $g_t^k = x_t^k - (x_t^k - AVG_\ell^*(x_1^k,...,x_{t-1}^k))^2$ for expert k at time t. Then for large enough T for any reward sequence $\boldsymbol{x}$ and any expert k we have for window size ℓ*

$$G_T(A,\boldsymbol{x}) \geq G_T(k,\boldsymbol{x}) - O\left(M^2\ell\sqrt{\frac{\log K}{T-\ell}}\right)$$

Proof: Using the best expert assumption and Lemma 1, we have

$$T\cdot G(k,\boldsymbol{x}) = \sum_{t=1}^{T}x_t^k - \sum_{t=1}^{T}(x_t^k - AVG_\ell^*(x_1^k,..,y_t^k))^2$$

$$\leq \sum_{t=1}^{T}\sum_{k'=1}^{K}w_t^{k'} x_t^{k'} - \sum_{t=1}^{T}\sum_{k'=1}^{K}w_t^{k'}(x_t^{k'} - AVG_\ell^*(x_1^{k'},..,x_t^{k'}))^2 + M\sqrt{T\log K}$$

$$\leq T\cdot G(A,\boldsymbol{x}) + 2TM^2\ell\sqrt{\frac{\log K}{T-\ell}} + M\sqrt{T\log K}$$

Dividing both sides by T yields the result.   □

Corollary 1. *Let A be a best expert algorithm that satisfies Definition 1 with instantaneous reward function $g_t^k = x_t^k - (x_t^k - AVG_\ell^*(x_1^k,...,x_{t-1}^k))^2$. Then for large enough T we have for any expert k and fixed window size $\ell = O(\log T)$*

$$G(A,\boldsymbol{x}) \geq G(k,\boldsymbol{x}) - \tilde{O}\left(M^2\sqrt{\frac{\log K}{T}}\right)$$

7   Empirical Results

We conclude by showing the results of some simulations of the algorithms and measures discussed. The data set used in these experiments consists of the closing prices on the 1632 trading days between January 4, 1999 and June 29, 2005 of the 469 S&P 500 stocks that remained in the index for the duration of the period.

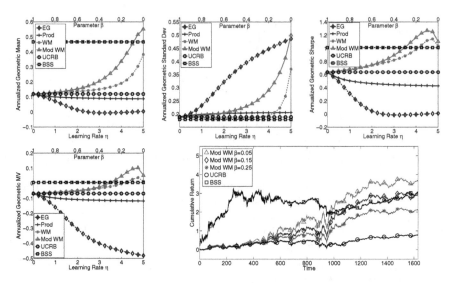

Fig. 1. Top Row and Bottom Left: Annualized geometric mean, standard deviation, Sharpe ratio, and MV of each algorithm plus the UCRB portfolio and the best single stock at the end of the 1632 day period. **Bottom Right:** Cumulative geometric return of the modified WM, the best single stock at each time step, and the UCRB portfolio.

We implemented the exponential gradient (EG) algorithm of Hembold et al. [6], Prod [5], weighted majority [7, 4], and the modified best experts algorithm presented in Section 6 using weighted majority as the black box. For the modified version of WM, we used a fixed window average size $\ell = 40$. Other values of ℓ yield similar performance results.

The first four plots in Figure 1 show the annualized geometric mean, standard deviation, Sharpe ratio, and MV of the four algorithms along with those of the uniform constant rebalanced portfolio (UCRB) and the best single stock (BSS) with respect to each performance measure. Note that the x axis ranges over values of the learning rate η for EG and Prod and values of the parameter β for both versions of WM making direct comparisons at particular parameter values difficult. However, it is clear that on this data set, WM and the modified WM algorithm outperform EG and Prod for all parameter settings. In fact, EG and Prod are outperformed by both the best single stock and the uniform constant rebalanced portfolio. This may be due to the large number of stocks available; similar behavior has been noted by [3] and [1]. Additionally, our modified WM outperforms the best expert with respect to geometric mean, Sharpe ratio, and MV when WM's β parameter is small.

The final plot shows the cumulative geometric return (i.e. $\sum_{t=1}^{T} \log(1 + r_t)$ where r_t is return as defined in Section 2) as a function of time T for our modified version of WM with three different β values, the best single stock at each time step, and the uniform constant rebalanced portfolio. At early times, there exist single stocks which can outperform the algorithm, but as T increases, our modified version of WM surpasses any individual stock.

References

1. A. Agarwal, E. Hazan, S. Kale, and R. E. Schapire. Algorithms for Portfolio Management based on the Newton Method, *ICML*, 2006.
2. Z. Bodie, A. Kane, and A. J. Marcus. Portfolio Performance Evaluation, Investments, 4th edition, Irwin McGraw-Hill, 1999.
3. A. Borodin, R. El-Yaniv, and V. Gogan. Can We Learn to Beat the Best Stock, *JAIR*, 21: 579–594, 2004.
4. N. Cesa-Bianchi, Y. Freund, D. Haussler, D. Helmbold, R.E. Schapire, and M.K. Warmuth. How to Use Expert Advice, *J. of the ACM*, 44(3): 427-485, 1997.
5. N. Cesa-Bianchi, Y. Mansour, and G. Stoltz. Improved Second-Order Bounds for Prediction with Expert Advice, *COLT*, 217–232, 2005.
6. D.P. Helmbold, R.E. Schapire, Y. Singer, and M.K. Warmuth. On-line portfolio selection using multiplicative updates, *Mathematical Finance*, 8(4): 325–347, 1998.
7. N. Littlestone and M. K. Warmuth. The Weighted Majority Algorithm, *Information and Computation*, 108(2): 212-261, 1994.
8. H. Markowitz. Portfolio Selection, *The Journal of Finance*, 7(1):77–91, 1952.
9. W. F. Sharpe. Mutual Fund Performance, *The Journal of Business*, Vol 39, Number 1, part 2: Supplement on Security Prices, 119-138, 1966.
10. M. K. Warmuth and D. Kuzmin. Online Variance Minimization, *COLT*, 2006.

A   Proof of Theorem 1

We define an *m-segment sequence* as a sequence described by expert rewards at m times, $n_1 < \ldots < n_m$, such that for all $i \in \{1, \ldots, m\}$, every expert's reward in the time segment $[n_{i-1} + 1, n_i]$ is constant, i.e. $\forall t \in [n_{i-1} + 1, n_i], \forall k \in \mathcal{K}, x_t^k = x_{n_i}^k$. where $n_0 = 0$. We say that an algorithm has a *fixed policy* in the ith segment if the weights that the algorithm places on each expert remain constant between times $n_{i-1} + 1$ and n_i. The following lemma states that an algorithm with maximal Sharpe ratio at time n_i uses a fixed policy at every segment prior to i.

Lemma 2. *Let x be an m-segment reward sequence. Let A_i^r (for $i \le m$) be the set of algorithms that have average reward r on x at time n_i. Then an algorithm $A \in A_i^r$ with minimal standard deviation has a fixed policy in every segment prior to i. The optimal Sharpe ratio at time n_i is thus attained by an algorithm that has a fixed policy in every segment prior to i.*

The intuition behind this lemma is that switching weights within a segment can only result in higher variance without enabling an algorithm to achieve an average reward any higher than it would have been able to achieve using a fixed set of weights in this segment. The proof is omitted due to lack of space.

With this lemma, we are ready to prove Theorem 1. We will consider one specific 3-segment sequence with two experts and show that there is no algorithm that can have competitive ratio bigger than 0.71 at both times n_2 and n_3 on this sequence. The three segments are of equal length. The rewards for expert 1 are .05, .01, and .05 in intervals 1, 2, and 3 respectively. The rewards for expert 2 are .011, .009, and .05. [2] The Sharpe ratio of the algorithm will be compared to the Sharpe ratio of the best expert at times n_2 and n_3. Analyzing the sequence we observe that the best expert at time n_2 is expert 2 with Sharpe ratio 10. The best expert at n_3 is expert 1 with Sharpe ratio approximately 1.95.

The intuition behind this construction is that in order for the algorithm to have a good competitive ratio at time n_2 it cannot put too much weight on expert 1 and must put significant weight on expert 2. However, putting significant weight on expert 2 prevents the algorithm from being competitive in time n_3 where it must have switched completely to expert 1 to maintain a good Sharpe ratio. The remainder of the proof formalizes this notion.

Suppose first that the average reward of the algorithm on the lower bound Sharpe sequence x at time n_2 is at least .012. The reward in the second segment can be at most .01, so if the average reward at time n_2 is $.012 + z$ where z is positive constant smaller than .018, then the standard deviation of the algorithm at n_2 is at least $.002 + z$. This implies that the algorithm's Sharpe ratio is at most $\frac{.012+z}{.002+z}$, which is at most 6. Comparing this to the Sharpe ratio of 10 obtained by expert 2, we see that the algorithm can have a competitive ratio no higher than 0.6, or equivalently the algorithm's regret is at least 4.

Suppose instead that the average reward of the algorithm on x at time n_2 is less than .012. Note that the Sharpe ratio of expert 1 at time n_3 is approximately $\frac{.03667}{.018} > 1.94$. In order to obtain a bound that holds for any algorithm with average reward at most .012 at time n_2, we consider the algorithm A which has reward of .012 in every time step and clearly outperforms any other algorithm.[3] The average reward of A for the third segment must be .05 as it is the reward of both experts. Now we can compute its average and standard deviation $\bar{R}_{n_3}(A, x) \approx 2.4667$ and $\sigma_{n_3}(A, x) \approx 1.79$. The Sharpe ratio of A is then approximately 1.38, and we find that A has a competitive ratio at time n_3 that is at most 0.71 or equivalently its regret is at least 0.55.

The lower bound sequence that we used here can be further improved to obtain a competitive ratio of .5. The improved sequence is of the form $n, 1, n$ for the first expert's rewards, and $1 + 1/n, 1 - 1/n, n$ for the second expert's rewards. As n approaches infinity, the competitive ratio of the Sharpe ratio tested on two checkpoints at n_2 and n_3 approaches .5.

B   Proof of Theorem 2

Recall that we are considering a two expert scenario. Until time n, expert 1 receives a reward of 2 with probably 1/2 and a reward of 0 with probability 1/2. From n to $2n$, he always receives 1. Expert 2 always receives 1/4. Recall that we refer to the set of sequences that can be generated by this distribution as S.

In this analysis we use a form of Azuma's inequality, which we present here for sake of completeness. Note that we cannot use standard Chernoff bound since we would like to provide bounds on the behavior of adaptive algorithms.

---

[2] Note that since the Sharpe ratio is a unitless measure, we could scale the rewards in this sequence by any positive constant factor and the proof would still hold.

[3] Of course such an algorithm cannot exist for this sequence.

Lemma 3 (Azuma). *Let $\zeta_0, \zeta_1, ..., \zeta_n$ be a martingale sequence such that for each i, $1 \leq i \leq n$, we have $|\zeta_i - \zeta_{i-1}| \leq c_i$ where the constant c_i may depend on i. Then for $n \geq 1$ and any $\epsilon > 0$*

$$Pr\left[|\zeta_n - \zeta_0| > \epsilon\right] \leq 2e^{-\frac{\epsilon^2}{2\sum_{i=1}^{n} c_i^2}}$$

Now we define two martingale sequences, $y_t(\boldsymbol{x})$ and $z_t(A, \boldsymbol{x})$. The first counts the difference between the number of times expert 1 receives a reward of 2 and the number of times expert 1 receives a reward of 0 on a given sequence $\boldsymbol{x} \in S$. The second counts the difference between the weights that algorithm A places on expert 1 when expert 1 receives a reward of 2 and the weights placed on expert 1 when expert 1 receives a reward of 0. We define $y_0(\boldsymbol{x}) = z_0(A, \boldsymbol{x}) = 0$ for all $\boldsymbol{x}$ and A.

$$y_{t+1}(\boldsymbol{x}) = \begin{cases} y_t(\boldsymbol{x}) + 1, & x_{t+1}^1 = 2 \\ y_t(\boldsymbol{x}) - 1, & x_{t+1}^1 = 0 \end{cases}, \quad z_{t+1}(A, \boldsymbol{x}) = \begin{cases} z_t(A, \boldsymbol{x}) + w_{t+1}^1, & x_{t+1}^1 = 2 \\ z_t(A, \boldsymbol{x}) - w_{t+1}^1, & x_{t+1}^1 = 0 \end{cases}$$

In order to simplify notation throughout the rest of this section, we will often drop the parameters and write y_t and z_t when A and $\boldsymbol{x}$ are clear from context.

Recall that $\bar{R}_t(A, \boldsymbol{x})$ is the average reward of an algorithm A on sequence $\boldsymbol{x}$ at time t. We denote the *expected* average reward at time t as $\bar{R}_t(A, D) = E_{\boldsymbol{x} \sim D}\left[\bar{R}_t(A, \boldsymbol{x})\right]$, where D is the distribution over rewards.

Next we define a set of sequences that are "close" to the balanced sequence on which the algorithm A will have a high reward, and subsequently show that for algorithms with high expected average reward this set is not empty.

Definition 2. *Let A be any algorithm and δ any positive constant. Then the set S_A^δ is the set of sequences $\boldsymbol{x} \in S$ that satisfy (1) $|y_n(\boldsymbol{x})| \leq \sqrt{2n \ln(2n)}$, (2) $|z_n(A, \boldsymbol{x})| \leq \sqrt{2n \ln(2n)}$, (3) $\bar{R}_n(A, \boldsymbol{x}) \geq 1/4 + \delta - O(1/n)$.*

Lemma 4. *Let δ be any positive constant and A be an algorithm such that $\bar{R}_n(A, D) \geq 1/4 + \delta$. Then S_A^δ is not empty.*

Proof: Since y_n and z_n are martingale sequences, we can apply Azuma's inequality to show that $\Pr[y_n \geq \sqrt{2n \ln(2n)}] < 1/n$ and $\Pr[z_n \geq \sqrt{2n \ln(2n)}] < 1/n$. Thus, since rewards are bounded by a constant value in our construction (namely 2), the contribution of sequences for which y_n or z_n are larger than $\sqrt{2n \ln(2n)}$ to the expected average reward is bounded by $O(1/n)$. This implies that if there exists an algorithm A such that $\bar{R}_n(A, D) \geq 1/4 + \delta$, then there exists a sequence $\boldsymbol{x}$ for which the $\bar{R}_n(A, \boldsymbol{x}) \geq 1/4 + \delta - O(1/n)$ and both y_n and z_n are bounded by $\sqrt{2n \ln(2n)}$. □

Now we would like to analyze the performance of an algorithm for some sequence $\boldsymbol{x}$ in S_A^δ. We first analyze the balanced sequence where $y_n = 0$ with a balanced algorithm (so $z_n = 0$), and then show how the analysis easily extends to sequences in the set S_A. In particular, we will first show that for the balanced sequence the optimal policy in terms of the objective function achieved has one fixed policy in times $[1, n]$ and another fixed policy in times $[n + 1, 2n]$. Due to lack of space the proof, which is similar but slightly more complicated than the proof of Lemma 2, is omitted.

Lemma 5. *Let $x \in S$ be a sequence with $y_n = 0$ and let A_0^x be the set of algorithms for which $z_n = 0$ on x. Then the optimal algorithm in A_0^x with respect to the objective function $MV(A, x)$ has a fixed policy in times $[1, n]$ and a fixed policy in times $[n + 1, 2n]$.*

Now that we have characterized the optimal algorithm for the balanced setting, we will analyze its performance. The next lemma (proof omitted) connects the average reward to the standard deviation on balanced sequences by using the fact that on balanced sequences algorithms behave as they are "expected."

Lemma 6. *Let $x \in S$ be a sequence with $y_n = 0$, and let A_0^x be the set of algorithms with $z_n = 0$ on x. For any positive constant δ, if $A \in A_0^x$ and $\bar{R}_n(A, x) = 1/4 + \delta$, then $\sigma_n(A, x) \geq \frac{4\delta}{3}$.*

The following is a bound on the objective function at time $2n$ given high reward at time n. The proof (again omitted) uses the fact the added standard deviation is at least as large as the added average reward and thus cancels it.

Lemma 7. *Let x be any sequence and A any algorithm. If $\bar{R}_n(A, x) = 1/4 + \delta$, then $MV_{2n}(A, x) \leq 1/4 + \delta$ for any positive constant δ.*

Recall that the best expert at time n is expert 2 with reward $1/4$ and standard deviation 0, and the best expert at time $2n$ is expert 1 with average reward 1 and standard deviation $1/\sqrt{2}$. Using this knowledge in addition to Lemmas 6 and 7, we obtain the following proposition for the balanced sequence:

Proposition 1. *Let $x \in S$ be a sequence with $y_n = 0$, and let A_0^x be the set of algorithms with $z_n = 0$ for s. If $A \in A_0^x$, then A has a constant regret at either time n or time $2n$ or at both.*

We are now ready to return to the non-balanced setting in which y_n and z_n may take on values other than 0. Here we use the fact that there exists a sequence in S for which the average reward is at least $1/4 + \delta - O(1/n)$ and for which y_n and z_n are small. The next lemma shows that standard deviation of an algorithm A on sequences in S_A^δ is high at time n. The proof, which is omitted, uses the fact that such sequences and algorithm can be changed with almost no effect on average reward and standard deviation to balanced sequence, for which we know the standard deviation of any algorithm must be high.

Lemma 8. *Let δ be any positive constant, A be any algorithm, and x be a sequence in S_A^δ. Then $\sigma_n(A, x) \geq \frac{4\delta}{3} - O\left(\sqrt{\ln(n)/n}\right)$.*

We are ready to prove the main theorem of the section.

Proof: [Theorem 2] Let δ be any positive constant. If $\bar{R}_n(A, D) < 1/4 + \delta$, then there must be a sequence $x \in S$ with $y_n \leq \sqrt{2n \ln(2n)}$ and $\bar{R}_n(A, x) < 1/4 + \delta$. Then the regret of A at time $2n$ will be at least $1 - 1/\sqrt{2} - 1/4 - \delta - O(1/n)$.

If, on the other hand, $\bar{R}_n(A, D) \geq 1/4 + \delta$, then by Lemma 4 there exists a sequence $x \in S$ such that $\bar{R}_n(A, x) \geq 1/4 + \delta - O(1/n)$. By Lemma 8, $\sigma_n(A, x) \geq 4/3\delta - O\left(\sqrt{\ln(n)/n}\right)$, and thus the algorithm has regret at time n of at least $\delta/3 - O\left(\sqrt{\ln(n)/n}\right)$. This shows that for any δ we have that either the regret at time n is constant or the regret at time $2n$ is constant. $\qquad\square$

C Proof of Theorem 4

The following facts about the behavior of $\ln(1+z)$ for small z will be useful.

Lemma 9. *For any $L > 2$ and any v, y, and z such that $|v|$, $|y|$, $|v+y|$, and $|z|$ are all bounded by $1/L$ we have the following*

$$z - \frac{(3L+2)z^2}{6L} < \ln(1+z) < z - \frac{(3L-2)z^2}{6L}$$

$$\ln(1+v) + \frac{Ly}{L+1} < \ln(1+v+y) < \ln(1+v) + \frac{Ly}{L-1}$$

Similar to the analysis in [5], we bound $\ln\frac{\tilde{W}_{n+1}}{\tilde{W}_1}$ from above and below.

Lemma 10. *For the algorithm Prod with $\eta = 1/(LM) \leq 1/4$ where $L > 2$,*

$$\ln\frac{\tilde{W}_{n+1}}{\tilde{W}_1} \leq \frac{\eta L R_n(A, \boldsymbol{x})}{L-1} - \frac{\eta^2(3L-2)nVar_n(A, \boldsymbol{x})}{6L}$$

at any time n for sequence $\boldsymbol{x}$ with the absolute value of rewards bounded by M.

Proof: Similarly to [5] we obtain,

$$\ln\frac{\tilde{W}_{n+1}}{\tilde{W}_1} = \sum_{t=1}^{n}\ln\frac{\tilde{W}_{t+1}}{\tilde{W}_t} = \sum_{t=1}^{n}\ln\left(\sum_{k=1}^{K}\frac{\tilde{w}_t^k}{\tilde{W}_t}(1+\eta x_t^k)\right) = \sum_{t=1}^{n}\ln(1+\eta x_t^A)$$

$$= \sum_{t=1}^{n}\ln(1+\eta(x_t^A - \bar{R}_n(A, \boldsymbol{x}) + \bar{R}_n(A, \boldsymbol{x})))$$

Now using Lemma 9 twice we obtain the proof.   □

Next we bound $\ln\frac{\tilde{W}_{n+1}}{\tilde{W}_1}$ from below. The proof is based on similar arguments to the previous lemma and the observation made in [5] that $\ln\frac{\tilde{W}_{n+1}}{\tilde{W}_1} \geq \ln\left(\frac{\tilde{w}_{n+1}^k}{K}\right)$, and is thus omitted.

Lemma 11. *For the algorithm Prod with $\eta = 1/LM$ where $L > 2$, for any expert $k \in \mathcal{K}$ the following is satisfied*

$$\ln\frac{\tilde{W}_{n+1}}{\tilde{W}_1} \geq -\ln K + \frac{\eta L R_n(k, \boldsymbol{x})}{L+1} - \frac{\eta^2(3L+2)nVar_n(k, \boldsymbol{x})}{6L}$$

at any time n for any sequence $\boldsymbol{x}$ with rewards absolute values bounded by M.

Combining the two lemmas we obtain Theorem 4.

Leading Strategies
in Competitive On-Line Prediction

Vladimir Vovk

Computer Learning Research Centre, Department of Computer Science
Royal Holloway, University of London, Egham, Surrey TW20 0EX, UK
vovk@cs.rhul.ac.uk

Abstract. We start from a simple asymptotic result for the problem of
on-line regression with the quadratic loss function: the class of continuous limited-memory prediction strategies admits a "leading prediction
strategy", which not only asymptotically performs at least as well as any
continuous limited-memory strategy but also satisfies the property that
the excess loss of any continuous limited-memory strategy is determined
by how closely it imitates the leading strategy. More specifically, for any
class of prediction strategies constituting a reproducing kernel Hilbert
space we construct a leading strategy, in the sense that the loss of any
prediction strategy whose norm is not too large is determined by how
closely it imitates the leading strategy. This result is extended to the loss
functions given by Bregman divergences and by strictly proper scoring
rules.

> For the only way to compete is to
> imitate the leader...
>
> ———————————————
>
> Jacques Ellul

1 Introduction

Suppose $\mathcal{F}$ is a normed function class of prediction strategies (the "benchmark
class"). It is well known that, under some restrictions on $\mathcal{F}$, there exists a "master
prediction strategy" (sometimes also called a "universal strategy") that performs
almost as well as the best strategies in $\mathcal{F}$ whose norm is not too large (see,
e.g., [6, 2]). The "leading prediction strategies" constructed in this paper satisfy
a stronger property: the loss of any prediction strategy in $\mathcal{F}$ whose norm is
not too large exceeds the loss of a leading strategy by the divergence between
the predictions output by the two prediction strategies. Therefore, the leading
strategy implicitly serves as a standard for prediction strategies F in $\mathcal{F}$ whose
norm is not too large: such a prediction strategy F suffers a small loss to the
degree that its predictions resemble the leading strategy's predictions, and the
only way to compete with the leading strategy is to imitate it.

J.L. Balcázar, P.M. Long, and F. Stephan (Eds.): ALT 2006, LNAI 4264, pp. 214–228, 2006.
© Springer-Verlag Berlin Heidelberg 2006

We start the formal exposition with a simple asymptotic result (Proposition 1 in §2) asserting the existence of leading strategies in the problem of on-line regression with the quadratic loss function for the class of continuous limited-memory prediction strategies. To state a non-asymptotic version of this result (Proposition 2) we introduce several general definitions that are used throughout the paper. In the following two sections Proposition 2 is generalized in two directions, to the loss functions given by Bregman divergences (§3) and by strictly proper scoring rules (§4). Competitive on-line prediction typically avoids making any stochastic assumptions about the way the observations are generated, but in §5 we consider, mostly for comparison purposes, the case where observations are generated stochastically. That section contains most of the references to the related literature, although there are bibliographical remarks scattered throughout the paper. Some proofs and proof sketches are given in §6, and the rest can be found in the full version of this paper, [31]. The final section, §7, discusses possible directions of further research.

There are many techniques for constructing master strategies, such as gradient descent, strong and weak aggregating algorithms, following the perturbed leader, defensive forecasting, to mention just a few. In this paper we will use defensive forecasting (proposed in [26] and based on [34, 27] and much earlier work by Levin, Foster, and Vohra). The master strategies constructed using defensive forecasting automatically satisfy the stronger properties required of leading strategies; on the other hand, it is not clear whether leading strategies can be constructed using other techniques.

2   On-Line Quadratic-Loss Regression

Our general prediction protocol is:

ON-LINE PREDICTION PROTOCOL
FOR $n = 1, 2, \ldots$:
    Reality announces $x_n \in \mathbf{X}$.
    Predictor announces $\mu_n \in \mathbf{P}$.
    Reality announces $y_n \in \mathbf{Y}$.
END FOR.

At the beginning of each round n Forecaster is given some side information x_n relevant to predicting the following observation y_n, after which he announces his prediction μ_n. The side information is taken from the *information space* $\mathbf{X}$, the observations from the *observation space* $\mathbf{Y}$, and the predictions from the *prediction space* $\mathbf{P}$. The error of prediction is measured by a *loss function* $\lambda : \mathbf{Y} \times \mathbf{P} \to \mathbb{R}$, so that $\lambda(y_n, \mu_n)$ is the loss suffered by Predictor on round n.

A *prediction strategy* is a strategy for Predictor in this protocol. More explicitly, each prediction strategy F maps each sequence

$$s = (x_1, y_1, \ldots, x_{n-1}, y_{n-1}, x_n) \in \mathbf{S} := \bigcup_{n=1}^{\infty} (\mathbf{X} \times \mathbf{Y})^{n-1} \times \mathbf{X} \qquad (1)$$

to a prediction $F(s) \in \mathbb{R}$; we will call $\mathbf{S}$ the *situation space* and its elements *situations*. We will sometimes use the notation

$$s_n := (x_1, y_1, \ldots, x_{n-1}, y_{n-1}, x_n) \in \mathbf{S}, \tag{2}$$

where x_i and y_i are Reality's moves in the on-line prediction protocol.

In this section we will always assume that $\mathbf{Y} = [-Y, Y]$ for some $Y > 0$, $[-Y, Y] \subseteq \mathbf{P} \subseteq \mathbb{R}$, and $\lambda(y, \mu) = (y - \mu)^2$; in other words, we will consider the problem of on-line quadratic-loss regression (with the observations bounded in absolute value by a known constant Y).

Asymptotic Result

Let k be a positive integer. We say that a prediction strategy F is *order k Markov* if $F(s_n)$ depends on (2) only via $x_{\max(1,n-k)}, y_{\max(1,n-k)}, \ldots, x_{n-1}, y_{n-1}, x_n$. More explicitly, F is order k Markov if and only if there exists a function

$$f : (\mathbf{X} \times \mathbf{Y})^k \times \mathbf{X} \to \mathbf{P}$$

such that, for all $n > k$ and all (2),

$$F(s_n) = f(x_{n-k}, y_{n-k}, \ldots, x_{n-1}, y_{n-1}, x_n).$$

A *limited-memory* prediction strategy is a prediction strategy which is order k Markov for some k. (The expression "Markov strategy" being reserved for "order 0 Markov strategy".)

Proposition 1. *Let $\mathbf{Y} = \mathbf{P} = [-Y, Y]$ and $\mathbf{X}$ be a metric compact. There exists a strategy for Predictor that guarantees*

$$\frac{1}{N} \sum_{n=1}^{N} (y_n - \mu_n)^2 + \frac{1}{N} \sum_{n=1}^{N} (\mu_n - \phi_n)^2 - \frac{1}{N} \sum_{n=1}^{N} (y_n - \phi_n)^2 \to 0 \tag{3}$$

as $N \to \infty$ for the predictions ϕ_n output by any continuous limited-memory prediction strategy.

The strategy whose existence is asserted by Proposition 1 is a leading strategy in the sense discussed in §1: the average loss of a continuous limited-memory strategy F is determined by how well it manages to imitate the leading strategy. And once we know the predictions made by F and by the leading strategy, we can find the excess loss of F over the leading strategy without need to know the actual observations.

Leading Strategies for Reproducing Kernel Hilbert Spaces

In this subsection we will state a non-asymptotic version of Proposition 1. Since $\mathbf{P} = \mathbb{R}$ is a vector space, the sum of two prediction strategies and the product of a scalar (i.e., real number) and a prediction strategy can be defined pointwise:

$$(F_1 + F_2)(s) := F_1(s) + F_2(s), \quad (cF)(s) := cF(s), \quad s \in \mathbf{S}.$$

Let $\mathcal{F}$ be a Hilbert space of prediction strategies (with the pointwise operations of addition and multiplication by scalar). Its *embedding constant* $\mathbf{c}_{\mathcal{F}}$ is defined by

$$\mathbf{c}_{\mathcal{F}} := \sup_{s \in \mathbf{S}} \sup_{F \in \mathcal{F}: \|F\|_{\mathcal{F}} \leq 1} |F(s)|. \tag{4}$$

We will be interested in the case $\mathbf{c}_{\mathcal{F}} < \infty$ and will refer to $\mathcal{F}$ satisfying this condition as *reproducing kernel Hilbert spaces (RKHS) with finite embedding constant*. (More generally, $\mathcal{F}$ is said to be an *RKHS* if the internal supremum in (4) is finite for each $s \in \mathbf{S}$.) In our informal discussions we will be assuming that $\mathbf{c}_{\mathcal{F}}$ is a moderately large constant.

Proposition 2. *Let* $\mathbf{Y} = [-Y, Y]$, $\mathbf{P} = \mathbb{R}$, *and* $\mathcal{F}$ *be an RKHS of prediction strategies with finite embedding constant* $\mathbf{c}_{\mathcal{F}}$. *There exists a strategy for Predictor that guarantees*

$$\left| \sum_{n=1}^{N} (y_n - \mu_n)^2 + \sum_{n=1}^{N} (\mu_n - \phi_n)^2 - \sum_{n=1}^{N} (y_n - \phi_n)^2 \right|$$
$$\leq 2Y\sqrt{\mathbf{c}_{\mathcal{F}}^2 + 1}\,(\|F\|_{\mathcal{F}} + Y)\sqrt{N}, \qquad \forall N \in \{1, 2, \ldots\} \; \forall F \in \mathcal{F}, \tag{5}$$

where ϕ_n *are* F*'s predictions,* $\phi_n := F(s_n)$.

For an F whose norm is not too large (i.e., F satisfying $\|F\|_{\mathcal{F}} \ll N^{1/2}$), (5) shows that

$$\frac{1}{N}\sum_{n=1}^{N} (y_n - \phi_n)^2 \approx \frac{1}{N}\sum_{n=1}^{N} (y_n - \mu_n)^2 + \frac{1}{N}\sum_{n=1}^{N} (\mu_n - \phi_n)^2.$$

Proposition 1 is obtained by applying Proposition 2 to large ("universal") RKHS. The details are given in [31], and here we will only demonstrate this idea with a simple but non-trivial example. Let k and m be positive integer constants such that $m > k/2$. A prediction strategy F will be included in $\mathcal{F}$ if its predictions ϕ_n satisfy

$$\phi_n = \begin{cases} 0 & \text{if } n \leq k \\ f(y_{n-k}, \ldots, y_{n-1}) & \text{otherwise,} \end{cases}$$

where f is a function from the Sobolev space $W^{m,2}([-Y, Y]^k)$ (see, e.g., [1] for the definition and properties of Sobolev spaces); $\|F\|_{\mathcal{F}}$ is defined to be the Sobolev norm of f. Every continuous function of $(y_{n-k}, \ldots, y_{n-1})$ can be arbitrarily well approximated by functions in $W^{m,2}([-Y, Y]^k)$, and so $\mathcal{F}$ is a suitable class of prediction strategies if we believe that neither $x_1, \ldots, x_n$ nor $y_1, \ldots, y_{n-k-1}$ are useful in predicting y_n.

Very Large Benchmark Classes

Some interesting benchmark classes of prediction strategies are too large to equip with the structure of RKHS [30]. However, an analogue of Proposition 2 can also be proved for some Banach spaces $\mathcal{F}$ of prediction strategies (with the pointwise operations of addition and multiplication by scalar) for which the constant $\mathbf{c}_{\mathcal{F}}$ defined by (4) is finite. The *modulus of convexity* of a Banach space U is defined as the function

$$\delta_U(\epsilon) := \inf_{\substack{u,v \in S_U \\ \|u-v\|_U = \epsilon}} \left(1 - \left\|\frac{u+v}{2}\right\|_U\right), \quad \epsilon \in (0, 2],$$

where $S_U := \{u \in U \mid \|u\|_U = 1\}$ is the unit sphere in U.

The existence of leading strategies (in a somewhat weaker sense than in Proposition 2) is asserted in the following result.

Proposition 3. *Let $\mathbf{Y} = [-Y, Y]$, $\mathbf{P} = \mathbb{R}$, and $\mathcal{F}$ be a Banach space of prediction strategies having a finite embedding constant $\mathbf{c}_{\mathcal{F}}$ (see (4)) and satisfying*

$$\forall \epsilon \in (0, 2] : \delta_{\mathcal{F}}(\epsilon) \geq (\epsilon/2)^p/p$$

for some $p \in [2, \infty)$. There exists a strategy for Predictor that guarantees

$$\left|\sum_{n=1}^{N} (y_n - \mu_n)^2 + \sum_{n=1}^{N} (\mu_n - \phi_n)^2 - \sum_{n=1}^{N} (y_n - \phi_n)^2\right|$$

$$\leq 40Y\sqrt{\mathbf{c}_{\mathcal{F}}^2 + 1}\,(\|F\|_{\mathcal{F}} + Y)\,N^{1-1/p}, \qquad \forall N \in \{1, 2, \ldots\}\ \forall F \in \mathcal{F}, \quad (6)$$

where ϕ_n are F's predictions.

The example of a benchmark class of prediction strategies given after Proposition 2 but with f ranging over the Sobolev space $W^{s,p}([-Y, Y]^k)$, $s > k/p$, is covered by this proposition. The parameter s describes the "degree of regularity" of the elements of $W^{s,p}$, and taking sufficiently large p we can reach arbitrarily irregular functions in the Sobolev hierarchy.

3   Predictions Evaluated by Bregman Divergences

A *predictable process* is a function F mapping the situation space $\mathbf{S}$ to $\mathbb{R}$, $F : \mathbf{S} \to \mathbb{R}$. Notice that for any function $\psi : \mathbf{P} \to \mathbb{R}$ and any prediction strategy F the composition $\psi(F)$ (mapping each situation s to $\psi(F(s))$) is a predictable process; such compositions will be used in Theorems 1–3 below. A Hilbert space $\mathcal{F}$ of predictable processes (with the usual pointwise operations) is called an *RKHS with finite embedding constant* if (4) is finite.

The notion of Bregman divergence was introduced in [5], and is now widely used in competitive on-line prediction (see, e.g., [14, 3, 15, 17, 7]). Suppose $\mathbf{Y} = \mathbf{P} \subseteq \mathbb{R}$ (although it would be interesting to extend Theorem 1 to the case where

$\mathbb{R}$ is replaced by any Euclidean, or even Hilbert, space). Let Ψ and Ψ' be two real-valued functions defined on $\mathbf{Y}$. The expression

$$d_{\Psi,\Psi'}(y, z) := \Psi(y) - \Psi(z) - \Psi'(z)(y - z), \quad y, z \in \mathbf{Y}, \tag{7}$$

is said to be the corresponding *Bregman divergence* if $d_{\Psi,\Psi'}(y, z) > 0$ whenever $y \neq z$. (Bregman divergence is usually defined for y and z ranging over a Euclidean space.) In all our examples Ψ will be a strictly convex continuously differentiable function and Ψ' its derivative, in which case we abbreviate $d_{\Psi,\Psi'}$ to d_{Ψ}.

We will be using the standard notation

$$\|f\|_{C(A)} := \sup_{y \in A} |f(y)|,$$

where A is a subset of the domain of f.

Theorem 1. *Suppose* $\mathbf{Y} = \mathbf{P}$ *is a bounded subset of* $\mathbb{R}$. *Let* $\mathcal{F}$ *be an RKHS of predictable processes with finite embedding constant* $\mathbf{c}_{\mathcal{F}}$ *and* Ψ, Ψ' *be real-valued functions on* $\mathbf{Y} = \mathbf{P}$. *There exists a strategy for Predictor that guarantees, for all prediction strategies* F *and* $N = 1, 2, \ldots,$

$$\left| \sum_{n=1}^{N} d_{\Psi,\Psi'}(y_n, \mu_n) + \sum_{n=1}^{N} d_{\Psi,\Psi'}(\mu_n, \phi_n) - \sum_{n=1}^{N} d_{\Psi,\Psi'}(y_n, \phi_n) \right|$$
$$\leq \operatorname{diam}(\mathbf{Y})\sqrt{\mathbf{c}_{\mathcal{F}}^2 + 1}\left(\|\Psi'(F)\|_{\mathcal{F}} + \|\Psi'\|_{C(\mathbf{Y})}\right)\sqrt{N}, \tag{8}$$

where ϕ_n *are* F's *predictions.*

The expression $\|\Psi'(F)\|_{\mathcal{F}}$ in (8) is interpreted as ∞ when $\Psi'(F) \notin \mathcal{F}$; in this case (8) holds vacuously. Similar conventions will be made in all following statements.

Two of the most important Bregman divergences are obtained from the convex functions $\Psi(y) := y^2$ and $\Psi(y) := y \ln y + (1 - y)\ln(1 - y)$ (negative entropy, defined for $y \in (0, 1)$); they are the quadratic loss function

$$d_{\Psi}(y, z) = (y - z)^2 \tag{9}$$

and the relative entropy (also known as the Kullback–Leibler divergence)

$$d_{\Psi}(y, z) = D(y \,\|\, z) := y \ln \frac{y}{z} + (1 - y)\ln \frac{1 - y}{1 - z}, \tag{10}$$

respectively. If we apply Theorem 1 to them, (9) leads (assuming $\mathbf{Y} = [-Y, Y]$) to a weaker version of Proposition 2, with the right-hand side of (8) twice as large as that of (5), and (10) leads to the following corollary.

Corollary 1. *Let* $\epsilon \in (0, 1/2)$, $\mathbf{Y} = \mathbf{P} = [\epsilon, 1 - \epsilon]$, *and the loss function be*

$$\lambda(y, \mu) = D(y \,\|\, \mu)$$

(defined in (10)). Let $\mathcal{F}$ be an RKHS of predictable processes with finite embedding constant $\mathbf{c}_{\mathcal{F}}$. There exists a strategy for Predictor that guarantees, for all prediction strategies F,

$$\left| \sum_{n=1}^{N} \lambda(y_n, \mu_n) + \sum_{n=1}^{N} \lambda(\mu_n, \phi_n) - \sum_{n=1}^{N} \lambda(y_n, \phi_n) \right|$$
$$\leq \sqrt{\mathbf{c}_{\mathcal{F}}^2 + 1} \left(\left\| \ln \frac{F}{1-F} \right\|_{\mathcal{F}} + \ln \frac{1-\epsilon}{\epsilon} \right) \sqrt{N}, \qquad \forall N \in \{1, 2, \ldots\},$$

where ϕ_n are F's predictions.

The log likelihood ratio $\ln \frac{F}{1-F}$ appears because $\Psi'(y) = \ln \frac{y}{1-y}$ in this case.

Analogously to Proposition 2, Theorem 1 (as well as Theorems 2–3 in the next section) can be easily generalized to Banach spaces of predictable processes. One can also state asymptotic versions of Theorems 1–3 similar to Proposition 1; and the continuous limited-memory strategies of Proposition 1 could be replaced by the equally interesting classes of continuous stationary strategies (as in [29]) or Markov strategies (possibly discontinuous, as in [28]). We will have to refrain from pursuing these developments in this paper.

4   Predictions Evaluated by Strictly Proper Scoring Rules

In this section we consider the case where $\mathbf{Y} = \{0, 1\}$ and $\mathbf{P} \subseteq [0, 1]$. Every loss function $\lambda : \mathbf{Y} \times \mathbf{P} \to \mathbb{R}$ will be extended to the domain $[0, 1] \times \mathbf{P}$ by the formula

$$\lambda(p, \mu) := p\lambda(1, \mu) + (1 - p)\lambda(0, \mu);$$

intuitively, $\lambda(p, \mu)$ is the expected loss of the prediction μ when the probability of $y = 1$ is p. Let us say that a loss function λ is a *strictly proper scoring rule* if

$$\forall p, \mu \in \mathbf{P} : p \neq \mu \implies \lambda(p, p) < \lambda(p, \mu)$$

(it is optimal to give the prediction equal to the true probability of $y = 1$ when the latter is known and belongs to $\mathbf{P}$). In this case the function

$$d_\lambda(\mu, \phi) := \lambda(\mu, \phi) - \lambda(\mu, \mu)$$

can serve as a measure of difference between predictions μ and ϕ: it is non-negative and is zero only when $\mu = \phi$. (Cf. [11], §4.)

The *exposure* of a loss function λ is defined as

$$\text{Exp}_\lambda(\mu) := \lambda(1, \mu) - \lambda(0, \mu), \quad \mu \in \mathbf{P}.$$

Theorem 2. *Let $\mathbf{Y} = \{0, 1\}$, $\mathbf{P} \subseteq [0, 1]$, λ be a strictly proper scoring rule, and $\mathcal{F}$ be an RKHS of predictable processes with finite embedding constant $\mathbf{c}_{\mathcal{F}}$. There* *exists a strategy for Predictor that guarantees, for all prediction strategies F and all $N = 1, 2, \ldots$,*

$$\left| \sum_{n=1}^{N} \lambda(y_n, \mu_n) + \sum_{n=1}^{N} d_\lambda(\mu_n, \phi_n) - \sum_{n=1}^{N} \lambda(y_n, \phi_n) \right|$$
$$\leq \frac{\sqrt{c_\mathcal{F}^2 + 1}}{2} \left(\|\mathrm{Exp}_\lambda(F)\|_\mathcal{F} + \|\mathrm{Exp}_\lambda\|_{C(\mathbf{P})} \right) \sqrt{N}, \quad (11)$$

where ϕ_n are F's predictions.

Two popular strictly proper scoring rules are the quadratic loss function $\lambda(y, \mu) := (y - \mu)^2$ and the log loss function

$$\lambda(y, \mu) := \begin{cases} -\ln \mu & \text{if } y = 1 \\ -\ln(1 - \mu) & \text{if } y = 0. \end{cases}$$

Applied to the quadratic loss function, Theorem 2 becomes essentially a special case of Proposition 2. For the log loss function we have $d_\lambda(\mu, \phi) = D(\mu \| \phi)$, and so we obtain the following corollary.

Corollary 2. *Let $\epsilon \in (0, 1/2)$, $\mathbf{Y} = \{0, 1\}$, $\mathbf{P} = [\epsilon, 1 - \epsilon]$, λ be the log loss function, and $\mathcal{F}$ be an RKHS of predictable processes with finite embedding constant $c_\mathcal{F}$. There exists a strategy for Predictor that guarantees, for all prediction strategies F,*

$$\left| \sum_{n=1}^{N} \lambda(y_n, \mu_n) + \sum_{n=1}^{N} D(\mu_n \| \phi_n) - \sum_{n=1}^{N} \lambda(y_n, \phi_n) \right|$$
$$\leq \frac{\sqrt{c_\mathcal{F}^2 + 1}}{2} \left(\left\| \ln \frac{F}{1 - F} \right\|_\mathcal{F} + \ln \frac{1 - \epsilon}{\epsilon} \right) \sqrt{N}, \quad \forall N \in \{1, 2, \ldots\},$$

where ϕ_n are F's predictions.

A weaker version (with the bound twice as large) of Corollary 2 would be a special case of Corollary 1 were it not for the restriction of the observation space $\mathbf{Y}$ to $[\epsilon, 1 - \epsilon]$ in the latter. Using methods of [26], it is even possible to get rid of the restriction $\mathbf{P} = [\epsilon, 1 - \epsilon]$ in Corollary 2. Since the log loss function plays a fundamental role in information theory (the cumulative loss corresponds to the code length), we state this result as our next theorem.

Theorem 3. *Let $\mathbf{Y} = \{0, 1\}$, $\mathbf{P} = (0, 1)$, λ be the log loss function, and $\mathcal{F}$ be an RKHS of predictable processes with finite embedding constant $c_\mathcal{F}$. There exists a strategy for Predictor that guarantees, for all prediction strategies F,*

$$\left| \sum_{n=1}^{N} \lambda(y_n, \mu_n) + \sum_{n=1}^{N} D(\mu_n \| \phi_n) - \sum_{n=1}^{N} \lambda(y_n, \phi_n) \right|$$
$$\leq \frac{\sqrt{c_\mathcal{F}^2 + 1.8}}{2} \left(\left\| \ln \frac{F}{1 - F} \right\|_\mathcal{F} + 1 \right) \sqrt{N}, \quad \forall N \in \{1, 2, \ldots\},$$

where ϕ_n are F's predictions.

5   Stochastic Reality and Jeffreys's Law

In this section we revert to the quadratic regression framework of §2 and assume $\mathbf{Y} = \mathbf{P} = [-Y, Y]$, $\lambda(y, \mu) = (y - \mu)^2$. (It will be clear that similar results hold for Bregman divergences and strictly proper scoring rules, but we stick to the simplest case since our main goal in this section is to discuss the related literature.)

Proposition 4. *Suppose* $\mathbf{Y} = \mathbf{P} = [-Y, Y]$. *Let F be a prediction strategy and* $y_n \in [-Y, Y]$ *be generated as* $y_n := F(s_n) + \xi_n$ *(remember that s_n are defined by (2)), where the noise random variables ξ_n have expected value zero given s_n. For any other prediction strategy G, any $N \in \{1, 2, \ldots\}$, and any $\delta \in (0, 1)$,*

$$\left| \sum_{n=1}^{N} (y_n - \phi_n)^2 + \sum_{n=1}^{N} (\phi_n - \mu_n)^2 - \sum_{n=1}^{N} (y_n - \mu_n)^2 \right| \leq 4Y^2 \sqrt{2 \ln \frac{2}{\delta}} \sqrt{N} \quad (12)$$

with probability at least $1 - \delta$, where ϕ_n are F's predictions and μ_n are G's predictions.

Combining Proposition 4 with Proposition 2 we obtain the following corollary.

Corollary 3. *Suppose* $\mathbf{Y} = \mathbf{P} = [-Y, Y]$. *Let $\mathcal{F}$ be an RKHS of prediction strategies with finite embedding constant $\mathbf{c}_\mathcal{F}$, G be a prediction strategy whose predictions μ_n are guaranteed to satisfy (5) (a "leading prediction strategy"), F be a prediction strategy in $\mathcal{F}$, and $y_n \in [-Y, Y]$ be generated as $y_n := F(s_n) + \xi_n$, where the noise random variables ξ_n have expected value zero given s_n. For any $N \in \{1, 2, \ldots\}$ and any $\delta \in (0, 1)$, the conjunction of*

$$\left| \sum_{n=1}^{N} (y_n - \mu_n)^2 - \sum_{n=1}^{N} (y_n - \phi_n)^2 \right|$$
$$\leq Y \sqrt{\mathbf{c}_\mathcal{F}^2 + 1} \left(\|F\|_\mathcal{F} + Y \right) \sqrt{N} + 2Y^2 \sqrt{2 \ln \frac{2}{\delta}} \sqrt{N} \quad (13)$$

and

$$\sum_{n=1}^{N} (\phi_n - \mu_n)^2 \leq Y \sqrt{\mathbf{c}_\mathcal{F}^2 + 1} \left(\|F\|_\mathcal{F} + Y \right) \sqrt{N} + 2Y^2 \sqrt{2 \ln \frac{2}{\delta}} \sqrt{N} \quad (14)$$

holds with probability at least $1 - \delta$, where ϕ_n are F's predictions and μ_n are G's predictions.

We can see that if the "true" (in the sense of outputting the true expectations) strategy F belongs to the RKHS $\mathcal{F}$ and $\|F\|_\mathcal{F}$ is not too large, not only the loss of the leading strategy will be close to that of the true strategy, but their predictions will be close as well.

Jeffreys's Law

In the rest of this section we will explain the connection of this paper with the phenomenon widely studied in probability theory and the algorithmic theory of randomness and dubbed "Jeffreys's law" by Dawid [9, 12]. The general statement of "Jeffreys's law" is that two successful prediction strategies produce similar predictions (cf. [9], §5.2). To better understand this informal statement, we first discuss two notions of success for prediction strategies.

As argued in [33], there are (at least) two very different kinds of predictions, which we will call "S-predictions" and "D-predictions". Both S-predictions and D-predictions are elements of $[-Y, Y]$ (in our current context), and the prefixes "S-" and "D-" refer to the way in which we want to evaluate their quality. S-predictions are Statements about Reality's behaviour, and they are successful if they withstand attempts to falsify them; standard means of falsification are statistical tests (see, e.g., [8], Chapter 3) and gambling strategies ([23]; for a more recent exposition, see [21]). D-predictions do not claim to be falsifiable statements about Reality; they are Decisions deemed successful if they lead to a good cumulative loss.

As an example, let us consider the predictions ϕ_n and μ_n in Proposition 4. The former are S-predictions; they can be rejected if (12) fails to happen for a small δ (the complement of (12) can be used as the critical region of a statistical test). The latter are D-predictions: we are only interested in their cumulative loss. If ϕ_n are successful ((12) holds for a moderately small δ) and μ_n are successful (in the sense of their cumulative loss being close to the cumulative loss of the successful S-predictions ϕ_n; this is the best that can be achieved as, by (12), the latter cannot be much larger than the former), they will be close to each other, in the sense $\sum_{n=1}^{N}(\phi_n - \mu_n)^2 \ll N$. We can see that Proposition 4 implies a "mixed" version of Jeffreys's law, asserting the proximity of S-predictions and D-predictions.

Similarly, Corollary 3 is also a mixed version of Jeffreys's law: it asserts the proximity of the S-predictions ϕ_n (which are part of our falsifiable model $y_n = \phi_n + \xi_n$) and the D-predictions μ_n (successful in the sense of leading to a good cumulative loss; cf. (5)).

Proposition 2 immediately implies two "pure" versions of Jeffreys's laws for D-predictions:

– if a prediction strategy F with $\|F\|_{\mathcal{F}}$ not too large performs well, in the sense that its loss is close to the leading strategy's loss, F's predictions will be similar to the leading strategy's predictions; more precisely,

$$\sum_{n=1}^{N}(\phi_n - \mu_n)^2 \leq \sum_{n=1}^{N}(y_n - \phi_n)^2 - \sum_{n=1}^{N}(y_n - \mu_n)^2$$
$$+ 2Y\sqrt{c_{\mathcal{F}}^2 + 1}\left(\|F\|_{\mathcal{F}} + Y\right)\sqrt{N};$$

– therefore, if two prediction strategies F_1 and F_2 with $\|F_1\|_{\mathcal{F}}$ and $\|F_2\|_{\mathcal{F}}$ not too large perform well, in the sense that their loss is close to the leading strategy's loss, their predictions will be similar.

It is interesting that the leading strategy can be replaced by a master strategy for the second version: if F_1 and F_2 gave very different predictions and both performed almost as well as the master strategy, the mixed strategy $(F_1 + F_2)/2$ would beat the master strategy; this immediately follows from

$$\left(\frac{\phi_1 + \phi_2}{2} - y\right)^2 = \frac{(\phi_1 - y)^2 + (\phi_2 - y)^2}{2} - \left(\frac{\phi_1 - \phi_2}{2}\right)^2,$$

where ϕ_1 and ϕ_2 are F_1's and F_2's predictions, respectively, and y is the observation.

The usual versions of Jeffreys's law are, however, statements about S-predictions. The quality of S-predictions is often evaluated using universal statistical tests (as formalized by Martin-Löf [19]) or universal gambling strategies (Levin [18], Schnorr [20]). For example, Theorem 7.1 of [10] and Theorem 3 of [24] state that if two computable S-prediction strategies are both successful, their predictions will asymptotically agree. Earlier, somewhat less intuitive, statements of Jeffreys's law were given in terms of absolute continuity of probability measures: see, e.g., [4] and [16]. Solomonoff [22] proved a version of Jeffreys's law that holds "on average" (rather than for individual sequences).

This paper is, to my knowledge, the first to state a version of Jeffreys's law for D-predictions (although a step in this direction was made in Theorem 8 of [25]).

6   Proofs

In this section we prove Propositions 2–3 and give proof sketches of Theorems 1–2. For the rest of the proofs, see [31].

Proof of Propositions 2 and 3

Noticing that

$$\left| \sum_{n=1}^{N} (y_n - \mu_n)^2 + \sum_{n=1}^{N} (\mu_n - \phi_n)^2 - \sum_{n=1}^{N} (y_n - \phi_n)^2 \right|$$

$$= 2 \left| \sum_{n=1}^{N} (\phi_n - \mu_n)(y_n - \mu_n) \right|$$

$$\leq 2 \left| \sum_{n=1}^{N} \mu_n (y_n - \mu_n) \right| + 2 \left| \sum_{n=1}^{N} \phi_n (y_n - \mu_n) \right|, \quad (15)$$

we can use the results of [32], §6, asserting the existence of a prediction strategy producing predictions $\mu_n \in [-Y, Y]$ that satisfy

$$\left| \sum_{n=1}^{N} \mu_n \left(y_n - \mu_n \right) \right| \leq Y^2 \sqrt{\mathbf{c}_{\mathcal{F}}^2 + 1} \sqrt{N} \tag{16}$$

(see (24) in [32]; this a special case of good calibration) and

$$\left| \sum_{n=1}^{N} \phi_n \left(y_n - \mu_n \right) \right| \leq Y \sqrt{\mathbf{c}_{\mathcal{F}}^2 + 1} \, \|F\|_{\mathcal{F}} \sqrt{N} \tag{17}$$

(see (25) in [32]; this a special case of good resolution).

Replacing (16) and (17) with the corresponding statements for Banach function spaces ([30], (52) and (53)) we obtain the proof of Proposition 3.

Remark. In [32] we considered only prediction strategies F for which $F(s_n)$ depends on s_n (see (2)) via x_n; in the terminology of this paper these are (order 0) Markov strategies. It is easy to see that considering only Markov strategies does not lead to a loss of generality: if we redefine the object x_n as $x_n := s_n$, any prediction strategy will become a Markov prediction strategy.

Proof Sketch of Theorem 1

The proof is based on the *generalized law of cosines*

$$d_{\Psi, \Psi'} (y, \phi) = d_{\Psi, \Psi'} (\mu, \phi) + d_{\Psi, \Psi'} (y, \mu) - \left(\Psi'(\phi) - \Psi'(\mu) \right) (y - \mu) \tag{18}$$

(which follows directly from the definition (7)). From (18) we deduce

$$\left| \sum_{n=1}^{N} d_{\Psi, \Psi'} \left(y_n, \mu_n \right) + \sum_{n=1}^{N} d_{\Psi, \Psi'} \left(\mu_n, \phi_n \right) - \sum_{n=1}^{N} d_{\Psi, \Psi'} \left(y_n, \phi_n \right) \right|$$

$$= \left| \sum_{n=1}^{N} \left(\Psi'(\phi_n) - \Psi'(\mu_n) \right) \left(y_n - \mu_n \right) \right|$$

$$\leq \left| \sum_{n=1}^{N} \Psi'(\mu_n) \left(y_n - \mu_n \right) \right| + \left| \sum_{n=1}^{N} \Psi'(\phi_n) \left(y_n - \mu_n \right) \right|. \tag{19}$$

The rest of the proof is based on generalizations of (16) and (17).

Proof Sketch of Theorem 2

The proof is similar to that of Theorem 1, with the role of the generalized law of cosines (18) played by the equation

$$\lambda(y, \phi) = a + \lambda(y, \mu) + b(y - \mu) \tag{20}$$

for some $a = a(\mu, \phi)$ and $b = b(\mu, \phi)$. Since y can take only two possible values, suitable a and b are easy to find: it suffices to solve the linear system

$$\begin{cases} \lambda(1, \phi) = a + \lambda(1, \mu) + b(1 - \mu) \\ \lambda(0, \phi) = a + \lambda(0, \mu) + b(-\mu). \end{cases}$$

Subtracting these equations we obtain $b = \text{Exp}(\phi) - \text{Exp}(\mu)$ (abbreviating Exp_λ to Exp), which in turn gives $a = d_\lambda(\mu, \phi)$. Therefore, (20) gives

$$\left| \sum_{n=1}^{N} \lambda(y_n, \mu_n) + \sum_{n=1}^{N} d_\lambda(\mu_n, \phi_n) - \sum_{n=1}^{N} \lambda(y_n, \phi_n) \right|$$

$$= \left| \sum_{n=1}^{N} (\text{Exp}(\phi_n) - \text{Exp}(\mu_n)) (y_n - \mu_n) \right|$$

$$\leq \left| \sum_{n=1}^{N} \text{Exp}(\mu_n) (y_n - \mu_n) \right| + \left| \sum_{n=1}^{N} \text{Exp}(\phi_n) (y_n - \mu_n) \right|. \quad (21)$$

The rest of the proof is based on different generalizations of (16) and (17).

7   Conclusion

The existence of master strategies (strategies whose loss is less than or close to the loss of any strategy with not too large a norm) can be shown for a very wide class of loss functions. On the contrary, leading strategies appear to exist for a rather narrow class of loss functions. It would be very interesting to delineate the class of loss functions for which a leading strategy does exist. In particular, does this class contain any loss functions except Bregman divergences and strictly proper scoring rules?

Even if a leading strategy does not exist, one might look for a strategy G such that the loss of any strategy F whose norm is not too large lies between the loss of G plus some measure of difference between F's and G's predictions and the loss of G plus another measure of difference between F's and G's predictions.

Acknowledgments

I am grateful to the anonymous referees for their comments. This work was partially supported by MRC (grant S505/65).

References

1. Robert A. Adams and John J. F. Fournier. *Sobolev Spaces*, volume 140 of *Pure and Applied Mathematics*. Academic Press, Amsterdam, second edition, 2003.
2. Peter Auer, Nicolò Cesa-Bianchi, and Claudio Gentile. Adaptive and self-confident on-line learning algorithms. *Journal of Computer and System Sciences*, 64:48–75, 2002.

3. Katy S. Azoury and Manfred K. Warmuth. Relative loss bounds for on-line density estimation with the exponential family of distributions. *Machine Learning*, 43:211–246, 2001.
4. David Blackwell and Lester Dubins. Merging of opinions with increasing information. *Annals of Mathematical Statistics*, 33:882–886, 1962.
5. Lev M. Bregman. The relaxation method of finding the common point of convex sets and its application to the solution of problems in convex programming. *USSR Computational Mathematics and Physics*, 7:200–217, 1967.
6. Nicolò Cesa-Bianchi, Philip M. Long, and Manfred K. Warmuth. Worst-case quadratic loss bounds for on-line prediction of linear functions by gradient descent. *IEEE Transactions on Neural Networks*, 7:604–619, 1996.
7. Nicolò Cesa-Bianchi and Gábor Lugosi. *Prediction, Learning, and Games*. Cambridge University Press, Cambridge, 2006.
8. David R. Cox and David V. Hinkley. *Theoretical Statistics*. Chapman and Hall, London, 1974.
9. A. Philip Dawid. Statistical theory: the prequential approach. *Journal of the Royal Statistical Society* A, 147:278–292, 1984.
10. A. Philip Dawid. Calibration-based empirical probability (with discussion). *Annals of Statistics*, 13:1251–1285, 1985.
11. A. Philip Dawid. Proper measures of discrepancy, uncertainty and dependence, with applications to predictive experimental design. Technical Report 139, Department of Statistical Science, University College London, November 1994. This technical report was revised (and its title was slightly changed) in August 1998.
12. A. Philip Dawid. Probability, causality and the empirical world: a Bayes–de Finetti–Popper–Borel synthesis. *Statistical Science*, 19:44–57, 2004.
13. Jacques Ellul. *The Technological Bluff*. Eerdmans, Grand Rapids, MI, 1990. Translated by Geoffrey W. Bromiley. The French original: *Le bluff technologique*, Hachette, Paris, 1988.
14. David P. Helmbold, Jyrki Kivinen, and Manfred K. Warmuth. Relative loss bounds for single neurons. *IEEE Transactions on Neural Networks*, 10:1291–1304, 1999.
15. Mark Herbster and Manfred K. Warmuth. Tracking the best linear predictor. *Journal of Machine Learning Research*, 1:281–309, 2001.
16. Yury M. Kabanov, Robert Sh. Liptser, and Albert N. Shiryaev. To the question of absolute continuity and singularity of probability measures (in Russian). *Matematicheskii Sbornik*, 104:227–247, 1977.
17. Jyrki Kivinen and Manfred K. Warmuth. Relative loss bounds for multidimensional regression problems. *Machine Learning*, 45:301–329, 2001.
18. Leonid A. Levin. On the notion of a random sequence. *Soviet Mathematics Doklady*, 14:1413–1416, 1973.
19. Per Martin-Löf. The definition of random sequences. *Information and Control*, 9:602–619, 1966.
20. Claus P. Schnorr. *Zufälligkeit und Wahrscheinlichkeit*. Springer, Berlin, 1971.
21. Glenn Shafer and Vladimir Vovk. *Probability and Finance: It's Only a Game!* Wiley, New York, 2001.
22. Ray J. Solomonoff. Complexity-based induction systems: comparisons and convergence theorems. *IEEE Transactions on Information Theory*, IT-24:422–432, 1978.
23. Jean Ville. *Etude critique de la notion de collectif*. Gauthier-Villars, Paris, 1939.
24. Vladimir Vovk. On a randomness criterion. *Soviet Mathematics Doklady*, 35:656–660, 1987.

25. Vladimir Vovk. Probability theory for the Brier game. *Theoretical Computer Science*, 261:57–79, 2001. Conference version in Ming Li and Akira Maruoka, editors, *Algorithmic Learning Theory*, volume 1316 of *Lecture Notes in Computer Science*, pages 323–338, 1997.

26. Vladimir Vovk. Defensive prediction with expert advice. In Sanjay Jain, Hans Ulrich Simon, and Etsuji Tomita, editors, *Proceedings of the Sixteenth International Conference on Algorithmic Learning Theory*, volume 3734 of *Lecture Notes in Artificial Intelligence*, pages 444–458, Berlin, 2005. Springer. Full version: Technical Report arXiv:cs.LG/0506041 "Competitive on-line learning with a convex loss function" (version 3), arXiv.org e-Print archive, September 2005.

27. Vladimir Vovk. Non-asymptotic calibration and resolution. In Sanjay Jain, Hans Ulrich Simon, and Etsuji Tomita, editors, *Proceedings of the Sixteenth International Conference on Algorithmic Learning Theory*, volume 3734 of *Lecture Notes in Artificial Intelligence*, pages 429–443, Berlin, 2005. Springer. A version of this paper can be downloaded from the arXiv.org e-Print archive (arXiv:cs.LG/0506004).

28. Vladimir Vovk. Competing with Markov prediction strategies. Technical report, arXiv.org e-Print archive, July 2006.

29. Vladimir Vovk. Competing with stationary prediction strategies. Technical Report arXiv:cs.LG/0607067, arXiv.org e-Print archive, July 2006.

30. Vladimir Vovk. Competing with wild prediction rules. In Gabor Lugosi and Hans Ulrich Simon, editors, *Proceedings of the Nineteenth Annual Conference on Learning Theory*, volume 4005 of *Lecture Notes in Artificial Intelligence*, pages 559–573, Berlin, 2006. Springer. Full version: Technical Report arXiv:cs.LG/0512059 (version 2), arXiv.org e-Print archive, January 2006.

31. Vladimir Vovk. Leading strategies in competitive on-line prediction. Technical Report arXiv:cs.LG/0607134, arXiv.org e-Print archive, July 2006. The full version of this paper.

32. Vladimir Vovk. On-line regression competitive with reproducing kernel Hilbert spaces. Technical Report arXiv:cs.LG/0511058 (version 2), arXiv.org e-Print archive, January 2006. Extended abstract in Jin-Yi Cai, S. Barry Cooper, and Angsheng Li, editors, *Theory and Applications of Models of Computation. Proceedings of the Third Annual Conference on Computation and Logic*, volume 3959 of *Lecture Notes in Computer Science*, pages 452–463, Berlin, 2006. Springer.

33. Vladimir Vovk. Predictions as statements and decisions. In Gabor Lugosi and Hans Ulrich Simon, editors, *Proceedings of the Nineteenth Annual Conference on Learning Theory*, volume 4005 of *Lecture Notes in Artificial Intelligence*, page 4, Berlin, 2006. Springer. Full version: Technical Report arXiv:cs.LG/0606093, arXiv.org e-Print archive, June 2006.

34. Vladimir Vovk, Akimichi Takemura, and Glenn Shafer. Defensive forecasting. In Robert G. Cowell and Zoubin Ghahramani, editors, *Proceedings of the Tenth International Workshop on Artificial Intelligence and Statistics*, pages 365–372. Society for Artificial Intelligence and Statistics, 2005. Available electronically at http://www.gatsby.ucl.ac.uk/aistats/.

Hannan Consistency in On-Line Learning in Case of Unbounded Losses Under Partial Monitoring[*][**]

Chamy Allenberg[1], Peter Auer[2], László Györfi[3], and György Ottucsák[3]

[1] School of Computer Science
Tel Aviv University
Tel Aviv, Israel, 69978
chamy_a@netvision.net.il

[2] Chair for Information Technology
University of Leoben
Leoben, Austria, A-8700
auer@unileoben.ac.at

[3] Department of Computer Science and Information Theory
Budapest University of Technology and Economics,
Magyar Tudósok körútja 2., Budapest, Hungary, H-1117
{gyorfi, oti}@szit.bme.hu

Abstract. In this paper the sequential prediction problem with expert advice is considered when the loss is unbounded under partial monitoring scenarios. We deal with a wide class of the partial monitoring problems: the combination of the label efficient and multi-armed bandit problem, that is, where the algorithm is only informed about the performance of the *chosen* expert with probability $\varepsilon \leq 1$. For bounded losses an algorithm is given whose expected regret scales with the square root of the loss of the best expert. For unbounded losses we prove that Hannan consistency can be achieved, depending on the growth rate of the average squared losses of the experts.

1 Introduction

In on-line (often referred also as sequential) prediction problems in general, an algorithm has to perform a sequence of actions. After each action, the algorithm suffers some loss, depending on the response of the environment. Its goal is to minimize its cumulative loss over a sufficiently long period of time. In the adversarial setting no probabilistic assumption is made on how the losses corresponding to different actions are generated. In particular, the losses may depend on the previous actions of the algorithm, whose goal is to perform well relative to a set of experts for any possible behavior of the environment. More precisely, the aim of the algorithm is to achieve asymptotically the same average loss (per round) as the best expert.

---

[*] We would like to thank Gilles Stoltz and András György for useful comments.

[**] This research was supported in part by the Hungarian Inter-University Center for Telecommunications and Informatics (ETIK).

J.L. Balcázar, P.M. Long, and F. Stephan (Eds.): ALT 2006, LNAI 4264, pp. 229–243, 2006.

In most of the machine learning literature, one assumes that the loss is bounded, and such a bound is known in advance, when designing an algorithm. In many applications, including regression problems (Györfi and Lugosi [9]) or routing in communication networks (cf. György and Ottucsák [11]) the loss is unbounded. In the latter one the algorithm tries to minimize the average end-to-end loss between two dedicated nodes of the network, where the loss can be any quality of service measures, e.g. delay or the number of hops. The delay can be arbitrarily large in case of nearly exponential delay distributions or link failures or substantially changing traffic scenarios. The main aim of this paper is to show Hannan consistency of on-line algorithms for unbounded losses under partial monitoring.

The first theoretical results concerning sequential prediction (decision) are due to Blackwell [2] and Hannan [12], but they were rediscovered by the learning community only in the 1990's, see, for example, Vovk [16], Littlestone and Warmuth [14] and Cesa-Bianchi et al. [3]. These results show that it is possible to construct algorithms for on-line (sequential) decision that predict almost as well as the best expert. The main idea of these algorithms is the same: after observing the past performance of the experts, in each step the decision of a randomly chosen expert is followed such that experts with superior past performance are chosen with higher probability.

However, in certain type of problems it is not possible to obtain all the losses corresponding to the decisions of the experts. Throughout the paper we use this framework in which the algorithm has a limited access to the losses. For example, in the so called multi-armed bandit problem the algorithm has only information on the loss of the chosen expert, and no information is available about the loss it would have suffered had it made a different decision (see, e.g., Auer et al. [1], Hart and Mas Colell [13]). Another example is label efficient prediction, where it is expensive to obtain the losses of the experts, and therefore the algorithm has the option to query this information (see Cesa-Bianchi et. al [5]). Finally the combination of the label efficient and the multi-armed bandit problem, where after choosing a decision, the algorithm learns its own loss if and only if it asks for it (see György and Ottucsák [11]).

Cesa-Bianchi et. al. [7] studied second-order bounds for exponentially weighted average forecaster and they analyzed the expected regret of the algorithm in full monitoring and in partial monitoring cases when the bound of the loss function is unknown. Poland and Hutter [15] dealt with unbounded losses in bandit setting and an algorithm was presented based on the follow the perturbed leader method, however we managed to improve significantly their result.

2   Sequential Prediction and Partial Monitoring Models

The on-line decision problem considered in this paper is described as follows. Suppose an algorithm has to make a sequence of actions. At each time instant $t = 1, 2, \ldots$, an action $a_t \in \mathcal{A}$ is made, where $\mathcal{A}$ denotes the action space. Then, based on the state of the environment $y_t \in \mathcal{Y}$, where $\mathcal{Y}$ is some state space, the algorithm suffers some loss $\ell(a_t, y_t)$ with loss function $\ell : \mathcal{A} \times \mathcal{Y} \to \mathbb{R}^+$.

The performance of the algorithm is evaluated relative to a set of experts, and its goal is to perform asymptotically as well as the best expert. Formally, given N experts, at each time instant t, for every $i = 1, \ldots, N$, expert i chooses an action $f_{i,t} \in \mathcal{A}$, and suffers loss $\ell(f_{i,t}, y_t)$. We assume that the action space is finite, therefore we consider algorithms that follow the advice of one of the experts, that is, $f_{I_t,t}$ for some I_t, where $I_t \in \{1, \ldots, N\}$ is a random variable. The distribution of I_t is generated by the algorithm. I_t only depends on the past losses $\ell(f_{i,t-1}, y_t), \ldots, \ell(f_{i,1}, y_1)$ for all i and the earlier choices of the algorithm $I_{t-1}, \ldots, I_1$. For convenience we use the notations $\ell_{i,t}$ instead of $\ell(f_{i,t}, y_t)$ and $\ell_{I_t,t}$ instead of $\ell(f_{I_t,t}, y_t)$.

Formally, at each time instance $t = 1, 2, \ldots$,

1. the environment decides on the losses $\ell_{i,t} \geq 0$ of the experts $i \in \{1, \ldots, N\}$,
2. the algorithm chooses an expert $I_t \in \{1, \ldots, N\}$,
3. the algorithm suffers loss $\ell_{I_t,t}$,
4. the algorithm receives some feedback on his loss and the losses of the experts.

After n rounds the loss of the algorithm and the loss of the experts are

$$\widehat{L}_n = \sum_{t=1}^{n} \ell_{I_t,t} \quad \text{and} \quad L_{i,n} = \sum_{t=1}^{n} \ell_{i,t},$$

and the performance of the algorithm is measured by its regret, $\widehat{L}_n - \min_i L_{i,n}$, or by its regret per round, $\frac{1}{n}\left(\widehat{L}_n - \min_i L_{i,n}\right)$. An algorithm is Hannan consistent [12], if

$$\limsup_{n \to \infty} \frac{1}{n}\left(\widehat{L}_n - \min_i L_{i,n}\right) \leq 0 \qquad a.s.$$

The performance of any expert algorithm obviously depends on how much information is available to the algorithm about the experts' and its own performance. Next we show the most important classes of partial monitoring according to the amount of the information available to the algorithm.

- **Full information** (FI) case: the algorithm knows the losses $\ell_{i,t}$ of all experts.
- **Multi-armed bandit** (MAB) problem: only the loss of the chosen expert is revealed to the algorithm, i.e., only $\ell_{I_t,t}$ is known.
- **Label efficient** (LE) setting: the algorithm tosses a coin S_t whether to query for the losses.[1] If $S_t = 1$ (with probability ε_t) then the algorithm knows all $\ell_{i,t}$, $i = 1, \ldots, n$, otherwise it does not.
- **Combination of the label efficient and multi-armed bandit** (LE+MAB) setting: the algorithm queries with probability ε_t only about the loss of the chosen expert, $\ell_{I_t,t}$.

Throughout the paper we focus on problem LE+MAB because all of the other problems mentioned above are "easier": if an algorithm is Hannan consistent for problem LE+MAB, then it is Hannan consistent for the other cases, too.

---

[1] It is easy to see that in order to achieve a nontrivial performance, the algorithm must use randomization in determining whether the losses should be revealed or not (cf. Cesa-Bianchi and Lugosi [4]).

3   The Algorithm

In problem LE+MAB, the algorithm learns its own loss only if it chooses to query it, and it cannot obtain information on the loss of any other expert. For querying its loss the algorithm uses a sequence $S_1, S_2, \ldots$ of independent Bernoulli random variables such that

$$\mathbb{P}(S_t = 1) = \varepsilon_t,$$

and asks for the loss $\ell_{I_t,t}$ of the chosen expert I_t if $S_t = 1$, which for constant $\varepsilon_t = \varepsilon$ is identical to the label efficient algorithms in Cesa-Bianchi *et al.* [5]. We denote by LE(ε_t) the label efficient problem with time-varying parameter ε_t.

We will derive sufficient conditions for Hannan consistency for the combination of the time-varying label efficient and multi-armed bandit problem (LE(ε_t)+MAB) and then we will show that this condition can be adapted straightforwardly to the other cases.

For problem LE(ε_t)+MAB we use algorithm GREEN with time-varying learning rate η_t. Algorithm GREEN is a variant of the weighted majority (WM) algorithm of Littlestone and Warmuth [14] and it was named after the known phrase: "The neighbor's grass is greener", since GREEN assumes that the experts it did not choose had the best possible payoff (the zero loss).

Denote by $p_{i,t}$ the probability of choosing action i at time t in case of the original WM algorithm, that is,

$$p_{i,t} = \frac{e^{-\eta_t \widetilde{L}_{i,t-1}}}{\sum_{j=1}^N e^{-\eta_t \widetilde{L}_{j,t-1}}},$$

where $\widetilde{L}_{i,t}$ is so called cumulative estimated loss, which we will specify later. Algorithm GREEN uses modified probabilities $\widetilde{p}_{i,t}$ which can be calculated from $p_{i,t}$,

$$\widetilde{p}_{i,t} = \begin{cases} 0 & \text{if } p_{i,t} < \gamma_t, \\ c_t \cdot p_{i,t} & \text{if } p_{i,t} \geq \gamma_t, \end{cases}$$

where c_t is the normalizing factor and $\gamma_t \geq 0$ is a time-varying threshold. Finally, the algorithm uses estimated losses which are given by

$$\widetilde{\ell}_{i,t} = \begin{cases} \frac{\ell_{i,t}}{\widetilde{p}_{i,t}\varepsilon_t} & \text{if } I_t = i \text{ and } S_t = 1; \\ 0 & \text{otherwise,} \end{cases}$$

based on György and Ottucsák [11]. Therefore, the estimated loss is an unbiased estimate of the true loss with respect to its natural filtration, that is,

$$\mathbb{E}_t\left[\widetilde{\ell}_{i,t}\right] \stackrel{\text{def}}{=} \mathbb{E}\left[\widetilde{\ell}_{i,t} \big| S_1^{t-1}, I_1^{t-1}\right] = \ell_{i,t},$$

where $S_1^{t-1} \stackrel{\text{def}}{=} S_1, \ldots, S_{t-1}$ and $I_1^{t-1} \stackrel{\text{def}}{=} I_1, \ldots, I_{t-1}$. The cumulative estimated loss of an expert is given by $\widetilde{L}_{i,n} = \sum_{t=1}^n \widetilde{\ell}_{i,t}$. The resulting algorithm is given in Figure 1.

In all theorems in the sequel we assume that $\ell_{i,t}$ may be a random variable depending on I_1^{t-1} and S_1^{t-1}.

Algorithm GREEN

Let $\eta_1, \eta_2, \ldots > 0$, $\varepsilon_1, \varepsilon_2, \ldots > 0$ and $\gamma_1, \gamma_2, \ldots \geq 0$.

Initialization: $\widetilde{L}_{i,0} = 0$ for all $i = 1, \ldots, N$.

For each round $t = 1, 2, \ldots$

(1) Calculate the probability distribution

$$p_{i,t} = \frac{e^{-\eta_t \widetilde{L}_{i,t-1}}}{\sum_{i=1}^{N} e^{-\eta_t \widetilde{L}_{i,t-1}}} \qquad i = 1, \ldots, N \;.$$

(2) Calculate the modified probabilities

$$\widetilde{p}_{i,t} = \begin{cases} 0 & \text{if } p_{i,t} < \gamma_t, \\ c_t \cdot p_{i,t} & \text{if } p_{i,t} \geq \gamma_t, \end{cases}$$

where $c_t = 1/\sum_{p_{i,t} \geq \gamma_t} p_{i,t}$.

(3) Select an action $I_t \in \{1, \ldots, N\}$ according to $\widetilde{\mathbf{p}}_\mathbf{t} = (\widetilde{p}_{1,t}, \ldots, \widetilde{p}_{N,t})$.

(4) Draw a Bernoulli random variable S_t such that $\mathbb{P}(S_t = 1) = \varepsilon_t$.

(5) Compute the estimated loss for all $i = 1, \ldots, N$

$$\widetilde{\ell}_{i,t} = \begin{cases} \frac{\ell_{i,t}}{\widetilde{p}_{i,t}\varepsilon_t} & \text{if } I_t = i \text{ and } S_t = 1; \\ 0 & \text{otherwise.} \end{cases}$$

(6) For all $i = 1, \ldots, N$ update the cumulative estimated loss

$$\widetilde{L}_{i,t} = \widetilde{L}_{i,t-1} + \widetilde{\ell}_{i,t}.$$

Fig. 1. Algorithm GREEN for LE(ε_t)+MAB

4   Bounds on the Expected Regret

Theorem 1. *If $\ell_{i,t}^2 \leq t^\nu$ and $\varepsilon_t \geq t^{-\beta}$ for all t, then for all n the expected loss of algorithm* GREEN *with $\gamma_t = 0$ and $\eta_t = 2\sqrt{\frac{\ln N}{N}} \cdot t^{-(1+\nu+\beta)/2}$ is bounded by*

$$\mathbb{E}\left[\widehat{L}_n\right] - \min_i \mathbb{E}\left[L_{i,n}\right] \leq 2\sqrt{(N \ln N)}(n+1)^{(1+\nu+\beta)/2}.$$

If the individual losses are bounded by a constant, a much stronger result can be obtained.

Theorem 2. *If $\ell_{i,t} \in [0,1]$ and $\varepsilon_t = \varepsilon$ for all t, then for all n with $\min_i L_{i,n} \leq B$ the expected loss of algorithm* GREEN *with $\gamma_t = \gamma = \frac{1}{N(B\varepsilon+2)}$ and $\eta_t = \eta = 2\sqrt{\frac{\ln N}{N}\frac{\varepsilon}{B}}$ is bounded by*

$$\mathbb{E}\left[\widehat{L}_n\right] - \min_i \mathbb{E}\left[L_{i,n}\right] \leq 4\sqrt{\frac{B}{\varepsilon}N \ln N} + \frac{N \ln N + 2}{\varepsilon} + \frac{N \ln(\varepsilon B + 1)}{\varepsilon}.$$

Remark 1. The improvement in Theorem 2 is significant, since it bounds the regret of the algorithm in terms of the loss of the best action and not in respect to the number of rounds. For example, Theorem 1 is void for $\min_i L_{i,n} \ll \sqrt{n}$ whereas Theorem 2 still gives a nearly optimal bound[2].

Remark 2. If the magnitude of the losses is not known a-priori, the doubling trick can be used to set the parameter ν in Theorem 1 and the parameter B in Theorem 2 with no significant change in the bounds. The generalization of Theorem 2 to losses in $[a, b]$ is straightforward.

For the proofs we introduce the notations

$$\check{\ell}_t = \sum_{i=1}^{N} \widetilde{p}_{i,t}\widetilde{\ell}_{i,t}, \quad \overline{\ell}_t = \sum_{i=1}^{N} p_{i,t}\widetilde{\ell}_{i,t}, \quad \text{and} \quad \overline{L}_n = \sum_{t=1}^{n} \overline{\ell}_t.$$

Then

$$\widehat{L}_n - \min_i L_{i,n} = \left(\widehat{L}_n - \overline{L}_n\right) + \left(\overline{L}_n - \min_i \widetilde{L}_{i,n}\right) + \left(\min_i \widetilde{L}_{i,n} - \min_i L_{i,n}\right). \quad (1)$$

Lemma 1. *For any sequence of losses $\ell_{i,t} \geq 0$,*

$$\widehat{L}_n - \overline{L}_n \leq \sum_{t=1}^{n}\left(\ell_{I_t,t} - \check{\ell}_t\right) + \sum_{t=1}^{n} N\gamma_t \check{\ell}_t.$$

Proof.   Since $p_{I_t,t}/\widetilde{p}_{I_t,t} = 1/c_t = \sum_{j:p_{j,t}\geq\gamma_t} p_{j,t} = 1 - \sum_{j:p_{j,t}<\gamma_t} p_{j,t} \geq 1 - N\gamma_t$ we have

$$\overline{\ell}_t = \sum_{i=1}^{N} p_{i,t}\widetilde{\ell}_{i,t} = p_{I_t,t}\widetilde{\ell}_{I_t,t} \geq (1 - N\gamma_t)\widetilde{p}_{I_t,t}\widetilde{\ell}_{I_t,t} = (1 - N\gamma_t)\check{\ell}_t.$$

Thus

$$\widehat{L}_n - \overline{L}_n = \sum_{t=1}^{n} \ell_{I_t,t} - \sum_{t=1}^{n}\overline{\ell}_t \leq \sum_{t=1}^{n}\left(\ell_{I_t,t} - \check{\ell}_t\right) + \sum_{t=1}^{n} N\gamma_t\check{\ell}_t.$$

$\square$

For bounding $\overline{L}_n - \min_i \widetilde{L}_{i,n}$ we use of the following lemma.

Lemma 2 (Cesa-Bianchi et al. [6]). *Consider any nonincreasing sequence of $\eta_1, \eta_2, \ldots$ positive learning rates and any sequences $\widetilde{\boldsymbol{\ell}}_1, \widetilde{\boldsymbol{\ell}}_2, \ldots \in \mathbb{R}_+^N$ of loss vectors. Define the function Φ by*

$$\Phi(\mathbf{p}_t, \eta_t, -\widetilde{\boldsymbol{\ell}}_t) = \sum_{i=1}^{N} p_{i,t}\widetilde{\ell}_{i,t} + \frac{1}{\eta_t}\ln\sum_{i=1}^{N} p_{i,t}e^{-\eta_t\widetilde{\ell}_{i,t}},$$

where $\mathbf{p}_t = (p_{1,t}, p_{2,t}, \ldots, p_{N,t})$ the probability vector of the WM algorithm. Then, for Algorithm GREEN

$$\overline{L}_n - \min_i \widetilde{L}_{i,n} \leq \left(\frac{2}{\eta_{n+1}} - \frac{1}{\eta_1}\right)\ln N + \sum_{t=1}^{n}\Phi(\mathbf{p}_t, \eta_t, -\widetilde{\boldsymbol{\ell}}_t).$$

---

[2] For $\varepsilon = 1$ optimality follows from the lower bound on the regret in [1].

Lemma 3. *With the notation of Lemma 2 we get for algorithm* GREEN,

$$\Phi(\mathbf{p}_t, \eta_t, -\widetilde{\boldsymbol{\ell}}_t) \leq \frac{\eta_t}{2\varepsilon_t} \sum_{i=1}^{N} \ell_{i,t}\widetilde{\ell}_{i,t}.$$

Proof.

$$\Phi(\mathbf{p}_t, \eta_t, -\widetilde{\boldsymbol{\ell}}_t) = \sum_{i=1}^{N} p_{i,t}\widetilde{\ell}_{i,t} + \frac{1}{\eta_t} \ln \sum_{i=1}^{N} p_{i,t} e^{-\eta_t \widetilde{\ell}_{i,t}}$$

$$\leq \sum_{i=1}^{N} p_{i,t}\widetilde{\ell}_{i,t} + \frac{1}{\eta_t} \ln \sum_{i=1}^{N} p_{i,t} \left(1 - \eta_t \widetilde{\ell}_{i,t} + \frac{\eta_t^2 \widetilde{\ell}_{i,t}^2}{2}\right) \qquad (2)$$

$$\leq \sum_{i=1}^{N} p_{i,t}\widetilde{\ell}_{i,t} + \frac{1}{\eta_t} \ln \left(1 - \eta_t \sum_{i=1}^{N} p_{i,t}\widetilde{\ell}_{i,t} + \frac{\eta_t^2}{2} \sum_{i=1}^{N} p_{i,t}\widetilde{\ell}_{i,t}^2\right)$$

$$\leq \frac{\eta_t}{2} \sum_{i=1}^{N} p_{i,t}\widetilde{\ell}_{i,t}^2 \leq \frac{\eta_t}{2\varepsilon_t} \sum_{i=1}^{N} \ell_{i,t}\widetilde{\ell}_{i,t} \qquad (3)$$

where (2) holds because of $e^{-x} \leq 1 - x + x^2/2$ for $x \geq 0$, and (3) follows from the fact that $\ln(1 + x) \leq x$ for all $x > -1$, and from the definition of $\widetilde{\ell}_{i,t}$ in algorithm GREEN. □

Lemma 4. *For any sequence of $\ell_{i,t}$ the loss of algorithm* GREEN *is bounded by*

$$\mathbb{E}\left[\widehat{L}_n\right] - \min_i \mathbb{E}\left[L_{i,n}\right] \leq N \sum_{t=1}^{n} \gamma_t \mathbb{E}\left[\ell_{I_t,t}\right] + \frac{2\ln N}{\eta_{n+1}} + \sum_{i=1}^{N}\sum_{t=1}^{n} \frac{\eta_t \mathbb{E}\left[\ell_{i,t}\widetilde{\ell}_{i,t}\right]}{2\varepsilon_t} \qquad (4)$$

$$= N \sum_{t=1}^{n} \gamma_t \mathbb{E}\left[\ell_{I_t,t}\right] + \frac{2\ln N}{\eta_{n+1}} + \sum_{i=1}^{N}\sum_{t=1}^{n} \frac{\eta_t \mathbb{E}\left[\ell_{i,t}^2\right]}{2\varepsilon_t}.$$

Proof. From (1) and Lemmas 1–3, we get

$$\widehat{L}_n - \min_i L_{i,n} \leq \sum_{t=1}^{n} \left(\ell_{I_t,t} - \check{\ell}_t\right) + \sum_{t=1}^{n} N\gamma_t \check{\ell}_t + \left(\frac{2}{\eta_{n+1}} - \frac{1}{\eta_1}\right) \ln N$$

$$+ \sum_{t=1}^{n} \frac{\eta_t}{2\varepsilon_t} \sum_{i=1}^{N} \ell_{i,t}\widetilde{\ell}_{i,t} + \left(\min_i \widetilde{L}_{i,n} - \min_i L_{i,n}\right).$$

Since $\mathbb{E}_t[\ell_{I_t,t}] = \sum_{i=1}^{N} \widetilde{p}_{i,t}\ell_{i,t} = \sum_{i=1}^{N} \widetilde{p}_{i,t}\mathbb{E}_t\left[\check{\ell}_{i,t}\right] = \mathbb{E}_t[\check{\ell}_t]$ and $\mathbb{E}\left[\min_i \widetilde{L}_{i,n}\right] \leq \min_i \mathbb{E}\left[\widetilde{L}_{i,n}\right] = \min_i \mathbb{E}[L_{i,n}]$, taking expectations gives (4). The second line of the lemma follows from $\mathbb{E}_t\left[\widetilde{\ell}_{i,t}\right] = \ell_{i,t}$. □

Proof of Theorem 1. By simple calculation from Lemma 4.   □

Proof of Theorem 2. Let $T_i = \max\{0 \leq t \leq n : p_{i,t} \geq \gamma\}$ be the last round which contributes to $\tilde{L}_{i,n}$. Therefore,

$$\gamma \leq p_{i,T_i} = \frac{e^{-\eta \tilde{L}_{i,T_i}}}{\sum_{j=1}^{N} e^{-\eta \tilde{L}_{j,T_i}}} < \frac{e^{-\eta \tilde{L}_{i,T_i}}}{e^{-\eta \tilde{L}_{i^*,n}}},$$

where $i^* = \arg\min_i L_{i,n}$. After rearranging we obtain

$$\tilde{L}_{i,T_i} \leq \tilde{L}_{i^*,n} + \frac{\ln(1/\gamma)}{\eta}$$

and since $\tilde{L}_{i,n} = \tilde{L}_{i,T_i}$ we get that $\tilde{L}_{i,n} \leq \tilde{L}_{i^*,n} + \frac{\ln(1/\gamma)}{\eta}$. Plugging this bound into (4) and using $\ell_{i,t} \in [0,1]$ we get

$$\mathbb{E}\left[\widehat{L}_n\right] - \min_i \mathbb{E}\left[L_{i,n}\right] \leq \gamma N \mathbb{E}\left[\widehat{L}_n\right] + \frac{2\ln N}{\eta} + N\frac{\eta}{2\varepsilon}\left(\mathbb{E}\left[L_{i^*,n}\right] + \frac{\ln(1/\gamma)}{\eta}\right).$$

Solving for $\mathbb{E}\left[\widehat{L}_n\right]$ we find

$$\mathbb{E}\left[\widehat{L}_n\right] \leq \frac{1}{1 - \gamma N}\left[\min_i \mathbb{E}\left[L_{i,n}\right] + \frac{2\ln N}{\eta} + N\frac{\eta}{2\varepsilon}\left(\mathbb{E}\left[L_{i^*,n}\right] + \frac{\ln(1/\gamma)}{\eta}\right)\right].$$

For $\gamma = \frac{1}{N(\varepsilon B + 2)}$ we have $\frac{\min_i \mathbb{E}[L_{i,n}]}{1 - \gamma N} \leq \min_i \mathbb{E}[L_{i,n}] + \frac{1}{\varepsilon}$ and $\frac{1}{1 - \gamma N} \leq 2$, which implies

$$\mathbb{E}\left[\widehat{L}_n\right] \leq \min_i \mathbb{E}\left[L_{i,n}\right] + \frac{1}{\varepsilon} + \frac{4\ln N}{\eta} + N\frac{\eta}{\varepsilon}\left(\mathbb{E}\left[L_{i^*,n}\right] + \frac{\ln N}{\eta} + \frac{\ln(\varepsilon B + 2)}{\eta}\right)$$

and, by simple calculation, the statement of the theorem.   □

5   Hannan Consistency

In this section we derive the sufficient conditions of Hannan consistency under partial monitoring for algorithm GREEN using time-varying parameters in case when the bound of the loss is unknown in advance, or when the loss is unbounded.

The next result shows sufficient conditions of Hannan consistency of Algorithm GREEN.

Theorem 3. *Algorithm* GREEN *is run for the combination of the label efficient and multi armed bandit problem. There exist constants $c < \infty$ and $0 \leq \nu < 1$ such that for each n*

$$\max_{1 \leq i \leq N} \frac{1}{n} \sum_{t=1}^{n} \ell_{i,t}^2 < cn^\nu.$$

For some constant $\rho > 0$ choose the parameters of the algorithm as:
$$\gamma_t = t^{-\alpha}/N; \quad (\nu + \rho)/2 \leq \alpha \leq 1,$$

$$\eta_t = t^{-1+\delta}; \quad 0 < \delta \leq 1 - \nu - \alpha - \beta - \rho$$

and

$$\varepsilon_t = \varepsilon_0 t^{-\beta}; \quad 0 < \varepsilon_0 \leq 1 \quad and \quad 0 \leq \beta \leq 1 - \nu - \alpha - \delta - \rho.$$

Then Algorithm GREEN *is Hannan consistent, that is,*

$$\limsup_{n \to \infty} \frac{1}{n} \left(\widehat{L}_n - \min_i L_{i,n} \right) \leq 0 \qquad a.s.$$

Remark 3. (Unknown ν) If ν is unknown in advance, then define a set of infinite number of experts. The experts use Algorithm 1 with different parameter ν. Since $0 \leq \nu < 1$, instead of ν we can use ν_k, a quantization of the $[0, 1)$ interval. Let $\{\nu_k\}$ is a monotonically increasing sequence which goes to 1 and let q_k be an arbitrary distribution over the set of k such that $q_k > 0$ for all k. Then using exponential weighting with time-varying learning rate in case of unbounded losses, the difference between the average loss of the (combined) algorithm and the average loss of the best expert vanishes asymptotically [10][Lemma 1]. Therefore the algorithm reaches Hannan consistency.

Remark 4. We derive the consequences of the theorem in special cases:

- **FI:** With a slight modification of the proof and fixing $\beta = 0$ ($\varepsilon_t = 1$) and $\gamma_t = 0$ we get the following condition for the losses in full information case:

$$\max_{1 \leq i \leq N} \frac{1}{n} \sum_{t=1}^{n} \ell_{i,t}^2 \leq O\left(n^{1-\delta-\rho}\right).$$

- **MAB:** we fix $\beta = 0$ ($\varepsilon_t = 1$). Choose $\gamma_t = t^{-1/3}$ for all t. Then the condition is for the losses

$$\max_{1 \leq i \leq N} \frac{1}{n} \sum_{t=1}^{n} \ell_{i,t}^2 \leq O\left(n^{2/3-\delta-\rho}\right).$$

- **LE(ε_t):** With a slight modification of the proof and fixing $\gamma_t = 0$ we get the following condition for the loss function in label efficient case:

$$\max_{1 \leq i \leq N} \frac{1}{n} \sum_{t=1}^{n} \ell_{i,t}^2 \leq O\left(n^{1-\beta-\delta-\rho}\right).$$

- **LE(ε_t)+MAB:** This is the most general case. Let $\gamma_t = t^{-1/3}$. Then the bound is

$$\max_{1 \leq i \leq N} \frac{1}{n} \sum_{t=1}^{n} \ell_{i,t}^2 \leq O\left(n^{2/3-\beta-\delta-\rho}\right).$$

Remark 5. (Convergence rate) With a slight extension of Lemma 5 we can retrieve the ν dependent almost sure convergence rate of the algorithm. The rate is

$$\frac{1}{n}\left(\widehat{L}_n - \min_i L_{i,n}\right) \leq O(n^{\nu/2-1/2}) \qquad a.s.$$

in the FI and the LE cases with optimal choice of the parameters and in the MAB and the LE+MAB cases it is

$$\frac{1}{n}\left(\widehat{L}_n - \min_i L_{i,n}\right) \leq O(n^{\nu/2-1/3}) \qquad a.s.$$

Remark 6. (Minimum amount of query rate in $\text{LE}(\varepsilon_t)$) Denote

$$\mu(n) = \sum_{t=1}^{n} \varepsilon_t$$

the expected query rate, that is, the expected number of queries that can be issued up to time n. Assume that the average of the loss function has a constant bound, i.e., $\nu = 0$. With a slight modification of the proof of Theorem 3 and choosing

$$\eta_t = \frac{\log\log\log t}{t} \quad \text{and} \quad \varepsilon_t = \frac{\log\log t}{t}$$

we obtain the condition for Hannan consistency, such that

$$\mu(n) = \log n \log\log n,$$

which is the same as that of to Cesa-Bianchi *et al.* [5].

6 Proof

In order to prove Theorem 3, we split the proof into three lemmas by telescope as before:

$$\frac{1}{n}\widehat{L}_n - \frac{1}{n}\min_i L_{i,n}$$

$$= \underbrace{\frac{1}{n}\left(\widehat{L}_n - \overline{L}_n\right)}_{\text{Lemma 6}} + \underbrace{\frac{1}{n}\left(\overline{L}_n - \min_i \widetilde{L}_{i,n}\right)}_{\text{Lemma 7}} + \underbrace{\frac{1}{n}\left(\min_i \widetilde{L}_{i,n} - \min_i L_{i,n}\right)}_{\text{Lemma 8}}. \qquad (5)$$

Combine sequentially Lemma 6, Lemma 7 and Lemma 8 to prove Theorem 3. We will show separately the almost sure convergence of the three terms on the right-hand side. In the sequel, we need the following lemma which is the key of the proof of Theorem 3:

Lemma 5. *Let $\{Z_t\}$ a martingale difference sequence. Let*

$$h_t \mathbb{E}\left[k_t\right] \geq \mathbf{Var}(Z_t)$$

where

$$h_t = 1/t^a$$

for all $t = 1, 2, \ldots$ and

$$K_n = \frac{1}{n} \sum_{t=1}^{n} k_t \leq Cn^b$$

and $0 \leq b < 1$ and $b - a < 1$. Then

$$\lim_{n \to \infty} \frac{1}{n} \sum_{t=1}^{n} Z_t = 0 \qquad a.s.$$

Proof. By the strong law of large numbers for martingale differences due to Chow [8], if $\{Z_t\}$ a martingale difference sequence with

$$\sum_{t=1}^{\infty} \frac{\mathbf{Var}(Z_t)}{t^2} < \infty \tag{6}$$

then

$$\lim_{n \to \infty} \frac{1}{n} \sum_{t=1}^{n} Z_t = 0 \qquad a.s.$$

We have to verify (6). Because of $k_t = tK_t - (t-1)K_{t-1}$, and $\frac{h_t}{t} - \frac{h_{t+1}t}{(t+1)^2} \geq 0$ we have that

$$\sum_{t=1}^{n} \frac{\mathbf{Var}(Z_t)}{t^2} \leq \sum_{t=1}^{n} \frac{h_t \mathbb{E}\left[k_t\right]}{t^2} = \sum_{t=1}^{n} \frac{h_t \mathbb{E}\left[(tK_t - (t-1)K_{t-1})\right]}{t^2}$$

$$= \frac{h_n \mathbb{E}\left[K_n\right]}{n} + \sum_{t=1}^{n-1} \left(\frac{h_t}{t} - \frac{h_{t+1}t}{(t+1)^2} \right) \mathbb{E}\left[K_t\right]$$

$$\leq \frac{n^{-a}Cn^b}{n} + \sum_{t=1}^{n-1} \left(\frac{t^{-a}}{t} - \frac{(t+1)^{-a}t}{(t+1)^2} \right) Ct^b$$

which is bounded by conditions. $\qquad\square$

Now we are ready to prove one by one the almost sure convergence of the terms in (5).

Lemma 6. *Under the conditions of the Theorem 3,*

$$\lim_{n \to \infty} \frac{1}{n} \left(\widehat{L}_n - \overline{L}_n \right) = 0 \qquad a.s.$$

Proof. First we use Lemma 1, that is

$$\widehat{L}_n - \overline{L}_n \leq \sum_{t=1}^{n} \left(\ell_{I_t, t} - \check{\ell}_t \right) + \sum_{t=1}^{n} N\gamma_t \check{\ell}_t = \sum_{t=1}^{n} Z_t + \sum_{t=1}^{n} N\gamma_t \check{\ell}_t. \tag{7}$$

Below we show separately, that both sums in (7) divided by n converge to zero almost surely. First observe that $\{Z_t\}$ is a martingale difference sequence with respect to I_1^{t-1} and S_1^{t-1}. Observe that I_t is independent from S_t therefore we get the following bound for the variance of Z_t:

$$\mathbf{Var}(Z_t) = \mathbb{E}\left[Z_t^2\right] = \mathbb{E}\left[(\ell_{I_t,t} - \check{\ell}_t)^2\right] \leq \frac{1}{\varepsilon_t}\mathbb{E}\left[\sum_{i=1}^N \ell_{i,t}^2\right] \overset{\text{def}}{=} h_t \mathbb{E}\left[k_t\right],$$

where $h_t = 1/\varepsilon_t$ and $k_t = \sum_{i=1}^N \ell_{i,t}^2$. Then applying Lemma 5 we obtain

$$\lim_{n\to\infty} \frac{1}{n}\sum_{t=1}^n Z_t = 0 \quad a.s.$$

Next we show that the second sum in (7) divided by n goes to zero almost surely, that is,

$$\frac{1}{n}\sum_{t=1}^n N\gamma_t\check{\ell}_t = \frac{1}{n}\sum_{t=1}^n \frac{S_t}{\varepsilon_t}\ell_{I_t,t}N\gamma_t = \frac{1}{n}\sum_{t=1}^n R_t + \frac{1}{n}\sum_{t=1}^n \ell_{I_t,t}N\gamma_t \to 0 \quad (n\to\infty)$$

$$(8)$$

where R_t is a martingale difference sequence respect to S_1^{t-1} and I_1^t. Bounding the variance of R_t, we obtain

$$\mathbf{Var}(R_t) \leq N^2\frac{\gamma_t^2}{\varepsilon_t}\mathbb{E}\left[\sum_{i=1}^N \ell_{i,t}^2\right].$$

Then using Lemma 5 with parameters $h_t = \gamma_t^2/\varepsilon_t$ and $k_t = \sum_{i=1}^N \ell_{i,t}^2$ we get

$$\lim_{n\to\infty} \frac{1}{n}\sum_{t=1}^n R_t = 0 \quad a.s.$$

The proof is finished by showing, that the second sum in (8) goes to zero. i.e.,

$$\lim_{n\to\infty} \frac{1}{n}\sum_{t=1}^n \ell_{I_t,t}N\gamma_t = \lim_{n\to\infty} N\sum_{i=1}^N \frac{1}{n}\sum_{t=1}^n \ell_{i,t}\gamma_t = 0.$$

Introduce $K_{i,n} = \frac{1}{n}\sum_{t=1}^n \ell_{i,t}$ then for all i

$$\frac{1}{n}\sum_{t=1}^n \ell_{i,t}\gamma_t = \frac{1}{n}\sum_{t=1}^n (tK_{i,t} - (t-1)K_{i,t-1})\gamma_t$$

$$= K_{i,n}\gamma_n + \frac{1}{n}\sum_{t=1}^{n-1}(\gamma_t - \gamma_{t+1})tK_{i,t}$$

$$\leq K_{i,n}\gamma_n + \frac{1}{n}\sum_{t=1}^{n-1}\gamma_t K_{i,t} \qquad (9)$$

$$\leq \sqrt{c}\frac{1}{N}n^{\nu/2-\alpha} + \frac{1}{nN}\sum_{t=1}^{n-1}t^{\nu/2-\alpha}\sqrt{c} \to 0 \qquad (10)$$

where the (9) holds because $(\gamma_t - \gamma_{t+1})t \leq \gamma_t$ and (10) follows from $K_{i,n} \leq \sqrt{cn^\nu}$, the definition of the parameters and $\alpha \geq (\nu + \rho)/2$. $\qquad\square$

Lemma 7 yields the relation between $\overline{L}_n$ and $\min_i \widetilde{L}_{i,n}$.

Lemma 7. *Under the conditions of Theorem 3,*

$$\limsup_{n\to\infty} \frac{1}{n}\left(\overline{L}_n - \min_i \widetilde{L}_{i,n}\right) \leq 0 \qquad a.s.$$

Proof. We start by applying Lemma 2, that is,

$$\overline{L}_n - \min_i \widetilde{L}_{i,n} \leq \frac{2\ln N}{\eta_{n+1}} + \sum_{t=1}^n \Phi(\mathbf{p}_t, \eta_t, -\widetilde{\boldsymbol{\ell}}_t). \tag{11}$$

To bound the quantity of $\Phi(\mathbf{p}_t, \eta_t, -\widetilde{\boldsymbol{\ell}}_t)$, our starting point is (3). Moreover,

$$\frac{\eta_t}{2}\sum_{i=1}^N p_{i,t}\widetilde{\ell}_{i,t}^2 = \frac{\eta_t}{2}\sum_{i=1}^N p_{i,t}\frac{\ell_{i,t}^2}{\widetilde{p}_{i,t}^2\varepsilon_t^2}S_t\mathbb{I}_{\{I_t=i\}} \leq \frac{\eta_t}{2\gamma_t\varepsilon_t}\frac{S_t}{\varepsilon_t}\ell_{I_t,t}^2 \leq \frac{\eta_t}{2\gamma_t\varepsilon_t}\frac{S_t}{\varepsilon_t}\sum_{i=1}^N \ell_{i,t}^2 \tag{12}$$

where the first inequality comes from $p_{I_t,t} \geq \gamma_t$. Combining this bound with (11), dividing by n and taking the limit superior we get

$$\limsup_{n\to\infty}\frac{1}{n}\left(\overline{L}_n - \min_i \widetilde{L}_{i,n}\right) \leq \limsup_{n\to\infty}\frac{2\ln N}{n\eta_{n+1}} + \limsup_{n\to\infty}\frac{1}{n}\sum_{t=1}^n\frac{\eta_t}{2\gamma_t\varepsilon_t}\frac{S_t}{\varepsilon_t}\sum_{i=1}^N \ell_{i,t}^2.$$

Let analyze separately the two terms on the right-hand side. The first term is zero because of the assumption of the Theorem 3. Concerning the second term, similarly to Lemma 6 we can split S_t/ε_t as follows: let us

$$\frac{S_t}{\varepsilon_t}\frac{\eta_t}{2\gamma_t\varepsilon_t}\sum_{i=1}^N \ell_{i,t}^2 = Z_t + \frac{\eta_t}{2\gamma_t\varepsilon_t}\sum_{i=1}^N \ell_{i,t}^2, \tag{13}$$

where Z_t is a martingale difference sequence. The variance is

$$\mathbf{Var}(Z_t) = \mathbb{E}\left[\frac{\eta_t^2 S_t}{\gamma_t^2\varepsilon_t^2}\left(\sum_{i=1}^N \ell_{i,t}^2\right)^2\right] = \frac{\eta_t^2}{\varepsilon_t\gamma_t^2}\mathbb{E}\left[\left(\sum_{i=1}^N \ell_{i,t}^2\right)^2\right].$$

Application of Lemma 5 with $h_t = \frac{\eta_t^2}{\varepsilon_t\gamma_t^2}$ and $k_t = \left(\sum_{i=1}^N \ell_{i,t}^2\right)^2$ yields

$$\lim_{n\to\infty}\frac{1}{n}\sum_{t=1}^n Z_t = 0 \qquad a.s.$$

where we used that

$$\frac{1}{n}\sum_{t=1}^n k_t \leq \frac{1}{n}\left(\sum_{t=1}^n \sqrt{k_t}\right)^2 \leq N^2c^2n^{1+2\nu}.$$

Finally, we have to prove that the sum of the second term in (13) goes to zero, that is,

$$\limsup_{n\to\infty} \frac{1}{n}\sum_{t=1}^{n}\sum_{i=1}^{N}\frac{\eta_t}{2\gamma_t\varepsilon_t}\ell_{i,t}^2 = 0$$

for which we use same argument as in Lemma 6. Introduce $K_{i,n} = \frac{1}{n}\sum_{t=1}^{n}\ell_{i,t}^2$ then we get

$$\frac{1}{n}\sum_{t=1}^{n}\ell_{i,t}^2\frac{\eta_t}{2\gamma_t\varepsilon_t} = K_{i,n}\frac{\eta_n}{2\gamma_n\varepsilon_n} + \frac{1}{n}\sum_{t=1}^{n-1}\left(\frac{\eta_t}{2\gamma_t\varepsilon_t} - \frac{\eta_{t+1}}{2\gamma_{t+1}\varepsilon_{t+1}}\right)tK_{i,t}$$

$$\leq K_{i,n}\frac{\eta_n}{2\gamma_n\varepsilon_n} + \frac{1}{n}\sum_{t=1}^{n-1}\frac{\eta_t}{2\gamma_t\varepsilon_t}K_{i,t}$$

$$\leq Ncn^{\nu-1+\alpha+\beta+\delta} + \frac{1}{n}\sum_{t=1}^{n-1}Nct^{\nu-1+\alpha+\beta+\delta} \to 0$$

because of $K_{i,n} \leq cn^{\nu}$ and $\nu < 1 - \alpha - \beta - \delta - \rho$. $\square$

Finally, the last step is to analyze the difference between the estimated loss and the true loss.

Lemma 8. *Under the conditions of Theorem 3,*

$$\lim_{n\to\infty} \frac{1}{n}\left(\min_i \widetilde{L}_{i,n} - \min_j L_{j,n}\right) = 0 \qquad a.s.$$

Proof. First, bound the difference of the minimum of the true and the estimated loss. Obviously,

$$\frac{1}{n}\left(\min_i \widetilde{L}_{i,n} - \min_j L_{j,n}\right) \leq \sum_{i=1}^{N}\left|\frac{1}{n}\left(\widetilde{L}_{i,n} - L_{i,n}\right)\right| = \sum_{i=1}^{N}\left|\frac{1}{n}\sum_{t=1}^{n}(\widetilde{\ell}_{i,t} - \ell_{i,t})\right|$$

$$= \sum_{i=1}^{N}\left|\frac{1}{n}\sum_{t=1}^{n}Z_{i,t}\right|,$$

where $Z_{i,t}$ is martingale difference sequence for all i. As earlier, we use Lemma 5. First we bound $\mathbf{Var}(Z_{i,t})$ as follows

$$\mathbf{Var}(Z_{i,t}) = \mathbb{E}\widetilde{\ell}_{i,t}^2 \leq \frac{\mathbb{E}\left[\sum_{i=1}^{N}\ell_{i,t}^2\right]}{\varepsilon_t\gamma_t}. \tag{14}$$

Applying Lemma 5 with parameters $k_t = \sum_{i=1}^{N}\ell_{i,t}^2$ and $h_t = \frac{1}{\varepsilon_t\gamma_t}$, for each i

$$\lim_{n\to\infty} \frac{1}{n}\sum_{t=1}^{n}Z_{i,t} = 0 \qquad a.s.$$

therefore

$$\lim_{n\to\infty} \sum_{i=1}^{N} \left| \frac{1}{n} \sum_{t=1}^{n} Z_{i,t} \right| = 0 \qquad a.s.$$

$\square$

References

1. P. Auer, N. Cesa-Bianchi, Y. Freund, and R. E. Schapire. Gambling in a rigged casino: the adversial multi-armed bandit problem. In *Proceedings of the 36th Annual Symposium on Foundations of Computer Science, FOCS 1995*, pages 322–331, Washington, DC, USA, Oct. 1995. IEEE Computer Society Press, Los Alamitos, CA.

2. D. Blackwell. An analog of the minimax theorem for vector payoffs. *Pacific Journal of Mathematics*, 6:1–8, 1956.

3. N. Cesa-Bianchi, Y. Freund, D. P. Helmbold, D. Haussler, R. Schapire, and M. K. Warmuth. How to use expert advice. *Journal of the ACM*, 44(3):427–485, 1997.

4. N. Cesa-Bianchi and G. Lugosi. *Prediction, Learning, and Games*. Cambridge University Press, Cambridge, 2006.

5. N. Cesa-Bianchi, G. Lugosi, and G. Stoltz. Minimizing regret with label efficient prediction. *IEEE Trans. Inform. Theory*, IT-51:2152–2162, June 2005.

6. N. Cesa-Bianchi, Y. Mansour, and G. Stoltz. Improved second-order bounds for prediction with expert advice. In *COLT 2005*, pages 217–232, 2005.

7. N. Cesa-Bianchi, Y. Mansour, and G. Stoltz. Improved second-order bounds for prediction with expert advice, 2006. (submitted).

8. Y. S. Chow. Local convergence of martingales and the law of large numbers. *Annals of Mathematical Statistics*, 36:552–558, 1965.

9. L. Györfi and G. Lugosi. Strategies for sequential prediction of stationary time series. In M. Dror, P. L'Ecuyer, and F. Szidarovszky, editors, *Modelling Uncertainty: An Examination of its Theory, Methods and Applications*, pages 225–248. Kluwer Academic Publishers, 2001.

10. L. Györfi and Gy. Ottucsák. Sequential prediction of unbounded stationary time series, 2006. (submitted).

11. A. György and Gy. Ottucsák. Adaptive routing using expert advice. *The Computer Journal*, 49(2):180–189, 2006.

12. J. Hannan. Approximation to bayes risk in repeated plays. In M. Dresher, A. Tucker, and P. Wolfe, editors, *Contributions to the Theory of Games*, volume 3, pages 97–139. Princeton University Press, 1957.

13. S. Hart and A. Mas-Colell. A simple adaptive procedure leading to correlated equilibrium. *Econometria*, 68(5):181–200, 2002.

14. N. Littlestone and M. K. Warmuth. The weighted majority algorithm. *Information and Computation*, 108:212–261, 1994.

15. J. Poland and M. Hutter. Defensive universal learning with experts. In *Proc. 16th International Conf. on Algorithmic Learning Theory, ALT 2005*, pages 356–370, Singapore, 2005. Springer, Berlin.

16. V. Vovk. Aggregating strategies. In *Proceedings of the 3rd Annual Workshop on Computational Learning Theory*, pages 372–383, Rochester, NY, Aug. 1990. Morgan Kaufmann.

General Discounting Versus Average Reward

Marcus Hutter

IDSIA / RSISE / ANU / NICTA /
http://www.hutter1.net

Abstract. Consider an agent interacting with an environment in cycles. In every interaction cycle the agent is rewarded for its performance. We compare the average reward U from cycle 1 to m (average value) with the future discounted reward V from cycle k to ∞ (discounted value). We consider essentially arbitrary (non-geometric) discount sequences and arbitrary reward sequences (non-MDP environments). We show that asymptotically U for $m \to \infty$ and V for $k \to \infty$ are equal, provided both limits exist. Further, if the effective horizon grows linearly with k or faster, then the existence of the limit of U implies that the limit of V exists. Conversely, if the effective horizon grows linearly with k or slower, then existence of the limit of V implies that the limit of U exists.

1 Introduction

We consider the reinforcement learning setup [RN03, Hut05], where an agent interacts with an environment in cycles. In cycle k, the agent outputs (acts) a_k, then it makes observation o_k and receives reward r_k, both provided by the environment. Then the next cycle $k+1$ starts. For simplicity we assume that agent and environment are deterministic.

Typically one is interested in action sequences, called plans or policies, for agents that result in high reward. The simplest reasonable measure of performance is the total reward sum or equivalently the average reward, called average value $U_{1m} := \frac{1}{m}[r_1 + ... + r_m]$, where m should be the lifespan of the agent. One problem is that the lifetime is often not known in advance, e.g. often the time one is willing to let a system run depends on its displayed performance. More serious is that the measure is indifferent to whether an agent receives high rewards early or late if the values are the same.

A natural (non-arbitrary) choice for m is to consider the limit $m \to \infty$. While the indifference may be acceptable for finite m, it can be catastrophic for $m = \infty$. Consider an agent that receives no reward until its first action is $a_k = b$, and then once receives reward $\frac{k-1}{k}$. For finite m, the optimal k to switch from action a to b is $k_{opt} = m$. Hence $k_{opt} \to \infty$ for $m \to \infty$, so the reward maximizing agent for $m \to \infty$ actually always acts with a, and hence has zero reward, although a value arbitrarily close to 1 would be achievable. (Immortal agents are lazy [Hut05, Sec.5.7]). More seriously, in general the limit $U_{1\infty}$ may not even exist.

Another approach is to consider a moving horizon. In cycle k, the agent tries to maximize $U_{km} := \frac{1}{m-k+1}[r_k + ... + r_m]$, where m increases with k, e.g. $m = k + h - 1$

J.L. Balcázar, P.M. Long, and F. Stephan (Eds.): ALT 2006, LNAI 4264, pp. 244–258, 2006.
© Springer-Verlag Berlin Heidelberg 2006

with h being the horizon. This naive truncation is often used in games like chess (plus a heuristic reward in cycle m) to get a reasonably small search tree. While this can work in practice, it can lead to inconsistent optimal strategies, i.e. to agents that change their mind. Consider the example above with $h=2$. In every cycle k it is better first to act a and then b ($U_{km} = r_k + r_{k+1} = 0 + \frac{k}{k+1}$), rather than immediately b ($U_{km} = r_k + r_{k+1} = \frac{k-1}{k} + 0$), or a,a ($U_{km} = 0 + 0$). But entering the next cycle $k+1$, the agent throws its original plan overboard, to now choose a in favor of b, followed by b. This pattern repeats, resulting in no reward at all.

The standard solution to the above problems is to consider geometrically=exponentially discounted reward [Sam37, BT96, SB98]. One discounts the reward for every cycle of delay by a factor $\gamma < 1$, i.e. one considers the future discounted reward sum $V_{k\gamma} := (1-\gamma)\sum_{i=k}^{\infty}\gamma^{i-k}r_i$, which models a preference towards early rewards. The $V_{1\gamma}$ maximizing policy is consistent in the sense that its actions $a_k, a_{k+1},...$ coincide with the optimal policy based on $V_{k\gamma}$. At first glance, there seems to be no arbitrary lifetime m or horizon h, but this is an illusion. $V_{k\gamma}$ is dominated by contributions from rewards $r_k...r_{k+O(\ln\gamma^{-1})}$, so has an effective horizon $h^{eff} \approx \ln\gamma^{-1}$. While such a sliding effective horizon does not cause inconsistent policies, it can nevertheless lead to suboptimal behavior. For every (effective) horizon, there is a task that needs a larger horizon to be solved. For instance, while $h^{eff} = 5$ is sufficient for tic-tac-toe, it is definitely insufficient for chess. There are elegant closed form solutions for Bandit problems, which show that for any $\gamma < 1$, the Bayes-optimal policy can get stuck with a suboptimal arm (is not self-optimizing) [BF85, KV86].

For $\gamma \to 1$, $h^{eff} \to \infty$, and the defect decreases. There are various deep papers considering the limit $\gamma \to 1$ [Kel81], and comparing it to the limit $m \to \infty$ [Kak01]. The analysis is typically restricted to ergodic MDPs for which the limits $\lim_{\gamma \to 1}V_{1\gamma}$ and $\lim_{m \to \infty}U_{1m}$ exist. But like the limit policy for $m \to \infty$, the limit policy for $\gamma \to 1$ can display very poor performance, i.e. we need to choose $\gamma < 1$ fixed in advance (but how?), or consider higher order terms [Mah96, AA99]. We also cannot consistently adapt γ with k. Finally, the value limits may not exist beyond ergodic MDPs.

In the computer science literature, geometric discount is essentially assumed for convenience without outer justification (sometimes a constant interest rate or probability of surviving is quoted [KLM96]). In the psychology and economics literature it has been argued that people discount a one day=cycle delay in reward more if it concerns rewards now rather than later, e.g. in a year (plus one day) [FLO02]. So there is some work on "sliding" discount sequences $W_{k\gamma} \propto \gamma_0 r_k + \gamma_1 r_{k+1} + ...$ One can show that this also leads to inconsistent policies if γ is non-geometric [Str56, VW04].

Is there any non-geometric discount leading to consistent policies? In [Hut02] the generally discounted value $V_{k\gamma} := \frac{1}{\Gamma_k}\sum_{i=k}^{\infty}\gamma_i r_i$ with $\Gamma_k := \sum_{i=k}^{\infty}\gamma_i < \infty$ has been introduced. It is well-defined for arbitrary environments, leads to consistent policies, and e.g. for quadratic discount $\gamma_k = 1/k^2$ to an increasing effective horizon (proportionally to k), i.e. the optimal agent becomes increasingly farsighted in a consistent way, leads to self-optimizing policies in ergodic (kth-order) MDPs in general, Bandits in particular, and even beyond MDPs. See [Hut02] for these and [Hut05] for more results. The only other serious analysis of general discounts we are aware of is in [BF85], but their analysis is limited to Bandits and so-called regular discount. This discount has bounded effective horizon, so also does not lead to self-optimizing policies.

The *asymptotic* total average performance $U_{1\infty}$ and future discounted performance $V_{\infty\gamma}$ are of key interest. For instance, often we do not know the exact environment in advance but have to *learn* it from past experience, which is the domain of reinforcement learning [SB98] and adaptive control theory [KV86]. Ideally we would like a learning agent that performs *asymptotically* as well as the optimal agent that knows the environment in advance.

Contents and main results. The subject of study of this paper is the relation between $U_{1\infty}$ and $V_{\infty\gamma}$ for *general discount* γ and *arbitrary environment*. The importance of the performance measures U and V, and general discount γ has been discussed above. There is also a clear need to study general environments beyond ergodic MDPs, since the real world is neither ergodic (e.g. losing an arm is irreversible) nor completely observable.

The only restriction we impose on the discount sequence γ is summability ($\Gamma_1 < \infty$) so that $V_{k\gamma}$ exists, and monotonicity ($\gamma_k \geq \gamma_{k+1}$). Our main result is that if both limits $U_{1\infty}$ and $V_{\infty\gamma}$ exist, then they are necessarily equal (Section 7, Theorem 19). Somewhat surprisingly this holds for *any* discount sequence γ and *any* environment (reward sequence r), whatsoever.

Note that limit $U_{1\infty}$ may exist or not, independent of whether $V_{\infty\gamma}$ exists or not. We present examples of the four possibilities in Section 2. Under certain conditions on γ, existence of $U_{1\infty}$ implies existence of $V_{\infty\gamma}$, or vice versa. We show that if (a quantity closely related to) the effective horizon grows linearly with k or faster, then existence of $U_{1\infty}$ implies existence of $V_{\infty\gamma}$ and their equality (Section 5, Theorem 15). Conversely, if the effective horizon grows linearly with k or slower, then existence of $V_{\infty\gamma}$ implies existence of $U_{1\infty}$ and their equality (Section 6, Theorem 17). Note that apart from discounts with oscillating effective horizons, this implies (and this is actually the path used to prove) the first mentioned main result. In Sections 3 and 4 we define and provide some basic properties of average and discounted value, respectively.

2   Example Discount and Reward Sequences

In order to get a better feeling for general discount sequences, effective horizons, average and discounted value, and their relation and existence, we first consider various examples.

Notation
- In the following we assume that $i,k,m,n \in I\!N$ are natural numbers.
- Let $\underline{F} := \underline{\lim}_n F_n = \lim_{k\to\infty} \inf_{n>k} F_n$ denote the limit inferior and
- $\overline{F} := \overline{\lim}_n F_n = \lim_{k\to\infty} \sup_{n>k} F_n$ the limit superior of F_n.
- $\forall' n$ means for all but finitely many n.

- Let $\boldsymbol{\gamma} = (\gamma_1, \gamma_2, \ldots)$ denote a summable discount sequence in the sense that
- $\Gamma_k := \sum_{i=k}^{\infty} \gamma_i < \infty$ and $\gamma_k \in I\!\!R^+ \ \forall k$.
- Further, $\boldsymbol{r} = (r_1, r_2, \ldots)$ is a bounded reward sequence w.l.g. $r_k \in [0,1] \ \forall k$.
- Let constants $\alpha, \beta \in [0,1]$, boundaries $0 \leq k_1 < m_1 < k_2 < m_2 < k_3 < \ldots$,
- total average value $U_{1m} := \frac{1}{m} \sum_{i=1}^{m} r_i$ (see Definition 10) and
- future discounted value $V_{k\gamma} := \frac{1}{\Gamma_k} \sum_{i=k}^{\infty} \gamma_i r_i$ (see Definition 12).

The derived theorems also apply to general bounded rewards $r_i \in [a,b]$ by linearly rescaling $r_i \rightsquigarrow \frac{r_i - a}{b - a} \in [0,1]$ and $U \rightsquigarrow \frac{U-a}{b-a}$ and $V \rightsquigarrow \frac{V-a}{b-a}$.

Discount sequences and effective horizons. Rewards r_{k+h} give only a small contribution to $V_{k\gamma}$ for large h, since $\gamma_{k+h} \xrightarrow{h \to \infty} 0$. More important, the whole reward tail from $k+h$ to ∞ in $V_{k\gamma}$ is bounded by $\frac{1}{\Gamma_k}[\gamma_{k+h} + \gamma_{k+h+1} + \ldots]$, which tends to zero for $h \to \infty$. So effectively $V_{k\gamma}$ has a horizon h for which the cumulative tail weight Γ_{k+h}/Γ_k is, say, about $\frac{1}{2}$, or more formally $h_k^{eff} := \min\{h \geq 0 : \Gamma_{k+h} \leq \frac{1}{2}\Gamma_k\}$. The closely related quantity $h_k^{quasi} := \Gamma_k/\gamma_k$, which we call the quasi-horizon, will play an important role in this work. The following table summarizes various discounts with their properties.

Discounts	γ_k	Γ_k	h_k^{eff}	h_k^{quasi}	$k\gamma_k/\Gamma_k \to ?$
finite ($k \leq m$)	1	$m - k + 1$	$\frac{1}{2}(m-k+1)$	$m - k + 1$	$\frac{k}{m-k+1}$
geometric	$\gamma^k, \ 0 \leq \gamma < 1$	$\frac{\gamma^k}{1-\gamma}$	$\frac{\ln 2}{\ln \gamma^{-1}}$	$\frac{1}{1-\gamma}$	$(1-\gamma)k \to \infty$
quadratic	$\frac{1}{k(k+1)}$	$\frac{1}{k}$	k	$k+1$	$\frac{k}{k+1} \to 1$
power	$k^{-1-\varepsilon}, \ \varepsilon > 0$	$\sim \frac{1}{\varepsilon}k^{-\varepsilon}$	$\sim (2^{1/\varepsilon}-1)k$	$\sim \frac{k}{\varepsilon}$	$\sim \varepsilon \quad \to \varepsilon$
harmonic$_\approx$	$\frac{1}{k\ln^2 k}$	$\sim \frac{1}{\ln k}$	$\sim k^2$	$\sim k\ln k$	$\sim \frac{1}{\ln k} \to 0$

For instance, the standard discount is geometric $\gamma_k = \gamma^k$ for some $0 \leq \gamma < 1$, with constant effective horizon $\frac{\ln(1/2)}{\ln \gamma}$. (An agent with $\gamma = 0.95$ can/will not plan farther than about 10-20 cycles ahead). Since in this work we allow for general discount, we can even recover the average value U_{1m} by choosing $\gamma_k = \{ \begin{smallmatrix} 1 \ \text{for} \ k \leq m \\ 0 \ \text{for} \ k > m \end{smallmatrix} \}$. A power discount $\gamma_k = k^{-\alpha}$ ($\alpha > 1$) is very interesting, since it leads to a linearly increasing effective horizon $h_k^{eff} \propto k$, i.e. to an agent whose farsightedness increases proportionally with age. This choice has some appeal, as it avoids preselection of a global time-scale like m or $\frac{1}{1-\gamma}$, and it seems that humans of age k years usually do not plan their lives for more than, perhaps, the next k years. It is also the boundary case for which $U_{1\infty}$ exists if and only if $V_{\infty\gamma}$ exists.

Example reward sequences. Most of our (counter)examples will be for binary reward $\boldsymbol{r} \in \{0,1\}^\infty$. We call a maximal consecutive subsequence of ones a 1-run. We denote start, end, and length of the nth run by k_n, $m_n - 1$, and $A_n = m_n - k_n$, respectively. The following 0-run starts at m_n, ends at $k_{n+1} - 1$, and has length $B_n = k_{n+1} - m_n$. The (non-normalized) discount sum in 1/0-run n is denoted by a_n / b_n, respectively. The following definition and two lemmas facilitate the discussion of our examples. The proofs contain further useful relations.

Definition 1 (Value for binary rewards). *Every binary reward sequence* $\boldsymbol{r} \in \{0,1\}^\infty$ *can be defined by the sequence of change points* $0 \leq k_1 < m_1 < k_2 < m_2 < \ldots$ *with* $r_k = 1$ *iff there is an* n *for which* $k_n \leq k < m_n\}$.

The intuition behind the following lemma is that the relative length A_n of a 1-run and the following 0-run B_n (previous 0-run B_{n-1}) asymptotically provides a lower (upper) limit of the average value U_{1m}.

Lemma 2 (Average value for binary rewards). *For binary r of Definition 1, let $A_n := m_n - k_n$ and $B_n := k_{n+1} - m_n$ be the lengths of the nth 1/0-run. Then*

$$\text{If } \frac{A_n}{A_n + B_n} \to \alpha \quad \text{then} \quad \underline{U}_{1\infty} = \lim_n U_{1,k_n-1} = \alpha$$

$$\text{If } \frac{A_n}{B_{n-1} + A_n} \to \beta \quad \text{then} \quad \overline{U}_{1\infty} = \lim_n U_{1,m_n-1} = \beta$$

In particular, if $\alpha = \beta$, then $U_{1\infty} = \alpha = \beta$ exists.

Proof. The elementary identity $U_{1m} = U_{1,m-1} + \frac{1}{m}(r_m - U_{1,m-1}) \gtrless U_{1,m-1}$ if $r_m = \{{1 \atop 0}\}$ implies

$$U_{1k_n} \leq U_{1m} \leq U_{1,m_n-1} \text{ for } k_n \leq m < m_n$$

$$U_{1,k_{n+1}-1} \leq U_{1m} \leq U_{1,m_n} \text{ for } m_n \leq m < k_{n+1}$$

$$\Rightarrow \quad \inf_{n \geq n_0} U_{1k_n} \leq U_{1m} \leq \sup_{m \geq n_0} U_{1,m_n-1} \quad \forall m \geq k_{n_0}$$

$$\Rightarrow \quad \lim_n U_{1k_n} = \underline{U}_{1\infty} \leq \overline{U}_{1\infty} = \overline{\lim_n} U_{1,m_n-1} \qquad (1)$$

The $\geq$ direction in the equalities in the last line holds, since (U_{1k_n}) and (U_{1,m_n-1}) are subsequences of (U_{1m}). Now

$$\text{If } \frac{A_n}{A_n + B_n} \geq \alpha \, \forall n \quad \text{then} \quad U_{1,k_n-1} = \frac{A_1 + \ldots + A_{n-1}}{A_1 + B_1 + \ldots + A_{n-1} + B_{n-1}} \geq \alpha \, \forall n \qquad (2)$$

This implies $\inf_n \frac{A_n}{A_n + B_n} \leq \inf_n U_{1,k_n-1}$. If the condition in (2) is initially (for a finite number of n) violated, the conclusion in (2) still holds asymptotically. A standard argument along these lines shows that we can replace the inf by a $\underline{\lim}$, i.e.

$$\underline{\lim_n} \frac{A_n}{A_n + B_n} \leq \underline{\lim_n} U_{1,k_n-1} \quad \text{and similarly} \quad \overline{\lim_n} \frac{A_n}{A_n + B_n} \geq \overline{\lim_n} U_{1,k_n-1}$$

Together this shows that $\lim_n U_{1,k_n-1} = \alpha$ exists, if $\lim_n \frac{A_n}{A_n + B_n} = \alpha$ exists. Similarly

$$\text{If } \frac{A_n}{B_{n-1} + A_n} \geq \beta \, \forall n \quad \text{then} \quad U_{1,m_n-1} = \frac{A_1 + \ldots + A_n}{B_0 + A_1 + \ldots + B_{n-1} + A_n} \geq \beta \, \forall n \qquad (3)$$

where $B_0 := 0$. This implies $\inf_n \frac{A_n}{B_{n-1} + A_n} \leq \inf_n U_{1,m_n-1}$, and by an asymptotic refinement of (3)

$$\underline{\lim_n} \frac{A_n}{B_{n-1} + A_n} \leq \underline{\lim_n} U_{1,m_n-1} \quad \text{and similarly} \quad \overline{\lim_n} \frac{A_n}{B_{n-1} + A_n} \geq \overline{\lim_n} U_{1,m_n-1}$$

Together this shows that $\lim_n U_{1,m_n-1} = \beta$ exists, if $\lim_n \frac{A_n}{B_{n-1} + A_n} = \beta$ exists. ∎

Similarly to Lemma 2, the asymptotic ratio of the discounted value a_n of a 1-run and the discount sum b_n of the following (b_{n-1} of the previous) 0-run determines the upper (lower) limits of the discounted value $V_{k\gamma}$.

Lemma 3 (Discounted value for binary rewards). *For binary r of Definition 1, let $a_n := \sum_{i=k_n}^{m_n-1} \gamma_i = \Gamma_{k_n} - \Gamma_{m_n}$ and $b_n := \sum_{i=m_n}^{k_{n+1}-1} \gamma_i = \Gamma_{m_n} - \Gamma_{k_{n+1}}$ be the discount sums of the nth 1/0-run. Then*

$$\text{If } \frac{a_{n+1}}{b_n + a_{n+1}} \to \alpha \quad \text{then} \quad \underline{V}_{\infty\gamma} = \lim_n V_{m_n\gamma} = \alpha$$

$$\text{If } \frac{a_n}{a_n + b_n} \to \beta \quad \text{then} \quad \overline{V}_{\infty\gamma} = \lim_n V_{k_n\gamma} = \beta$$

In particular, if $\alpha = \beta$, then $V_{\infty\gamma} = \alpha = \beta$ exists.

Proof. The proof is very similar to the proof of Lemma 2. The elementary identity $V_{k\gamma} = V_{k+1,\gamma} + \frac{\gamma_k}{\Gamma_k}(r_k - V_{k+1,\gamma}) \gtrless V_{k+1,\gamma}$ if $r_k = \{^1_0\}$ implies

$$V_{m_n\gamma} \leq V_{k\gamma} \leq V_{k_n\gamma} \text{ for } k_n \leq k \leq m_n$$

$$V_{m_n\gamma} \leq V_{k\gamma} \leq V_{k_{n+1}\gamma} \text{ for } m_n \leq k \leq k_{n+1}$$

$$\Rightarrow \quad \inf_{n \geq n_0} V_{m_n\gamma} \leq V_{k\gamma} \leq \sup_{m \geq n_0} V_{k_n\gamma} \quad \forall k \geq k_{n_0}$$

$$\Rightarrow \quad \lim_n V_{m_n\gamma} = \underline{V}_{\infty\gamma} \leq \overline{V}_{\infty\gamma} = \overline{\lim_n} V_{k_n\gamma} \tag{4}$$

The $\geq$ in the equalities in the last line holds, since $(V_{k_n\gamma})$ and $(V_{m_n\gamma})$ are subsequences of $(V_{k\gamma})$. Now if $\frac{a_n}{a_n+b_n} \geq \beta \ \forall n \geq n_0$ then $V_{k_n\gamma} = \frac{a_n + a_{n+1} + \dots}{a_n + b_n + a_{n+1} + b_{n+1} + \dots} \geq \beta$ $\forall n \geq n_0$. This implies

$$\varliminf_n \frac{a_n}{a_n+b_n} \leq \varliminf_n V_{k_n\gamma} \quad \text{and similarly} \quad \varlimsup_n \frac{a_n}{a_n+b_n} \geq \varlimsup_n V_{k_n\gamma}$$

Together this shows that $\lim_n V_{k_n\gamma} = \beta$ exists, if $\lim_n \frac{a_n}{a_n+b_n} = \beta$ exists. Similarly if $\frac{a_{n+1}}{b_n+a_{n+1}} \geq \alpha \ \forall n \geq n_0$ then $V_{m_n\gamma} = \frac{a_{n+1} + a_{n+2} + \dots}{b_n + a_{n+1} + b_{n+1} + a_{n+2} + \dots} \geq \alpha$ $\forall n \geq n_0$. This implies

$$\varliminf_n \frac{a_{n+1}}{b_n+a_{n+1}} \leq \varliminf_n V_{m_n\gamma} \quad \text{and similarly} \quad \varlimsup_n \frac{a_{n+1}}{b_n+a_{n+1}} \geq \varlimsup_n V_{m_n\gamma}$$

Together this shows that $\lim_n V_{m_n\gamma} = \alpha$ exists, if $\lim_n \frac{a_{n+1}}{b_n+a_{n+1}} = \alpha$ exists. ∎

Example 4 ($U_{1\infty} = V_{\infty\gamma}$). Constant rewards $r_k \equiv \alpha$ is a trivial example for which $U_{1\infty} = V_{\infty\gamma} = \alpha$ exist and are equal.

A more interesting example is $r = 1^1 0^2 1^3 0^4 \dots$ of linearly increasing 0/1-run-length with $A_n = 2n-1$ and $B_n = 2n$, for which $U_{1\infty} = \frac{1}{2}$ exists. For quadratic discount $\gamma_k = \frac{1}{k(k+1)}$, using $\Gamma_k = \frac{1}{k}$, $h_k^{quasi} = k+1 = \Theta(k)$, $k_n = (2n-1)(n-1) + 1$, $m_n = (2n-1)n+1$, $a_n = \Gamma_{k_n} - \Gamma_{m_n} = \frac{A_n}{k_n m_n} \sim \frac{1}{2n^3}$, and $b_n = \Gamma_{m_n} - \Gamma_{k_{n+1}} = \frac{B_n}{m_n k_{n+1}} \sim \frac{1}{2n^3}$, we also get $V_{\infty\gamma} = \frac{1}{2}$. The values converge, since they average over increasingly many 1/0-runs, each of decreasing weight.

Example 5 (simple $U_{1\infty} \neq V_{\infty\gamma}$). Let us consider a very simple example with alternating rewards $r = 101010\dots$ and geometric discount $\gamma_k = \gamma^k$. It is immediate that $U_{1\infty} = \frac{1}{2}$ exists, but $\underline{V}_{\infty\gamma} = V_{2k,\gamma} = \frac{\gamma}{1+\gamma} < \frac{1}{1+\gamma} = V_{2k-1,\gamma} = \overline{V}_{\infty\gamma}$.

Example 6 ($U_{1\infty} \neq V_{\infty\gamma}$). Let us reconsider the more interesting example $r = 1^1 0^2 1^3 0^4 \dots$ of linearly increasing 0/1-run-length with $A_n = 2n-1$ and $B_n = 2n$ for which $U_{1\infty} = \frac{1}{2}$ exists, as expected. On the other hand, for geometric discount $\gamma_k =$

γ^k, using $\Gamma_k = \frac{\gamma^k}{1-\gamma}$ and $a_n = \Gamma_{k_n} - \Gamma_{m_n} = \frac{\gamma^{k_n}}{1-\gamma}[1 - \gamma^{A_n}]$ and $b_n = \Gamma_{m_n} - \Gamma_{k_{n+1}} = \frac{\gamma^{m_n}}{1-\gamma}[1 - \gamma^{B_n}]$, i.e. $\frac{b_n}{a_n} \sim \gamma^{A_n} \to 0$ and $\frac{a_{n+1}}{b_n} \sim \gamma^{B_n} \to 0$, we get $\underline{V}_{\infty\gamma} = \alpha = 0 < 1 = \beta = \overline{V}_{\infty\gamma}$. Again, this is plausible since for k at the beginning of a long run, $V_{k\gamma}$ is dominated by the reward $0/1$ in this run, due to the bounded effective horizon of geometric γ.

Example 7 ($V_{\infty\gamma} \not\Rightarrow U_{1\infty}$). Discounted may not imply average value on sequences of exponentially increasing run-length like $r = 1^1 0^2 1^4 0^8 1^{16}...$ with $A_n = 2^{2n-2} = k_n$ and $B_n = 2^{2n-1} = m_n$ for which $\underline{U}_{1\infty} = \frac{A_n}{A_n+B_n} = \frac{1}{3} < \frac{2}{3} = \frac{A_n}{B_{n-1}+A_n} = \overline{U}_{1\infty}$, i.e. $U_{1\infty}$ does not exist. On the other hand, $V_{\infty\gamma}$ exists for a discount with super-linear horizon like $\gamma_k = [k \ln^2 k]^{-1}$, since an increasing number of runs contribute to $V_{k\gamma}$: $\Gamma_k \sim \frac{1}{\ln k}$, hence $\Gamma_{k_n} \sim \frac{1}{(2n-2)\ln 2}$ and $\Gamma_{m_n} \sim \frac{1}{(2n-1)\ln 2}$, which implies $a_n = \Gamma_{k_n} - \Gamma_{m_n} \sim [4n^2 \ln 2]^{-1} \sim \Gamma_{m_n} - \Gamma_{k_{n+1}} = b_n$, i.e. $V_{\infty\gamma} = \frac{1}{2}$ exists.

Example 8 (Non-monotone discount γ, $U_{1\infty} \neq V_{\infty\gamma}$). Monotonicity of γ in Theorems 15, 17, and 19 is necessary. As a simple counter-example consider alternating rewards $r_{2k} = 0$ with arbitrary γ_{2k} and $r_{2k-1} = 1$ with $\gamma_{2k-1} = 0$, which implies $V_{k\gamma} \equiv 0$, but $U_{1\infty} = \frac{1}{2}$.

The above counter-example is rather simplistic. One may hope equivalence to hold on smoother γ like $\frac{\gamma_{k+1}}{\gamma_k} \to 1$. The following example shows that this condition alone is not sufficient. For a counter-example one needs an oscillating γ of constant relative amplitude, but increasing wavelength, e.g. $\gamma_k = [2 + \cos(\pi\sqrt{2k})]/k^2$. For the sequence $r = 1^1 0^2 1^3 0^4...$ of Example 6 we had $U_{1\infty} = \frac{1}{2}$. Using $m_n = \frac{1}{2}(2n - \frac{1}{2})^2 + \frac{7}{8}$ and $k_{n+1} = \frac{1}{2}(2n + \frac{1}{2})^2 + \frac{7}{8}$, and replacing the sums in the definitions of a_n and b_n by integrals, we get $a_n \sim \frac{1}{n^3}[\frac{1}{2} - \frac{1}{\pi}]$ and $b_n \sim \frac{1}{n^3}[\frac{1}{2} + \frac{1}{\pi}]$, which implies that $V_{\infty\gamma} = \frac{1}{2} - \frac{1}{\pi}$ exists, but differs from $U_{1\infty} = \frac{1}{2}$.

Example 9 (Oscillating horizon). It is easy to construct a discount γ for which $\sup_k \frac{\Gamma_k}{k\gamma_k} = \infty$ and $\sup_k \frac{k\gamma_k}{\Gamma_k} = \infty$ by alternatingly patching together discounts with super- and sub-linear quasi-horizon h_k^{quasi}. For instance choose $\gamma_k \propto \gamma^k$ geometric until $\frac{\Gamma_k}{k\gamma_k} < \frac{1}{n}$, then $\gamma_k \propto \frac{1}{k \ln^2 k}$ harmonic until $\frac{\Gamma_k}{k\gamma_k} > n$, then repeat with $n \rightsquigarrow n+1$. The proportionality constants can be chosen to insure monotonicity of γ. For such γ neither Theorem 15 nor Theorem 17 is applicable, only Theorem 19.

3   Average Value

We now take a closer look at the (total) average value U_{1m} and relate it to the future average value U_{km}, an intermediate quantity we need later. We recall the definition of the average value:

Definition 10 (Average value, U_{1m}). Let $r_i \in [0,1]$ be the reward at time $i \in I\!N$. Then $U_{1m} := \frac{1}{m}\sum_{i=1}^{m} r_i \in [0,1]$ is the average value from time 1 to m, and $U_{1\infty} := \lim_{m\to\infty} U_{1m}$ the average value if it exists.

We also need the average value $U_{km} := \frac{1}{m-k+1}\sum_{i=k}^{m} r_i$ from k to m and the following Lemma.

Lemma 11 (Convergence of future average value, $U_{k\infty}$). *For $k_m \leq m \to \infty$ and every k we have*

$$U_{1m} \to \alpha \quad \Leftrightarrow \quad U_{km} \to \alpha \quad \begin{array}{l} \Rightarrow \quad U_{k_m m} \to \alpha \quad \text{if} \quad \sup_m \frac{k_m-1}{m} < 1 \\ \Leftarrow \quad U_{k_m m} \to \alpha \end{array}$$

The first equivalence states the obvious fact (and problem) that any finite initial part has no influence on the average value $U_{1\infty}$. Chunking together many $U_{k_m m}$ implies the last $\Leftarrow$. The $\Rightarrow$ only works if we average in $U_{k_m m}$ over sufficiently many rewards, which the stated condition ensures ($r = 101010...$ and $k_m = m$ is a simple counter-example). Note that $U_{k m_k} \to \alpha$ for $m_k \geq k \to \infty$ implies $U_{1m_k} \to \alpha$, but not necessarily $U_{1m} \to \alpha$ (e.g. in Example 7, $U_{1m_k} = \frac{1}{3}$ and $\frac{k-1}{m_k} \to 0$ imply $U_{k m_k} \to \frac{1}{3}$ by (5), but $U_{1\infty}$ does not exist).

Proof. The trivial identity $mU_{1m} = (k-1)U_{1,k-1} + (m-k+1)U_{km}$ implies $U_{km} - U_{1m} = \frac{k-1}{m-k+1}(U_{1m} - U_{1,k-1})$ implies

$$|U_{km} - U_{1m}| \leq \frac{|U_{1m} - U_{1,k-1}|}{\frac{m}{k-1} - 1} \tag{5}$$

$\Leftrightarrow$) The numerator is bounded by 1, and for fixed k and $m \to \infty$ the denominator tends to ∞, which proves $\Leftrightarrow$.

$\Rightarrow$) We choose (small) $\varepsilon > 0$, m_ε large enough so that $|U_{1m} - \alpha| < \varepsilon \; \forall m \geq m_\varepsilon$, and $m \geq \frac{m_\varepsilon}{\varepsilon}$. If $k := k_m \leq m_\varepsilon$, then (5) is bounded by $\frac{1}{1/\varepsilon - 1}$. If $k := k_m > m_\varepsilon$, then (5) is bounded by $\frac{2\varepsilon}{1/c - 1}$, where $c := \sup_k \frac{k_m-1}{m} < 1$. This shows that $|U_{k_m m} - U_{1m}| = O(\varepsilon)$ for large m, which implies $U_{k_m m} \to \alpha$.

$\Leftarrow$) We partition the time-range $\{1...m\} = \bigcup_{n=1}^{L}\{k_{m_n}...m_n\}$, where $m_1 := m$ and $m_{n+1} := k_{m_n} - 1$. We choose (small) $\varepsilon > 0$, m_ε large enough so that $|U_{k_m m} - \alpha| < \varepsilon \; \forall m \geq m_\varepsilon$, $m \geq \frac{m_\varepsilon}{\varepsilon}$, and l so that $k_{m_l} \leq m_\varepsilon \leq m_l$. Then

$$U_{1m} = \frac{1}{m}\left[\sum_{n=1}^{l} + \sum_{n=l+1}^{L}\right](m_n - k_{m_n} + 1)U_{k_{m_n} m_n}$$

$$\leq \frac{1}{m}\sum_{n=1}^{l}(m_n - k_{m_n} + 1)(\alpha + \varepsilon) + \frac{m_{l+1} - k_{m_L} + 1}{m}$$

$$\leq \frac{m_1 - k_{m_l} + 1}{m}(\alpha + \varepsilon) + \frac{k_{m_l}}{m} \leq (\alpha + \varepsilon) + \varepsilon$$

Similarly $\quad U_{1m} \geq \frac{m_1 - k_{m_l} + 1}{m}(\alpha - \varepsilon) \geq \frac{m - m_\varepsilon}{m}(\alpha - \varepsilon) \geq (1 - \varepsilon)(\alpha - \varepsilon)$

This shows that $|U_{1m} - \alpha| \leq 2\varepsilon$ for sufficiently large m, hence $U_{1m} \to \alpha$. ∎

4   Discounted Value

We now take a closer look at the (future) discounted value $V_{k\gamma}$ for general discounts γ, and prove some useful elementary asymptotic properties of discount γ_k and normalizer Γ_k. We recall the definition of the discounted value:

Definition 12 (Discounted value, $V_{k\gamma}$). *Let $r_i \in [0,1]$ be the reward and $\gamma_i \geq 0$ a discount at time $i \in \mathbb{N}$, where γ is assumed to be summable in the sense that $0 < \Gamma_k := \sum_{i=k}^{\infty} \gamma_i < \infty$. Then $V_{k\gamma} := \frac{1}{\Gamma_k} \sum_{i=k}^{\infty} \gamma_i r_i \in [0,1]$ is the γ-discounted future value and $V_{\infty\gamma} := \lim_{k \to \infty} V_{k\gamma}$ its limit if it exists.*

We say that γ is *monotone* if $\gamma_{k+1} \leq \gamma_k \forall k$. Note that monotonicity and $\Gamma_k > 0$ $\forall k$ implies $\gamma_k > 0$ $\forall k$ and convexity of Γ_k.

Lemma 13 (Discount properties, γ/Γ).

$$i) \quad \frac{\gamma_{k+1}}{\gamma_k} \to 1 \quad \Leftrightarrow \quad \frac{\gamma_{k+\Delta}}{\gamma_k} \to 1 \quad \forall \Delta \in \mathbb{N}$$

$$ii) \quad \frac{\gamma_k}{\Gamma_k} \to 0 \quad \Leftrightarrow \quad \frac{\Gamma_{k+1}}{\Gamma_k} \to 1 \quad \Leftrightarrow \quad \frac{\Gamma_{k+\Delta}}{\Gamma_k} \to 1 \quad \forall \Delta \in \mathbb{N}$$

Furthermore, (i) implies (ii), but not necessarily the other way around (even not if γ is monotone).

Proof. $(i) \Rightarrow \frac{\gamma_{k+\Delta}}{\gamma_k} = \prod_{i=k}^{\Delta-1} \frac{\gamma_{i+1}}{\gamma_i} \xrightarrow{k \to \infty} 1$, since Δ is finite.
$(i) \Leftarrow$ Set $\Delta = 1$.
(ii) The first equivalence follows from $\Gamma_k = \gamma_k + \Gamma_{k+1}$. The proof for the second equivalence is the same as for (i) with γ replaced by Γ.
$(i) \Rightarrow (ii)$ Choose $\varepsilon > 0$. (i) implies $\frac{\gamma_{k+1}}{\gamma_k} \geq 1 - \varepsilon$ $\forall' k$ implies

$$\Gamma_k = \sum_{i=k}^{\infty} \gamma_i = \gamma_k \sum_{i=k}^{\infty} \prod_{j=k}^{i-1} \frac{\gamma_{i+1}}{\gamma_i} \geq \gamma_k \sum_{i=k}^{\infty} (1-\varepsilon)^{i-k} = \gamma_k/\varepsilon$$

hence $\frac{\gamma_k}{\Gamma_k} \leq \varepsilon$ $\forall' k$, which implies $\frac{\gamma_k}{\Gamma_k} \to 0$.
$(i) \nLeftarrow (ii)$ Consider counter-example $\gamma_k = 4^{-\lceil \log_2 k \rceil}$, i.e. $\gamma_k = 4^{-n}$ for $2^{n-1} < k \leq 2^n$. Since $\Gamma_k \geq \sum_{i=2^n}^{\infty} \gamma_i = 2^{-n-1}$ we have $0 \leq \frac{\gamma_k}{\Gamma_k} \leq 2^{1-n} \to 0$, but $\frac{\gamma_{k+1}}{\gamma_k} = \frac{1}{4} \nrightarrow 1$ for $k = 2^n$. ∎

5   Average Implies Discounted Value

We now show that existence of $\lim_m U_{1m}$ can imply existence of $\lim_k V_{k\gamma}$ and their equality. The necessary and sufficient condition for this implication to hold is roughly that the effective horizon grows linearly with k or faster. The auxiliary quantity U_{km} is in a sense closer to $V_{k\gamma}$ than U_{1m} is, since the former two both average from k (approximately) to some (effective) horizon. If γ is sufficiently smooth, we can chop the area under the graph of $V_{k\gamma}$ (as a function of k) "vertically" approximately into a sum of average values, which implies

Proposition 14 (Future average implies discounted value, $U_\infty \Rightarrow V_{\infty\gamma}$). *Assume $k \leq m_k \to \infty$ and monotone γ with $\frac{\gamma_{m_k}}{\gamma_k} \to 1$. If $U_{km_k} \to \alpha$, then $V_{k\gamma} \to \alpha$.*

The proof idea is as follows: Let $k_1 = k$ and $k_{n+1} = m_{k_n} + 1$. Then for large k we get

$$V_{k\gamma} = \frac{1}{\Gamma_k} \sum_{n=1}^{\infty} \sum_{i=k_n}^{m_{k_n}} \gamma_i r_i \approx \frac{1}{\Gamma_k} \sum_{n=1}^{\infty} \gamma_{k_n}(k_{n+1} - k_n) U_{k_n m_{k_n}}$$

$$\approx \frac{\alpha}{\Gamma_k} \sum_{n=1}^{\infty} \gamma_{k_n}(k_{n+1} - k_n) \approx \frac{\alpha}{\Gamma_k} \sum_{n=1}^{\infty} \sum_{i=k_n}^{m_{k_n}} \gamma_i = \alpha$$

The (omitted) formal proof specifies the approximation error, which vanishes for $k \to \infty$.

Actually we are more interested in relating the (total) average value $U_{1\infty}$ to the (future) discounted value $V_{k\gamma}$. The following (first main) Theorem shows that for linearly or faster increasing quasi-horizon, we have $V_{\infty\gamma} = U_{1\infty}$, provided the latter exists.

Theorem 15 (Average implies discounted value, $U_{1\infty} \Rightarrow V_{\infty\gamma}$).
Assume $\sup_k \frac{k\gamma_k}{\Gamma_k} < \infty$ *and monotone* γ. *If* $U_{1m} \to \alpha$, *then* $V_{k\gamma} \to \alpha$.

For instance, quadratic, power and harmonic discounts satisfy the condition, but faster-than-power discount like geometric do not. Note that Theorem 15 does not imply Proposition 14.

The intuition of Theorem 15 for binary reward is as follows: For U_{1m} being able to converge, the length of a run must be small compared to the total length m up to this run, i.e. $o(m)$. The condition in Theorem 15 ensures that the quasi-horizon $h_k^{quasi} = \Omega(k)$ increases faster than the run-lengths $o(k)$, hence $V_{k\gamma} \approx U_{k\Omega(k)} \approx U_{1m}$ (Lemma 11) asymptotically averages over many runs, hence should also exist. The formal proof "horizontally" slices $V_{k\gamma}$ into a weighted sum of average rewards U_{1m}. Then $U_{1m} \to \alpha$ implies $V_{k\gamma} \to \alpha$.

Proof. We represent $V_{k\gamma}$ as a δ_j-weighted mixture of U_{1j}'s for $j \geq k$, where $\delta_j := \gamma_j - \gamma_{j+1} \geq 0$. The condition $\infty > c \geq \frac{k\gamma_k}{\Gamma_k} =: c_k$ ensures that the excessive initial part $\propto U_{1,k-1}$ is "negligible". It is easy to show that

$$\sum_{j=i}^{\infty} \delta_j = \gamma_i \quad \text{and} \quad \sum_{j=k}^{\infty} j\delta_j = (k-1)\gamma_k + \Gamma_k$$

We choose some (small) $\varepsilon > 0$, and m_ε large enough so that $|U_{1m} - \alpha| < \varepsilon \; \forall m \geq m_\varepsilon$. Then, for $k > m_\varepsilon$ we get

$$V_{k\gamma} = \frac{1}{\Gamma_k} \sum_{i=k}^{\infty} \gamma_i r_i = \frac{1}{\Gamma_k} \sum_{i=k}^{\infty} \sum_{j=i}^{\infty} \delta_j r_i = \frac{1}{\Gamma_k} \sum_{j=k}^{\infty} \sum_{i=k}^{j} \delta_j r_i$$

$$= \frac{1}{\Gamma_k} \sum_{j=k}^{\infty} \delta_j [j U_{1j} - (k-1)U_{1,k-1}]$$

$$\lessgtr \frac{1}{\Gamma_k} \sum_{j=k}^{\infty} \delta_j [j(\alpha \pm \varepsilon) - (k-1)(\alpha \mp \varepsilon)]$$

$$= \frac{1}{\Gamma_k}[(k-1)\gamma_k + \Gamma_k](\alpha \pm \varepsilon) - \frac{1}{\Gamma_k}\gamma_k(k-1)(\alpha \mp \varepsilon)$$

$$= \alpha \pm \left(1 + \frac{2(k-1)\gamma_k}{\Gamma_k}\right)\varepsilon \lessgtr \alpha \pm (1 + 2c_k)\varepsilon$$

i.e. $|V_{k\gamma} - \alpha| < (1 + 2c_k)\varepsilon \leq (1 + 2c)\varepsilon \; \forall k > m_\varepsilon$, which implies $V_{k\gamma} \to \alpha$. ∎

Theorem 15 can, for instance, be applied to Example 4. Examples 5, 6, and 8 demonstrate that the conditions in Theorem 15 cannot be dropped. The following proposition shows more strongly, that the sufficient condition is actually necessary (modulo monotonicity of γ), i.e. cannot be weakened.

Proposition 16 ($U_{1\infty} \not\Rightarrow V_{\infty\gamma}$). *For every monotone γ with* $\sup_k \frac{k\gamma_k}{\Gamma_k} = \infty$, *there are r for which $U_{1\infty}$ exists, but not $V_{\infty\gamma}$.*

The proof idea is to construct a binary r such that all change points k_n and m_n satisfy $\Gamma_{k_n} \approx 2\Gamma_{m_n}$. This ensures that $V_{k_n\gamma}$ receives a significant contribution from 1-run n, i.e. is large. Choosing $k_{n+1} \gg m_n$ ensures that $V_{m_n\gamma}$ is small, hence $V_{k\gamma}$ oscillates. Since the quasi-horizon $h_k^{quasi} \neq \Omega(k)$ is small, the 1-runs are short enough to keep U_{1m} small so that $U_{1\infty} = 0$.

Proof. The assumption ensures that there exists a sequence m_1, m_2, m_3, ... for which

$$\frac{m_n\gamma_{m_n}}{\Gamma_{m_n}} \geq n^2 \quad \text{We further (can) require } \Gamma_{m_n} < \tfrac{1}{2}\Gamma_{m_{n-1}+1} \quad (m_0 := 0)$$

For each m_n we choose k_n such that $\Gamma_{k_n} \approx 2\Gamma_{m_n}$. More precisely, since Γ is monotone decreasing and $\Gamma_{m_n} < 2\Gamma_{m_n} \leq \Gamma_{m_{n-1}+1}$, there exists (a unique) k_n in the range $m_{n-1} < k_n < m_n$ such that $\Gamma_{k_n+1} < 2\Gamma_{m_n} \leq \Gamma_{k_n}$. We choose a binary reward sequence with $r_k = 1$ iff $k_n \leq k < m_n$ for some n. This implies

$$n^2 \leq \frac{m_n\gamma_{m_n}}{\Gamma_{m_n}} = \frac{m_n}{m_n - k_n - 1} \frac{(m_n - k_n - 1)\gamma_{m_n}}{\Gamma_{m_n}}$$

$$\leq \frac{m_n}{m_n - k_n - 1} \frac{\Gamma_{k_n+1} - \Gamma_{m_n}}{\Gamma_{m_n}} \leq \frac{m_n}{m_n - k_n - 1}$$

$$\implies \frac{m_n - k_n}{m_n} = \frac{m_n - k_n - 1}{m_n} + \frac{1}{m_n} \leq \frac{1}{n^2} + \frac{\gamma_{m_n}}{\Gamma_{m_n}}\frac{1}{n^2} \leq \frac{2}{n^2}$$

$$\implies U_{1m_n} \leq \frac{1}{m_n}[k_l - 1] + \frac{1}{m_n}\sum_{n'=l}^{n}[m_{n'} - k_{n'}] \leq \frac{k_l}{m_n} + \sum_{n'=l}^{n}\frac{m_{n'} - k_{n'}}{m_{n'}}$$

$$\leq \frac{k_l}{m_n} + \sum_{n'=l}^{n}\frac{2}{n'^2} \leq \frac{k_l}{m_n} + \frac{2}{l - 1}$$

hence by (1) we have $\overline{U}_{1\infty} = \overline{\lim}_n U_{1,m_n-1} \leq \frac{2}{l-1}$ $\forall l$, hence $U_{1\infty} = 0$. On the other hand

$$\Gamma_{k_n}V_{k_n\gamma} = [\Gamma_{k_n} - \Gamma_{m_n}] + \Gamma_{m_n}V_{m_n\gamma} \quad \Rightarrow \quad \frac{1 - V_{k_n\gamma}}{1 - V_{m_n\gamma}} = \frac{\Gamma_{m_n}}{\Gamma_{k_n}} \leq \tfrac{1}{2}$$

This shows that $V_{k\gamma}$ cannot converge to an $\alpha < 1$. Theorem 19 and $U_{1\infty} = 0$ implies that $V_{k\gamma}$ can also not converge to 1, hence $V_{\infty\gamma}$ does not exist. ∎

6   Discounted Implies Average Value

We now turn to the converse direction that existence of $V_{\infty\gamma}$ can imply existence of $U_{1\infty}$ and their equality, which holds under a nearly converse condition on the discount: Roughly, the effective horizon has to grow linearly with k or slower.

Theorem 17 (Discounted implies average value, $V_{\infty\gamma} \Rightarrow U_{1\infty}$).
Assume $\sup_k \frac{\Gamma_k}{k\gamma_k} < \infty$ *and monotone* γ*. If* $V_{k\gamma} \to \alpha$*, then* $U_{1m} \to \alpha$*.*

For instance, power or faster and geometric discounts satisfy the condition, but harmonic does not. Note that power discounts satisfy the conditions of Theorems 15 *and* 17, i.e. $U_{1\infty}$ exists iff $V_{\infty\gamma}$ in this case.

The intuition behind Theorem 17 for binary reward is as follows: The run-length needs to be small compared to the quasi-horizon, i.e. $o(h_k^{quasi})$, to ensure convergence of $V_{k\gamma}$. The condition in Theorem 17 ensures that the quasi-horizon $h_k^{quasi} = O(k)$ grows at most linearly, hence the run-length $o(m)$ is a small fraction of the sequence up to m. This ensures that U_{1m} ceases to oscillate. The formal proof slices U_{1m} in "curves" to a weighted mixture of discounted values $V_{k\gamma}$. Then $V_{k\gamma} \to \alpha$ implies $U_{1m} \to \alpha$.

Proof. We represent U_{km} as a ($0 \leq b_j$-weighted) mixture of $V_{j\gamma}$ for $k \leq j \leq m$. The condition $c := \sup_k \frac{\Gamma_k}{k\gamma_k} < \infty$ ensures that the redundant tail $\propto V_{m+1,\gamma}$ is "negligible". Fix k large enough so that $|V_{j\gamma} - \alpha| < \varepsilon \ \forall j \geq k$. Then

$$\sum_{j=k}^{m} b_j(\alpha \mp \varepsilon) \lessgtr \sum_{j=k}^{m} b_j V_{j\gamma} = \sum_{j=k}^{m} \frac{b_j}{\Gamma_j} \sum_{i=j}^{m} \gamma_i r_i + \sum_{j=k}^{m} \frac{b_j}{\Gamma_j} \sum_{i=m+1}^{\infty} \gamma_i r_i \qquad (6)$$

$$= \sum_{i=k}^{m} \left(\sum_{j=k}^{i} \frac{b_j}{\Gamma_j} \right) \gamma_i r_i + \left(\sum_{j=k}^{m} \frac{b_j}{\Gamma_j} \right) \Gamma_{m+1} V_{m+1,\gamma}$$

In order for the first term on the r.h.s. to be a uniform mixture, we need

$$\sum_{j=k}^{i} \frac{b_j}{\Gamma_j} = \frac{1}{\gamma_i} \frac{1}{m-k+1} \qquad (k \leq i \leq m) \qquad (7)$$

Setting $i=k$ and, respectively, subtracting an $i \rightsquigarrow i-1$ term we get

$$\frac{b_k}{\Gamma_k} = \frac{1}{\gamma_k} \frac{1}{m-k+1} \quad \text{and} \quad \frac{b_i}{\Gamma_i} = \left(\frac{1}{\gamma_i} - \frac{1}{\gamma_{i-1}} \right) \frac{1}{m-k+1} \geq 0 \quad \text{for} \quad k < i \leq m$$

So we can evaluate the b-sum in the l.h.s. of (6) to

$$\sum_{j=k}^{m} b_j = \frac{1}{m-k+1} \left[\sum_{j=k+1}^{m} \left(\frac{\Gamma_j}{\gamma_j} - \frac{\Gamma_j}{\gamma_{j-1}} \right) + \frac{\Gamma_k}{\gamma_k} \right]$$

$$= \frac{1}{m-k+1} \left[\sum_{j=k}^{m} \left(\frac{\Gamma_j}{\gamma_j} - \frac{\Gamma_{j+1}}{\gamma_j} \right) + \frac{\Gamma_{m+1}}{\gamma_m} \right]$$

$$= 1 + \frac{\Gamma_{m+1}}{\gamma_m(m-k+1)} =: 1 + c_m \qquad (8)$$

where we shifted the sum index in the second equality, and used $\Gamma_j - \Gamma_{j+1} = \gamma_j$ in the third equality. Inserting (7) and (8) into (6) we get

$$(1+c_m)(\alpha \mp \varepsilon) \lessgtr \sum_{i=k}^{m} \frac{1}{m-k+1} r_i + \frac{\Gamma_{m+1}}{\gamma_m(m-k+1)} V_{m+1,\gamma} \lessgtr U_{km} + c_m(\alpha \pm \varepsilon)$$

Note that the excess c_m over unity in (8) equals the coefficient of the tail contribution $V_{m+1,\gamma}$. The above bound shows that

$$|U_{km} - \alpha| \leq (1 + 2c_m)\varepsilon \leq (1 + 4c)\varepsilon \quad \text{for} \quad m \geq 2k$$

Hence $U_{m/2,m} \to \alpha$, which implies $U_{1m} \to \alpha$ by Lemma 11. ∎

Theorem 17 can, for instance, be applied to Example 4. Examples 7 and 8 demonstrate that the conditions in Theorem 17 cannot be dropped. The following proposition shows more strongly, that the sufficient condition is actually necessary, i.e. cannot be weakened.

Proposition 18 ($V_{\infty\gamma} \nRightarrow U_{1\infty}$). *For every monotone γ with $\sup_k \frac{\Gamma_k}{k\gamma_k} = \infty$, there are r for which $V_{\infty\gamma}$ exists, but not $U_{1\infty}$.*

Proof. The assumption ensures that there exists a sequence $k_1, k_2, k_3, \ldots$ for which

$$\frac{k_n \gamma_{k_n}}{\Gamma_{k_n}} \leq \frac{1}{n^2} \quad \text{We further choose} \quad k_{n+1} > 8k_n$$

We choose a binary reward sequence with $r_k = 1$ iff $k_n \leq k < m_n := 2k_n$.

$$V_{k_n\gamma} = \frac{1}{\Gamma_{k_n}} \sum_{l=n}^{\infty} \gamma_{k_l} + \ldots + \gamma_{2k_l - 1} \leq \frac{1}{\Gamma_{k_n}} \sum_{l=n}^{\infty} k_l \gamma_{k_l}$$

$$\leq \sum_{l=n}^{\infty} \frac{k_l \gamma_{k_l}}{\Gamma_{k_l}} \leq \sum_{l=n}^{\infty} \frac{1}{l^2} \leq \frac{1}{n-1} \to 0$$

which implies $V_{\infty\gamma} = 0$ by (4). In a sense the 1-runs become asymptotically very sparse. On the other hand,

$$U_{1,m_n-1} \geq \tfrac{1}{m_n}[r_{k_n} + \ldots + r_{m_n-1}] = \tfrac{1}{m_n}[m_n - k_n] = \tfrac{1}{2} \quad \text{but}$$
$$U_{1,k_{n+1}-1} \leq \tfrac{1}{k_{n+1}-1}[r_1 + \ldots + r_{m_n-1}] \leq \tfrac{1}{8k_n}[m_n - 1] \leq \tfrac{1}{4},$$

hence $U_{1\infty}$ does not exist. ∎

7   Average Equals Discounted Value

Theorem 15 and 17 together imply for nearly all discount types (all in our table) that $U_{1\infty} = V_{\infty\gamma}$ if $U_{1\infty}$ and $V_{\infty\gamma}$ both exist. But Example 9 shows that there are γ for which simultaneously $\sup_k \frac{\Gamma_k}{k\gamma_k} = \infty$ *and* $\sup_k \frac{k\gamma_k}{\Gamma_k} = \infty$, i.e. neither Theorem 15, nor Theorem 17 applies. This happens for quasi-horizons that grow alternatingly super- and sub-linear. Luckily, it is easy to also cover this missing case, and we get the remarkable result that $U_{1\infty}$ equals $V_{\infty\gamma}$ if both exist, for *any* monotone discount sequence γ and *any* reward sequence r, whatsoever.

Theorem 19 (Average equals discounted value, $U_{1\infty} = V_{\infty\gamma}$).
Assume monotone γ and that $U_{1\infty}$ and $V_{\infty\gamma}$ exist. Then $U_{1\infty} = V_{\infty\gamma}$.

Proof. Case 1, $\sup_k \frac{\Gamma_k}{k\gamma_k} < \infty$: By assumption, there exists an α such that $V_{k\gamma} \to \alpha$. Theorem 17 now implies $U_{1m} \to \alpha$, hence $U_{1\infty} = V_{\infty\gamma} = \alpha$.

Case 2, $\sup_k \frac{\Gamma_k}{k\gamma_k} = \infty$: This implies that there is an infinite subsequence $k_1 < k_2 < k_3,...$ for which $\Gamma_{k_i}/k_i\gamma_{k_i} \to \infty$, i.e. $c_{k_i} := k_i\gamma_{k_i}/\Gamma_{k_i} \le c < \infty$. By assumption, there exists an α such that $U_{1m} \to \alpha$. If we look at the proof of Theorem 15, we see that it still implies $|V_{k_i\gamma} - \alpha| < (1+c_{k_i})\varepsilon \le (1+2c)\varepsilon$ on this subsequence. Hence $V_{k_i\gamma} \to \alpha$. Since we assumed existence of the limit $V_{k\gamma}$ this shows that the limit necessarily equals α, i.e. again $U_{1\infty} = V_{\infty\gamma} = \alpha$. ∎

Considering the simplicity of the statement in Theorem 19, the proof based on the proofs of Theorems 15 and 17 is remarkably complex. A simpler proof, if it exists, probably avoids the separation of the two (discount) cases.

Example 8 shows that the monotonicity condition in Theorem 19 cannot be dropped.

8 Discussion

We showed that asymptotically, discounted and average value are the same, provided both exist. This holds for essentially arbitrary discount sequences (interesting since geometric discount leads to agents with bounded horizon) and arbitrary reward sequences (important since reality is neither ergodic nor MDP). Further, we exhibited the key role of power discounting with linearly increasing effective horizon. First, it separates the cases where existence of $U_{1\infty}$ implies/is-implied-by existence of $V_{\infty\gamma}$. Second, it neither requires nor introduces any artificial time-scale; it results in an increasingly farsighted agent with horizon proportional to its own age. In particular, we advocate the use of quadratic discounting $\gamma_k = 1/k^2$. All our proofs provide convergence rates, which could be extracted from them. For simplicity we only stated the asymptotic results. The main theorems can also be generalized to probabilistic environments. Monotonicity of γ and boundedness of rewards can possibly be somewhat relaxed. A formal relation between effective horizon and the introduced quasi-horizon may be interesting.

References

[AA99]   K. E. Avrachenkov and E. Altman. Sensitive discount optimality via nested linear programs for ergodic Markov decision processes. In *Proceedings of Information Decision and Control 99*, pages 53–58, Adelaide, Australia, 1999. IEEE.

[BF85]   D. A. Berry and B. Fristedt. *Bandit Problems: Sequential Allocation of Experiments*. Chapman and Hall, London, 1985.

[BT96]   D. P. Bertsekas and J. N. Tsitsiklis. *Neuro-Dynamic Programming*. Athena Scientific, Belmont, MA, 1996.

[FLO02]   S. Frederick, G. Loewenstein, and T. O'Donoghue. Time discounting and time preference: A critical review. *Journal of Economic Literature*, 40:351–401, 2002.

[Hut02]   M. Hutter. Self-optimizing and Pareto-optimal policies in general environ-
           ments based on Bayes-mixtures. In *Proc. 15th Annual Conf. on Computa-
           tional Learning Theory (COLT'02)*, volume 2375 of *LNAI*, pages 364–379,
           Sydney, 2002. Springer, Berlin.

[Hut05]   M. Hutter. *Universal Artificial Intelligence: Sequential Decisions based
           on Algorithmic Probability.*   Springer, Berlin, 2005.   300 pages,
           http://www.idsia.ch/~marcus/ai/uaibook.htm.

[Kak01]   S. Kakade. Optimizing average reward using discounted rewards. In *Proc.
           14th Conf. on Computational Learning Theory (COLT'01)*, volume 2111 of
           LNCS, pages 605–615, Amsterdam, 2001. Springer.

[Kel81]   F. P. Kelly.   Multi-armed bandits with discount factor near one: The
           Bernoulli case. *Annals of Statistics*, 9:987–1001, 1981.

[KLM96]   L. P. Kaelbling, M. L. Littman, and A. W. Moore. Reinforcement learning:
           a survey. *Journal of Artificial Intelligence Research*, 4:237–285, 1996.

[KV86]   P. R. Kumar and P. P. Varaiya. *Stochastic Systems: Estimation, Identifi-
           cation, and Adaptive Control.* Prentice Hall, Englewood Cliffs, NJ, 1986.

[Mah96]   S. Mahadevan. Sensitive discount optimality: Unifying discounted and aver-
           age reward reinforcement learning. In *Proc. 13th International Conference
           on Machine Learning*, pages 328–336. Morgan Kaufmann, 1996.

[RN03]   S. J. Russell and P. Norvig. *Artificial Intelligence. A Modern Approach.*
           Prentice-Hall, Englewood Cliffs, NJ, 2nd edition, 2003.

[Sam37]   P. Samuelson. A note on measurement of utility. *Review of Economic
           Studies*, 4:155–161, 1937.

[SB98]   R. S. Sutton and A. G. Barto. *Reinforcement Learning: An Introduction.*
           MIT Press, Cambridge, MA, 1998.

[Str56]   R. H. Strotz. Myopia and inconsistency in dynamic utility maximization.
           Review of Economic Studies, 23:165–180, 1955–1956.

[VW04]   N. Vieille and J. W. Weibull. Dynamic optimization with non-exponential
           discounting: On the uniqueness of solutions. Technical Report WP No. 577,
           Department of Economics, Boston Univeristy, Boston, MA, 2004.

The Missing Consistency Theorem for Bayesian Learning: Stochastic Model Selection

Jan Poland⋆

Graduate School of Information Science and Technology
Hokkaido University, Japan
jan@ist.hokudai.ac.jp
http://www-alg.ist.hokudai.ac.jp/~jan

Abstract. Bayes' rule specifies how to obtain a posterior from a class of hypotheses endowed with a prior and the observed data. There are three principle ways to use this posterior for predicting the future: marginalization (integration over the hypotheses w.r.t. the posterior), MAP (taking the a posteriori most probable hypothesis), and stochastic model selection (selecting a hypothesis at random according to the posterior distribution). If the hypothesis class is countable and contains the data generating distribution, strong consistency theorems are known for the former two methods, asserting almost sure convergence of the predictions to the truth as well as loss bounds. We prove the first corresponding results for stochastic model selection. As a main technical tool, we will use the concept of a potential: this quantity, which is always positive, measures the total possible amount of future prediction errors. Precisely, in each time step, the expected potential decrease upper bounds the expected error. We introduce the *entropy potential* of a hypothesis class as its worst-case entropy with regard to the true distribution. We formulate our results in the online classification framework, but they are equally applicable to the prediction of non-i.i.d. sequences.

1 Introduction

Bayesian learning is one of the theoretically best-founded and practically most successful induction principles at all, with numerous important applications in science. Establishing consistency, i.e., proving that a certain algorithm converges to the correct behavior after some initial errors, and also bounding the number of these errors, is one of the most fundamental duties of statistics and theoretical computer science.

A Bayesian learner starts with a class of hypotheses about the behavior of the particular "world" he is operating in[1]. This class is endowed with a *prior*,

---

⋆ This work was supported by JSPS 21st century COE program C01.

[1] We'll spend a large portion of this paper on general countably infinite hypothesis classes. Although such classes are typically computationally infeasible, this is interesting and important to study, as we will discuss at the end of this introduction.

J.L. Balcázar, P.M. Long, and F. Stephan (Eds.): ALT 2006, LNAI 4264, pp. 259–273, 2006.

i.e., each hypothesis is assigned a prior belief probability such that these probabilities sum up to one (or integrate up to one, if the hypothesis class is continuously parameterized). It is helpful to interpret the prior just as a belief and *not* probabilistically, i.e. we assume no sampling mechanism that selects hypotheses according to the prior.

After observing some data, the learner uses Bayes' rule to obtain the *posterior*. If we ask the learner to give a prediction about the next observation, he has three different principle ways to compute this prediction:

1. *Marginalization*, that is, summing (or integrating) over the hypothesis class w.r.t. the posterior and using the resulting mixture prediction.
2. *Maximum a posteriori (MAP) model selection*, that is, selecting the hypothesis with the highest posterior probability and predicting according to this model. This is closely related to the important *minimum description length (MDL) principle*.
3. *Stochastic model selection*, which consists of *randomly* sampling a hypothesis according to the posterior and predicting as does this hypothesis. Note that we use the terms "model" and "hypothesis" interchangeably. Thus, stochastic model selection defines a randomized learner, in contrast to the previous two ones which, for given data, obviously yield deterministic outputs.

All these three Bayesian predictors are both theoretically and practically very important. Marginalization directly corresponds to Bayes' principle (without fixing a particular model), but integrating over the model class may be computationally expensive, and the mixture may be outside the range of all model outputs. If, for efficiency or output range or other reasons, we are interested in just one model's predictions, MAP/MDL or stochastic model selection are the choice, the latter being preferable if the MAP/MDL estimator might be biased. Many practical learning methods (e.g. for artificial neural networks) are approximations to MAP or stochastic model selection. Also, some fundamental recent theoretical progress is associated with stochastic model selection, namely active learning using "query by committee" [1] and the PAC-Bayesian theorems [2].

In this work, we will consider the framework of *online learning*, where the learner is asked for a prediction after each piece of data he observes, i.e., after each discrete time step $t = 1, 2, 3, \ldots$ Our results apply for both the popular classification setup, where the learner gets some input and has to predict the corresponding label, and the sequence prediction setup where there are no inputs. Since classification is more important in practice, we will formulate all results in this framework, they immediately transfer to sequence prediction.

In case of *proper learning*, i.e., if the data is generated by some distribution contained in the model class, strong consistency theorems are known for online prediction by both marginalization and MAP or MDL. Pioneering work has been, among others, [3,4] for marginalization and [5] for MDL/MAP. In the case of a *discrete* model class, particularly nice assertions have been proven for marginalization and MDL/MAP, stating *finite bounds* on the expected cumulative quadratic prediction error, and implying *almost sure convergence* of the predictions to the truth. For marginalization, this is Solomonoff's theorem [6], while for MDL/MAP the bounds have been obtained only recently [7, 8].

In this work, we will show the first bounds of this type for a Bayesian stochastic model selection learner on a discrete model class. By doing so, we prove the first consistency theorems for such a learner to our knowledge, and we complete the proof of the following important fact: *All Bayesian learners based on countable hypothesis class are consistent with probability one under the proper learning assumption.* More precisely, we will complete the proof of the following theorem.

Theorem 1. *Consider an online classification setup, i.e., there is a sequence of inputs $z_1, z_2, \ldots$ in an arbitrary input space $\mathcal{Z}$ generated by any mechanism. The sequence of labels $x_1, x_2, \ldots$ in some finite label space or alphabet $\mathcal{X}$ is generated by a probability distribution $\mu(\cdot|z)$ on $\mathcal{X}$, the notation indicates that μ depends on the input z. There is a countable hypothesis or model class $\mathcal{C}$, endowed with a prior $w = (w_\nu)_{\nu \in \mathcal{C}}$, and containing the true distribution μ. Since $\mu \in \mathcal{C}$, it makes sense to speak about the true prior weight w_μ. For some observation history $h_{<t} = (z_1, x_1, z_2, x_2, \ldots, z_{t-1}, x_{t-1})$ and current input z_t, define*

$\xi(\cdot|z_t, h_{<t})$ = *the predictive distribution (on $\mathcal{X}$) obtained by marginalization,*

$\varrho(\cdot|z_t, h_{<t})$ = *the predictive distribution due to the MAP predictor, and*

$\Xi(\cdot|z_t, h_{<t})$ = *the predictive distribution given by stochastic model selection*

(see Section 2 for more technical details and definitions, in particular the definition of Ξ, while ϱ will not be formally specified here, please see [8]). Then the following bounds hold on the expected cumulative quadratic error (expectation is w.r.t. μ and, in case of stochastic model selection, also w.r.t. the internal randomization of Ξ, and all of the subsequent logarithms are natural):

$$\sum_{t=1}^{\infty} \mathbf{E} \sum_{x \in \mathcal{X}} \left(\xi(x|z_t, h_{<t}) - \mu(x|z_t) \right)^2 \leq \log w_\mu^{-1}, \tag{1}$$

$$\sum_{t=1}^{\infty} \mathbf{E} \sum_{x \in \mathcal{X}} \left(\varrho(x|z_t, h_{<t}) - \mu(x|z_t) \right)^2 \leq O(w_\mu^{-1}), \tag{2}$$

$$\sum_{t=1}^{\infty} \mathbf{E} \sum_{x \in \mathcal{X}} \left(\Xi(x|z_t, h_{<t}) - \mu(x|z_t) \right)^2 \leq O(\log w_\mu^{-1} \Pi(w)). \tag{3}$$

Here, $\Pi(w)$ is the entropy potential *of the (prior of the) model class, defined as*

$$\Pi((w_\nu)_{\nu \in \mathcal{N}}) = \sup \left\{ H\left(\left(\tfrac{\tilde{w}_\nu}{\sum_{\nu'} \tilde{w}_{\nu'}} \right)_\nu \right) : \tilde{w}_\mu = w_\mu \wedge \tilde{w}_\nu \leq w_\nu \ \forall \nu \in \mathcal{C} \setminus \{\mu\} \right\}, \tag{4}$$

with H being the ordinary entropy function. These error bounds imply in particular almost sure convergence of the respective predictive probabilities to the true probabilities $\mu(x|z_t)$, for all $x \in \mathcal{X}$.

The same bounds hold for the setup of non-i.i.d. sequence prediction [8].

Assertion (1) has been proven in [6] for the binary case (see [9] for a much more accessible proof and Section 2 below for a slightly different one); (2) is due to

[7], while (3) will be shown in this paper. The reader will immediately notice the different quality of the bounds on the r.h.s.: By Kraft's inequality, the bound $\log w_\mu^{-1}$ (1) corresponds to the description length for μ within a *prefix code*, where for all hypotheses there are codewords of length of the negative log of the respective weight. This is an excellent and non-improvable error bound, in contrast to the second one for MDL/MAP, which is exponentially larger. This quantity is generally huge and therefore may be interpreted asymptotically, but its direct use for applications is questionable. Fortunately, bounds of logarithmic order can be proven in many important cases [5, 10]. For stochastic model selection, we will study the magnitute of the entropy potential in Section 5, showing that this quantity is of order $\log w_\mu^{-1}$ provided that the weights do not decay too slowly. Hence, in these favorable cases, the bound of (3) is $O\big((\log w_\mu^{-1})^2\big)$. However, $\Pi(w)$ is always bounded by $H \cdot w_\mu^{-1}$ (with H being the ordinary entropy of the model class).

The bounds in Theorem 1 do not only imply consistency with probability one, but also performance guarantees w.r.t. *arbitrary bounded loss functions*:

Corollary 2. *For each input z, let $\ell(\cdot, \cdot|z) : (\hat{x}, x) \mapsto \ell(\hat{x}, x|z) \in [0, 1]$ be a loss function known to the learner, depending on the true outcome x and the prediction $\hat{x}$ (ℓ may also depend on the time, but we don't complicate notation by making this explicit). Let $\ell_{<\infty}^\mu$ be the cumulative loss of a predictor knowing the true distribution μ, where the predictions are made in a Bayes optimal way (i.e. choosing the prediction $\arg\min_{\hat{x}} \mathbf{E}_{x\sim\mu}\ell(\hat{x}, x|z_t)$ for current input z_t), and $\ell_{<\infty}^\Xi$ be the corresponding quantity for the stochastic model selection learner. Then the loss of the learner is bounded by*

$$\mathbf{E}\ell_{<\infty}^\Xi \le \mathbf{E}\ell_{<\infty}^\mu + O\big(\log w_\mu^{-1}\Pi(w)\big) + O\big(\sqrt{\log w_\mu^{-1}\Pi(w)\mathbf{E}\ell_{<\infty}^\mu}\big). \tag{5}$$

Corresponding assertions hold for the Bayes mixture [11] and MAP [8]. The proof of this statement follows from Theorem 1 by using techniques as in [8, Lemma 24–26]. The bound may seem weak to a reader familiar with another learning model, *prediction with expert advice*, which has received quite some attention since [12, 13]. Algorithms of this type are based on a class of experts rather than hypotheses, and proceed by randomly selecting experts according to a (non-Bayesian) posterior based on past performance of the experts. It is straightforward to use a hypothesis as an expert. Thus the experts theorems (for instance [14, Theorem 8(i)]) imply a bound similar to (5), but *without any assumption on the data generating process* μ, instead the bounds are relative to the best expert (hypothesis) in hindsight $\hat{\nu}$ (and moreover with $\log w_{\hat{\nu}}^{-1}\Pi(w)$ replaced by $\log w_{\hat{\nu}}^{-1}$). So the experts bounds are stronger, which does not necessarily imply that the experts algorithms are better: bounds like (5) are derived in the worst case over all loss functions, and in this worst case Bayesian learning is not better than experts learning, even under the proper learning assumption. However, experts algorithms do not provide estimates for the probabilities, which Bayesian algorithms do provide: in many practically relevant cases learning probabilities does yield superior performance.

The proofs in this work are based on the method of *potential functions*. A potential quantifies the current state of learning, such that the expected error in the next step does not exceed the expected decrease of the potential function in the next step. If we then can bound the cumulative decrease of the potential function, we obtain the desired bounds. The potential method used here has been inspired by similar idea in prediction with expert advice [15], the proof techniques are however completely different. We will in particular introduce the *entropy potential*, already stated in (4), which may be interpreted as the worst-case entropy of the model class under all admissible transformations of the weights, where the weight of the true distribution is kept fixed. The entropy potential is possibly a novel definition in this work.

Before starting the technical presentation, we discuss the limitations of our online learning setup. A Bayesian online learner defined in the straightforward way is computationally inefficient, if in each time step the full posterior is computed: Thus, marginalization, MAP/MDL, and stochastic model selection are equally inefficient in a naive implementation, and even generally uncomputable in case of a countable model class. On the other hand, many practical and efficient learning methods (e.g. training of an artificial neural network) are approximations to MAP/MDL and stochastic model selection. Moreover, bounds for the online algorithm also imply bounds for the *offline* variant, if additional assumptions (i.i.d.) on the process generating the inputs are satisfied. Also, in some cases one can sample efficiently from a probability distribution without knowing the complete distribution.

But the most important contribution of this paper is theoretical, as it clarifies the learning behavior of all three variants of Baysian learning in the ideal case. Also, countable hypothesis classes constitute the limit of what is computationally feasible at all, for this reason they are a core concept in Algorithmic Information Theory [16]. Proving corresponding results for the likewise important case of continuously parameterized model classes is, to our knowledge, an open problem.

As already indicated, the dependence of the bound (3) on w_μ^{-1} is logarithmic if the prior weights decay sufficiently rapidly (precisely polynomially), but linear in the worst case. This implies the practical recommendation of using a prior with light tails together with stochastic model selection.

The remainder of this paper is structured as follows. In the next section, we will introduce the notation and, in order to introduce the methods, prove Solomonoff's result with a potential function. In Section 3, we consider stochastic model selection and prove the main auxiliary result. Section 4 defines the entropy potential and proves bounds for general countable model class. In Section 5 we turn to the question how large the newly defined entropy potential can be.

2   Setup and Bayes Mixture

We work in a general discrete Bayesian online classification framework with stochastic concepts. All our theorems and proofs carry over to the prediction of non-i.i.d. sequences (this setup is defined e.g. in [8], compare also Remark 4).

Let $\mathcal{X} = \{1 \ldots |\mathcal{X}|\}$ be a finite alphabet, $\mathcal{Z}$ be an arbitrary set of possible inputs, and $\mathcal{C} = \nu_1, \nu_2, \ldots$ be a finite or countable model class. Each model $\nu \in \mathcal{C}$ specifies probability distributions[2] on $\mathcal{X}$ for all inputs $z \in \mathcal{Z}$, i.e. ν is a function

$$\nu : z \mapsto \big(\nu(x|z)\big)_{x \in \mathcal{X}} \text{ where } \nu(x|z) \geq 0 \text{ and } \sum_{x \in \mathcal{X}} \nu(x|z) = 1. \tag{6}$$

Each $\nu \in \mathcal{C}$ is assigned a prior weight $w_\nu > 0$, where $\sum_{\nu \in \mathcal{C}} w_\nu = 1$. (We need not consider models with zero prior weight, as they don't have any impact for anything of what follows.) In order to make clear that we talk of the prior or *initial* weight, opposed to a posterior weight, we will sometimes write w_ν^{init} instead of w_ν.

We assume that there is one data generating or *true* distribution $\mu \in \mathcal{C}$. Then the online classification proceeds in discrete time $t = 1, 2, \ldots$: An input z_t is generated by an arbitrary mechanism. The learner must compute a guess $\big(p(x)\big)_{x \in \mathcal{X}}$ (where $\sum_{x \in \mathcal{X}} p(x) = 1$) for the current probability vector $\big(\mu(x|z_t)\big)_{x \in \mathcal{X}}$. An outcome $x_t \in \mathcal{X}$ is sampled according to $\big(\mu(x|z_t)\big)$ and revealed to the learner (note that the probabilities $\big(\mu(x|z_t)\big)$ are *not* revealed).

After each observation x_t, we may update the weights w_ν by Bayes' rule, thus obtaining, after time $t - 1$ and before time t, the posterior weights

$$w_\nu(h_{<t}) = w_\nu(h_{1:t-1}) = w_\nu(z_{1:t-1}, x_{1:t-1}) = \frac{w_\nu \prod_{i=1}^{t-1} \nu(x_i|z_i)}{\sum_{\nu' \in \mathcal{C}} w_{\nu'} \prod_{i=1}^{t-1} \nu'(x_i|z_i)},$$

where $h_{<t} = (z_{<t}, x_{<t}) = (z_1, x_1, z_2, x_2, \ldots, z_{t-1}, x_{t-1})$ denotes the history. Then, in the Bayesian sense it is optimal to estimate the current probabilities according to the *Bayes mixture*, i.e., marginalization:

$$\xi(x|z_t, h_{<t}) = \sum_{\nu \in \mathcal{C}} w_\nu(h_{<t}) \nu(x|z_t).$$

Example 3. Assume that $\mathcal{X}$ is binary and $\mathcal{Z}$ contains only a single element. In this case the observations are *Bernoulli* trials, i.e. they result from fair or unfair coin flips. $\mathcal{C}$ specifies the set of possible coins we consider, and it is well-known that all posterior weights but the weight of the true coin will converge to zero almost surely for $t \to \infty$. With the set of coins $\mathcal{C} \cong \{\frac{1}{4}, \frac{1}{2}, \frac{3}{4}\}$ and the true coin being the fair one, it is easy to see that this example gives a lower bound $\Omega(-\log w_\mu)$ on the expected quadratic error of Bayes mixture and stochastic model selection predictions, namely the l.h.s. expressions of (9) and (12), respectively.

Remark 4. The inputs z_t are not necessary for the proofs. Thus we could as well work in an input-less *sequence prediction* setup, which is common for Solomonoff

---

[2] We don't consider *semimeasures* which are common in Algorithmic Information Theory and used by e.g. [6, 8, 9], as our methods below rely on normalized probability distributions. This restriction can be possibly lifted to some extent, however we do not expect the consequences to be very interesting (see also Example 20).

induction (Theorem 5 below). We decided to keep the inputs, as stochastic model selection is usually considered in a classification setup. We incorporate the inputs into the history $h_{<t}$, thus they don't complicate the notation.

Solomonoff's [6] remarkable universal induction result tightly bounds the performance guarantee for the marginalization learner with an arbitrary input sequence z_t. For introductory purpose, we prove it here in the classification setup. We use an appropriate *potential function*, thereby slightly modifying the proof from [9].

Theorem 5. (Solomonoff's universal induction result) *Assume that the data generating distribution is contained in the model class, i.e. $\mu \in C$. Define the complexity potential as*

$$\mathcal{K}(h_{<t}) = -\log w_\mu(h_{<t}). \qquad (7)$$

For any current input z_t and any history $h_{<t}$, this potential satisfies

$(i) \quad \mathcal{K}(h_{<t}) \geq 0,$

$(ii) \quad \mathcal{K}(h_{<t}) - \mathbf{E}_{x_t \sim \mu(\cdot|z_t)} \mathcal{K}(h_{1:t}) \geq \sum_{x \in \mathcal{X}} \left(\mu(x|z_t) - \xi(x|z_t, h_{<t}) \right)^2. \qquad (8)$

By summing up the expectation of (ii) while observing (i), we immediately obtain Solomonoff's assertion for arbitrary sequence of inputs $z_1, z_2, \ldots$:

$$\sum_{t=1}^{\infty} \mathbf{E} \|\mu - \xi\|_2^2 := \sum_{t=1}^{\infty} \mathbf{E} \|\mu(\cdot|z_t) - \xi(\cdot|z_t, h_{<t})\|_2^2 \leq \mathcal{K}^{\text{init}} = -\log w_\mu^{\text{init}}, \qquad (9)$$

where expectation is with respect to μ, and the squared 2-norm of a vector $v \in \mathbb{R}^{|\mathcal{X}|}$ is defined as usual, $\|v\|_2^2 = \sum_i v_i^2$. (Note the abbreviation $\|\mu - \xi\|$ introduced in the context of the expected sum here.) As we will see in the proof of Theorem 9, this implies that the marginal (Bayes mixture) probabilities ξ converge to the true probabilities μ almost surely.

Proof. Clearly, (i) holds. In order to show (ii), we observe that $w_\mu(h_{1:t}) = w_\mu(h_{<t}) \frac{\mu(x_t|z_t)}{\xi(x_t|z_t, h_{<t})}$. Then, simplifying the notation by suppressing the history $h_{<t}$ and the current input z_t (e.g. $\mathcal{K}$ stands for $\mathcal{K}(h_{<t})$),

$$\mathcal{K} - \mathbf{E}\mathcal{K}(x) = \mathcal{K} - \sum_{x \in \mathcal{X}} \mu(x) \left(\mathcal{K} - \log \frac{\mu(x)}{\xi(x)} \right) = D\left[\mu(\cdot|z_t) \| \xi(\cdot|z_t, h_{<t}) \right].$$

The r.h.s. here is called *Kullback-Leibler divergence*. By the following lemma it is an upper bound for $\sum_{x \in \mathcal{X}} \left(\mu(x|z_t) - \xi(x|z_t, h_{<t}) \right)^2$.   □

Lemma 6. *For two probability distributions μ and ρ on $\mathcal{X}$, we have*

$$\sum_{a \in \mathcal{X}} \left(\mu(a) - \rho(a) \right)^2 \leq \sum_{a \in \mathcal{X}} \mu(a) \log \frac{\mu(a)}{\rho(a)}.$$

This well known inequality is proven for instance in [9, Sec.3.9.2].

By Kraft's inequality, the complexity $\mathcal{K}$ of μ can be interpreted as μ's description length. Thus, Solomonoff's theorem asserts that the predictive complexity (measured in terms of the quadratic error) coincides with the descriptive complexity, if the data is rich enough to distinguish the models. Then $\mathcal{K}$ can be viewed as the *state of learning* in the discrete model class. Observe that only the *expected* progress, i.e. decrease of $\mathcal{K}$, is positive. The actual progress depends on the outcome of x_t and is positive if and only if $\mu(x_t) \geq \xi(x_t)$. If the probability vectors μ and ξ coincide, then – according to this potential function – no learning takes place for any observation, as then $\mathcal{K}(x_t) = \mathcal{K}$ for all x_t. Hence, the complexity potential $\mathcal{K}$ need not always be a good choice to describe the learning state.

Example 7. Consider a binary alphabet and a model class containing three distributions ν_1, ν_2, ν_3, predicting $\nu_i(1|z) = \frac{i}{4}$ for some input z. Suppose $\mu = \nu_2$, i.e. the true probability is $\frac{1}{2}$. Then we cannot measure the learning progress after the observation in terms of $\mathcal{K}$. However, there should be a progress, and indeed there is one, if we consider the *entropy* of the model class. This will become clear with Lemma 8.

3   Stochastic Model Selection

Here is another case where the complexity potential $\mathcal{K}$ is not appropriate to quantify the state of learning. In *stochastic model selection*, the current prediction vector $\Xi(\cdot|z_t, h_{<t})$ is obtained by randomly sampling a model according to the current weights $w_\nu(h_{<t})$ and using this model's prediction, i.e.

$$\Xi(\cdot|z_t, h_{<t}) = \nu_J(\cdot|z_t) \text{ where } \mathbf{P}(J = i) = w_{\nu_i}(h_{<t}).$$

Hence, Ξ is a random variable depending on the sampled index J. The following lemma gives a first indication for a suitable potential function for learning with stochastic model selection.

Lemma 8. *Assume that the current entropy of the model class,*

$$\mathcal{H}(h_{<t}) = -\sum_{\nu \in \mathcal{C}} w_\nu(h_{<t}) \log w_\nu(h_{<t}),$$

is finite. Then, for any input z_t,

$$\mathcal{H}(h_{<t}) - \mathbf{E}_{x_t \sim \xi(\cdot|z_t, h_{<t})} \mathcal{H}(h_{1:t}) = \sum_{\nu \in \mathcal{C}} w_\nu(h_{<t}) \sum_{x \in \mathcal{X}} \nu(x|z_t) \log \frac{\nu(x|z_t)}{\xi(x|z_t, h_{<t})}$$

$$\geq \sum_{\nu \in \mathcal{C}} w_\nu(h_{<t}) \sum_{x \in \mathcal{X}} \left(\nu(x|z_t) - \xi(x|z_t, h_{<t})\right)^2 =: \mathbf{E}\|\Xi - \xi\|_2^2.$$

Proof. The equality is straightforward computation. Then use Lemma 6 for the inequality.   □

Unfortunately, the l.h.s. of the above inequality contains an expectation w.r.t. ξ instead of μ. Since on the other hand μ governs the process and generally differs from ξ, the entropy $\mathcal{H}$ is not directly usable as a potential for the Ξ's deviation from its mean ξ. The following theorem demonstrates an easy fix, which however exponentially blows up the potential.

Theorem 9. (Predictive performance of stochastic model selection, loose bound) *Assume that $\mu \in \mathcal{C}$. Define the potential $\mathcal{P}_E(h_{<t}) = \mathcal{H}(h_{<t}) \exp\left(\mathcal{K}(h_{<t})\right) = \mathcal{H}(h_{<t})/w_\mu(h_{<t})$. Then, for any history $h_{<t}$ and any current input z_t,*

$$\mathcal{P}_E(h_{<t}) - \mathbf{E}_{x_t \sim \mu(\cdot|z_t)} \mathcal{P}_E(h_{1:t}) \geq \mathbf{E}\big\| \Xi(\cdot|z_t, h_{<t}) - \xi(\cdot|z_t, h_{<t}) \big\|_2^2. \tag{10}$$

Consequently, with $\mathcal{H}^{\mathrm{init}} = -\sum_{\nu \in \mathcal{C}} w_\nu^{\mathrm{init}} \log w_\nu^{\mathrm{init}}$ denoting the initial entropy,

$$\sum_{t=1}^{\infty} \mathbf{E}\big\| \Xi - \xi \big\|_2^2 \leq \mathcal{P}_E^{\mathrm{init}} = \mathcal{H}^{\mathrm{init}}/w_\mu^{\mathrm{init}}, \tag{11}$$

$$\sum_{t=1}^{\infty} \mathbf{E}\big\| \Xi - \mu \big\|_2^2 \leq -\log(w_\mu^{\mathrm{init}}) + \mathcal{H}^{\mathrm{init}}/w_\mu^{\mathrm{init}} + 2\sqrt{-\mathcal{H}^{\mathrm{init}} \log(w_\mu^{\mathrm{init}})/w_\mu^{\mathrm{init}}}, \tag{12}$$

and the predictions by Ξ converge to the true probabilities μ almost surely.

Proof. Recall $w_\mu(h_{1:t}) = w_\mu(h_{<t}) \frac{\mu(x_t|z_t)}{\xi(x_t|z_t, h_{<t})}$. Since always $1/w_\mu(h_{<t}) \geq 1$, using Lemma 8 we obtain (10) by

$$\mathcal{P}_E(h_{<t}) - \sum_{x \in \mathcal{X}} \mu(x|z_t) \mathcal{P}_E(h_{1:t}) = \tfrac{1}{w_\mu(h_{<t})} \Big(\mathcal{H}(h_{<t}) - \sum_{x \in \mathcal{X}} \xi(x|z_t, h_{<t}) \mathcal{H}(h_{1:t}) \Big)$$

$$\geq \mathbf{E}\big\| \Xi(\cdot|z_t, h_{<t}) - \xi(\cdot|z_t, h_{<t}) \big\|_2^2.$$

Summing the expectation up yields (11). Using this together with (9) and the triangle inequality $\sqrt{\sum \mathbf{E}\big\| \Xi - \mu \big\|_2^2} \leq \sqrt{\sum \mathbf{E}\big\| \Xi - \xi \big\|_2^2} + \sqrt{\sum \mathbf{E}\big\| \xi - \mu \big\|_2^2}$, we conclude (12). Finally, almost sure convergence follows from

$$\mathbf{P}\Big(\exists t \geq n : s_t \geq \varepsilon \Big) = \mathbf{P}\Big(\bigcup_{t \geq n} \{s_t \geq \varepsilon\} \Big) \leq \sum_{t \geq n} \mathbf{P}(s_t \geq \varepsilon) \leq \frac{1}{\varepsilon} \sum_{t=n}^{\infty} \mathbf{E}s_t \xrightarrow{n \to \infty} 0$$

for each $\varepsilon > 0$, with $s_t = \mathbf{E}\big\| \Xi(\cdot|z_t, h_{<t}) - \mu(\cdot|z_t, h_{<t}) \big\|_2^2$.   □

In particular, this theorem shows that the entropy of a model class, if it is initially finite, necessarily remains finite almost surely. Moreover, it establishes almost sure asymptotic consistency of prediction by stochastic model selection in our Bayesian framework. However, it does not provide meaningful error bounds for all but very small model classes, since the r.h.s. of the bound is exponential in the complexity, hence possibly huge.

Before continuing to show better bounds, we demonstrate that the entropy is indeed a lower bound for any successful potential function for stochastic model selection.

Example 10. Let the alphabet be binary. Let $w_\mu = 1 - \frac{1}{n}$, in this way $\mathcal{K} \approx \frac{1}{n}$ and can be made arbitrary small for large $n \in \mathbb{N}$. Fix a target entropy $H_0 \in \mathbb{N}$ and set $K = 2^{nH_0}$. Choose a model class that consists of the true distribution, always predicting $\frac{1}{2}$, and K other distributions with the same prior weight $1/(nK)$. In this way, the entropy of the model class is indeed close to $H_0 \log 2$. Let the input set be $\mathcal{Z} = \{1 \ldots nH_0\}$, and let $\nu_b(1|z) = b_z$, where b_z is the zth bit of ν's index b in binary representation. Then it is not hard to see that on the input stream $z_{1:nH_0} = 1, 2, \ldots nH_0$ always $\mu = \xi$. Moreover, at each time, $E\|\Xi - \mu\|_2^2 = 1/(4n)$. Therefore the cumulative error is $H_0/4$, i.e. of order of the entropy. Note that this error, which can be chosen arbitrarily large, is achievable for arbitrarily small complexity $\mathcal{K}$.

In the proof of Theorem 9, we used only one "wasteful" inequality, namely $1/w_\mu(h_{<t}) \geq 1$. The following lemma will be our main tool for obtaining better bounds.

Lemma 11. (Predictive performance of stochastic model selection, main auxiliary result) *Suppose that we have some function $B(h_{<t})$, depending on the history, with the following properties:*

(i) $B(h_{<t}) \geq \mathcal{H}(h_{<t})$ *(dominates the entropy),*

(ii) $\mathbf{E}_{x_t \sim \mu(\cdot|z_t)} B(h_{1:t}) \leq B(h_{<t})$ *(decreases in expectation),*

(iii)   *the value of $B(h_{<t})$ can be approximated arbitrarily close by restricting to a finite model class.*

Then, for any history and current input, the potential function defined by

$$\mathcal{P}(h_{<t}) = \left[\mathcal{K}(h_{<t}) + \log(1 + \mathcal{H}(h_{<t})) \right](1 + B(h_{<t}))$$

satisfies

$$\mathcal{P}(h_{<t}) - \mathbf{E}_{x_t \sim \mu(\cdot|z_t)} \mathcal{P}(h_{1:t}) \geq \mathcal{H}(h_{<t}) - \mathbf{E}_{x_t \sim \xi(\cdot|z_t, h_{<t})} \mathcal{H}(h_{1:t}). \quad (13)$$

Proof. Because of (iii), we need to prove the lemma only for finite model class, the countable case then follows by approximation. In this way we avoid dealing with a Lagrangian on an infinite dimensional space below.

Again we drop all dependencies on the history $h_{<t}$ and the current input z_t from the notation. Then observe that in the inequality chain

$$\mathcal{K} + \log(1 + \mathcal{H}) - \sum_{x \in \mathcal{X}} \mu(x) \left[\mathcal{K}(x) + \log(1 + \mathcal{H}(x)) \right] \frac{1 + B(x)}{1 + B}$$

$$\geq \mathcal{K} + \log(1 + \mathcal{H}) - \sum_{x \in \mathcal{X}} \frac{\mu(x)(1 + B(x))}{\sum_{x'} \mu(x')(1 + B(x'))} \left[\mathcal{K}(x) + \log(1 + \mathcal{H}(x)) \right] \quad (14)$$

$$\geq \frac{\sum_\nu w_\nu \sum_x \nu(x) \log \frac{\nu(x)}{\xi(x)}}{1 + B}, \quad (15)$$

(14) follows from assumption (ii), so that we only need to show (15) in order to complete the proof. We will demonstrate an even stronger assertion:

$$\log(1 + \mathcal{H}) - \sum_{x \in \mathcal{X}} \tilde{\mu}_x \big[\log(1 + \mathcal{H}(x)) - \log \tfrac{\mu(x)}{\xi(x)} \big] \geq \frac{\sum_\nu w_\nu \sum_x \nu(x) \log \frac{\nu(x)}{\xi(x)}}{1 + B} \quad (16)$$

for any probability vector $\tilde{\mu} = (\tilde{\mu}_x)_{x \in \mathcal{X}} \in [0, 1]^{|\mathcal{X}|}$ with $\sum_x \tilde{\mu}_x = 1$.

It is sufficient to prove (16) for all stationary points of the Lagrangian and all boundary points. In order to cover all of the boundary, we allow $\tilde{\mu}_x = 0$ for all x in some subset $\mathcal{X}_0 \subsetneq \mathcal{X}$ ($\mathcal{X}_0$ may be empty). Let $\tilde{\mathcal{X}} = \mathcal{X} \setminus \mathcal{X}_0$ and define $\xi(\tilde{\mathcal{X}}) = \sum_{x \in \tilde{\mathcal{X}}} \xi(x)$, $\xi(\mathcal{X}_0) = 1 - \xi(\tilde{\mathcal{X}})$, and $\tilde{\xi}(x) = \xi(x)/\xi(\tilde{\mathcal{X}})$. Then (16) follows from

$$f(\tilde{\mu}) = \log(1 + \mathcal{H}) - \sum_{x \in \tilde{\mathcal{X}}} \tilde{\mu}_x \big(\tilde{V}(x) - \log \tfrac{\mu(x)}{\tilde{\xi}(x)} \big) \geq \frac{\sum_\nu w_\nu \sum_x \nu(x) \log \frac{\nu(x)}{\xi(x)}}{1 + B}, \quad (17)$$

where $\tilde{V}(x) = \log(1 - \sum_\nu \frac{w_\nu \nu(x)}{\tilde{\xi}(x)} \log \frac{w_\nu \nu(x)}{\xi(x)})$.

We now identify the stationary points of the Lagrangian

$$\mathcal{L}(\tilde{\mu}, \lambda) = f(\tilde{\mu}) - \lambda \big(\sum_x \tilde{\mu}_x - 1 \big).$$

The derivative of $\mathcal{L}$ w.r.t. all $\tilde{\mu}_x$ vanishes only if

$$\lambda = -\tilde{V}(x) + \log \tfrac{\mu(x)}{\tilde{\xi}(x)} \text{ for all } x \in \tilde{\mathcal{X}}. \quad (18)$$

This implies $\mu(x) = \tilde{\xi}(x) e^{\lambda + \tilde{V}(x)}$, and, since the $\mu(x)$ sum up to one, $1 = e^\lambda \sum_x \tilde{\xi}(x) e^{\tilde{V}(x)}$. This can be reformulated as $\lambda = -\log \big[\sum_x \tilde{\xi}(x) e^{\tilde{V}(x)} \big]$. Using this and (18), (17) is transformed to

$$\frac{\sum_{\nu \in \mathcal{C}} w_\nu \sum_{x \in \mathcal{X}} \nu(x) \log \frac{\nu(x)}{\xi(x)}}{1 + B} \leq \log(1 + \mathcal{H}) + \lambda \quad (19)$$

$$= \log(1 - \sum_{\nu \in \mathcal{C}} w_\nu \log w_\nu) - \log \big[1 - \sum_{x \in \tilde{\mathcal{X}}} \tilde{\xi}(x) \sum_{\nu \in \mathcal{C}} \frac{w_\nu \nu(x)}{\xi(x)} \log \frac{w_\nu \nu(x)}{\xi(x)} \big].$$

The arguments of both outer logarithms on the r.h.s. of (19) are at most $1 + B$: For the left one this holds by assumption (i), $\mathcal{H} \leq B$, and for the right one also by (i) because $\mathbf{E}_{x \sim \xi} \mathcal{H}(x) \leq \mathcal{H}$. Since for $x \leq y \leq 1 + B$ we have $\log(y) - \log(x) \geq \frac{y - x}{1 + B}$, (19) follows from

$$\sum_{\nu \in \mathcal{C}} w_\nu \sum_{x \in \mathcal{X}_0} \nu(x) \log \frac{\nu(x)}{\xi(x)} \leq -\sum_{\nu \in \mathcal{C}} w_\nu \sum_{x \in \mathcal{X}_0} \nu(x) \log w_\nu.$$

But this relation is true by Jensen's inequality:

$$\sum_{\nu \in \mathcal{C}} \sum_{x \in \mathcal{X}_0} \frac{w_\nu \nu(x)}{\xi(\mathcal{X}_0)} \log \frac{w_\nu \nu(x)}{\xi(x)} \leq \log \big(\sum_{\nu \in \mathcal{C}} \sum_{x \in \mathcal{X}_0} \frac{w_\nu \nu(x)}{\xi(\mathcal{X}_0)} \cdot \frac{w_\nu \nu(x)}{\xi(x)} \big) \leq 0,$$

since the $\frac{w_\nu \nu(x)}{\xi(\mathcal{X}_0)}$ sum up to one and always $\frac{w_\nu \nu(x)}{\xi(x)} \leq 1$ holds. $\square$

We now present a simple application of this result for finite model classes.

Theorem 12. (Predictive performance of stochastic model selection for finite model class) *Suppose that $\mathcal{C}$ consists of $N \in \mathbb{N}$ models, one of them is μ. Let*

$$\mathcal{P}_F(h_{<t}) = \big[\mathcal{K}(h_{<t}) + \log(1 + \mathcal{H}(h_{<t}))\big](1 + \log N).$$

Then $\mathcal{P}_F(h_{<t}) - \mathbf{E}_{x_t \sim \mu}\mathcal{P}_F(h_{1:t}) \geq \mathcal{H}(h_{<t}) - \sum_{x \in \mathcal{X}} \xi(x|z_t, h_{<t})\mathcal{H}(h_{1:t})$ holds for any history $h_{<t}$ and current input z_t, Consequently,

$$\sum_{t=1}^{\infty} \mathbf{E}\|\Xi - \xi\|_2^2 \leq \mathcal{P}_F^{\text{init}} = (1 + \log N)\big[\log(1 + \mathcal{H}^{\text{init}}) - \log(w_\mu^{\text{init}})\big]. \qquad (20)$$

Proof. Since the entropy of a class with N elements is at most $\log N$, this follows directly from Lemma 11. □

4   Entropy Potential and Countable Classes

We now generalize Theorem 12 to arbitrary countable model classes. First note that there is one very convenient fact about the potential function proofs so far: (8), (10), and (13) all are *local* assertions, i.e. for a single time instance and history. If the local expected error is bounded by the expected potential decrease, then the desired consequence on the cumulative error holds.

The entropy cannot be directly used as B in Lemma 11, since it may increase under μ-expectation. Intuitively, the problem is the following: There could be a false model with a quite large weight, such that the entropy is kept "artificially" low. If this false model is now refuted with high probability by the next observation, then the entropy may (drastically) increase. An instance is constructed in the following example. Afterwards, we define the *entropy potential*, which does not suffer from this problem.

Example 13. Fix binary alphabet and let $\tilde{\mathcal{C}}$ and $\tilde{\mathcal{Z}}$ be model class and input space of Example 10. Let $\mathcal{C} = \tilde{\mathcal{C}} \cup \{\nu_{\text{fool}}\}$, $\mathcal{Z} = \tilde{\mathcal{Z}} \cup \{0\}$, $w_{\text{fool}} = 1 - \frac{1}{m}$, and the rest of the prior of mass $\frac{1}{m}$ be distributed to the other models as in Example 10. Also the true distribution remains the same one. If the input sequence is $z_{1:nH_0+1} = 0, 1, \ldots nH_0$, and $\nu_{\text{fool}}(1|0) = 0$ while $\nu(1|0) = 1$ for all other ν, then like before the cumulative error is (even more than) $H_0/4$, while the entropy can be made arbitrarily small for large m.

Definition 14. (Entropy potential) *Let $H\big((w_\nu)_{\nu \in \mathcal{C}}\big) = -\sum_\nu w_\nu \log w_\nu$ be the entropy function. The μ-entropy potential (or short entropy potential) of a model class $\mathcal{C}$ containing the true distribution μ is, as already stated in (4),*

$$\Pi\big((w_\nu)_{\nu \in \mathcal{N}}\big) = \sup \Big\{ H\big((\tfrac{\tilde{w}_\nu}{\sum_{\nu'} \tilde{w}_{\nu'}})_\nu\big) : \tilde{w}_\mu = w_\mu \wedge \tilde{w}_\nu \leq w_\nu \ \forall \nu \in \mathcal{C} \setminus \{\mu\} \Big\}. \quad (21)$$

Clearly, $\Pi \geq \mathcal{H}$. According to Theorem 9, Π is necessarily finite if $\mathcal{H}$ is finite, so the supremum can be replaced by a maximum. Note that the entropy potential is finitely approximable in the sense of *(iii)* in Lemma 11.

Because of space limitations, we state the next two results without proofs. The first one characterizing Π is rather technical and useful for proving the second one, which asserts that Π decreases in expectation and therefore paves the way to proving the main theorem of this paper.

Proposition 15. (Characterization of Π) *For $S \subset C$, let $w(S) = \sum_{\nu \in S} w_\nu$. There is exactly one subset $A \subset C$ with $\mu \in A$, such that*

$$- \log w_\nu > L(A) := - \sum_{\nu' \in A} \frac{w_{\nu'}}{w(A)} \log w_{\nu'} \quad \Longleftrightarrow \quad \nu \in A \setminus \{\mu\}. \qquad (22)$$

We call A the set of active *models (in Π). Then, with $\tilde{w}_\nu = \exp(-L(A))$ for $\nu \in C \setminus A$, $\tilde{w}_\nu = w_\nu$ for $\nu \in A$, and $k = |C \setminus A|$, we have*

$$\Pi = \Pi\big((w_\nu)_{\nu \in C}\big) = H\big((\tfrac{\tilde{w}_\nu}{\sum_{\nu'} \tilde{w}_{\nu'}})_{\nu \in \mathcal{N}}\big)$$
$$= \log\big(k + w(A)e^{L(A)}\big). \qquad (23)$$

Moreover, this is scaling invariant in the weights, i.e. (22) yields the correct active set and (23) gives the correct value for weights that are not normalized, if these unnormalized weights are also used for computing $w(A)$ and $L(A)$.

Theorem 16. *For any history $h_{<t}$ and current input z_t,*

$$\sum_{x_t \in \mathcal{X}} \mu(x_t | z_t) \Pi(h_{1:t}) \leq \Pi(h_{<t}).$$

where the posterior entropy potential is defined as $\Pi(h_{<t}) := \Pi\big([w_\nu(h_{<t})]_{\nu \in C}\big)$.

This is the proof idea: The l.h.s. is a function of all $\nu(x|z_t)$ for all $\nu \in C \setminus \{\mu\}$ and $x \in \mathcal{X}$. It is possible to prove that the maximum of the l.h.s. is attained if $\nu(x|z_t) = \mu(x|z_t)$ for all $\nu \in C \setminus \{\mu\}$ and $x \in \mathcal{X}$, which immediately implies the assertion. To this aim, one first shows that the maximum can be only attained if in all $1 + |\mathcal{X}|$ sets of weights w, $\big(w\nu(x|z_t)\big)_{x \in \mathcal{X}}$ the same models are *active* (see Proposition 15). After that, the assertion can be proven.

The previous theorem, together with Lemma 11, immediately implies the main result of this paper, Theorem 1 (3). More precisely, it reads as follows.

Theorem 17. (Predictive performance of stochastic model selection) *For countable model class C containing the true distribution μ, define the potential as*

$$\mathcal{P}(h_{<t}) = \big[\mathcal{K}(h_{<t}) + \log(1 + \mathcal{H}(h_{<t}))\big](1 + \Pi(h_{<t})).$$

Then, for any history $h_{<t}$ and current input z_t,

$$\mathcal{P}(h_{<t}) - \mathbf{E}_{x_t \sim \mu(\cdot|z_t)} \mathcal{P}(h_{1:t}) \geq \mathcal{H}(h_{<t}) - \mathbf{E}_{x_t \sim \xi(\cdot|z_t, g_{<t})} \mathcal{H}(h_{1:t}), \text{ and thus}$$

$$\sum_{t=1}^{\infty} \mathbf{E}\big\|\Xi - \xi\big\|_2^2 \leq \mathcal{P}^{\text{init}} = (1 + \Pi^{\text{init}})\big[\log(1 + \mathcal{H}^{\text{init}}) - \log(w_\mu^{\text{init}})\big]. \qquad (24)$$

5   The Magnitude of the Entropy Potential

In this section, we will answer the question how large the newly defined quantity, the entropy potential, can grow. We start with a general statement that establishes both an upper and lower bound.

Proposition 18. *The μ-entropy potential is always bounded by*

$$\Pi \leq \frac{\mathcal{H}}{w_\mu}.$$

There are cases where this bound is sharp up to a factor, and also the cumulative quadratic error is of the same order:

$$\sum_{t=1}^{\infty} \mathbf{E}\|\Xi - \xi\|_2^2 = \Omega(\Pi) = \Omega\left(\frac{\mathcal{H}}{w_\mu}\right). \tag{25}$$

Proof. With A denoting the active set (see Proposition 15), we have that

$$\mathcal{H} \geq - \sum_{\nu \in A} w_\nu \log w_\nu = w(A)L(A) \geq w_\mu L(A) \geq w_\mu \Pi.$$

In order to see that this bound is sharp in general, consider the case of Example 13 and choose large $m, n > 1$ and $H_0 := m$. Then $\mathcal{H} \approx \log 2$, $w_\mu \approx \frac{1}{m}$, and $\Pi \approx H_0 \log 2 \approx \mathcal{H}/w_\mu$. Moreover, as seen above, the expected cumulative quadratic error is roughly $\frac{1}{4}H_0$. Hence, for this model class and prior, (25) holds.   □

Proposition 18 gives a worst-case bound which is of course not satisfactory: Using it in Theorem 17, the resulting bound becomes no better than that of Theorem 9. Fortunately, in case of light tails, i.e., if the weights are not decaying too slowly, the entropy potential is of order $\log w_\mu^{-1}$.

Proposition 19. *If w_ν decays exponentially, $\Pi = O(-\log w_\mu)$ holds. For simplicity, we may identify ν with its index in an enumeration, then exponential decay is reads as $w_\nu = O(\alpha^\nu)$ for some $\alpha \in (0,1)$.*

If w_ν decays inverse polynomially, that is, $w_\nu = O(\nu^{-b})$ for $b > 1$, we have $\Pi = O\left(-\frac{b^2}{b-1}\log w_\mu\right)$.

This proposition is easily verified. However, in the case of slowly decaying weights of order $\nu^{-1}(\log \nu)^{-b}$ for $b > 2$, we have $\Pi = \Omega(w_\mu^{-\frac{1}{b+1}})$.

The entropy potential is infinite with the usual definition of a *universal model class* [16]. But with a slight modification of the prior, it becomes finite. Hence we can obtain a universal induction result for stochastic model selection:

Example 20. Consider a model class $\mathcal{C}$ corresponding to the set of programs on a universal Turing machine. For $\nu \in \mathcal{C}$, let $w_\nu \sim 2^{-K(\nu)}/K(\nu)^2$, where K denotes the prefix Kolmogorov complexity – it is shown e.g. in [16] how to obtain such a construction. Then $\mathcal{H} = O(1)$, and Theorem 17 implies consistency of universal stochastic model selection with this prior and normalization. Had we chosen the usual "canonical" weights $w_\nu \sim 2^{-K(\nu)}$, then $\mathcal{H} \cong \sum K(\nu)2^{-K(\nu)} = \infty$, since K is the smallest possible code length to satisfy the Kraft inequality, and any smaller growth must necessarily result in an infinite sum. Hence the bound for universal stochastic model selection is infinite with the usual prior.

References

1. Freund, Y., Seung, H.S., Shamir, E., Tishby, N.: Selective sampling using the query by committee algorithm. Machine Learning **28** (1997) 133
2. McAllester, D.: PAC-bayesian stochastic model selection. Machine Learning **51** (2003) 5–21
3. Blackwell, D., Dubins, L.: Merging of opinions with increasing information. Annals of Mathematical Statistics **33** (1962) 882–887
4. Clarke, B.S., Barron, A.R.: Information-theoretic asymptotics of Bayes methods. IEEE Trans. Inform. Theory **36** (1990) 453–471
5. Rissanen, J.J.: Fisher Information and Stochastic Complexity. IEEE Trans. Inform. Theory **42** (1996) 40–47
6. Solomonoff, R.J.: Complexity-based induction systems: comparisons and convergence theorems. IEEE Trans. Inform. Theory **24** (1978) 422–432
7. Poland, J., Hutter, M.: Convergence of discrete MDL for sequential prediction. In: 17th Annual Conference on Learning Theory (COLT). (2004) 300–314
8. Poland, J., Hutter, M.: Asymptotics of discrete MDL for online prediction. IEEE Transactions on Information Theory **51** (2005) 3780–3795
9. Hutter, M.: Universal Artificial Intelligence: Sequential Decisions based on Algorithmic Probability. Springer, Berlin (2004)
10. Poland, J., Hutter, M.: On the convergence speed of MDL predictions for Bernoulli sequences. In: International Conference on Algorithmic Learning Theory (ALT). (2004) 294–308
11. Hutter, M.: Convergence and loss bounds for Bayesian sequence prediction. IEEE Trans. Inform. Theory **49** (2003) 2061–2067
12. Littlestone, N., Warmuth, M.K.: The weighted majority algorithm. In: 30th Annual Symposium on Foundations of Computer Science, Research Triangle Park, North Carolina, IEEE (1989) 256–261
13. Vovk, V.G.: Aggregating strategies. In: Proc. Third Annual Workshop on Computational Learning Theory, Rochester, New York, ACM Press (1990) 371–383
14. Hutter, M., Poland, J.: Adaptive online prediction by following the perturbed leader. Journal of Machine Learning Research **6** (2005) 639–660
15. Cesa-Bianchi, N., Lugosi, G.: Potential-based algorithms in on-line prediction and game theory. Machine Learning **51** (2003) 239–261
16. Li, M., Vitányi, P.M.B.: An introduction to Kolmogorov complexity and its applications. 2nd edn. Springer (1997)

Is There an Elegant Universal
Theory of Prediction?

Shane Legg

Dalle Molle Institute for Artificial Intelligence*
Galleria 2, Manno-Lugano 6928
Switzerland
shane@idsia.ch

Abstract. Solomonoff's inductive learning model is a powerful, universal and highly elegant theory of sequence prediction. Its critical flaw is
that it is incomputable and thus cannot be used in practice. It is sometimes suggested that it may still be useful to help guide the development
of very general and powerful theories of prediction which are computable.
In this paper it is shown that although powerful algorithms exist, they
are necessarily highly complex. This alone makes their theoretical analysis problematic, however it is further shown that beyond a moderate
level of complexity the analysis runs into the deeper problem of Gödel
incompleteness. This limits the power of mathematics to analyse and
study prediction algorithms, and indeed intelligent systems in general.

1   Introduction

Solomonoff's model of induction rapidly learns to make optimal predictions for
any computable sequence, including probabilistic ones [13, 14]. It neatly brings
together the philosophical principles of Occam's razor, Epicurus' principle of
multiple explanations, Bayes theorem and Turing's model of universal computation into a theoretical sequence predictor with astonishingly powerful properties.
Indeed the problem of sequence prediction could well be considered solved [9, 8],
if it were not for the fact that Solomonoff's theoretical model is incomputable.

Among computable theories there exist powerful general predictors, such as
the Lempel-Ziv algorithm [5] and Context Tree Weighting [18], that can learn
to predict some complex sequences, but not others. Some prediction methods,
based on the Minimum Description Length principle [12] or the Minimum Message Length principle [17], can even be viewed as computable approximations
of Solomonoff induction [10]. However in practice their power and generality are
limited by the power of the compression methods employed, as well as having a
significantly reduced data efficiency as compared to Solomonoff induction [11].

Could there exist elegant computable prediction algorithms that are in some
sense universal? Unfortunately this is impossible, as pointed out by Dawid
[4]. Specifically, he notes that for any statistical forecasting system there exist

---

* This work was funded by the grant SNF 200020-107616.

J.L. Balcázar, P.M. Long, and F. Stephan (Eds.): ALT 2006, LNAI 4264, pp. 274–287, 2006.

sequences which are not calibrated. Dawid also notes that a forecasting system for a family of distributions is necessarily more complex than any forecasting system generated from a single distribution in the family. However, he does not deal with the complexity of the sequences themselves, nor does he make a precise statement in terms of a specific measure of complexity, such as Kolmogorov complexity. The impossibility of forecasting has since been developed in considerably more depth by V'yugin [16], in particular he proves that there is an efficient randomised procedure producing sequences that cannot be predicted (with high probability) by computable forecasting systems.

In this paper we study the prediction of computable sequences from the perspective of Kolmogorov complexity. The central question we look at is the prediction of sequences which have bounded Kolmogorov complexity. This leads us to a new notion of complexity: rather than the length of the shortest program able to generate a given sequence, in other words Kolmogorov complexity, we take the length of the shortest program able to learn to predict the sequence. This new complexity measure has the same fundamental invariance property as Kolmogorov complexity, and a number of strong relationships between the two measures are proven. However in general the two may diverge significantly. For example, although a long random string that indefinitely repeats has a very high Kolmogorov complex, this sequence also has a relatively simple structure that even a simple predictor can learn to predict.

We then prove that some sequences, however, can only be predicted by very complex predictors. This implies that very general prediction algorithms, in particular those that can learn to predict all sequences up to a given Kolmogorov complex, must themselves be complex. This puts an end to our hope of there being an extremely general and yet relatively simple prediction algorithm. We then use this fact to prove that although very powerful prediction algorithms exist, they cannot be mathematically discovered due to Gödel incompleteness. Given how fundamental prediction is to intelligence, this result implies that beyond a moderate level of complexity the development of powerful artificial intelligence algorithms can only be an experimental science.

2   Preliminaries

An *alphabet* $\mathcal{A}$ is a finite set of 2 or more elements which are called *symbols*. In this paper we will assume a binary alphabet $\mathbb{B} := \{0, 1\}$, though all the results can easily be generalised to other alphabets. A *string* is a finite ordered n-tuple of symbols denoted $x := x_1 x_2 \ldots x_n$ where $\forall i \in \{1, \ldots, n\}$, $x_i \in \mathbb{B}$, or more succinctly, $x \in \mathbb{B}^n$. The 0-tuple is denoted λ and is called the *null string*. The expression $\mathbb{B}^{\leq n}$ has the obvious interpretation, and $\mathbb{B}^* := \bigcup_{n \in \mathbb{N}} \mathbb{B}^n$. The length *lexicographical* ordering is a total order on $\mathbb{B}^*$ defined as $\lambda < 0 < 1 < 00 < 01 < 10 < 11 < 000 < 001 < \cdots$. A *substring* of x is defined $x_{j:k} := x_j x_{j+1} \ldots x_k$ where $1 \leq j \leq k \leq n$. By $|x|$ we mean the length of the string x, for example, $|x_{j:k}| = k - j + 1$. We will sometimes need to encode a natural number as a string. Using simple encoding techniques it can be shown that there exists a computable injective function $f : \mathbb{N} \to \mathbb{B}^*$ where no string in the range of f is a prefix of any other, and $\forall n \in \mathbb{N} : |f(n)| \leq \log_2 n + 2 \log_2 \log_2 n + 1 = O(\log n)$.

Unlike strings which always have finite length, a *sequence* ω is an infinite list of symbols $x_1 x_2 x_3 \ldots \in \mathbb{B}^\infty$. Of particular interest to us will be the class of sequences which can be generated by an algorithm executed on a universal Turing machine:

Definition 1. *A* **monotone universal Turing machine** $\mathcal{U}$ *is defined as a universal Turing machine with one unidirectional input tape, one unidirectional output tape, and some bidirectional work tapes. Input tapes are read only, output tapes are write only, unidirectional tapes are those where the head can only move from left to right. All tapes are binary (no blank symbol) and the work tapes are initially filled with zeros. We say that $\mathcal{U}$ outputs/computes a sequence ω on input p, and write $\mathcal{U}(p) = \omega$, if $\mathcal{U}$ reads all of p but no more as it continues to write ω to the output tape.*

We fix $\mathcal{U}$ and define $\mathcal{U}(p, x)$ by simply using a standard coding technique to encode a program p along with a string $x \in \mathbb{B}^*$ as a single input string for $\mathcal{U}$.

Definition 2. *A sequence $\omega \in \mathbb{B}^\infty$ is a* **computable binary sequence** *if there exists a program $q \in \mathbb{B}^*$ that writes ω to a one-way output tape when run on a monotone universal Turing machine $\mathcal{U}$, that is, $\exists q \in \mathbb{B}^* : \mathcal{U}(q) = \omega$. We denote the set of all computable sequences by $\mathcal{C}$.*

A similar definition for strings is not necessary as all strings have finite length and are therefore trivially computable.

Definition 3. *A* **computable binary predictor** *is a program $p \in \mathbb{B}^*$ that on a universal Turing machine $\mathcal{U}$ computes a total function $\mathbb{B}^* \to \mathbb{B}$.*

For simplicity of notation we will often write $p(x)$ to mean the function computed by the program p when executed on $\mathcal{U}$ along with the input string x, that is, $p(x)$ is short hand for $\mathcal{U}(p, x)$. Having $x_{1:n}$ as input, the objective of a predictor is for its output, called its *prediction*, to match the next symbol in the sequence. Formally we express this by writing $p(x_{1:n}) = x_{n+1}$.

As the algorithmic prediction of incomputable sequences, such as the halting sequence, is impossible by definition, we only consider the problem of predicting computable sequences. To simplify things we will assume that the predictor has an unlimited supply of computation time and storage. We will also make the assumption that the predictor has unlimited data to learn from, that is, we are only concerned with whether or not a predictor can learn to predict in the following sense:

Definition 4. *We say that a predictor p can* **learn to predict** *a sequence $\omega := x_1 x_2 \ldots \in \mathbb{B}^\infty$ if there exists $m \in \mathbb{N}$ such that $\forall n \geq m : p(x_{1:n}) = x_{n+1}$.*

The existence of m in the above definition need not be constructive, that is, we might not know when the predictor will stop making prediction errors for a given sequence, just that this will occur eventually. This is essentially "next value" prediction as characterised by Barzdin [1], which follows from Gold's notion of identifiability in the limit for languages [7].

Definition 5. *Let $P(\omega)$ be the set of all predictors able to learn to predict ω. Similarly for sets of sequences $S \subset \mathbb{B}^\infty$, define $P(S) := \bigcap_{\omega \in S} P(\omega)$.*

A standard measure of complexity for sequences is the length of the shortest program which generates the sequence:

Definition 6. *For any sequence $\omega \in \mathbb{B}^\infty$ the monotone* **Kolmogorov complexity** *of the sequence is,*

$$K(\omega) := \min_{q \in \mathbb{B}^*} \{|q| : \mathcal{U}(q) = \omega\},$$

where $\mathcal{U}$ is a monotone universal Turing machine. If no such q exists, we define $K(\omega) := \infty$.

It can be shown that this measure of complexity depends on our choice of universal Turing machine $\mathcal{U}$, but only up to an additive constant that is independent of ω. This is due to the fact that a universal Turing machine can simulate any other universal Turing machine with a fixed length program.

In essentially the same way as the definition above we can define the Kolmogorov complexity of a string $x \in \mathbb{B}^n$, written $K(x)$, by requiring that $\mathcal{U}(q)$ halts after generating x on the output tape. For an extensive treatment of Kolmogorov complexity and some of its applications see [10] or [2].

As many of our results will have the above property of holding within an additive constant that is independent of the variables in the expression, we will indicate this by placing a small plus above the equality or inequality symbol. For example, $f(x) \stackrel{+}{<} g(x)$ means that that $\exists c \in \mathbb{R}, \forall x : f(x) < g(x) + c$. When using standard "Big O" notation this is unnecessary as expressions are already understood to hold within an independent constant, however for consistency of notation we will use it in these cases also.

3   Prediction of Computable Sequences

The most elementary result is that every computable sequence can be predicted by at least one predictor, and that this predictor need not be significantly more complex than the sequence to be predicted.

Lemma 1. $\forall \omega \in \mathcal{C}, \exists p \in P(\omega) : K(p) \stackrel{+}{<} K(\omega).$

Proof. As the sequence ω is computable, there must exist at least one algorithm that generates ω. Let q be the shortest such algorithm and construct an algorithm p that "predicts" ω as follows: Firstly the algorithm p reads $x_{1:n}$ to find the value of n, then it runs q to generate $x_{1:n+1}$ and returns x_{n+1} as its prediction. Clearly p perfectly predicts ω and $|p| < |q| + c$, for some small constant c that is independent of ω and q.   □

Not only can any computable sequence be predicted, there also exist very simple predictors able to predict arbitrarily complex sequences:

Lemma 2. *There exists a predictor p such that $\forall n \in \mathbb{N}, \exists \omega \in \mathcal{C} : p \in P(\omega)$ and $K(\omega) > n$.*

Proof. Take a string x such that $K(x) = |x| \geq 2n$, and from this define a sequence $\omega := x0000\dots$. Clearly $K(\omega) > n$ and yet a simple predictor p that always predicts 0 can learn to predict ω.   □

The predictor used in the above proof is very simple and can only "learn" sequences that end with all 0's, albeit where the initial string can have arbitrarily high Kolmogorov complexity. It may seem that this is due to sequences that are initially complex but where the "tail complexity", defined $\liminf_{i \to \infty} K(\omega_{i:\infty})$, is zero. This is not the case:

Lemma 3. *There exists a predictor p such that $\forall n \in \mathbb{N}, \exists \omega \in \mathcal{C} : p \in P(\omega)$ and $\liminf_{i \to \infty} K(\omega_{i:\infty}) > n$.*

Proof. A predictor p for eventually periodic sequences can be defined as follows: On input $\omega_{1:k}$ the predictor goes through the ordered pairs $(1, 1), (1, 2), (2, 1), (1, 3), (2, 2), (3, 1), (1, 4), \dots$ checking for each pair (a, b) whether the string $\omega_{1:k}$ consists of an initial string of length a followed by a repeating string of length b. On the first match that is found p predicts that the repeating string continues, and then p halts. If $a + b > k$ before a match is found, then p outputs a fixed symbol and halts. Clearly $K(p)$ is a small constant and p will learn to predict any sequence that is eventually periodic.

For any $(m, n) \in \mathbb{N}^2$, let $\omega := x(y^*)$ where $x \in \mathbb{B}^m$, and $y \in \mathbb{B}^n$ is a random string, that is, $K(y) = n$. As ω is eventually periodic $p \in P(\omega)$ and also we see that $\liminf_{i \to \infty} K(\omega_{i:\infty}) = \min\{K(\omega_{m+1:\infty}), K(\omega_{m+2:\infty}), \dots, K(\omega_{m+n:\infty})\}$.

For any $k \in \{1, \dots, n\}$ let q_k^* be the shortest program that can generate $\omega_{m+k:\infty}$. We can define a halting program q_k' that outputs y where this program consists of q_k^*, n and k. Thus, $|q_k'| = |q_k^*| + O(\log n) = K(\omega_{k:\infty}) + O(\log n)$. As $n = K(y) \leq |q_k'|$, we see that $K(\omega_{k:\infty}) > n - O(\log n)$. As n and k are arbitrary the result follows.   □

Using a more sophisticated version of this proof it can be shown that there exist predictors that can learn to predict arbitrary regular or primitive recursive sequences. Thus we might wonder whether there exists a computable predictor able to learn to predict all computable sequences. Unfortunately, no universal predictor exists, indeed for every predictor there exists a sequence which it cannot predict at all:

Lemma 4. *For any predictor p there constructively exists a sequence $\omega := x_1 x_2 \dots \in \mathcal{C}$ such that $\forall n \in \mathbb{N} : p(x_{1:n}) \neq x_{n+1}$ and $K(\omega) \overset{+}{<} K(p)$.*

Proof. For any computable predictor p there constructively exists a computable sequence $\omega = x_1 x_2 x_3 \dots$ computed by an algorithm q defined as follows: Set

$x_1 = 1 - p(\lambda)$, then $x_2 = 1 - p(x_1)$, then $x_3 = 1 - p(x_{1:2})$ and so on. Clearly $\omega \in \mathcal{C}$ and $\forall n \in \mathbb{N} : p(x_{1:n}) = 1 - x_{n+1}$.

Let p^* be the shortest program that computes the same function as p and define a sequence generation algorithm q^* based on p^* using the procedure above. By construction, $|q^*| = |p^*| + c$ for some constant c that is independent of p^*. Because q^* generates ω, it follows that $K(\omega) \leq |q^*|$. By definition $K(p) = |p^*|$ and so $K(\omega) \overset{+}{<} K(p)$.   □

Allowing the predictor to be probabilistic does not fundamentally avoid the problem of Lemma 4. In each step, rather than generating the opposite to what will be predicted by p, instead q attempts to generate the symbol which p is least likely to predict given $x_{1:n}$. To do this q must simulate p in order to estimate $\Pr(p(x_{1:n}) = 1 | x_{1:n})$. With sufficient simulation effort, q can estimate this probability to any desired accuracy for any $x_{1:n}$. This produces a computable sequence ω such that $\forall n \in \mathbb{N} : \Pr(p(x_{1:n}) = x_{n+1} | x_{1:n})$ is not significantly greater than $\frac{1}{2}$, that is, the performance of p is no better than a predictor that makes completely random predictions.

As probabilistic prediction complicates things without avoiding this fundamental problem, in the remainder of this paper we will consider only deterministic predictors. This will also allow us to see the roots of this problem as clearly as possible. With the preliminaries covered, we now move on to the central problem considered in this paper: Predicting sequences of limited Kolmogorov complexity.

4   Prediction of Simple Computable Sequences

As the computable prediction of any computable sequence is impossible, a weaker goal is to be able to predict all "simple" computable sequences.

Definition 7. *For $n \in \mathbb{N}$, let $\mathcal{C}_n := \{\omega \in \mathcal{C} : K(\omega) \leq n\}$. Further, let $P_n := P(\mathcal{C}_n)$ be the set of predictors able to learn to predict all sequences in $\mathcal{C}_n$.*

Firstly we establish that prediction algorithms exist that can learn to predict all sequences up to a given complexity, and that these predictors need not be significantly more complex than the sequences they can predict:

Lemma 5. $\forall n \in \mathbb{N}, \exists p \in P_n : K(p) \overset{+}{<} n + O(\log n)$.

Proof. Let $h \in \mathbb{N}$ be the number of programs of length n or less which generate infinite sequences. Build the value of h into a prediction algorithm p constructed as follows:

In the kth prediction cycle run in parallel all programs of length n or less until h of these programs have each produced $k + 1$ symbols of output. Next predict according to the $k + 1^{th}$ symbol of the generated string whose first k symbols is consistent with the observed string. If two generated strings are consistent with the observed sequence (there cannot be more than two as the strings are binary and have length $k + 1$), pick the one which was generated by the program that occurs first in a lexicographical ordering of the programs. If no generated output is consistent, give up and output a fixed symbol.

For sufficiently large k, only the h programs which produce infinite sequences will produce output strings of length k. As this set of sequences is finite, they can be uniquely identified by finite initial strings. Thus for sufficiently large k the predictor p will correctly predict any computable sequence ω for which $K(\omega) \leq n$, that is, $p \in P_n$.

As there are $2^{n+1} - 1$ possible strings of length n or less, $h < 2^{n+1}$ and thus we can encode h with $\log_2 h + 2\log_2 \log_2 h = n + 1 + 2\log_2(n+1)$ bits. Thus, $K(p) < n+1+2\log_2(n+1)+c$ for some constant c that is independent of n. $\Box$

Can we do better than this? Lemmas 2 and 3 shows us that there exist predictors able to predict at least some sequences vastly more complex than themselves. This suggests that there might exist simple predictors able to predict arbitrary sequences up to a high complexity. Formally, could there exist $p \in P_n$ where $n \gg K(p)$? Unfortunately, these simple but powerful predictors are not possible:

Theorem 1. $\forall n \in \mathbb{N} : p \in P_n \Rightarrow K(p) \overset{+}{>} n$.

Proof. For any $n \in \mathbb{N}$ let $p \in P_n$, that is, $\forall \omega \in \mathcal{C}_n : p \in P(\omega)$. By Lemma 4 we know that $\exists \omega' \in \mathcal{C} : p \notin P(\omega')$. As $p \notin P(\omega')$ it must be the case that $\omega' \notin \mathcal{C}_n$, that is, $K(\omega') \geq n$. From Lemma 4 we also know that $K(p) \overset{+}{>} K(\omega')$ and so the result follows. $\Box$

Intuitively the reason for this is as follows: Lemma 4 guarantees that every simple predictor fails for at least one simple sequence. Thus if we want a predictor that can learn to predict all sequences up to a moderate level of complexity, then clearly the predictor cannot be simple. Likewise, if we want a predictor that can predict all sequences up to a high level of complexity, then the predictor itself must be very complex. Thus, even though we have made the generous assumption of unlimited computational resources and data to learn from, only very complex algorithms can be truly powerful predictors.

These results easily generalise to notions of complexity that take computation time into consideration. As sequences are infinite, the appropriate measure of time is the time needed to generate or predict the next symbol in the sequence. Under any reasonable measure of time complexity, the operation of inverting a single output from a binary valued function can be performed with little cost. If C is any complexity measure with this property, it is trivial to see that the proof of Lemma 4 still holds for C. From this, an analogue of Theorem 1 for C easily follows.

With similar arguments these results also generalise in a straightforward way to complexity measures that take space or other computational resources into account. Thus, the fact that extremely powerful predictors must be very complex, holds under any measure of complexity for which inverting a single bit is inexpensive.

5   Complexity of Prediction

Another way of viewing these results is in terms of an alternate notion of sequence complexity defined as the size of the smallest predictor able to learn to predict the sequence. This allows us to express the results of the previous sections more concisely. Formally, for any sequence ω define the complexity measure,

$$\dot{K}(\omega) := \min_{p \in \mathbb{B}^*}\{|p| : p \in P(\omega)\},$$

and $\dot{K}(\omega) := \infty$ if $P(\omega) = \varnothing$. Thus, if $\dot{K}(\omega)$ is high then the sequence ω is complex in the sense that only complex prediction algorithms are able to learn to predict it. It can easily be seen that this notion of complexity has the same invariance to the choice of reference universal Turing machine as the standard Kolmogorov complexity measure.

It may be tempting to conjecture that this definition simply describes what might be called the "tail complexity" of a sequence, that is, $\dot{K}(\omega)$ is equal to $\liminf_{i \to \infty} K(\omega_{i:\infty})$. This is not the case. In the proof of Lemma 3 saw that there exists a single predictor capable of learning to predict any sequence that consists of a repeating string, and thus for these sequences $\dot{K}$ is bounded. It was further shown that there exist sequences of this form with arbitrarily high tail complexity. Clearly then tail complexity and $\dot{K}$ cannot be equal in general.

Using $\dot{K}$ we can now rewrite a number of our previous results much more succinctly. From Lemma 1 it immediately follows that,

$$\forall \omega : 0 \le \dot{K}(\omega) \overset{+}{<} K(\omega).$$

From Lemma 2 we know that $\exists c \in \mathbb{N}, \forall n \in \mathbb{N}, \exists \omega \in \mathcal{C}$ such that $\dot{K}(\omega) < c$ and $K(\omega) > n$, that is, $\dot{K}$ can attain the lower bound above within a small constant, no matter how large the value of K is. The sequences for which the upper bound on $\dot{K}$ is tight are interesting as they are the ones which demand complex predictors. We prove the existence of these sequences and look at some of their properties in the next section.

The complexity measure $\dot{K}$ can also be generalised to sets of sequences, for $S \subset \mathbb{B}^\infty$ define $\dot{K}(S) := \min_p\{|p| : p \in P(S)\}$. This allows us to rewrite Lemma 5 and Theorem 1 as simply,

$$\forall n \in \mathbb{N} : n \overset{+}{<} \dot{K}(\mathcal{C}_n) \overset{+}{<} n + O(\log n).$$

This is just a restatement of the fact that the simplest predictor capable of predicting all sequences up to a Kolmogorov complexity of n, has itself a Kolmogorov complexity of roughly n.

Perhaps the most surprising thing about $\dot{K}$ complexity is that this very natural definition of the complexity of a sequence, as viewed from the perspective of prediction, does not appear to have been studied before.

6   Hard to Predict Sequences

We have already seen that some individual sequences, such as the repeating string used in the proof of Lemma 3, can have arbitrarily high Kolmogorov complexity but nevertheless can be predicted by trivial algorithms. Thus, although these sequences contain a lot of information in the Kolmogorov sense, in a deeper sense their structure is very simple and easily learnt.

What interests us in this section is the other extreme; individual sequences which can only be predicted by complex predictors. As we are only concerned with prediction in the limit, this extra complexity in the predictor must be some kind of special information which cannot be learnt just through observing the sequence. Our first task is to show that these difficult to predict sequences exist.

Theorem 2. $\forall n \in \mathbb{N}, \exists \omega \in \mathcal{C} : n \overset{+}{<} \dot{K}(\omega) \overset{+}{<} K(\omega) \overset{+}{<} n + O(\log n)$.

Proof. For any $n \in \mathbb{N}$, let $Q_n \subset \mathbb{B}^{<n}$ be the set of programs shorter than n that are predictors, and let $x_{1:k} \in \mathbb{B}^k$ be the observed initial string from the sequence ω which is to be predicted. Now construct a meta-predictor $\hat{p}$:

By dovetailing the computations, run in parallel every program of length less than n on every string in $\mathbb{B}^{\leq k}$. Each time a program is found to halt on all of these input strings, add the program to a set of "candidate prediction algorithms", called $\tilde{Q}_n^k$. As each element of Q_n is a valid predictor, and thus halts for all input strings in $\mathbb{B}^*$ by definition, for every n and k it eventually will be the case that $|\tilde{Q}_n^k| = |Q_n|$. At this point the simulation to approximate Q_n terminates. It is clear that for sufficiently large values of k all of the valid predictors, and only the valid predictors, will halt with a single symbol of output on all tested input strings. That is, $\exists r \in \mathbb{N}, \forall k > r : \tilde{Q}_n^k = Q_n$.

The second part of the $\hat{p}$ algorithm uses these candidate prediction algorithms to make a prediction. For $p \in \tilde{Q}_n^k$ define $d^k(p) := \sum_{i=1}^{k-1} |p(x_{1:i}) - x_{i+1}|$. Informally, $d^k(p)$ is the number of prediction errors made by p so far. Compute this for all $p \in \tilde{Q}_n^k$ and then let $p_k^* \in \tilde{Q}_n^k$ be the program with minimal $d^k(p)$. If there is more than one such program, break the tie by letting p_k^* be the lexicographically first of these. Finally, $\hat{p}$ computes the value of $p_k^*(x_{1:k})$ and then returns this as its prediction and halts.

By Lemma 4, there exists $\omega' \in \mathcal{C}$ such that $\hat{p}$ makes a prediction error for every k when trying to predict ω'. Thus, in each cycle at least one of the finitely many predictors with minimal d^k makes a prediction error and so $\forall p \in Q_n : d^k(p) \to \infty$ as $k \to \infty$. Therefore, $\nexists p \in Q_n : p \in P(\omega')$, that is, no program of length less than n can learn to predict ω' and so $n \leq \dot{K}(\omega')$. Further, from Lemma 1 we know that $\dot{K}(\omega') \overset{+}{<} K(\omega')$, and from Lemma 4 again, $K(\omega') \overset{+}{<} K(\hat{p})$.

Examining the algorithm for $\hat{p}$, we see that it contains some fixed length program code and an encoding of $|Q_n|$, where $|Q_n| < 2^n - 1$. Thus, using a standard encoding method for integers, $K(\hat{p}) \overset{+}{<} n + O(\log n)$.

Chaining these together we get, $n \overset{+}{<} \dot{K}(\omega') \overset{+}{<} K(\omega') \overset{+}{<} K(\hat{p}) \overset{+}{<} n + O(\log n)$, which proves the theorem.   □

This establishes the existence of sequences with arbitrarily high $\dot{K}$ complexity which also have a similar level of Kolmogorov complexity. Next we establish a fundamental property of high $\dot{K}$ complexity sequences: they are extremely difficult to compute.

For an algorithm q that generates $\omega \in \mathcal{C}$, define $t_q(n)$ to be the number of computation steps performed by q before the nth symbol of ω is written to the output tape. For example, if q is a simple algorithm that outputs the sequence $010101\ldots$, then clearly $t_q(n) = O(n)$ and so ω can be computed quickly. The following theorem proves that if a sequence can be computed in a reasonable amount of time, then the sequence must have a low $\dot{K}$ complexity:

Lemma 6. $\forall \omega \in \mathcal{C}$, if $\exists q : \mathcal{U}(q) = \omega$ and $\exists r \in \mathbb{N}, \forall n > r : t_q(n) < 2^n$, then $\dot{K}(\omega) \overset{+}{=} 0$.

Proof. Construct a prediction algorithm $\tilde{p}$ as follows:
On input $x_{1:n}$, run all programs of length n or less, each for 2^{n+1} steps. In a set W_n collect together all generated strings which are at least $n + 1$ symbols long and where the first n symbols match the observed string $x_{1:n}$. Now order the strings in W_n according to a lexicographical ordering of their generating programs. If $W_n = \varnothing$, then just return a prediction of 1 and halt. If $|W_n| > 1$ then return the $n + 1^{th}$ symbol from the first sequence in the above ordering.

Assume that $\exists q : \mathcal{U}(q) = \omega$ such that $\exists r \in \mathbb{N}, \forall n > r : t_q(n) < 2^n$. If q is not unique, take q to be the lexicographically first of these. Clearly $\forall n > r$ the initial string from ω generated by q will be in the set W_n. As there is no lexicographically lower program which can generate ω within the time constraint $t_q(n) < 2^n$ for all $n > r$, for sufficiently large n the predictor $\tilde{p}$ must converge on using q for each prediction and thus $\tilde{p} \in P(\omega)$. As $|\tilde{p}|$ is clearly a fixed constant that is independent of ω, it follows then that $\dot{K}(\omega) < |\tilde{p}| \overset{+}{=} 0$.   □

We could replace the 2^n bound in the above result with any monotonically growing computable function, for example, 2^{2^n}. In any case, this does not change the fundamental result that sequences which have a high $\dot{K}$ complexity are practically impossible to compute. However from our theoretical perspective these sequences present no problem as they can be predicted, albeit with immense difficulty.

7   The Limits of Mathematical Analysis

One way to interpret the results of the previous sections is in terms of constructive theories of prediction. Essentially, a constructive theory of prediction $\mathcal{T}$, expressed in some sufficiently rich formal system $\mathcal{F}$, is in effect a description of a prediction algorithm with respect to a universal Turing machine which implements the required parts of $\mathcal{F}$. Thus from Theorems 1 and 2 it follows that if we want to have a predictor that can learn to predict all sequences up to a high level of Kolmogorov complexity, or even just predict individual sequences which have high $\dot{K}$ complexity, the constructive theory of prediction that we base our predictor on must be very complex. Elegant and highly general constructive theories of prediction simply do not exist, even if we assume unlimited computational resources. This is in marked contrast to Solomonoff's highly elegant but non-constructive theory of prediction.

Naturally, highly complex theories of prediction will be very difficult to mathematically analyse, if not practically impossible. Thus at some point the development of very general prediction algorithms must become mainly an experimental endeavour due to the difficulty of working with the required theory. Interestingly, an even stronger result can be proven showing that beyond some point the mathematical analysis is in fact impossible, even in theory:

Theorem 3. *In any consistent formal axiomatic system $\mathcal{F}$ that is sufficiently rich to express statements of the form "$p \in P_n$", there exists $m \in \mathbb{N}$ such that for all $n > m$ and for all predictors $p \in P_n$ the true statement "$p \in P_n$" cannot be proven in $\mathcal{F}$.*

In other words, even though we have proven that very powerful sequence prediction algorithms exist, beyond a certain complexity it is impossible to find any of these algorithms using mathematics. The proof has a similar structure to Chaitin's information theoretic proof [3] of Gödel incompleteness theorem for formal axiomatic systems [6].

Proof. For each $n \in \mathbb{N}$ let T_n be the set of statements expressed in the formal system $\mathcal{F}$ of the form "$p \in P_n$", where p is filled in with the complete description of some algorithm in each case. As the set of programs is denumerable, T_n is also denumerable and each element of T_n has finite length. From Lemma 5 and Theorem 1 it follows that each T_n contains infinitely many statements of the form "$p \in P_n$" which are true.

Fix n and create a search algorithm s that enumerates all proofs in the formal system $\mathcal{F}$ searching for a proof of a statement in the set T_n. As the set T_n is recursive, s can always recognise a proof of a statement in T_n. If s finds any such proof, it outputs the corresponding program p and then halts.

By way of contradiction, assume that s halts, that is, a proof of a theorem in T_n is found and p such that $p \in P_n$ is generated as output. The size of the algorithm s is a constant (a description of the formal system $\mathcal{F}$ and some proof enumeration code) as well as an $O(\log n)$ term needed to describe n. It follows then that $K(p) \overset{+}{<} O(\log n)$. However from Theorem 1 we know that $K(p) \overset{+}{>} n$. Thus, for sufficiently large n, we have a contradiction and so our assumption of the existence of a proof must be false. That is, for sufficiently large n and for all $p \in P_n$, the true statement "$p \in P_n$" cannot be proven within the formal system $\mathcal{F}$.   □

The exact value of m depends on our choice of formal system $\mathcal{F}$ and which reference machine $\mathcal{U}$ we measure complexity with respect to. However for reasonable choices of $\mathcal{F}$ and $\mathcal{U}$ the value of m would be in the order of 1000. That is, the bound m is certainly not so large as to be vacuous.

8   Discussion

Solomonoff induction is an elegant and extremely general model of inductive learning. It neatly brings together the philosophical principles of Occam's razor, Epicurus' principle of multiple explanations, Bayes theorem and Turing's model of universal computation into a theoretical sequence predictor with astonishingly powerful properties. If theoretical models of prediction can have such elegance and power, one cannot help but wonder whether similarly beautiful and highly general computable theories of prediction are also possible.

What we have shown here is that there does not exist an elegant constructive theory of prediction for computable sequences, even if we assume unbounded computational resources, unbounded data and learning time, and place moderate bounds on the Kolmogorov complexity of the sequences to be predicted. Very powerful computable predictors are therefore necessarily complex. We have further shown that the source of this problem is computable sequences which are extremely expensive to compute. While we have proven that very powerful prediction algorithms which can learn to predict these sequences exist, we have also proven that, unfortunately, mathematical analysis cannot be used to discover these algorithms due to problems of Gödel incompleteness.

These results can be extended to more general settings, specifically to those problems which are equivalent to, or depend on, sequence prediction. Consider, for example, a reinforcement learning agent interacting with an environment [15, 8]. In each interaction cycle the agent must choose its actions so as to maximise the future rewards that it receives from the environment. Of course the agent cannot know for certain whether or not some action will lead to rewards in the future, thus it must predict these. Clearly, at the heart of reinforcement learning lies a prediction problem, and so the results for computable predictors presented in this paper also apply to computable reinforcement learners. More specifically, from Theorem 1 it follows that very powerful computable reinforcement learners are necessarily complex, and from Theorem 3 it follows that it is impossible to discover extremely powerful reinforcement learning algorithms mathematically. These relationships are illustrated in Figure 1.

It is reasonable to ask whether the assumptions we have made in our model need to be changed. If we increase the power of the predictors further, for example by providing them with some kind of an oracle, this would make the predictors even more unrealistic than they currently are. Clearly this goes against our goal of finding an elegant, powerful and general prediction theory that is more realistic in its assumptions than Solomonoff's incomputable model. On the other hand, if we weaken our assumptions about the predictors' resources to make them more realistic, we are in effect taking a subset of our current class of predictors. As such, all the same limitations and problems will still apply, as well as some new ones.

It seems then that the way forward is to further restrict the problem space. One possibility would be to bound the amount of computation time needed

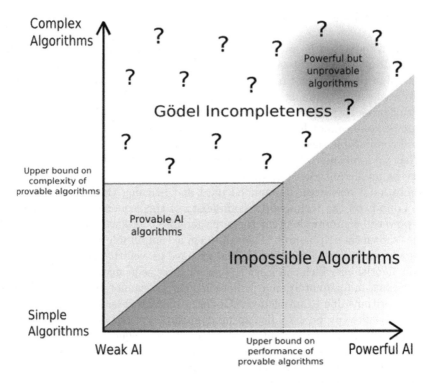

Fig. 1. Theorem 1 rules out simple but powerful artificial intelligence algorithms, as indicated by the greyed out region on the lower right. Theorem 3 upper bounds how complex an algorithm can be before it can no longer be proven to be a powerful algorithm. This is indicated by the horizontal line separating the region of provable algorithms from the region of Gödel incompleteness.

to generate the next symbol in the sequence. However if we do this without restricting the predictors' resources then the simple predictor from Lemma 6 easily learns to predict any such sequence and thus the problem of prediction in the limit has become trivial. Another possibility might be to bound the memory of the machine used to generate the sequence, however this makes the generator a finite state machine and thus bounds its computation time, again making the problem trivial.

Perhaps the only reasonable solution would be to add additional restrictions to both the algorithms which generate the sequences to be predicted, and to the predictors. We may also want to consider not just learnability in the limit, but also how quickly the predictor is able to learn. Of course we are then facing a much more difficult analysis problem.

Acknowledgements. I would like to thank Marcus Hutter, Alexey Chernov, Daniil Ryabko and Laurent Orseau for useful discussions and advice during the development of this paper.

References

1. J. M. Barzdin. Prognostication of automata and functions. *Information Processing*, 71:81–84, 1972.
2. C. S. Calude. *Information and Randomness*. Springer, Berlin, 2nd edition, 2002.
3. G. J. Chaitin. Gödel's theorem and information. *International Journal of Theoretical Physics*, 22:941–954, 1982.
4. A. P. Dawid. Comment on The impossibility of inductive inference. *Journal of the American Statistical Association*, 80(390):340–341, 1985.
5. M. Feder, N. Merhav, and M. Gutman. Universal prediction of individual sequences. *IEEE Trans. on Information Theory*, 38:1258–1270, 1992.
6. K. Gödel. Über formal unentscheidbare Sätze der principia mathematica und verwandter systeme I. *Monatshefte für Matematik und Physik*, 38:173–198, 1931. [English translation by E. Mendelsohn: "On undecidable propositions of formal mathematical systems". In M. Davis, editor, *The undecidable*, pages 39–71, New York, 1965. Raven Press, Hewlitt].
7. E. Mark Gold. Language identification in the limit. *Information and Control*, 10(5):447–474, 1967.
8. M. Hutter. *Universal Artificial Intelligence: Sequential Decisions based on Algorithmic Probability*. Springer, Berlin, 2005. 300 pages, http://www.idsia.ch/~marcus/ai/uaibook.htm.
9. M. Hutter. On the foundations of universal sequence prediction. In *Proc. 3rd Annual Conference on Theory and Applications of Models of Computation (TAMC'06)*, volume 3959 of *LNCS*, pages 408–420. Springer, 2006.
10. M. Li and P. M. B. Vitányi. *An introduction to Kolmogorov complexity and its applications*. Springer, 2nd edition, 1997.
11. J. Poland and M. Hutter. Convergence of discrete MDL for sequential prediction. In *Proc. 17th Annual Conf. on Learning Theory (COLT'04)*, volume 3120 of *LNAI*, pages 300–314, Banff, 2004. Springer, Berlin.
12. J. J. Rissanen. Fisher Information and Stochastic Complexity. *IEEE Trans. on Information Theory*, 42(1):40–47, January 1996.
13. R. J. Solomonoff. A formal theory of inductive inference: Part 1 and 2. *Inform. Control*, 7:1–22, 224–254, 1964.
14. R. J. Solomonoff. Complexity-based induction systems: comparisons and convergence theorems. *IEEE Trans. Information Theory*, IT-24:422–432, 1978.
15. R. Sutton and A. Barto. *Reinforcement learning: An introduction*. Cambridge, MA, MIT Press, 1998.
16. V. V. V'yugin. Non-stochastic infinite and finite sequences. *Theoretical computer science*, 207:363–382, 1998.
17. C. S. Wallace and D. M. Boulton. An information measure for classification. *Computer Jrnl.*, 11(2):185–194, August 1968.
18. F.M.J. Willems, Y.M. Shtarkov, and Tj.J. Tjalkens. The context-tree weighting method: Basic properties. *IEEE Transactions on Information Theory*, 41(3), 1995.

Learning Linearly Separable Languages

Leonid Kontorovich[1], Corinna Cortes[2], and Mehryar Mohri[3,2]

[1] Carnegie Mellon University
5000 Forbes Avenue, Pittsburgh, PA 15213
[2] Google Research,
1440 Broadway, New York, NY 10018
[3] Courant Institute of Mathematical Sciences,
251 Mercer Street, New York, NY 10012

Abstract. This paper presents a novel paradigm for learning languages that consists of mapping strings to an appropriate high-dimensional feature space and learning a separating hyperplane in that space. It initiates the study of the linear separability of automata and languages by examining the rich class of piecewise-testable languages. It introduces a high-dimensional feature map and proves piecewise-testable languages to be linearly separable in that space. The proof makes use of word combinatorial results relating to subsequences. It also shows that the positive definite kernel associated to this embedding can be computed in quadratic time. It examines the use of support vector machines in combination with this kernel to determine a separating hyperplane and the corresponding learning guarantees. It also proves that all languages linearly separable under a regular finite cover embedding, a generalization of the embedding we used, are regular.

1 Motivation

The problem of learning regular languages, or, equivalently, finite automata, has been extensively studied over the last few decades.

Finding the smallest automaton consistent with a set of accepted and rejected strings was shown to be NP-complete by Angluin [1] and Gold [12]. Pitt and Warmuth [21] further strengthened these results by showing that even an approximation within a polynomial function of the size of the smallest automaton is NP-hard. These results imply the computational intractability of the general problem of passively learning finite automata within many learning models, including the mistake bound model of Haussler et al. [14] or the PAC-learning model of Valiant [16]. This last negative result can also be directly derived from the fact that the VC-dimension of finite automata is infinite.

On the positive side, Trakhtenbrot and Barzdin [24] showed that the smallest finite automaton consistent with the input data can be learned exactly provided that a uniform complete sample is provided, whose size is exponential in that of the automaton. The worst case complexity of their algorithm is exponential but a better average-case complexity can be obtained assuming that the topology and the labeling are selected randomly [24] or even that the topology is selected adversarially [9].

J.L. Balcázar, P.M. Long, and F. Stephan (Eds.): ALT 2006, LNAI 4264, pp. 288–303, 2006.

The model of identification in the limit of automata was introduced and discussed by Gold [11]. Deterministic finite automata were shown not to be identifiable in the limit from positive examples [11]. But positive results were given for the identification in the limit of the families of k-reversible languages [2] and subsequential transducers [20]. Some restricted classes of probabilistic automata such as acyclic probabilistic automata were also shown by Ron et al. to be efficiently learnable [22].

There is a wide literature dealing with the problem of learning automata and we cannot survey all these results in such a short space. Let us mention however that the algorithms suggested for learning automata are typically based on a state-merging idea. An initial automaton or prefix tree accepting the sample strings is first created. Then, starting with the trivial partition with one state per equivalence class, classes are merged while preserving an invariant congruence property. The automaton learned is obtained by merging states according to the resulting classes. Thus, the choice of the congruence determines the algorithm.

This work departs from this established paradigm in that it does not use the state-merging technique. Instead, it initiates the study of the linear separation of automata or languages by mapping strings to an appropriate high-dimensional feature space and learning a separating hyperplane, starting with the rich class of *piecewise-testable languages*.

Piecewise-testable languages form a non-trivial family of regular languages. They have been extensively studied in formal language theory [18] starting with the work of Imre Simon [23]. A language L is said to be *n-piecewise-testable*, $n \in \mathbb{N}$, if whenever u and v have the same subsequences of length at most n and u is in L, then v is also in L. A language L is said to be *piecewise testable* if it is n-piecewise-testable for some $n \in \mathbb{N}$.

For a fixed n, n-piecewise-testable languages were shown to be identifiable in the limit by García and Ruiz [10]. The class of n-piecewise-testable languages is finite and thus has finite VC-dimension. To the best of our knowledge, there has been no learning result related to the full class of piecewise-testable languages.

This paper introduces an embedding of all strings in a high-dimensional feature space and proves that piecewise-testable languages are finitely linearly separable in that space, that is linearly separable with a finite-dimensional weight vector. The proof is non-trivial and makes use of deep word combinatorial results relating to subsequences. It also shows that the positive definite kernel associated to this embedding can be computed in quadratic time. Thus, the use of support vector machines in combination with this kernel and the corresponding learning guarantees are examined. Since the VC-dimension of the class of piecewise-testable languages is infinite, it is not PAC-learnable and we cannot hope to derive PAC-style bounds for this learning scheme. But, the finite linear separability of piecewise-testable helps us derive weaker bounds based on the concept of the margin.

The linear separability proof is strong in the sense that the dimension of the weight vector associated with the separating hyperplane is finite. This is related to the fact that a *regular finite cover* is used for the separability of piecewise testable languages. This leads us to study the general problem of separability with other finite regular covers. We prove that languages separated with such regular finite covers are necessarily regular.

The paper is organized as follows. Section 2 introduces some preliminary definitions and notations related to strings, automata, and piecewise-testable languages. Section 3 presents the proof of the finite linear separability of piecewise-testable languages using a subsequence feature mapping. The subsequence kernel associated to this feature mapping is shown to be efficiently computable in Section 4. Section 5 uses margin bounds to examine how the support vector machine algorithm combined with the subsequence kernel can be used to learn piecewise-testable languages. Section 6 examines the general problem of separability with regular finite covers and shows that all languages separated using such covers are regular.

2   Preliminaries

In all that follows, Σ represents a finite alphabet. The length of a string $x \in \Sigma^*$ over that alphabet is denoted by $|x|$ and the complement of a subset $L \subseteq \Sigma^*$ by $\overline{L} = \Sigma^* \setminus L$. For any string $x \in \Sigma^*$, we denote by $x[i]$ the ith symbol of x, $i \leq |x|$. More generally, we denote by $x[i : j]$, the substring of contiguous symbols of x starting at $x[i]$ and ending at $x[j]$.

A string x is a *subsequence* of $y \in \Sigma^*$ if x can be derived from y by erasing some of y's characters. We will write $x \sqsubseteq y$ to indicate that x is a subsequence of y. The relation $\sqsubseteq$ defines a partial order over Σ^*. For $x \in \Sigma^n$, the *shuffle ideal* of x is defined as the set of all strings containing x as a subsequence:

$$\text{III}(x) = \{u \in \Sigma^* : x \sqsubseteq u\} = \Sigma^* x[1] \Sigma^* \ldots \Sigma^* x[n] \Sigma^*.$$

The definition of piecewise-testable languages was given in the previous section. An equivalent definition is the following: a language is *piecewise-testable* (PT for short) if it is a finite Boolean combination of shuffle ideals [23].

We will often use the *subsequence feature mapping* $\phi : \Sigma^* \to \mathbb{R}^{\mathbb{N}}$ which associates to $x \in \Sigma^*$ a vector $\phi(x) = (y_u)_{u \in \Sigma^*}$ whose non-zero components correspond to the subsequences of x and are all equal to one:[1]

$$y_u = \begin{cases} 1 & \text{if } u \sqsubseteq x, \\ 0 & \text{otherwise.} \end{cases} \tag{1}$$

3   Linear Separability of Piecewise-Testable Languages

This section shows that any piecewise-testable language is finitely linearly separable for the subsequence feature mapping.

We will show that every piecewise-testable language is given by some *decision list* of shuffle ideals (a rather special kind of Boolean function). This suffices to

---

[1] Elements $u \in \Sigma^*$ can be used as indices since Σ^* and $\mathbb{N}$ are isomorphic.

prove the finite linear separability of piecewise-testable languages since decision lists are known to be linearly separable Boolean functions [3].

We will say that a string $u \in \Sigma^*$ is *decisive* for a language $L \subseteq \Sigma^*$, if $\text{III}(u) \subseteq L$ or $\text{III}(u) \subseteq \overline{L}$. The string u is said to be *positive-decisive* for L when $\text{III}(u) \subseteq L$ (*negative-decisive* when $\text{III}(u) \subseteq \overline{L}$). Note that when u is positive-decisive (negative-decisive),

$$x \in \text{III}(u) \Rightarrow x \in L \quad (\text{resp. } x \in \text{III}(u) \Rightarrow x \notin L). \tag{2}$$

Lemma 1 (Decisive strings). *Let $L \subseteq \Sigma^*$ be a piecewise-testable language, then there exists a decisive string $u \in \Sigma^*$ for L.*

Proof. We will prove that this property (existence of a decisive string) holds for shuffle ideals and that it is preserved under the Boolean operations (negation, intersection, union). This will imply that it holds for all finite Boolean combinations of shuffle ideals, i.e., for all PT languages.

By definition, a shuffle ideal $\text{III}(u)$ admits u as a decisive string. It is also clear that if u is decisive for some PT language L, then u is also decisive for $\overline{L}$. Thus, the existence of a decisive string is preserved under negation. For the remainder of the proof, L_1 and L_2 will denote two PT languages over Σ.

If u_1 is positive-decisive for L_1 and u_2 is positive-decisive for L_2, $\text{III}(u_1) \cap \text{III}(u_2) \subseteq L = L_1 \cap L_2$. $\text{III}(u_1) \cap \text{III}(u_2)$ is not empty since it contains, for example, $u_1 u_2$. For any string $u \in \text{III}(u_1) \cap \text{III}(u_2)$, $\text{III}(u) \subseteq \text{III}(u_1) \cap \text{III}(u_2)$, thus any such u is positive-decisive for L. Similarly, when u_1 is negative-decisive for L_1 and u_2 negative-decisive for L_2 any $u \in \text{III}(u_1) \cup \text{III}(u_2)$ is negative-decisive for $L = L_1 \cap L_2$. Finally, if u_1 is positive-decisive for L_1 and u_2 negative-decisive for L_2 then any $u \in \text{III}(u_2)$ is negative-decisive for $L = L_1 \cap L_2 \subseteq L_1$. This shows that the existence of a decisive string is preserved under intersection.

The existence of a decisive string is also preserved under union. If u_1 is positive-decisive for L_1 and u_2 positive-decisive for L_2, then any $u \in \text{III}(u_1) \cup \text{III}(u_2)$ is positive-decisive for $L = L_1 \cup L_2$. Similarly, when u_1 is negative-decisive for L_1 and u_2 negative-decisive for L_2, any $u \in \text{III}(u_1) \cap \text{III}(u_2) \neq \emptyset$ is negative-decisive for $L = L_1 \cup L_2$. Lastly, if u_1 is positive-decisive for L_1 and u_2 is negative-decisive for L_2 then any $u \in \text{III}(u_1)$ is positive-decisive for $L = L_1 \cup L_2$. $\qquad \square$

We say that u is *minimally decisive* for L if it admits no proper subsequence $v \sqsubseteq u$ that is decisive for L.

Lemma 2 (Finiteness of the set of minimally-decisive strings). *Let $L \subseteq \Sigma^*$ be a PT language and let $D \subseteq \Sigma^*$ be the set of all minimally decisive strings for L, then D is a finite set.*

Proof. Observe that D is a *subsequence-free* subset of Σ^*: no element of D is a proper subsequence of another. Thus, the finiteness of D follows directly from Theorem 1 below. $\qquad \square$

The following result, on which Lemma 2 is based, is a non-trivial theorem of word combinatorics which was originally discovered, in different forms, by Higman [15] in 1952 and Haines [13] in 1969. The interested reader could refer to [19, Theorem 2.6] for a modern presentation.

Theorem 1 ([13, 15]). *Let Σ be a finite alphabet and $L \subseteq \Sigma^*$ a language containing no two distinct strings x and y such that $x \sqsubseteq y$. Then L is finite.*

The definitions and the results just presented can be generalized to decisiveness modulo a set V: we will say that a string u is *decisive modulo some* $V \subseteq \Sigma^*$ if $V \cap \text{III}(u) \subseteq L$ or $V \cap \text{III}(u) \subseteq \overline{L}$. As before, we will refer to the two cases as *positive-* and *negative-decisiveness modulo* V and similarly define *minimally decisive strings modulo* V. These definitions coincide with ordinary decisiveness when $V = \Sigma^*$.

Lemma 3 (Finiteness of the set of minimally-decisive strings modulo V). *Let $L, V \subseteq \Sigma^*$ be two PT languages and let $D \subseteq \Sigma^*$ be the set of all minimally decisive strings for L modulo V, then D is a non-empty finite set.*

Proof. Lemma 1 on the existence of decisive strings can be generalized straightforwardly to the case of decisiveness modulo a PT language V: if $L, V \subseteq \Sigma^*$ are PT and $V \neq \emptyset$, then there exists $u \in V$ such that u is decisive modulo V for L. Indeed, by Lemma 1, for any language of the form $\text{III}(s)$ there exists a decisive string $u \in V \cap \text{III}(s)$. The generalization follows by replacing $\text{III}(X)$ with $V \cap \text{III}(X)$ in the proof of Lemma 1.

Similarly, in view of Lemma 2, it is clear that there can only be finitely many minimally decisive strings for L modulo V. □

Theorem 2 (PT decision list). *If $L \subseteq \Sigma^*$ is PT then L is equivalent to some finite decision list Δ over shuffle ideals.*

Proof. Consider the sequence of PT languages $V_1, V_2, \ldots$ defined according to the following process:

- $V_1 = \Sigma^*$.
- When $V_i \neq \emptyset$, V_{i+1} is constructed from V_i in the following way. Let $D_i \subseteq V_i$ be the nonempty and finite set of minimally decisive strings u for L modulo V_i. The strings in D_i are either all positive-decisive modulo V_i or all negative-decisive modulo V_i. Indeed, if $u \in D_i$ is positive-decisive and $v \in D_i$ is negative-decisive then $uv \in \text{III}(u) \cap \text{III}(v)$, which generates a contradiction. Define σ_i as $\sigma_i = 1$ when all strings of D_i are positive-decisive, $\sigma_i = 0$ when they are negative-decisive modulo V_i and define V_{i+1} by:

$$V_{i+1} = V_i \setminus \text{III}(D_i), \tag{3}$$

with $\text{III}(D_i) = \bigcup_{u \in D_i} \text{III}(u)$.

We show that this process terminates, that is $V_{N+1} = \emptyset$ for some $N > 0$. Assume the contrary. Then, the process generates an infinite sequence $D_1, D_2, \ldots$. Construct an infinite sequence $X = (x_n)_{n \in \mathbb{N}}$ by selecting a string $x_n \in D_n$ for any $n \in \mathbb{N}$. By construction, $D_{n+1} \subseteq \overline{\text{III}(D_n)}$ for all $n \in \mathbb{N}$, thus all strings

x_n are necessarily distinct. Define a new sequence $(y_n)_{n\in\mathbb{N}}$ by: $y_1 = x_1$ and $y_{n+1} = x_{\psi(n)}$, where $\psi : \mathbb{N} \to \mathbb{N}$ is defined for all $n \in \mathbb{N}$ by:

$$\psi(n) = \begin{cases} \min\{k \in \mathbb{N} : \{y_1, \ldots, y_n, x_k\} \text{ is subsequence-free}\}, & \text{if such a } k \text{ exists,} \\ \infty & \text{otherwise.} \end{cases} \tag{4}$$

We cannot have $\psi(n) \neq \infty$ for all $n > 0$ since the set $Y = \{y_1, y_2, \ldots\}$ would then be (by construction) subsequence-free and infinite. Thus, $\psi(n) = \infty$ for some $n > 0$. But then any x_k, $k \in \mathbb{N}$, is a subsequence of an element of $\{y_1, \ldots, y_n\}$. Since the set of subsequences of $\{y_1, \ldots, y_n\}$ is finite, this would imply that X is finite and lead to a contradiction.

Thus, there exists an integer $N > 0$ such that $V_{N+1} = \emptyset$ and the process described generates a finite sequence $D = (D_1, \ldots, D_N)$ of nonempty sets as well as a sequence $\sigma = (\sigma_i) \in \{0, 1\}^N$. Let Δ be the decision list

$$(\text{III}(D_1), \sigma_1), \ldots, (\text{III}(D_N), \sigma_N). \tag{5}$$

Let $\Delta_n : \Sigma^* \to \{0, 1\}$, $n = 1, \ldots, N$, be the mapping defined for all $x \in \Sigma^*$ by:

$$\forall x \in \Sigma^*, \quad \Delta_n(x) = \begin{cases} \sigma_n & \text{if } x \in \text{III}(D_n), \\ \Delta_{n+1}(x) & \text{otherwise,} \end{cases} \tag{6}$$

with $\Delta_{N+1}(x) = \sigma_N$. It is straightforward to verify that Δ_n coincides with the characteristic function of L over $\bigcup_{i=1}^n \text{III}(D_i)$. This follows directly from the definition of decisiveness. In particular, since

$$V_n = \bigcap_{i=1}^{n-1} \overline{\text{III}(D_i)} \tag{7}$$

and $V_{N+1} = \emptyset$,

$$\bigcup_{i=1}^N \text{III}(D_i) = \Sigma^*, \tag{8}$$

and Δ coincides with the characteristic function of L everywhere. $\square$

Using this result, we show that a PT language is linearly separable with a finite-dimensional weight vector.

Corollary 1. *For any PT language L, there exists a weight vector $w \in \mathbb{R}^{\mathbb{N}}$ with finite support such that $L = \{x : \text{sgn}(\langle w, \phi(x)\rangle) > 0\}$, where ϕ is the subsequence feature mapping.*

Proof. Let L be a PT language. By Theorem 2, there exists a decision list $(\text{III}(D_1), \sigma_1), \ldots, (\text{III}(D_N), \sigma_N)$ equivalent to L where each D_n, $n = 1, \ldots, N$, is a finite set. We construct a weight vector $w = (w_u)_{u\in\Sigma^*} \in \mathbb{R}^{\mathbb{N}}$ by starting with $w = 0$ and modifying its coordinates as follows:

$$\forall u \in D_n, \quad w_u = \begin{cases} +(|\displaystyle\sum_{\{v\in\bigcup_{i=n+1}^N D_i : w_v < 0\}} w_v| + 1) & \text{if } \sigma_i = 1, \\ -(|\displaystyle\sum_{\{v\in\bigcup_{i=n+1}^N D_i : w_v > 0\}} w_v| + 1) & \text{otherwise,} \end{cases} \tag{9}$$

in the order $n = N, N - 1, \ldots, 1$. By construction, the decision list is equivalent to $\{x : \text{sgn}(\langle w, \phi(x) \rangle) > 0\}$. Since each D_n, $n = 1, \ldots, N$, is finite, the weight vector w has only a finite number of non-zero coordinates. □

The dimension of the feature space associated to ϕ is infinite, the next section shows that the kernel associated to ϕ can be computed efficiently however.

4   Efficient Kernel Computation

The positive definite symmetric kernel K associated to the subsequence feature mapping ϕ is defined by:

$$\forall x, y \in \Sigma^*, \quad K(x, y) = \langle \phi(x), \phi(y) \rangle = \sum_{u \in \Sigma^*} [\![u \sqsubseteq x]\!] \, [\![u \sqsubseteq y]\!], \qquad (10)$$

where $[\![P]\!]$ represents the 0-1 truth value of the predicate P. Thus, $K(x, y)$ counts the number of subsequences common to x and y, without multiplicity.

This subsequence kernel is closely related to but distinct from the one defined by Lodhi et al. [17]. Indeed, the kernel of Lodhi et al. counts the number of occurrences of subsequences common to x and y. Thus, for example $K(abc, acbc) = 8$, since the cardinal of the set of common subsequences of abc and $acbc$, $\{\epsilon, a, b, c, ab, ac, bc, abc\}$, is 8. But, the kernel of Lodhi et al. (without penalty factor) would instead associate the value 9 to the pair $(abc, acbc)$.

A string with n distinct symbols has at least 2^n possible subsequences, so a naive computation of $K(x, y)$ based on the enumeration of the subsequences of x and y is inefficient. We will show however that $K(x, y)$ can be computed in quadratic time, $O(|\Sigma||x||y|)$, using a method suggested by Derryberry [8] which turns out to be somewhat similar to that of Lodhi et al.

For any symbol $a \in \Sigma$ and a string $u \in \Sigma^*$, define $\text{last}_a(u)$ to be 0 if a does not occur in u and the largest index i such that $u[i] = a$ otherwise. For $x, y \in \Sigma^*$, define K' by:

$$\forall x, y \in \Sigma^*, \quad K'(x, y) = \sum_{u \in \Sigma^+} [\![u \sqsubseteq x]\!] \, [\![u \sqsubseteq y]\!]. \qquad (11)$$

Thus, $K'(x, y)$ is the number of nonempty subsequences without multiplicity common to x and y. For any $a \in \Sigma$, define K_a by:

$$\forall x, y \in \Sigma^*, \quad K_a(x, y) = \sum_{u \in \Sigma^* a} [\![u \sqsubseteq x]\!] \, [\![u \sqsubseteq y]\!] \qquad (12)$$

be the number of such subsequences ending in a. Then, by definition of K',

$$\forall x, y \in \Sigma^*, \quad K'(x, y) = \sum_{a \in \Sigma} K_a(x, y). \qquad (13)$$

By definition, if a does not appear in x and or y, then $K_a(x, y) = 0$. Otherwise, let ua be a common subsequence of x and y with $u \neq \emptyset$, then u is a non-empty subsequence of x and y. Thus,

$$K_a(x, y) = \begin{cases} 0 & \text{if } \text{last}_a(x) = 0 \text{ or } \text{last}_a(y) = 0 \\ 1 + K'(x[1 : \text{last}_a(x) - 1], y[1 : \text{last}_a(y) - 1]) & \text{otherwise,} \end{cases} \quad (14)$$

where the addition of 1 in the last equation accounts for the common subsequence $ua = a$ with $u = \epsilon$ which is not computed by K'. The subsequence kernel K, which does count the empty string ϵ as a common subsequence, is given by $K(x, y) = K'(x, y) + 1$. A straightforward recursive algorithm based on Equation 14 can be used to compute K in time $O(|\Sigma'||x||y|)$, where $\Sigma' \subseteq \Sigma$ is the alphabet reduced to the symbols appearing in x and y.

The kernel of Lodhi et al. [17] was shown to be a specific instance of a rational kernel over the $(+, \times)$ semiring [6]. Similarly, it can be shown that the subsequence kernel just examined is related to rational kernels over the $(+, \times)$ semiring.

5   Learning Linearly Separable Languages

This section deals with the problem of learning PT languages. In previous sections, we showed that using the subsequence feature mapping ϕ, or equivalently a subsequence kernel K that can be computed efficiently, PT languages are finitely linearly separable.

These results suggest the use of a linear separation learning technique such as support vector machines (SVM) combined with the subsequence kernel K for learning PT languages [5, 7, 25]. In view of the estimate of the complexity of the subsequence kernel computation presented in the previous section, the complexity of the algorithm for a sample of size m where $x_{\max}$ is the longest string is in $O(\text{QP}(m)) + m^2 |x_{\max}|^2 |\Sigma|)$, where $\text{QP}(m)$ is the cost of solving a quadratic programming problem of size m, which is at most $O(m^3)$.

We will use the standard margin bound to analyze the behavior of that algorithm. Note however that since the VC-dimension of the set of PT languages is infinite, PAC-learning is not possible and we need to resort to a weaker guarantee.

Let $(x_1, y_1), \ldots, (x_m, y_m) \in X \times \{-1, +1\}$ be a sample extracted from a set X ($X = \Sigma^*$ when learning languages). The margin ρ of a hyperplane with weight vector $w \in \mathbb{R}^N$ over this sample is defined by:

$$\rho = \inf_{i=1,\ldots,m} \frac{y_i \langle w, \phi(x_i) \rangle}{\|w\|}.$$

The sample is linearly separated by w iff $\rho > 0$. Note that our definition holds even for infinite-size samples.

The linear separation result shown for the class of PT languages is in fact strong. Indeed, for any weight vector $w \in \mathbb{R}^N$, let $\text{supp}(w) = \{i : w_i \neq 0\}$ denote the support of w, then the following property holds for PT languages.

Definition 1. *Let C be a concept class defined over a set X. We will say that a concept $c \in C$ is* finitely linearly separable, *if there exists a mapping $\phi : X \to \{0, 1\}^N$ and a weight vector $w \in \mathbb{R}^N$ with finite support, $|\text{supp}(w)| < \infty$, such that*

$$c = \{x \in X : \langle w, \phi(x) \rangle > 0\}. \quad (15)$$

The concept class C is said to be finitely linearly separable *if all $c \in C$ are finitely linearly separable for the same mapping ϕ.*

Note that in general a linear separation in an infinite-dimensional space does not guarantee a strictly positive margin ρ. Points in an infinite-dimensional space may be arbitrarily close to the separating hyperplane and their infimum distance could be zero. However, finitely linear separation does guarantee a strictly positive margin.

Proposition 1. *Let C be a class of concepts defined over a set X that is finitely linearly separable using the mapping $\phi : X \to \{0,1\}^{\mathbb{N}}$ and a weight vector $w \in \mathbb{R}^{\mathbb{N}}$. Then, the margin ρ of the hyperplane defined by w is strictly positive, $\rho > 0$.*

Proof. By assumption, the support of w is finite. For any $x \in X$, let $\phi'(x)$ be the projection of $\phi(x)$ on the span of w, $\mathrm{span}(w)$. Thus, $\phi'(x)$ is a finite-dimensional vector for any $x \in X$ with discrete coordinates in $\{0,1\}$. Thus, the set of $S = \{\phi'(x) : x \in X\}$ is finite. Since for any $x \in X$, $\langle w, \phi(x) \rangle = \langle w, \phi'(x) \rangle$, the margin is defined over a finite set:

$$\rho = \inf_{x \in X} \frac{y_x \langle w, \phi'(x) \rangle}{\|w\|} = \min_{z \in S} \frac{y_x \langle w, z \rangle}{\|w\|} > 0, \tag{16}$$

and is thus strictly positive. $\square$

The following general margin bound holds for all classifiers consistent with the training data [4].

Theorem 3 (Margin bound). *Define the class $\mathcal{F}$ of real-valued functions on the ball of radius R in $\mathbb{R}^n$ as*

$$\mathcal{F} = \{x \mapsto \langle w, x \rangle : \|w\| \leq 1, \|x\| \leq R\}. \tag{17}$$

There is a constant α_0 such that, for all distributions D over X, with probability at least $1 - \delta$ over m independently generated examples, if a classifier $\mathrm{sgn}(f)$, with $f \in \mathcal{F}$, has margin at least ρ on the training examples, then the generalization error of $\mathrm{sgn}(f)$ is no more than

$$\frac{\alpha_0}{m} \left(\frac{R^2}{\rho^2} \log^2 m + \log(\frac{1}{\delta}) \right). \tag{18}$$

Note that the notion of linear separability with a finite sample may be weak. Any sample of size m can be trivially made linearly separable by using an embedding $\phi : X \to \{0,1\}^{\mathbb{N}}$ mapping each point x to a distinct dimension. However, the support of the weight vector increases with the size of the sample and is not bounded. Also, the margin ρ for such a mapping is $\frac{1}{2\sqrt{m}}$ and thus goes to zero as m increases, and the ratio $(R/\rho)^2$, where $R = 1$ is the radius of the sphere containing the sample points, is $(R/\rho)^2 = 4m$. Thus, such trivial linear separations do not guarantee convergence. The bound of Theorem 3 is not effective with that value of $(R/\rho)^2$.

But, the result of the previous sections guarantee linear separability for samples of infinite size with strictly positive margin.

Theorem 4. *Let C be a finitely linearly separable concept class over X with a feature mapping $\phi : X \rightarrow \{0,1\}^{\mathbb{N}}$. Define the class $\mathcal{F}$ of real-valued functions on the ball of radius R in $\mathbb{R}^n$ as*

$$\mathcal{F} = \{x \mapsto \langle w, \phi(x) \rangle : \|w\| \leq 1, \|\phi(x)\| \leq R\}. \tag{19}$$

There is a constant α_0 such that, for all distributions D over X, for any concept $c \in C$, there exists $\rho_0 > 0$ such that with probability at least $1 - \delta$ over m independently generated examples according to D, there exists a classifier $\mathrm{sgn}(f)$, with $f \in \mathcal{F}$, with margin at least ρ_0 on the training examples, and generalization error no more than

$$\frac{\alpha_0}{m} \left(\frac{R^2}{\rho_0^2} \log^2 m + \log(\frac{1}{\delta}) \right). \tag{20}$$

Proof. Fix a concept $c \in C$. By assumption, c is finitely linearly separable by some hyperplane. By Proposition 1, the corresponding margin ρ_0 is strictly positive, $\rho_0 > 0$. ρ_0 is less than or equal to the margin of the optimal hyperplane ρ separating c from $X \setminus c$ based on the m examples.

Since the full sample X is linearly separable, so is any subsample of size m. Let $f \in \mathcal{F}$ be the linear function corresponding to the optimal hyperplane over a sample of size m drawn according to D. Then, the margin of f is at least as large as ρ since not all points of X are used to define f. Thus, the margin of f is greater than or equal to ρ_0 and the statement follows Theorem 3. □

Theorem 4 applies directly to the case of PT languages. Observe that in the statement of the theorem, ρ_0 depends on the particular concept c learned but does not depend on the sample size m.

Note that the linear separating hyperplane with finite-support weight vector is not necessarily an optimal hyperplane. The following proposition shows however that when the mapping ϕ is surjective the optimal hyperplane has the same property.

Proposition 2. *Let $c \in C$ be a finitely linearly separable concept with the feature mapping $\phi : X \rightarrow \{0,1\}^{\mathbb{N}}$ and weight vector w with finite support, $|\mathrm{supp}(w)| < \infty$, such that $\phi(X) = \mathbb{R}^{\mathbb{N}}$. Assume that ϕ is surjective, then the weight vector $\hat{w}$ corresponding to the optimal hyperplane for c has also a finite support and $\mathrm{supp}(\hat{w}) \subseteq \mathrm{supp}(w)$.*

Proof. Assume that $\hat{w}_i \neq 0$ for some $i \notin \mathrm{supp}(w)$. We first show that this implies the existence of two points $x_- \notin c$ and $x_+ \in c$ such that $\phi(x_-)$ and $\phi(x_+)$ differ only by their ith coordinate.

Let ϕ' be the mapping such that for all $x \in X$, $\phi'(x)$ differs from $\phi(x)$ only by the ith coordinate and let $\hat{w}'$ be the vector derived from $\hat{w}$ by setting the ith coordinate to zero. Since ϕ is surjective, thus $\phi^{-1}(\phi'(x)) \neq \emptyset$. If x and any $x' \in \phi^{-1}(\phi'(x))$ are in the same class for all $x \in X$, then

$$\mathrm{sgn}(\langle \hat{w}, \phi(x) \rangle) = \mathrm{sgn}(\langle \hat{w}, \phi'(x) \rangle). \tag{21}$$

Fix $x \in X$. Assume for example that $[\phi'(x)]_i = 0$ and $[\phi(x)]_i = 1$, then $\langle \hat{w}, \phi'(x) \rangle = \langle \hat{w}', \phi(x) \rangle$. Thus, in view of Equation 21,

$$\text{sgn}(\langle \hat{w}, \phi(x) \rangle) = \text{sgn}(\langle \hat{w}, \phi'(x) \rangle) = \text{sgn}(\langle \hat{w}', \phi(x) \rangle). \tag{22}$$

We obtain similarly that $\text{sgn}(\langle \hat{w}, \phi(x) \rangle) = \text{sgn}(\langle \hat{w}', \phi(x) \rangle)$ when $[\phi'(x)]_i = 1$ and $[\phi(x)]_i = 0$. Thus, for all $x \in X$, $\text{sgn}(\langle \hat{w}, \phi(x) \rangle) = \text{sgn}(\langle \hat{w}', \phi(x) \rangle)$. This leads to a contradiction, since the norm of the weight vector for the optimal hyperplane is the smallest among all weight vectors of separating hyperplanes.

This proves the existence of the $x_- \notin c$ and $x_+ \in c$ with $\phi(x_-)$ and $\phi(x_+)$ differing only by their ith coordinate.

But, since $i \notin \text{supp}(w)$, for two such points $x_- \notin c$ and $x_+ \in c$, $\langle w, \phi(x_-) \rangle = \langle w, \phi(x_+) \rangle$. This contradicts the status of $\text{sgn}(\langle w, \phi(x) \rangle)$ as a linear separator. Thus, our original hypothesis cannot hold: there exists no $i \notin \text{supp}(w)$ such that $\hat{w}_i \neq 0$ and the support of $\hat{w}$ is included in that of w.   □

In the following, we will give another analysis of the generalization error of SVMs for finitely separable hyperplanes using the following bound of Vapnik based on the number of essential support vectors:

$$\text{E}[error(h_m)] \leq \frac{\text{E}[(\frac{R_{m+1}}{\rho_{m+1}})^2]}{m+1}, \tag{23}$$

where h_m is the optimal hyperplane hypothesis based on a sample of m points, $error(h_m)$ the generalization error of that hypothesis, R_{m+1} the smallest radius of a set of essential support vectors of an optimal hyperplane defined over a set of $m+1$ points, and ρ_{m+1} its margin.

Let c be a finitely separable concept. When the mapping ϕ is surjective, by Proposition 2, the weight vector $\hat{w}$ of the optimal separating hyperplane for c has finite support and the margin ρ_0 is positive $\rho_0 > 0$. Thus, the smallest radius of a set of essential support vectors for that hyperplane is $R = \sqrt{N(c)}$ where $N(c) = |\text{supp}(\hat{w})|$. If R_{m+1} tends to R when m tends to infinity, then for all $\epsilon > 0$, there exists M_ϵ such that for $m > M_\epsilon$, $R^2(m) \leq N(c) + \epsilon$. In view of Equation 23 the expectation of the generalization error of the optimal hyperplane based on a sample of size m is bounded by

$$\text{E}[error(h_m)] \leq \frac{\text{E}[(\frac{R_{m+1}}{\rho_{m+1}})^2]}{m+1} \leq \frac{N(c) + \epsilon}{\rho_0^2(m+1)}. \tag{24}$$

This upper bound varies as $\frac{1}{m}$.

6   Finite Cover with Regular Languages

In previous sections, we introduced a feature mapping ϕ, the subsequence mapping, for which PT languages are finitely linearly separable. The subsequence mapping can be defined in terms of the set of shuffle ideals of all strings,

$U_u = \mathrm{III}(u)$, $u \in \Sigma^*$. A string x can belong only to a finite number of shuffle ideals U_u, which determine the non-zero coordinates of $\phi(x)$. This leads us to consider other such mappings based on other regular sets U_u and investigate the properties of languages linearly separated for such mappings. The main result of this section is that all such linearly separated languages are regular.

6.1   Definitions

Let $U_n \subseteq \Sigma^*$, $n \in \mathbb{N}$, be a countable family of sets, such any string $x \in \Sigma^*$ lies in at least one and at most finitely many U_n. Thus, for all $x \in \Sigma^*$,

$$1 \le \sum_n \psi_n(x) < \infty,$$

where ψ_n is the characteristic function of U_n:

$$\psi_n(x) = \begin{cases} 1 & \text{if } x \in U_n \\ 0 & \text{otherwise.} \end{cases}$$

Any such family $(U_n)_{n \in \mathbb{N}}$ is called a *finite cover* of Σ^*. If additionally, each U_n is a regular set and Σ^* is a member of the family, we will say that $(U_n)_{n \in \mathbb{N}}$ is a *regular finite cover* (RFC).

Any finite cover $(U_n)_{n \in \mathbb{N}}$ naturally defines a positive definite symmetric kernel K over Σ^* given by:

$$\forall x, y \in \Sigma^*, \quad K(x, y) = \sum_n \psi_n(x) \psi_n(y).$$

Its finiteness, symmetry, and positive definiteness follow its construction as a dot product. $K(x, y)$ counts the number of common sets U_n that x and y belong to.

We may view $\psi(x)$ as an infinite-dimensional vector in the space $\mathbb{R}^{\mathbb{N}}$, in which case we can write $K(x, y) = \langle \psi(x), \psi(y) \rangle$. We will say that ψ is an *RFC-induced embedding*. Any weight vector $w \in \mathbb{R}^{\mathbb{N}}$ defines a language $L(w)$ given by:

$$L(w) = \{x \in \Sigma^* : \langle w, \psi(x) \rangle > 0\}.$$

Note that since Σ^* is a member of every RFC, $K(x, y) \ge 1$.

6.2   Main Result

The main result of this section is that any finitely linearly separable language under an RFC embedding is regular. The converse is clearly false. For a given RFC, not all regular languages can be defined by some separating hyperplane. A simple counterexample is provided with the RFC $\{\emptyset, U, \Sigma^* \setminus U, \Sigma^*\}$ where U is some regular language. For this RFC, U, its complement, Σ^*, and the empty set are linearly separable but no other regular language is.

Theorem 5. *Let $\psi : \Sigma^* \to \{0, 1\}^{\mathbb{N}}$ be an RFC-induced embedding and let $w \in \mathbb{R}^{\mathbb{N}}$ be a finitely supported weight vector. Then, the language $L(w) = \{x \in \Sigma^* : \langle w, \psi(x) \rangle > 0\}$ is regular.*

Proof. Let $f : \Sigma^* \to \mathbb{R}$ be the function defined by:

$$f(x) = \langle w, \psi(x) \rangle = \sum_{i=1}^{N} w_i \psi_i(x), \tag{25}$$

where the weights $w_i \in \mathbb{R}$ and the integer $N = |\operatorname{supp}(w)|$ are independent of x. Observe that f can only take on finitely many real values $\{r_k : k = 1, \ldots, K\}$. Let $L_{r_k} \subseteq \Sigma^*$ be defined by

$$L_{r_k} = f^{-1}(r_k). \tag{26}$$

A subset $I \subseteq \{1, 2, \ldots, N\}$ is said to be r_k-*acceptable* if $\sum_{i \in I} w_i = r_k$. Any such r_k-acceptable set corresponds to a set of strings $L_I \subseteq \Sigma^*$ such that

$$L_I = \left(\bigcap_{i \in I} \psi_i^{-1}(1) \right) \setminus \left(\bigcup_{i \in \{1, \ldots, N\} \setminus I} \psi_i^{-1}(1) \right) = \left(\bigcap_{i \in I} U_i \right) \setminus \left(\bigcup_{i \in \{1, \ldots, N\} \setminus I} U_i \right).$$

Thus, L_I is regular because each U_i is regular by definition of the RFC. Each L_{r_k} is the union of finitely many r_k-acceptable L_I's, and L is the union of the L_{r_k} for positive r_k. $\qquad \square$

Theorem 5 provides a representation of regular languages in terms of some subsets of $\mathbb{R}^N$. Although we present a construction for converting this representation to a more familiar one such as a finite automaton, our construction is not necessarily efficient. Indeed, for some r_k there may be exponentially many r_k-acceptable L_Is. This underscores the specific feature of our method. Our objective is to learn regular languages efficiently using some representation, not necessarily automata.

6.3   Representer Theorem

Let $S = \{x_j : j = 1, \ldots, m\} \subseteq \Sigma^*$ be a finite set of strings and $\alpha \in \mathbb{R}^m$. The pair (S, α) defines a language $L(S, \alpha)$ given by:

$$L(S, \alpha) = \{x \in \Sigma^* : \sum_{j=1}^{m} \alpha_j K(x, x_j) > 0\}. \tag{27}$$

Let $w = \sum_{j=1}^{m} \alpha_j \psi(x_j)$. Since each $\psi(x_j)$ has only a finite number of non-zero components, the support of w is finite and by Theorem 5, $L(S, \alpha)$ can be seen to be regular. Conversely, the following result holds.

Theorem 6. *Let* $\psi : \Sigma^* \to \{0, 1\}^N$ *be an RFC-induced embedding and let* $w \in \mathbb{R}^N$ *be a finitely supported weight vector. Let* $L(w)$ *be defined by* $L(w) = \{x \in \Sigma^* : \langle w, \psi(x) \rangle > 0\}$. *Then, there exist* (x_j), $j = 1, \ldots, m$, *and* $\alpha \in \mathbb{R}^m$ *such that* $L(w) = L(S, \alpha) = \{x \in \Sigma^* : \sum_{j=1}^{m} \alpha_j K(x, x_j) > 0\}$.

Proof. Without loss of generality, we can assume that no cover set $U_n \neq \Sigma^*$, U_n is fully contained in a finite union of the other cover sets $U_{n'}$, $U_{n'} \neq \Sigma^*$. Otherwise, the corresponding feature component can be omitted for linear separation. Now, for any $U_n \neq \Sigma^*$, let $x_n \in U_n$ be a string that does not belong to any finite union of $U_{n'}$, $U_{n'} \neq \Sigma^*$. For $U_n = \Sigma^*$, choose an arbitrary string $x_n \in \Sigma^*$. Then, by definition of the x_n,

$$\langle w, \psi(x) \rangle = \sum_{j=1}^{m} w_j K(x, x_j). \tag{28}$$

This proves the claim. □

This result shows that any finitely linearly separable language can be inferred from a finite sample.

6.4 Further Characterization

It is natural to ask what property of finitely supported hyperplanes is responsible for their inducing regular languages. In fact, Theorem 5 is readily generalized:

Theorem 7. *Let $f : \Sigma^* \to \mathbb{R}$ be a function such that there exist an integer $N \in \mathbb{N}$ and a function $g : \{0, 1\}^N \to \mathbb{R}$ such that*

$$\forall x \in \Sigma^*, \quad f(x) = g(\psi_1(x), \psi_2(x), \dots, \psi_N(x)), \tag{29}$$

Thus, the value of f depends on a fixed finite number of components of ψ. Then, for any $r \in \mathbb{R}$, the language $L = \{x \in \Sigma^* : f(x) = r\}$ is regular.

Proof. Since f is a function of finitely many binary variables, its range is finite. From here, the proof proceeds exactly as in the proof of Theorem 5, with identical definitions for $\{r_k\}$ and L_{r_k}. □

This leads to the following corollary.

Corollary 2. *Let $f : \Sigma^* \to \mathbb{R}$ be a function satisfying the conditions of Theorem 7. Then, for any $r \in \mathbb{R}$, the languages $L_1 = \{x \in \Sigma^* : f(x) > r\}$ and $L_2 = \{x \in \Sigma^* : f(x) < r\}$ are regular.*

7 Conclusion

We introduced a new framework for learning languages that consists of mapping strings to a high-dimensional feature space and seeking linear separation in that space. We applied this technique to the non-trivial case of PT languages and showed that this class of languages is indeed linearly separable and that the corresponding subsequence kernel can be computed efficiently.

Many other classes of languages could be studied following the same ideas. This could lead to new results related to the problem of learning families of languages or classes of automata.

Acknowledgments

Much of the work by Leonid Kontorovich was done while visiting the Hebrew University, in Jerusalem, Israel, in the summer of 2003. Many thanks to Yoram Singer for providing hosting and guidance at the Hebrew University. Thanks also to Daniel Neill and Martin Zinkevich for helpful discussions. This work was supported in part by the IST Programme of the European Community, under the PASCAL Network of Excellence, IST-2002-506778. The research at CMU was supported in part by NSF ITR grant IIS-0205456. This publication only reflects the authors' views. Mehryar Mohri's work was partially funded by the New York State Office of Science Technology and Academic Research (NYSTAR).

References

1. Dana Angluin. On the complexity of minimum inference of regular sets. *Information and Control*, 3(39):337–350, 1978.
2. Dana Angluin. Inference of reversible languages. *Journal of the ACM (JACM)*, 3(29):741–765, 1982.
3. Martin Anthony. Threshold Functions, Decision Lists, and the Representation of Boolean Functions. Neurocolt Technical report Series NC-TR-96-028, Royal Holloway, University of London, 1996.
4. Peter Bartlett and John Shawe-Taylor. Generalization performance of support vector machines and other pattern classifiers. In *Advances in kernel methods: support vector learning*, pages 43–54. MIT Press, Cambridge, MA, USA, 1999.
5. Bernhard E. Boser, Isabelle Guyon, and Vladimir N. Vapnik. A training algorithm for optimal margin classifiers. In *Proceedings of the Fifth Annual Workshop of Computational Learning Theory*, volume 5, pages 144–152, Pittsburg, 1992. ACM.
6. Corinna Cortes, Patrick Haffner, and Mehryar Mohri. Rational Kernels: Theory and Algorithms. *Journal of Machine Learning Research (JMLR)*, 5:1035–1062, 2004.
7. Corinna Cortes and Vladimir N. Vapnik. Support-Vector Networks. *Machine Learning*, 20(3):273–297, 1995.
8. Jonathan Derryberry, 2004. Private communication.
9. Yoav Freund, Michael Kearns, Dana Ron, Ronitt Rubinfeld, Robert E. Schapire, and Linda Sellie. Efficient learning of typical finite automata from random walks. In *STOC '93: Proceedings of the twenty-fifth annual ACM symposium on Theory of computing*, pages 315–324, New York, NY, USA, 1993. ACM Press.
10. Pedro García and José Ruiz. Learning k-testable and k-piecewise testable languages from positive data. *Grammars*, 7:125–140, 2004.
11. E. Mark Gold. Language identification in the limit. *Information and Control*, 50(10):447–474, 1967.
12. E. Mark Gold. Complexity of automaton identification from given data. *Information and Control*, 3(37):302–420, 1978.
13. L. H. Haines. On free monoids partially ordered by embedding. *Journal of Combinatorial Theory*, 6:35–40, 1969.
14. David Haussler, Nick Littlestone, and Manfred K. Warmuth. Predicting $\{0, 1\}$-Functions on Randomly Drawn Points. In *Proceedings of the first annual workshop on Computational learning theory (COLT 1988)*, pages 280–296, San Francisco, CA, USA, 1988. Morgan Kaufmann Publishers Inc.

15. George Higman. Ordering by divisibility in abstract algebras. *Proceedings of The London Mathematical Society*, 2:326–336, 1952.
16. Micheal Kearns and Umesh Vazirani. *An Introduction to Computational Learning Theory*. The MIT Press, 1997.
17. Huma Lodhi, John Shawe-Taylor, Nello Cristianini, and Chris Watkins. Text classification using string kernels. In Todd K. Leen, Thomas G. Dietterich, and Volker Tresp, editors, *NIPS 2000*, pages 563–569. MIT Press, 2001.
18. M. Lothaire. *Combinatorics on Words*, volume 17 of *Encyclopedia of Mathematics and Its Applications*. Addison-Wesley, 1983.
19. Alexandru Mateescu and Arto Salomaa. *Handbook of Formal Languages, Volume 1: Word, Language, Grammar*, chapter Formal languages: an Introduction and a Synopsis, pages 1–39. Springer-Verlag New York, Inc., New York, NY, USA, 1997.
20. José Oncina, Pedro García, and Enrique Vidal. Learning subsequential transducers for pattern recognition interpretation tasks. *IEEE Trans. Pattern Anal. Mach. Intell.*, 15(5):448–458, 1993.
21. Leonard Pitt and Manfred Warmuth. The minimum consistent DFA problem cannot be approximated within any polynomial. *Journal of the Assocation for Computing Machinery*, 40(1):95–142, 1993.
22. Dana Ron, Yoram Singer, and Naftali Tishby. On the learnability and usage of acyclic probabilistic finite automata. *Journal of Computer and System Sciences*, 56(2):133–152, 1998.
23. Imre Simon. Piecewise testable events. In *Automata Theory and Formal Languages*, pages 214–222, 1975.
24. Boris A. Trakhtenbrot and Janis M. Barzdin. *Finite Automata: Behavior and Synthesis*, volume 1 of *Fundamental Studies in Computer Science*. North-Holland, Amsterdam, 1973.
25. Vladimir N. Vapnik. *Statistical Learning Theory*. John Wiley & Sons, 1998.

Smooth Boosting Using an Information-Based Criterion

Kohei Hatano

Department of Informatics, Kyushu University
hatano@i.kyushu-u.ac.jp

Abstract. Smooth boosting algorithms are variants of boosting methods which handle only smooth distributions on the data. They are proved to be noise-tolerant and can be used in the "boosting by filtering" scheme, which is suitable for learning over huge data. However, current smooth boosting algorithms have rooms for improvements: Among non-smooth boosting algorithms, real AdaBoost or InfoBoost, can perform more efficiently than typical boosting algorithms by using an information-based criterion for choosing hypotheses. In this paper, we propose a new smooth boosting algorithm with another information-based criterion based on Gini index. we show that it inherits the advantages of two approaches, smooth boosting and information-based approaches.

1 Introduction

In recent years, huge data have become available due to the development of computers and the Internet. As size of such huge data can reach hundreds of gigabytes in knowledge discovery and machine learning tasks, it is important to make knowledge discovery or machine learning algorithms scalable. Sampling is one of effective techniques to deal with large data. There are many results on sampling techniques [23, 5] and applications to data mining tasks such as decision tree learning [7], support vector machine [2], and boosting [5, 6].

Especially, boosting is simple and efficient learning method among machine learning algorithms. The basic idea of boosting is to learn many slightly accurate hypotheses (or *weak hypotheses*) with respect to different distributions over the data, and to combine them into a highly accurate one. Originally, boosting was invented under the *boosting by filtering* framework [21, 10] (or the filtering framework), where the booster can sample examples randomly from the whole instance space. On the other hand, in the *boosting by subsampling* framework [21, 10] (or, the subsampling framework), the booster is given a bunch of examples in advance. Of course, the subsampling framework is more suitable when the size of data is relatively small. But, for large data, there are two advantages of the filtering framework over the subsampling framework. First, the space complexity is reduced as the booster "filters" examples and accepts only necessary ones (See, e.g., [10]). The second advantage is that the booster can automatically determine the sufficient sample size. Note that it is not trivial to determine the

J.L. Balcázar, P.M. Long, and F. Stephan (Eds.): ALT 2006, LNAI 4264, pp. 304–318, 2006.

sufficient sample size a priori in the subsampling framework. So the boosting by filtering framework seems to fit learning over huge data. However, early boosting algorithms [21, 10] which work in the filtering framework were not practical, because they were not "adaptive", i.e., they need the prior knowledge on the accuracy of weak hypotheses.

MadaBoost, a modification of AdaBoost [11], is the first adaptive boosting algorithm which works in the filtering framework [6]. Combining with adaptive sampling methods [5], MadaBoost is shown to be more efficient than AdaBoost over huge data, while keeping the prediction accuracy. By its nature of updating scheme, MadaBoost is categorized as one of "smooth" boosting algorithms [12, 25, 14], where the name, smooth boosting, comes from the fact that these boosting algorithms only deal with smooth distributions over data (In contrast, for example, AdaBoost might construct exponentially skew distributions over data). Smoothness of distributions enables boosting algorithms to sample data efficiently. Also, smooth boosting algorithms have theoretical guarantees for noise tolerance in the various noisy learning settings, such as statistical query model [6] malicious noise model [25] and agnostic boosting [14].

However, there seems still room for improvements on smooth boosting. A non-smooth boosting algorithm, InfoBoost [1] (which is a special form of real AdaBoost [22]), performs more efficiently than other boosting algorithms in the boosting by subsampling framework. More precisely, given hypotheses with error $1/2 - \gamma/2$, typical boosting algorithms take $O((1/\gamma^2) \log(1/\varepsilon))$ iterations to learn a $(1 - \varepsilon)$-accurate hypothesis. On the other hand, InfoBoost learns in from $O((1/\gamma) \log(1/\varepsilon))$ to $O((1/\gamma^2) \log(1/\varepsilon))$ iterations by taking advantage of the situation when weak hypotheses have low false positive error [15, 16]. So InfoBoost can be more efficient at most by $O(1/\gamma)$ times.

The main difference between InfoBoost and other boosting algorithms such as AdaBoost or MadaBoost is the criterion for choosing weak hypotheses. Typical boosting algorithms are designed to choose hypotheses whose errors are minimum with respect to given distributions. In contrast, InfoBoost uses an information-based criterion to choose weak hypotheses. The criterion was previously proposed by Kearns and Mansour in the context of decision tree learning [18], and also applied to boosting algorithms using branching programs [19, 26]. But, so far, no smooth algorithm has such the nice property of InfoBoost.

In this paper, we propose a new smooth boosting algorithm, *GiniBoost*, which uses another information-based criterion based on *Gini index* [3]. GiniBoost learns in $O(1/\varepsilon\Delta)$ iterations, where we call Δ the "pseudo gain" of weak hypotheses (that will be defined later). As Δ varies from γ^2 to γ, our bound on iterations is potentially smaller than the $O(1/\varepsilon\gamma^2)$ bound which are achieved by previous smooth boosting algorithms [6, 25]. Unfortunately though, we have not given such a refined analysis as done for InfoBoost yet. Then, we propose an adaptive sampling procedure to estimate pseudo gains and apply GiniBoost in the filtering framework. Preliminary experiments show that GiniBoost improves MadaBoost in the filtering framework over large data.

2   Preliminaries

2.1   Learning Model

We adapt the PAC learning model [27]. Let $\mathcal{X}$ be an *instance space* and let $\mathcal{Y} = \{-1, +1\}$ be a set of labels. We assume an unknown *target function* $f : \mathcal{X} \to \mathcal{Y}$. Further we assume that f is contained in a known class $\mathcal{F}$ of functions from $\mathcal{X}$ to $\mathcal{Y}$. Let D be an unknown distribution over $\mathcal{X}$. The learner has an access to the *example oracle* $\mathrm{EX}(f, D)$. When given a call from the learner, $\mathrm{EX}(f, D)$ returns an *example* $(\boldsymbol{x}, f(\boldsymbol{x}))$ where each instance $\boldsymbol{x}$ is drawn randomly according to D. Let $\mathcal{H}$ be a hypothesis space, or a set of functions from $\mathcal{X}$ to $\mathcal{Y}$. We assume that $\mathcal{H} \supset \mathcal{F}$. For any distribution D over $\mathcal{X}$, *error* of hypothesis $h \in \mathcal{H}$ is defined as $\mathrm{err}_D(h) \stackrel{\text{def}}{=} \mathrm{Pr}_D\{h(\boldsymbol{x}) \neq f(\boldsymbol{x})\}$. Let S be a *sample*, a set of examples $((\boldsymbol{x}_1, f(\boldsymbol{x}_1)), \ldots, (\boldsymbol{x}_m, f(\boldsymbol{x}_m)))$. For any sample S, *training error* of hypothesis $h \in \mathcal{H}$ is defined as $\widehat{\mathrm{err}}_S(h) \stackrel{\text{def}}{=} |\{(\boldsymbol{x}_i, f(\boldsymbol{x}_i) \in S \mid h(\boldsymbol{x}_i) \neq f(\boldsymbol{x}_i)\}|/|S|$.

We say that learning algorithm A is a *strong learner* for $\mathcal{F}$ if and only if, for any $f \in \mathcal{F}$ and any distribution D, given ε, δ $(0 < \varepsilon, \delta < 1)$, a hypothesis space $\mathcal{H}$, and access to the example oracle $\mathrm{EX}(f, D)$ as inputs, A outputs a hypothesis $h \in \mathcal{H}$ such that $\mathrm{err}_D(h) = \mathrm{Pr}_D\{h(x) \neq f(x)\} \leq \varepsilon$ with probability at least $1-\delta$. We also consider a weaker learner. Specifically, we say that learning algorithm A is a *weak leaner*[1] for $\mathcal{F}$ if and only if, for any $f \in \mathcal{F}$, given a hypothesis space $\mathcal{H}$, and access to the example oracle $\mathrm{EX}(f, D)$ as inputs, A outputs a hypothesis $h \in \mathcal{H}$ such that $\mathrm{err}_D(h) \leq 1/2 - \gamma/2$ for a fixed γ $(0 < \gamma < 1)$. Note that $\mathrm{err}_D(h) = 1/2 - \gamma/2$ if and only if $r = \sum_{\boldsymbol{x} \in \mathcal{X}} f(\boldsymbol{x})h(\boldsymbol{x})D(\boldsymbol{x})$.

2.2   Boosting Approach

Schapire proved that the strong and weak learnability are equivalent to each other for the first time [21]. Especially the technique to construct a strong learner by using a weak learner is called "boosting". Basic idea of boosting is the following: First, the booster trains a weak learner with respect to different distributions $D_1, \ldots, D_T$ over the domain $\mathcal{X}$, and gets different "weak" hypotheses $h_1, \ldots, h_T$ such that $\mathrm{err}_{D_t}(h_t) \leq 1/2 - \gamma_t/2$ for each $t = 1, \ldots, T$. Then the booster combines weak hypotheses $h_1, \ldots, h_T$ into a final hypotheses h_{final} satisfying $\mathrm{err}_D(h_{final}) \leq \varepsilon$.

In the subsampling framework, the booster calls $EX(f, D)$ for a number of times and obtains a sample $S = ((\boldsymbol{x}_1, f(\boldsymbol{x}_1)), \ldots, (\boldsymbol{x}_m, f(\boldsymbol{x}_m)))$ in advance. Then the booster constructs the final hypothesis h_{final} with its training error $\widehat{\mathrm{err}}_S(h_{final}) \leq \varepsilon$ by training the weak learner over the given sample S. The error $\mathrm{err}_D(h_{final})$ can be estimated by using arguments on VC-dimension or margin (E.g., see [11] or [20], respectively). For example, for typical boosting algorithms,

---

[1] In the original definition of [21], the weak learning algorithm is allowed to output a hypothesis h with $\mathrm{err}_D(h) > 1/2 - \gamma/2$ with probability at most δ as well. But in our definition we omit δ to make our discussion simple. Of course, we can use the original definition, while our analysis becomes slightly more complicated.

$\text{err}_D(h_{final}) \leq \widehat{\text{err}}_S(h_{final}) + \tilde{O}(\sqrt{T \log |\mathcal{W}|/m})$ [2] with high probability, where T is the size of the final hypotheses, i.e., the number of weak hypotheses combined in h_{final}. So, assuming that $|\mathcal{W}|$ is finite, the sample and space complexity are $\tilde{O}(1/\gamma^2 \varepsilon^2)$, respectively.

In the filtering framework, on the other hand, the booster deal with the whole instance space $\mathcal{X}$ through $\text{EX}(f, D)$. By using statistics obtained from calls to $\text{EX}(f, D)$, the booster tries to minimize $\text{err}_D(h_{final})$ directly. Then, it can be shown that the sample complexity is $\tilde{O}(1/\gamma^4 \varepsilon^2)$, but the space complexity is $\tilde{O}(1/\gamma^2)$ (in which the factor $\log(1/\varepsilon)$ is hidden) by using e.g., [6] and [5].

Smooth boosting algorithms generates only such distributions $D_1, \ldots, D_t$ that are "smooth" with respect to the original distribution D. We define the following measure of smoothness.

Definition 1. Let D and D' be any distributions over $\mathcal{X}$. We say that D' is λ-smooth with respect to D if $\max_{\boldsymbol{x} \in \mathcal{X}} D'(\boldsymbol{x})/D(\boldsymbol{x}) \leq \lambda$.

The smoothness parameter λ has crucial roles in robustness of boosting algorithms [6, 25, 14]. Also, it affects the efficiency of sampling methods.

2.3 Our Assumption and Technical Goal

In the rest of the paper, we assume that the learner is given a finite set $\mathcal{W}$ of hypotheses such that for any distribution D' over $\mathcal{X}$, there exists a hypothesis $h \in \mathcal{W}$ satisfying $\text{err}_{D'}(h) \leq 1/2 - \gamma/2$. Now our technical goal is to construct an efficient smooth boosting algorithm which works in both the subsampling and the filtering framework.

3 Boosting by Subsampling

In this section, we propose our boosting algorithm in the subsampling framework.

3.1 Derivation

First of all, we derive our algorithm. It is well known that many of boosting algorithms can be viewed as greedy minimizers of loss functions [13]. More precisely, it can be viewed that they minimize particular loss functions that bound the training errors. The derivation of our algorithm is also explained simply in terms of its loss function.

Suppose that the learner is given a sample $S = \{(\boldsymbol{x}_1, f(\boldsymbol{x}_1)), \ldots, (\boldsymbol{x}_m, f(\boldsymbol{x}_m))\}$, a set $\mathcal{W}$ of hypotheses, and the current final hypothesis $H_t(\boldsymbol{x}) = \sum_{j=1}^{t} \alpha_j h_j(\boldsymbol{x})$, where each $h_j \in \mathcal{W}$ and $\alpha_j \in \mathbb{R}$ for $j = 1, \ldots, t$. The training error of $H_t(\boldsymbol{x})$ over S is defined by $\widehat{\text{err}}(\text{sign}(H_t)) = \frac{1}{m} \sum_{i=1}^{m} I(-f(\boldsymbol{x}_i)H_t(\boldsymbol{x}_i))$, where $I(a) = 1$ if $a > 1$ and $I(a) = 0$, otherwise. We assume a function $L : \mathbb{R} \to [0, +\infty)$ such that $I(a) \leq L(a)$ for any $a \in \mathbb{R}$. Then, by definition, $\widehat{\text{err}}(\text{sign}(H_t)) \leq$

---
[2] In the $\tilde{O}(g(n))$ notation, we neglect $poly(\log(n))$ terms.

$\frac{1}{m}\sum_{i=1}^{m}L(-f(\boldsymbol{x}_i)H_t(\boldsymbol{x}_i))$. If the function L is convex, the upperbound of the training error have a global minimum. Given a new hypothesis $h \in \mathcal{W}$, a typical boosting algorithm assigns α to h that minimizes a particular loss function. For example, AdaBoost solves the following minimization problem:

$$\min_{\alpha\in\mathbb{R}}\frac{1}{m}\sum_{i=1}^{m}L_{exp}(-f(\boldsymbol{x}_i)\{H_t(\boldsymbol{x}_i)+\alpha h(\boldsymbol{x}_i)\}),$$

where its loss function is given by *exponential loss*, $L_{exp}(x) = e^x$. The solution is given analytically as $\alpha = \frac{1}{2}\ln\frac{1+\gamma}{1-\gamma}$, where $\gamma = \sum_{i=1}^{m}f(\boldsymbol{x}_i)h(\boldsymbol{x}_i)D_t(\boldsymbol{x}_i)$, and $D_t(\boldsymbol{x}_i) = \frac{\exp(-f(\boldsymbol{x}_i)H(\boldsymbol{x}_i))}{\sum_{i=1}^{m}\exp(-f(\boldsymbol{x}_i)H(\boldsymbol{x}_i))}$. InfoBoost is designed to minimize the same loss function L_{exp} as AdaBoost, but it uses a slightly different form of the final hypothesis $H_t(\boldsymbol{x}) = \sum_{j=1}^{r}\alpha_j(h_j(\boldsymbol{x}))h_j(\boldsymbol{x})$, where $\alpha_j(z) = \alpha_j[+1]$ if $z \geq 0$, $\alpha_j(z) = \alpha_j[+1]$, otherwise $(\alpha_j[\pm 1] \in \mathbb{R})$. The main difference is that InfoBoost assigns coefficients for each prediction $+1$ and -1 of a hypothesis. Then, the minimization problem of InfoBoost is given as:

$$\min_{\alpha[+1],\alpha[-1]\in\mathbb{R}}\frac{1}{m}\sum_{i=1}^{m}L_{exp}(-f(\boldsymbol{x})\{H_t(\boldsymbol{x})+\alpha(h(\boldsymbol{x}))h(\boldsymbol{x})\}).$$

This problem also has the analytical solution: $\alpha[\pm 1] = \frac{1}{2}\ln\frac{1+\gamma[\pm 1]}{1-\gamma[\pm 1]}$, $\gamma[\pm 1] = \frac{\sum_{i:h(\boldsymbol{x}_i)=\pm 1}f(\boldsymbol{x}_i)h(\boldsymbol{x}_i)D_t(\boldsymbol{x}_i)}{\sum_{i:h(\boldsymbol{x}_i)=\pm 1}D(\boldsymbol{x}_i)}$, and $D_t(\boldsymbol{x}_i) = \frac{\exp(-f(\boldsymbol{x}_i)H_t(\boldsymbol{x}_i))}{\sum_{i=1}^{m}\exp(-f(\boldsymbol{x}_i)H_t(\boldsymbol{x}_i))}$. Curiously, this derivation makes InfoBoost choose a hypothesis that maximizes information gain, where the entropy function is defined not by Shannon's entropy function $E_{Shannon}(p) = -p\log p - (1-p)\log(1-p)$, but by the entropy function $E_{KM}(p) = 2\sqrt{p(1-p)}$ proposed by Kearns and Mansour [18] (See [26] for details). MadaBoost is formulated as the same minimization problem of AdaBoost, except that its loss function is replaced with $L_{mada}(x) = e^x$, if $x \leq 0$, $L_{mada}(x) = x$, otherwise.

Now combining the derivations of InfoBoost and MadaBoost in a straightforward way, our boosting algorithm is given by

$$\min_{\alpha[+1],\alpha[-1]\in\mathbb{R}}\frac{1}{m}\sum_{i=1}^{m}L_{mada}(-f(\boldsymbol{x}_i)\{H_t(\boldsymbol{x}_i)+\alpha(h(\boldsymbol{x}_i))h(\boldsymbol{x}_i)\}). \qquad (1)$$

Since the solution cannot be obtained analytically, we minimize an upperbound of (1). The way of our approximation is a modification of the technique used for AdaFlat [14]. By using Taylor expansion (see Lemma 3 in Appendix for a proof) we have $L_{mada}(x+a) \leq L_{mada}(a) + L'_{mada}(a)(x+x^2)$.

Let

$$\ell(x) = L'_{mada}(x) = \begin{cases} 1, & x \geq 0 \\ e^x, & x < 0. \end{cases}$$

Then we get

$$\frac{1}{m}\sum_{i=1}^{m} L_{mada}(-f(\boldsymbol{x}_i)H_t(\boldsymbol{x}_i)) - \frac{1}{m}\sum_{i=1}^{m} L_{mada}(-f(\boldsymbol{x}_i)H_{t+1}(\boldsymbol{x}_i))$$

$$\geq \frac{1}{m}\sum_{i=1}^{m}\{f(\boldsymbol{x}_i)h_t(\boldsymbol{x}_i)\alpha[h(\boldsymbol{x}_i)]\ell(-f(\boldsymbol{x}_i)H_t(\boldsymbol{x}_i)) - \alpha[h(\boldsymbol{x}_i)]^2\ell(-f(\boldsymbol{x}_i)H_t(\boldsymbol{x}_i))\}$$

$$\stackrel{\text{def}}{=} \Delta L_t(h).$$

By solving the equations $\partial \Delta L_t(h)/\partial \alpha_t[b] = 0$ for $b = \pm 1$, we see that $\Delta L_t(h)$ is maximized if $\alpha_t[b] = \gamma_t[b](h)/2$, where

$$\gamma_t[b](h) = \frac{\sum_{i:h(\boldsymbol{x}_i)=b} h(\boldsymbol{x}_i)f(\boldsymbol{x}_i)D_t(\boldsymbol{x}_i)}{\sum_{i:h(\boldsymbol{x}_i)=b} D_t(\boldsymbol{x}_i)}, \quad \text{and } D_t(\boldsymbol{x}_i) = \frac{\ell(-f(\boldsymbol{x}_i)H_t(\boldsymbol{x}_i))}{\sum_{i=1}^{m} \ell(-f(\boldsymbol{x}_i)H_t(\boldsymbol{x}_i))}.$$

By substituting $\alpha_t[b] = \gamma_t[b](h)/2$ for $b = \pm 1$, we get

$$\Delta L_t(h) = \frac{\mu_t}{4}\left\{p_t(h)\gamma_t[+1](h)^2 + (1 - p_t(h))\gamma_t[-1](h)^2\right\} \tag{2}$$

where $\mu_t = \frac{\sum_{i=1}^{m} \ell(-f(\boldsymbol{x}_i)H_t(\boldsymbol{x}_i))}{m}$, and $p_t(h) = \Pr_{D_t}\{h(\boldsymbol{x}_i) = +1\}$.

Our derivation implies a new criterion to choose a weak hypothesis. That is, we choose $h \in \mathcal{W}$ that maximizes

$$\Delta_t(h) = p_t(h)\gamma_t[+1](h)^2 + (1 - p_t(h))\gamma_t[-1](h)^2.$$

We call the quantity *pseudo gain* of hypothesis h with respect to f and D_t. Now we motivate the pseudo gain in the following way. Let $\varepsilon_t[\pm 1](h) = \Pr_{D_t}\{f(\boldsymbol{x}_i) = \mp 1 | h(\boldsymbol{x}_i) = \pm 1\}$. Note that $\gamma_t[\pm 1](h) = 1 - 2\varepsilon_t[\pm 1](h)$. Then

$$1 - \Delta_t(h)$$
$$= p_t(h)\{1 - (1 - 2\varepsilon_t[+1](h))^2\} + (1 - p_t)\{1 - (1 - 2\varepsilon_t[-1](h))^2\}$$
$$= p_t(h) \cdot 4\varepsilon_t[+1](h)(1 - \varepsilon_t[+1](h)) + (1 - p_t(h)) \cdot 4\varepsilon_t[-1](h)(1 - \varepsilon_t[-1](h)),$$

which can be interpreted as the conditional entropy of f given h with respect to D_t, where the entropy is defined by *Gini index* $E_{Gini}(p) = 4p(1 - p)$ [3] (See other entropy measures in Figure 1 for comparison). So, maximizing the pseudo gain is equivalent to maximizing the information gain defined with Gini index.

3.2 Our Algorithm

Based on our derivation we propose GiniBoost. The description of our modification is given in Figure 2. To make our notation simple, we denote $p_t(h_t) = p_t$, $\gamma_t[\pm 1](h_t) = \gamma_t[\pm 1]$, and $\Delta_t(h_t) = \Delta_t$.

First, we show that the smoothness of distributions D_t.

Proposition 1. During the execution of GiniBoost, each distribution D_t $(t \geq 1)$ is $1/\varepsilon$-smooth with respect to D_1, the uniform distribution over S.

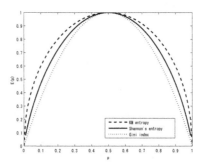

Fig. 1. Plots of three entropy functions, KM entropy (upper) $E_{KM}(p) = 2\sqrt{p(1-p)}$, Shannon's entropy (middle) $E_{Shannon}(p) = -p \log p - (1-p) \log(1-p)$, and Gini index (lower) $E_{Gini}(p) = 4p(1-p)$

Proof. Note that, during the while-loops, $\mu_t \geq \text{err}_S(h_{final}) > \varepsilon$. Therefore, for any i, $D_t(i)/D_1(i) = \ell(-f(\boldsymbol{x}_i)H_t(\boldsymbol{x}_i))/\mu_t < 1/\varepsilon$.   □

It is already shown that smoothness $1/\varepsilon$ is optimal, i.e., there is no boosting algorithm that achieves the smoothness less than $1/\varepsilon$ [25, 14].

Next, we prove the time complexity of GiniBoost.

Theorem 2. Suppose that, during the while-loops, $\text{err}_{D_t}(h_t) \leq 1/2 - \gamma_t/2 \leq 1/2 - \gamma/2$ for some $\gamma > 0$. Then, GiniBoost outputs a final hypothesis h_{final} satisfying $\widehat{\text{err}}_S(h_{final}) \leq \varepsilon$ within $T = O\left(1/\varepsilon\Delta\right)$ iterations, where $\Delta = \min_{t=1,\dots,T} \Delta_t$ and $\Delta \geq \gamma^2$.

Proof. By our derivation of GiniBoost, for any $T \geq 1$, the training error $\widehat{\text{err}}(H_T)$ is less than $1 - \sum_{t=1}^{T} \Delta L_t(h_t)$. As in the proof of Proposition 1, $\mu_t \geq \varepsilon$. So we have $\Delta L_t(h_t) \geq \varepsilon\Delta/4$ and thus $\widehat{\text{err}}_S(h_{final}) \leq \varepsilon$ if $T = 4/\varepsilon\Delta$. Finally, by Jensen's inequality, $\Delta_t \geq p_t\gamma_t[+1]^2 + (1-p_t)\gamma_t[-1]^2 \geq \gamma_t^2 \geq \gamma^2$, which proves $\Delta \geq \gamma^2$.   □

Remark. We discuss the efficiency of other boosting algorithms and GiniBoost. GiniBoost runs in $O(1/\varepsilon\gamma^2)$ iterations in the worst case. But, since the pseudo gain Δ ranges from γ^2 to γ, our bound $O(1/\varepsilon\Delta)$ is potentially smaller. Smooth boosting algorithms MadaBoost [6] and SmoothBoost [25] run in $O(1/\varepsilon\gamma^2)$ iterations as well. However, the former needs a technical assumption in their analysis that $\gamma_t \geq \gamma_{t+1}$ for each iteration t. Also the latter is not adaptive, i.e., it needs the prior knowledge of $\gamma > 0$. On the other hand, GiniBoost is adaptive and does not need such the technical assumption. AdaFlat [14] is another smooth boosting algorithm which is adaptive, but it takes $O(1/\varepsilon^2\gamma^2)$ iterations. Finally, AdaBoost [11] achieves $O(\log(1/\varepsilon)/\gamma^2)$ bound and the bound is optimal [10]. But AdaBoost might construct exponentially skew distributions. It is shown that a combination of boosting algorithms ("boosting tandems approach" [9, 14]) can achieve $O(\log(1/\varepsilon)/\gamma^2)$ with smoothness $\tilde{O}(1/\varepsilon)$. Yet, it is still open whether a single adaptive boosting algorithm can learn in $O(\log(1/\varepsilon)/\gamma^2)$ iterations while keeping the optimal smoothness $1/\varepsilon$.

GiniBoost

Given: $S = ((x_1, f(x_1)), ..., (x_m, f(x_m)))$, and ε $(0 < \varepsilon < 1)$

1. $D_1(i) \leftarrow 1/m$; $(i = 1, ..., m)$ $H_0(x) \leftarrow 0$; $t \leftarrow 1$;
2. **while** $\widehat{\mathrm{err}}_S(h_{final}) > \varepsilon$ **do**
   a) $h_t \leftarrow \arg\max\limits_{h \in W} \Delta_t(h)$;
   b) $\alpha_t[\pm 1] \leftarrow \gamma_t[\pm 1]/2$; Let $\alpha_t(z) = \alpha_t[+1]$ if $z > 0$, o.w. let $\alpha_t(z) = \alpha_t[-1]$;
   c) $H_{t+1}(x) \leftarrow H_t(x) + \alpha_t(h_t(x))h_t(x)$;
   d) Define the next distribution D_{t+1} as
   $$D_{t+1}(i) = \frac{\ell(-f(x_i)H_{t+1}(x_i))}{\sum_{i=1}^{m} \ell(-f(x_i)H_{t+1}(x_i))};$$
   e) $t \leftarrow t + 1$;
   end-while
3. Output the final hypothesis $h_{final}(x) = \mathrm{sign}\,(H_{t+1}(x))$.

Fig. 2. GiniBoost

4   Boosting by Filtering

In this section, we propose GiniBoost$_{filt}$ in the filtering framework. Let

$$D_t(x) = \frac{D(x)\ell(-f(x)H_t(x))}{\sum_{x \in \mathcal{X}} D(x)\ell(-f(x)H_t(x))}.$$

We define $\mu_t = \sum_{x \in \mathcal{X}} D(x)\ell(-f(x)H_t(x))$,. We denote $\hat{a}$ as the empirical estimate of the parameter a given a sample S_t. The description of GiniBoost$_{filt}$ is given in Figure 3.

The following property of FiltEX can be immediately verified.

Proposition 3. Fix any iteration t, (i) FiltEX outputs $(x, f(x))$, where x is drawn according to D_t, and (ii) the probability that FiltEX outputs an example is at least $\mu_t \geq \mathrm{err}_D(\mathrm{sign}(H_t))$.

Then, we prove a multiplicative tail bound on the estimate $\hat{\Delta}_t(h)$ of the pseudo gain.

Lemma 1. Fix any $t \geq 1$. Let $\hat{\Delta}_t(h) = \hat{p}_t(h)\hat{\gamma}_t[+1](h)^2 + (1 - \hat{p}_t(h))\hat{\gamma}_t[-1](h)^2$ be the empirical estimate of $\Delta_t(h)$ given S_t. Then it holds for any ε $(0 < \varepsilon < 1)$ that

$$\Pr_{D^m}\{\hat{\Delta}_t(h) \geq (1 + \varepsilon)\Delta_t(h)\} \leq b_1 e^{-\frac{\varepsilon^2 \Delta_t m}{c_1}}, \tag{3}$$

and

$$\Pr_{D^m}\{\hat{\Delta}_t(h) \leq (1 - \varepsilon)\Delta_t(h)\} \leq b_1 e^{-\frac{\varepsilon^2 \Delta_t m}{c_2}}, \tag{4}$$

where $b_1 \leq 8$, $c_1 \leq 600$, and $c_2 \leq 64$.

GiniBoost$_{\mathrm{filt}}(\varepsilon, \delta, \mathcal{W})$

1. Let $H_1(x) = 0$; $t \leftarrow 1$; $\delta_1 \leftarrow \delta/8$;
   $S_1' \leftarrow \frac{18\log(1/\delta_1)}{\varepsilon}$ random examples drawn by EX(f, D);
2. **while** $\widehat{\mathrm{err}}_{S_t'}(\mathrm{sign}(H_t)) \geq \frac{2\varepsilon}{3}$ **do**
   $(h_t, S_t) \leftarrow$ HSelect$(1/2, \delta_t)$;
   $(\hat{\gamma}_t[+1], \hat{\gamma}_t[-1]) \leftarrow$ empirical estimates over S_t;
   $\alpha_t[\pm 1] \leftarrow \hat{\gamma}_t[\pm 1]/2$;
   $H_{t+1}(x) \leftarrow H_t(x) + \alpha_t(h_t(x))h_t(x)$;
   $t \leftarrow t + 1$; $\delta_t \leftarrow \delta/(4t(t+1))$;
   $S_t' \leftarrow \frac{18\log(1/\delta_t)}{\varepsilon}$ random examples drawn by EX(f, D);
   end-while
3. Output the final hypothesis $h_{final}(x) = \mathrm{sign}\,(H_t(x))$;

FiltEX()

do
   $(x, f(x)) \leftarrow$ EX(f, D);
   $r \leftarrow$ uniform random number over $[0, 1]$;
   if $r < \ell(-f(x)H_t(x))$ **then return** $(x, f(x))$;
end-do

HSelect(ε, δ)

$m \leftarrow 0$; $S \leftarrow \emptyset$; $i \leftarrow 1$; $\Delta_g \leftarrow 1/2$; $\delta' \leftarrow \delta/(2|\mathcal{W}|)$;
do
   $(x, f(x)) \leftarrow$ FiltEX();
   $S \leftarrow S \cup (x, f(x))$; $m \leftarrow m + 1$;
   if $m = \left\lceil \frac{c_1 \ln \frac{b_1}{\delta'}}{\varepsilon^2 \Delta_g} \right\rceil$ **then**
      Let $\hat{\Delta}_t(h)$ be the empirical estimate of $\Delta_t(h)$ over S for each $h \in \mathcal{W}$;
      if $\exists h \in \mathcal{W}$, $\hat{\Delta}_t(h) \geq \Delta_g$ **then** return h and S;
      else $\Delta_g \leftarrow \Delta_g/2$; $i \leftarrow i + 1$; $\delta \leftarrow \delta/(i(i+1)|\mathcal{W}|)$;
   end-if
end-do

Fig. 3. GiniBoost$_{\mathrm{filt}}$

The proof of Lemma 1 is omitted and given in the technical report version of our paper [17]. Then, we analyze our adaptive sampling procedure HSelect. Let $\Delta_t^* = \max_{h' \in \mathcal{W}} \Delta_t(h')$. We prove the following lemma. The proof is also given in [17] .

Lemma 2. Fix any $t \geq 1$. Then, with probability at least $1 - \delta$, (i) HSelect(ε, δ) outputs a hypothesis $h \in \mathcal{W}$ such that $\Delta_t(h) > (1 - \varepsilon)\Delta_t^*$, and (ii) the number of calls of $EX(f, D)$ is

$$O\left(\frac{\log \frac{1}{\delta} + \log |\mathcal{W}| + \log\log \frac{1}{\Delta_t^*}}{\varepsilon^2 \Delta_t^*}\right).$$

Finally we obtain the following theorem.

Theorem 4. With probability at least $1 - \delta$,

(i) GiniBoost$_{\text{filt}}$ outputs the final hypothesis h_{final} such that $\text{err}_D(h_{final}) \leq \varepsilon$,
(ii) GiniBoost$_{\text{filt}}$ terminates in $T = O(1/\varepsilon\Delta)$ iterations,
(iii) the number of calls of $EX(f, D)$ is

$$O\left(\frac{\log\frac{1}{\delta} + \log\frac{1}{\varepsilon\Delta} + \log|\mathcal{W}| + \log\log\frac{1}{\Delta}}{\varepsilon^2\Delta^2} \cdot \left(\log\frac{1}{\delta} + \log\frac{1}{\varepsilon\Delta}\right)\right), \text{ and}$$

(iv) the space complexity is

$$O\left(\frac{\log\frac{1}{\delta} + \log\frac{1}{\varepsilon\Delta} + \log|\mathcal{W}| + \log\log\frac{1}{\Delta}}{\Delta}\right),$$

where $\Delta_t \geq \Delta \geq \gamma^2$.

Proof. We say that GiniBoost fails at iteration t if one of the following event occurs: (a) HSelect fails, i.e., it does not meet the conditions (i) or (ii) in Lemma 2, (b) FiltEX calls $EX(f, D)$ for more than $(6/\varepsilon)M_t \log(1/\delta_t)$ times at iteration t, where M_t is denoted as the number of calls for FiltEX, (c) $\text{err}_D(\text{sign}(H_t)) > \varepsilon$ and $\widehat{\text{err}}_{S'_t}(\text{sign}(H_t)) < 2\varepsilon/3$, or (d) $\text{err}_D(\text{sign}(H_t)) < \varepsilon/2$ and $\widehat{\text{err}}_{S'_t}(\text{sign}(H_t)) > 2\varepsilon/3$. Note that, by Proposition 3, Lemma 2 and an application of Chernoff bound, the probability of each event (a), ..., (d) is at most δ_t, respectively. So the probability that GiniBoost fails is at most $4\delta_t$ at each iteration t. Then, during T iterations, GiniBoost fails at some iteration is at most $\sum_{t=1}^{T} 4\delta_t = \delta - \delta/(T+1) < \delta$. Now suppose that GiniBoost does not fail during T iterations. Then, we have $\text{err}_D(h_{final}) \leq 1 - \sum_{i=t}^{T}(1/8)\Delta_t^*$ by using the similar argument in the proof of Theorem 2, and thus GiniBoost $\text{err}_D(h_{final}) \leq \varepsilon/2$ in $T = 16/(\varepsilon\Delta)$ iterations. Then, since GiniBoost does not fail during T iterations, $\widehat{\text{err}}_{S'_t}(\text{sign}(H_t)) < 2\varepsilon/3$ at iteration $T + 1$ and GiniBoost outputs h_{final} with $\text{err}_D(h_{final}) \leq \varepsilon/2$ and terminates. The total number of calls of $EX(f, D)$ in $T = O(1/\varepsilon\Delta)$ iterations is $O(T \cdot M_T(1/\varepsilon)\log(1/\delta_T))$ with probability $1 - \delta$ and by combining with Lemma 2, we complete the proof.   □

5   Improvement on Sampling

While Lemma 1 gives a theoretical guarantee without any assumption, the bound has the constant factor $c_1 = 600$, which is too large to apply the lemma in practice. In this section, we derive a practical tail bound on the pseudo gain by using the central limit theorem. We say that a sequence of random variables $\{X_i\}$ is *asymptotically normal* with mean μ_i and variance σ_i^2 (we write X_i is $AN(\mu_i, \sigma_i^2)$ for short) if $(X_i - \mu_i)/\sigma_i$ converges to $N(0, 1)$ in distribution [3]. The central limit

---

[3] Let $F_1(x), \ldots, F_m(x)$, and $F(x)$ be distribution functions. Let $X_1, \ldots, X_m$, and X be corresponding random variables, respectively. X_m converges to X in distribution if $\lim_{m \to \infty} F_m(x) = F(x)$.

theorem states that, for independent random variables $X_1, \ldots, X_m$ from the same distribution with mean μ and variance σ^2, $\sum_{i=1}^{m} X_i/m$ is $AN(\mu, \sigma^2/m)$. In particular, we use the multivariate version of the central limit theorem.

Theorem 5 ([24]). Let $\mathbf{X_1}, \ldots, \mathbf{X_m}$ be i.i.d. random vectors with mean $\boldsymbol{\mu}$ and covariance matrix $\boldsymbol{\Sigma}$. Then, $\sum_{i=1}^{m} \mathbf{X}_i/m$ is $AN(\boldsymbol{\mu}, \boldsymbol{\Sigma})$.

Fix any hypothesis $h \in \mathcal{W}$, and distribution D_t over $\mathcal{X}$. Let $X \in \{0, 1\}$ and $Y \in \{-1, +1\}$ be random variables, induced by an independent random draw of $\boldsymbol{x} \in \mathcal{X}$ under D_t, such that $X = 1$ if $h(\boldsymbol{x}) = +1$, otherwise $X = 0$ and $Y = f(\boldsymbol{x})h_t(\boldsymbol{x})$, respectively. Then the pseudo gain $\Delta_t(h)$ can be written as $E(X) \cdot \{E(XY)/E(X)\}^2 + E(\bar{X}) \cdot \{E(\bar{X}Y)/E(\bar{X})\}^2$, where $\bar{X} = 1 - X$. Our empirical estimate of the pseudo gain is $Z = (\sum_{i=1}^{m} X_i Y_i/m)^2/(\sum_{i=1}^{m} X_i/m) + (\sum_{i=1}^{m} \bar{X}_i Y_i/m)^2/(\sum_{i=1}^{m} \bar{X}_i/m)$. The following theorem guarantees that a combination of sequences of asymptotically normal random variables is also asymptotically normal (Theorem 3.3A in [24]).

Theorem 6 ([24]). Suppose that $\mathbf{X} = (X^{(1)}, \ldots, X^{(k)})$ is $AN(\boldsymbol{\mu}, b\boldsymbol{\Sigma})$, with $\boldsymbol{\Sigma}$ a covariance matrix and $b \to 0$. Let $g(\mathbf{x}) = (g_1(\mathbf{x}), \ldots, g_n(\mathbf{x}))$, $\mathbf{x} = (x_1, \ldots, x_k)$, be a vector-valued function for which each component function $g_i(\mathbf{x})$ is real-valued and has a nonzero differential at $\mathbf{x} = \boldsymbol{\mu}$. Then, $g(\mathbf{X})$ is $AN(g(\boldsymbol{\mu}), b^2 \mathbf{D} \boldsymbol{\Sigma} \mathbf{D}')$, where

$$\mathbf{D} = \left[\frac{\partial g_i}{\partial x_j} \Big|_{\mathbf{x}=\boldsymbol{\mu}} \right]_{n \times k}.$$

By using Theorem 5 and 6 for $\mathbf{X_m} = (\sum_{i=1}^{m} X_i/m, \sum_{i=1}^{m} X_i Y_i/m, \sum_{i=1}^{m} \bar{X}_i Y_i/m)$ and $g(u, v, w) = v^2/u + w^2/(1-u)$, we get the following result.

Corollary 7. $Z = \dfrac{(\sum_{i=1}^{m} X_i Y_i/m)^2}{\sum_{i=1}^{m} X_i/m} + \dfrac{(\sum_{i=1}^{m} \bar{X}_i Y_i/m)^2}{\sum_{i=1}^{m} X_i/m}$ is $AN(\mu_z, \sigma_z^2)$, where $\mu_z = \dfrac{E(XY)^2}{E(X)} + \dfrac{E(\bar{X}Y)^2}{E(\bar{X})}$, and $\sigma_z^2 \leq 4\mu_z/m$.

The proof is given in [17]. When the given sample is large enough, we may be able to use the central limit theorem. Then

$$\Pr\left\{ \frac{Z - \mu_z}{\sigma_z} \leq \varepsilon \right\} \approx \Phi(\varepsilon),$$

where $\Phi(x) = \int_{-\infty}^{x} (1/\sqrt{2\pi}) e^{-\frac{1}{2}y^2} dy$. Since $1 - \Phi(x) \leq 1/(x\sqrt{2\pi}) e^{-\frac{1}{2}x^2}$ (see, e.g.,[8]),

$$\Pr\{Z - \mu_z > \varepsilon\mu_z\} = \Pr\left\{ \frac{Z - \mu_z}{\sigma_z} > \frac{\varepsilon\mu_z}{\sigma_z} \right\} \lesssim \frac{\sigma_z}{\varepsilon\mu_z\sqrt{2\pi}} e^{-\frac{\varepsilon^2 \mu_z^2}{2\sigma_z^2}}$$

$$< \frac{2}{\sqrt{2\pi\varepsilon^2\mu_z m}} e^{-\frac{\varepsilon^2 \mu_z m}{8}}. \quad (5)$$

Substituting

$$m = \frac{8\left(\ln\frac{1}{\delta\sqrt{2\pi}} - \frac{1}{2}\ln\ln\frac{1}{\delta\sqrt{2\pi}}\right)}{\varepsilon^2\mu_z}$$

to inequality (5), we obtain $\Pr\{Z - \mu_z > \varepsilon\mu_z\} < \delta$. Note that the same argument holds for $\Pr\{Z \leq (1 - \varepsilon)\mu_z\}$. Therefore, we can replace the estimate of sample size $m = \frac{c_1 \ln(b_1/\delta)}{\varepsilon^2 \Delta_g}$ in HSelect with $m = \frac{8\left(\ln\frac{1}{\delta\sqrt{2\pi}} - \frac{1}{2}\ln\ln\frac{1}{\delta\sqrt{2\pi}}\right)}{\varepsilon^2 \Delta_g}$ and this modification makes HSelect more practical.

6   Experimental Results

In this section, we show our preliminary experimental results in the filtering framework. We apply GiniBoost and MadaBoost for text categorization tasks on a collection of Reuters news (Reuters-21578 [4]). We use the modified Apte split which contains about $10,000$ news documents labeled with topics. We choose five major topics and for each topics, we let boosting algorithms classify whether a news document belongs to the topic or not. As weak hypotheses, we prepare about $30,000$ decision stumps corresponding to words.

We evaluate algorithms using cross validation in a random fashion, as done in [4]. For each topic, we split the data randomly into a training data with probability 0.7 and a test data with probability 0.3. We prepare 10 pairs of such training and test data. We train algorithms over the training data until they sample $1,000,000$ examples in total, and then we evaluate them over the test data. The results are averaged over 10 trials and 5 topics. We conduct our experiments on a computer with a CPU Xeon 3.8GHz using 8 Gb of memory under Linux.

We consider two versions of GiniBoost in our experiments. The first version is the original one which we described in Section 3. The second version is a slight modification of the original one, in which we use $\alpha_t[\pm 1] = \gamma_t[\pm 1]$. We call this version GiniBoost2.

We run GiniBoost with HSelect(ε, δ), where parameter $\varepsilon = 0.75$ and $\delta = 0.1$ are fixed. Also, we run MadaBoost with geometric AdaSelect [5] whose parameters are $s = 2$, $\varepsilon = 0.5$ and $\delta = 0.1$. Note that, in this setting, we demand both HSelect and AdaSelect to output a weak hypothesis h_t with $\gamma_t^2 \geq (1/4)\max_{h' \in \mathcal{W}} \gamma_t(h')^2$. In the following experiments, we use the approximation based on the central limit theorem, described in Section 5.

The results are shown in Table 1 and Figure 4, As indicated, GiniBoost and GiniBoost2 improve the performance of MadaBoost. We also run AdaBoost (without sampling) for 100 iterations, where AdaBoost processes about 1,000,000 examples. Then, GiniBoost is about three times faster than AdaBoost, while improving the accuracy. The main reason why filtering-based algorithms save time would be that they use rejection sampling. By using rejection sampling,

---

[4] http://www.daviddlewis.com/resources/testcollections/reuters21578

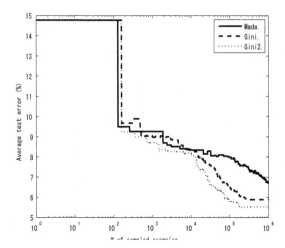

Fig. 4. Test errors (%) of boosting algorithms for Reuters-21578 data. The test errors are averaged over topics.

Table 1. Summary of experiments over Reuters-2158

	# of sampled examples	# of accepted examples	time (sec.)	test error (%)
Ada.	N/A	N/A	1349	5.6
Mada.	1,032,219	157,320	493	6.7
Gini.	1,039,943	156,856	408	5.8
Gini2.	1,027,874	140,916	359	5.5

filtering-based algorithms keep only accepted examples in hand. Since the number of accepted example is much smaller than that of the whole given sample, we can find weak hypotheses faster over accepted examples than over the given sample.

In particular, GiniBoost uses fewer accepted examples than MadaBoost. mainly because they use different criteria. Roughly speaking, MadaBoost takes $\tilde{O}(1/\gamma_t^2)$ accepted examples in order to estimate γ_t. On the other hand, in order to estimate Δ_t, GiniBoost takes $\tilde{O}(1/\Delta_t)$ accepted examples, which is smaller than $\tilde{O}(1/\gamma_t^2)$. This consideration would explain why GiniBoost is faster than MadaBoost.

7   Summary and Future Work

In this paper, we propose a smooth boosting algorithm that uses an information-based criterion based on Gini index for choosing hypotheses. Our preliminary experiments show that our algorithm performs well in the filtering framework. As future work, we further investigate the connections between boosting and information-based criteria. Also, we will conduct experiments over much huge data in the filtering framework.

Acknowledgments

I would like to thank Prof. Masayuki Takeda of Kyushu University for his various support. I thank Prof. Osamu Wannabe and Prof. Eiji Takimoto for their discussion. I also thank anonymous referees for their helpful comments. This work is supported in part by the 21st century COE program at Graduate School of Information Science and Electrical Engineering in Kyushu University.

References

1. J. A. Aslam. Improving algorithms for boosting. In *Proc. 13th Annu. Conference on Comput. Learning Theory*, pages 200–207, 2000.
2. Jose L. Balcazar, Yang Dai, and Osamu Watanabe. Provably fast training algorithms for support vector machines. In *Proceedings of IEEE International Conference on Data Mining (ICDM'01)*, pages 43–50, 2001.
3. L. Breiman, J. H. Friedman, R. A. Olshen, and C. J. Stone. *Classification and Regression Trees*. Wadsworth International Group, 1984.
4. Sanjoy Dasgupta and Philip M. Long. Boosting with diverse base classifers. In *Proceedings of the 16th Annual Conference on Learning Theory and 7th Kernel Workshop*, pages 273–287, 2003.
5. C. Domingo, R. Gavaldà, and O. Watanabe. Adaptive sampling methods for scaling up knowledge discovery algorithms. *Data Mining and Knowledge Discovery*, 6(2):131–152, 2002.
6. C. Domingo and O. Watanabe. MadaBoost: A modification of AdaBoost. In *Proceedings of 13th Annual Conference on Computational Learning Theory*, pages 180–189, 2000.
7. P. Domingos and G. Hulten. Mining high-speed data streams. In *Proceedings of the Sixth ACM International Conference on Knowledge Discovery and Data Mining*, pages 71–80, 2000.
8. W. Feller. *An introduction to probability theory and its applications*. Wiley, 1950.
9. Y. Freund. An improved boosting algorithm and its implications on learning complexity. In *Proc. 5th Annual ACM Workshop on Computational Learning Theory*, pages 391–398. ACM Press, New York, NY, 1992.
10. Y. Freund. Boosting a weak learning algorithm by majority. *Information and Computation*, 121(2):256–285, 1995.
11. Y. Freund and R. E. Schapire. A decision-theoretic generalization of on-line learning and an application to boosting. *Journal of Computer and System Sciences*, 55(1):119–139, 1997.
12. Yoav Freund. An adaptive version of the boost by majority algorithm. In *COLT '99: Proceedings of the twelfth annual conference on Computational learning theory*, pages 102–113, 1999.
13. J. Friedman, T. Hastie, and R. Tibshirani. Additive logistic regression: a statistical view of boosting. *Annals of Statisitics*, 2:337–374, 2000.
14. D. Gavinsky. Optimally-smooth adaptive boosting and application to agnostic learning. *Journal of Machine Learning Research*, 2003.
15. K. Hatano and M. K. Warmuth. Boosting versus covering. In *Advances in Neural Information Processing Systems 16*, 2003.

16. K. Hatano and O. Watanabe. Learning r-of-k functions by boosting. In *Proceedings of the 15th International Conference on Algorithmic Learning Theory*, pages 114–126, 2004.
17. Kohei Hatano. Smooth boosting using an information-based criterion. Technical Report DOI-TR-225, Department of Informatics, Kyushu University, 2006.
18. M. Kearns and Y. Mansour. On the boosting ability of top-down decision tree learning algorithms. *Journal of Computer and System Sciences*, 58(1):109–128, 1999.
19. Yishay Mansour and David A. McAllester. Boosting using branching programs. *Journal of Computer and System Sciences*, 64(1):103–112, 2002.
20. R. E. Schapire, Y. Freund, P. Bartlett, and W. S. Lee. Boosting the margin: a new explanation for the effectiveness of voting methods. *The Annals of Statistics*, 26(5):1651–1686, 1998.
21. Robert E. Schapire. The strength of weak learnability. *Machine Learning*, 5(2):197–227, 1990.
22. Robert E. Schapire and Yoram Singer. Improved boosting algorithms using confidence-rated predictions. *Machine Learning*, 37(3):297–336, 1999.
23. Tobias Scheffer and Stefan Wrobel. Finding the most interesting patterns in a database quickly by using sequential sampling. *Journal of Machine Learning Research*, 3:833–862, 2003.
24. R. J. Serfling. *Approximation theorems of mathematical statistics*. Wiley, 1980.
25. R. A. Servedio. Smooth boosting and learning with malicious noise. In *14th Annual Conference on Computational Learning Theory*, pages 473–489, 2001.
26. Eiji Takimoto, Syuhei Koya, and Akira Maruoka. Boosting based on divide and merge. In *Proceedings of the 15th International Conference on Algorithmic Learning Theory*, pages 127–141, 2004.
27. L. G. Valiant. A theory of the learnable. *Communications of the ACM*, 27(11):1134–1142, 1984.

Appendix

Lemma 3. Let $L(x) = x + 1$, if $x > 0$ and e^x, otherwise. Then it holds for any $a \in \mathbb{R}$ and any $x \in [-1, +1]$ that

$$L(x + a) \leq L(a) + L'(a)x + L'(a)x^2.$$

Proof. For any $x \in [-1, 1]$, let $g_x(a) = L(a) + L'(a)(x + x^2) - L(x + a)$. We consider the following cases. (Case 1: $x + a, a \leq 0$) We have $g_x(a) = e^a(1 + x + x^2 - e^x) \geq 0$, as $e^x \leq 1 + x + x^2$ for $x \in [-1, 1]$. (Case 2: $x + a, a \geq 0$) It is immediate to see that $g_x(a) = x^2 \geq 0$. (Case 3: $x + a < 0$, and $a > 0$) It holds that $g_x(a) = 1 + a + x + x^2 - e^{x+a} \geq 0$ since $g'_x(a) = 1 - e^{x+a} > 0$ and $g_x(0) = 1 + x + x^2 - e^x \geq 0$. (Case 4: $x + a > 0$, and $a < 0$) By using the fact that $1 + x + x^2 \geq e^x$ for $x \in [-1, 1]$, we have $g_x(a) = e^a(1 + x + x^2) - (x + a + 1) \geq e^{x+a} - (1 + x + a) \geq 0$. $\square$

Large-Margin Thresholded Ensembles for Ordinal Regression: Theory and Practice

Hsuan-Tien Lin and Ling Li

Learning Systems Group, California Institute of Technology, USA
htlin@caltech.edu, ling@caltech.edu

Abstract. We propose a thresholded ensemble model for ordinal regression problems. The model consists of a weighted ensemble of confidence functions and an ordered vector of thresholds. We derive novel large-margin bounds of common error functions, such as the classification error and the absolute error. In addition to some existing algorithms, we also study two novel boosting approaches for constructing thresholded ensembles. Both our approaches not only are simpler than existing algorithms, but also have a stronger connection to the large-margin bounds. In addition, they have comparable performance to SVM-based algorithms, but enjoy the benefit of faster training. Experimental results on benchmark datasets demonstrate the usefulness of our boosting approaches.

1 Introduction

Ordinal regression resides between multiclass classification and metric regression in the area of supervised learning. They have many applications in social science and information retrieval to match human preferences. In an ordinal regression problem, examples are labeled with a set of $K \geq 2$ discrete ranks, which, unlike general class labels, also carry ordering preferences. However, ordinal regression is not exactly the same as common metric regression, because the label set is of finite size and metric distance between ranks is undefined.

Several approaches for ordinal regression were proposed in recent years from a machine learning perspective. For example, Herbrich et al. [1] designed an algorithm with support vector machines (SVM). Other SVM formulations were first studied by Shashua and Levin [2], and some improved ones were later proposed by Chu and Keerthi [3]. Crammer and Singer [4] generalized the perceptron learning rule for ordinal regression in an online setting. These approaches are all extended from well-known binary classification algorithms [5]. In addition, they share a common property in predicting: the discrete rank comes from thresholding a continuous potential value, which represents an ordering preference. Ideally, examples with higher ranks should have higher potential values.

In the special case of $K = 2$, ordinal regression is similar to binary classification [6]. If we interpret the similarity from the other side, the confidence function for a binary classifier can be naturally used as an ordering preference. For example, Freund et al. [7] proposed a boosting algorithm, RankBoost, that constructs an ensemble of those confidence functions to form a better ordering preference.

J.L. Balcázar, P.M. Long, and F. Stephan (Eds.): ALT 2006, LNAI 4264, pp. 319–333, 2006.

However, RankBoost was not specifically designed for ordinal regression. Hence, some efforts are needed when applying RankBoost for ordinal regression.

In this work, we combine the ideas of thresholding and ensemble learning to propose a thresholded ensemble model for ordinal regression. In our model, potential values are computed from an ensemble of confidence functions, and then thresholded to rank labels. It is well-known that ensemble is useful and powerful in approximating complex functions for classification and metric regression [8]. Our model shall inherit the same advantages for ordinal regression. Furthermore, we define margins for the thresholded ensemble model, and derive novel large-margin bounds of its out-of-sample error. The results indicate that large-margin thresholded ensembles could generalize well.

Algorithms for constructing thresholded ensembles are also studied. We not only combine RankBoost with a thresholding algorithm, but also propose two simpler boosting formulations, named ordinal regression boosting (ORBoost). ORBoost formulations have stronger connections with the large-margin bounds that we derive, and are direct generalizations to the famous AdaBoost algorithm [9]. Experimental results demonstrate that ORBoost formulations share some good properties with AdaBoost. They usually outperform RankBoost, and have comparable performance to SVM-based algorithms.

This paper is organized as follows. Section 2 introduces ordinal regression, as well as the thresholded ensemble model. Large-margin bounds for thresholded ensembles are derived in Sect. 3. Then, an extended RankBoost algorithm and two ORBoost formulations, which construct thresholded ensembles, are discussed in Sect. 4. We show the experimental results in Sect. 5, and conclude in Sect. 6.

2   Thresholded Ensemble Model for Ordinal Regression

In an ordinal regression problem, we are given a set of training examples $S = \{(x_n, y_n)\}_{n=1}^{N}$, where each input vector $x_n \in \mathbb{R}^D$ is associated with an ordinal label (i.e., rank) y_n. We assume that y_n belongs to a set $\{1, 2, \ldots, K\}$. The goal is to find an ordinal regression rule $G(x)$ that predicts the rank y of an unseen input vector x. For a theoretic setting, we shall assume that all input-rank pairs are drawn i.i.d. from some unknown distribution $\mathcal{D}$.

The setting above looks similar to that of a multiclass classification problem. Hence, a general classification error,[1]

$$E_C(G, \mathcal{D}) = \mathcal{E}_{(x,y)\sim\mathcal{D}}[\![G(x) \neq y]\!],$$

can be used to measure the performance of G. However, the classification error does not consider the ordering preference of the ranks. One naive interpretation of the ordering preference is as follows: for an example (x, y) with $y = 4$, if $G_1(x) = 3$ and $G_2(x) = 1$, G_1 is preferred over G_2 on that example. A common practice to encode such preference is to use the absolute error:

$$E_A(G, \mathcal{D}) = \mathcal{E}_{(x,y)\sim\mathcal{D}} |G(x) - y|.$$

---

[1] $[\![\cdot]\!] = 1$ when the inner condition is true, and 0 otherwise.

Next, we propose the thresholded ensemble model for ordinal regression. As the name suggests, the model has two components: a vector of thresholds, and an ensemble of confidence functions.

Thresholded models are widely used for ordinal regression [3,4]. The thresholds can be thought as estimated scales that reflect the discrete nature of ordinal regression. The ordinal regression rule, denoted as $G_{H,\theta}$, is illustrated in Fig. 1. Here $H(x)$ computes the potential value of x, and θ is a $(K-1)$ dimensional ordered vector that contains the thresholds $(\theta_1 \leq \theta_2 \leq \cdots \leq \theta_{K-1})$. We shall denote $G_{H,\theta}$ as G_θ when H is clear from the context. Then, if we let $\theta_0 = -\infty$ and $\theta_K = \infty$, the ordinal regression rule is

$$G_\theta(x) = \min\{k\colon H(x) \leq \theta_k\} = \max\{k\colon H(x) > \theta_{k-1}\} = 1 + \sum_{k=1}^{K-1} [\![H(x) > \theta_k]\!].$$

In the thresholded ensemble model, we take an ensemble of confidence functions to compute the potentials. That is,

$$H(x) = H_T(x) = \sum_{t=1}^{T} \alpha_t h_t(x), \quad \alpha_t \in \mathbb{R}.$$

We shall assume that the confidence function h_t comes from a hypothesis set $\mathcal{H}$, and has an output range $[-1, 1]$. A special case of the confidence function, which only outputs -1 or 1, would be called a binary classifier. Each confidence function reflects a possibly imperfect ordering preference. The ensemble linearly combines the ordering preferences with α. Note that we allow α_t to be any real value, which means that it is possible to reverse the ordering preference of h_t in the ensemble when necessary.

Ensemble models in general have been successfully used for classification and metric regression [8]. They not only introduce more stable predictions through the linear combination, but also provide sufficient power for approximating complex functions. These properties shall be inherited by the thresholded ensemble model for ordinal regression.

3   Large-Margin Bounds for Thresholded Ensembles

Margin is an important concept in structural risk minimization [10]. Many large-margin error bounds were proposed based on the intuition that large margins lead to good generalization. They are typically of the form

$$E_1(G, \mathcal{D}) \leq E_2(G, \mathcal{S}_u, \Delta) + \text{complexity term}.$$

Here $E_1(G, \mathcal{D})$ is the generalization error of interest, such as $E_A(G, \mathcal{D})$. $\mathcal{S}_u$ denotes the uniform distribution on the set $\mathcal{S}$, and $E_2(G, \mathcal{S}_u, \Delta)$ represents some training error with margin Δ, which will be further explained in this section.

For ordinal regression, Herbrich et al. [1] derived a large-margin bound for a thresholded ordinal regression rule G. Unfortunately the bound is quite restricted

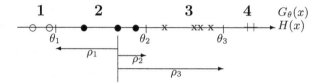

Fig. 1. The thresholded model and the margins of a correctly-predicted example

since it requires that $E_2(G, \mathcal{S}_u, \Delta) = 0$. In addition, the bound uses a definition of margin that has $O(N^2)$ terms, which makes it more complicated to design algorithms that relate to the bound. Another bound was derived by Shashua and Levin [2]. The bound is based on a margin definition of only $O(KN)$ terms, and is applicable to the thresholded ensemble model. However, the bound is loose when T, the size of the ensemble, is large, because its complexity term grows with T.

In this section, we derive novel large-margin bounds of different error functions for the thresholded ensemble model. The bounds are extended from the results of Schapire et al. [11]. Our bounds are based on a margin definition of $O(KN)$ terms. Similar to the results of Schapire et al., our bounds do not require $E_2(G, \mathcal{S}_u, \Delta) = 0$, and their complexity terms do not grow with T.

3.1   Margins

The margins with respect to a thresholded model are illustrated in Fig. 1. Intuitively, we expect the potential value $H(x)$ to be in the correct interval $(\theta_{y-1}, \theta_y]$, and we want $H(x)$ to be far from the boundaries (thresholds):

Definition 1. *Consider a given thresholded ensemble $G_\theta(x)$.*

1. The margin of an example (x, y) with respect to θ_k is defined as

$$\rho_k(x, y) = \begin{cases} H(x) - \theta_k, & \text{if } y > k; \\ \theta_k - H(x), & \text{if } y \le k. \end{cases}$$

2. The normalized margin $\bar{\rho}_k(x, y)$ is defined as

$$\bar{\rho}_k(x, y) = \rho_k(x, y) \bigg/ \left(\sum_{t=1}^{T} |\alpha_t| + \sum_{k=1}^{K-1} |\theta_k| \right).$$

Definition 1 is similar to the definition by Shashua and Levin [2], which is analogous to the definition of margins in binary classification. A negative $\rho_k(x, y)$ would indicate an incorrect prediction.

For each example (x, y), we can obtain $(K - 1)$ margins from Definition 1. However, two of them are of the most importance. The first one is $\rho_{y-1}(x, y)$, which is the margin to the left (lower) boundary of the correct interval. The other is $\rho_y(x, y)$, which is the margin to the right (upper) boundary. We will give them special names: the left-margin $\rho_L(x, y)$, and the right-margin $\rho_R(x, y)$. Note that by definition, $\rho_L(x, 1) = \rho_R(x, K) = \infty$.

Δ-classification error: Next, we take a closer look at the error functions for thresholded ensemble models. If we make a minor assumption that the degenerate cases $\bar{\rho}_R(x, y) = 0$ are of an infinitesimal probability,

$$E_C(G_\theta, \mathcal{D}) = \mathcal{E}_{(x,y)\sim\mathcal{D}}[\![G_\theta(x) \neq y]\!]$$
$$= \mathcal{E}_{(x,y)\sim\mathcal{D}}[\![\bar{\rho}_L(x, y) \leq 0 \text{ or } \bar{\rho}_R(x, y) \leq 0]\!].$$

The definition could be generalized by expecting both margins to be larger than Δ. That is, define the Δ-classification error as

$$E_C(G_\theta, \mathcal{D}, \Delta) = \mathcal{E}_{(x,y)\sim\mathcal{D}}[\![\bar{\rho}_L(x, y) \leq \Delta \text{ or } \bar{\rho}_R(x, y) \leq \Delta]\!].$$

Then, $E_C(G_\theta, \mathcal{D})$ is just a special case with $\Delta = 0$.

Δ-boundary error: The "or" operation of $E_C(G_\theta, \mathcal{D}, \Delta)$ is not easy to handle in the proof of the coming bounds. An alternative choice is the Δ-boundary error:

$$E_B(G_\theta, \mathcal{D}, \Delta) = \mathcal{E}_{(x,y)\sim\mathcal{D}} \begin{cases} [\![\bar{\rho}_R(x, y) \leq \Delta]\!], & \text{if } y = 1; \\ [\![\bar{\rho}_L(x, y) \leq \Delta]\!], & \text{if } y = K; \\ \frac{1}{2} \cdot ([\![\bar{\rho}_L(x, y) \leq \Delta]\!] + [\![\bar{\rho}_R(x, y) \leq \Delta]\!]), & \text{otherwise.} \end{cases}$$

The Δ-boundary error and the Δ-classification error are equivalent up to a constant. That is, for any $(G_\theta, \mathcal{D}, \Delta)$,

$$\tfrac{1}{2}E_C(G_\theta, \mathcal{D}, \Delta) \leq E_B(G_\theta, \mathcal{D}, \Delta) \leq E_C(G_\theta, \mathcal{D}, \Delta). \tag{1}$$

Δ-absolute error: We can analogously define the Δ-absolute error as

$$E_A(G_\theta, \mathcal{D}, \Delta) = \mathcal{E}_{(x,y)\sim\mathcal{D}} \sum_{k=1}^{K-1} [\![\bar{\rho}_k(x, y) \leq \Delta]\!].$$

Then, if we assume that the degenerate cases $\rho_k(x, y) = 0$ happen with an infinitesimal probability, $E_A(G_\theta, \mathcal{D})$ is just a special case with $\Delta = 0$.

3.2   Large-Margin Bounds

An important observation for deriving our bounds is that E_B and E_A can be written with respect to an additional sampling of k. For example,

$$E_A(G_\theta, \mathcal{D}, \Delta) = (K - 1)\mathcal{E}_{(x,y)\sim\mathcal{D},k\sim\{1,...,K-1\}_u}[\![\bar{\rho}_k(x, y) \leq \Delta]\!].$$

Equivalently, we can define a distribution $\hat{\mathcal{D}}$ by $\mathcal{D}$ and $\{1, \ldots, K-1\}_u$ to generate the tuple (x, y, k). Then $E_A(G_\theta, \mathcal{D})$ is simply the portion of nonpositive $\bar{\rho}_k(x, y)$ under $\hat{\mathcal{D}}$. Consider an extended training set $\hat{\mathcal{S}} = \{(x_n, y_n, k)\}$

with $N(K-1)$ elements. Each element is a possible outcome from $\hat{\mathcal{D}}$. Note, however, that these elements are not all independent. For example, $(x_n, y_n, 1)$ and $(x_n, y_n, 2)$ are dependent. Thus, we cannot directly use the whole $\hat{\mathcal{S}}$ as a set of i.i.d. outcomes from $\hat{\mathcal{D}}$.

Fortunately, some subsets of $\hat{\mathcal{S}}$ contain independent outcomes from $\hat{\mathcal{D}}$. One way to extract such subsets is to choose one k_n from $\{1, \ldots, K-1\}_u$ for each example (x_n, y_n) independently. The subset would be named $\mathcal{T} = \{(x_n, y_n, k_n)\}_{n=1}^{N}$. Then, we can obtain a large-margin bound of the absolute error:

Theorem 1. *Consider a set $\mathcal{H}$, which contains only binary classifiers, is negation-complete,[2] and has VC-dimension d. Let $\delta > 0$, and $N > d + K - 1 = \hat{d}$. Then with probability at least $1 - \delta$ over the random choice of the training set $\mathcal{S}$, every thresholded ensemble $G_\theta(x)$, where the associated H is constructed with $h \in \mathcal{H}$, satisfies the following bound for all $\Delta > 0$:*

$$E_A(G_\theta, \mathcal{D}) \le E_A(G_\theta, \mathcal{S}_u, \Delta) + O\left(\frac{K}{\sqrt{N}}\left(\frac{\hat{d}\log^2(N/\hat{d})}{\Delta^2} + \log\frac{1}{\delta}\right)^{1/2}\right).$$

Proof. The key is to reduce the ordinal regression problem to a binary classification problem, which consists of training examples derived from $(x_n, y_n, k_n) \in \mathcal{T}$:

$$(X_n, Y_n) = \begin{cases} ((x_n, 1_{k_n}), +1), & \text{if } y_n > k_n; \\ ((x_n, 1_{k_n}), -1), & \text{if } y_n \le k_n, \end{cases} \tag{2}$$

where 1_m is a vector of length $(K-1)$ with a single 1 at the m-th dimension and 0 elsewhere. The test examples are constructed similarly with $(x, y, k) \sim \hat{\mathcal{D}}$. Then, large-margin bounds for the ordinal regression problem can be inferred from those for the binary classification problem, as shown in Appendix A. □

Similarly, if we look at the boundary error,

$$E_B(G_\theta, \mathcal{D}, \Delta) = \mathcal{E}_{(x,y)\sim\mathcal{D}, k\sim\mathcal{B}_y}[\bar{\rho}_k(x,y) \le \Delta],$$

for some distribution $\mathcal{B}_y$ on $\{L, R\}$. Then, a similar proof leads to

Theorem 2. *For the same conditions as of Theorem 1,*

$$E_B(G_\theta, \mathcal{D}) \le E_B(G_\theta, \mathcal{S}_u, \Delta) + O\left(\frac{1}{\sqrt{N}}\left(\frac{\hat{d}\log^2(N/\hat{d})}{\Delta^2} + \log\frac{1}{\delta}\right)^{1/2}\right).$$

Then, a large-margin bound of the classification error can immediately be derived by applying (1).

Corollary 1. *For the same conditions as of Theorem 1,*

$$E_C(G_\theta, \mathcal{D}) \le 2E_C(G_\theta, \mathcal{S}_u, \Delta) + O\left(\frac{1}{\sqrt{N}}\left(\frac{\hat{d}\log^2(N/\hat{d})}{\Delta^2} + \log\frac{1}{\delta}\right)^{1/2}\right).$$

---

[2] $h \in \mathcal{H} \iff (-h) \in \mathcal{H}$, where $(-h)(x) = -(h(x))$ for all x.

Similar bounds can be derived with another large-margin theorem [11, Theorem 4] when $\mathcal{H}$ contains confidence functions rather than binary classifiers. These bounds provide motivations for building algorithms with margin-related formulations.

4   Boosting Algorithms for Thresholded Ensembles

The bounds in the previous section are applicable to thresholded ensembles generated from any algorithms. One possible algorithm, for example, is an SVM-based approach [3] with special kernels [12]. In this section, we focus on another branch of approaches: boosting. Boosting approaches can iteratively grow the ensemble $H(x)$, and have been successful in classification and metric regression [8]. Our study includes an extension to the RankBoost algorithm [7] and two novel formulations that we propose.

4.1   RankBoost for Ordinal Regression

RankBoost [7] constructs a weighted ensemble of confidence functions based on the following large-margin concept: for each pair (i, j) such that $y_i > y_j$, the difference between their potential values, $H_t(x_i) - H_t(x_j)$, is desired to be positive and large. Thus, in the t-th iteration, the algorithm chooses (h_t, α_t) to approximately minimize

$$\sum_{y_i > y_j} e^{-H_{t-1}(x_i) - \alpha_t h_t(x_i) + H_{t-1}(x_j) + \alpha_t h_t(x_j)}. \tag{3}$$

Our efforts in extending RankBoost for ordinal regression are discussed as follows:

Computing α_t: Two approaches can be used to determine α_t in RankBoost [7]:

1. Obtain the optimal α_t by numerical search (confidence functions) or analytical solution (binary classifiers).
2. Minimize an upper bound of (3).

If $h_t(x_n)$ is monotonic with respect to y_n, the optimal α_t obtained from approach 1 is ∞, and one single h_t would dominate the ensemble. This situation not only makes the ensemble less stable, but also limits its power. For example, if $(y_n, h_t(x_n))$ pairs for four examples are $(1, -1)$, $(2, 0)$, $(3, 1)$, and $(4, 1)$, ranks 3 and 4 on the last two examples cannot be distinguished by h_t. We have frequently observed such a degenerate situation, called *partial matching*, in real-world experiments, even when h_t is as simple as a decision stump. Thus, we shall use approach 2 for our experiments. Note, however, that when partial matching happens, the magnitude of α_t from approach 2 can still be relatively large, and may cause numerical difficulties.

Obtaining θ: After RankBoost computes a potential function $H(x)$, a reasonable way to obtain the thresholds based on training examples is

$$\theta = \operatorname{argmin}_\vartheta E_A(G_\vartheta, S_u). \tag{4}$$

The combination of RankBoost and the absolute error criterion (4) would be called RankBoost-AE. The optimal range of ϑ_k can be efficiently determined by dynamic programming. For simplicity and stability, we assign θ_k to be the middle value in the optimal range. The algorithm that aims at E_C instead of E_A can be similarly derived.

4.2 Ordinal Regression Boosting with Left-Right Margins

The idea of ordinal regression boosting comes from the definition of margins in Sect. 3. As indicated by our bounds, we want the margins to be as large as possible. To achieve this goal, our algorithms, similar to AdaBoost, work on minimizing the exponential margin loss.

First, we introduce a simple formulation called ordinal regression boosting with left-right margins (ORBoost-LR), which tries to minimize

$$\sum_{n=1}^{N} \left[e^{-\rho_L(x_n, y_n)} + e^{-\rho_R(x_n, y_n)} \right]. \tag{5}$$

The formulation can be thought as maximizing the soft-min of the left- and right-margins. Similar to RankBoost, the minimization is performed in an iterative manner. In each iteration, a confidence function h_t is chosen, its weight α_t is computed, and the vector θ is updated. If we plug in the margin definition to (5), we can see that the iteration steps should be designed to approximately minimize

$$\sum_{n=1}^{N} \left[\varphi_n e^{\alpha_t h_t(x_n) - \theta_{y_n}} + \varphi_n^{-1} e^{\theta_{y_n-1} - \alpha_t h_t(x_n)} \right], \tag{6}$$

where $\varphi_n = e^{H_{t-1}(x_n)}$. Next, we discuss these three steps in detail.

Choosing h_t: Mason et al. [13] explained AdaBoost as a gradient descent technique in function space. We derive ORBoost-LR using the same technique. We first choose a confidence function h_t that is close to the negative gradient:

$$h_t = \underset{h \in \mathcal{H}}{\operatorname{argmin}} \sum_{n=1}^{N} h(x_n) \left(\varphi_n e^{-\theta_{y_n}} - \varphi_n^{-1} e^{\theta_{y_n-1}} \right).$$

This step can be performed with the help of another learning algorithm, called the base learner.

Computing α_t: Similar to RankBoost, we minimize an upper bound of (6), which is based on a piece-wise linear approximation of e^x for $x \in [-1, 0]$ and $x \in [0, 1]$. The bound can be written as $W_+ e^\alpha + W_- e^{-\alpha}$, with

$$W_+ = \sum_{h_t(x_n)>0} h_t(x_n)\varphi_n e^{-\theta_{y_n}} - \sum_{h_t(x_n)<0} h_t(x_n)\varphi_n^{-1} e^{\theta_{y_n-1}},$$

$$W_- = \sum_{h_t(x_n)>0} h_t(x_n)\varphi_n^{-1} e^{\theta_{y_n-1}} - \sum_{h_t(x_n)<0} h_t(x_n)\varphi_n e^{-\theta_{y_n}}.$$

Then, the optimal α_t for the bound can be computed by $\frac{1}{2} \log \frac{W_-}{W_+}$.

Note that the upper bound is equal to (6) if $h_t(x_n) \in \{-1, 0, 1\}$. Thus, when h_t is a binary classifier, the optimal α_t can be exactly determined. Another remark here is that α_t is finite under some mild conditions which make both W_+ and W_- positive. Thus, unlike RankBoost, ORBoost-LR rarely sets α_t to ∞.

Updating θ: Note that when the pair (h_t, α_t) is fixed, (6) can be reorganized as $\sum_{k=1}^{K-1} W_{k,+} e^{\theta_k} + W_{k,-} e^{-\theta_k}$. Then, each θ_k can be computed analytically, uniquely, and independently. However, when each θ_k is updated independently, the thresholds may not be ordered. Hence, we propose to add an additional ordering constraint to (6). That is, choosing θ by solving

$$\min_{\vartheta} \sum_{k=1}^{K-1} W_{k,+} e^{\vartheta_k} + W_{k,-} e^{-\vartheta_k} \tag{7}$$
$$\text{s.t. } \vartheta_1 \le \vartheta_2 \le \cdots \le \vartheta_{K-1}.$$

An efficient algorithm for solving (7) can be obtained from by a simple modification of the pool adjacent violators algorithm(PAV) for isotonic regression [14].

Combination of the steps: ORBoost-LR works by combining the three steps above sequentially in each iteration. Note that after h_t is determined, α_t and θ_t can be either jointly optimized, or cyclically updated. However, we found that joint or cyclic optimization does not always introduce better performance, and could sometimes cause ORBoost-LR to overfit. Thus, we only execute each step once in each iteration.

4.3   Ordinal Regression Boosting with All Margins

ORBoost with all margins (ORBoost-All) operates on

$$\sum_{n=1}^{N} \sum_{k=1}^{K-1} e^{-\rho_k(x_n, y_n)} \tag{8}$$

instead of (6). The derivations for the three steps are almost the same as ORBoost-LR. We shall just make some remarks.

Updating θ: When using (8) to update the thresholds, we have proved that each θ_k can be updated uniquely and independently, while still being ordered [5]. Thus, we do not need to implement the PAV algorithm for ORBoost-All.

Relationship between algorithm and theory: A simple relation is that for any Δ, $e^{-A\bar{\rho}_k(x_n, y_n)}$ is an upper bound of $e^{-A\Delta} \cdot [\![\bar{\rho}_k(x_n, y_n) \le \Delta]\!]$. If we take A to be the normalization term of $\bar{\rho}_k$, we can see that

- ORBoost-All works on minimizing an upper bound of $E_A(G_\theta, \mathcal{S}_u, \Delta)$.
- ORBoost-LR works to minimizing an upper bound of $E_B(G_\theta, \mathcal{S}_u, \Delta)$, or $\frac{1}{2} E_C(G_\theta, \mathcal{S}_u, \Delta)$.

ORBoost-All not only minimizes an upper bound, but provably also minimizes the term $E_A(G_\theta, \mathcal{S}_u, \Delta)$ exponentially fast with a sufficiently strong choice of h_t. The proof relies on an extension of the training error theorem of AdaBoost [11, Theorem 5]. Similar proof can be used for ORBoost-LR.

Connection to other algorithms: ORBoost approaches are direct generalizations of AdaBoost using the gradient descent optimization point of view. In the special case of $K = 2$, both ORBoost approaches are almost the same as AdaBoost with an additional term θ_1. Note that the term θ_1 can be thought as the coefficient of a constant classifier. Interestingly, Rudin et al. [6] proved the connection between RankBoost and AdaBoost when including a constant classifier in the ensemble. Thus, when $K = 2$, RankBoost-EA, ORBoost-LR, and ORBoost-All, all share some similarity with AdaBoost.

ORBoost formulations also have connections with SVM-based algorithms. In particular, ORBoost-LR has a counterpart of SVM with explicit constraints (SVM-EXC), and ORBoost-All is related to SVM with implicit constraints (SVM-IMC) [3]. These connections follow closely with the links between Ada-Boost and SVM [12, 15].

5   Experiments

In this section, we compare the three boosting formulations for constructing the thresholded ensemble model. We also compare these formulations with SVM-based algorithms.

Two sets of confidence functions are used in the experiments. The first one is the set of perceptrons $\{\text{sign}(w^T x + b) : w \in \mathbb{R}^D, b \in \mathbb{R}\}$. The RCD-bias algorithm is known to work well with AdaBoost [16], and is adopted as our base learner.

The second set is $\{\tanh(w^T x + b) : w^T w + b^2 = \gamma^2\}$, which contains normalized sigmoid functions. Note that sigmoid functions smoothen the output of perceptrons, and the smoothness is controlled by the parameter γ. We use a naive base learner for normalized sigmoid functions as follows: RCD-bias is first performed to get a perceptron. Then, the weights and bias of the perceptron are normalized, and the outputs are smoothened. Throughout the experiments we use $\gamma = 4$, which was picked with a few experimental runs on some datasets.

5.1   Artificial Dataset

We first verify that the idea of the thresholded ensemble model works with an artificial 2-D dataset (Fig. 2(a)). Figure 2(b) depicts the separating boundaries of the thresholded ensemble of 200 perceptrons constructed by ORBoost-All. By combining perceptrons, ORBoost-All works reasonably well in approximating the nonlinear boundaries. A similar plot can be obtained with ORBoost-LR. RankBoost-AE cannot perform well on this dataset due to numerical difficulties (see Subsect. 4.1) after only 5 iterations.

If we use a thresholded ensemble of 200 normalized sigmoid functions, it is observed that ORBoost-All, ORBoost-LR, and RankBoost-AE perform similarly.

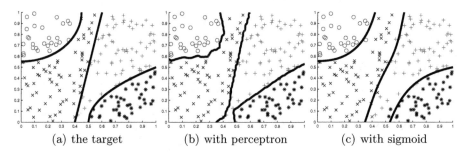

(a) the target   (b) with perceptron   (c) with sigmoid

Fig. 2. An artificial 2-D dataset and the learned boundaries with ORBoost-All

The result of ORBoost-All (Fig. 2(c)) shows that the separating boundaries are much smoother because each sigmoid function is smooth. As we shall discuss later, the smoothness can be important for some ordinal regression problems.

5.2   Benchmark Datasets

Next, we perform experiments with eight benchmark datasets[3] that were used by Chu and Keerthi [3]. The datasets are quantized from some metric regression datasets. We use the same $K = 10$, the same "training/test" partition ratio, and also average the results over 20 trials. Thus, we can compare RankBoost and ORBoost fairly with the SVM-based results of Chu and Keerthi [3].

The results on the abalone dataset with T up to 2000 are given in Fig. 3. The training errors are shown in the top plots, while the test errors are shown in the bottom plots. Based on these results, we have several remarks:

RankBoost vs. ORBoost: RankBoost-AE can usually decrease both the training classification and the training absolute errors faster than ORBoost algorithms. However, such property often lead to consistently worse test error than both ORBoost-LR and ORBoost-All. An explanation is that although the Rank-Boost ensemble orders the training examples well, the current estimate of θ is not used to decide (h_t, α_t). Thus, the two components (H_T, θ) of the thresholded ensemble model are not jointly considered, and the greediness in constructing only H_T results in overfitting. In contrast, ORBoost-LR and ORBoost-All take into consideration the current θ in choosing (h_t, α_t) and the current H_T in updating θ. Hence, a better pair of (H_T, θ) could be obtained.

ORBoost-LR vs. ORBoost-All: Both ORBoost formulations inherit a good property from AdaBoost: not very vulnerable to overfitting. ORBoost-LR is better on test classification errors, while ORBoost-All is better on test absolute errors. This is partially justified by our discussion in Subsect. 4.3 that the two formulations minimize different margin-related upper bounds. A similar observation was made by Chu and Keerthi [3] on SVM-EXC and SVM-IMC algorithms. Note, however, that ORBoost-LR with perceptrons minimizes the

---

[3] Pyrimdines, machineCPU, boston, abalone, bank, computer, california, and census.

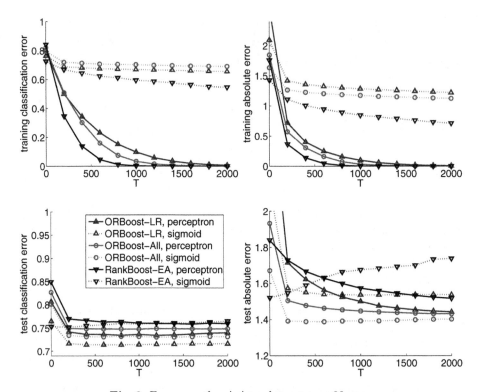

Fig. 3. Errors on the abalone dataset over 20 runs

training classification error slower than ORBoost-All on this dataset, because the additional ordering constraint of θ in ORBoost-LR slows down the convergence.

Perceptron vs. sigmoid: Formulations with sigmoid functions have consistently higher training error, which is due to the naive choice of base learner and the approximation of α_t. However, the best test performance is also achieved with sigmoid functions. One possible reason is that the abalone dataset is quantized from a metric regression dataset, and hence contains some properties such as smoothness of the boundaries. If we only use binary classifiers like perceptrons, as depicted in Fig. 2(b), the boundaries would not be as smooth, and more errors may happen. Thus, for ordinal regression datasets that are quantized from metric regression datasets, smooth confidence functions may be more useful than discrete binary classifiers.

We list the mean and standard errors of all test results with $T = 2000$ in Tables 1 and 2. Consistent with the results on the abalone dataset, RankBoost-AE almost always performs the worst; ORBoost-LR is better on classification errors, and ORBoost-All is slightly better on absolute errors. When compared with SVM-IMC on classification errors and SVM-EXC on absolute errors [3], both ORBoost formulations have similar errors as the SVM-based algorithms. Note, however, that ORBoost formulations with perceptrons or sigmoid functions

Table 1. Test classification error of ordinal regression algorithms

data	RankBoost-AE		ORBoost-LR		ORBoost-All		SVM-EXC [3]
set	perceptron	sigmoid	perceptron	sigmoid	perceptron	sigmoid	
pyr.	0.758±0.015	0.767±0.020	**0.731±0.019**	**0.731±0.018**	0.744±0.019	0.735±0.017	0.752±0.014
mac.	0.717±0.022	0.669±0.011	**0.610±0.009**	0.633±0.011	**0.605±0.010**	0.625±0.014	0.661±0.012
bos.	0.603±0.006	0.578±0.008	0.580±0.006	**0.549±0.007**	0.579±0.006	0.558±0.006	0.569±0.006
aba.	0.759±0.001	0.765±0.002	0.740±0.002	**0.716±0.002**	0.749±0.002	0.731±0.002	0.736±0.002
ban.	0.805±0.001	0.822±0.001	0.767±0.001	0.777±0.002	0.771±0.001	0.776±0.001	**0.744±0.001**
com.	0.598±0.002	0.616±0.001	0.498±0.001	0.491±0.001	0.499±0.001	0.505±0.001	**0.462±0.001**
cal.	0.741±0.001	0.690±0.001	0.628±0.001	**0.605±0.001**	0.626±0.001	0.618±0.001	0.640±0.001
cen.	0.808±0.001	0.780±0.001	0.718±0.001	**0.694±0.001**	0.722±0.001	0.701±0.001	0.699±0.000

(results that are within one standard error of the best are marked in bold)

Table 2. Test absolute error of ordinal regression algorithms

data	RankBoost-AE		ORBoost-LR		ORBoost-All		SVM-IMC [3]
set	perceptron	sigmoid	perceptron	sigmoid	perceptron	sigmoid	
pyr.	1.619±0.078	1.590±0.077	**1.340±0.049**	1.402±0.052	1.360±0.046	1.398±0.052	**1.294±0.046**
mac.	1.573±0.191	1.282±0.034	**0.897±0.019**	0.985±0.018	**0.889±0.019**	0.969±0.025	0.990±0.026
bos.	0.842±0.014	0.829±0.014	0.788±0.013	**0.758±0.015**	0.791±0.013	0.777±0.015	**0.747±0.011**
aba.	1.517±0.005	1.738±0.008	1.442±0.004	1.537±0.007	1.432±0.003	1.403±0.004	**1.361±0.003**
ban.	1.867±0.004	2.183±0.007	1.507±0.002	1.656±0.005	1.490±0.002	1.539±0.002	**1.393±0.002**
com.	0.841±0.003	0.945±0.004	0.631±0.002	0.634±0.003	0.626±0.002	0.634±0.002	**0.596±0.002**
cal.	1.528±0.006	1.251±0.004	1.042±0.004	0.956±0.002	0.977±0.002	**0.942±0.002**	1.008±0.001
cen.	2.008±0.006	1.796±0.005	1.305±0.003	1.262±0.003	1.265±0.002	**1.198±0.002**	1.205±0.002

(results that are within one standard error of the best are marked in bold)

are much faster. On the census dataset, which contains 6000 training examples, it takes about an hour for ORBoost to finish one trial. But SVM-based approaches, which include a time-consuming automatic parameter selection step, need more than four days. With the comparable performance and significantly less computational cost, ORBoost could be a useful tool for large datasets.

6 Conclusion

We proposed a thresholded ensemble model for ordinal regression, and defined margins for the model. Novel large-margin bounds of common error functions were proved. We studied three algorithms for obtaining thresholded ensembles. The first algorithm, RankBoost-AE, combines RankBoost and a thresholding algorithm. In addition, we designed two new boosting approaches, ORBoost-LR and ORBoost-All, which have close connections with the large-margin bounds. ORBoost formulations are direct extensions of AdaBoost, and inherit its advantage of being less venerable to overfitting.

Experimental results demonstrated that ORBoost formulations have superior performance over RankBoost-AE. In addition, they are comparable to SVM-based algorithms in terms of test error, but enjoy the advantage of faster training. These properties make ORBoost formulations favorable over SVM-based algorithms on large datasets.

ORBoost formulations can be equipped with any base learners for confidence functions. In this work, we studied the perceptrons and the normalized sigmoid functions. Future work could be exploring other confidence functions for OR-Boost, or extending other boosting approaches to perform ordinal regression.

Acknowledgment

We thank Yaser S. Abu-Mostafa, Amrit Pratap, and the anonymous reviewers for helpful comments. Hsuan-Tien Lin is supported by the Caltech Division of Engineering and Applied Science Fellowship.

References

1. Herbrich, R., Graepel, T., Obermayer, K.: Large margin rank boundaries for ordinal regression. In: Advances in Large Margin Classifiers. MIT Press (2000) 115–132
2. Shashua, A., Levin, A.: Ranking with large margin principle: Two approaches. In: Advances in Neural Information Processing Systems 15, MIT Press (2003) 961–968
3. Chu, W., Keerthi, S.S.: New approaches to support vector ordinal regression. In: Proceedings of ICML 2005, Omnipress (2005) 145–152
4. Crammer, K., Singer, Y.: Online ranking by projecting. Neural Computation **17** (2005) 145–175
5. Li, L., Lin, H.T.: Ordinal regression by extended binary classification. Under review (2007)
6. Rudin, C., Cortes, C., Mohri, M., Schapire, R.E.: Margin-based ranking meets boosting in the middle. In: Learning Theory: COLT 2005, Springer-Verlag (2005) 63–78
7. Freund, Y., Iyer, R., Shapire, R.E., Singer, Y.: An efficient boosting algorithm for combining preferences. Journal of Machine Learning Research **4** (2003) 933–969
8. Meir, R., Rätsch, G.: An introduction to boosting and leveraging. In: Advanced Lectures on Machine Learning. Springer-Verlag (2003) 118–183
9. Freund, Y., Schapire, R.E.: Experiments with a new boosting algorithm. In: Machine Learning: ICML 1996, Morgan Kaufmann (1996) 148–156
10. Vapnik, V.N.: The Nature of Statistical Learning Theory. Springer-Verlag (1995)
11. Schapire, R.E., Freund, Y., Bartlett, P., Lee, W.S.: Boosting the margin: A new explanation for the effectiveness of voting methods. The Annals of Statistics **26** (1998) 1651–1686
12. Lin, H.T., Li, L.: Infinite ensemble learning with support vector machines. In: Machine Learning: ECML 2005, Springer-Verlag (2005) 242–254
13. Mason, L., Baxter, J., Bartlett, P., Frean, M.: Functional gradient techniques for combining hypotheses. In: Advances in Large Margin Classifiers. MIT Press (2000) 221–246
14. Robertson, T., Wright, F.T., Dykstra, R.L.: Order Restricted Statistical Inference. John Wiley & Sons (1988)
15. Rätsch, G., Mika, S., Schölkopf, B., Müller, K.R.: Constructing boosting algorithms from SVMs: An application to one-class classification. IEEE Transactions on Pattern Analysis and Machine Intelligence **24** (2002) 1184–1199
16. Li, L.: Perceptron learning with random coordinate descent. Technical Report CaltechCSTR:2005.006, California Institute of Technology (2005)

A   Proof of Theorem 1

As shown in (2), we first construct a transformed binary problem. Then, the problem is modeled by an ensemble function $F(x)$ defined on a base space

$$\mathcal{F} = \mathcal{H} \cup \{s_k\}_{k=1}^{K-1}.$$

Here $s_k(X) = -\operatorname{sign}(X_{D+k} - 0.5)$ is a decision stump on dimension $(D+k)$. It is not hard to show that the VC-dimension of $\mathcal{F}$ is no more than $\hat{d} = d + K - 1$.

Without loss of generality, we normalize $G_\theta(x)$ such that $\sum_{t=1}^{T} |\alpha_t| + \sum_{k=1}^{K-1} |\theta_k|$ is 1. Then, consider the associated ensemble function

$$F(X) = \sum_{t=1}^{T} \alpha_t h_t(X) + \sum_{k=1}^{K-1} \theta_k s_k(X).$$

An important property for the transform is that for every (X, Y) derived from the tuple (x, y, k), $YF(X) = \bar{\rho}_k(x, y)$.

Because $\mathcal{T}$ contains N i.i.d. outcomes from $\hat{\mathcal{D}}$, the large-margin theorem [11, Theorem 2] states that with probability at least $1 - \delta/2$ over the choice of $\mathcal{T}$,

$$\mathcal{E}_{(x,y,k)\sim\hat{\mathcal{D}}}[YF(X) \le 0] \le$$

$$\frac{1}{N} \sum_{n=1}^{N} [\![Y_n F(X_n) \le \Delta]\!] + O\left(\frac{1}{\sqrt{N}} \left(\frac{\hat{d}\log^2(N/\hat{d})}{\Delta^2} + \log\frac{1}{\delta}\right)^{1/2}\right). \quad (9)$$

Since $YF(X) = \bar{\rho}_k(x, y)$, the left-hand-side is $\frac{1}{K-1} E_A(G_\theta, \mathcal{D})$.

Let $b_n = [\![Y_n F(X_n) \le \Delta]\!] = [\![\bar{\rho}_{k_n}(x_n, y_n) \le \Delta]\!]$, which is a Boolean random variable. An extended Chernoff bound shows that when each b_n is chosen independently, with probability at least $1 - \delta/2$ over the choice of b_n,

$$\frac{1}{N} \sum_{n=1}^{N} b_n \le \frac{1}{N} \sum_{n=1}^{N} \mathcal{E}_{k_n\sim\{1,\cdots,K-1\}_u} b_n + O\left(\frac{1}{\sqrt{N}} \left(\log\frac{1}{\delta}\right)^{1/2}\right). \quad (10)$$

The desired result can be obtained by combining (9) and (10), with a union bound and $\mathcal{E}_{k_n\sim\{1,\cdots,K-1\}_u} b_n = \frac{1}{K-1} E_A(G_\theta, S_u, \Delta)$.   □

Asymptotic Learnability of Reinforcement Problems with Arbitrary Dependence[*]

Daniil Ryabko and Marcus Hutter

IDSIA, Galleria 2, CH-6928 Manno-Lugano, Switzerland
{daniil, marcus}@idsia.ch
http://www.idsia.ch/~{daniil, marcus}

Abstract. We address the problem of reinforcement learning in which observations may exhibit an arbitrary form of stochastic dependence on past observations and actions, i.e. environments more general than (PO) MDPs. The task for an agent is to attain the best possible asymptotic reward where the true generating environment is unknown but belongs to a known countable family of environments. We find some sufficient conditions on the class of environments under which an agent exists which attains the best asymptotic reward for any environment in the class. We analyze how tight these conditions are and how they relate to different probabilistic assumptions known in reinforcement learning and related fields, such as Markov Decision Processes and mixing conditions.

1 Introduction

Many real-world "learning" problems (like learning to drive a car or playing a game) can be modelled as an agent π that interacts with an environment μ and is (occasionally) rewarded for its behavior. We are interested in agents which perform well in the sense of having high long-term reward, also called the value $V(\mu,\pi)$ of agent π in environment μ. If μ is known, it is a pure (non-learning) computational problem to determine the optimal agent $\pi^\mu := \text{argmax}_\pi V(\mu,\pi)$. It is far less clear what an "optimal" agent means, if μ is unknown. A reasonable objective is to have a single policy π with high value simultaneously in many environments. We will formalize and call this criterion *self-optimizing* later.

Learning approaches in reactive worlds. Reinforcement learning, sequential decision theory, adaptive control theory, and active expert advice, are theories dealing with this problem. They overlap but have different core focus: Reinforcement learning algorithms [SB98] are developed to learn μ or directly its value. Temporal difference learning is computationally very efficient, but has slow asymptotic guarantees (only) in (effectively) small observable MDPs. Others have faster guarantee in finite state MDPs [BT99]. There are algorithms [EDKM05] which are optimal for any finite connected POMDP, and this is apparently the largest class of environments considered. In sequential decision theory, a Bayes-optimal agent π^* that maximizes $V(\xi,\pi)$ is considered, where ξ is

---

[*] This work was supported by the Swiss NSF grant 200020-107616.

J.L. Balcázar, P.M. Long, and F. Stephan (Eds.): ALT 2006, LNAI 4264, pp. 334–347, 2006.

a mixture of environments $\nu \in \mathcal{C}$ and $\mathcal{C}$ is a class of environments that contains the true environment $\mu \in \mathcal{C}$ [Hut05]. Policy π^* is self-optimizing in an arbitrary (e.g. non-POMDP) class $\mathcal{C}$, provided $\mathcal{C}$ allows for self-optimizingness [Hut02]. Adaptive control theory [KV86] considers very simple (from an AI perspective) or special systems (e.g. linear with quadratic loss function), which sometimes allow computationally and data efficient solutions. Action with expert advice [dFM04, PH05, PH06, CBL06] constructs an agent (called master) that performs nearly as well as the best agent (best expert in hindsight) from some class of experts, in *any* environment ν. The important special case of passive sequence prediction in arbitrary unknown environments, where the actions=predictions do not affect the environment is comparably easy [Hut03, HP04].

The difficulty in active learning problems can be identified (at least, for countable classes) with *traps* in the environments. Initially the agent does not know μ, so has asymptotically to be forgiven in taking initial "wrong" actions. A well-studied such class are ergodic MDPs which guarantee that, from any action history, every state can be (re)visited [Hut02].

What's new. The aim of this paper is to characterize as general as possible classes $\mathcal{C}$ in which self-optimizing behaviour is possible, more general than POMDPs. To do this we need to characterize classes of environments that forgive. For instance, exact state recovery is unnecessarily strong; it is sufficient being able to recover high rewards, from whatever states. Further, in many real world problems there is no information available about the "states" of the environment (e.g. in POMDPs) or the environment may exhibit long history dependencies.

Rather than trying to model an environment (e.g. by MDP) we try to identify the conditions sufficient for learning. Towards this aim, we propose to consider only environments in which, after any arbitrary finite sequence of actions, the best value is still achievable. The performance criterion here is asymptotic average reward. Thus we consider such environments for which there exists a policy whose asymptotic average reward exists and upper-bounds asymptotic average reward of any other policy. Moreover, the same property should hold after any finite sequence of actions has been taken (no traps).

Yet this property in itself is not sufficient for identifying optimal behavior. We require further that, from any sequence of k actions, it is possible to return to the optimal level of reward in $o(k)$ steps. (The above conditions will be formulated in a probabilistic form.) Environments which possess this property are called *value-stable*.

We show that for any countable class of value-stable environments there exists a policy which achieves best possible value in any of the environments from the class (i.e. is *self-optimizing* for this class). We also show that strong value-stability is in a certain sense necessary.

We also consider examples of environments which possess strong value-stability. In particular, any ergodic MDP can be easily shown to have this property. A mixing-type condition which implies value-stability is also demonstrated. Finally, we provide a construction allowing to build examples of value-stable environments which are not isomorphic to a finite POMDP, thus demonstrating that the class of value-stable environments is quite general.

It is important in our argument that the class of environments for which we seek a self-optimizing policy is countable, although the class of all value-stable environments is uncountable. To find a set of conditions necessary and sufficient for learning which do not rely on countability of the class is yet an open problem. However, from a computational perspective countable classes are sufficiently large (e.g. the class of all computable probability measures is countable).

Contents. The paper is organized as follows. Section 2 introduces necessary notation of the agent framework. In Section 3 we define and explain the notion of value-stability, which is central in the paper. Section 4 presents the theorem about self-optimizing policies for classes of value-stable environments, and illustrates the applicability of the theorem by providing examples of strongly value-stable environments. In Section 5 we discuss necessity of the conditions of the main theorem. Section 6 provides some discussion of the results and an outlook to future research. The formal proof of the main theorem is given in the appendix, while Section 4 contains only intuitive explanations.

2   Notation and Definitions

We essentially follow the notation of [Hut02, Hut05].

Strings and probabilities. We use letters $i,k,l,m,n \in I\!N$ for natural numbers, and denote the cardinality of sets S by $\#S$. We write $\mathcal{X}^*$ for the set of finite strings over some alphabet $\mathcal{X}$, and $\mathcal{X}^\infty$ for the set of infinite sequences. For a string $x \in \mathcal{X}^*$ of length $\ell(x) = n$ we write $x_1 x_2 ... x_n$ with $x_t \in \mathcal{X}$ and further abbreviate $x_{k:n} := x_k x_{k+1} ... x_{n-1} x_n$ and $x_{<n} := x_1 ... x_{n-1}$. Finally, we define $x_{k..n} := x_k + ... + x_n$, provided elements of $\mathcal{X}$ can be added.

We assume that sequence $\omega = \omega_{1:\infty} \in \mathcal{X}^\infty$ is sampled from the "true" probability measure μ, i.e. $\mathbf{P}[\omega_{1:n} = x_{1:n}] = \mu(x_{1:n})$. We denote expectations w.r.t. μ by $\mathbf{E}$, i.e. for a function $f : \mathcal{X}^n \to I\!R$, $\mathbf{E}[f] = \mathbf{E}[f(\omega_{1:n})] = \sum_{x_{1:n}} \mu(x_{1:n}) f(x_{1:n})$. When we use probabilities and expectations with respect to other measures we make the notation explicit, e.g. $\mathbf{E}_\nu$ is the expectation with respect to ν. Measures ν_1 and ν_2 are called *singular* if there exists a set A such that $\nu_1(A) = 0$ and $\nu_2(A) = 1$.

The agent framework is general enough to allow modelling nearly any kind of (intelligent) system [RN95]. In cycle k, an agent performs *action* $y_k \in \mathcal{Y}$ (output) which results in *observation* $o_k \in \mathcal{O}$ and *reward* $r_k \in \mathcal{R}$, followed by cycle $k+1$ and so on. We assume that the action space $\mathcal{Y}$, the observation space $\mathcal{O}$, and the reward space $\mathcal{R} \subset I\!R$ are finite, w.l.g. $\mathcal{R} = \{0,...,r_{max}\}$. We abbreviate $z_k := y_k r_k o_k \in \mathcal{Z} := \mathcal{Y} \times \mathcal{R} \times \mathcal{O}$ and $x_k = r_k o_k \in \mathcal{X} := \mathcal{R} \times \mathcal{O}$. An agent is identified with a (probabilistic) *policy* π. Given *history* $z_{<k}$, the probability that agent π acts y_k in cycle k is (by definition) $\pi(y_k|z_{<k})$. Thereafter, *environment* μ provides (probabilistic) reward r_k and observation o_k, i.e. the probability that the agent perceives x_k is (by definition) $\mu(x_k|z_{<k}y_k)$. Note that policy and environment are allowed to depend on the complete history. We do not make any MDP

or POMDP assumption here, and we don't talk about states of the environment, only about observations. Each (policy,environment) pair (π,μ) generates an I/O sequence $z_1^{\pi\mu}z_2^{\pi\mu}....$ Mathematically, history $z_{1:k}^{\pi\mu}$ is a random variable with probability

$$\mathbf{P}[z_{1:k}^{\pi\mu} = z_{1:k}] \;=\; \pi(y_1)\cdot\mu(x_1|y_1)\cdot...\cdot\pi(y_k|z_{<k})\cdot\mu(x_k|z_{<k}y_k)$$

Since value maximizing policies can always be chosen deterministic, there is no real need to consider probabilistic policies, and henceforth we consider deterministic policies p. We assume that $\mu\in\mathcal{C}$ is the true, but unknown, environment, and $\nu\in\mathcal{C}$ a generic environment.

3   Setup

For an environment ν and a policy p define random variables (lower and upper average value)

$$\overline{V}(\nu,p) \;:=\; \limsup_{m}\left\{\tfrac{1}{m}r_{1..m}^{p\nu}\right\} \quad\text{and}\quad \underline{V}(\nu,p) \;:=\; \liminf_{m}\left\{\tfrac{1}{m}r_{1..m}^{p\nu}\right\}$$

where $r_{1..m}:=r_1+...+r_m$. If there exists a constant V such that

$$\overline{V}(\nu,p) \;=\; \underline{V}(\nu,p) \;=\; V \text{ a.s.}$$

then we say that the limiting average value exists and denote it by $V(\nu,p)=:V$.

An environment ν is *explorable* if there exists a policy p_ν such that $V(\nu,p_\nu)$ exists and $\overline{V}(\nu,p)\leq V(\nu,p_\nu)$ with probability 1 for every policy p. In this case define $V_\nu^*:=V(\nu,p_\nu)$.

A policy p is *self-optimizing* for a set of environments $\mathcal{C}$ if $V(\nu,p)=V_\nu^*$ for every $\nu\in\mathcal{C}$.

Definition 1 (value-stable environments). *An explorable environment ν is (strongly) value-stable if there exist a sequence of numbers $r_i^\nu \in [0,r_{max}]$ and two functions $d_\nu(k,\varepsilon)$ and $\varphi_\nu(n,\varepsilon)$ such that $\tfrac{1}{n}r_{1..n}^\nu \to V_\nu^*$, $d_\nu(k,\varepsilon)=o(k)$, $\sum_{n=1}^{\infty}\varphi_\nu(n,\varepsilon)<\infty$ for every fixed ε, and for every k and every history $z_{<k}$ there exists a policy $p=p_\nu^{z_{<k}}$ such that*

$$\mathbf{P}\left(r_{k..k+n}^\nu - r_{k..k+n}^{p\nu} > d_\nu(k,\varepsilon) + n\varepsilon \mid z_{<k}\right) \leq \varphi_\nu(n,\varepsilon). \tag{1}$$

First of all, this condition means that the strong law of large numbers for rewards holds uniformly over histories $z_{<k}$; the numbers r_i^ν here can be thought of as expected rewards of an optimal policy. Furthermore, the environment is "forgiving" in the following sense: from any (bad) sequence of k actions it is possible (knowing the environment) to recover up to $o(k)$ reward loss; to recover means to reach the level of reward obtained by the optimal policy which from the beginning was taking only optimal actions. That is, suppose that a person A has made k possibly suboptimal actions and after that "realized" what the true environment was and how to act optimally in it. Suppose that a person B was

from the beginning taking only optimal actions. We want to compare the performance of A and B on first n steps after the step k. An environment is strongly value stable if A can catch up with B except for $o(k)$ gain. The numbers r_i^ν can be thought of as expected rewards of B; A can catch up with B up to the reward loss $d_\nu(k,\varepsilon)$ with probability $\varphi_\nu(n,\varepsilon)$, where the latter does not depend on past actions and observations (the law of large numbers holds uniformly).

In the next section after presenting the main theorem we consider examples of families of strongly-values stable environments.

4   Main Results

In this section we present the main self-optimizingness result along with an informal explanation of its proof, and illustrate the applicability of this result with examples of classes of value-stable environments.

Theorem 2 (value-stable⇒self-optimizing). *For any countable class $\mathcal{C}$ of strongly value-stable environments, there exists a policy which is self-optimizing for $\mathcal{C}$.*

A formal proof is given in the appendix; here we give some intuitive justification. Suppose that all environments in $\mathcal{C}$ are deterministic. We will construct a self-optimizing policy p as follows: Let ν^t be the first environment in $\mathcal{C}$. The algorithm assumes that the true environment is ν^t and tries to get ε-close to its optimal value for some (small) ε. This is called an exploitation part. If it succeeds, it does some exploration as follows. It picks the first environment ν^e which has higher average asymptotic value than ν^t ($V_{\nu^e}^* > V_{\nu^t}^*$) and tries to get ε-close to this value acting optimally under ν^e. If it can not get close to the ν^e-optimal value then ν^e is not the true environment, and the next environment can be picked for exploration (here we call "exploration" successive attempts to exploit an environment which differs from the current hypothesis about the true environment and has a higher average reward). If it can, then it switches to exploitation of ν^t, exploits it until it is ε'-close to $V_{\nu^t}^*$, $\varepsilon' < \varepsilon$ and switches to ν^e again this time trying to get ε'-close to V_{ν^e}; and so on. This can happen only a finite number of times if the true environment is ν^t, since $V_{\nu^t}^* < V_{\nu^e}^*$. Thus after exploration either ν^t or ν^e is found to be inconsistent with the current history. If it is ν^e then just the next environment ν^e such that $V_{\nu^e}^* > V_{\nu^t}^*$ is picked for exploration. If it is ν^t then the first consistent environment is picked for exploitation (and denoted ν^t). This in turn can happen only a finite number of times before the true environment ν is picked as ν^t. After this, the algorithm still continues its exploration attempts, but can always keep within $\varepsilon_k \to 0$ of the optimal value. This is ensured by $d(k) = o(k)$.

The probabilistic case is somewhat more complicated since we can not say whether an environment is "consistent" with the current history. Instead we test each environment for consistency as follows. Let ξ be a mixture of all environments in $\mathcal{C}$. Observe that together with some fixed policy each environment μ can be considered as a measure on $\mathcal{Z}^\infty$. Moreover, it can be shown that (for any fixed policy) the ratio $\frac{\nu(z_{<n})}{\xi(z_{<n})}$ is bounded away from zero if ν is the true environment μ and tends to zero if ν is singular with μ (in fact, here singularity is a probabilistic analogue of inconsistency). The exploration part of the algorithm ensures that at least one of the environments ν^t and ν^e is singular with ν on the current history, and a succession of tests $\frac{\nu(z_{<n})}{\xi(z_{<n})} \geq \alpha_s$ with $\alpha_s \to 0$ is used to exclude such environments from consideration.

The next proposition provides some conditions on mixing rates which are sufficient for value-stability; we do not intend to provide sharp conditions on mixing rates but rather to illustrate the relation of value-stability with mixing conditions.

We say that a stochastic process h_k, $k \in \mathbb{N}$ satisfies strong α-mixing conditions with coefficients $\alpha(k)$ if (see e.g. [Bos96])

$$\sup_{n \in \mathbb{N}} \sup_{B \in \sigma(h_1,\ldots,h_n), C \in \sigma(h_{n+k},\ldots)} |\mathbf{P}(B \cap C) - \mathbf{P}(B)\,\mathbf{P}(C)| \leq \alpha(k),$$

where $\sigma()$ stands for the sigma-algebra generated by the random variables in brackets. Loosely speaking, mixing coefficients α reflect the speed with which the process "forgets" about its past.

Proposition 3 (mixing conditions). *Suppose that an explorable environment ν is such that there exist a sequence of numbers r_i^ν and a function $d(k)$ such that $\frac{1}{n} r_{1..n}^\nu \to V_\nu^*$, $d(k) = o(k)$, and for each $z_{<k}$ there exists a policy p such that the sequence $r_i^{p\nu}$ satisfies strong α-mixing conditions with coefficients $\alpha(k) = \frac{1}{k^{1+\varepsilon}}$ for some $\varepsilon > 0$ and*

$$r_{k..k+n}^\nu - \mathbf{E}\left(r_{k..k+n}^{p\nu} \mid z_{<k}\right) \leq d(k)$$

for any n. Then ν is value-stable.

Proof. Using the union bound we obtain

$$\mathbf{P}\left(r_{k..k+n}^\nu - r_{k..k+n}^{p\nu} > d(k) + n\varepsilon\right)$$
$$\leq I\left(r_{k..k+n}^\nu - \mathbf{E}\,r_{k..k+n}^{p\nu} > d(k)\right) + \mathbf{P}\left(\left|r_{k..k+n}^{p\nu} - \mathbf{E}\,r_{k..k+n}^{p\nu}\right| > n\varepsilon\right).$$

The first term equals 0 by assumption and the second term for each ε can be shown to be summable using [Bos96, Thm.1.3]: For a sequence of uniformly bounded zero-mean random variables r_i satisfying strong α-mixing conditions the following bound holds true for any integer $q \in [1, n/2]$:

$$\mathbf{P}\left(|r_{1..n}| > n\varepsilon\right) \leq ce^{-\varepsilon^2 q/c} + cq\alpha\left(\frac{n}{2q}\right)$$

for some constant c; in our case we just set $q = n^{\frac{\varepsilon}{2+\varepsilon}}$.　　□

(PO)MDPs. Applicability of Theorem 2 and Proposition 3 can be illustrated on (PO)MDPs. We note that self-optimizing policies for (uncountable) classes of finite ergodic MDPs and POMDPs are known [BT99, EDKM05]; the aim of the present section is to show that value-stability is a weaker requirement than the requirements of these models, and also to illustrate applicability of our results.

We call μ a (stationary) *Markov decision process* (MDP) if the probability of perceiving $x_k \in \mathcal{X}$, given history $z_{<k}y_k$ only depends on $y_k \in \mathcal{Y}$ and x_{k-1}. In this case $x_k \in \mathcal{X}$ is called a *state*, $\mathcal{X}$ the *state space*. An MDP μ is called *ergodic* if there exists a policy under which every state is visited infinitely often with probability 1. An MDP with a stationary policy forms a Markov chain.

An environment is called a (finite) *partially observable MDP* (POMDP) if there is a sequence of random variables s_k taking values in a finite space $\mathcal{S}$ called the state space, such that x_k depends only on s_k and y_k, and s_{k+1} is independent of $s_{<k}$ given s_k. Abusing notation the sequence $s_{1:k}$ is called the underlying Markov chain. A POMDP is called *ergodic* if there exists a policy such that the underlying Markov chain visits each state infinitely often with probability 1.

In particular, any ergodic POMDP ν satisfies strong α-mixing conditions with coefficients decaying exponentially fast in case there is a set $H \subset \mathcal{R}$ such that $\nu(r_i \in H) = 1$ and $\nu(r_i = r | s_i = s, y_i = y) \neq 0$ for each $y \in \mathcal{Y}, s \in \mathcal{S}, r \in H, i \in \mathbb{N}$. Thus for any such POMDP ν we can use Proposition 3 with $d(k, \varepsilon)$ a constant function to show that ν is strongly value-stable:

Corollary 4 (POMDP⇒value-stable). *Suppose that a POMDP ν is ergodic and there exists a set $H \subset \mathcal{R}$ such that $\nu(r_i \in H) = 1$ and $\nu(r_i = r | s_i = s, y_i = y) \neq 0$ for each $y \in \mathcal{Y}, h \in \mathcal{S}, r \in H$, where $\mathcal{S}$ is the finite state space of the underlying Markov chain. Then ν is strongly value-stable.*

However, it is illustrative to obtain this result for MDPs directly, and in a slightly stronger form.

Proposition 5 (MDP⇒value-stable). *Any finite-state ergodic MDP ν is a strongly value-stable environment.*

Proof. Let $d(k, \varepsilon) = 0$. Denote by μ the true environment, let $z_{<k}$ be the current history and let the current state (the observation x_k) of the environment be $a \in \mathcal{X}$, where $\mathcal{X}$ is the set of all possible states. Observe that for an MDP there is an optimal policy which depends only on the current state. Moreover, such a policy is optimal for any history. Let p_μ be such a policy. Let r_i^μ be the expected reward of p_μ on step i. Let $l(a,b) = \min\{n : x_{k+n} = b | x_k = a\}$. By ergodicity of μ there exists a policy p for which $\mathbf{E}l(b,a)$ is finite (and does not depend on k). A policy p needs to get from the state b to one of the states visited by an optimal policy, and then acts according to p_μ. Let $f(n) := \frac{n r_{\max}}{\log n}$. We have

$$\mathbf{P}\left(|r_{k..k+n}^\mu - r_{k..k+n}^{p\mu}| > n\varepsilon\right) \leq \sup_{a \in \mathcal{X}} \mathbf{P}\left(|\mathbf{E}\left(r_{k..k+n}^{p_\mu \mu} | x_k = a\right) - r_{k..k+n}^{p\mu}| > n\varepsilon\right)$$

$$\leq \sup_{a,b \in \mathcal{X}} \mathbf{P}(l(a,b) > f(n)/r_{\max})$$

$$+ \sup_{a,b \in \mathcal{X}} \mathbf{P}\left(\left|\mathbf{E}\left(r_{k..k+n}^{p_\mu \mu} | x_k = a\right) - r_{k+f(n)..k+n}^{p_\mu \mu}\right| > n\varepsilon - f(n) \,\Big|\, x_{k+f(n)} = a\right)$$

$$\leq \sup_{a,b \in \mathcal{X}} \mathbf{P}(l(a,b) > f(n)/r_{\max})$$

$$+ \sup_{a \in \mathcal{X}} \mathbf{P}\left(\left|\mathbf{E}\left(r_{k..k+n}^{p_\mu \mu} | x_k = a\right) - r_{k..k+n}^{p_\mu \mu}\right| > n\varepsilon - 2f(n) \,\Big|\, x_k = a\right).$$

In the last term we have the deviation of the reward attained by the optimal policy from its expectation. Clearly, both terms are bounded exponentially in n.   □

In the examples above the function $d(k,\varepsilon)$ is a constant and $\varphi(n,\varepsilon)$ decays exponentially fast. This suggests that the class of value-stable environments stretches beyond finite (PO)MDPs. We illustrate this guess by the construction that follows.

An example of a value-stable environment: Infinitely armed bandit. Next we present a construction of environments which can not be modelled as finite POMDPs but are value-stable. Consider the following environment ν. There is a countable family $\mathcal{C}' = \{\zeta_i : i \in I\!N\}$ of *arms*, that is, sources generating i.i.d. rewards 0 and 1 (and, say, empty observations) with some probability δ_i of the reward being 1. The action space $\mathcal{Y}$ consists of three actions $\mathcal{Y} = \{g, u, d\}$. To get the next reward from the current arm ζ_i an agent can use the action g. At the beginning the current arm is ζ_0 and then the agent can move between arms as follows: it can move one arm "up" using the action u or move "down" to the first environment using the action d. The reward for actions u and d is 0.

Clearly, ν is a POMDP with countably infinite number of states in the underlying Markov chain, which (in general) is not isomorphic to a finite POMDP.

Claim. The environment ν just constructed is value-stable.

Proof. Let $\delta = \sup_{i \in I\!N} \delta_i$. Clearly, $\overline{V}(\nu, p') \leq \delta$ with probability 1 for any policy p'. A policy p which, knowing all the probabilities δ_i, achieves $\overline{V}(\nu, p) = \underline{V}(\nu, p) = \delta =: V_\nu^*$ a.s., can be easily constructed. Indeed, find a sequence ζ_j', $j \in I\!N$, where for each j there is $i =: i_j$ such that $\zeta_j' = \zeta_i$, satisfying $\lim_{j \to \infty} \delta_{i_j} = \delta$. The policy p should carefully exploit one by one the arms ζ_j, staying with each arm long enough to ensure that the average reward is close to the expected reward with ε_j probability, where ε_j quickly tends to 0, and so that switching between arms has a negligible impact on the average reward. Thus ν can be shown to be explorable. Moreover, a policy p just sketched can be made independent on (observation and) rewards.

Furthermore, one can modify the policy p (possibly allowing it to exploit each arm longer) so that on each time step t (from some t on) we have $j(t) \leq \sqrt{t}$, where $j(t)$ is the number of the current arm on step t. Thus, after any actions-perceptions history $z_{<k}$ one needs about $\sqrt{k}$ actions (one action u and enough actions d) to catch up with p. So, (1) can be shown to hold with $d(k,\varepsilon) = \sqrt{k}$, r_i the expected reward of p on step i (since p is independent of rewards, $r_i^{p\nu}$ are independent), and the rates $\varphi(n,\varepsilon)$ exponential in n.   □

In the above construction we can also allow the action d to bring the agent $d(i) < i$ steps down, where i is the number of the current environment ζ, according to some (possibly randomized) function $d(i)$, thus changing the function $d_\nu(k,\varepsilon)$ and possibly making it non-constant in ε and as close as desirable to linear.

5   Necessity of Value-Stability

Now we turn to the question of how tight the conditions of strong value-stability are. The following proposition shows that the requirement $d(k,\varepsilon) = o(k)$ in (1) can not be relaxed.

Proposition 6 (necessity of $d(k,\varepsilon) = o(k)$). *There exists a countable family of deterministic explorable environments $\mathcal{C}$ such that*

- *for any $\nu \in \mathcal{C}$ for any sequence of actions $y_{<k}$ there exists a policy p such that*

$$r^{\nu}_{n..k+n} = r^{p\nu}_{k..k+n} \text{ for all } n \geq k,$$

  where r^{ν}_i are the rewards attained by an optimal policy p_ν (which from the beginning was acting optimally), but
- *for any policy p there exists an environment $\nu \in \mathcal{C}$ such that $\underline{V}(\nu,p) < V^*_\nu$.*

Clearly, each environment from such a class $\mathcal{C}$ satisfies the value stability conditions with $\varphi(n,\varepsilon) \equiv 0$ except $d(k,\varepsilon) = k \neq o(k)$.

Proof. There are two possible actions $y_i \in \{a,b\}$, three possible rewards $r_i \in \{0,1,2\}$ and no observations.

Construct the environment ν_0 as follows: if $y_i = a$ then $r_i = 1$ and if $y_i = b$ then $r_i = 0$ for any $i \in I\!N$.

For each i let n_i denote the number of actions a taken up to step i: $n_i := \#\{j \leq i : y_j = a\}$. For each $s > 0$ construct the environment ν_s as follows: $r_i(a) = 1$ for any i, $r_i(b) = 2$ if the longest consecutive sequence of action b taken has length greater than n_i and $n_i \geq s$; otherwise $r_i(b) = 0$.

Suppose that there exists a policy p such that $\underline{V}(\nu_i,p) = V^*_{\nu_i}$ for each $i > 0$ and let the true environment be ν_0. By assumption, for each s there exists such n that

$$\#\{i \leq n : y_i = b, r_i = 0\} \geq s > \#\{i \leq n : y_i = a, r_i = 1\}$$

which implies $\underline{V}(\nu_0,p) \leq 1/2 < 1 = V^*_{\nu_0}$.   □

It is also easy to show that the *uniformity* of convergence in (1) can not be dropped. That is, if in the definition of value-stability we allow the function $\varphi(n,\varepsilon)$ to depend additionally on the past history $z_{<k}$ then Theorem 2 does not hold. This can be shown with the same example as constructed in the proof of Proposition 6, letting $d(k,\varepsilon) \equiv 0$ but instead allowing $\varphi(n,\varepsilon,z_{<k})$ to take values 0 and 1 according to the number of actions a taken, achieving the same behaviour as in the example provided in the last proof.

Finally, we show that the requirement that the class $\mathcal{C}$ to be learnt is countable can not be easily withdrawn. Indeed, consider the following simple class of environments. An environment is called *passive* if the observations and rewards are independent of actions. Sequence prediction task is a well-studied (and perhaps the only reasonable) class of passive environments: in this task an agent gets the reward 1 if $y_i = o_{i+1}$ and the reward 0 otherwise. Clearly, any *deterministic* passive environment ν is strongly value-stable with $d_\nu(k,\varepsilon) \equiv 1$, $\varphi_\nu(n,\varepsilon) \equiv 0$ and $r_i^\nu = 1$ for all i. Obviously, the class of all deterministic passive environments is not countable. Since for every policy p there is an environment on which p errs exactly on each step,

Claim. The class of all deterministic passive environments can not be learned.

6   Discussion

We have proposed a set of conditions on environments, called value-stability, such that any countable class of value-stable environments admits a self-optimizing policy. It was also shown that these conditions are in a certain sense tight. The class of all value-stable environments includes ergodic MDPs, certain class of finite POMDPs, passive environments, and (provably) other and more environments. So the novel concept of value-stability allows to characterize self-optimizing environment classes, and proving value-stability is typically much easier than proving self-optimizingness directly.

We considered only countable environment classes $\mathcal{C}$. From a computational perspective such classes are sufficiently large (e.g. the class of all computable probability measures is countable). On the other hand, countability excludes continuously parameterized families (like all ergodic MDPs), common in statistical practice. So perhaps the main open problem is to find under which conditions the requirement of countability of the class can be lifted. Ideally, we would like to have some necessary and sufficient conditions such that the class of all environments that satisfy this condition admits a self-optimizing policy.

Another question concerns the uniformity of forgetfulness of the environment. Currently in the definition of value-stability (1) we have the function $\varphi(n,\varepsilon)$ which is the same for all histories $z_{<k}$, that is, both for all actions histories $y_{<k}$ and observations-rewards histories $x_{<k}$. Probably it is possible to differentiate between two types of forgetfulness, one for actions and one for perceptions. In particular, any countable class of passive environments (i.e. such that perceptions are independent of actions) is learnable, suggesting that uniform forgetfulness in perceptions may not be necessary.

References

[Bos96]   D. Bosq. *Nonparametric Statistics for Stochastic Processes.* Springer, 1996.

[BT99]   R. I. Brafman and M. Tennenholtz. A general polynomial time algorithm for near-optimal reinforcement learning. In *Proc. 17th International Joint Conference on Artificial Intelligence (IJCAI-01)*, pages 734–739, 1999.

[CBL06]   N. Cesa-Bianchi and G. Lugosi. *Prediction, Learning, and Games.* Cambridge University Press, 2006. in preparation.

[CS04]   I. Csiszar and P.C. Shields. Notes on information theory and statistics. In *Foundations and Trends in Communications and Information Theory*, 2004.

[Doo53]   J. L. Doob. *Stochastic Processes*. John Wiley & Sons, New York, 1953.

[EDKM05]   E. Even-Dar, S. M. Kakade, and Y. Mansour. Reinforcement learning in POMDPs without resets. In *IJCAI*, pages 690–695, 2005.

[HP04]   M. Hutter and J. Poland. Prediction with expert advice by following the perturbed leader for general weights. In *Proc. 15th International Conf. on Algorithmic Learning Theory (ALT'04)*, volume 3244 of *LNAI*, pages 279–293, Padova, 2004. Springer, Berlin.

[Hut02]   M. Hutter. Self-optimizing and Pareto-optimal policies in general environments based on Bayes-mixtures. In *Proc. 15th Annual Conference on Computational Learning Theory (COLT 2002)*, Lecture Notes in Artificial Intelligence, pages 364–379, Sydney, Australia, July 2002. Springer.

[Hut03]   M. Hutter. Optimality of universal Bayesian prediction for general loss and alphabet. *Journal of Machine Learning Research*, 4:971–1000, 2003.

[Hut05]   M. Hutter. *Universal Artificial Intelligence: Sequential Decisions based on Algorithmic Probability*. Springer, Berlin, 2005. 300 pages, http://www.idsia.ch/~marcus/ai/uaibook.htm.

[KV86]   P. R. Kumar and P. P. Varaiya. *Stochastic Systems: Estimation, Identification, and Adaptive Control*. Prentice Hall, Englewood Cliffs, NJ, 1986.

[PH05]   J. Poland and M. Hutter. Defensive universal learning with experts. In *Proc. 16th International Conf. on Algorithmic Learning Theory (ALT'05)*, volume 3734 of *LNAI*, pages 356–370, Singapore, 2005. Springer, Berlin.

[PH06]   J. Poland and M. Hutter. Universal learning of repeated matrix games. In *Conference Benelearn'06 and GTDT workshop at AAMAS'06*, Ghent, 2006.

[dFM04]   D. Pucci de Farias and N. Megiddo. How to combine expert (and novice) advice when actions impact the environment? In Sebastian Thrun, Lawrence Saul, and Bernhard Schölkopf, editors, *Advances in Neural Information Processing Systems 16*. MIT Press, Cambridge, MA, 2004.

[RN95]   S. J. Russell and P. Norvig. *Artificial Intelligence. A Modern Approach*. Prentice-Hall, Englewood Cliffs, 1995.

[SB98]   R. Sutton and A. Barto. *Reinforcement learning: An introduction*. Cambridge, MA, MIT Press, 1998.

A   Proof of Theorem 2

A self-optimizing policy p will be constructed as follows. On each step we will have two polices: p^t which exploits and p^e which explores; for each i the policy p either takes an action according to p^t ($p(z_{<i}) = p^t(z_{<i})$) or according to p^e ($p(z_{<i}) = p^e(z_{<i})$), as will be specified below. When the policy p has been defined up to a step k, each environment μ, endowed with this policy, can be considered as a measure on $\mathcal{Z}^k$. We assume this meaning when we use environments as measures on $\mathcal{Z}^k$ (e.g. $\mu(z_{<i})$).

In the algorithm below, i denotes the number of the current step in the sequence of actions-observations. Let $n = 1$, $s = 1$, and $j^t = j^e = 0$. Let also $\alpha_s = 2^{-s}$ for $s \in I\!N$. For each environment ν, find such a sequence of real numbers ε_n^ν that $\varepsilon_n^\nu \to 0$ and $\sum_{n=1}^\infty \varphi_\nu(n, \varepsilon_n^\nu) \leq \infty$.

Let $1: I\!N \to C$ be such a numbering that each $\nu \in C$ has infinitely many indices. For all $i > 1$ define a measure ξ as follows

$$\xi(z_{<i}) = \sum_{\nu \in C} w_\nu \nu(z_{<i}),$$

where $w_\nu \in R$ are (any) such numbers that $\sum_\nu w_\nu = 1$ and $w_\nu > 0$ for all $\nu \in C$.

Define T. On each step i let

$$T \equiv T_i := \left\{ \nu \in C : \frac{\nu(z_{<i})}{\xi(z_{<i})} \geq \alpha_s \right\}$$

Define ν^t. Set ν^t to be the first environment in T with index greater than $1(j^t)$. In case this is impossible (that is, if T is empty), increment s, (re)define T and try again. Increment j^t.

Define ν^e. Set ν^e to be the first environment with index greater than $1(j^e)$ such that $V_{\nu^e}^* > V_{\nu^t}^*$ and $\nu^e(z_{<k}) > 0$, if such an environment exists. Otherwise proceed one step (according to p^t) and try again. Increment j^e.

Consistency. On each step i (re)define T. If $\nu^t \notin T$, define ν^t, increment s and iterate the infinite loop. (Thus s is incremented only if ν^t is not in T or if T is empty.)

Start the **infinite loop**. Increment n.

Let $\delta := (V_{\nu^e}^* - V_{\nu^t}^*)/2$. Let $\varepsilon := \varepsilon_n^{\nu^t}$. If $\varepsilon < \delta$ set $\delta = \varepsilon$. Let $h = j^e$.

Prepare for exploration.

Increment h. The index h is incremented with each next attempt of exploring ν^e. Each attempt will be at least h steps in length.

Let $p^t = p_{\nu^t}^{y_{<i}}$ and set $p = p^t$.

Let i_h be the current step. Find k_1 such that

$$\frac{i_h}{k_1} V_{\nu^t}^* \leq \varepsilon/8 \tag{2}$$

Find $k_2 > 2i_h$ such that for all $m > k_2$

$$\left| \frac{1}{m - i_h} r_{i_h+1..m}^{\nu^t} - V_{\nu^t}^* \right| \leq \varepsilon/8. \tag{3}$$

Find k_3 such that

$$hr_{max}/k_3 < \varepsilon/8. \tag{4}$$

Find k_4 such that for all $m > k_4$

$$\frac{1}{m} d_{\nu^e}(m, \varepsilon/4) \leq \varepsilon/8, \quad \frac{1}{m} d_{\nu^t}(m, \varepsilon/8) \leq \varepsilon/8 \quad \text{and} \quad \frac{1}{m} d_{\nu^t}(i_h, \varepsilon/8) \leq \varepsilon/8. \tag{5}$$

Moreover, it is always possible to find such $k > \max\{k_1, k_2, k_3, k_4\}$ that

$$\frac{1}{2k} r_{k..3k}^{\nu^e} \geq \frac{1}{2k} r_{k..3k}^{\nu^t} + \delta. \tag{6}$$

Iterate up to the step k.

Exploration. Set $p^e = p_{\nu^e}^{y<n}$. Iterate h steps according to $p = p^e$. Iterate further until either of the following conditions breaks

(i) $\left| r_{k..i}^{\nu^e} - r_{k..i}^{p\nu} \right| < (i-k)\varepsilon/4 + d_{\nu^e}(k, \varepsilon/4)$,

(ii) $i < 3k$.

(iii) $\nu^e \in T$.

Observe that either (i) or (ii) is necessarily broken.

If on some step ν^t is excluded from T then the infinite loop is iterated. If after exploration ν^e is not in T then redefine ν^e and **iterate the infinite loop**. If both ν^t and ν^e are still in T then **return** to "Prepare for exploration" (otherwise the loop is iterated with either ν^t or ν^e changed).
End of the infinite loop and the algorithm.

Let us show that with probability 1 the "Exploration" part is iterated only a finite number of times in a row with the same ν^t and ν^e.

Suppose the contrary, that is, suppose that (with some non-zero probability) the "Exploration" part is iterated infinitely often while $\nu^t, \nu^e \in T$. Observe that (1) implies that the ν^e-probability that (i) breaks is not greater than φ_{ν_e} $(i-k, \varepsilon/4)$; hence by Borel-Cantelli lemma the event that (i) breaks infinitely often has probability 0 under ν^e.

Suppose that (i) holds almost every time. Then (ii) should be broken except for a finite number of times. We can use (2), (3), (5) and (6) to show that with probability at least $1 - \varphi_{\nu^t}(k - i_h, \varepsilon/4)$ under ν^t we have $\frac{1}{3k} r_{1..3k}^{p\nu^t} \geq V_{\nu^t}^* + \varepsilon/2$. Again using Borel-Cantelli lemma and $k > 2i_h$ we obtain that the event that (ii) breaks infinitely often has probability 0 under ν^t.

Thus (at least) one of the environments ν^t and ν^e is singular with respect to the true environment ν given the described policy and current history. Denote this environment by ν'. It is known (see e.g. [CS04, Thm.26]) that if measures μ and ν are mutually singular then $\frac{\mu(x_1,...,x_n)}{\nu(x_1,...,x_n)} \to \infty$ μ-a.s. Thus

$$\frac{\nu'(z_{<i})}{\nu(z_{<i})} \to 0 \ \nu\text{-a.s.} \tag{7}$$

Observe that (by definition of ξ) $\frac{\nu(z_{<i})}{\xi(z_{<i})}$ is bounded. Hence using (7) we can see that

$$\frac{\nu'(z_{<i})}{\xi(z_{<i})} \to 0 \ \nu\text{-a.s.}$$

Since s and α_s are not changed during the exploration phase this implies that on some step ν' will be excluded from T according to the "consistency" condition, which contradicts the assumption. Thus the "Exploration" part is iterated only a finite number of times in a row with the same ν^t and ν^e.

Observe that s is incremented only a finite number of times since $\frac{\nu'(z_{<i})}{\xi(z_{<i})}$ is bounded away from 0 where ν' is either the true environment ν or any environment from $\mathcal{C}$ which is equivalent to ν on the current history. The latter follows

from the fact that $\frac{\xi(z_{\le i})}{\nu(z_{< i})}$ is a submartingale with bounded expectation, and hence, by the submartingale convergence theorem (see e.g. [Doo53]) converges with ν-probability 1.

Let us show that from some step on ν (or an environment equivalent to it) is always in T and selected as ν^t. Consider the environment ν^t on some step i. If $V_{\nu^t}^* > V_\nu^*$ then ν^t will be excluded from T since on any optimal for ν^t sequence of actions (policy) measures ν and ν^t are singular. If $V_{\nu^t}^* < V_\nu^*$ than ν^e will be equal to ν at some point, and, after this happens sufficient number of times, ν^t will be excluded from T by the "exploration" part of the algorithm, s will be decremented and ν will be included into T. Finally, if $V_{\nu^t}^* = V_\nu^*$ then either the optimal value V_ν^* is (asymptotically) attained by the policy p_t of the algorithm, or (if p_{ν^t} is suboptimal for ν) $\frac{1}{i} r_{1..i}^{p\nu^t} < V_{\nu^t}^* - \varepsilon$ infinitely often for some ε, which has probability 0 under ν^t and consequently ν^t is excluded from T.

Thus, the exploration part ensures that all environments not equivalent to ν with indices smaller than $\imath(\nu)$ are removed from T and so from some step on ν^t is equal to (an environment equivalent to) the true environment ν.

We have shown in the "Exploration" part that $n \to \infty$, and so $\varepsilon_n^{\nu^t} \to 0$. Finally, using the same argument as before (Borel-Cantelli lemma, (i) and the definition of k) we can show that in the "exploration" and "prepare for exploration" parts of the algorithm the average value is within $\varepsilon_n^{\nu^t}$ of $V_{\nu^t}^*$ provided the true environment is (equivalent to) ν^t.   □

Probabilistic Generalization of Simple Grammars and Its Application to Reinforcement Learning

Takeshi Shibata[1], Ryo Yoshinaka[2], and Takashi Chikayama[1]

[1] Department of Electronic Engineering, the University of Tokyo
{shibata, chikayama}@logos.t.u-tokyo.ac.jp
[2] Graduate School of Interdisciplinary Information Studies, the University of Tokyo
ry@iii.u-tokyo.ac.jp

Abstract. Recently, some non-regular subclasses of context-free grammars have been found to be efficiently learnable from positive data. In order to use these efficient algorithms to infer probabilistic languages, one must take into account not only equivalences between languages but also probabilistic generalities of grammars. The probabilistic generality of a grammar G is the class of the probabilistic languages generated by probabilistic grammars constructed on G. We introduce a subclass of simple grammars (SGs), referred as to unifiable simple grammars (USGs), which is a superclass of an efficiently learnable class, right-unique simple grammars (RSGs). We show that the class of RSGs is unifiable within the class of USGs, whereas SGs and RSGs are not unifiable within the class of SGs and RSGs, respectively. We also introduce simple context-free decision processes, which are a natural extension of finite Markov decision processes and intuitively may be thought of a Markov decision process with stacks. We propose a reinforcement learning method on simple context-free decision processes, as an application of the learning and unification algorithm for RSGs from positive data.

1 Introduction

In grammatical inference in the limit from positive data, there is a trade-off between the richness of the language class and the efficiency of the algorithm. Although some general conditions on learning grammars from only positive data have been found [1, 2] and are well-known, these conditions only establishes the existence of a learning algorithm, and does not say anything about its efficiency. Preceding research has proposed several efficient algorithms that identify some subclasses of context-free languages [2, 6]. In particular, recent studies [10, 12, 13] have found some nonregular context-free languages that are efficiently learnable from positive data. Yoshinaka has proposed a polynomial-time algorithm that learns a subclass of context-free grammars, called *right-unique simple grammars* (RSGs) [13], which is a superclass of very simple grammars (VSGs) found as a efficiently learnable class by Yokomori [12].

J.L. Balcázar, P.M. Long, and F. Stephan (Eds.): ALT 2006, LNAI 4264, pp. 348–362, 2006.

Both the classes of RSGs and VSGs are subclasses of simple grammars (SGs). In this paper, we consider the properties and the unification methods of the subclasses of probabilistic simple grammars. In learning these subclasses from positive examples, since if the grammar is not probabilistic, the problem becomes the classical problem of grammatical inference from positive data, it may seem that there is no problem: first infer the target grammar from positive data, and then determine the probabilities of production rules by using a statistical method. However, this solution is not sufficient because although the inferred grammar generates the correct language, there is not necessarily some probability assignment of production rules on the inferred grammar such that it generates the correct probabilistic language. For example, let us consider CFGs G and G' whose rules are $\{S \to aS|b\}$ and $\{S' \to aA'|b, A' \to aA'|b\}$ respectively. Then it is obviously impossible for G to generate the same probabilistic language as G' if $\Pr(S' \to aA') \neq \Pr(A' \to aA')$, although $L(G) = L(G')$.

In Section 3, we introduce the notion of the *probabilistic generality* of simple grammars (SGs), where the class of SGs is a superclass of RSGs and VSGs. Probabilistic generality of a grammar is defined as the set of the probabilistic languages generated by probabilistic grammars that are obtained by assigning probabilities to the production rules of the grammar. We show that, for the class of SGs and the class of RSGs, there exist two grammars whose languages are equivalent, and for which the probabilistic generality of any grammar in the same class is not larger than both of them.

In Section 4, a new subclass of SGs called *unifiable simple grammars (USGs)* is introduced. The class of USGs is a superclass of RSGs. We show that for any two USGs that generate the same language, there is a USG whose probabilistic generality is larger than the two. This implies that all RSGs whose languages are equivalent can be unified to one USG, since the number of those RSGs is finite.

In Section 5, we give an application for which the results of this paper are required. We introduce context-free decision processes, which are an extension of finite Markov decision processes (MDPs), and introduce a modified Q-learning algorithm for their optimisation. A simple context-free decision process intuitively may be thought of a finite MDP with stacks. The class of RSGs is sufficiently large so that context-free decision processes based on RSGs include all episodic finite MDPs. We use Yoshinaka's learning method to output all the minimal grammars that can generate the histories, then construct a USG by unifying the output RSGs, and use the extended Q-learning for learning optimal decisions.

2   Preliminaries

First, we outline some standard notation and definitions.

A context-free grammar is denoted by $\langle V, \Sigma, R, S \rangle$, where V is a finite set of *nonterminal symbols*, Σ is a finite set of *terminal symbols*, $R \subset V \times (V \cup \Sigma)^*$ is a finite set of *production rules* and $S \in V$ is the *start symbol*. Let $G = \langle V, \Sigma, R, S \rangle$ be a CFG. We write $XAZ \Rightarrow_G XYZ$ iff $A \to Y \in R$ and $X, Z \in (V \cup \Sigma)^*$, and $\Rightarrow_G^*$ denotes the reflective and transitive closure of $\Rightarrow_G$. When G is clearly identified, we write simply $\Rightarrow$ instead of $\Rightarrow_G$. G is said to be *reduced* iff for all $A \in V$, there are some $x, y, z \in \Sigma^*$ such that $S \overset{*}{\Rightarrow} xAz \overset{*}{\Rightarrow} xyz$. The language of G, $L(G)$, is defined as $\{x \in \Sigma^* \mid S \overset{*}{\Rightarrow} x\}$. Let $L(G, X) = \{x \in \Sigma^* \mid X \overset{*}{\Rightarrow} x\}$, where $X \in (V \cup \Sigma)^*$. When G is clearly identified, we write simply $L(X)$ instead of $L(G, X)$. For $A \in V$, let R_A indicate $\{A \to X \in R\}$.

Let ε denote the empty sequence and $|x|$ denote the length of a sequence x. For a set V, let $|V|$ denote the number of the elements in V. For a CFG $G = \langle V, \Sigma, R, S \rangle$, let $|G|$ denote $\sum_{A \to X \in R} |AX|$.

Hereafter, let terminal symbols and nonterminal symbols be denoted by a, b, c, $\cdots$ and $A, B, C, \cdots$ respectively, and finite sequences of terminals symbols and of nonterminal symbols be denoted by $\cdots, x, y, z$ and $\alpha, \beta, \gamma, \cdots$ respectively.

Subclasses of CFGs we discuss in this paper are defined below.

Definition 1. *A CFG $G = \langle V, \Sigma, R, S \rangle$ is called a* simple grammar (SG) *iff G is Greibach normal form, and*

$$A \to a\alpha \in R \text{ and } A \to a\beta \in R \text{ imply } \alpha = \beta.$$

An SG G is called a right-unique simple grammar (RSG) *iff*

$$A \to a\alpha \in R \text{ and } B \to a\beta \in R \text{ imply } \alpha = \beta.$$

An SG G is called a very simple grammar (VSG) *iff*

$$A \to a\alpha \in R \text{ and } B \to a\beta \in R \text{ imply } \alpha = \beta \text{ and } A = B.$$

An RSG G is normal form *iff it is reduced, and for all $C \in V$, $A \to a\alpha C\beta, B \to a'\alpha'C\beta' \in R$ implies $a = a'$, $\alpha = \alpha'$, $\beta = \beta'$ and $C \neq S$.*

CFGs in GNF $G = \langle V, \Sigma, R, S \rangle$ and $H = \langle V', \Sigma, R', S' \rangle$ are equivalent *modulo renaming nonterminals* iff there is a bijection $\phi : V \to V'$ such that $\phi(S) = S'$, $A \to a\alpha \in R$ iff $\phi(A) \to a\hat{\phi}(\alpha) \in R'$ where $\hat{\phi}$ is the unique homomorphic extension of ϕ.

While the class of SGs is not learnable in the limit from positive data, for both the class of VSGs and the class of RSGs, there are the efficient learning algorithms, which satisfy conservativeness and consistency and output grammars in polynomial time in the size of the input positive examples.

Those algorithms for VSGs and RSGs are based on the following strategy. Let $\mathcal{C}$ be either the class of VSGs or the class of RSGs. Let positive presentation of the target grammar in $\mathcal{C}$ be $s_1, s_2, \cdots$, and output grammars be $G_1, G_2, \cdots$. For each i-th input of positive data, if s_i is in $L(G_{i-1})$ then $G_i := G_{i-1}$, otherwise $G_i := G$, where $G \in \mathcal{C}$ such that $\{s_1, \cdots, s_i\} \subset L(G)$ and $L(G)$ is minimal, namely, $\forall G' \in \mathcal{C}[L(G') \subsetneq L(G)$ implies $\{s_1, \cdots, s_i\} \not\subset L(G')]$. $\mathcal{C}$ has finite thickness, namely, for any finite language $D = \{s_1, \ldots, s_i\}$, at most finitely many (modulo renaming nonterminals) grammars G in $\mathcal{C}$ generate a language including D.

A function $\#_G : \Sigma^* \to \{-1, 0, \cdots\}$ for $G = \langle V, \Sigma, R, S \rangle \in \mathcal{C}$ is defined as $\#_G(\varepsilon) = 0$, $\#_G(a) = |\alpha| - 1$, where $A \to a\alpha \in R$ for some $A \in V$, and

$\#(ax) = \#(a) + \#(x)$. Note that $\#(a)$ is well-defined due to the definition of the class $\mathcal{C}$. Since $D \subset L(G)$ implies that $\#_G(s) = -1$ for all $s \in D$ and $\#_G(t) \geq 0$ for each proper prefix t of s, the number of possible $\#$s for D is finite. When a possible $\#$ is given, it is easy to determine the minimal grammar in $\{G \in \mathcal{C} \mid \#_G = \#\}$. The algorithm outputs a minimal grammar among those minimal grammars.

Although Yoshinaka's algorithm can decide the inclusion of every two RSGs G and H in polynomial time in $|G| + |H|$, since the number of possible $\#$s can be exponential in $|\Sigma|$, those algorithm is also in exponential time in $|\Sigma|$.

Let $G = \langle V, \Sigma, R, S \rangle$ be an SG. A *probability assignment* P on G is a map from R to $[0, 1]$ such that $\sum_{r \in R_A} P(r) = 1$ for all $A \in V$, where $R_A = \{A \to a\alpha \in R\}$. A *probabilistic simple grammar (PSG)* is a pair $\langle G, P \rangle$, where P is probability assignment on an SG G. $\langle G, P \rangle$ is *reduced* iff G is reduced and $P(r) \neq 0$ for all $r \in R$.

When G is an SG, every $x \in L(G)$ has a unique sequence of production rules that are used in the left-most derivation of $S \overset{*}{\Rightarrow}_G x$. Let us denote that sequence by $r(G, x, 1), \cdots, r(G, x, |x|)$. Then, the *probabilistic language* of a PSG $\langle G, P \rangle$, $\Pr(\cdot | \langle G, P \rangle) : \Sigma^* \to [0, 1]$, is defined as

$$\Pr(x | \langle G, P \rangle) = \begin{cases} \prod_{i=1}^{|x|} P(r(G, x, i)) & \text{if } x \in L(G), \\ 0 & \text{otherwise.} \end{cases}$$

We define similarly that $\Pr(x | \langle G, P \rangle, A) = \prod_{i=1}^{|x|} P(r(A, x, i))$ if $x \in L(G, A)$, otherwise 0, where $r(G, A, x, 1) \cdots r(G, A, x, |x|)$ are the sequence of rules used in the derivation $A \overset{*}{\Rightarrow}_G x$.

3   Probabilistic Generality of Subclasses of Simple Grammars

Definition 2. *The* generality *of an SG G is defined as*

$$\mathbb{K}(G) = \{\Pr(\cdot | \langle G, P \rangle) | P \text{ is a probability assignment on } G\}.$$

G is more general than *an SG H iff* $\mathbb{K}(G) \subset \mathbb{K}(H)$.

The following lemma establishes requirements for $\mathbb{K}(G) \subset \mathbb{K}(H)$.

Lemma 1. *Let $G = \langle V, \Sigma, R, S \rangle$ and $H = \langle V', \Sigma, R', S' \rangle$ be reduced SGs. $\mathbb{K}(G) \subset \mathbb{K}(H)$ iff $L(G) = L(H)$ and there is some map $\psi : V'_{\geq 2} \to V$ such that $\forall A \in V'_{\geq 2} \forall x \in \Sigma^* [S' \overset{*}{\Rightarrow}_H xA\alpha$ implies $S \overset{*}{\Rightarrow}_G x\psi(A)\beta]$, where $V'_{\geq 2} = \{A \in V' \mid |R'_A| \geq 2\}$.*

Definition 3. *Let $\mathcal{C}$ and $\mathcal{D}$ be subclasses of SGs. $\mathcal{C}$ is* unifiable within *$\mathcal{D}$ iff for all $G_1, G_2 \in \mathcal{C}$ such that $L(G_1) = L(G_2)$, there is $H \in \mathcal{D}$ such that $\mathbb{K}(G_1) \cup \mathbb{K}(G_2) \subset \mathbb{K}(H)$.*

The main purpose of this paper is to construct an SG G_* that is more general than a finite number of given RSGs whose languages are equivalent. However, neither the class of SGs nor the class of RSGs is unifiable within itself, as we demonstrate in what follows. In the following, we say that $\mathcal{C}$ is *unifiable* when $\mathcal{C}$ is unifiable within $\mathcal{C}$.

Proposition 1. *The class of SGs is not unifiable.*

Proof. Let $G = \langle V, \Sigma, R, S \rangle$ and $G' = \langle V', \Sigma, R', S' \rangle$ be SGs, whose rules are, respectively,

$\{S \to aAB,\ A \to aB|b|c,\ B \to aAB|bC_1|cC_2,\ C_1 \to aB|b|c,\ C_2 \to aB|b|c\}$ and
$\{S' \to aB'A',\ A' \to aB'|b|c,\ B' \to aA'B'|bC_1'|cC_2',\ C_1' \to aB'|b|c,\ C_2' \to aB'|b|c\}$.

First we show that $L(G) = L(G')$. G and G' are isomorphic if we disregard the rules $S \to aAB$ and $S \to aB'A'$. Clearly

$$L(A) = L(C_1) = L(C_2) = L(A') = L(C_1') = L(C_2'), \text{ and } L(B) = L(B').$$

Moreover, it is not hard to see that for every $x \in \Sigma^*$ and $\gamma \in \{A\}^*$, the following are equivalent:

- $AA \overset{*}{\Rightarrow}_G x\alpha$ with $\phi(\alpha) = \gamma$ for some $\alpha \in V^*$,
- $B \overset{*}{\Rightarrow}_G x\beta$ with $\phi(\beta) = \gamma$ for some $\beta \in V^*$,

where $\phi : V^* \to \{A\}^*$ is the homomorphism such that $\phi(A) = \phi(C_1) = \phi(C_2) = A$ and $\phi(B) = AA$. Therefore, $L(AA) = L(B) = L(B') = L(A'A')$, and thus $L(S) = L(S')$.

Second, we show that no SG H is more general than both G and G'. Let $H = \langle V_H, \Sigma, R_H, S_H \rangle$ be an SG such that $L(H) = L(G) = L(G')$. Since $a^{2n}b^{2n+2} \in L(G)$, there are $D_n \in V_H$ and $\alpha_n \in V_H^*$ such that

$$S_H \overset{*}{\Rightarrow}_H a^{2n} D_n \alpha_n \overset{*}{\Rightarrow} a^{2n}b^{2n+2}$$

for each $n \in \mathbb{N}$. Since V_H is finite, we can find $m, n \in \mathbb{N}$ such that $m < n$ and $D_m = D_n$. Let k and E be such that $D_m = D_n \overset{*}{\Rightarrow}_H b^{k-1}E \Rightarrow b^k$, $\alpha_m \overset{*}{\Rightarrow}_H b^{2m+2-k}$ and $\alpha_n \overset{*}{\Rightarrow}_H b^{2n+2-k}$. Note that $k \le 2m+2 < 2n+2$. Since $a^{2n}b^{k-1}cb^{2n+2-k} \in L(G) = L(H)$, we have $E \to c\gamma \in R$ and

$$S_H \overset{*}{\Rightarrow}_H a^{2n} D_n \alpha_n \overset{*}{\Rightarrow} a^{2n}b^{k-1}E\alpha_n \Rightarrow a^{2n}b^{k-1}c\gamma\alpha_n \overset{*}{\Rightarrow} a^{2n}b^{k-1}cb^{2n+2-k}.$$

Since H is an SG, $b^{2n+2-k} \in L(\gamma\alpha_n) \cap L(\alpha_n)$ implies $\gamma = \varepsilon$. Therefore, we have

$$S_H \overset{*}{\Rightarrow}_H a^{2n} D_n \alpha_n \overset{*}{\Rightarrow} a^{2n}b^k \alpha_n, \qquad S_H \overset{*}{\Rightarrow}_H a^{2n} D_n \alpha_n \overset{*}{\Rightarrow} a^{2n}b^{k-1}c\alpha_n.$$

Since $k < 2n+2$, $\alpha_n \neq \varepsilon$. If $k = 2j+1 < 2n+2$, then

$$S \overset{*}{\Rightarrow}_G a^{2n}b^k C_1 B^{n-j}, \qquad S \overset{*}{\Rightarrow}_G a^{2n}b^{k-1}c C_2 B^{n-j}.$$

By Lemma 1, H is not more general than G. Similarly, if $k = 2j+2 < 2n+2$, then H is not more general than G'. $\square$

The class of RSGs is also not unifiable. Let us consider the finite language $L = (a|b)(c|d)(e|f) = \{ace, acf, ade, adf, bce, bcf, bde, bdf\}$. In normal form, any RSG that generates L is equivalent, modulo renaming nonterminals, to either $G = \langle V, \Sigma, R, S \rangle$ or $H = \langle V', \Sigma, R', S \rangle$, whose rules are, respectively,

$$\{S \rightarrow aA|bB, \ A \rightarrow cC|dD, \ B \rightarrow cC|dD, \ C \rightarrow e|f, \ D \rightarrow e|f\} \text{ or}$$
$$\{S \rightarrow aA_0A_1|bB_0B_1, \ A_0 \rightarrow c|d, \ B_0 \rightarrow c|d, \ A_1 \rightarrow e|f, \ B_1 \rightarrow e|f\}.$$

$|R_A| = |R'_{A'}| = 2$ for all $A \in V$ and $A' \in V'$. $S \overset{*}{\Rightarrow}_G acC$ and $S \overset{*}{\Rightarrow}_G adD$, while $S \overset{*}{\Rightarrow}_H acA_1$ and $S \overset{*}{\Rightarrow}_H adA_1$. Thus $\mathbb{K}(G) \not\subset \mathbb{K}(H)$ from Lemma 1. On the other hand, $S \overset{*}{\Rightarrow}_G acC$ and $S \overset{*}{\Rightarrow}_G bcC$, while $S \overset{*}{\Rightarrow}_H acA_1$ and $S \overset{*}{\Rightarrow}_H bcB_1$. Thus $\mathbb{K}(H) \not\subset \mathbb{K}(G)$. It follows that there is no RSG I such that $L(I) = L$, $\mathbb{K}(G) \subset \mathbb{K}(I)$ and $\mathbb{K}(H) \subset \mathbb{K}(I)$ from Lemma 9.

4   A Unifiable Subclass of Simple Grammars

In this section, we introduce *unifiable simple grammars (USGs)*. The class of USGs is unifiable and is a superclass of the class of RSGs. This implies that the class of RSGs is unifiable within the class of USGs. This is the main result of this paper.

Let $G = \langle V, \Sigma, R, S \rangle$ be an SG. Let $\sigma_G(A) = \{a \in \Sigma \mid A \rightarrow a\alpha \in R\}$ for $A \in V$. We write $A \overset{\sigma}{\sim} B$ iff $\sigma_G(A) = \sigma_G(B)$. $\overset{\sigma}{\sim}$ is an equivalence relation, thus let $\overline{A}$ denote the equivalence class containing A, i.e., $\overline{A} = \{A' \in V \mid A' \overset{\sigma}{\sim} A\}$. We also introduce the notation $\overline{U} = \{A' \in V \mid \exists A \in U, A' \in \overline{A}\}$ and $\overline{A_1 \cdots A_m} = \overline{A_1} \cdots \overline{A_m}$, where $U \subset V$.

Definition 4. *An SG G is a Unifiable Simple Grammar (USG) iff*

$$\overline{A} = \overline{B}, \ A \rightarrow a\alpha \in R \text{ and } B \rightarrow a\beta \in R \text{ imply } \overline{\alpha} = \overline{\beta}.$$

For a USG $G = \langle V, \Sigma, R, S \rangle$, we define a USG $G/\sigma = \langle V/\sigma, \Sigma, R/\sigma, \overline{S} \rangle$ as

$$V/\sigma = \{\overline{A} \mid A \in V\}$$
$$R/\sigma = \{\overline{A} \rightarrow a\overline{B_1} \ldots \overline{B_n} \mid A \rightarrow aB_1 \ldots B_n \in R\}$$

USGs $G = \langle V, \Sigma, R, S \rangle$ and $H = \langle V', \Sigma, R', S' \rangle$ are *σ-isomorphic* iff G/σ and H/σ are equivalent modulo renaming nonterminals. From the definition of USGs, G/σ is also a USG and $L(G/\sigma) = L(G)$.

To show the USGs are unifiable, we define *neighbourhood pairs* for a USG, and eliminate them keeping its generality. The intuitive meaning of neighbourhood pairs can be seen in Lemma 3. For all USGs G and H that have no neighbourhood pair, $L(G) = L(H)$ implies that G is σ-isomorphic to H (Lemma 7). If G and H are σ-isomorphic, it is easy to unify them (Lemma 8).

Definition 5. *The upstream of* $A \in V$ *is defined as* $\mathsf{up}_G(A) = \{B \in V \mid B \stackrel{*}{\Rightarrow} xA\}$, *and* $\mathsf{up}_G(U) = \bigcup_{A \in U} \mathsf{up}_G(A)$ *where* $U \subset V$.

Let us define $W(U_1, U_2) \subset V^*$ as

$$W(U_1, U_2) = \{\alpha \in V^* \mid \forall A \in U_1[\alpha = \alpha' A \beta \text{ imply } \exists B \in U_2[\beta = B\beta']]\}$$

Lemma 2. $\alpha\beta \in W(U_1, U_2)$ *iff*

$$\begin{cases} \alpha', \beta' \in W(U_1, U_2) & \text{if } \alpha = \alpha' A, \ \beta = B\beta' \text{ and } (A, B) \in (U_1, U_2) \\ \alpha, \beta \in W(U_1, U_2) & \text{otherwise} \end{cases}$$

Definition 6. *A pair* $\langle U_1, U_2 \rangle \in \mathcal{P}(V) \times \mathcal{P}(V)$ *is called a* neighbourhood pair *iff the following conditions hold.*

1. $U_1 \cap U_2 = \varnothing$.
2. $\exists A \in V \ (\ U_1 = \mathsf{up}(\overline{A})\ )$.
3. $\exists A \in V \ (\ U_2 = \overline{A}\ )$.
4. $S \notin U_1$.
5. *For all* $A \to a\alpha \in R$,
   - $A \in U_1$ *implies* $\alpha B \in W(U_1, U_2)$ *for some* $B \in U_2$.
   - $A \notin U_1$ *implies* $\alpha \in W(U_1, U_2)$.

The following Lemma 3 and Lemma 4 can be proven by induction on $|x|$.

Lemma 3. $\langle U_1, U_2 \rangle$ *is an neighbourhood pair iff conditions 1, 2 and 3 in Definition 6, as well as the following condition, hold.*

- $S \stackrel{*}{\Rightarrow} x\alpha$ *implies* $\alpha \in W(U_1, U_2)$ *for all* x.

Definition 7. *Let* $\langle U_1, U_2 \rangle$ *be an neighbourhood pair of a USG* $G = \langle V, \Sigma, R, S \rangle$. *We define a map* $\phi_{U_1, U_2} : W(U_1, U_2) \to V'^*$, *where* $V' = (V - U_1) \cup (U_1 \times U_2)$, *by*

- $\phi_{U_1, U_2}(\varepsilon) = \varepsilon$.
- $\phi_{U_1, U_2}(A\beta) = \begin{cases} A_B \phi_{U_1, U_2}(\beta') & \text{if } A \in U_1 \text{ and } \beta = B\beta', \\ A\phi_{U_1, U_2}(\beta) & \text{otherwise.} \end{cases}$

$\Phi(G, \langle U_1, U_2 \rangle)$ *denotes the USG obtained by eliminating useless nonterminals and rules from the USG* $\langle V', \Sigma, R', S \rangle$, *where*

$$R' = \{\ A \to a\phi_{U_1, U_2}(\alpha) \mid A \to a\alpha \in R \text{ and } A \in V - U_1\ \}$$
$$\cup \{\ A_B \to a\phi_{U_1, U_2}(\alpha B) \mid A \to a\alpha \in R \text{ and } A_B \in U_1 \times U_2\ \}$$

Note that ϕ_{U_1, U_2} is a bijection.

Lemma 4. *Let* $G' = \Phi(G, \langle U_1, U_2 \rangle)$. *For all* x, α *and* β *such that* $\beta = \phi_{U_1, U_2}(\alpha)$,

$$S \stackrel{*}{\Rightarrow}_G x\alpha \quad \text{iff} \quad S \stackrel{*}{\Rightarrow}_{G'} x\beta.$$

Lemma 5. *Let* $\langle U_1, U_2 \rangle$ *be an neighbourhood pair of a USG* G. $\Phi(G, \langle U_1, U_2 \rangle)$ *is more general than* G.

Algorithm 1. Transformation of USGs

Require: G is a USG.
  while There exists an neighbourhood pair $\langle U_1, U_2 \rangle$ in G. **do**
    $G := \Phi(G, \langle U_1, U_2 \rangle)$.
  end while
  return $G_o := G$.

Proof. Let $\psi : V' \to V$ where $V' = (V - U_1) \cup (U_1 \times U_2)$ be defined as $\psi(A) = A$ for $A \in V - U_1$ and $\psi(A_B) = A$ for $A_B \in U_1 \times U_2$. By Lemma 4, ψ satisfies the condition in Lemma 1.   □

Lemma 6. *Algorithm 1 terminates for all $G \in USGs$.*

Proof. Let $\langle U_1, U_2 \rangle$ be an neighbourhood pair of G, $H = \langle V_H, \Sigma, R_H, S_H \rangle$ denote $\Phi(G, \langle U_1, U_2 \rangle)$, and $G' = \langle V_{G'}, \Sigma, R_{G'}, S_{G'} \rangle$ denote G/σ. The following claims are easy to prove but useful for what follows:

- $\langle U_1/\sigma, U_2/\sigma \rangle$ is an neighbourhood pair of G', and $\Phi(G', \langle U_1/\sigma, U_2/\sigma \rangle)$ is equivalent to H/σ modulo renaming nonterminals.

$$
\begin{array}{ccc}
G & \xrightarrow{\;\Phi(\cdot,\langle U_1,U_2\rangle)\;} & H \\
{\scriptstyle /\sigma}\downarrow & & \downarrow{\scriptstyle /\sigma} \quad \text{modulo renaming} \\
& & \qquad\quad \text{nonterminals} \\
G' & \xrightarrow{\;\Phi(\cdot,\langle U_1/\sigma,U_2/\sigma\rangle)\;} & H'
\end{array}
$$

Let $H' = \langle V_{H'}, \Sigma, R_{H'}, S_{H'} \rangle$ denote $\Phi(G', \langle U_1/\sigma, U_2/\sigma \rangle)$.
- G has no neighbourhood pair if G' has no neighbourhood pair.
- There is a trivial bijection π from $V_{G'}$ to $V_{H'}$ such that $\sigma_{G'}(A) = \sigma_{H'}(\pi(A))$.

We define $p(G', A) \in V_{G'}^*$ for $A \in V_{G'}$ as the longest sequence in $\{\gamma \in V_{G'}^* \mid \forall x \, [S_{G'} \overset{*}{\Rightarrow} xA\alpha \text{ implies } A\alpha = \gamma\alpha']\}$. From Lemma 3, if $|p(G', A)| = 1$ for all $A \in V_{G'}$, there is no neighbourhood pair in G'. Thus, it is enough to prove that

$$
\sum_{A \in V_{G'}} |p(H', \pi(A))| < \sum_{A \in V_{G'}} |p(G', A)|, \tag{1}
$$

from the second claim noted above. In the following, let us denote $\phi_{U_1/\sigma, U_2/\sigma}$ as ϕ. From Lemma 4, we have $p(H', \pi(A)) = \phi(p(G', A))$. It is obvious that $\phi(p(G', A)) \leq p(G', A)$ for all $A \in V_{G'}$ from the definition of $p(G', A)$.

When $A \in U_1/\sigma$, since $p(G', A)$ is written as $AB\beta$, where $\{B\} = U_2/\sigma$, $\phi(p(G', A)) = A_B\phi(\beta)$. Thus $|\phi(p(G', A))| = 1 + |\phi(\beta)| \leq 1 + |\beta| = -1 + |AB\beta|$. Consequently, we obtain Eq. 1.   □

Since the above proof shows that the number of loop is less than $|G/\sigma|^2$, it is easy to prove that $|G_o|$ is $O(|G|^{|G/\sigma|^2})$, while $|G_o/\sigma|$ is $O(|G/\sigma|^3)$, where G_o is the output USG of Alg.1. This implies that the time complexity of finding neighbourhood pairs are $O(|G/\sigma|^6)$ in all. Thus the time complexity of Alg.1 is also $O(|G|^{|G|^2})$ when concerning only $|G|$. Let the ambiguity $\mathsf{amb}(G)$ of a USG G be defined as $|\{H/\sigma$ modulo renaming of nonterminals $\mid H \in \mathrm{USGs}, L(H) = L(G)\}|$. Since $|G_o|$ is limited to $O(|G|^{\mathsf{amb}(G)})$, the time complexity of Alg.1 is limited to $O(|G|^{\max\{\mathsf{amb}(G),6\}})$.

Lemma 7. *Let two USGs G_o and H_o have no neighbourhood pair. If $L(G_o) = L(H_o)$, then G_o and H_o are σ-isomorphic.*

Proof. Let $G = \langle V, \Sigma, R, S \rangle$ and $H = \langle V', \Sigma, R', S' \rangle$ denote G_o/σ and H_o/σ, respectively. It is sufficient to show that $L(G) = L(H)$ implies that G and H are equivalent modulo renaming nonterminals. Note that $\overline{A} = \{A\}$ for all $A \in V$, and thus $\sigma_G(A) = \sigma_G(A')$ implies $A = A'$.

First, we prove that $\sigma_G(A) = \sigma_H(B)$ implies $L(G, A) = L(H, B)$ for all $A \in V$ and $B \in V$. When $\sigma_G(A) = \sigma_H(B)$,

$$\forall x\, [S \overset{*}{\Rightarrow}_G xA\alpha \text{ iff } S \overset{*}{\Rightarrow}_H xB\beta],$$

since $L(G) = L(H)$. Thus $y \in L(G, A)$ implies that, for some $z \in L(H, B)$, z is a prefix of y or y is a prefix of z (if not so, $L(G) \neq L(H)$). We may assume that y is a prefix of z. Suppose that y is a *proper* prefix of z, i.e., $A \overset{*}{\Rightarrow}_G y$ and $B \overset{*}{\Rightarrow}_H yC\gamma$, then we have

$$\exists yC\gamma\, \forall x\, [S \overset{*}{\Rightarrow}_G xy\alpha \text{ iff } S \overset{*}{\Rightarrow}_H xyC\gamma\beta].$$

It follows that $\alpha = D\alpha$ for all x, where $D \in V$ and $\sigma_G(D) = \sigma_H(C)$. Thus there exists some D such that, for all x, $S \overset{*}{\Rightarrow}_G xA\alpha$ implies $\alpha = D\alpha$. For $A' \in \mathsf{up}_G(A)$, we also have, for all x, $S \overset{*}{\Rightarrow}_G xA'\alpha$ implies $\alpha = D\alpha$, because $S \overset{*}{\Rightarrow}_G xA'\alpha \overset{*}{\Rightarrow} xzA\alpha$ for some z. Thus, by Lemma 3, $\langle \mathsf{up}_G(A), \{D\} \rangle$ is an neighbourhood pair of G. Clearly, G_o has some neighbourhood pair iff G has some neighbourhood pair. This is a contradiction. Thus $y \in L(G, A)$ implies $y \in L(G, B)$ and vice versa, so $L(G, A) = L(G, B)$.

Second, we show that G and H are equivalent modulo renaming nonterminals. Let $\sigma_G(A) = \sigma_H(B)$, $A \to a\alpha \in R$ and $B \to a\beta \in R'$.

If $\alpha = \varepsilon$, $\beta = \varepsilon$ since $L(G, A) = L(H, B)$. If $\alpha = A_1 \cdots A_m$ and $m \geq 1$, we may assume that $\beta = B_1 \cdots B_n$ and $n \geq m$. Let us prove that $\sigma_G(A_i) = \sigma_H(B_i)$ by induction on i. For the base, $\sigma_G(A_1) = \sigma_H(B_1)$ since $L(G, A) = L(H, B)$. If $\sigma_G(A_1) = \sigma_H(B_1)$, $\cdots$ and $\sigma_G(A_i) = \sigma_H(B_i)$, then $L(G, A_1 \cdots A_i) = L(H, B_1 \cdots B_i)$. It follows that $\sigma_G(A_{i+1}) = \sigma_H(B_{i+1})$, since $L(G, A) = L(H, B)$. We have also $n = m$, since $L(G, A_1 \cdots A_m) = L(H, B_1 \cdots B_m)$ and $L(G, A) = L(H, B)$. $\square$

Let $G_1 = \langle V_1, \Sigma, R_1, S_1 \rangle$ and $G_2 = \langle V_2, \Sigma, R_2, S_2 \rangle$ be USGs for which $L(G_1) = L(G_2)$, neither having any neighbourhood pairs . Let

$$\begin{aligned}
V' &= \{\, (A_1, A_2) \in V_1 \times V_2 \mid s_{G_1}(A_1) = s_{G_2}(A_2) \},\\
R' &= \{\, (A_1, A_2) \to a(B_{1,1}, B_{2,1}) \cdots (B_{1,m}, B_{2,m}) \mid (A_1, A_2) \in V',\\
&\qquad A_1 \to aB_{1,1} \cdots B_{1,m} \in R_1 \text{ and } A_n \to aB_{2,1} \cdots B_{2,m} \in R_2 \,\},\\
S_* &= (S_1, S_2).
\end{aligned}$$

The USG G_*, obtained by *parallelizing* G_1 and G_2, is defined as $\langle V_*, \Sigma, R_*, S_* \rangle$, where V_* and R_* are arrived at by eliminating the useless nonterminals and rules from V' and R', respectively.

Lemma 8. G_* *is more general than* G_1 *and* G_2.

Proof. Let $\pi_i : V_* \to V_i$ be a map such that $\pi_i(A_1, A_2) = A_i$. From Lemma 7, $A_1 \to a\alpha_1 \in R_1$ iff $A_* \to a\alpha_* \in R_*$, $\pi_1(A_*) = A_1$ and $\pi_1(\alpha_*) = \alpha_1$. It follows that $S_* \overset{*}{\Rightarrow}_{G_*} x\alpha_*$ implies $S_i \overset{*}{\Rightarrow}_{G_i} x\pi_i(\alpha_*)$ for all x.   □

Theorem 1. *The class of USGs is unifiable.*

Proof. Let USGs G_0 and H_0 be output by Algorithm 1 for the input USGs G and H, with $L(G) = L(H)$. G_0 and H_0 are more general than G and H, respectively, by Lemma 5. Therefore G_* obtained by parallelizing G_0 and H_0 is more general than G and H.   □

For every RSL, there is a finite number of RSGs, modulo renaming nonterminals, that exactly generate the RSL. Moreover, it is easy to prove the following lemma.

Lemma 9. *For every RSG H, there is an RSG G in normal form, where G is σ-isomorphic to H and more general than H.*

It is easy to modify Yoshinaka's learning algorithm so that, for a given RSG G, it enumerates all RSGs in normal form that generate the same language as G. In that learning algorithm. From the above theorem, we have the following:

Theorem 2. *For every RSG G, we can construct a USG G_* such that for any RSG H with $L(H) = L(G)$, it holds that $\mathbb{K}(H) \subset \mathbb{K}(G_*)$. $|G_*|$ is $O(m(G)^{2\mathsf{amb}(G)})$, where $m(G) = \max\{|H| \mid H$ is an RSG and $L(G) = L(H)\}$.*

5   Application to Reinforcement Learning

At first, let us introduce simple context-free decision processes, which are a natural extension of finite-state Markov decision processes.

Definition 8. *Let $G = \langle V, \Sigma, R, S \rangle$ be an SG. $G_{U,P,C} = \langle V, \Sigma, R, S, U, P, C \rangle$ is a simple context-free decision process iff U, P, C are the following set and functions.*

- *U is a finite set of actions.*
- *P is a map from $R \times U$ to $[0,1]$, called a probability assignment, where $\forall u \in U, \forall A \in V[\sum_{r \in R_A} P(r, u) = 1]$ holds.*
- *C is a map from Σ to $(-\infty, \infty)$, called reward.*

Hereafter, if G is an SG or an RSG, simple context-free decision processes $G_{U,P,C}$ are called an SG-DP or an RSG-DP, respectively.

Corresponding to a given SG-DP $G_{U,P,C}$, the sequence of discrete random variables is given as $X_1, Y_1, X_2, Y_2, \cdots$, where the domains of X_i and Y_i are $\Sigma^* V^*$ and U respectively, and $X_1 = S$. The following properties hold.

$$\Pr(X_t = x_t \alpha_t | X_1 = S, Y_1 = u_1, \cdots, X_{t-1} = x_{t-1}\alpha_{t-1}, Y_{t-1} = u_{t-1})$$

$$= \Pr(X_t = x_t \alpha_t | X_{t-1} = x_{t-1}\alpha_{t-1}, Y_{t-1} = u_{t-1})$$

$$= \begin{cases} P(r, u_{t-1}) & \text{if } x_{t-1}\alpha_{t-1} \Rightarrow_G x_t \alpha_t \text{ with the rule } r \\ 1 & \text{if } x_{t-1} = x_t \text{ and } \alpha_{t-1} = \alpha_t = \varepsilon \\ 0 & \text{otherwise} \end{cases}$$

An SG-DP $G_{U,P,C}$ is called an *episodic finite Markov decision process* iff $G = \langle V, \Sigma, R, S \rangle$ is reduced and can be expressed in the form:

for some $n \geq 1$, $k \geq 0$ and $V_1, \cdots, V_{n+k} \subset V$,

$$V = \{A_1 (= S), \cdots, A_n\}, \quad \Sigma = \{a_1, \cdots, a_{n+k}\},$$

$$R = \{A \rightarrow a_j A_j | A \in V_j, j = 1, \cdots, n\} \cup \{A \rightarrow a_{n+j} | A \in V_{n+j}, j = 1, \cdots, k\}$$

The above definition is obviously equivalent to the usual definition of episodic finite MDPs. Note that G is an RSG whenever $G_{U,P,C}$ is an episodic finite MDP.

Let $G_{U,P,C} = \langle V, \Sigma, R, S, U, P, C \rangle$ be an SG-DP. A map $\mu : V \rightarrow U$ is called a *policy*. One of the main purpose of reinforcement learning is to determine the policy μ so as to maximise the expectation of the total reward from S. The *value function* $J : V \rightarrow (-\infty, \infty)$ under μ is defined as

$$J_\mu(A) = \sum_{x \in L(G,A)} \Pr(x | \langle G, P_\mu \rangle, A) \sum_{i=1}^{|x|} C(a_i),$$

where $x = a_1 \cdots a_{|x|}$, and P_μ is the probability assignment of G under μ, namely, for $B \rightarrow b\beta \in R$, $P_\mu(B \rightarrow b\beta) = P(B \rightarrow b\beta, \mu(A))$.

Let $M(G_{U,P,C}, \mu)$ be a $(|V|, |V|)$ matrix whose element $M(G_{U,P,C}, \mu)_{ij}$ represents the expectation of the number of A_j derivable in one step from A_i under μ, where $V = \{A_1, A_2, \cdots, A_{|V|}\}$. It is known that P_μ is consistent if $\rho(M(G_{U,P,C}, \mu)) < 1$, where $\rho(M)$ is the spectral radius of M [11].

When $\rho(M(G_{U,P,C}, \mu)) < 1$ for any $\mu \in \pi$, where π is the set of all policies, the *optimal value function* $J_* : V \rightarrow (-\infty, \infty)$ can be defined as $J_*(A) = \max_{\mu \in \pi} J_\mu(A)$. There exists some policy μ_* such that $J_{\mu_*}(A) = J_*(A)$ for all $A \in V$, called an *optimal policy*. The *optimal action-value function* $Q_* : V \times U \rightarrow \mathbb{R}$ are also defined as $Q_*(A, u) = \sum_{A \rightarrow aB_1 \cdots B_k \in R_A} P(A \rightarrow aB_1 \cdots B_k, u)(C(a) + \sum_{i=1}^{k} J_*(B_i))$. Note that the above definitions are a natural extension of the usual definitions on reinforcement learning whose discounting factor equals 1.

Let $G_{U,P,C} = \langle V, \Sigma, R, S, U, P, C \rangle$ be an SG-DP, and $H = \langle V', \Sigma, R', S' \rangle$ be an SG such that $\mathbb{K}(G) \subset \mathbb{K}(H)$. Let $\psi : V'_{\geq 2} \rightarrow V$ be some map that satisfies the property in Lemma 1. We can construct P', a probabilistic assignment of H, such that, for $A \rightarrow a\alpha \in R'$ and $u \in U$, $P'(A \rightarrow a\alpha, u) = P(\psi(A) \rightarrow a\beta, u)$ if $A \in V'_{\geq 2}$, otherwise $P'(A \rightarrow a\alpha, u) = 1$. We have the following:

Theorem 3. *Assume that $\rho(M(G_{U,P,C}, \mu)) < 1$ for all $\mu \in \pi(V, U)$, Q_t defined by the following iteration (Q-Learning) converges to the optimal action-value function of $H_{U,P',C}$ as $t \to \infty$ w.p. 1.*

$$Q_{t+1}(A_t, u_t) := (1 - \mathsf{k}_t)Q_t(A_t, u_t) + \mathsf{k}_t(C(a) + \sum_{i=1}^{k} \max_{v \in U} Q_t(B_i, v)), \qquad (2)$$

where the rule $A_t \to aB_1 \cdots B_k \in R'$ is randomly chosen with probability $P(\psi(A_t) \to a\beta, u_t)$ if $A_t \in V'_{\geq 2}$, otherwise 1. $\mathsf{k}_t \in [0, 1]$ is a random variable depending on A_t and u_t, called a step-size parameter. *We assume that A_t, u_t and k_t satisfy the following conditions for all $(A, u) \in V' \times U$; $\sum_{\{t \in \mathbb{N} | (A_t, u_t) = (A, u)\}} \mathsf{k}_t^2 < \infty$, $\sum_{\{t \in \mathbb{N} | (A_t, u_t) = (A, u)\}} \mathsf{k}_t = \infty$.*

Proof. By the definition of P', We may assume that $G = H$ and ψ is the identity map. If $G = H$, the convergence of the Q-Learning method in the above theorem is proved by modifying the contraction mapping and the weighted norm in [4]. $\square$

Now, we explain the relationship between learning an SG from positive data and Q-Learning on an SG-DP, and the necessity of probabilistic unification. We identify elements of Σ with observations and nonterminal symbols with unobservable states. The division of a process into observable and unobservable states follows the same scheme as appears in partially observable Markov decision processes (POMDPs) [7]. The difference from POMDPs is that nonterminal symbols are unobservable in SG-DPs but are determined if its grammar is known. In order to use the extended Q-learning method (Eq. 2), we must identify the sequence of nonterminals that corresponds to observations. We can regard histories of observations as positive data. Thus we can use the extended Q-learning method (Eq. 2) after identifying the grammar from histories of observations.

We assume that the class of environments belongs to the class of RSG-DPs, instead of to the class of SG-DPs, because the class of RSGs is of the most suitable size among subclasses of SGs. The class of RSGs is large enough to include all episodic finite MDPs, while also small enough to be learnable from positive data efficiently. Moreover, the class of RSGs is a probabilistic unifiable class within the class of USGs. Recall other subclasses of SGs we mentioned in this paper; the class of VSGs are efficiently learnable but VSG-DPs do not include all episodic finite MDPs, USGs are learnable from positive data but no efficient learning algorithm for them is known, and SGs are not even learnable from positive data.

Alg. 2 is a learning method for one episode in order to optimize the policy for RSG-DPs when the grammars are unknown. Let $G_{U,P,C} = \langle V, \Sigma, R, S, U, P, C \rangle$ be an RSG-DP (unknown). Let Env be a oracle function from {prefixes of $L(G)$} $\times U$ to $\Sigma \cup \{\varepsilon\}$. $\mathsf{Env}(x, u) = \varepsilon$ if $x \in L(G)$, otherwise, $\mathsf{Env}(x, u) = a$ such that a is randomly chosen with probability $P(A \to a\alpha, u)$, where $S \overset{*}{\Rightarrow} xA$. As the initial parameters, let the USG H, Q_H and Hist be as follows. $H = \langle V', \Sigma, R', S \rangle$, where $V' = \{[a] | a \in \Sigma\} \cup \{S\}$ and $R' = \{[a] \to b[b], S \to b[b] \mid a, b \in \Sigma\}$. $Q_H(A, u) = 0$ for all $A \in V$ and $u \in U$, where $Q_H : V \times U \to (-\infty, \infty)$.

Hist $:= \varnothing$. Let $\mathsf{Str}(H, Q_H) : \{\text{prefixes of } L(H)\} \to U$ be some *strategy* e.g., ε-greedy strategy [9].

By the definition of the learnability from positive data, it holds that, for some $n \in \mathbb{N}$, for all $m > n$, $H_m = H_n$ and $\mathbb{K}(G) \subset \mathbb{K}(H_n)$, where H_n is the inferred grammar at the n-th episode. Thus, by Theorem 3, Q_{H_n} converges to the optimal action-value function.

Algorithm 2. A reinforcement learning for one episode on RSG-DP

Require: $H = \langle V, \Sigma, R, S \rangle$ is an USG and $Q_H : V \times U \to (-\infty, \infty)$.
  $x := \varepsilon$ and $u := \mathsf{Str}(H, Q_H)(x)$.
  while $(a := \mathsf{Env}(x, u)) \neq \varepsilon$ **do**
    if $S \overset{*}{\Rightarrow}_H xA\alpha \Rightarrow xa\beta\alpha$ **then**
        Update $Q_H(A, u)$ according to Eq. 2, $u := \mathsf{Str}(H, Q_H)(xa)$, and $x := xa$.
    else
        $x := xa$. u is randomly chosen under the uniform distribution on U.
    end if
  end while
  Hist $:=$ Hist $\cup \{x\}$.
  if $x \notin L(H)$ **then**
    $\mathcal{G}$ = all the RSGs in normal form generated by the algorithm for learning RSGs
    from Hist.
    $H :=$ [the USG obtained by unifying all the RSGs in $\mathcal{G}$], with Q_H initialized to 0.
  end if

Finally, as an example of an RSG-DP and an application of the unification algorithm, we consider the problem of maximizing total reward under some conditions. An agent starts from the position $s = (1, 2)$ on the map (Fig. 1), and can move left, right, up or down, unless there is a wall in that direction. It costs 1 (-1 as a reward) per single step, and the agent is allowed to occupy a location either $f_+ = (5, 6)$ or $f_- = (5, 2)$ at most one time. When reaching to the goal $g = (9, 2)$, if the agent has passed through f_+, it observes h_+ w.p. 0.9 or h_- w.p. 0.1, whereas if the agent has passed through f_-, it observes h_+ w.p. 0.1 or h_- w.p. 0.9. The observation of h_+ implies that the agent gets 100 as a reward, and of h_- implies that it gets 50. In this case, the RSG $G = \langle V, \Sigma, R, S \rangle$ is written as follows. $\Sigma = \mathsf{Map} \cup \{h_+, h_-\}$, $V = \{[a, 0] \mid a \in \mathsf{Map} \text{ and } a \neq g\} \cup \{[f_\pm, 1], S\}$, and

$$R = \{[a, 0] \to b[b, 0] \mid b \in \mathsf{mov}(a) \text{ and } b \notin \{f_+, f_-, g\}\}$$
$$\cup \{[a, 0] \to b[b, 0][b, 1] \mid b \in \mathsf{mov}(a) \text{ and } b \in \{f_+, f_-\}\}$$
$$\cup \{[a, 0] \to g \mid g \in \mathsf{mov}(a)\} \cup \{[f_+, 1] \to h_\pm, \ [f_-, 1] \to h_\pm, \ S \to s[s, 0]\},$$

where $\mathsf{Map} = \{(i, j) \mid (i, j) \text{ is a reachable position on the map.}\}$, and $\mathsf{mov}(i, j)$ denotes a set of positions where the agent can move from (i, j) in one step. For example, $\mathsf{mov}(S) = \{(1, 1), (2, 3), (2, 2)\}$, $\mathsf{mov}(f_+) = \{(6, 6)\}$ and $\mathsf{mov}(g) = \varnothing$.

There is another RSG $H = \langle V' \Sigma, R', S \rangle$ such that $L(G) = L(H)$, where $V' = \{[a, 0] \mid a \in \mathsf{Map}\} \cup \{S\}$ and $R' = \{[a, 0] \to b[b, 0] \mid b \in \mathsf{mov}(a)\} \cup$

$\{S \rightarrow s[s,0], [g,0] \rightarrow h_\pm\}$. Note that the RSG-DP based on H is an episodic finite MDP.

G and H are all the RSGs in normal form whose language is equivalent to $L(G)$, thus both G and H, and only G and H are output by the learning algorithm of RSGs from positive data. The USG $G_* = \langle V_*, \Sigma, R_*, S_* \rangle$ transformed from G by Alg. 1 is as follows. $V_* = \{[a,0] \mid a \in \mathsf{West}\} \cup \{[a,0]_\pm \mid a \in \mathsf{East}\} \cup \{[f_\pm, 0]_\pm, S_*\}$, and

$$R_* = \{[a,0] \rightarrow b[b,0] \mid b \in \mathsf{mov}(a) \text{ and } b \in \mathsf{West}\}$$
$$\cup\{[a,0]_\pm \rightarrow b[b,0]_\pm \mid b \in \mathsf{mov}(a) \text{ and } b \in \mathsf{East}\}$$
$$\cup\{[a,0]_\pm \rightarrow g[f_\pm, 1] \mid g \in \mathsf{mov}(a)\}$$
$$\cup\{[(4,4\pm2),0] \rightarrow f_\pm[f_\pm,0]_\pm, [f_+,1] \rightarrow h_\pm, [f_-,1] \rightarrow h_\pm, S \rightarrow s[s,0]\},$$

where $\mathsf{East} = \{(i,j) \in \mathsf{Map} \mid j \geq 6, (i.j) \neq g\}$, $\mathsf{West} = \{(i,j) \in \mathsf{Map} \mid j \leq 4\}$, and $[a,0]_\pm$ denote $[a,0]_{[f_\pm,1]}$. Table 1 shows the neighbourhood pair and changed rules for each loop in Alg. 1 for G.

Table 1. Neighbourhood pairs in Alg. 1 for G

Loop	U_1	U_2	New rules obtained by $\Phi(\cdot, \langle U_1, U_2 \rangle)$
1	$\{[f_+,0]\}$	$\{[f_\pm,1]\}$	$\{[(4,6),0] \rightarrow f_+[f_+,0]_+, [f_+,0]_+ \rightarrow (6,6)[(6,6),0][f_+,1]\}$
2	$\{[f_-,0]\}$	$\{[f_\pm,1]\}$	$\{[(4,2),0] \rightarrow f_-[f_-,0]_-, [f_-,0]_- \rightarrow (6,2)[(6,2),0][f_-,1]\}$
3	$\{[a,0] \mid a \in \mathsf{East}\}$	$\{[f_\pm,1]\}$	$\{[f_\pm,0]_\pm \rightarrow [(6,4\pm2),0]\}\cup$ $\{[a,0]_\pm \rightarrow b[b,0]_\pm \mid b \in \mathsf{mov}(a) \text{ and } b \in \mathsf{East}\}\cup$ $\{[a,0]_\pm \rightarrow g[f_\pm,1] \mid g \in \mathsf{mov}(a)\}$

G_* is σ-isomorphic to H and clearly $\mathbb{K}(H) \subset \mathbb{K}(G_*)$. Thus $\mathbb{K}(G_*)$ is more general than both G and H. Note that G_* is not an RSG but a USG.

The optimal length of episode of this problem is 16 when the agent is through f_+, and thus the maximum total reward is 79. Fig. 2 is an experiment of Alg. 2 on the above problem. It demonstrates that the agent approaches the optimal path and obtains maximum total reward after the grammatical inference and the unification are complete at approximately the 200th episode. In Fig. 3 our

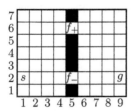

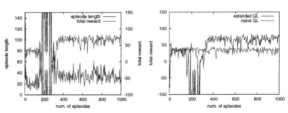

Fig. 1. Example problem of RSG-DP

Fig. 2. Total reward and episode length

Fig. 3. Comparison of QL and SG-QL methods

method is comparing to the naive Q-Learning method, in which the environment is assumed to be an episodic finite MDP (same as H). The total reward obtained by the naive Q-Learning method is approximately 40, indicating that the agent passed through f_-.

References

1. Angluin, D.: Inductive inference of formal languages from positive data. Information and Control **45** (1980) 117–135
2. Angluin, D.: Inference of reversible languages. Journal of the Association for Computing Machinery **29** (1982) 741–765
3. Barto, A. G. and Mahadevan, S.: Recent advances in hierarchical reinforcement learning. Discrete Event Dynamic Systems: Theory and Applications **13** (2003) 41–77
4. Bertsekas, D. P. and Tsitsiklis, J. N.: Neuro-dynamic Programming. Athena Scientific (1996) Sec. 5.6
5. Hirshfeld, Y and Jerrum, M. and Moller, F.: A polynomial algorithm for deciding bisimilarity of normed context-free processes. Theoretical Computer Science **158** (1996) 143–159
6. Kobayashi, S. : Iterated transductions and efficient learning from positive data: A unifying view. In Proceedings of the 5th International Colloquium on Grammatical Inference, **1891** in Lecture Notes in Computer Science (2000) 157–170
7. Kaelbling, L. P. , Littman, M. L. and Cassandra, A. R.: Planning and acting in partially observable stochastic domains. Artificial Intelligence **101** (1998) 99–134
8. Sakakibara, Y.: Recent advances of grammatical inference. Theoretical Computer Science **185** (1997) 15–45
9. Sutton, R. S. and Barto, A. G.: Reinforcement Learning: An Introduction. MIT Press (1998)
10. Wakatsuki, M. Teraguchi, K. and Tomita, E.: Polynomial time identification of strict deterministic restricted one-counter automata in some class from positive data. Proceedings of the 7th International Colloquium on Grammatical Inference **3264** in Lecture Notes in Computer Science (2004) 260–272
11. Wetherell, C.S.: Probabilistic languages: A review and some open questions. Computing Surveys, **12** No. 4 (1980) 361–379
12. Yokomori, T.: Polynomial-time identification of very simple grammars from positive data. Theoretical Computer Science **298** (2003) 179–206
13. Yoshinaka, R.: Polynomial-Time Identification of an Extension of Very Simple Grammars from Positive Data. Proceedings of the 8th International Colloquium on Grammatical Inference **4201** in Lecture Notes in Computer Science (2006)

Unsupervised Slow Subspace-Learning from Stationary Processes

Andreas Maurer

Adalbertstr. 55
D-80799 München
andreasmaurer@compuserve.com

Abstract. We propose a method of unsupervised learning from stationary, vector-valued processes. A low-dimensional subspace is selected on the basis of a criterion which rewards data-variance (like PSA) and penalizes the variance of the velocity vector, thus exploiting the short-time dependencies of the process. We prove error bounds in terms of the β-mixing coefficients and consistency for absolutely regular processes. Experiments with image recognition demonstrate the algorithms ability to learn geometrically invariant feature maps.

1 Introduction

Some work has been done to extend the results of learning theory from independent, identically distributed input variables to more general stationary processes ([19], [8], [16]). For suitably mixing processes this extension is possible, with an increase in sample complexity caused by dependencies which slow down the estimation process. But some of these dependencies also provide important information on the environment generating the process and can be turned from a curse to a blessing, in particular in the case of unsupervised learning, when side information is scarce and the sample complexity is not as painfully felt.

Consider a stationary stochastic process modeling the evolution of complex sensory signals by a sequence of zero-mean random variables X_t taking values in a Hilbert-space H. Let $\mathcal{P}_d$ be the class of d-dimensional orthogonal projections in H. From observation of $X_0, ..., X_m$ we seek to find some $P \in \mathcal{P}_d$ such that the projected stimulus PX on average captures the significance implied by the primary stimulus $X \in H$. To guide this search we will invoke two principles of common sense.

The first principle states that *significant signals should have a large variance.* In view of the zero-mean assumption this classical idea suggests to maximize $\mathbb{E}\left[\|PX_0\|^2\right]$, which coincides with the objective of PSA[1]([9], [10], [15]) seeking to give the perspective with the broadest view of the distribution.

---

[1] Principal Subspace Analysis, sometimes Principal Component Analysis (PCA) is used synonymously.

J.L. Balcázar, P.M. Long, and F. Stephan (Eds.): ALT 2006, LNAI 4264, pp. 363–377, 2006.
© Springer-Verlag Berlin Heidelberg 2006

The second principle, the principle of *slowness* (introduced by Földiak [2], promoted and developed by Wiskott [17]), states that *sensory signals vary more quickly than their significance*. Consider the visual impressions caused by a familiar complex object, like a tree on the side of the road or a person acting in a movie. Any motion or deformation of the object will cause rapid changes in the states of retinal photoreceptors (or pixel-values). Yet the identities of the tree and the person in the movie remain unchanged. When a person speaks, the communicated ideas vary much more slowly than individual phonemes, let alone the air pressure amplitudes of the transmitted sound signal.

The slowness principle suggests to minimize $\mathbb{E}\left[\left\|P\dot{X}_0\right\|^2\right]$ (here $\dot{X}$ is the velocity process $\dot{X}_t = X_t - X_{t-1}$), and combining both principles leads to the objective function

$$L_\alpha(P) = \mathbb{E}\left[\alpha \|PX_0\|^2 - (1-\alpha)\left\|P\dot{X}_0\right\|^2\right],$$

to be maximized, where the parameter $\alpha \in [0,1]$ controls the trade-off between two potentially conflicting goals. In section 4 we will further justify the use of this objective function and show that for $\alpha \in (0,1)$ maximizing L_α minimizes an error bound for a simple classification algorithm on a generic class of classification problems, and that $\sqrt{\alpha}$ can be interpreted as a scale-parameter. When there is no ambiguity we write $L = L_\alpha$.

As the details of the process X are generally unknown, the optimization has to rely on an empirical basis. Let $(X)_0^m = (X_0, ..., X_m)$ be $m+1$ consecutive observations of the process X and define an empirical analogue $\hat{L}(P)$ of the objective function L

$$\hat{L}(P) = \frac{1}{m}\sum_{i=1}^m \left(\alpha\|PX_i\|^2 - (1-\alpha)\left\|P\dot{X}_i\right\|^2\right).$$

We now propose to seek $P \in \mathcal{P}_d$ to maximize $\hat{L}(.)$. This optimization problem, its analysis, algorithmic implementation and preliminary experimental tests are the contributions of this paper.

Existence of Solutions. We will require the general boundedness assumption that $\|X_t\| \leq 1/2$ a.s. Define an operator T on H by

$$Tz = \mathbb{E}\left[\alpha\langle z, X\rangle X - (1-\alpha)\left\langle z, \dot{X}\right\rangle \dot{X}\right] \text{ for } z \in H. \tag{1}$$

Then $T = \alpha C_X - (1-\alpha)C_{\dot{X}}$, where C_X and $C_{\dot{X}}$ are the covariance operators corresponding to X and $\dot{X}$ respectively. The empirical counterpart to T is $\hat{T}$ defined by

$$\hat{T}z = \frac{1}{m}\sum_{i=1}^m \left(\alpha\langle z, X_i\rangle X_i - (1-\alpha)\left\langle z, \dot{X}_i\right\rangle \dot{X}_i\right). \tag{2}$$

The operators T and $\hat{T}$ are central objects of the proposed method. They are both symmetric and compact, T is trace-class and $\hat{T}$ has finite rank. If $\alpha \in (0,1)$ they will tend to have both positive and negative eigenvalues. The following Theorem (see section 2) shows that a solution of our optimization problem can be obtained by projecting onto a dominant eigenspace of $\hat{T}$.

Theorem 1. *Fix $\alpha \in [0,1]$ and let $\hat{\lambda}_1 \geq \hat{\lambda}_2 \geq ... \geq 0$ be the nonnegative eigenvalues of $\hat{T}$, and (e_i) the sequence of associated eigenvectors. Then*

$$\max_{P \in \mathcal{P}_d} \hat{L}(P) = \sum_{i=1}^{d} \hat{\lambda}_i,$$

the maximum being attained when P is the orthogonal projection onto the span of $e_1, ..., e_d$.

This leads to a straightforward batch algorithm: Observe and store a realization of $(X_0, ..., X_m)$, construct $\hat{T}$, find eigenvectors and eigenvalues and project onto the span of d orthonormal eigenvectors corresponding to the largest eigenvalues.

Such a solution P need not be unique. In fact, if $\alpha = 0$ and $\dim(H) = \infty$, then $\hat{T}$ is a nonpositive operator with infinite dimensional nullspace, and there is an infinity of mutually orthogonal solutions, from which an arbitrary choice must be made. This can hardly be the way to extract meaningful signals, and the utility of the objective function with $\alpha = 0$ is questionable for high-dimensional input spaces. Except for very pathological cases, this extreme degeneracy is absent in the case $\alpha > 0$. In the generic, noisy case all nonzero eigenvalues will be distinct and if m is large then there are more than d positive eigenvalues of $\hat{T}$, so that the solution will be unique.

Estimation. Having found P to maximize $\hat{L}(.)$, can we be confident that $L(P)$ is also nearly maximal, and how does this confidence improve with the sample size?

These questions are complicated by the interdependence of observations, in particular by the possibility of being trapped for longer periods of time. Since we want to estimate an expectation on the basis of a temporal average, some sort of ergodicity property of the process X will be relevant. Our bounds are expressed in terms of the mixing coefficients $\beta(a)$, which roughly bound the interdependence of past and future variables separated by a time interval of duration a. Combining the techniques developed in [11] and [19] we arrive at the following result:

Theorem 2. *With the assumptions already introduced above, fix $\delta > 0$ and let $m, a \in \mathbb{N}$, $a < m/2$ and $l = \lfloor m/2a \rfloor$ and $\beta(a) < \delta/(2l)$. Then with probability greater $1 - \delta$ in the sample $(X)_0^m = (X_0, ..., X_m)$ we have*

$$\sup_{P \in \mathcal{P}_d} \left| \hat{L}(P) - L(P) \right| \leq \frac{4}{\sqrt{l}} \left(\sqrt{d} + \sqrt{\frac{1}{2} \ln \frac{1}{\delta/2 - l\beta(a-1)}} \right).$$

If the mixing coefficients β are known, then the right hand side can be minimized with an appropriate choice of a, which in general depends on the sample size (or *total learning time*) m. For easy interpretation assume $\beta(a) = 0$ for $a \geq a_0$. Then we can interpret a_0 as the mixing time beyond which all correlations vanish. If we set $a = a_0 + 1$ above, the resulting bound resembles the bound for the iid case with an effective sample size $l = \lfloor m/(2(a_0 + 1)) \rfloor$. This shows the ambiguous role of temporal dependencies: Over short time intervals they are beneficial, providing us with information which allows us to go beyond PSA by using the slowness principle. Over long periods of time they get in the way of mixing and become detrimental to learning.

Often the mixing coefficients are unknown, but one knows (or assumes or hopes) that X is absolutely regular, that is $\beta(a) \to 0$ as $a \to \infty$. We can then still establish learnability in the sense of convergence in probability:

Theorem 3. *If X is absolutely regular then for every $\epsilon > 0$ we have*

$$\lim_{m \to \infty} \Pr \left\{ \sup_{P \in \mathcal{P}_d} \left| \hat{L}(P) - L(P) \right| > \epsilon \right\} = 0.$$

We will prove both theorems in section 3.

A major problem caused by large observation times is the accumulating memory requirement to store the sample data, as long as we adhere to the batch algorithm sketched above. For this reason we use an online-algorithm for our experiments in image processing. The algorithm, a modification of an algorithm introduced by Oja [9], is briefly introduced in section 5. We apply it either directly to the image data or to train the second layer of a two-layered radial-basis-function network.

The experiments reported in section 6 involve processes with specific geometric invariants: Consider rapidly rotating views of a slowly changing scene. The projection returned by our algorithm then performs well as a preprocessor for rotation invariant recognition. An analogous behaviour was observed for scale-invariance, and it might be conjectured that similar mechanisms could account for the ubiquity of scale invariant perception in biological vision.

A similar technique has been proposed by Wiskott [17]. It is missing an analogue of a positive variance term in the objective function. The problem of potentially trivial solutions is circumnavigated by an orthonormalization prescription (whitening) of the covariance matrix prior to the subspace search, which then essentially seeks out a minimal subspace of the velocity covariance. In high (or infinite) dimensions minimal subspace analysis of (compact positive) operators should cause the above-mentioned degeneracy problem, because the eigenvalues will concentrate at zero. In [17] a corresponding problem is in fact mentioned. Also the orthonormalization increases the norms of the input vectors as the dimension grows, making it difficult to analyse the generalisation behaviour. In our approach all these problems are eliminated by a positive variance term, corresponding to $\alpha > 0$.

2   Preliminaries

For the next sections H will be a real separable infinite-dimensional Hilbert space with norm $\|.\|$ and inner product $\langle .,. \rangle$. In practice H will be finite dimensional, but as the dimension is large and should not enter into our results we may as well assume infinite-dimensionality, which will also eliminate some complications.

2.1   Hilbert Schmidt Operators

With H_2 we denote the real vector space of symmetric operators on H satisfying $\sum_{i=1}^{\infty} \|Te_i\|^2 < \infty$ for every orthonormal basis $(e_i)_{i=1}^{\infty}$ of H. For $S, T \in H_2$ the number $\langle S, T \rangle_2 = Tr(TS)$ defines an inner product on H_2, making it into a Hilbert space with norm $\|T\|_2 = \langle T, T \rangle_2^{1/2}$. The members of H_2 are compact and called Hilbert-Schmidt operators (see Reed and Simon [12] for background on functional analysis). For every $v \in H$ we define an operator Q_v by

$$Q_v x = \langle x, v \rangle\, v \text{ for all } x \in H.$$

The set of d-dimensional, orthogonal projections in H is denoted with $\mathcal{P}_d$. The following facts are easily verified (see [5]):

Lemma 1. *Let* $x, y \in H$ *and* $P \in \mathcal{P}_d$. *Then (i)* $Q_x \in H_2$ *and* $\|Q_x\|_2 = \|x\|^2$, *(ii)* $\langle Q_x, Q_y \rangle_2 = \langle x, y \rangle^2$, *(iii)* $\langle P, Q_x \rangle_2 = \|Px\|^2$ *and (iv)* $\|P\|_2 = \sqrt{d}$.

In terms of the Q-operators we can rewrite the operators T and $\hat{T}$ in (1) and (2) as

$$T = \mathbb{E}\left[\alpha Q_X - (1 - \alpha)\, Q_{\dot{X}}\right] \text{ and } \hat{T} = \frac{1}{m} \sum_{i=1}^{m} \left(\alpha Q_{X_i} - (1 - \alpha)\, Q_{\dot{X}_i}\right).$$

Using (iii) above, the objective functionals $L(.)$ and $\hat{L}(.)$ become

$$L(P) = \langle T, P \rangle_2 \text{ and } \hat{L}(P) = \left\langle \hat{T}, P \right\rangle_2.$$

Let $\hat{\lambda}_1 \geq \hat{\lambda}_2 \geq ... \geq 0$ be any nonincreasing enumeration of the nonnegative eigenvalues of $\hat{T}$, counting multiplicities, and (e_i) a corresponding orthonormal sequence of eigenvectors. Note that the sequence is necessarily infinite because $\hat{T}$ has finite rank and thus an infinite-dimensional null-space. Now let $P \in \mathcal{P}_d$. Since P has the eigenvalue 1 with multiplicity d and all its other eigenvalues are zero, it follows from Horn's theorem [14, Theorem 1.15] that

$$\left\langle \hat{T}, P \right\rangle_2 \leq \sum_{i=1}^{d} \hat{\lambda}_i.$$

If P is the projection onto the span of $e_1, ..., e_d$ then this becomes an equality. This shows that any such maximal projection P is also a maximizer for $\hat{L}(P)$ and that

$$\max_{P \in \mathcal{P}_d} \hat{L}(P) = \sum_{i=1}^{d} \hat{\lambda}_i,$$

thus proving Theorem 1.

These arguments are fairly standard, but in the infinite dimensional case there are some pitfalls resulting from non-positivity. For example the above is not generally true for the operator T corresponding to the true objective functional L, because it may happen that T has fewer than d nonnegative eigenvalues, or none at all. Since all negative eigenvalues converge to 0, the supremum might not be attained.

2.2   Mixing Coefficients and Inequalities

Let $\xi = \{\xi_t\}_{t \in \mathbb{Z}}$ be a stationary stochastic process with values in a measurable space (Ω, Σ) and with law μ. For $A \subseteq \mathbb{Z}$ let σ_A denote the σ-algebra generated by the variables ξ_t with $t \in A$, and use μ_A to denote the marginal distribution of μ on (Ω^A, σ_A).

Definition 1. *For $k \in \mathbb{N}$ define the mixing coefficient*

$$\beta_\xi(k) = \mathbb{E}\left[\sup\left\{\left|\mu\left(B|\sigma_{\{t:t\leq l\}}\right) - \mu(B)\right| : B \in \sigma_{\{t:t\geq l+k\}}\right\}\right].$$

The process ξ is called absolutely regular or β-mixing if $\beta_\xi(k) \to 0$ as $k \to \infty$.

The interpretation is as follows: The random variable

$$\sup\left\{\left|\mu\left(B|\sigma_{\{t:t\leq l\}}\right) - \mu(B)\right| : B \in \sigma_{\{t:t\geq l+k\}}\right\}$$

gives the largest change in the probability of any future event B occurring when a specific realization of the past is unveiled. It therefore measures the maximal dependence of the future $\{t \geq l + k\}$ on the past $\{t \leq l\}$, as a function of the past. Taking the expectation of this variable leads to a quantity which is itself independent of the past but takes the probabilities of different realizations of the past into account (see the book by Rio [13] for a general theory of weakly dependent processes). From this definition one can prove the following (Yu [19]):

Lemma 2. *Let $\xi = \{\xi_t\}_{t \in \mathbb{Z}}$ be stationary with values in a measurable space (Ω, Σ) and $B \in \sigma_{\{1,...,m\}}$. Then*

$$\left|\mu_{\{1,...,m\}}(B) - \left(\mu_{\{1\}}\right)^m(B)\right| \leq (m-1)\beta_\xi(1).$$

We will also need the following lemma of Vidyasagar [16, Lemma 3.1]:

Lemma 3. *Suppose $\beta(k) \downarrow 0$ as $k \to \infty$. It is possible to choose a sequence $\{a_m\}$ such that $a_m \leq m$, and with $l_m = \lfloor m/a_m \rfloor$ we have that $l_m \to \infty$ while $l_m \beta(a_m) \to 0$ as $m \to \infty$.*

3   Generalization

We first prove a general result for vector-valued processes. For two subsets $V, W \subseteq H$ of a Hilbert space H we introduce the following notation

$$\|V\| = \sup_{v \in V} \|v\| \quad \text{and} \quad |\langle V, W \rangle| = \sup_{v \in V, w \in W} |\langle v, w \rangle|.$$

Theorem 4. *Let* $V, W \subset H$ *and* $X = \{X_t\}_{t \in \mathbb{Z}}$ *a stationary, mean zero process with values in* V.

1. Fix $\delta > 0$ *and let* $m, a \in \mathbb{N}$, $a < m/2$ *and* $l = \lfloor m/2a \rfloor$ *and* $\beta(a) < \delta/(2l)$. *Then with probability greater than* $1 - \delta$ *we have*

$$\sup_{w \in W} \left| \frac{1}{m} \sum_{i=1}^{m} \langle w, X_i \rangle \right| \leq \frac{2}{\sqrt{l}} \left(\|V\| \|W\| + |\langle V, W \rangle| \sqrt{\frac{1}{2} \ln \frac{1}{\delta/2 - l\beta_X(a)}} \right).$$

2. If X *is absolutely regular then for every* $\epsilon > 0$

$$\Pr \left\{ \sup_{w \in W} \left| \frac{1}{m} \sum_{i=1}^{m} \langle w, X_i \rangle \right| > \epsilon \right\} \to 0 \text{ as } m \to \infty.$$

If we let W be the unit ball in H we immediately obtain the following

Corollary 1. *Under the first assumptions of Theorem 4 we have with probability greater* $1 - \delta$ *that*

$$\left\| \frac{1}{m} \sum_{i=1}^{m} X_i \right\| \leq \frac{2 \|V\|}{\sqrt{l}} \left(1 + \sqrt{\frac{1}{2} \ln \frac{1}{\delta/2 - l\beta_X(a)}} \right).$$

If in addition X_t *is absolutely regular then* $\|(1/m) \sum_{i=1}^{m} X_i\| \to 0$ *in probability.*

Here is a practical reformulation with trivial proof:

Corollary 2. *Theorem 4 and Corollary 1 remain valid if the mean-zero assumption is omitted,* X_i *is replaced by* $X_i - \mathbb{E}[X_1]$ *and* $\|V\|$ *and* $|\langle V, W \rangle|$ *are replaced by* $2 \|V\|$ *and* $2 |\langle V, W \rangle|$ *respectively.*

To prove Theorem 4 we first establish an analogous result for iid X_i (essentially following [11]) and then adapt it to dependent variables.

Lemma 4. *Let* $V, W \subset H$ *be and* $X_1, ..., X_m$ *iid zero-mean random variables with values in* V. *Then for* ϵ *and* m *such that* $\|W\| \|V\| < \sqrt{m}\epsilon$ *we have*

$$\Pr \left\{ \sup_{w \in W} \left| \frac{1}{m} \sum_{i=1}^{m} \langle w, X_i \rangle \right| > \epsilon \right\} \leq \exp \left(\frac{-(\sqrt{m}\epsilon - \|V\| \|W\|)^2}{2 |\langle V, W \rangle|^2} \right).$$

Proof. Consider the average $\bar{\mathbf{X}} = (1/m) \sum_1^m X_i$. With Jensen's inequality and using independence we obtain

$$\left(\mathbb{E}\left[\|\bar{\mathbf{X}}\|\right]\right)^2 \leq \mathbb{E}\left[\|\bar{\mathbf{X}}\|^2\right] = \frac{1}{m^2}\sum_{i=1}^m \mathbb{E}\left[\|X_i\|^2\right] \leq \|V\|^2/m.$$

Now let $f : V^m \to \mathbb{R}$ be defined by $f(\mathbf{x}) = \sup_{w \in W} |(1/m)\sum_1^m \langle w, x_i \rangle|$. We have to bound the probability that $f > \epsilon$. By Schwartz' inequality and the above bound we have

$$\mathbb{E}\left[f(\mathbf{X})\right] = \mathbb{E}\left[\sup_{w \in W} |\langle w, \bar{\mathbf{X}}\rangle|\right] \leq \|W\|\,\mathbb{E}\left[\|\bar{\mathbf{X}}\|\right] \leq \left(1/\sqrt{m}\right)\|W\|\,\|V\|. \qquad (3)$$

Let $\mathbf{x} \in V^m$ be arbitrary and $\mathbf{x}' \in V^m$ be obtained by modifying a coordinate x_k of $\mathbf{x}$ to be an arbitrary $x_k' \in V$. Then

$$|f(\mathbf{x}) - f(\mathbf{x}')| \leq \frac{1}{m}\sup_{w \in W}|\langle w, x_k\rangle - \langle w, x_k'\rangle| \leq \frac{2}{m}|\langle V, W\rangle|.$$

By (3) and the bounded-difference inequality (see [7]) we obtain for $t > 0$

$$\Pr\left\{f(\mathbf{X}) > \frac{\|W\|\,\|V\|}{\sqrt{m}} + t\right\} \leq \Pr\left\{f(\mathbf{X}) - \mathbb{E}\left[f(\mathbf{X})\right] > t\right\} \leq \exp\left(\frac{-mt^2}{2|\langle V, W\rangle|^2}\right).$$

The conclusion follows from setting $t = \epsilon - (1/\sqrt{m})\|W\|\,\|V\|$ ∎

The proof of Theorem 4 now uses the techniques introduced by Yu [19] (see also Meir [8] and Lozano et al [3]).

Proof (of Theorem 4). Select a time-scale $a \in \mathbb{N}$, $2a < m$ and represent the discrete time axis as an alternating sequence of blocks

$$\mathbb{Z} = \left(..., H_{-1}, T_{-1}, H_0, T_0, H_1, T_1, ..., H_k, T_k, ...\right),$$

where each of the H_k and T_k has length a,

$$H_k = \{2ka, ..., 2ka + a - 1\} \text{ and } T_k = \{(2k+1)a, ..., (2k+1)a + a - 1\}.$$

We now define the blocked processes X^H and X^T with values in $\mathrm{co}(V)$ by $X_t^H = (1/a)\sum_{j \in H_t} X_j$ and $X_t^T = (1/a)\sum_{j \in T_t} X_j$. By stationarity the X_i^H and X_i^T are identically distributed and themselves stationary. Because of the gaps of size a we have $\beta_{X^H}(1) = \beta_{X^T}(1) = \beta_X(a)$. We can now write

$$(1, ..., m) = \left(H_1, T_1, H_2, T_2, ..., H_l, T_l, R\right),$$

where the number l of block-pairs is chosen so as to minimize the size of the remainder R, so $l = \lfloor m/(2a) \rfloor$ and $|R| < 2a$. For arbitrary $\epsilon > 0$ we obtain

$$\Pr\left\{ \sup_{w\in W} \left| \frac{1}{2al} \sum_{i=1}^{2al} \langle w, X_i \rangle \right| > \epsilon \right\}$$

$$= \Pr\left\{ \sup_{w\in W} \left| \frac{1}{2l} \sum_{i=1}^{l} \langle w, X_i^H \rangle + \frac{1}{2l} \sum_{i=1}^{l} \langle w, X_i^T \rangle \right| > \epsilon \right\}$$

$$\leq \Pr\left\{ \sup_{w\in W} \left| \frac{1}{2l} \sum_{i=1}^{l} \langle w, X_i^H \rangle \right| + \sup_{w\in W} \left| \frac{1}{2l} \sum_{i=1}^{l} \langle w, X_i^T \rangle \right| > \epsilon \right\}$$

$$= 2\Pr\left\{ \sup_{w\in W} \left| \frac{1}{l} \sum_{i=1}^{l} \langle w, X_i^H \rangle \right| > \epsilon \right\}$$

$$\leq 2\exp\left(\frac{-\left(\sqrt{l}\epsilon - \|V\|\,\|W\| \right)^2}{2\,|\langle V, W\rangle|^2} \right) + 2l\beta_X(a).$$

The last inequality follows from the mixing Lemma 2, $\beta_{X^H}(1) = \beta_X(a)$, the iid case Lemma 4 and the fact that $\|\mathrm{co}(V)\| = \|V\|$ and $|\langle \mathrm{co}(V), W\rangle| = |\langle V, W\rangle|$. To deal with the remainder R, note that

$$\Pr\left\{ \sup_{w\in W} \left| \frac{1}{m} \sum_{i=1}^{m} \langle w, X_i \rangle \right| > \epsilon \right\} \leq \Pr\left\{ \sup_{w\in W} \left| \frac{1}{2al} \sum_{i=1}^{2al} \langle w, X_i \rangle \right| + \frac{\|V\|\,\|W\|}{l} > \epsilon \right\}.$$

We thus obtain

$$\Pr\left\{ \sup_{w\in W} \left| \frac{1}{m} \sum_{i=1}^{m} \langle w, X_i \rangle \right| > \epsilon \right\}$$

$$\leq 2\exp\left(\frac{-\left(\sqrt{l}\epsilon - \left(1 + \frac{1}{\sqrt{l}}\right)\|V\|\,\|W\| \right)^2}{2\,|\langle V, W\rangle|^2} \right) + 2l\beta_X(a). \tag{4}$$

Solving for ϵ and using $\left(1 + 1/\sqrt{l}\right) \leq 2$ gives the first conclusion.

If X is absolutely regular then $\beta(a) \downarrow 0$ as $a \to \infty$. Choosing a subsequence a_m as in Lemma 3 we have $l_m = \lfloor m/(2a) \rfloor \to \infty$ and $l_m \beta(a_m) \to 0$. Substituting l_m for l and a_m for a above, the bound (4) will go to zero as $m \to \infty$, which proves the second conclusion. ∎

Now it is easy to prove the bounds in the introduction by applying Theorem 4 to the stationary operator-valued stochastic process

$$A_t = \alpha Q_{X_t} - (1 - \alpha) Q_{\dot{X}_t}, \tag{5}$$

which we reinterpret as a vector-valued process with values in the Hilbert space H_2 of Hilbert-Schmidt operators. Note that $T = \mathbb{E}[A_1]$ and $\hat{T} = (1/m)\sum_{1}^{m} A_i$.

Proof (of Theorem 2 and   Theorem 3). : First note that $\beta_A(a) = \beta_X(a-1)$, because A_t depends also on X_{t-1}, and that A is absolutely regular if X is. Set $W = \mathcal{P}_d$ and define $V \subset H_2$ by

$$V = \{\alpha Q_x - (1-\alpha) Q_x : \|x\| \le 1 \text{ and } \|y\| \le 1\}.$$

Then $A_t \in V$ a.s. By Lemma 1 (i), V is contained in the unit ball in H_2 and

$$|\langle V, W \rangle_2| = \sup_{P \in \mathcal{P}_d} \sup \{|\langle P, \alpha Q_x - (1-\alpha) Q_x \rangle_2| : \|x\| \le 1, \ \|y\| \le 1\}$$

$$\le \sup_{P \in \mathcal{P}_d} \sup \left\{ \alpha \|Px\|^2 + (1-\alpha) \|Py\|^2 \right\} \le 1.$$

By Lemma 1 (iv) $\|W\|_2 = \sqrt{d}$. We also have

$$\sup_{P \in \mathcal{P}_d} \left| \hat{L}(P) - L(P) \right| = \sup_{P \in \mathcal{P}_d} \left| \frac{1}{m} \sum_{i=1}^{m} \langle P, A_i - \mathbb{E}[A_1] \rangle_2 \right|.$$

Applying Corollary 2 to the process $A_t - \mathbb{E}[A_1]$ gives both Theorem 2 and 3. ∎

4   A Generic Error Bound

Now we show that maximizing L minimizes an error-bound for all classification tasks posessing a certain continuity property. We fix a stationary process $\xi = \{\xi_t\}_{t \in \mathbb{Z}}$ with values in a measurable space (Ω, Σ), law μ and marginal distributions μ_I for $I \subset \mathbb{Z}$.

Definition 2. *Let ξ be as above. An (at most) countable partition $\Omega = \bigcup_k E_k$ of Ω into disjoint measurable E_k is continuous w.r.t. X if for all k and all $A, B \subseteq E_k$ we have*

$$\mu_{\{0\}}(A) \mu_{\{0\}}(B) \le \mu_{\{0,1\}}(A, B).$$

So knowledge that E_k occurs at time 0 increases the probability at time 1 for any event A implying E_k. For an example let Ω be the unit interval, $\{E_k\}$ any partition of Ω into intervals of diameter less than $1/2$ and X_t a Gaussian random walk with periodic boundary conditions. Unlike the mixing properties relevant for generalization, the notion of continuity is concerned only with process dependencies on a microscopic time-scale.

We now assume that the process X has the form $X_t = \phi \circ \xi_t$, where $\phi : \Omega \to H$ is a a feature map with $\|\phi\| \le 1/2$ and $\mathbb{E}[\phi \circ \xi_t] = 0$. One easily verifies $\beta_X(k) \le \beta_\xi(k)$, for all k. The feature map ϕ may hide important information such as labels, for example if $\Omega = \mathcal{X} \times \mathcal{Y}$ and $\phi(x, y) = \psi(x)$.

Suppose now that $\{E_k\}$ is a partition of Ω, with each E_k defining some pattern class. Given a pair (ω_1, ω_2) drawn from $\mu_{\{0\}}^2$ we have to decide if ω_1 and ω_2 belong to the same class, that is to decide if there is some k such that $x \in E_k$

and $y \in E_k$. In the absence of other known structure we use a simple metric decision rule based on the projected input and the distance threshold $\sqrt{\alpha}$.

ω_1 and ω_2 are in the same class iff $\|P\phi(\omega_1) - P\phi(\omega_2)\|^2 < \alpha$.

Error bounds for this rule can be converted into error bounds for simple metric classifiers, whenever we are provided with examples for the various E_k.

Theorem 5. *With ξ, ϕ and X as above and $\alpha \in (0,1)$, if $\{E_k\}$ is continuous w.r.t. ξ, then the error probability for the above rule, as ω_1 and ω_2 are drawn independently from $\mu_{\{0\}}$, is bounded by*

$$Err \leq \frac{1}{1-\alpha} \left(1 - \frac{2}{\alpha}L_\alpha(P)\right) - R$$

where $R = \sum_k \left(\mu_{\{0\}}(E_k)\right)^2$.

The theorem implies a rule to select the trade-off parameter α: It should be chosen to minimize the first term in the bound above, so α should be close to 0, but a positive value for $L_\alpha(P)$ should still be obtained, corresponding to positive eigenvalues of the operator T.

Proof. We use the notation $\Delta = \Delta(\omega_1, \omega_2) := \|P\phi(\omega_1) - P\phi(\omega_2)\|^2$. Then

$$Err = \sum_{k,l:k\neq l} \mathbb{E}_{\mu_{\{0\}}^2}\left[1_{\Delta<\alpha}1_{E_k \times E_l}\right] + \sum_k \mathbb{E}_{\mu_{\{0\}}^2}\left[1_{\Delta\geq\alpha}1_{E_k \times E_k}\right]$$

$$= \mathbb{E}_{\mu_{\{0\}}^2}\left[1_{\Delta<\alpha}\right] + 2\sum_k \mathbb{E}_{\mu_{\{0\}}^2}\left[1_{\Delta\geq\alpha}1_{E_k \times E_k}\right] - R$$

$$\leq \mathbb{E}_{\mu_{\{0\}}^2}\left[\frac{1-\Delta}{1-\alpha}\right] + 2\sum_k \mathbb{E}_{\mu_{\{0\}}^2}\left[\frac{\Delta}{\alpha}1_{E_k \times E_k}\right] - R$$

$$\leq \frac{1}{1-\alpha} - \frac{1}{1-\alpha}\mathbb{E}_{\mu_{\{0\}}^2}\left[\Delta\right] + \frac{2}{\alpha}\sum_k \mathbb{E}_{\mu_{\{0,1\}}}\left[\Delta\, 1_{E_k \times E_k}\right] - R.$$

The first inequality uses the bounds $1_{\Delta<\alpha} \leq (1 - \Delta)/(1-\alpha)$ and $1_{\Delta\geq\alpha} \leq \Delta/\alpha$, which hold since $\Delta \in [0,1]$. The other inequality uses the continuity property of the E_k-system, because for any nonnegative function $g = g(\omega_1, \omega_2)$ and any k we have

$$\mathbb{E}_{\mu_{\{0\}}^2}\left[g\, 1_{E_k \times E_k}\right] \leq \mathbb{E}_{\mu_{\{0,1\}}}\left[g\, 1_{E_k \times E_k}\right],$$

as can be shown directly from Definition 2 by an approximation with simple functions. Now we use

$$\sum_k \mathbb{E}_{\mu_{\{0,1\}}}\left[\Delta\, 1_{E_k \times E_k}\right] \leq \mathbb{E}_{\mu_{\{0,1\}}}\left[\Delta\right] = \mathbb{E}\left[\left\|P\dot{X}_1\right\|^2\right] = \mathbb{E}\left[\left\|P\dot{X}_0\right\|^2\right]$$

and the identity $\mathbb{E}_{\mu_{\{0\}}^2}\left[\Delta\right] = 2\mathbb{E}\left[\|PX_0\|^2\right]$, which follows from the mean-zero assumption, to obtain

$$Err \leq \frac{1}{1-\alpha} - \frac{2}{1-\alpha}\mathbb{E}\left[\|PX_0\|^2\right] + \frac{2}{\alpha}\mathbb{E}\left[\left\|P\dot{X}_0\right\|^2\right] - R \qquad \blacksquare$$

5   An Online Algorithm

In practice H will be finite-dimensional. If the process X is slowly mixing, the learning time m can be quite large, leading to excessive storage requirements for any kind of batch algorithm. For this reason we used an online algorithm for principal subspace analysis, to which every successive realization of the operator valued variable $A_t = (1 - \alpha) Q_{X_t} - \alpha Q_{\dot{X}_t}$ was fed, for $t = 1, ..., m$. This takes us somewhat astray from the results proved in this paper, and would require a different analysis in terms of stochastic approximation theory (see Benveniste et al [1]), an analysis which we cannot provide at this point. The principal goal of our first experiments was to test the value of our objective function L.

If $\mathbf{v} = (v_1, ..., v_d)$ is an orthonormal basis for the range of some $P \in \mathcal{P}_d$, the Oja-Karhunen flow [9], is given by the ordinary differential equation

$$\dot{v}_k = (I - P_\mathbf{v}) T v_k,$$

where $P_\mathbf{v}$ is the projection onto the span of the v_k. If T is symmetric it has been shown by Yan et al [18] that a solution $\mathbf{v}(t)$ to this differential equation will remain forever on the Stiefel-manifold of orthonormal sets if the initial condition is orthonormal, and that it will converge to a dominant eigenspace of T for almost all initial conditions. Discretizing gives the update rule

$$v_k(t + 1) = v_k(t) + \eta(t) \left(I - P_{\mathbf{v}(t)}\right) T v_k(t),$$

where $\eta(t)$ is a learning rate. Unfortunately a careful analysis shows that the Stiefel manifold becomes unstable if T is not positive. The simplest solution to this problem lies in orthonormalization. This is what we do, but there are more elegant techniques and different flows have been proposed (see e.g. [4]) to extract dominant eigenspaces for general symmetric operators. We now replace $T = E[A_t]$ by the process variable A_t to obtain the final rule

$$v_k(t + 1) = v_k(t) + \eta(t) \left(I - P_{\mathbf{v}(t)}\right) \left((1 - \alpha) Q_{X_t} - \alpha Q_{\dot{X}_t}\right) v_k(t), \qquad (6)$$

which, together with the orthonormalization prescription, gives the algorithm used in our experiments. The update rule (6) can be considered a combination of Hebbian learning of input data with anti-Hebbian learning of input velocity.

6   Experiments

We applied our technique to train a preprocessor for image recognition. In all these experiments we used the output dimension $d = 10$, and the trade-off parameter $\alpha = 0.8$.

To train the algorithm we generated different input processes ξ to produce sequences of 28x28-pixel, gray-scale images, normalized to unity in the euclidean norm of $\mathbb{R}^{28 \times 28}$. These processes are described below.

We considered two possible architectures for the preprocessor: In the linear case we used the pixel vectors directly as inputs to our algorithm, that is $X = \xi$ and $H = \mathbb{R}^{28 \times 28}$.

In the nonlinear case (RBF) we used our algorithm to train the second layer of a two-layered radial-basis-function network. In an initial training phase a large number (2000) of prototypes π_i for the first layer were chosen from the process ξ at time intervals larger than the mixing time and kept fixed afterwards. Define a kernel κ on $\mathbb{R}^{28 \times 28} \times \mathbb{R}^{28 \times 28}$ by

$$\kappa\left(\zeta_1, \zeta_2\right) = \exp\left(-\beta \left\|\pi_j - \xi\right\|_{28 \times 28}^2\right),$$

where in practice we always use $\beta = 4$. The first network layer then implements the (randomly chosen) nonlinear map $\tau : \mathbb{R}^{28 \times 28} \to \mathbb{R}^{2000}$ given by

$$\tau\left(\xi\right)_k = \sum_{j=1}^{2000} G_{kj}^{-1/2} \kappa\left(\pi_j, \xi\right), \text{ for } \xi \in \mathbb{R}^{28 \times 28},$$

where G is the Gramian $G_{ij} = \kappa\left(\pi_i, \pi_j\right)$, which is generically non-singular. The transformation through $G_{kj}^{-1/2}$ is chosen to ensure that $\langle \tau\left(\pi_i\right), \tau\left(\pi_j\right)\rangle_{2000} = \kappa\left(\pi_i, \pi_j\right)$. We then applied the algorithm to the output of the first layer, so $X = \tau\left(\xi\right)$ and $H = \mathbb{R}^{2000}$.

The processes are designed to train specific geometric invariants. Fix a large image I with periodic boundary conditions. At any time t the 28x28-process image ξ_t is a mapped subimage of I and completely described by four parameters: The position $\mathbf{x}_t = (x_t, y_t)$ of ξ_t within the source image, a rotation angle r_t and a scale s_t in the interval $[1/2, 3/2]$. We can thus write $\xi_t = \xi\left(\mathbf{x}_t, r_t, s_t\right)$ and we initialize to $\xi_0 = \xi\left(\mathbf{0}, 0, 1\right)$. Given ξ_t we find ξ_{t+1} by

$$\xi_{t+1} = \xi\left(\mathbf{x}_t + D\mathbf{x}, r_t + Dr, s_t + Ds\right),$$

where it is understood that the additions on $\mathbf{x}_t$ and r_t respect the periodic boundary conditions, and the addition on s_t restricts to the interval $[1/2, 3/2]$. The $D\mathbf{x}, Dr, Ds$ are random variables defining the essential geometric properties of the process. Here we report two cases, corresponding to the training of rotation and scale invariance. There were no experiments with translation invariance yet.

To train rotation invariance: The distribution of Dr is uniform on $[-\pi, \pi]$ and the distribution of Ds is uniform on $[-0.01, 0.01]$. Rapidly changing orientation, small changes in scale.

To train scale invariance: The distribution of Dr is uniform on $[-0.01, 0.01]$ and the distribution of Ds is uniform on $[-1, 1]$. Rapidly changing scale, small changes in orientation.

The choice of the distribution of $D\mathbf{x}$ is critical, with qualitative aspects of the exploration-exploitation dilemma. If we chose $\mathcal{N}\left(0, \sigma^2\right)$ (normal, centered with width σ) the centers of ξ will take a random walk with average stepsize σ. If

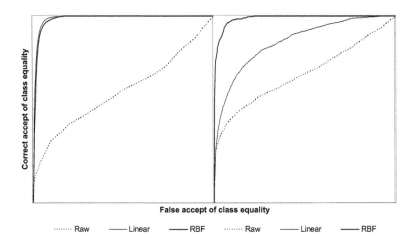

Fig. 1. ROC curves for the metric as a detector of class-equality for (left) rotation- and (right) scale-invariant character recognition

σ is large (rapid exploration) the translation obliterates the effect of rotation or scaling, we loose continuity and the performance degrades. If σ is small (intense exploitation) the mixing time becomes large, causing exessive total learning times. We used $\sigma = 1/2$ in pixel units. With these parameter settings and a dynamic learning rate of $\eta(t) = \frac{10^2}{10^4+t}$ the system was trained on $m = 10^6$ observations.

The performance of the resulting preprocessors is tested on a real life problem, the rotation- (scale-)-invariant recognition of characters. To this end two test-sets were prepared containing images of the digits 0-8 (0-9) in 100 randomly chosen states of orientation (scaling between $1/2$ and $3/2$).

An important criterion for the quality of a preprocessor is the ability of the distance between preprocessed examples to serve as a detector for class-equality. Figure 1 shows corresponding receiver-operating-characteristics. The area under these curves then estimates the probability that for four independently drawn examples $\|a_1 - b_1\|_{10} \leq \|a_2 - b_2\|_{10}$, given that a_1 and b_1 belong to the same, and a_2 and b_2 to different classes. We also give a practical measure by recording the error rate of a *single-example-per-class* nearest-neighbour classifier, trained on a randomly selected example for each pattern class, *Error* in the following table.

Invariance Type	Method used	ROC-Area	Error
	Raw Data	0.597	0.716
Rotation	Linear	0.987	0.126
	RBF	0.983	0.138
	Raw Data	0.690	0.508
Scaling	Linear	0.866	0.421
	RBF	0.989	0.100

In the case of rotation invariance, the linear preprocessor architecture even slightly outperformed the RBF network. The latter showed stable good performance in both cases.

References

1. A. Benveniste, M. Métevier, Pierre Priouret. *Adaptive Algorithms and Stochastic Approximations.* Springer, 1987.
2. P. Földiák. Learning invariance from transformation sequences. *Neural Computation*, 3: 194-200, 1991.
3. A. C. Lozano, S. R. Kulkarni, R. E. Shapire. Convergence and consistency of regularized boosting algorithms with stationary, β-mixing observations. *Advances in Neural Information Processing Systems* 18, 2006.
4. J.H. Manton, U. Helmke, I.M.Y. Mareels. A dual purpose principal and minor component flow. *Systems & Control Letters* 54: 759-769, 2005.
5. A. Maurer, Bounds for linear multi-task learning. *JMLR*, 7:117–139, 2006.
6. A. Maurer, Generalization Bounds for Subspace Selection and Hyperbolic PCA. *Subspace, Latent Structure and Feature Selection. LNCS* 3940: 185-197, Springer, 2006.
7. Colin McDiarmid, Concentration, in *Probabilistic Methods of Algorithmic Discrete Mathematics*, p. 195-248. Springer, Berlin, 1998.
8. R. Meir. Nonparametric time series prediction through adaptive model selection. *Machine Learning*, 39, 5-34, 2000.
9. E. Oja. Principal component analysis. *The Handbook of Brain Theory and Neural Networks*. M. A. Arbib ed. MIT Press, 910-913, 2002.
10. S.Mika, B.Schölkopf, A.Smola, K.-R.Müller, M.Scholz and G.Rätsch. Kernel PCA and De-noising in Feature Spaces, in *Advances in Neural Information Processing Systems* 11, 1998.
11. J. Shawe-Taylor, N. Christianini, Estimating the moments of a random vector, *Proceedings of GRETSI 2003 Conference*, I: 47–52, 2003.
12. M. Reed, B. Simon. *Functional Analysis*, part I of *Methods of Mathematical Physics, Academic Press*, 1980.
13. E. Rio. *Théorie asymptotique des processus aléatoires faiblement dépendants.* Springer 2000.
14. B. Simon. *Trace Ideals and Their Applications.* Cambridge University Press, London, 1979
15. J. Shawe-Taylor, C.K.I. Williams, N. Cristianini, J.S. Kandola: On the eigenspectrum of the Gram matrix and the generalization error of kernel-PCA. *IEEE Transactions on Information Theory* 51(7): 2510-2522, 2005.
16. M. Vidyasagar, *Learning and generalization with applications to neural networks.* Springer, London, 2003.
17. L. Wiskott, T. Sejnowski. Slow feature analysis: Unsupervised learning of invariances. *Neural Computation*, 14: 715-770, 2003.
18. W. Yan, U. Helmke, J.B. Moore. Global analysis of Oja's flow for neural networks. *IEEE Trans. on Neural Networks* 5,5: 674-683, 1994.
19. B. Yu. Rate of convergence for empirical processes of stationary mixing sequences. Annals of Probability 22, 94-116, 1994.

Learning-Related Complexity of Linear Ranking Functions

Atsuyoshi Nakamura

Graduate School of Information Science and Technology, Hokkaido University
Kita 14, Nishi 9, Kita-ku, Sapporo 060-0814, Japan
atsu@main.ist.hokudai.ac.jp

Abstract. In this paper, we study learning-related complexity of *linear ranking functions* from n-dimensional Euclidean space to $\{1, 2, ..., k\}$. We show that their *graph dimension*, a kind of measure for PAC learning complexity in the multiclass classification setting, is $\Theta(n+k)$. This graph dimension is significantly smaller than the graph dimension $\Omega(nk)$ of the class of $\{1, 2, ..., k\}$-valued decision-list functions naturally defined using $k-1$ linear discrimination functions. We also show a risk bound of learning linear ranking functions in the ordinal regression setting by a technique similar to that used in the proof of an upper bound of their graph dimension.

1 Introduction

A *linear ranking function* we study in this paper is a function from the n-dimensional Euclidean space $\Re^n$ to the set of ranks $\{1, 2, ..., k\}$ represented by $k-1$ parallel hyperplanes in $\Re^n$ that separate the domains of two consecutive ranks. This function is a simple one represented by $n+k-1$ real parameters, and the class of linear ranking functions is one of the most popular function classes studied in *ordinal regression*.

Ordinal regression is a kind of multiclass classification problem in which there is a linear ordering among the values of a class attribute. Problems of learning human preference [7, 8] are often formalized as this kind of problem.

Recently, some learning algorithms of linear ranking functions have been developed from the viewpoint of large margin principle [5, 10, 11]. However, there have been few studies on learning-related complexity specific to those functions. The only study[1] we know is a *ranking loss* analysis of an online learning algorithm derived from the perceptron algorithm by Crammer and Singer [3], where *ranking loss* of predicted rank $\hat{i}$ for true rank i is $|\hat{i} - i|$.

In this paper, we study learning-related complexity of the class of linear ranking functions. On this issue, Rajaram et al. [10] already proved that *VC dimension* of this class is the same as that of the class of linear discrimination functions. However, it seems not to be appropriate to compare a class of $\{-1, 1\}$-valued

---

[1] In [11], a certain risk bound was shown using Vapnik's theorem [12, p.84], but there seems to be some problem in their application of the theorem. See Remark 2.

J.L. Balcázar, P.M. Long, and F. Stephan (Eds.): ALT 2006, LNAI 4264, pp. 378–392, 2006.
© Springer-Verlag Berlin Heidelberg 2006

functions with a class of $\{1, 2, ..., k\}$-valued functions ($k > 2$) by VC dimension. For such comparison, *graph dimension* [9], which is an extension of VC dimension for $\{1, 2, ..., k\}$-valued functions, appears to be appropriate. In this paper, we show a difference between graph dimensions for the above two classes; that is, the graph dimension of the class of linear ranking functions is $\Theta(n + k)$, while that of the class of linear discrimination functions is $\Theta(n)$.

For comparison's sake, we also analyze the graph dimension of the class of *decision-list* functions represented by $k - 1$ linear discrimination functions $g_1, g_2, ..., g_{k-1}$ that determine the function value for $\mathbf{x}$ by the smallest index i that satisfies $g_i(\mathbf{x}) = 1$. What motivated us to study this comparison was the following simple questions asked by our colleagues: "Why don't you learn a linear ranking function by decomposing it into $k - 1$ learning problems of a linear discrimination function? It is possible for the separator between ranks i and $i + 1$ to be learned using all the instances of more than rank i as positive and using the others as negative, isn't it?" Giving priority to a smaller rank for the overlapped domains of different ranks, functions learned by this method can be seen as the above decision lists. The answer to the above questions is that the complexity of the class of linear ranking functions is significantly smaller than that of the class of such decision lists and, as a result, the number of instances necessary to learn for the former is smaller than that for the latter. Actually, we show that the graph dimension of the latter is $\Omega(nk)$, while the former is $\Theta(n + k)$ as described above. In the problem of predicting the user's ratings for items, initial prediction performance for new users is an important issue, and learners with small sample complexity are preferable for quick acquisition of the user's preference.

According to the theorem proved by Ben-David et al. [1], sample complexity of PAC learning of $\{1, 2, ..., k\}$-valued functions in the multiclass classification setting is linearly upper-bounded by graph dimension. Therefore, we can obtain sample complexity upper bounds from our graph dimension upper bounds by applying their theorem.

Actually, their theorem is implied by Vapnik's more general theorem [12, p.84], which includes the settings of not only classification but also regression. The graph dimension of the class LR of linear ranking functions is equal to the VC dimension of the set of *indicators* of the function class defined by LR using the *zero-one loss function*. An upper bound of the VC dimension of the set of *indicators* of the function class defined by LR using the *L1 loss function* instead of the zero-one loss function is also shown by a similar argument used to prove an upper bound of graph dimension of LR. From the upper bound, we obtain a risk bound of learning LR in the ordinal regression setting.

This paper is organized as follows. In Section 2, two function classes, the class LR of linear ranking functions and the class DL$_\mathcal{L}$ of decision lists with condition function class $\mathcal{L}$, where $\mathcal{L}$ is the class of linear discrimination functions, are defined. Analyses of the two function classes by VC dimension and graph dimension are described in Section 3. In Section 4, risk bounds on learning LR are shown in two settings, the multiclass classification setting and the ordinal regression setting. Conclusions are given in Section 5.

2   Linear Ranking Functions

Let K denote the set $\{1, 2, ..., k\}$. In this paper, we consider functions from $\Re^n$ to K. A *linear ranking function* is a function $f : R^n \rightarrow K$ defined as

$$f(\mathbf{x}) = \min_{r \in K}\{r : \mathbf{w} \cdot \mathbf{x} - b_r < 0\},$$

where $\mathbf{w} \in \Re^n$, $\mathbf{b} = (b_1, b_2, ..., b_{k-1})$ with $b_1 \le b_2 \le ... \le b_{k-1}$ and $b_k = \infty$. Let LR denote the class of linear ranking functions.

For comparison, we consider a larger function class. Let $\mathcal{B}$ denote a class of functions from $\Re^n$ to $\{-1, 1\}$. For arbitrary $g_1, g_2, ..., g_{k-1} \in \mathcal{B}$ and $g_k \equiv 1$, consider a kind of decision list $\mathrm{dl}[g_1, g_2, ..., g_{k-1}] : R^n \rightarrow K$ defined as

$$\mathrm{dl}[g_1, g_2, ..., g_{k-1}](\mathbf{x}) = \min\{i : g_i(\mathbf{x}) = 1\}.$$

We call functions defined like this *decision lists with condition function class $\mathcal{B}$*. Let $\mathrm{DL}_{\mathcal{B}}$ denote the class of them. As condition function classes, here, we only consider the class $\mathcal{L}$ of *linear discrimination functions* f, namely, a function represented by

$$f(\mathbf{x}) = \begin{cases} 1 & \text{if } \mathbf{w} \cdot \mathbf{x} < b \\ -1 & \text{if } \mathbf{w} \cdot \mathbf{x} \ge b \end{cases}$$

using $\mathbf{w} \in \Re^n$ and $b \in \Re$. We call vector $\mathbf{w}$ a *normal vector* of f. Note that $\mathrm{DL}_{\mathcal{L}} \supseteq \mathrm{LR}$.

3   Complexity of LR

3.1   VC Dimension Analysis

Let $\mathcal{F}$ denote a class of functions from $X(= \Re^n)$ to K. Let l denote an arbitrary natural number. For $S = (\mathbf{x}_1, \mathbf{x}_2, ..., \mathbf{x}_l) \in X^l$ and $f \in \mathcal{F}$, define $f_S \in K^l$ as $(f(\mathbf{x}_1), f(\mathbf{x}_2), ..., f(\mathbf{x}_l))$. Function set $\Pi_{\mathcal{F}}(S)$ is defined as the set of functions in $\mathcal{F}$ with the restricted domain S, namely, defined as follows:

$$\Pi_{\mathcal{F}}(S) = \{f_S : f \in \mathcal{F}\}.$$

Set $S \subseteq X^l$ is said to be *shattered* by $\mathcal{F}$ if $|\Pi_{\mathcal{F}}(S)| = k^l$ or $\Pi_{\mathcal{F}}(S) = K^l$, where $|\cdot|$ is the number of elements in a set. Furthermore, define $\Pi_{\mathcal{F}}(l)$ as follows:

$$\Pi_{\mathcal{F}}(l) = \max_{S \in X^l} |\Pi_{\mathcal{F}}(S)|.$$

VC dimension $d_V(\mathcal{F})$ of $\mathcal{F}$ is defined[2] as the maximum number of elements among the sets that are shattered by $\mathcal{F}$ [1, 10], namely, defined as follows:

$$d_V(\mathcal{F}) = \max\{l : \Pi_{\mathcal{F}}(l) = k^l\}.$$

---

[2] $d_V(\mathcal{F})$ is called *ranking dimension* in [10].

Note that this definition of VC dimension coincides with the original definition by Vapnik and Chervonenkis [13] when $k = 2$.

The next proposition holds trivially.

Proposition 1.

$$d_V(DL_\mathcal{B}) \leq d_V(\mathcal{B})$$

By Proposition 1 and LR $\subseteq$ DL$_\mathcal{L}$,

$$d_V(\text{LR}) \leq d_V(\mathcal{L}) \tag{1}$$

holds. In [10], it was shown that both sides in Inequality (1) are equal.

Theorem 1 (Rajaram et al. [10]).

$$d_V(LR) = d_V(\mathcal{L})$$

Thus, $d_V(\text{LR}) = d_V(\text{DL}_\mathcal{L})$ holds, which means that no difference in the two function classes appears by VC dimension analysis.

3.2   Graph Dimension Analysis

As another extension of VC dimension for K-valued function classes, Natarajan considered *graph dimension* defined as follows.

Let function δ denote a $\{-1, 1\}$-valued function on $K \times K$ defined as

$$\delta(i, j) = \begin{cases} 1 \text{ if } i = j \\ -1 \text{ otherwise.} \end{cases}$$

Let l denote an arbitrary natural number. For $S = (\mathbf{x}_1, \mathbf{x}_2, ..., \mathbf{x}_l) \in X^l$, $I = (i_1, i_2, ..., i_l) \in K^l$ and $f \in \mathcal{F}$, define $f_{I,S} \in \{-1, 1\}^l$ as

$$(\delta(f(\mathbf{x}_1), i_1), \delta(f(\mathbf{x}_2), i_2), ..., \delta(f(\mathbf{x}_l), i_l)).$$

Let $\Pi_{I,\mathcal{F}}(S)$ denote $\{f_{I,S} : f \in \mathcal{F}\}$. Then, define $\Pi_\mathcal{F}^G(l)$ as follows:

$$\Pi_\mathcal{F}^G(l) = \max_{S \in X^l, I \in K^l} |\Pi_{I,\mathcal{F}}(S)|.$$

Graph dimension $d_G(\mathcal{F})$ of K-valued function class $\mathcal{F}$ [1, 9] is defined as follows:

$$d_G(\mathcal{F}) = \max\{l : \Pi_\mathcal{F}^G(l) = 2^l\}.$$

From the definition of graph dimension, the graph dimension of K-valued function class $\mathcal{F}$ on X can be seen as the VC dimension of $\{-1, 1\}$-valued function class $\mathcal{F}_\delta$ on $X \times K$ defined as follows

$$\mathcal{F}_\delta = \{h_f : h_f(\mathbf{x}, i) \stackrel{def}{=} \delta(f(\mathbf{x}), i), f \in \mathcal{F}\}. \tag{2}$$

3.3 Graph Dimension of DL$_\mathcal{C}$

The following lemma is a slight modification of Lemma 3.2.3 [2] proved by Blumer et al. The proof of Lemma 1 is similar to that of their lemma and is omitted. Note that $\{-1,1\}$-valued function classes $\mathcal{B}_1, \mathcal{B}_2, ..., \mathcal{B}_s$ can be different classes that have the same VC dimension.

Lemma 1. *For $s \geq 1$, let $\mathcal{B}_1, \mathcal{B}_2, ..., \mathcal{B}_s$ be $\{-1,1\}$-valued function classes on X with $d_V(\mathcal{B}_1) = d_V(\mathcal{B}_2) = \cdots = d_V(\mathcal{B}_s) = d < \infty$. Let $\mathcal{C} = \{\min_{i=1}^s f_i : f_i \in \mathcal{B}_i, 1 \leq i \leq s\}$. Then, $d_V(\mathcal{C}) < 2ds \log_2(3s)$.*

Theorem 2. $d_G(DL_\mathcal{B}) < d_V(\mathcal{B})k(k+1)\log_2(3k)$

Proof. Let $I = (i_1, i_2, ..., i_l) \in K^l$ and $S = (\mathbf{x}_1, \mathbf{x}_2, ..., \mathbf{x}_l)$. Let $l_s = |\{j : i_j = s\}|$ and define S_s as $(\mathbf{x}_{j_1}, \mathbf{x}_{j_2}, ..., \mathbf{x}_{j_{l_s}})$, where $j_1, j_2, ..., j_{l_s}$ are distinct elements in $\{j : i_j = s\}$. Let $I_s = (i_{j_1}, i_{j_2}, ..., i_{j_{l_s}})$. We show

$$|\varPi_{I,\text{DL}_\mathcal{B}}(S)| = 2^l \Rightarrow l_s < 2d_V(\mathcal{B})s \log_2(3s) \tag{3}$$

for all $1 \leq s \leq k$. Let

$$\mathcal{H}_s = \{h_{f,s} : h_{f,s}(\mathbf{x}) \overset{def}{=} \delta(f(\mathbf{x}), s), f \in \text{DL}_\mathcal{B}\}.$$

Note that $|\varPi_{I,\text{DL}_\mathcal{B}}(S)| = 2^l$ implies $|\varPi_{\mathcal{H}_s}(S_s)| = 2^{l_s}$. Note that $\mathcal{H}_s$ can be represented as follows:

$$\mathcal{H}_s = \begin{cases} \{\min_{i=1}^s g_i : g_i \in \overline{\mathcal{B}} \text{ for } 1 \leq i \leq s-1, g_s \in \mathcal{B}\} & \text{for } 1 \leq s < k \\ \{\min_{i=1}^{s-1} g_i : g_i \in \overline{\mathcal{B}}\} & \text{for } s = k, \end{cases}$$

where $\overline{\mathcal{B}} = \{-f : f \in \mathcal{B}\}$. By the fact that $d_V(\overline{\mathcal{B}}) = d_V(\mathcal{B})$ and Lemma 1,

$$l_s \leq d_V(\mathcal{H}_s) < 2d_V(\mathcal{B})s \log_2(3s).$$

Thus, (3) holds for all $1 \leq s \leq k$. Therefore,

$$d_G(\text{DL}_\mathcal{B}) < \sum_{s=1}^k 2d_V(\mathcal{B})s \log_2(3s) \leq k(k+1)d_V(\mathcal{B})\log_2(3k).$$

$\square$

Theorem 3. $n(k-1) \leq d_G(DL_\mathcal{C}) < (n+1)k(k+1)\log_2(3k)$

Proof. By Theorem 2 and the fact that $d_V(\mathcal{L}) = n+1$ [2], $d_G(\text{DL}_\mathcal{C}) \leq (n+1)k(k+1)\log_2(3k)$ holds.

Now we prove inequality $(k-1)n \leq d_G(\text{DL}_\mathcal{C})$. In $\Re^n = \{(x_1, x_2, ..., x_n) : x_i \in \Re\}$, consider subspace $X_0 = \{(0, x_2, ..., x_n) : x_i \in \Re\}$. Since X_0 is isomorphic to $\Re^{n-1}$, the VC dimension of the class of linear discrimination functions in X_0 is n. Let $S_0 \in X_0^n$ be a list of points shattered by the class of linear discrimination functions. Let S_i be a list of points made by moving S_0 in the direction of the x_1-axis by i. Consider list S with length $(k-1)n$ made by concatenating $S_1, S_2, ..., S_{k-1}$ and

$$I = (\underbrace{1, 1, ..., 1}_{n \text{ times}}, \underbrace{2, 2, ..., 2}_{n \text{ times}}, ..., \underbrace{k-1, k-1, ..., k-1}_{n \text{ times}}).$$

We show that $\Pi_{I,\mathrm{DL}\mathcal{L}}(S) = \{-1, 1\}^{(k-1)n}$. Let A be an arbitrary element in $\{-1, 1\}^{(k-1)n}$. In hyperplane $x_1 = i$, which contains S_i, there is a linear discrimination function g_i in $(n-1)$-dimensional Euclidean space such that $g_i(\mathbf{x}) = 1$ for $\mathbf{x} \in S_i$ if and only if the corresponding component in A is 1. Function g_i can be seen as a linear discrimination function $f_i : \Re^n \to \{-1, 1\}$ restricted in hyperplane $x_1 = i$. A normal vector $\mathbf{w}_i$ of such f_i can be as close to $(1, 0, 0, ..., 0)$ as you want, namely, it is possible that $f_i(\mathbf{x}) = -1$ ($\mathbf{w}_i \cdot \mathbf{x} \geq b_i$) for all elements $\mathbf{x}$ in $S_{i+1}, S_{i+2}, ..., S_{k-1}$. (See the figure below.)

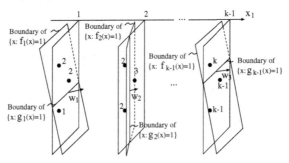

Then, for $f = \mathrm{dl}[f_1, f_2, ..., f_{k-1}]$, $f_{I,S} = A$ holds.   □

3.4   Graph Dimension of LR

Theorem 4. $d_G(LR) \geq n + k - 1$.

Proof. Like the proof of Theorem 3, consider a list $S_0 = (\mathbf{x}_1, \mathbf{x}_2, ..., \mathbf{x}_n)$ of n points in $\Re^n$ that are contained in hyperplane $x_1 = 1$ and shattered by linear discrimination functions. For $i = 1, 2, ..., k-1$, let $\mathbf{x}_{n+i} = \{(i+1, 0, 0, ..., 0)\}$. Let S be a list $(\mathbf{x}_1, \mathbf{x}_2, ..., \mathbf{x}_{n+k-1})$ of $n+k-1$ points in $\Re^n$ and let

$$I = (\underbrace{1, 1, ..., 1}_{n \text{ times}}, 2, 3, ..., k).$$

We show that $\Pi_{I,\mathrm{LR}}(S) = \{-1, 1\}^{n+k-1}$. Let $A = (a_1, a_2, ..., a_{n+k-1})$ be an arbitrary element in $\{-1, 1\}^{n+k-1}$. By similar reason argued in the proof of Theorem 3, there exist $\mathbf{w} \in \Re^n$ and $b_1 \leq b_2 \leq ... \leq b_{k-1}$ such that the linear ranking function $f(\mathbf{x}) = \min_{r \in K}\{r : \mathbf{w} \cdot \mathbf{x} - b_r < 0\}$ defined by these parameters $\mathbf{w}, b_1, b_2, ..., b_{k-1}$ satisfies that

$$f(\mathbf{x}_i) = \begin{cases} 1 & \text{if } i \leq n \text{ and } a_i = 1 \\ 2 & \text{if } i \leq n \text{ and } a_i = -1 \\ i - n + 1 & \text{if } n+1 \leq i \leq n+k-1. \end{cases}$$

Thus, when $(a_{n+1}, a_{n+2}, ..., a_{n+k-1}) = (1, 1, ..., 1)$, $f_{I,S} = A$ holds. In the case with $(a_{n+1}, a_{n+2}, ..., a_{n+k-1}) \neq (-1, -1, ..., -1)$, $f_{I,S} = A$ holds if thresholds $b_2, b_3, ..., b_{k-1}$ of f are changed to $b'_2, b'_3, ..., b'_{k-1}$ defined as follows:

$$b'_i = \begin{cases} b_i & \text{if } a_{n+i-1} = 1, i \neq i^* \\ b_{i+1} & \text{if } a_{n+i-1} = 1, i = i^* \\ b_{i-1} & \text{if } a_{n+i-1} = -1, i < i^* \\ b_{i+1} & \text{if } a_{n+i-1} = -1, i > i^*, \end{cases}$$

where $i^* = \max\{j : a_{n+j-1} = 1\}$. (See the figure below.)

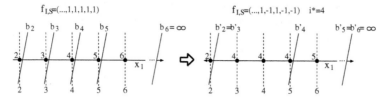

When $(a_{n+1}, a_{n+2}, ..., a_{n+k-1}) = (-1, -1, ..., -1)$, by choosing a vector $\mathbf{w}$ close to $(-1, 0, 0, ..., 0)$ and using thresholds with $b_1 = b_2 = \cdots = b_{k-1}$, we get a linear ranking function f that satisfies

$$f(\mathbf{x}_i) = \begin{cases} k & \text{if } i \leq n \text{ and } a_i = -1 \\ 1 & \text{otherwise.} \end{cases}$$

Then, $f_{I,S} = A$ holds.   □

To prove $d_G(\text{LR}) = O(n + k)$, we use notions and notations in the area of combinatorial geometry [4]. Let H be a finite set of hyperplanes in $\Re^d$. The *arrangement* $\mathcal{A}(H)$ of H is a dissection of $\Re^d$ into connected pieces of various dimensions defined by H. Let H be composed of m hyperplanes $h_1, h_2, ..., h_m$. Each $h_i \in H$ is represented as $g_i(\mathbf{x}) = 0$ using linear (or, more precisely, affine) function $g_i : \Re^d \to \Re$. For an arbitrary point p, the *face position vector*[3] $u(p)$ of p is defined as $(v_1(p), v_2(p), ..., v_m(p))$, where

$$v_i(p) = \begin{cases} +1 & \text{if } g_i(p) > 0 \\ 0 & \text{if } g_i(p) = 0 \\ -1 & \text{if } g_u(p) < 0. \end{cases}$$

The *binary position vector* of p is a binarized vector of $u(p)$ by replacing 0 with $+1$. A set of points with the same face position vector is called a *face*. A k-*flat* is defined as the affine hull of $k + 1$ affinely independent points. A face is called a *cell* if it is d-flat. An arrangement $\mathcal{A}(H)$ of $m \geq d$ hyperplanes in $\Re^d$ is called *simple* if any d hyperplanes of H have a unique point in common and if any $d+1$ hyperplanes have no point in common. When $m < d$, $\mathcal{A}(H)$ is called *simple* if the common intersection of the m hyperplanes is a $(d - m)$-*flat*.

---

[3] In [4], this is simply called a *position vector*. We added the word 'face' for distinguishing this from a *binary* position vector we introduced below.

Lemma 2. *Let H be a set of $m \geq d$ hyperplanes in $\Re^d$ such that $\mathcal{A}(H)$ is simple. Then, the number of distinct binary position vectors is equal to the number of cells.*

Proof. Assume that the face position vector $u(p)$ for point $p = (\pi_1, \pi_2, ..., \pi_d)$ has l zero-valued components and that the set of their indices is S. For $i \in S$, there exists a tiny value Δ such that the face position vector for point $p' = (\pi_1, \pi_2, ..., \pi_{i-1}, \pi_i + \Delta, \pi_{i+1}, ..., \pi_d)$ has $+1$ for its ith component and the same values for the other components by 'simple' assumption. By repeating this procedure, the number of zero-valued components can be reduced one by one and finally you can get a point q with $u(q)$ having no zero-valued component, namely, a point in a cell. The binary position vectors of p and q are trivially the same.   □

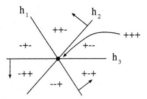

Fig. 1. Case in which the number of distinct binary vectors is larger than the number of cells. The directions of the arrows going out from hyperplanes indicate positive directions.

Remark 1. Note that Lemma 2 does not hold when $\mathcal{A}(H)$ is *not* simple. See Fig. 1.

Lemma 3 (A part of Lemma 1.2 in [4]). *Let H be a set of m hyperplanes in $\Re^d$ such that $\mathcal{A}(H)$ is simple. Then, the number of cells is*

$$\sum_{i=0}^{d} \binom{m}{i}.$$

Lemma 4. *For $a \geq 2e$, $ax \geq 2^x \Rightarrow x < 2\log_2 a$.*

Proof.

$$1 + \log_2 e < e$$
$$2\log_2 2e < 2e$$

Thus, for $a \geq 2e$,

$$2\log_2 a < a$$
$$2a\log_2 a < 2^{2\log_2 a}$$

This means $ax < 2^x$ at $x = 2\log_2 a$. Therefore, $x < 2\log_2 a$ must be hold to make $ax \geq 2^x$ hold.   □

Theorem 5. $d_G(LR) < 5(n + k - 1)$

Proof. Let $S = (\mathbf{x}_1, \mathbf{x}_2, ..., \mathbf{x}_l) \in X^l$ and $I = (i_1, i_2, ..., i_l) \in K^l$. Then, for an arbitrary $f \in LR$ defined by $\mathbf{w} \in \Re^n$ and $\mathbf{b} = (b_1, b_2, ..., b_{k-1}) \in \Re^{k-1}$,

$$\delta(f(\mathbf{x}_j), i_j) = \begin{cases} 1 & \text{if } \mathbf{w} \cdot \mathbf{x}_j - b_{i_j - 1} \geq 0 \text{ and } \mathbf{w} \cdot \mathbf{x}_j - b_{i_j} < 0 \\ -1 & \text{if } \mathbf{w} \cdot \mathbf{x}_j - b_{i_j - 1} < 0 \text{ or } \mathbf{w} \cdot \mathbf{x}_j - b_{i_j} \geq 0 \end{cases}$$

when $1 < i_j < k$,

$$\delta(f(\mathbf{x}_j), i_j) = \begin{cases} 1 & \text{if } \mathbf{w} \cdot \mathbf{x}_j - b_{i_j} < 0 \\ -1 & \text{if } \mathbf{w} \cdot \mathbf{x}_j - b_{i_j} \geq 0 \end{cases}$$

when $i_j = 1$, and

$$\delta(f(\mathbf{x}_j), i_j) = \begin{cases} 1 & \text{if } \mathbf{w} \cdot \mathbf{x}_j - b_{i_j - 1} \geq 0 \\ -1 & \text{if } \mathbf{w} \cdot \mathbf{x}_j - b_{i_j - 1} < 0 \end{cases}$$

when $i_j = k$.
Let

$$h_{j,i} = \{\mathbf{z} : \mathbf{z} \in \Re^{n+k-1}, \mathbf{z} \cdot (\mathbf{x}_j, \mathbf{1}_i) = 0\},$$

where $\mathbf{1}_i$ is a $(k - 1)$-dimensional vector of which component values are 0 except the ith one-valued component. Note that $\mathbf{z}$ in the definition of $h_{j,i}$ is a vector that corresponds to $(\mathbf{w}, \mathbf{b})$. Thus, $h_{j,i}$ is a hyperplane in $\Re^{n+k-1}$ with normal vector $(\mathbf{x}_j, \mathbf{1}_i)$, where the space $\Re^{n+k-1}$ can be seen as the functional space corresponding to LR. Consider a set H of hyperplanes defined by

$$H = \{h_{j,i_j} : 1 \leq j \leq l, i_j \neq k\} \cup \{h_{j,i_j - 1} : 1 \leq j \leq l, i_j \neq 1\}.$$

For $f, g \in LR$ defined by $(\mathbf{w}_f, \mathbf{b}_f), (\mathbf{w}_g, \mathbf{b}_g)$, respectively, if $f_{I,S} \neq g_{I,S}$, then the binary position vectors of $(\mathbf{w}_f, \mathbf{b}_f)$ and $(\mathbf{w}_g, \mathbf{b}_g)$ for H are different. Thus, the number of distinct binary position vectors for H must be at least 2^l in order that equation $|\Pi^G_{LR}(l)| = 2^l$ holds. The number of binary position vectors is maximized when $\mathcal{A}(H)$ is simple, and then it is equal to the number of cells by Lemma 2. Thus, by Lemma 3,

$$\sum_{i=0}^{d} \binom{m}{i} \geq 2^l,$$

where $d = n + k - 1$ and m is the number of hyperplanes in H, must hold. Define $\Phi_d(m)$ as $\sum_{i=0}^{d} \binom{m}{i}$, then Φ_d is increasing, so

$$\Phi_d(2l) \geq 2^l$$

must hold because $m \leq 2l$. Since $\Phi_d(m) \leq (em/d)^d$ by Proposition A2.1 in [2],

$$(2el/d)^d \geq 2^l$$

must hold. By replacing l with xd, this inequality becomes

$$(2ex)^d \geq 2^{xd},$$

which is equivalent to

$$2ex \geq 2^x. \tag{4}$$

To make (4) hold, x must be less than $2\log_2 2e < 5$ by Lemma 4. Thus,

$$l < 5d = 5(n + k - 1). \qquad \square$$

4   Risk Bounds on Learning LR

In this section, we show risk bounds on learning LR in two settings, the multi-class classification setting and the ordinal regression setting.

4.1   Vapnik's Framework of Risk Minimization

The learning framework we adopt here is Vapnik's framework of risk minimization. Vapnik considered the following general setting [12, p.20] of the learning problem, which generalizes all of the settings of classification, regression and density estimation.

Problem 1 (Vapnik's general setting of the learning problem). Let P be a probability measure on the space Z and let $\{Q(\cdot, \alpha) : \alpha \in \Lambda\}$ be a set of real-valued functions on Z parameterized by α. Given an i.i.d. sample $z_1, z_2, ..., z_l$, find $\alpha_0 \in \Lambda$ that minimize the risk functional

$$R(\alpha) = \int Q(z, \alpha) dP(z)$$

under the condition that the probability measure P is unknown.

In the classification and regression settings, the space Z is the product space of spaces X and Y, and we consider the class of functions $f \in \mathcal{F}$ from the space X to the space Y and real-valued loss function L on $Y \times Y$. Then, Q is defined by

$$Q((x, y), f) = L(f(x), y).$$

The loss function L is the zero-one loss $L_{0\text{-}1}$ defined as

$$L_{0\text{-}1}(y_1, y_2) = \begin{cases} 0 \text{ if } y_1 = y_2 \\ 1 \text{ if } y_1 \neq y_2 \end{cases}$$

in the classification settings, and the L1 loss L_{L1} defined as

$$L_{L1}(y_1, y_2) = |y_1 - y_2|$$

in our ordinal regression settings.

In order to generalize the result obtained for the set of $\{0,1\}$-valued functions to the set of real-valued functions, Vapnik considered a set of *indicators* $I(\cdot, \alpha, \beta), \alpha \in \Lambda, \beta \in (\inf_{z,\alpha} Q(z, \alpha), \sup_{z,\alpha} Q(z, \alpha))$ of the set of real-valued functions $Q(\cdot, \alpha), \alpha \in \Lambda$:

$$I(z, \alpha, \beta) = \theta(Q(z, \alpha) - \beta) \quad \text{where } \theta(x) = \begin{cases} 0 & \text{if } x < 0 \\ 1 & \text{if } x \geq 0. \end{cases}$$

Note that $I(z, \alpha, \beta) = Q(z, \alpha)$ for all $\beta \in (0,1)$ when $\{Q(\cdot, \alpha) : \alpha \in \Lambda\}$ is a set of $\{0,1\}$-valued functions.

Vapnik showed the following theorem for the set of totally bounded nonnegative functions.

Theorem 6 (Vapnik [12, p.84]). *Let $\{Q(\cdot, \alpha) : \alpha \in \Lambda\}$ be a set of nonnegative functions on Z whose range is bounded by B, and let h denote the VC dimension of the set of indicators of the function class. Let $z_1, z_2, ..., z_l$ be an i.i.d. sample drawn from Z according to an arbitrary unknown distribution. Define $R_{\text{emp}}(\alpha)$ as $(\sum_{i=1}^{l} Q(z_i, \alpha))/l$. Then, the following inequality holds with probability at least $1 - \delta$ simultaneously for all $\alpha \in \Lambda$:*

$$R(\alpha) \leq R_{\text{emp}}(\alpha) + \frac{B\mathcal{E}}{2}\left(1 + \sqrt{1 + \frac{4R_{\text{emp}}(\alpha)}{B\mathcal{E}}}\right),$$

where

$$\mathcal{E} = 4\frac{h(\ln(2l/h) + 1) - \ln(\delta/4)}{l}.$$

4.2   Error Probability Bounds in the Multi-class Classification Setting

Let $\mathcal{F}$ be a class of K-valued functions on X and let $\mathcal{F}_\delta$ denote the class of $\{-1, 1\}$-valued functions defined by (2). Define $\mathcal{F}_{L_{0\text{-}1}}$ as

$$\mathcal{F}_{L_{0\text{-}1}} = \{Q(\cdot, f) : Q((\mathbf{x}, i), f) \overset{def}{=} L_{0\text{-}1}(f(\mathbf{x}), i), f \in \mathcal{F}\}.$$

Then, trivially, $d_V(\mathcal{F}_{L_{0\text{-}1}}) = d_V(\mathcal{F}_\delta)$. Since $d_V(\mathcal{F}_\delta) = d_G(\mathcal{F})$, the following corollary of Theorem 6 is obtained.

Corollary 1. *Let $\mathcal{F}$ be a class of K-valued functions on X. Let $(\mathbf{x}_1, i_1), (\mathbf{x}_2, i_2), ..., (\mathbf{x}_l, i_l)$ be an i.i.d. sample drawn from $X \times K$ according to an arbitrary unknown distribution $\mathcal{D}$. Then, the following inequality holds with probability at least $1 - \delta$ simultaneously for all $f \in \mathcal{F}$:*

$$\Pr_{(x,i)\sim\mathcal{D}}(f(\mathbf{x}) \neq i) \leq \frac{m}{l} + \frac{\mathcal{E}}{2}\left(1 + \sqrt{1 + \frac{4m}{l\mathcal{E}}}\right),$$

where m is the number of instances $(\mathbf{x}_j, i_j)$ with $f(\mathbf{x}_j) \neq i_j$ and

$$\mathcal{E} = 4\frac{d_G(\mathcal{F})(\ln(2l/d_G(\mathcal{F})) + 1) - \ln(\delta/4)}{l}.$$

For $f : X \to K$, f is said to be an ϵ-close hypothesis when f satisfies that

$$\Pr_{(x,i) \sim \mathcal{D}}(f(\mathbf{x}) \neq i) < \epsilon.$$

The above corollary implies the following theorem proved by Ben-David et al. [1].

Theorem 7 (Ben-David et al. [1]). *Let $\mathcal{F}$ be a class of K-valued functions on X. Let $\mathcal{D}$ be an arbitrary unknown probabilistic distribution on $X \times K$. Then, there exists a constant value $c > 0$ such that, for given $0 < \epsilon, \delta < 1$, the probability that a hypothesis in $\mathcal{F}$ consistent with*

$$l \geq \frac{c}{\epsilon}\left(d_G(\mathcal{F})\log\frac{1}{\epsilon} + \log\frac{1}{\delta}\right) \tag{5}$$

instances randomly drawn according to $\mathcal{D}$ is ϵ-close is more than $1 - \delta$.

By Theorem 7 and the results shown in Section 3.2, the number of instances necessary to PAC-learn by a consistent hypothesis finder is $O(k + n)$ for LR and $O(nk^2 \log k)$ for $\mathrm{DL}_{\mathcal{L}}$ with respect to parameters k and n.

For given m instances in $\Re^n \times K$, a consistent linear ranking function from $\Re^n$ to K can be obtained in time polynomial to n, l and k by solving a linear programming problem composed of $n + k - 1$ variables and at most $2l$ constraints. Note that a linear programming problem can be solved in polynomial time by an algorithm such as Karmarkar's algorithm [6]. A consistent function in $\mathrm{DL}_{\mathcal{L}}$ can be also obtained in polynomial time by solving k learning problems of linear discrimination functions, which are known to be solved in polynomial time by linear programming [2].

4.3   Risk Bounds in the Ordinal Regression Setting

The set $\mathcal{F}_\theta$ of indicators of $\{Q(\cdot, f) : Q((\mathbf{x}, i), f) \overset{def}{=} L_{L1}(f(\mathbf{x}), i), f \in \mathcal{F}\}$ can be represented as follows:

$$\mathcal{F}_\theta = \{h_{f,\beta} : h_{f,\beta}(\mathbf{x}, i) \overset{def}{=} \theta(|f(\mathbf{x}) - i| - \beta), f \in \mathcal{F}, \beta \in (0, k - 1)\}.$$

Lemma 5. $d_V(LR_\theta) < 2(\log_2 e(k - 1))(n + k - 1)$

Proof. Let $S = (\mathbf{x}_1, \mathbf{x}_2, ..., \mathbf{x}_l) \in X^l$ and $I = (i_1, i_2, ..., i_l) \in K^l$. Then, for an arbitrary $f \in \mathrm{LR}$ defined by $\mathbf{w} \in \Re^n$ and $\mathbf{b} = (b_1, b_2, ..., b_{k-1}) \in \Re^{k-1}$,

$$\theta(|f(\mathbf{x}_j) - i_j| - \beta) = \begin{cases} 0 \text{ if } \mathbf{w} \cdot \mathbf{x}_j - b_{i_j - \lceil \beta \rceil} \geq 0 \text{ and } \mathbf{w} \cdot \mathbf{x}_j - b_{i_j + \lceil \beta \rceil - 1} < 0 \\ 1 \text{ if } \mathbf{w} \cdot \mathbf{x}_j - b_{i_j - \lceil \beta \rceil} < 0 \text{ or } \mathbf{w} \cdot \mathbf{x}_j - b_{i_j + \lceil \beta \rceil - 1} \geq 0 \end{cases}$$

when $\beta \leq i_j - 1$ and $\beta \leq k - i_j$,

$$\theta(|f(\mathbf{x}_j) - i_j| - \beta) = \begin{cases} 0 \text{ if } \mathbf{w} \cdot \mathbf{x}_j - b_{i_j + \lceil \beta \rceil - 1} < 0 \\ 1 \text{ if } \mathbf{w} \cdot \mathbf{x}_j - b_{i_j + \lceil \beta \rceil - 1} \geq 0 \end{cases}$$

when $\beta > i_j - 1$ and $\beta \leq k - i_j$,

$$\theta(|f(\mathbf{x}_j) - i_j| - \beta) = \begin{cases} 0 \text{ if } \mathbf{w} \cdot \mathbf{x}_j - b_{i_j - \lceil \beta \rceil} \geq 0 \\ 1 \text{ if } \mathbf{w} \cdot \mathbf{x}_j - b_{i_j - \lceil \beta \rceil} < 0 \end{cases}$$

when $\beta \leq i_j - 1$ and $\beta > k - i_j$, and

$$\theta(|f(\mathbf{x}_j) - i_j| - \beta) = 0$$

when $\beta > i_j - 1$ and $\beta > k - i_j$.

Let

$$H = \{h_{j,i} : 1 \leq j \leq l, 1 \leq i \leq k - 1\}$$

where

$$h_{j,i} = \{\mathbf{z} : \mathbf{z} \in \Re^{n+k-1}, \mathbf{z} \cdot (\mathbf{x}_j, \mathbf{1}_i) = 0\}$$

as defined in the proof of Theorem 5. By a similar discussion as that in the proof of Theorem 5,

$$\Phi_d(m) \geq 2^l,$$

where $d = n + k - 1$ and m is the number of hyperplanes in H, must hold. Since $m \leq (k - 1)l$,

$$\Phi_d((k - 1)l) \geq 2^l$$

must hold. Thus, a similar argument using Lemma 4 as that in the proof of Theorem 5 leads to

$$l < 2(\log_2 e(k - 1))(n + k - 1).$$

$\square$

Remark 2. Note that[4] $d_V(\mathrm{LR}_\theta) \geq n+k-1$ because $\mathrm{LR}_\theta \supseteq \mathrm{LR}_{L_{0\text{-}1}}$ and $d_V(\mathrm{LR}_{L_{0\text{-}1}}) = d_V(\mathrm{LR}_\delta) \geq n + k - 1$ by Theorem 4.

Corollary 2. *Let* $(\mathbf{x}_1, i_1), (\mathbf{x}_2, i_2), ..., (\mathbf{x}_l, i_l)$ *be an i.i.d. sample drawn from* $X \times K$ *according to an arbitrary unknown distribution* $\mathcal{D}$. *Then, the following inequality holds with probability at least* $1 - \delta$ *simultaneously for all* $f \in \mathrm{LR}$:

$$E_{(\mathbf{x},i) \sim \mathcal{D}}(|f(\mathbf{x}) - i|) \leq R_{\mathrm{emp}}(f) + \frac{(k-1)\mathcal{E}}{2}\left(1 + \sqrt{1 + \frac{4R_{\mathrm{emp}}(f)}{(k-1)\mathcal{E}}}\right),$$

where $R_{\mathrm{emp}}(f) = (\sum_{j=1}^{l} |f(\mathbf{x}_j) - i_j|)/l$,

$$\mathcal{E} = 4\frac{h(\ln(2l/h) + 1) - \ln(\delta/4)}{l} \text{ and } h = 2(\log_2 e(k - 1))(n + k - 1).$$

---

[4] In the process of obtaining a risk bound by applying Theorem 6 to the ordinal regression of LR, $d_V(\mathrm{LR}_\theta)$ was calculated as n in [11], which contradicts our result.

Remark 3. By Corollary 1, the following inequality holds with probability at least $1 - \delta$ simultaneously for all $f \in \text{LR}$:

$$E_{(\mathbf{x},i)\sim\mathcal{D}}(|f(\mathbf{x}) - i|) \le (k-1)Pr_{(x,i)\sim\mathcal{D}}(f(\mathbf{x}) \ne i) \le (k-1)\left(\frac{m}{l} + \frac{\mathcal{E}}{2}\left(1 + \sqrt{1 + \frac{4m}{l\mathcal{E}}}\right)\right),$$

where m is the number of instances $(\mathbf{x}_j, i_j)$ with $f(\mathbf{x}_j) \ne i_j$ and

$$\mathcal{E} = 4\frac{h(\ln(2l/h)) + 1) - \ln(\delta/4)}{l} \text{ and } h = 5(n + k - 1).$$

With respect to k and n, this bound is $O(k(n+k))$, which is better than $O(k(n+k)\log k)$, the bound obtained in Corollary 2.

5   Concluding Remarks

We showed that graph dimension of the class of linear ranking functions is $\Theta(n+k)$, which is asymptotically significantly smaller that the graph dimension $\Omega(nk)$ of the class of $\{1, 2, ..., k\}$-valued decision lists naturally defined using $k - 1$ linear discrimination functions. This difference causes the difference in sample complexity upper bounds for PAC learning of those classes. However, in order to show that sample complexities of the two learning problems are definitely different, their lower bounds should also be analyzed. Analyses of margin-based risk bounds in both the multiclass classification and ordinal regression settings would also be interesting.

Acknowledgments

The author would like to thank Prof. Mineichi Kudo and Jun Toyama for helpful discussions which led to this research.

References

1. S. Ben-David, Nicolo Cesa-Bianchi, D. Haussler and P. M. Long. Characterizations of Learnability for Classes of $\{0, ..., n\}$-Valued Functions. *Journal of Computer and System Sciences* 50, 1995, pp.74-86.
2. A. Blumer, A. Ehrenfeucht, D. Haussler and M. K. Warmuth. Learnability and the Vapnik-Chervonenkis Dimension. *Journal of the ACM* 36(4), 1989, pp.929-965.
3. K. Crammer and Y. Singer. Pranking with Ranking. *Advances in Neural Information Processing* 14, 2002, pp.641-647.
4. H. Edelsbrunner, Algorithms in Combinatorial Geometry, *Springer-Verlag*, Berlin Heidelberg, 1987.
5. R. Herbrich, T. Graepel and K. Obermayer. Large Margin Rank Boundaries for Ordinal Regression. Advances in Large Margin Classifiers, 2000, pp.115-132.
6. N. Karmarkar. A New Polynomial-Time Algorithm for Linear Programming. *Combinatorica* 4, 1984, PP.373-395.

7. A. Nakamura and N. Abe. Collaborative Filtering using Weighted Majority Prediction Algorithms. *Proceedings of the 15th International Conference on Machine Learning*, 1998, pp.395-403.

8. A. Nakamura, M. Kudo and A. Tanaka. Collaborative Filtering using Restoration Operators. *Proceedings of the 7th European Conference on Principles and Practice of Knowledge Discovery in Databases*, 2003, pp.339-349.

9. B. K. Natarajan. On Learning Sets and Functions. *Machine Learning* 4, 1989, pp.67-97.

10. S. Rajaram, A. Garg, X. S. Zhou and T. S. Huang. Classification Approach towards Ranking and Sorting Problems. *Proceedings of the 14th European Conference on Machine Learning, Lecture Notes in Artificial Intelligence* 2837, 2003, pp.301-312.

11. A. Shashua and A. Levin. Taxonomy of Large Margin Principle Algorithms for Ordinal Regression Problems. Technical Report 2002-39, Leibniz Center for Research, School of Computer Science and Eng., the Hebrew University of Jerusalem.

12. V. N. Vapnik. The Nature of Statistical Learning Theory (2nd Edition), *Springer-Verlag* New York, Inc., 1999.

13. V. N. Vapnik and A. Y. Chervonenkis. On the Uniform Convergence of Relative Frequencies of Events to Their Probabilities. *Theory Probab. Appl.* 16(2), 1971, pp.264-280.

Author Index

Lecture Notes in Artificial Intelligence (LNAI)

Vol. 4045: D. Barker-Plummer, R. Cox, N. Swoboda (Eds.), Diagrammatic Representation and Inference. XII, 301 pages. 2006.

Vol. 4031: M. Ali, R. Dapoigny (Eds.), Advances in Applied Artificial Intelligence. XXIII, 1353 pages. 2006.

Vol. 4029: L. Rutkowski, R. Tadeusiewicz, L.A. Zadeh, J.M. Zurada (Eds.), Artificial Intelligence and Soft Computing – ICAISC 2006. XXI, 1235 pages. 2006.

Vol. 4027: H.L. Larsen, G. Pasi, D. Ortiz-Arroyo, T. Andreasen, H. Christiansen (Eds.), Flexible Query Answering Systems. XVIII, 714 pages. 2006.

Vol. 4021: E. André, L. Dybkjær, W. Minker, H. Neumann, M. Weber (Eds.), Perception and Interactive Technologies. XI, 217 pages. 2006.

Vol. 4020: A. Bredenfeld, A. Jacoff, I. Noda, Y. Takahashi (Eds.), RoboCup 2005: Robot Soccer World Cup IX. XVII, 727 pages. 2006.

Vol. 4013: L. Lamontagne, M. Marchand (Eds.), Advances in Artificial Intelligence. XIII, 564 pages. 2006.

Vol. 4012: T. Washio, A. Sakurai, K. Nakajima, H. Takeda, S. Tojo, M. Yokoo (Eds.), New Frontiers in Artificial Intelligence. XIII, 484 pages. 2006.

Vol. 4008: J.C. Augusto, C.D. Nugent (Eds.), Designing Smart Homes. XI, 183 pages. 2006.

Vol. 4005: G. Lugosi, H.U. Simon (Eds.), Learning Theory. XI, 656 pages. 2006.

Vol. 3978: B. Hnich, M. Carlsson, F. Fages, F. Rossi (Eds.), Recent Advances in Constraints. VIII, 179 pages. 2006.

Vol. 3963: O. Dikenelli, M.-P. Gleizes, A. Ricci (Eds.), Engineering Societies in the Agents World VI. XII, 303 pages. 2006.

Vol. 3960: R. Vieira, P. Quaresma, M.d.G.V. Nunes, N.J. Mamede, C. Oliveira, M.C. Dias (Eds.), Computational Processing of the Portuguese Language. XII, 274 pages. 2006.

Vol. 3955: G. Antoniou, G. Potamias, C. Spyropoulos, D. Plexousakis (Eds.), Advances in Artificial Intelligence. XVII, 611 pages. 2006.

Vol. 3949: F. A. Savacı (Ed.), Artificial Intelligence and Neural Networks. IX, 227 pages. 2006.

Vol. 3946: T.R. Roth-Berghofer, S. Schulz, D.B. Leake (Eds.), Modeling and Retrieval of Context. XI, 149 pages. 2006.

Vol. 3944: J. Quiñonero-Candela, I. Dagan, B. Magnini, F. d'Alché-Buc (Eds.), Machine Learning Challenges. XIII, 462 pages. 2006.

Vol. 3930: D.S. Yeung, Z.-Q. Liu, X.-Z. Wang, H. Yan (Eds.), Advances in Machine Learning and Cybernetics. XXI, 1110 pages. 2006.

Vol. 3918: W.K. Ng, M. Kitsuregawa, J. Li, K. Chang (Eds.), Advances in Knowledge Discovery and Data Mining. XXIV, 879 pages. 2006.

Vol. 3913: O. Boissier, J. Padget, V. Dignum, G. Lindemann, E. Matson, S. Ossowski, J.S. Sichman, J. Vázquez-Salceda (Eds.), Coordination, Organizations, Institutions, and Norms in Multi-Agent Systems. XII, 259 pages. 2006.

Vol. 3910: S.A. Brueckner, G.D.M. Serugendo, D. Hales, F. Zambonelli (Eds.), Engineering Self-Organising Systems. XII, 245 pages. 2006.

Vol. 3904: M. Baldoni, U. Endriss, A. Omicini, P. Torroni (Eds.), Declarative Agent Languages and Technologies III. XII, 245 pages. 2006.

Vol. 3900: F. Toni, P. Torroni (Eds.), Computational Logic in Multi-Agent Systems. XVII, 427 pages. 2006.

Vol. 3899: S. Frintrop, VOCUS: A Visual Attention System for Object Detection and Goal-Directed Search. XIV, 216 pages. 2006.

Vol. 3898: K. Tuyls, P.J. 't Hoen, K. Verbeeck, S. Sen (Eds.), Learning and Adaption in Multi-Agent Systems. X, 217 pages. 2006.

Vol. 3891: J.S. Sichman, L. Antunes (Eds.), Multi-Agent-Based Simulation VI. X, 191 pages. 2006.

Vol. 3890: S.G. Thompson, R. Ghanea-Hercock (Eds.), Defence Applications of Multi-Agent Systems. XII, 141 pages. 2006.

Vol. 3885: V. Torra, Y. Narukawa, A. Valls, J. Domingo-Ferrer (Eds.), Modeling Decisions for Artificial Intelligence. XII, 374 pages. 2006.

Vol. 3881: S. Gibet, N. Courty, J.-F. Kamp (Eds.), Gesture in Human-Computer Interaction and Simulation. XIII, 344 pages. 2006.

Vol. 3874: R. Missaoui, J. Schmidt (Eds.), Formal Concept Analysis. X, 309 pages. 2006.

Vol. 3873: L. Maicher, J. Park (Eds.), Charting the Topic Maps Research and Applications Landscape. VIII, 281 pages. 2006.

Vol. 3864: Y. Cai, J. Abascal (Eds.), Ambient Intelligence in Everyday Life. XII, 323 pages. 2006.

Vol. 3863: M. Kohlhase (Ed.), Mathematical Knowledge Management. XI, 405 pages. 2006.

Vol. 3862: R.H. Bordini, M. Dastani, J. Dix, A.E.F. Seghrouchni (Eds.), Programming Multi-Agent Systems. XIV, 267 pages. 2006.

Vol. 3849: I. Bloch, A. Petrosino, A.G.B. Tettamanzi (Eds.), Fuzzy Logic and Applications. XIV, 438 pages. 2006.

Vol. 3848: J.-F. Boulicaut, L. De Raedt, H. Mannila (Eds.), Constraint-Based Mining and Inductive Databases. X, 401 pages. 2006.

Vol. 3847: K.P. Jantke, A. Lunzer, N. Spyratos, Y. Tanaka (Eds.), Federation over the Web. X, 215 pages. 2006.

Vol. 3835: G. Sutcliffe, A. Voronkov (Eds.), Logic for Programming, Artificial Intelligence, and Reasoning. XIV, 744 pages. 2005.

Vol. 3830: D. Weyns, H. V.D. Parunak, F. Michel (Eds.), Environments for Multi-Agent Systems II. VIII, 291 pages. 2006.

Vol. 3817: M. Faundez-Zanuy, L. Janer, A. Esposito, A. Satue-Villar, J. Roure, V. Espinosa-Duro (Eds.), Nonlinear Analyses and Algorithms for Speech Processing. XII, 380 pages. 2006.

Vol. 3814: M. Maybury, O. Stock, W. Wahlster (Eds.), Intelligent Technologies for Interactive Entertainment. XV, 342 pages. 2005.